The Definitive Handbook of Business Continuity Management

Second Edition

About the Editor

Andrew Hiles is a founding director of Kingswell International, a global consultancy in enterprise risk management (www.kingswell.net). He has over 30 years' international experience of business continuity planning, having conducted projects in some 60 countries. He was founder and, for some 15 years, chairman of the first international user group for business continuity professionals. He was founding director of the Business Continuity Institute (BCI) and was also a founding director of the World Food Safety Organization.

Andrew was a member of the committee establishing the British Standards Institution BSI 7799 Information Security standard (which has now evolved into ISO 27001). He has been a member of the advisory board of the Continuity Forum and an editorial board advisor to *Contingency Planning and Management* magazine (*CPM*) and to Continuity Central. He is a mentor under the BCI mentoring scheme.

He is the author of *Business Continuity – Best Practice* and *Enterprise Risk Assessment – Best Practices*, both published by Rothstein Associates (www.rothstein.com), and the *Guide to Risk Management* published by the Institute of Chartered Accountants of England and Wales. Andrew co-edited the first edition of this book, contributed to the *Guide to Business Continuity Management*, published for the Confederation of British Industry by Caspian Publishing, and to *Business Continuity Management*, published by the UK Institute of Directors and Department of Trade and Industry. One of his books was made the only required reading for a BC course at DePaul University, Chicago. He has over 300 published articles on business continuity to his credit.

Andrew is a speaker or chair at many international conferences and has delivered over 500 successful public and in-company workshops and training courses, as well as broadcasting on television, radio, webinars and podcasts.

He developed the Business Risk Management course for the 330 000 members of the American Institute of Certified Public Accountants and Business Continuity workshops for the UK Office of Government Commerce (the UK Cabinet Office's advisory service for the public sector). He presents training in the Americas; Eastern, Central and Western Europe; the Middle East; China; the Indian subcontinent; Australia; and the Pacific Rim for the world's leading training companies.

In 2004 Andrew was inducted into the prestigious Business Continuity Hall of Fame by *CPM* magazine in Washington DC as BC vendor practitioner.

The Definitive Handbook of Business Continuity Management

Second Edition

Edited by

Andrew Hiles FBCI
Director, Kingswell International Limited

John Wiley & Sons, Ltd

Other Wiley Editorial Offices

John Wiley & Sons Inc., 111 River Street, Hoboken, NJ 07030, USA

Jossey-Bass, 989 Market Street, San Francisco, CA 94103-1741, USA

Wiley-VCH Verlag GmbH, Boschstr. 12, D-69469 Weinheim, Germany

John Wiley & Sons Australia Ltd, 42 McDougall Street, Milton, Queensland 4064, Australia

John Wiley & Sons (Asia) Pte Ltd, 2 Clementi Loop #02-01, Jin Xing Distripark, Singapore 129809

John Wiley & Sons Canada Ltd, 6045 Freemont Blvd, Mississauga, ONT, L5R 4J3, Canada

Wiley also publishes its books in a variety of electronic formats. Some content that appears in print
may not be available in electronic books.

Anniversary Logo Design: Richard J. Pacifico

British Library Cataloguing in Publication Data

A catalogue record for this book is available from the British Library

ISBN 978-0-470-51638-6 (H/B)

Typeset in 10/12pt Garamond by SNP Best-set Typesetter Ltd, Hong Kong
Printed and bound in Great Britain by CPI Antony Rowe, Chippenham, Wiltshire

This book is dedicated to Murphy, an eternal optimist.

Contents

Contents

Contributors

TIM ARMIT
Director, Clifton Risk Management, UK
TimWArmit@aol.com

PETER BARNES FBCI
Principal, 2c Consulting, UK
peterbarnes@2c-consulting.com

GREGG C. BEATTY
Former Vice President, The Darien Group, USA
Email address withheld

LYNDON BIRD FBCI
Technical Director, Business Continuity Institute, UK
lyndon.bird@thebci.org

THOMAS CARROLL MBCS
Principal Consultant, Kingswell International, UK
tcarroll@kingswell.net

IAN CHARTERS FBCI
Consultant, UK
ianc@continuity.co.uk

MALCOLM CORNISH FBCI, FCA
Senior Consultant, Marsh, UK
malcolm.cornish@marsh.com

NEAL COURTNEY FBCI
Market Development Director – International Sales Europe, BELFOR Europe GmbH, Germany
neal.courtney@belfor.com

ALAN CRAIG MBCI
Director, Survive in Asia, Thailand
alan@survive.net

DENNIS C. HAMILTON FBCI
CEO Crisis Response Planning, Canada
Tel: 001 905-876-0229

DR ROBERT HEATH FBCI
Managing Director, Crisis Corp, UK/Australia
rjheath@compuserve.com

ANDREW HILES FBCI
Director, Kingswell International Limited, UK/International
ahiles@kingswell.net

DAVID HONOUR
Editor, Continuity Central, UK
dhonour@continuitycentral.com

JAYNE HOWE FBCI, MRP, CBRM
Managing Partner, The Howe Partnership, Canada
jayne.howe@sympatico.ca

ALLEN JOHNSON
Director, Scenaris, UK
Allen.Johnson@scenaris.co.uk

PAUL F. KIRVAN FBCI, CBCP, CISSP
*Senior Manager, Business Continuity Advisory Services, Prevalent Networks,
LLC, USA*
pkirvan@prevalent.net

MELVYN MUSSON FBCI
Business Continuity Planning Manager, Edward Jones, USA
melvyn.musson@edwardjones.com

MICHAEL O'HEHIR FBCI
*Former Director, Risk Management Solutions, PricewaterhouseCoopers,
Australia*
info@pwc.com

RANJIT KOVILINKAL RANAKRISHNAN
Freelance consultant, India
ranjit@pcsuae.com

ROLF VON RÖSSING FBCI
Partner, Advisory, KPMG Deutsche Treuhand-Gesellschaft AG, Germany
rvr@scmltd.com

DANNY ROWLAND
Director, Dispute-Resolution Limited, UK
dan@dispute-resolution.ltd.uk

PIPER-ANNA SHIELDS
*Head of Public Relations and Communications, SunGard Availability Services
(UK) Limited, UK/International*
International Piper.Shields@sungard.com

JILLIAN SIMMS
Director, Cornwood Consulting, UK
jillian@cornwood.co.uk

MICHAEL SMITH
Senior Product Development Manager – Communications, SunGard Availability Services (UK) Limited, UK/International
International Michael.Smith@sungard.com

GEERT VANCOPPENOLLE
Former Head of BCM, Accenture Europe
info@accenture.com

PETER VINEY
Director, Scenaris, UK
peter.viner@scenaris.co.uk

SATISH VISWANATHAN
*Practice Head for Strategic Planning within the Business Excellence Centre,
Dubai World, UAE*
viswanathan.satish@dubaiworld.ae

Foreword

Lyndon Bird FBCI – UK
www.thebci.org

As Technical Director of the Business Continuity Institute I am delighted both to contribute to the main knowledge section of the book and to write the foreword for what I believe to be a very important publication.

The first edition of *The Definitive Handbook of Business Continuity Management* set itself the challenge of getting many of the world's leading experts together in one publication. It succeeded very well, providing a wide range of views and challenging opinions. There were few articles that everyone agreed with entirely but none that were less than highly thought provoking. Neither the original edition nor this revised edition sets out to be a textbook for what is a diverse, rapidly evolving and at times still a controversial subject. Indeed, the BCI defines our mission as promoting 'the art and science of BCM on a worldwide basis'. Since when has art (or science for that matter) been uncontroversial? All serious subjects have a diverse range of professional opinion, each supported by highly committed, intelligent and articulate advocates.

Business continuity certainly fits this category, a sure sign that it is fast becoming a mainstream business discipline. It has its own standards, its own institutions, and its own influence on governments. It has a global reach and a resonance that is understood from Europe to America, from Asia to Africa. Its principles work for multinational corporations and small businesses, for public as well as private sector organizations and in all geographical and political terrains. Perhaps most of all it has its 'gurus' and thought leaders – many of whom are represented in this book.

I have known Andrew Hiles since around 1988, when we shared a vision of what the embryonic disaster recovery industry could become. I suspect that for both of us it has exceeded our expectations and this has much to do with changes we both strongly promoted. In particular the change of emphasis from IT disaster recovery to full business continuity in the early 1990s was crucial to its development. Along that route the Business Continuity Institute was formed in 1994 and has gone from strength to strength. From a small UK-based group of mainly consultants it is now a serious world name in business continuity. With nearly 4000 members in over 80 countries and a growing list of international chapters and forums, the BCI is increasingly being seen as a leading voice in world business continuity.

The Institute provides an internationally recognized certification scheme for business continuity professionals and all of its professional members will have undergone a rigorous admissions process to ensure they are highly competent in their areas of expertise.

Many of the contributors to this book are fellows or members of the BCI and the experience and wisdom they can bring to the subject is immense. The Business Continuity Institute is delighted to support it and suggest it is a book that no BCM professional, practitioner, consultant or vendor can afford to ignore.

Preface

David Honour

David is editor of http://www.continuitycentral.com, the global news, jobs and information portal for the business continuity profession.

The business continuity profession has come a long way since the first edition of *The Definitive Handbook of Business Continuity Management* was first published in 1999. Incidents, disasters and potential disasters have highlighted the need for business continuity. Defining events included:

- The 'Millennium Bug'
- Terrorist attacks in the United States (11 September 2001), in Madrid (March 2004), in London (7 July 2005) and in Mumbai (July 2006)
- The Buncefield industrial disaster (December 2005)
- Hurricanes Katrina and Rita during the 2005 Atlantic Hurricane Season
- The wide-area East Coast US, London and European power outages in 2003
- The SARS communicable disease outbreak in 2003.

These and many more incidents brought business continuity management to the attention of governments, regulators, analysts and boards. Business continuity, once a subject confined to the IT department, has now come of age as a management discipline that is taken seriously across all industry sectors as well as in central and local government around the world.

As well as awareness of business continuity increasing, the profession itself has changed. Business continuity has migrated to the boardroom with more forward thinking enterprises recognizing that business continuity commitment must start at the very top of the company. Boards set the direction and business continuity managers pick up the reins.

The need for an integrated approach to business continuity management has also been recognized. All business units or public sector departments need to make business continuity arrangements and these must be coordinated by a central management team to ensure consistency, integration, economies of scale and general efficiency. There is no room for a 'silo' approach in today's profession. Business continuity cannot be effective if different business units and departments simply 'do their own thing' without reference to each other and to the wider business. To do so not only risks the company spending much more than is necessary on business continuity, but also means that some threats and dependencies may go unnoticed.

Technology changes have advanced at incredible speed in the period since the first edition of this book. What was state of the art in 1999 is now confined to the dustbin of history. The communications revolution, led by the Internet and mobile communications technologies, has led to whole new ways of protecting businesses, as well as creating new single points of failure and new dependencies. The exponential growth in data produced and stored by businesses, as well as hand-in-hand growth in regulatory compliance which expects data to be stored for many years, has led to innovations in both online and offline data storage. New compression techniques and advances in storage management have added to the momentum in this area. And now companies are turning their gaze towards virtualization as the enabler of new and smarter IT continuity and disaster recovery solutions.

Finally, perhaps the most significant change that has taken place is the development of business continuity standards. In 1999, standards simply did not exist. *The Definitive Handbook of Business Continuity Management* was the first step in this process, providing the first comprehensive attempt to comprehensively capture thinking on business continuity best practices and to present a structured and practical resource for business continuity managers. Since then, formal standards have been introduced in the United States, Australia, Singapore and in the United Kingdom. An ISO international business continuity standard is also in the pipeline. This is expected to be available sometime before the end of 2009.

These standards are important for a variety of reasons:

- They establish an understanding of what business continuity management is and how a company should set about developing an effective business continuity plan.
- They allow the introduction of formal measurement schemes within organizations to help ensure the ongoing improvement of business continuity programmes.
- They allow internal and external benchmarking; allowing companies to assess how well they are doing when compared with their peers, and facilitating a general, if gradual, improvement in the quality of business continuity management across whole industry sectors.
- They are a concrete demonstration that business continuity has come of age and is accepted by the wider business community.

This new edition of *The Definitive Handbook of Business Continuity Management* will start where these standards finish. It will build upon the frameworks they have established to provide the most comprehensive and useful guide yet to the practicalities of business continuity management.

Introduction

Andrew Hiles FBCI – UK

Andrew is a Director of Kingswell International Limited, a global consultancy in all aspects of business risk management.

The past – and future

'Welcome to what we believe to be the most authoritative work on Business Continuity Planning yet produced.' These were the opening words to the introduction to the first edition of this book, written in 1999. But time changes, and things move on. Go back to 1989 and talk was about (IT) disaster recovery – restoration of IT operations after a hiatus. In 1999, the scope had widened to business continuity – ensuring mission-critical activities continued, without a (significant) break. Now, the focus is on a holistic approach to risk: enterprise risk management, encompassing all aspects of risk including supply chain issues. Dynamic, stakeholder-oriented companies are looking not just at alternative sites, but also at in-depth resilience and at in-state, out-of-state and out-of-continent solutions. Multinationals are seeking the same quality of business continuity wherever they operate – a challenge to the infrastructure of some emerging nations.

This new edition aims to reflect the changes in the range and level of threats and approaches to them. Some principles of continuity management do not change: but practices do.

Reaction time has shrunk: the growth of contact centres and Internet-based businesses means failure is immediately visible to the world at large. Reporting of failure or incident is instant and global. There is an ever-increasing dependence on fewer, larger, vendors. Just-in-time can too often be just-too-late. Outsourcing presents its own challenges: over 50% of outsourcing fails and over 50% of failures are resolved by changing the vendor. Visibility may be outsourced, but often risk cannot be. Technology platforms are ever more diverse and complex. Compliance requirements are ever more demanding – and sometimes seem in conflict.

Over the last few years, it seems disasters have intensified both in the number of incidents and in the number of organizations and people impacted. Deliberate acts, exemplified by the 7 August 1998 terrorist bombing that destroyed the American Embassy in Nairobi, killing and injuring thousands of people as well as damaging adjacent buildings, including the head offices of one of Kenya's biggest banks. Worse was to follow:

- The horror of 9/11 (2001) in the United States
- The Bali, Indonesia, bombing on 12 October 2002 that killed 202 people and injured a further 209 – followed by a less damaging bombing just three years later
- The Madrid, Spain, bombings in March 2004 that killed some 182 people and impacted the results of the election
- The 7/7 (2006) Underground rail bombings in London, UK
- The death of 180 people in the 11 July 2006 bombing of seven commuter trains in Mumbai, India.

The list goes on. The only common factor among these seemingly indiscriminate bombings is the courage and resilience shown by the victims, their families, their cities and their countries.

Natural or accidental disasters worldwide have also emphasized the truly international impact of apparently local disasters. The explosions at a petroleum storage depot at Buncefield, near London, UK, on 11 December 2005 created the biggest explosion and the biggest fire in Europe since the Second World War. It destroyed 5% of the UK's petrol stocks and impacted 600 businesses – 25 000 employees – though fortunately causing no deaths. Since the depot supplied London Heathrow airport, it caused havoc to international flight schedules.

Dependence on utilities is sometimes misplaced. The lights went out in Auckland, New Zealand, on 20 February 1998 when the cables supplying power from a hydroelectric plant to the city failed. Two thousand businesses were fighting to survive after weeks without power. Auckland University and the city's polytechnic told 24 000 students and staff to stay away. Port of Auckland authorities turned away ships and diverted thousands of refrigerated containers with perishable exports to other ports. Power was not fully restored until 27 March 1998. Maybe Auckland is simply unlucky. Failure of a 110 kV power line in Auckland on 12 June 2006 exposed the still fragile power grid, left 750 000 people without power and cost business an estimated $70 million in lost trade, according to the Employers and Manufacturers Association (Northern). But power failure can happen anywhere. On 14 August 2003 there was a wide-area power failure in the north-eastern USA and central Canada, affecting 50 million people – 'The Great American Blackout', while on 4 September 2004, Hurricane Frances was to blame for loss of power to five million people in Florida.

Equally, natural disasters seem to have grown in scale. Earthquakes in Turkey in August 1999 killed 2000 people and disrupted communications to and from the Middle East, while the earthquake on 8 October 2005 in the Kashmir region on the Indian–Pakistan border affected at least 5 million people and left some 87 000 dead and more than 3 million without homes. In the tsunami of 26 December 2004 some 300 000 souls died. In August 2005, Hurricane Katrina caused perhaps the biggest evacuation seen in the world in peacetime. The hurricane affected some 485 000 within New Orleans city and some 1.4 million in its greater metropolitan area. Damage ran to billions of dollars – much of it uninsured.

In the first edition of this book, we cited a number of examples of communications issues, still valid seven years later. During dramatic Chicago floods, the occupants of the upper floors of an office tower were working away unaware that lower floors were being evacuated – until advised by their London office! Terrorist explosions in London affected the international operations of some of the organizations situated in the area. A few years ago telecommunications downtime in the USA caused problems for the US subsidiaries of overseas companies.

The shortcomings in corporate governance highlighted the spate of legislation on corporate governance arising from growing requirements for corporate risk assessment and the protection of stakeholders' interests, especially following the Enron, WorldCom and similar financial scandals. Relevant international regulations include the Basel II requirements for financial institutions and International Accounting Standards (IAS). In the United States, the Food and Drugs Administration imposes requirements for traceability while in Europe Hazard Analysis Critical Control Point (HACCP) regulations require risk assessment from field to fork. Other requirements arise from the United States Health Insurance Portability and Accountability Act (HIPPA) of 1996, which requires protection of data. Requirements are also imposed in the United States by the United States Federal Reserve, Gramm-Leach-Bliley and the Sarbanes-Oxley Act and in the United Kingdom under the Combined Code, compliance with which is required for listing on the London Stock Exchange. Equally, insurance companies and customers are increasingly cynical about 'force majeure' clauses, considering that business continuity should be in place and that very few events are, in fact, totally outside the control of the claimant.

Theft is ever with us, and theft of data can cause major problems. SafeWare, a computer insurer, estimates that a computer is stolen in North America every 30 seconds. The cumulative cost totals $1.4 billion per year. More importantly, the value of the data on the units that go missing every year is estimated at $15 billion. One estimate states that more than 50% of computer thefts involve employees. Estimates are that 4 to 7% of computer thefts are committed by industrial spies, and that the units are stolen primarily for their data.

The business continuity industry has come of age, and increasingly organizations have been demanding a clear demonstration of the competence of its practitioners, expressed in professional memberships and qualifications. The editor was founding director of the Business Continuity Institute (BCI), formed in 1994 as a professional body for BC practitioners. The BCI worked with the Disaster Recovery Institute International (DRII) to create a common body of knowledge: 10 core competencies applied worldwide. Other organizations related to risk and continuity management include the International Risk Management Institute (IRMI) founded in Dallas in 1978 with an initial focus on insurance risk; the Association of Contingency Planners (ACP) initiated in California in 1983; as well as numerous local not-for-profit groups around the world.

The demand for more professionalism among practitioners saw a parallel demand for common standards for business continuity management. The Information Security standard ISO 17799 (the basis for ISO 27000) provided support for business continuity. In the United States National Fire Protection Association (NFPA) 1600 was first introduced in 2003. Similar initiatives were developed in other countries: for instance, in Australia 2004 saw the release of the Australian Prudential Regulation Authority (APRA) draft Prudential Standard on business continuity management for authorized deposit-taking institutions, general insurers and life insurance companies. APS 232 is now a mandatory requirement, while Australian Standard AS 4360 *Risk management* claims to be 'the international leader in providing generic guidance for every enterprise, large or small, public or private'.

The DRII/BCI common body of knowledge formed the basis of the BCI/British Standards Institution (BSI) Publicly Available Specification 56, providing guidelines for good BC practice. These guidelines in turn evolved into the BSI 25999 Standard for Business Continuity, set to become an international standard.

Equally, standards are being applied to vendors. The Business Continuity and Disaster Recovery Standard for Singapore was launched in 2004.

At the time of writing, there are over 50 international or national regulations, standards and guidelines relating to risk management and business continuity and dozens more relating to industry-specific risks.

The authors have helped to write or influence many of these. This book documents the skills of leading practitioners and helps to make those skills available to the widest possible audience.

The authors' experience of business continuity planning totals some 500 years and each of them is a distinguished authority on the subject. Increasingly business continuity planning is a global issue calling for global solutions. The author list also is truly international in its expertise.

For those of you new to the subject, their expertise is now yours. For those who are more experienced, we hope and expect that you will gain from the latest thinking, and challenging ideas presented to you.

An introduction to business continuity planning

Andrew Hiles FBCI

This introduction provides an overview of business continuity planning and subsequent chapters deal with specific topics in depth.

What is business continuity planning all about? Fundamentally, it seeks to mitigate the impact of a disaster by ensuring alternative mission-critical capability is available when disaster strikes. Business continuity planning seeks to preserve the assets of an organization in the event of a disaster: its capability to achieve its mission; its operational capability; its reputation and image; its customer base and market share; its profitability.

Most organizations are totally reliant on just a few key facilities: a head office building . . . a sophisticated production plant . . . a computer or telecommunications room . . . a contact centre . . . a website . . . enterprise resource management, workflow management, customer relationship management or supply chain management software or financial systems . . . they simply cannot operate without them.

All too often computers are the focus of disaster recovery planning – but it is no use recovering a stock control system if the warehouse has been destroyed, and it is no use catering for hardware failure if software problems deny access to electronic point of sale systems and close shops down. IT recovery remains important, but the growth of powerful PCs and distributed servers has simply complicated the issues. It has led to a situation where, in many organizations, deployment of additional equipment has been a reaction to an immediate capacity problem rather than a carefully planned strategy to improve resilience; where the real location of data is unclear; and where applications are so tightly integrated that it is extremely difficult to prioritize in a recovery situation. In some cases, loss of a single PC has caused bankruptcy.

While commercial recovery services are available for computing and administrative work positions, there are virtually no parallel services for warehouse or production facilities.

Business continuity planning requires a structured, methodical and comprehensive approach.

Buy-in is critical – from the most senior level possible. Awareness needs to be raised and commitment sought from all those likely to be involved in developing procedures or participating as team members. Senior managers need to allocate appropriate priority to the project – otherwise, the project will develop its own specific gravity: it will never rise to the top of the priority list, and never quite sink completely! Day-to-day business pressures have a habit of taking over and the project may never be completed. Realistic scope and deadlines are essential.

So, the project needs to be scoped. Is it to be a full crisis management plan, covering reputation management, together with contingency plans such as product recall, hostage, extortion, kidnap, attack on branches? Is it to cover all branches, or just the top 10? Is it to cover all customers, or just the 20% who generate the 80% of profit? Is it to cover all sites, or just head office? Is it intended to cover a local disaster, or a wide area disaster such as earthquake, floods or hurricanes?

Next we need to identify and validate the assumptions that are being made. For instance, do we assume our own skilled personnel are going to be available in a disaster? Many plans, perhaps a little rashly, assume this will be so. But if we do not assume our skilled staff will be available, many more detailed procedures will be required – the resulting plans will be a lot thicker and heavier!

Having scoped the plan and defined assumptions, we can develop the project plan. Business continuity planning is initially a project and needs to be handled with appropriate project disciplines until the project is signed off into the maintenance phase. It then becomes an ongoing programme.

A risk review will identify the key threats to a specific organization and the likelihood of them occurring. A critical component failure analysis will define where resilience is weak. Recommendations for reducing risk may result.

Sometimes the risk analysis will identify issues of information security and integrity. The reliability of management information is a key factor to business success: often, material errors exist and information integrity is compromized without the organization being aware of it. A review of information security procedures against international codes of practice can protect companies from major financial loss, especially when it comes to electronic trading opportunities.

Sometimes risk can be substantially reduced just by taking procedural action. In other cases, risk reduction may simply be included as a consideration in the capital programme. As the plant and infrastructure require renewal, it may be appropriate to reduce risk – often at little or no additional cost – for instance, by buying two lower capacity pieces of equipment rather than one high capacity item.

An insurance review may also be undertaken to establish areas which are, and which are not, covered. Insurance, however, does not buy back the business: it only provides money. And in some cases, the money comes later rather than sooner, with adverse implications for cashflow. We find that, for a variety of reasons, insurance typically only covers about 60% of the actual loss. Moreover, business interruption and loss of profits insurance eventually stops. Depending on your cover, this could be after six months.

In order fully to understand the impact of loss of service, a business impact analysis can be undertaken. This establishes what are the mission critical activities and, in cash and non-cash terms, their value to the business. It also identifies the time window in which recovery has to take place before loss becomes unsustainable (the recovery time objective).

The business impact analysis and risk analysis together provide an understanding of:

- The mission critical activities and assets of the business
- Crucial dependencies (including people, resources, skills and knowledge)
- The potential loss, in cash and non-cash terms (including loss of reputation and brand value)
- The time window in which recovery has to take place before losses become unsustainable (the recovery time objective)
- The point in time to which transactions or data has to be restored (recovery point objective)
- The extent to which the organization is prepared to tolerate risk (risk appetite)
- The documents and other materials that are vital to effective recovery.

Conducting a gap analysis by comparing the results of the business impact assessment with the results of the risk assessment may reveal a shortfall in capability. For instance, a four-hour recovery may be required, but maintenance contracts only require the maintenance vendor to be on site (not necessarily to fix the equipment) within four hours.

A full understanding of risks and impact will help in defining business continuity strategy and may result in changes to the scope of the business continuity plan. For instance, should the plan also cover critical research or development work?

During the business impact analysis we may also conduct a preliminary resource requirements analysis, which establishes when standby facilities and items of equipment are required, and in what timeframe, following the disaster.

The risk and impact analysis, together with the resource requirements, help to identify and justify an appropriate business continuity strategy. This strategy may be a 'mix and match' of various options, for instance:

- A 'bunker' approach, seeking to strengthen facilities to make them less vulnerable
- Business process re-engineering or process improvement, to reduce risks or to make the organization more resilient
- Increased replication and resilience that provides alternate capacity and capability in the event that the primary facility is lost
- Standby site and facilities, either in-company or from a commercial vendor, ranging from immediate availability ('hot') to longer term ('cold')
- Quick resupply of equipment
- Working from home

- Maintaining buffer stocks to cover the period during which production is lost
- Outsourcing or buying in goods or services normally produced in-company
- Insurance.

Basically, the quicker and bigger the restart capability, the more expensive it is likely to be in terms of capital or annual cost, or both. The cost of the recovery option has to be weighed against the impact of loss of service on the business.

Whatever the strategic option(s) selected, the business continuity plan is likely to comprise several elements:

- Immediate reaction procedures (incident management, disaster declaration, evacuation, damage assessment and limitation)
- Provision of emergency facility
- Resumption of business production under emergency arrangements
- Restoration of the permanent facility.

One of the key factors in determining whether an organization recovers from a disaster is the effectiveness of its backup arrangements – regular, off-site backup is essential for effective recovery. Frequently vital paper documentation is not backed up. The solution may lie in business process re-engineering, to computerize some of the paper-based operations so they can be backed up, or using a fire-protected and waterproof vault. A questionnaire may be designed to establish which documents are vital to organizational survival. Wherever practical, this questionnaire should comply with ISO 15489–52003 Records Management Standard. Other standards that influence how organizations manage information and records include the US Department of Defense's 5015.2 and MoReq. The MoReq Specification is a model specification of requirements for electronic records management systems (ERMS). This was produced by the European Commission and was designed to be easily used and to be applicable throughout Europe.

Equally, there may be other vital materials that should be replicated off-site – for instance, tools, jigs, patterns or samples.

Backlog management is also an important consideration: the longer the period of unavailability and the higher the transaction level, the greater is the possibility of accumulating an irretrievable backlog. Backlog planning and management are therefore vital to recovery. Sometimes more capacity is needed after a disaster – too often the assumption is that less capacity will do.

Often there are constraints on what the victim of the disaster is able to do. These may be because of legal or compliance requirements, or because of conditions imposed by emergency services, local authorities, the landlord or insurer. Such constraints need to be considered and factored into the plan.

A company can still go bankrupt following a successful recovery – if customers, stakeholders and influencers think the recovery has been a failure. Media and reputation management therefore plays a vital role in the business continuity plan.

Plans must be tested – and the more defects that are discovered, the better the test! Most plans 'fail' when first tested – there is always something that has not been considered. An effective testing programme therefore needs to be put in place, both to improve the plan and to exercise team members in their roles. Plan tests could include 'desktop tests', walkthrough and role-playing rehearsals against a scenario. Testing should be conducted to verify the effectiveness of each component of the plan, and to check that all dependencies have been covered. Exercise is also required so that BC team members can practise their functions under simulated disaster conditions. However, it is important not to be overambitious – the business must be protected during testing. Testing the business continuity plan should not cause the disaster! A review after each test will provide valuable feedback to improve the plan.

Whenever there is any change – in business emphasis, new products or services; in organization; in locations; in key personnel – its impact on the plan should be assessed and the plan updated if necessary. It pays to be prepared. Disaster can strike in any form, at any time. No organization is immune from a disaster – not even the best-run ones. But experience has shown that those with effective recovery plans are likely to survive, while those without do not.

How to use this book

Andrew Hiles FBCI – UK

This book is divided into the following parts:

Section One provides an executive overview of some of the strategic issues pertinent to business continuity planning and management.

Section Two covers planning for business continuity. It broadly follows the ten core competencies of business continuity – the common body of knowledge agreed by the Business Continuity Institute and the Disaster Recovery Institute International that form the foundations of effective business continuity planning and management. These form the basis for British Standards Institution BSI 25999 that is mooted to become an international standard for business continuity management.

Appendix 1 provides case studies. Some of these cases are industry classics, some are more recent. What they all have in common is lessons for us now, and in the future. The saddest thing about business continuity is that so few organizations learn from other organizations' mistakes and experiences. To quote just one example: the lessons of the UK Foot and Mouth epidemic of 1967 were completely ignored in the 2001 outbreak. Please, let us learn from history!

Appendix 2 gives some general guidance on various aspects of business continuity management, some light-hearted – but even they have a serious message.

Appendix 3 outlines certification standards for business continuity practitioners – the common body of knowledge, defining and amplifying the skill sets employed at Section Two.

Appendix 4 places BC in an international context and contains useful international contacts.

The book draws on expertise at the highest level, from practitioners around the world. We welcome their diversity, and the diversity of styles that they use. Each expert places his or her extensive experience openly and freely at your disposal. This volume carries truly international perspectives across all industries and the public sector.

Since each author is writing from their own experience, each chapter provides a self-contained element of the total fund of BC knowledge. Equally, Chapters 6 and 16 summarize recent standards while further practical detail is presented at more length in other chapters. It is inevitable that a degree of replication may take place – this is necessary for each author to put his or her own concepts into the appropriate framework and to present their own perspective. And whenever two experts are gathered together, you probably get three opinions. . . . There are many wrong ways of implementing BCM, and only a few variations on right ways. You may notice some differences of approach between the authors; however, if you follow the advice that most seems to match your situation, you are unlikely to fail.

It is not the sort of book that you necessarily read from beginning to end: it is a 'pick and mix' selection. We suggest you start with Section One, to put BCM into a strategic corporate context. As you move through each of the disciplines and activities outlined at Section Two, you may wish to pause after each chapter and dip into the complementary guideline notes at Appendix 2 and supporting case studies at Appendix 1.

For those of you who are new to BCM, we hope this will provide a fast track to ease the way and speed you to your goal of protecting your organization. For those of you who are more experienced BC practitioners, we hope that at least this book will consolidate your experience, reassure you and confirm your direction – and maybe show you a few new ideas or provide additional justification for your activities.

The ultimate aim for all of us is to create and embed BC and risk management practices in our (or our client's) organizations that mean 'business as usual – no matter what!'

Section One

Achieving and maintaining business continuity:
an executive overview

What are we planning for?

Geert Vancoppenolle – Belgium

1

Geert was formerly head of the Business Continuity Management practice of Accenture in Europe.

Introduction

Imagine that you have been asked to rebuild the business of the company that you work for in the immediate aftermath of a major disaster. Perhaps there has been a serious fire and you cannot make use of the existing IT infrastructure or of any other infrastructure elements within your current premises.

It is your responsibility to ensure that it should be possible to take orders within two hours. Customer deliveries must be possible within five days, except for your two most important customers for which it must be possible to deliver within the same day.

An immediate suggestion is that you will have to source your company's products from alternative plants within your company. These plants are not aware of the situation: moreover they may not have the capacity to modify production to cope with the scenario.

The customers, who are waiting for delivery, will flood you with questions regarding the affirmation of quality, accuracy and punctuality. Those who want to place orders will request guarantees of delivery. In the meantime, a number of suppliers will be waiting to deliver their goods, at the exact location that is unavailable to you.

Are you ready for it?

The example above might be what you are expected to do when your company is involved in a disaster. The event that caused the disaster could be anything: fire,

The Definitive Handbook of Business Continuity Management, Second Edition.
Edited by Andrew Hiles FBCI. © 2007 John Wiley & Sons Ltd.

power failure, unavailability of the IT infrastructure, evacuation of the installation and so on.

How long did it take to build your current business organization, providing customer service as it is doing today? The fact is that you have to plan to avoid or mitigate disasters before the event. Under extreme time pressures and the scrutiny of shareholders you must deal with all this in a crisis situation. I bet you wish you had prepared for this scenario!

This chapter poses the problem: What are we planning for through business continuity management? It not only defines 'disaster', but also explains outcomes and implications to our business organizations. The chapter is composed of four parts. The first part discusses the inherent dependencies and vulnerabilities of our business organizations. The second part discusses how unexpected events can lead to disaster and interrupt our business operations. The third part takes a look at what these disasters can do to our business: the damage, the impact and the business risks from operational interruptions. The last part asks the question about the objective of business continuity management: what should you expect to achieve through your business continuity plan?

Vulnerability of today's business organizations

Business organizations: who should plan for business continuity?

By 'business organizations', we do not only mean commercial organizations that manufacture and sell products or that provide, for instance, financial services. A business organization in this context is any organization that provides services or goods, either to individual customers, to other business organizations, or to the public.

Examples of such business organizations include manufacturers, distribution companies, sales organizations, transport organizations such as railroads or airlines, utility companies such as electricity production and distribution, water, gas and telecommunications, and community services such as tax services, justice, emergency services, government and so on. Although not all these organizations are established to make profit, they all provide some service to somebody else, and have all built an operational structure to enable them to do so. In the context of this chapter, they are all called business organizations.

As all these organizations are equally at risk from the effects of a disaster that interrupts their operations, they should consider business continuity management if they are to optimize their chances of successful resumption of business following an interruption.

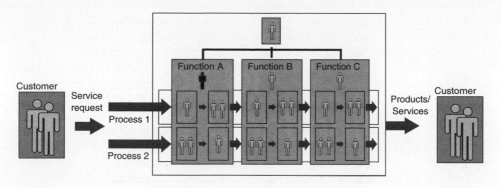

Figure 1.1—The business process

The business organizations of today

Driven by short cycle times, increased pressure to cut costs and to increase efficiency and customer orientation, today's organizations are organized around business processes to a greater extent than ever before. To deliver a product or a service to a customer, a chain of activities has to be performed. This chain of activities is called a business process (see Figure 1.1). Although in many organizations there is still a division into departments with a formal hierarchy, the actual business operations are typically organized and executed across departments, through these business processes, which are driven by information flows.

For the same reasons of efficiency and increased business value, companies are focusing themselves more and more on their activities where they can differentiate themselves in the market. For the other activities required to deliver the product or the service, many companies enter into partnerships with other organizations or outsource some of their activities. This means that the activities executed to deliver a product or a service to the customers extend beyond the boundaries of the company. Considering business processes, we have to look at the 'extended enterprise'.

Integrated organization

Each business organization always consists of three components (see Figure 1.2):

- Business processes – how products or services are delivered to the clients
- Participants – who participate in the execution of the business process
- Infrastructure and resources – used in the execution of the business process.

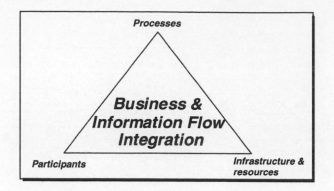

Figure 1.2—Elements of a business organization

These elements of the organization are integrated through information flows. Because of the high level of integration of business operations and information flows, it is difficult to separate any of these elements from the others. It is these elements together that allow an organization to execute its business operations. Also, when you think about how you will bring about the resumption of business after a disaster, you cannot separate any of the elements of the organization from the others. For instance, if you consider only IT, or just a single department, then you will probably not achieve business resumption, because you are overlooking the integration of dependencies throughout the organization.

Business dependencies and vulnerabilities

Each business process depends on a number of critical elements. In a business process a number of persons or departments are involved, who execute one or more activities and pass the resulting information on to the next participant in the business process.

A first dependency is human resources, where a minimum number is required with the appropriate skills and knowledge to be able to execute the business activities. Other dependencies are resources and infrastructure elements. These can be logistical resources, utilities, office infrastructure, manufacturing infrastructure, information technology or financial resources. Examples of logistical resources are loading and stocking areas, transport facilities, weighbridges and so on. The extent to which business operations depend on these critical items means that there is a higher vulnerability to business interruptions. These vulnerabilities include, for instance, single points of failures in the IT architecture and network. When such a component becomes unavailable, many or all of the critical information flows to support business operations are interrupted.

Within each business process, there are a number of key activities. When such key business activities can no longer be executed because of an unexpected event,

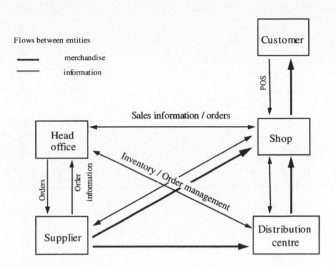

Figure 1.3—Retail replenishment

the result could be an interruption of the business process that is part of the value chain to the customer.

To illustrate this, let's take the example of the replenishment cycle of a super-market chain (Figure 1.3). In this case there is a complex information flow that starts from the POS terminals in the shops. Each shop sends daily information on the local stock levels to the head office. The information from all shops is consolidated and processed to issue orders to the suppliers. A second information flow provides input to the distribution centres, allowing them to plan the distribution to the shops. For each group of products, there are different supply cycles and deadlines within this replenishment cycle.

Continuity of the replenishment depends on this complex activity chain, where there is an integration of information flows and merchandise flows. Throughout the chain, several departments and locations interact on a regular basis. Within the chain, there are a number of subprocesses, each with its own dependencies and vulnerabilities, for example reception and transfer of goods for transport to the stores. The information flows go through a number of servers and networks.

Within business continuity management it is impossible to duplicate every process – this would be too expensive. Nor is it sufficient just to provide backup for one or more elements; as discussed above, due to the interdependencies, this would be insufficient to effectively recover the full process.

To be able to provide continuity of this complex cycle when an unexpected event interrupts the chain, the business continuity plan will have to organize the business process differently by using a limited alternative infrastructure and by temporarily redefining the cycle times and deadlines.

External dependencies

Business organizations are not only dependent on elements within the company. No business organization is an island. Each depends on a number of external resources and outside organizations. These external resources are often beyond its immediate control. Examples are electricity, water, telecommunications and so on. Although your organization cannot control the delivery of these services and therefore cannot prevent interruptions, it is your organization alone that can and will have to manage the impact on your business operations should these external dependencies fail. Likewise, the participants in the business processes are both internal and external to the company. Examples are suppliers, business partners, agents, distributors, banks, factors of invoices, insurers and public authorities.

The business activities that provide customer service extend beyond the company boundaries. The concept of 'extended enterprise' is very applicable. This means – again – that you are dependent on elements that are beyond your immediate control. You will have to handle the consequences to your business when they become unavailable.

These external dependencies are very critical for any company participating in a supply chain (Figure 1.4). These companies are, for instance, particularly dependent on a number of external information flows. Examples are order-entry and delivery notes, reception of invoices, payments to and from the bank, and ability to ship.

Companies are also dependent on the execution of business activities outside their own organization. This is especially true with the increased level of outsourcing and business partnerships. Examples of hi-tech outsourcing include information and communications technology, contact centres, web services and application services. Other services that are frequently outsourced are facilities management, security, cleaning, catering, transport, distribution, packaging, back-office functions and financial services. Although these external companies are responsible for their own business continuity management to resume their business, you are responsible for managing the impact on your business operations of a disaster within these companies.

Disaster can strike, within your organization as well

Unexpected events and incidents can become disasters

When one thinks of disaster, such examples as fire, flood, terrorist action, hurricane and so on immediately come to mind. Although there are regions where some of these threats are more real than elsewhere, the reality shows us that disasters come in a variety of guises. It does not have to be a large-scale event to

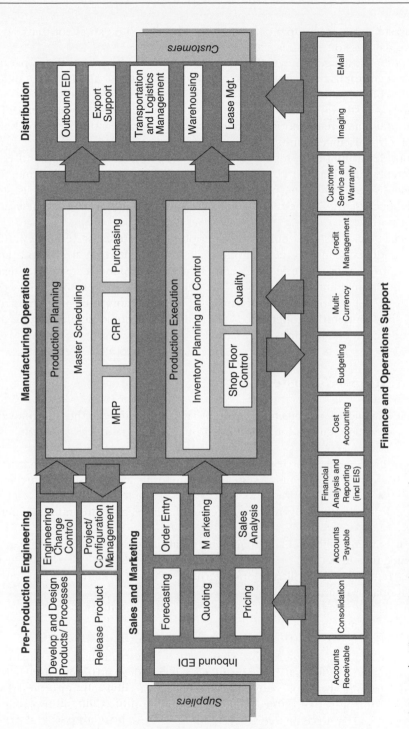

Figure 1.4—The complex business activity chain

mean disaster for your company. Neither does it have to be an event that causes extensive damage to the infrastructure.

Imagine, for instance, an event in your neighbourhood (your industry park or in the city centre) that requires an evacuation of the whole area until the problem is solved, which could be hours or even days. Your computers will still run, your telephones will still ring, and your business infrastructure will be unharmed. But you cannot use it. You cannot answer the telephone. You cannot enter the building. Such circumstances can be disastrous to your business.

Or consider a utilities company that starts a new service. But demand is so unexpectedly high that there is insufficient capacity to support the demand, and the service is reduced to the point of a business interruption. Is this a disaster? Probably, because the image will be damaged such that it will be extremely difficult to restore it.

Even small incidents, over only a short period, can create a disaster if they affect a key dependency. Consider the example of a fish farm, where an electricity failure of very short duration disturbed the temperature of the pools, causing the death or contamination of much of the stock. The effect was the loss of a breeding cycle of three years. Plenty of additional examples of events causing business interruptions can be found in the appendices at the end of this book, demonstrating that disasters do come in all shapes and sizes.

Classification of disasters

A possible classification of business disasters can be according to the type of event. Such classification includes the following groups:

- Acts of nature – e.g. hurricane, flood, etc.
- External man-made events – e.g. terrorism, evacuation, security intrusion, etc.
- Internal unintentional events – e.g. accidental loss of files, computer failure, etc.
- Internal intentional events – e.g. strike, sabotage, data deletion, financial wrong-doing, etc.
- Legal, regulatory, compliance or governance failure, which could be either intentional or unintentional
- Business failure – e.g. caused by inappropriate and unsuccessful business strategies or management.

Such classification has its merits in driving emergency plans and crisis management, where the event itself must be managed in order to protect people and assets, and to mitigate damage. When it comes to business continuity management, where the objective is to resume business operations, a different classification of disasters is more effective.

Some companies ask themselves if they should include the loss of the head office in the scope of the business continuity plan, especially as the probability of the destruction of the head office is considered to be low. Basically, this is the wrong, or at least an incomplete question. Your business continuity management should not be driven by eliminating risks according only to their probability but rather by considering what would be the effect and impact on your business if an unexpected event were to occur, whatever the event. In that sense, for business continuity management as a method of achieving business resumption, potential events and disasters could be better classified according to their business impact.

Such classification according to effect could be:

- Failure of an individual infrastructure element, including single points of failure
- Longer-term interruption of a critical information flow
- Longer-term interruption of a critical business activity chain or business process
- Local longer-term business interruption
- Complete business interruption.

Experience shows that, in many cases, the effect of an unexpected event cascades into larger impact levels. This again underlines why, for business continuity management to be effective, it must be driven in terms of managing the business impact, rather than handling the event. Many examples of this are to be found in the Appendix section of this book.

Disasters do happen

It is still a widespread belief that disasters only happen to others, and that the probability of a disaster is so low that investment in business continuity management cannot be justified with ease. However, statistics show that disasters do happen, and you could be the unfortunate victim today!

In 2004, the Gartner Group determined that the average cost of downtime worldwide was $42000 per hour. They also found that the average network experiences 175 hours of downtime each year. Even if an organization is far below the average downtime and is down for 100 hours in a year, that time would equate to potentially $4200000 in lost revenue.

A research report from the Yankee Group shows that more than half of the questioned companies lost over $1000 per hour because of system downtime. Another 9% indicated that their losses were $50000 or more per hour. Statistics suggest the average downtime event lasts 48 minutes.

And this is just IT.

As organizations have many more key dependencies that are not IT, the probability of business interruptions is in reality much higher. And when your organization is larger, you will have more key dependencies and vulnerabilities, hence it is more probable that your organization will suffer a business interruption at some point in time. Although smaller organizations have fewer dependencies, they are usually more important, hence an occurrence of a disaster here usually has a higher impact.

Another myth is that when a disaster happens, organizations are flexible enough to survive, even without a business continuity plan. On this topic, there is some variance in the statistics. But all mention a figure between 60% and 90% of companies without business continuity plans, and that suffer the loss of a key facility, go to the wall within 24 months of a disaster. And those that do survive typically never reach the same level of business that they would have obtained without the disaster occurring.

The business risks of unexpected events interrupting operations

Consequences of unexpected events interrupting operations

The immediate consequence of an unexpected event is the damage that it generates. This is the area where insurance can assist you in managing a disaster. In terms of business continuity, immediate physical damage is not the most important concern. Of greater importance is the impact on business operations, and how this can be overcome in order to resume the business and survive as a company.

Damage, impact and long-term effects

An unexpected event can cause damage to infrastructure elements and resources supporting business operations. Examples can be buildings, computers, networks, machinery, etc. The damage can be such that the infrastructure element is destroyed or unavailable for an extended period of time.

The direct consequences of such events can be twofold:

- Unavailability of infrastructure elements or resources
- Loss of information.

In terms of Business Continuity Management, it is important to make the distinction between damage caused by the event and the impact on the business because of the unavailability or the loss of information.

Next to the impact on business operations, one must also consider the long-term effects of such unexpected events. These are business impacts that are still felt long after the business has been resumed and operations have returned to normal. Examples are:

- Loss of market share
- Lower share price
- Lower credit rating
- Loss of brand value
- Loss of company image, public confidence and credibility
- Loss of key staff, who may move to competitors.

All these elements must be considered and will drive the business continuity management.

The direct impact: unavailability and loss of information

Alternative business operations

Unavailability of IT infrastructure has always been the focus of the traditional IT disaster recovery planning, which focused mainly on replacement or switching to alternative infrastructure. It is clear that it can rarely be cost justified to duplicate all your resources – priorities must be identified. It is often very difficult to decide how far one should go in these arrangements.

As it is rarely possible to duplicate the complete business infrastructure after a disaster, business operations will have to be organized with only limited infrastructure available. Executing the most critical business activities with this limited infrastructure and personnel is one of the fundamental challenges of business continuity management.

Very probably, given the limited infrastructure and resources, the information flows and the business operations will have to be reorganized in order to meet the business objectives at a minimum acceptable level.

Loss of information

After a disaster, one will typically restart from the last available backups (which have hopefully been stored off-site!) (see Figure 1.5). If you can restart from backups (many do not), this means that all transactions that had been entered

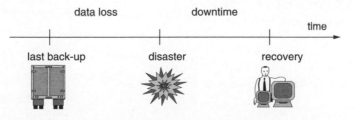

Figure 1.5—Typical IT recovery cycle

since the backups were taken will not be on the system after the restore. This information may well be lost. Also one must consider the synchronization of the data restored from different backups taken at different times. For instance, the backup of orders entered can be taken later than the backup of the financial systems, including the accounts receivable. It is as if your organization has gone back in time, but each system to a different time zone, and you have to match between time zones.

In addition to the time mismatch, the business events associated with the lost transactions will have been executed. For instance:

- Invoices will have been sent out
- Orders will have been received
- Goods will have been manufactured, lost or shipped
- Payments will have been made.

All this, but there may not be a trace of these events in the information systems. Even now, most organizations do not back up data in real time. Typically, there will be a periodic full image backup, followed by incremental backups of just the changed data. The changed data then needs to be applied to the last full image backup as part of the recovery process. Perhaps some of this information will be contained in incremental backups. But even with data mirroring, there will still be paper transactions that have not been entered in IT systems.

Thus a recovery point objective needs to be established – that is, the time to which data must be restored (e.g. start of day, end of day or some timed check-points throughout the day).

When analysing the impact of information loss, one must consider how that lost information can be retrieved:

- Would you be able to reconstitute this information within your organization (the paper audit trail could be burnt in the fire), or will you have to ask your customers, suppliers, trading partners and banks for assistance?
- How will that affect your reputation?
- How much effort will this information retrieval entail?
- In the meantime, can you continue your business operations?
- How can you integrate the retrieved information in your information systems, without re-executing the associated business events?
- Can you guarantee the integrity and completeness of the retrieved information?

Consider, for instance, an air cargo company. Consignments are tracked by a computer system. Restarting after a disaster from the last backup, in the worst case 24 hours old, means that information on all consignment movements in the last 24 hours would be lost. On top of that there may be no way of knowing from internal sources which consignments had been transported in that timeframe: loss of the systems might not cause the physical movement of consignments to stop. The company either has to recompose all transactions by manually collecting information from its worldwide agents and partners (nearly impossible to achieve completeness), or it has to perform a total inventory of all its warehouses and stop business operations until completion of the inventory.

Loss of information due to a disaster is not limited to data on computers. What about all the information stored in binders, folders (with, for instance, customer information), contracts, property deeds, the archives, the legally required vital records, the paper client files, the business knowledge spread over the place, etc. Depending on the event, part of this information can be lost too. You must also consider the potential impact on your business of losing this information.

The indirect impact: rippling effects on business operations

Each business process consists of a chain of activities that are executed typically by different departments. An unexpected event can interrupt a business activity, and/or interrupt an information flow supporting a business process. If the event is such that the business activity (or several activities) can no longer be executed, the impact could stretch out towards the entire business process.

Consider, for instance, in the process of handling requests for loans, that the business activity of checking the credit position of the requester can no longer be executed. Either the loan is granted without the credit verification, which creates a financial risk, or the entire business process is halted, which will increase the risk of losing business opportunities (the customer will go elsewhere). The business impact of unavailability of key supporting infrastructure or resources can have chain effects throughout the process and even on other business processes. An example is the case of a distribution environment, where the goods tracking is done through bar codes. If the scanning of incoming goods is not possible for a certain period of time, there will be an impact on the full process. Either the process of transfer of incoming and outgoing goods is continued, with risk of losing track of goods, or the goods transfer process is stopped, with all the consequences of shortage of storage capacity for other incoming goods and of not being able to deliver the goods in time. The business impact will largely increase, as soon as external parties become involved. The higher the external visibility of the event, the more considerable and long lasting the business impact will be.

The effect of an unexpected event impacting business operations can easily ripple through the company. Even a relatively small event in an environment where many activities depend on each other can have a tremendous impact. Consider, for instance, the replenishment process for a supermarket chain. A WAN failure at a bad time, which lasts long enough, can in the end create a logistical nightmare, impact customer satisfaction because of empty shelves, and create a large financial impact in an industry where net margins are already slim (Figure 1.6).

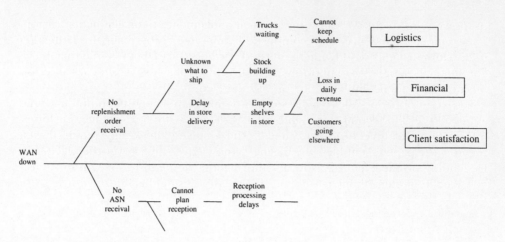

Figure 1.6—Effect diagram

As no organization is an island, the rippling effects of a business interruption can even go beyond the company's boundaries. This is particularly true for companies that are an integral component of a wider supply chain – that is most of us! If, because of a business interruption, you deliver late, your reliability may well be brought into question for a considerable period of time – often well after the actual crisis.

In some cases, when a company participating in a supply chain is hit by a disaster, this could ripple down throughout the supply chain. Each company within the chain will have to deal with the impact of this on its own business operations through its business continuity management.

The long-term impact: image, market position, growth or decline

Even long after you have recovered from a disaster, and have returned to normal business operations, you will feel long-term impact. Depending on how good your business continuity plan has proven to be, you will suffer some long-term impacts that can in the worst case even drive you out of business. These long-term impacts can include:

- Loss of customers
- Weakened financial position (for instance, reduced cash flow)
- Lost market share
- Loss of investor confidence
- Liabilities
- Eroded public image
- Etc.

Your share price is a good indicator of the degree of long-term impact. Typically, shortly after a disaster, as your shareholders learn about the disaster through the media, share price will drop. Depending on how positive the perception is of you coping with the disaster, the share price will rise. Whether it ever reaches the level it would have had without the disaster is a good indication of the long-term impact. This means that it is not only important to have an effective business continuity plan, but also that you must handle the outside world perception of the effectiveness of your plan. You will have to include media management and public relations as an integral component of an overall business continuity management strategy.

The importance of the public image of your company cannot be stressed enough. Even with the most effective and successful business resumption plan, if the public, investors, shareholders and so on get a negative perception, it could ruin all your efforts. Sound communication management, coupled with effective crisis management, is essential for survival beyond a disaster. For a company whose success is heavily dependent on its share price, the above-mentioned effect on share price alone should create a strong justification for investment in business continuity management.

In industries with intense competition, loss of customers or loss of market share might be something you will never recover from. Typically, this will generate a downsizing, and dependent on the flexibility of your organization, can even mean that you are pushed out of the market.

The business risks of an interruption in ICT operations becomes more critical every year. In 2006 Gartner EXP surveyed 1400 CIOs in more than 30 countries, representing more than US$90 billion in IT spending.[1] Marcus Blosch, vice president and research director at Gartner EXP, said:

> The survey results make it very clear that business expectations of IT have changed dramatically and executives are expecting their CIOs to move beyond concerns about cost, security and quality to help grow the business.

An unexpected event interrupting information flows or business operations can be considered a risk to the extent that it would create a material business risk for your company. A business risk is a threat that an event or action will adversely affect your organization's ability to successfully achieve its business objectives and execute its strategies – in other words the achievement of business mission. This implies that you have to look at IT or other business interruptions in the context of the key business risks for your company.

For example, a key business risk in the automotive components industry (and many other manufacturing industries) can be 'not being able to deliver parts where they are needed at the exact time they are needed'. In this industry, price and effectiveness are critical drivers that have enforced short cycle times through integrated logistics. Any disruption in business operations that would result in late

---

[1] *Growing IT's Contribution: The 2006 CIO Agenda*, Gartner EXP 2006.

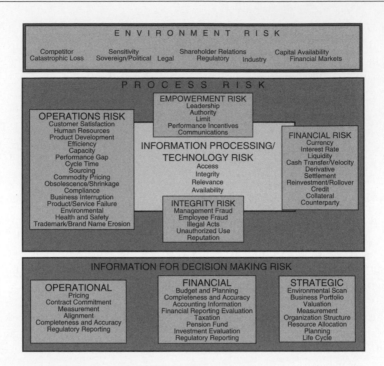

Figure 1.7—The Business Risk Model™. © Accenture

delivery or loss of efficiency is a key risk that subsequently must be covered in business continuity management for such companies.

When going through this exercise, it is important that you use a reference framework of business risks, specific for your business environment. Such a framework allows you not to dwell on symptoms or the obvious, but to focus on what is essential for your business success. An example of such framework is the Business Risk Model™, developed by Accenture for each industry segment (Figure 1.7).

Analysing your key business risks and performing a gap analysis with your current protection will allow you to set priorities. It also allows you to focus your investments towards those areas where you have the most benefit, namely covering the largest business risks for your company of an interruption in business operations.

Risk management: gamble or hedge?

Business continuity management is in the first place more about management of business interruption risks than about shopping around for solutions. The largest

✔ Assess risk
✔ Accept or reject risk
✔ Avoid risk, transfer risk or
   reduce risk to acceptable level
✔ Analyse performance gaps
✔ Act to improve

Figure 1.8—'The five As' of risk management

mistake one can make about business continuity management is thinking 'I have a business continuity plan, nothing can happen to me'. Every business continuity management is based on assumptions, and on risk management decisions. These include items such as maximum allowable downtime, disaster scenarios to include single point of failure assumptions, acceptance of certain risks and finding a balance between cost and benefits.

No business continuity management will ever cover all areas and all risks. The target is to cover the business risks that are key for your company, and to cover the business processes that are most critical for your business success. To reach that target, basically each business continuity management exercise is a risk management exercise, which is always based on the 'five As' of risk management (Figure 1.8).

By analysing the business risks of an interruption of business operations and the business impact, decisions can be made with regard to what level of risk can be accepted and what risks must be reduced to an acceptable level through business continuity management. It is important to realize that, when agreeing to accept a risk, this decision also includes acceptance of the consequences in the event that the worst happens.

Before going into defining solutions within a business continuity management, it is important that you do not make assumptions with a 'wet finger' approach. To return to the air cargo example, IT had assumed within its disaster recovery planning that restarting from yesterday's backup would be sufficient. We have discussed before what that meant in terms of loss of information and what would be the business impact.

It is important that risk management decisions are taken on an informed basis. Only in this way can a business continuity strategy be defined that will meet the business requirements and will cover the key risks. This is the difference between hedging and gambling: you gamble when you make assumptions, for instance, purely based on the probability of an event or based on 'gut feeling'. You hedge when you take risk management decisions based on a careful analysis of the business risk, on the potential business impact and on the key dependencies and vulnerabilities in perspective of your business objectives. Hedging is assessing the magnitude of the risks and taking informed and balanced decisions.

Business continuity management is about hedging the business risks of operational interruptions, deriving a business continuity strategy from this that meets the business objectives, and implementing this strategy.

Business continuity: what does survival mean to you?

So, you need business continuity management. It is a question of business survival. You want to manage the risks of a business interruption due to an unexpected event. But your business organization is complex. You cannot duplicate it all; this is just too expensive. Even duplicating only the most critical infrastructure is probably still very expensive and difficult to justify. Besides, what is critical and what is not, and to what level? Not all elements in your business organization are equally critical, yet they are interdependent because they are part of these activity chains.

What do you have to protect your business against? You cannot foresee all possible events. How far do you need to go? Where will you start? More important, where will you stop? How do you identify your priorities? How do you ensure that you invest in the right places? Could it be that you spend more than you should?

Before you actually start your business continuity management project, there is an important question to ask yourself: 'What is your objective, what do you want to obtain from your business continuity management?' At first sight, the answer is obvious: you want to be able to continue doing business after a disaster, to resume business activities and continue to serve your customers.

Consider the approach to business continuity management that you intend to take, and the project organization you intend to establish to build the plan. Compare the focus areas of that approach against what your objectives of business continuity management are.

Considering the different approaches to business continuity management that we see organizations apply, there are basically three kinds of objectives, each matching a different approach:

- Rebuild the infrastructure. Here the focus is on alternative facilities and sites and on solutions to minimize downtime of key infrastructure and systems.
- Resumption of business activities. The focus is on setting up an organization and the required facilities to enable key staff to resume their activities.
- Continuity in customer service at an acceptable level. The focus is on defining what level of customer service must be maintained throughout a disaster, and what is required to achieve that level of customer service.

The following sections discuss each of these objectives and approaches. They describe what are the benefits, what are the outcomes and what are the pitfalls or potential shortcomings of each of these.

Rebuilding the infrastructure

The objective in this approach is to rebuild the critical infrastructure that has been damaged in a disaster. The idea is that as soon as the damaged infrastructure is available again (albeit in a different location), the business activities can be resumed as before because the required infrastructure is the same.

Lists are created of mission critical activities including computer systems, networks, manufacturing infrastructure, contact centres, web services, office space and any other essential infrastructure elements. The selection of these critical infrastructure elements is based on a business impact analysis and a risk analysis. The maximum allowable downtime is defined (maximum acceptable outage and recovery time objective, which are usually the same), when required differentiated per group of infrastructure elements. With this list in hand and the determination of recovery time objective, alternative solutions are considered and a cost/benefit analysis is made. The critical success factor in this approach is to have a sufficient mission critical infrastructure duplicated so that business activities can be resumed in a similar way to how they were executed previously.

Once the solutions are selected, plans must be built to bring them into action. This is the mechanism to switch on these alternative systems and infrastructure elements. Because of cost considerations, we see the list of mission critical infrastructure elements very often trimmed down to the barest essentials (and sometimes less than that), for which the least costly option is chosen.

Although the thinking process in the beginning is business oriented through the business impact analysis, we very often see a too intense focus on systems and office space without sufficient verification as to whether business activities in the end can effectively be resumed. What we also see happen too often is that a reduced version of this approach is chosen to create a feeling of safety. Very often it is only the central IT system and communications that are considered within the scope of business continuity management, the concept being that without this system the company would not be able to survive a disaster. Consequently, the lowest cost options are considered in respect of hot-site or short-term delivery of a replacement system in the mistaken belief that this solution will ensure the company's survival. An example illustrating this is the replenishment cycle mentioned before. The company concerned decided to duplicate, through server mirroring, only the most critical within the chain of systems and networks supporting the replenishment information flow, without considering how the replenishment process would be resumed with only this single server available.

A further problem follows this narrow vision of protection of only the most critical infrastructure elements. This is in the testing component of the process. In many instances, testing focuses on making the alternative infrastructure available but too rarely considers the practical application of mission critical business activities based upon this limited infrastructure. Although the intention is correct, the outcome of this approach is infrastructure replacement, not necessarily business continuity. Relatively few companies can afford such an extensive duplication of infrastructure.

When a disaster does occur, we very often see these limited investments prove to be ineffective in providing business resumption. Stories abound of companies that went bankrupt even though their central computer system was recovered within hours of the disaster.

Resumption of business activities

Having witnessed the pitfalls of a purely infrastructure-oriented approach to business continuity management, many organizations have added the dimension of resumption of business activities to their approach.

Another key driver in the approach focusing on resumption of business activities is the awareness that central systems are only part of the infrastructure supporting the business activities. PC networks and client/server architectures have created critical dependencies throughout the enterprise. In this approach, the activities of the employees are considered. A list is made of what the mission critical activities are and what is required to be able to execute them. Again, a business impact analysis and risk analysis are instrumental in determining the level of criticality of these activities.

The result of this analysis is typically a scheme of what number of staff (and the associated office space and infrastructure) is required by what day after a disaster. The idea is to gradually resume the business activities elsewhere, starting with the most critical ones, until full business resumption or until the return to the old facilities is possible. The benefit of this approach is that it links business activities to required infrastructure, providing a much better guarantee for effective business resumption in the case of a disaster. The critical success factors of this approach are the criteria that are used to prioritize business activities.

The most important pitfall of this approach is that it very easily results in building departmental recovery plans, where each department within the company will build its plan to resume the critical business activities executed within its department but in isolation of the whole. What is missing here is business integration. For instance, one department is dependent on being provided with input from another department to execute one of its key activities. Perhaps the provision of that input is considered non-critical by the provider department but is absolutely crucial to the operation of the receiving department. Very often, departmental recovery plans lack a business process orientation, where business processes cross over a number of departments.

Another pitfall is that the criteria to define business criticality of the activities are not uniform over the departments, and/or are not linked to the business objectives or the key business drivers of the company. We often see business continuity plans using this approach focus much more on the business activities as objectives on their own, instead of focusing on the resumption of the key business activities to enable continuity in service delivery.

Continuity in customer service at an acceptable level

The continuity solution is the preferred (and sometimes the only) option for organizations having high volume, high value, transaction-based activities. Infrastructure replication and resilience is now generally considered essential for banking, dealing and online web-based businesses or contact centres and for telecommunications companies. For compliance reasons, many financial institutions have to follow this route. The more reliant the organization is on its technological infrastructure, the more likely it is that this approach will be followed.

When a CIO of a global bank was asked how they justified the massive spend on infrastructure resilience, he replied: 'It's simply part of the cost of being in business.' On another occasion, a CIO requested a consultant to find an Internet service provider that would guarantee 100% availability and be prepared to pay consequential cost if they failed to do so. 'No ISP will guarantee that,' responded the consultant, 'but why do you need it?' The CIO replied: 'Because we can lose a billion dollars in eight minutes.'

The case for infrastructure resilience can be powerful. Following 9/11, according to Fitch First Database, the Bank of New York lost some $900 million while Citigroup lost around $830 million. The UK Bishopsgate terrorist bomb in 1993 cost various UK banks a total of around $500 million.

For many other organizations, it may not be justifiable to duplicate all critical infrastructure, since that infrastructure alone does not provide business continuity. Moreover, it may be very difficult to obtain integrated business resumption through a mere resumption of individual business activities. In this case it is clear that selections will have to be made about what to replicate and that a structured approach to make these selections is the key to success. Making these selections is essentially business risk management, and is an executive level responsibility. It concerns the management of business interruption risks in the context of reaching the business objectives and safeguarding the key business drivers.

Typical management objectives of business continuity management are to:

● Provide continuity in customer service at a minimum acceptable level
● Limit the impact on the financial position of the company.

Defining what is the minimum level of customer service that is to be maintained throughout a disaster is critical in this approach. This requires a top-down analysis of business drivers and objectives, the key business processes supporting these business drivers and their key dependencies and vulnerabilities. In many cases, this will be determined by contractual commitments and service level agreements.

The goal of the business continuity plan is to build the business operational capability to reach these service levels. These will eventually include provision of alternative key infrastructure, resumption of key business processes and associated business activities, organization measures to execute the business resumption and many more.

Conclusion

Business continuity management is about being able to continue 'without missing a beat' or being prepared to rebuild your business organization after a disaster in order to provide continuity in customer service at a minimum acceptable level, to limit the impact on the financial position, and in the long term to survive as a business organization.

Today's business organizations are driven by business processes, which are chains of activities that are executed across departments. Each organization consists of an integration of business processes, the participants in these processes and the infrastructure and resources supporting these business processes. Within each business process, there are a number of critical dependencies, which can include: human resources, logistical infrastructure, information technology, key activities, and dependencies beyond the organization's boundaries. Unexpected events can at all times interrupt business operations. These do not have to be large-scale events or do not even have to cause extensive damage to mean a disaster to an organization.

Because unexpected events do come in all shapes and sizes, and considering the objective of business continuity management of being able to resume business operations, potential events and disasters can be better classified according to effect, rather than type of event. Statistics show that business interruptions do occur, more frequently than one would expect. They also show that you should be prepared if you want to optimize your chances to stay in business.

The effects of a disaster are not limited to the damage that it causes. They also include the business impact of unavailability and loss of information. The business effects and losses associated with extended interruptions of the critical business activities can be very high. Even after the resumption of business, the impact of a disaster can still be felt through loss of customers, a fall in the share price, and in an erosion of the organization's image, perception and credibility in the marketplace.

An unexpected event interrupting business operations can be considered a risk to the extent that it would materialize a key business risk for the organization. A business risk is a threat that an event or action will adversely affect the organization's ability to successfully achieve its business objectives and execute its strategies.

No business continuity management will ever be able to cover all business areas and all risks. The target is to cover the business risks that are key for your organization, and to cover the business processes that are essential for your business success. To reach that target, basically business continuity management is a business risk management exercise. It is important that risk management decisions are taken on an informed basis. Only in this way can a business continuity strategy be defined that will meet the business requirements and that will cover the key risks.

Business continuity management is about:

- Hedging the business risks of operational interruptions
- Forming a business continuity strategy from this that meets the business objectives
- Implementing this strategy.

Finally, it is very important to define your objective clearly: non-stop operations providing continuity in customer service, rebuilding the infrastructure, resuming business activities all at an acceptable service level. Having defined your objective, you have to apply an approach that meets that objective, and stay focused on that objective, throughout the business continuity management project.

What is a business continuity planning (BCP) strategy?

2

Mike O'Hehir – Australia

Michael O'Hehir was formerly Director, Global Risk Management Solutions, for PricewaterhouseCoopers in Sydney, Australia.

Introduction

The process of business continuity planning can be both time consuming and expensive. As a result, management will expect tangible benefits to be achieved by the process.

Corporate governance is the system in place to balance risk and entrepreneurial energy with appropriate internal control procedures to manage that risk. Directors and management are under increasing pressure to provide assurance on corporate governance standards both to organizational stakeholders and to regulatory authorities and must remain informed of the organization's risks and obligations. They will rely on processes and controls to ensure strategies are implemented to mitigate their exposures.

Business continuity planning defined

BCP may be defined as:

> the identification and protection of critical business processes and resources required to maintain an acceptable level of business, protecting those resources and preparing procedures to ensure the survival of the organization in times of business disruption.[1]

---

[1] *System Management Methodology – Disaster Contingency Planning*, Price Waterhouse, 1992.

The Definitive Handbook of Business Continuity Management, Second Edition.
Edited by Andrew Hiles FBCI. © 2007 John Wiley & Sons Ltd.

What is a BCP strategy?

A business continuity plan is a business management plan rather than a technical plan. Hence, contingency planning is based on the understanding of the organization, the tools that support the operations of the business, evaluating the loss of such tools, knowing who will handle a crisis situation and how they will do that.

It is essential in today's business environment for an organization to consider what should be done if a disaster were to have an impact upon the organization's normal business environment, as a minor, major or catastrophic disaster could bring substantial losses to any business. The issue of disaster recovery and business continuity planning must be addressed through the preparation of a disaster contingency and recovery plan.

The ongoing business is based on the assumption that the improved services, productivity and opportunities for growth provided by the current technology implemented within the organization will not decline. It is therefore important that the dependency of the organization on technology be considered by the organization in identifying the critical portions of the business.

Managers of the business are custodians of the business interests and responsibilities. They must practise good stewardship, which includes operating in a way that preserves profitability, stability and quality and advances the interests of customers, employees and investors. Management cannot be said to be fulfilling this duty if an unplanned event can jeopardize the survival of the organization. In addition, some legal mandates may have been issued, demanding that records of an organization be available at all times, regardless of the situation.

The following risks and issues are raised in the absence of effective BCP:

- Business interruption resulting in inability to serve the current customer base, erosion of customer base, lost opportunities, loss of goodwill and inability to compete
- Financial loss due to inability to process receivables, late payment penalties and missed discounts, inability to update account balances and lost or unrecorded sales
- Legal liability resulting from failure to satisfy contractual obligations
- Going out of business.

Just having addressed the issue of business continuity planning is not enough. A BCP project must involve the entire organization. Time and resources must be provided by management for the development, initial and ongoing testing and ongoing maintenance of the plan. Unless management commitment is displayed, the whole organization is involved and the plan development project is given a high priority, the project is likely to fail.

Disaster contingency plans in the past have generally addressed only computer-related disasters. However, this is too narrow a focus and all of the related activities must be addressed to ensure business continuity, including manual records and information.

Effective risk management and BCP drivers

It must also be decided how large an event the plan is to handle. If the organization is in an area where a regional disaster is likely, for example Southern California, which is subject to earthquakes, or central London, subject to terrorist activities, the plan should incorporate procedures to cope with loss of utilities and other outside services. If the organization is in an area where regional disasters are unlikely, the organization may choose to limit the plan to facility-related disaster planning. When a disaster is limited to a facility, help may be available from suppliers, authorities and the community.

The scope of the business recovery plan within the organization must also be determined. This will depend on the structure of the organization, such as a multiple or a single facility. The most important aspects of a successful approach to business continuity planning are paying attention to detail and addressing small sections at a time.

Objectives of a BCP strategy

The overall objectives of a business continuity project are as follows:

- Establish a framework for evaluating business processes that allows a focused approach to develop a business continuity plan through a well-structured and comprehensive methodology
- Develop a pragmatic, cost-effective and operable recovery plan that enables an organization to complete the critical business processes in the event of a major disruption to its business operations
- Minimize the impact of a disaster on an organization
- Have an effective recovery plan that is a relatively inexpensive form of insurance and a necessary cost of doing business for prudent organizations in today's environment
- Ensure effective risk management and the drivers of BCP: shareholder value, risk, reward and control.

Increasing shareholder value emerged as the key corporate requirement in a study among the *Financial Times* top 500 companies, commissioned by Price Waterhouse and carried out by the Harris Research Centre.

What is a BCP strategy?

Opportunities to enhance shareholder value exist in almost all companies. New tools and methodologies are now available to identify where these opportunities are and how they can be used to achieve sustainable increases in shareholder value. For instance, market analysts and institutional investors are increasingly adopting cashflow valuation approaches in making key investment decisions.

There are two sorts of mistakes a company can make: to destroy value by bad decisions and to miss the opportunity to create value by not making good decisions. While internal control is often better at preventing crisis than in guaranteeing long-run good performance, a balance of driving value and mitigating risks can satisfy shareholders.

Risk and reward

Shareholders understand value – that is, reward. Do they understand risk? Mr Paul Barrett, the Executive Director of the Business Council of Australia, wrote in the July 1995 *Business Council Bulletin* in his paper on corporate governance:

> As shareholders and lenders we entrust our capital to companies and their boards because we seek a higher return than we could achieve from a 'risk free' investment in Commonwealth securities.

This principle has not changed over the years. However, since then we have seen the Combined Code in the UK (a requirement for listing on the London Stock Exchange), Sarbanes-Oxley legislation in the United States and Basel II requirements for risk management in banking and finance. All these require careful evaluation of risk. The guiding principle implies that we expect boards and management to demonstrate entrepreneurship and dynamism, that is, to take risks. But what we also expect is that the risks will be well considered and well managed and that the risk profile of the enterprise will be widely understood.

There is clearly a much greater awareness today of the need to manage both the drivers of risk and the drivers of value.

Risk and control

In the past 20 years the global corporate landscape has been littered with the debris of risks that have gone awry: defaulted real estate loans; unsafe work practices; environmental disasters; failed contracts; millions of dollars of losses from imprudent investments in derivative exotica; Parmalat, WorldCom and Enron; the dot.com bubble; and incidents such as the loss of power to the city of Auckland. The pendulum appears to be swinging towards more control. How much is enough? Too much control will restrict an enterprise; conversely, without appropriate business controls, an organization may be exposed with devastating results.

Paul Barrett also stated:

> The worst possible outcome from the current focus on corporate governance would be if boards and management were to become risk averse.

The need for a structured business risk management process

Complementing the management of shareholder value is the management of risk. Risk management has become a widely used term for a common sense approach to the decision-making process concerning resources to avoid 'intolerable' outcomes. It depends on an assessment of risks and their associated probabilities, which in turn depends on experience, knowledge, value judgements, intuition and attitude to risk.

Risk management is now understood to encompass much more than just insurance. In wider terms, it translates a judgement on whether costs incurred by additional management controls are worth the avoidance of potential losses and costs. In the past risk management has been undertaken on a project basis. However, the combined effect of organizational, commercial and legislative changes means that this approach may no longer be adequate. Moreover, what is adequate to address the risks faced by the business today may not be so tomorrow.

For most organizations the need for a coordinated risk management capability has only become apparent in the past few years, and the techniques to manage this change are still in their infancy. Successful organizations recognize the importance of developing a coordinated risk management programme and acknowledge that risks occur and must be addressed.

Managing the exposures

A research report prepared by PricewaterhouseCoopers for the American Institute of Internal Auditors Research Foundation, titled *Improving Audit Committee Performances: What Works Best*, provides a useful summary of the source of risks:

> Business risks occur because of the volatile environments in which businesses operate and the nature of their operations.

Risks are diverse and arise from both external and internal sources. The research report cites external risks as including 'such matters as the state of the economy, or of the company's industry, and the legal and regulatory environment'. Internal risks include 'such factors as the nature of the company's operations and products, the control environment within the company (tone at the top), the adequacy of control systems, the financial strength or weakness of the company, the quality of the organization's accounting policies and procedures, and the quality of management'.

The multitude of risk areas where active risk management is necessary is illustrated in Figure 2.1.

The challenge is to control risk within acceptable limits without constraining operational effectiveness, business development opportunities or entrepreneurial spirit.

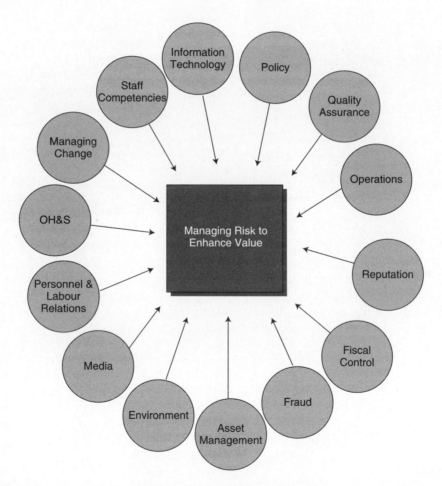

Figure 2.1—Areas where active risk management is necessary

What is management control?

The elements of management control are as follows. The control environment provides an atmosphere in which people conduct their activities and carry out their control responsibilities. IT serves as the foundation for the other components. Within this environment, management assesses risks to the achievement of specified objectives. Control activities are implemented to help ensure that management directives to address the risks are carried out. Meanwhile, relevant information is captured and communicated throughout the organization. The entire process is monitored and modified as conditions warrant.

Management control is thus the process of establishing controls to mitigate business risks.

The key elements of risk management comprise:

- The attitudes and attributes of the board or CEO (the 'tone at the top'), which establish the overall risk appetite and the risk control environment
- Analysis of external and internal risks, which potentially affect the achievement of objectives
- The controls established throughout an organization to mitigate risk
- The monitoring process, both in respect of the controls and the control system itself, which ensures that the system remains effective and dynamic.

These are demonstrated in Figure 2.2, which integrates risk management into the overall management process.

Classification of risk

Risk management has moved up the corporate management agenda. A growing multiplicity of business risks pushes multinationals to find more comprehensive approaches to managing them.

But what is business risk? Risk is a matter of perspective. Finance and operational managers, institutional and speculative investors, all see risk differently. It can mean any impediment, inside or outside the organization, to meeting business objectives. One report concludes: 'Business risk arises as much from the likelihood that something good won't happen as it does from the threat that something bad will happen.'[2]

The population of risks that an organization is exposed to can be divided into five core groups (Figure 2.3). These can be used as a starting point and over the course of the risk management measurement process should be further developed.

[2] *CFO-Architect of the Corporation's Future*, Price Waterhouse Financial and Cost Management Team, Wiley, 1997.

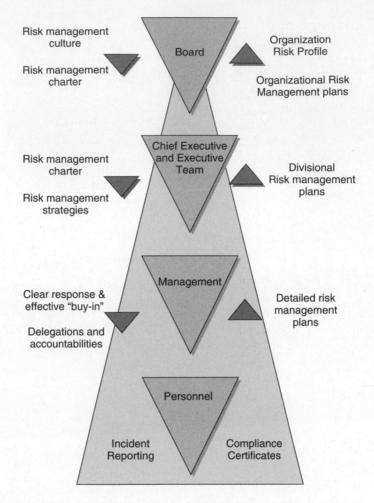

Figure 2.2—Risk management key roles and components

- **Strategic:** the risk of plans failing or succeeding
- **Financial:** the risk of financial controls failing or succeeding
- **Operational:** the risk of human error or achievement
- **Commercial:** the risk of relationships failing or succeeding
- **Technical:** the risk of physical assets failing/being damaged or enhanced.

Risk groups are not mutually exclusive. For example, human factors – prime drivers of operational risks – are significant in many strategic and financial risks. Also, companies carry their histories with them: a business may have accumulated liabilities or assets, bad or good practices, weak or strong relationships. Consider how past risks influence current exposures – and how risks of all types affect

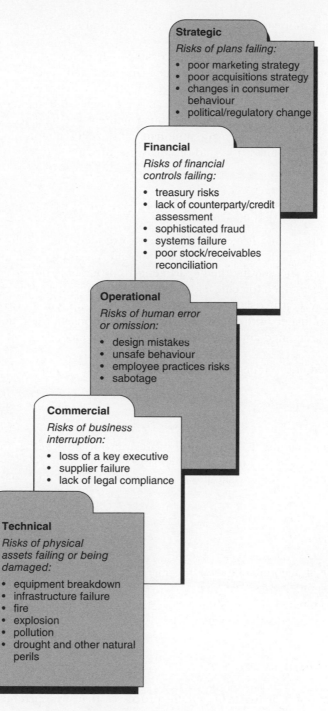

Strategic

Risks of plans failing:

- poor marketing strategy
- poor acquisitions strategy
- changes in consumer behaviour
- political/regulatory change

Financial

Risks of financial controls failing:

- treasury risks
- lack of counterparty/credit assessment
- sophisticated fraud
- systems failure
- poor stock/receivables reconciliation

Operational

Risks of human error or omission:

- design mistakes
- unsafe behaviour
- employee practices risks
- sabotage

Commercial

Risks of business interruption:

- loss of a key executive
- supplier failure
- lack of legal compliance

Technical

Risks of physical assets failing or being damaged:

- equipment breakdown
- infrastructure failure
- fire
- explosion
- pollution
- drought and other natural perils

Figure 2.3—Five core groups of risk

strategic direction and, ultimately, the company's ability to generate shareholder value in the future.

Until recently, companies managed risks largely in terms of possible solutions. An insurable risk might be the insurance manager's responsibility. If a risk seemed a financial control matter, the treasurer might deal with it. Risks touching on consumer relations might be managed as part of sales and marketing.

Today, functionally segregating risk management seems dated. The CFOs and other senior executives of many multinationals are learning to take a more integrated view of business risks and business risk management.

Management response to the risk profile

Management action will need to be taken to reduce the risk levels where they have been deemed unacceptably high, or alternatively to remove constraints where they are preventing the department from pursuing opportunities. Management responses need to be developed to improve the current processes and close the gap between the risk profile and the company's 'appetite for risk'. This action will be formulated into a risk management response in a framework, which ensures a disciplined approach to the future management of the risk as outlined below.

Embedded in the framework are some key issues as follows:

Policy

- A policy statement, authorized at an appropriate level, should codify the company's attitude to a particular risk.
- This policy statement should also prescribe the objectives of the company's risk response.

Accountability

- Individual accountability for the management of the risk should be clearly established.
- The nominated person should have the appropriate technical expertise and authority to effectively manage the risk.

Current business process

- A description of the management processes that are currently employed to manage the risk.

Future actions

- Recommended business processes that are to be implemented or refined to reduce the residual risk to an acceptable level.
- Responsibility and milestones are assigned.

Performance measures

- Key measures used by management to enable them to assess and monitor the effectiveness of the risk.
- The measures may be proactive or reactive. Proactive measures are best, as they tend to monitor risk preventive actions rather than risk detective actions.

Independent expert

- If appropriate, a suitably qualified independent expert (internal or external) assesses the adequacy of the risk response.
- The frequency of the review will depend upon the nature of the risk.

Contingency plan

- If appropriate, develop plans to manage or mitigate a major loss following the occurrence of an event.

BCP strategies for managing risk

The BCP process is as important as the plan itself

The process of building a business case for implementing business recovery plans is critical to the success of the process. The soundness of the business impact analysis methodology is characterized and supported by the following critical components:

- **BIA business case** – The business impact analysis or risk assessment processes are critical in building the business case to progress to future stages. Without a rigid methodology to gather the data to assess the risk environment, it may be difficult to get commitment to proceed.

- **Management support** – In the absence of management support for recovery planning, the project may stall, or at worst not even get off the ground. Ownership of the BCP process should rest with the senior executive levels of the organization and not in the domain of individuals whose main aim in life is an expansion of their empire. It is not a project for project's sake.
- **Enterprise-wide versus IT** – Be clear on the scope of the project. The continuity of business operations may be reliant on a range of dependencies, not just IT: e.g. manufacturing plant and equipment, key suppliers, personnel, vital records, operational systems.
- **Be realistic – risk versus cost** – Management may be prepared to accept certain levels of risk. The business case should be conscious of this and build a business case to progress to further stages based on a risk of occurrence versus cost of implementation of selected strategies.
- **The soundness of the financial impacts** – Data gathered during the BIA in the event of a loss or outage of business functionality can bring your business case undone. It is critical that user management provide written agreement and sign-off to the financial impact data they have provided, e.g. the impact on the business from revenue deferral after a disaster, as opposed to lost revenue, is significantly less. Be sure of the facts.
- **Formal sign-off and agreement** to findings from the BIA provides support from the business to the process. The business must own the process and recommendations. It must not be seen as a 'consultant-inspired' exercise.
- **Internal audit involvement provides an independent assessment.** An often-quoted description of an auditor is: 'An auditor is the person who comes in after the war is over and bayonets the wounded.' However, contrary to the myth, internal audit can be an ally in raising business continuity planning to the level of importance required within the organization. Often the internal audit department will have significant influence with management through regular reporting and meetings at board of director and audit committee level.

Adherence to legislative and compliance requirements

Is your organization adhering to the myriad of legislation or compliance, which requires your board of directors and management to identify and address the risks they face? Legal and compliance requirements are becoming too numerous to quote. Many are referred to elsewhere in this book.

If a disaster is going to happen it will more than likely occur at the worst possible time for an organization. Two classic Australian examples include:

- Victorian TAB (TabCorp) system crash on Melbourne Cup day 1996. 'The system crashed when the volume of transactions generated by cup bets, peaking at 300 a second, exposed faults in the disk logging. . . . As a result, TabCorp's earnings were down about A$2 million from 1995' (MIS February 1997).

- 'A major disaster with the Australian Stock Exchange's SEATS computer trading system dampened the financial euphoria over the Coalition victory and over-shadowed a strong rally on the bond market. The share market failed to trade at 10.00 a.m. and was down for two-and-half hours due to the breakdown in the electronic trading system'[3] Macquarie Equities managing director . . . said the meltdown would cost his company thousands of dollars because of settlement problems.'[4]

In developing a scenario around which an organization's business impact analysis and risk assessment will be performed, it is important to consider a range of scenarios. These should include incidents as well as a worst-case event. This will provide management with the basis upon which to assess the risks and the likely impacts should an incident or disaster occur.

The plan should reflect the changing business environment

If the plan is not up to date and does not reflect the current business environment then you might as well not have a plan. The plan should allow for changes in the business environment, and procedures should be in place to ensure it is updated in a timely manner.

Responsibility for ensuring the plan is up to date should be assigned. This should include:

- Issuing updated versions of the plan
- Maintaining a record of who has copies and for retrieving outdated versions
- Implementing mechanisms to facilitate maintenance of the plan whenever the business environment changes.

The contingency plan must be updated regularly in order to reduce the risks associated with disruptions. The contingency plan should contain sufficient update procedures to ensure that any changes to the organization or its information systems environment are accurately and promptly reflected in the plan. Specifically, mechanisms should be in place for:

- Changes of personnel – particularly changes to management, user and information systems personnel

[3] *Sydney Morning Herald*, 5 March 1996.
[4] *Australian Financial Review*, 5 March 1996.

- Systems changes – including changes to hardware, software, telecommunications equipment and security requirements
- Consider including business continuity in all due diligence assignments
- Key support services – are they still available?
- Has the business been involved in mergers, acquisitions, divestments that may impact the plan?
- Have new processes and operations commenced or some ceased? Have customer commitments and supplier relationships changed?

Adequacy of insurance coverage

Does your organization have adequate business interruption insurance and if so does it:

- Incorporate adequate indemnity periods?
- Allow for future business growth (or shrinkage)?
- Consider the nature of the disaster on all business components?
- Consider the contractual arrangements with customers and suppliers?
- Provide for loss of physical access to the business?

Statistics vary on uninsured losses, but figures have been published varying from 90 to 30% of total loss following a disaster not being covered by insurance.

Document management and control

Procedures should be established to ensure all changes that affect the operation of critical and necessary business processes are communicated for inclusion in the plan document. The steps involved in maintaining the plan should be documented, including any approval and logging procedures required.

To keep the information in the plan current, it will be necessary to continually incorporate alterations into the plan. It may be best to schedule regular updates to the distributed copies of the plan while having an on-site and off-site copy (both in hard and soft copy form) that incorporates all changes as they are made.

Once any alteration is made to the plan, those involved in that aspect of the plan must be notified and all copies must be updated and distributed. Any old procedures must be destroyed to ensure there is no confusion.

The key components in ensuring an up-to-date and controlled document are:

- Identify triggers for planned and unplanned maintenance, e.g. new business processes or acquisitions, personnel changes, new technology, etc.

- Prepare procedures for notification from critical departments in the event of changes in their business processes
- Prepare a schedule for regular review of the plan. This may encompass a re-evaluation of the risks and threats to the organization, random samples of adherence to procedures, etc.
- Document procedures for incorporating new business processes into the plan
- Prepare procedures to incorporate alterations into the plan. This must be performed in a structured fashion and all copies should be version and number controlled
- Determine a distribution list for the plan. Plans should be issued with an identifying code to ensure all copies have been updated and distributed. Prepare procedures for distribution of plan alterations to ensure all appropriate sections are replaced and distributed
- Prepare procedures to ensure that the plan is independently reviewed on a regular basis. This can be conducted by auditors and/or senior management to ensure the plan is relevant and accurate.

Identify and evaluate all threats

There are many threats which can disrupt an organization's business operations. The identification and evaluation of threats is necessary to prepare prevention and recovery procedures. Threat identification also provides a number of other advantages. It:

- Identifies where preventive measures are required
- Highlights previously unnoticed susceptibility that needs to be addressed by plans and procedures
- Can increase the awareness of staff to threats and evidence of those threats becoming problems
- Can also provide a stronger sense of purpose in staff related to the preparation of the continuity plan as they realize the importance of such a project
- Can highlight interdependencies between departments and result in better interdepartment cooperation to protect shared vulnerabilities
- Identifies where cost sharing is possible for threat prevention systems.

Threats can be categorized under the following headings:

- Water
- Fire
- Service failure
- Mechanical breakdown or software failure

- Accidental or deliberate damage to property and assets
- Personnel problems
- Supply chain failure
- Environmental/facility-wide damage
- Wide area disaster (e.g. flood, earthquake, hurricane, tsunami).

A common threat to an organization's information system's assets may come from inadequate protection of company data and information. The risks associated with unauthorized activity of this nature and the potential impacts are often not considered in the development of recovery plans.

The business impact analysis/risk assessment phase provides an excellent opportunity for an organization also to evaluate its logical security environment. The loss, destruction and/or disclosure of company data and information may have far more significant consequences and should be included for consideration in the continuity process.

Recurring themes from major disasters

Key lessons learned from recovery attempts during recent disasters demonstrate the importance of the human element in continuity planning. Other lessons 'relate to the absolute necessity of realistic testing of recovery plans, the need for clearly articulated communication links, and the need for explicit knowledge of environmental dependencies. Each of these was a recurring theme among the experience of several South Florida organizations during Hurricane Andrew.'[5] The four recurring themes they identified were:

Recurring themes in Hurricane Andrew disaster recovery

1. Human element:

    - Establish payroll policies for period of disruption
    - Establish policies to assist employees' families
    - Plan to proceed with recovery efforts without some personnel as a result of personal losses experienced by employees
    - Plan to locate key personnel before, during, and after disruption

2. Testing:

    - Must be realistic
    - Must be recurring/ongoing

[5] *Information Systems Audit & Control Association Journal*, 1, 1994.

- Must acknowledge all dependencies on external support or environmental constraints which might be affected by widespread disaster

3. Communications:

   - Access to public service announcements as a means of communication may not be feasible
   - Reliance on radio broadcasts may be dependent on existence of radio towers
   - Plan structure for communications – pre-numbered memos and dated voice mail
   - Do not rely on cellular phones – land lines were more stable during Hurricane Andrew

4. External dependencies:

   - Consider possibility of limited access to assets and business due to road and/or waterway damage/blockage
   - Reciprocal agreements should consider the likelihood of shared loss experiences among participants
   - Set realistic expectations of access to common carriers for transport of key personnel and data
   - Do not rely on delivery of services such as water, sewerage, power and gas or on availability of fuels.

Training is not the same as testing

This is often the most overlooked component of business continuity planning. Much effort is put into developing, testing and maintaining the plan but often personnel are not adequately trained in all aspects of plan activation.

Significant business disruption can be caused by overreaction to an alarm. Staff should be appropriately trained to recognize and discern between incidents and disasters, enabling them to make rational decisions. It is not unfeasible to imagine a diligent employee triggering the fire suppression system, after an alert, resulting in the dumping of litres of water over critical IT components. Appropriate training would, however, enable the employee to identify the real urgency of the situation and therefore make rational decisions regarding alternative actions to be taken. An incident of this nature recently occurred in Australia, resulting in an A$90 million ambit insurance claim for damages, business interruption and so on.

Fail-safe systems are a myth

In most cases (perhaps with the exception of defence systems) there are no regulations on how computer software systems should be specified, developed, implemented and controlled – even though lives and economies increasingly depend upon them. Consider the following:[6]

- The pilots of a Boeing 747 began their descent into Seattle Tacoma airport on 11 August 1995. Checking their instruments, they notified the control tower of their position. Then . . . nothing. A computer software failure knocked out the radio communications facilities of US air traffic control across an area of more than 500 000 square kilometres, leaving all commercial aircraft above Washington State . . . flying in complete isolation for more than a minute. Those who could not contact a military air base fell back on 'visual systems' – i.e. looking out of the window to see if any other planes were about. The software in this incident was part of a state-of-the-art system, just two months old, which cost US$1.4 billion.
- During the filming of *Babe* in the Southern Highlands of New South Wales, the animatronic pig, which was being operated by radio in the middle of the field, suddenly began behaving strangely, its legs kicking and jerking. Next day the Bowral police arrived. Every time the pig was operated, police radios were blacked out in an area of 120 square kilometres.
- At Melbourne's Tullamarine Airport, police thought a professional hacker must have been blocking pilot communication channels. When they identified the source of the interference it turned out to be an ordinary VCR in a home beneath the flight path.
- Although other engineers – mechanical, electrical, civil – operate under much more onerous regulatory constraints, anyone can develop a computer system regardless of experience, competence or resources.

How much of our lives is dependent upon computer systems? Consider:

- Nuclear power plants
- Air traffic control
- Traffic light grids
- Rail networks
- Freeway fog and speed limit signs
- Hospital drug administration
- Patient monitoring
- Braking systems on some cars
- Weather forecasting
- Stock exchanges.

Have you included business continuity planning as a mandatory phase of your organization's project or new product lifecycle? If not, then you should.

[6] *Sydney Morning Herald*, 18 May 1996.

Conclusion

Effective contingency planning requires the commitment of significant financial and human resources for situations that may never even occur. Nevertheless, prudent management recognizes that preparatory measures can make the difference between business survival and business failure.

A crisis management perspective of business continuity

Robert Heath – UK/Australia

3

Dr Robert Heath is an internationally respected counselling, organizational and managerial psychologist. Australian born, he is Managing Director of Crisis Corp Ltd based in London.

Crises: background

Crises are many and varied: to cite just a few potential crises:

- Workplace violence
- Danger to life, health or safety
- Kidnap/hostage
- Terrorist action
- Fraud/financial malpractice
- Product tampering/recall
- Extortion
- Ethics issues
- CEO succession
- Racism/sexism litigation
- Takeovers
- Email abuse
- Loss of communications or technology
- Evidence of lack of corporate governance
- Compliance failure
- Inappropriate published remarks by senior executives.

Any of these may lead to adverse publicity, which, in itself, may be a crisis.

Lessons from those involved in crises and crisis planners indicate that many organizations need to improve in the following areas:

The Definitive Handbook of Business Continuity Management, Second Edition.
Edited by Andrew Hiles FBCI. © 2007 John Wiley & Sons Ltd.

- Internal awareness
- Communications
- Exercises and training
- Vulnerability/risk analysis
- Information technology resilience and disaster recovery
- Planning
- Business continuity.

Given this background, we need to clearly understand the current concepts involved in business continuity management and crisis management.

Business continuity management (BCM) has a number of equivalent titles – the key ones being business recovery management, business recovery planning and business continuity planning. The names suggest the central concern: planning to recover from a disruption to the normal function of an organization. Consequently, conventional BCM processes involve reacting to the consequences of a given situation. This reaction can include a range of approaches from seamless recovery (developing ways in which processes, information systems and facilities may be recovered with imperceptible disruption) through to rebuilding (planning for detailed reconstruction activities that may take months or years to complete). Traditional BCM emerged from information technology concerns regarding failures in computer and information management systems. As a result, the focus of attention was firmly placed on:

- Reacting to failure or loss of system or operational capability
- Physical and tangible events
- Returning any disruption or failure or loss to a normal function as soon as possible.

This conventional approach involved undertaking risk and impact analysis, developing reactive recovery strategies and training staff to implement these strategies when needed.

Traditionally, crisis management (CM) also involved reacting to a critical situation. In conventional crisis management, this reaction placed most attention on responding to the stimulus event (onset management) and dealing with the impacts on people and resources inflicted by that stimulus event (impact management). Many of these early approaches placed some emphasis on pre-crisis planning and post-crisis recovery management, with an even smaller emphasis on any form of reducing exposure to crisis situations. CM emerged from general situation management requirements – mainly drawn from military applications (battlefield and campaign management) and community disaster responses from paramilitary organizations (police, fire fighting and paramedic). Consequently, traditional crisis management involved:

- Response (onset and impact) management of the crisis situation as the crisis unfolds

- Tangible and intangible situations
- Recovering an organization to pre-event levels of functioning.

This conventional approach involved undertaking risk and impact analysis, developing reactive response and recovery strategies, and training staff to implement these strategies when needed.

This evolution of BCM and CM shows two clear differences. These were:

1. Where BCM primarily waited until the situation consequences were known, CM was involved in dealing with the situation as it emerged (response management).
2. Where BCM had a specific focus on planning for, and managing, recovery from tangible and physical disruption, CM had a broader design that included response and recovery management.

As these points indicate, BCM fits under the umbrella of CM activities as the important component called recovery management.

Links between BCM and CM are more complex than this look at their traditional and conventional forms suggests. Both approaches now involve more detailed attention to searching for sources of risk, threat and hazard (and the consequent impacts on an organization) and greater emphasis on risk management and organizational resilience. Both approaches accept the need for greater pre-disruption management and preparation or readiness. Many BCM practitioners have realized that the conventional BCM approach does not cover less physical situations such as action by pressure groups, assaults on an organization's image and reputation, or the effects of 'white collar' crime.

CM practitioners now place greater emphasis on the areas of crisis reduction, improving preparedness and on recovery management. In this sense, BCM still fits under the broad umbrella of CM activities. Moreover, CM more easily addresses the different skill demands made by the less tangible situations to which organizations and their management may be exposed. Contemporary CM is likely to adopt an even-handed approach to pre-crisis, crisis and post-crisis management in what can be seen as an RRRR (or four R) action approach:

- Reduction
- Readiness
- Response
- Recovery.

As a result, CM seeks to eliminate, modify, or reduce exposure to crisis situations as much as developing response management and recovery management plans. Within most CM approaches, however, is an understanding that three transition points exist in the CM domain. At each of these three points, the personnel (and even overall management) may transfer from one set of people to another. The three transition points are:

1. From pre-crisis to crisis management
2. From crisis onset to crisis impact management
3. From crisis impact management to recovery management.

In pre-crisis management, CM activities are focused on prevention and prepared-ness activities. Consequently, many people involved are engineers and other spe-cialists, planners, project managers and trainers. While many respondents may assist in planning and participate in training, the activities involved differ from those activities required to deal with an actual crisis.

Within crisis response management there may exist two different clusters of management activities. The first cluster of activities involves confronting the emerging crisis situation in an effort to resolve the crisis before any significant damage arises. The second cluster involves dealing with the impacts of the crisis on the organization and people, so that the damage sustained is minimized.

The third transition point involves transferring emphasis from dealing with the crisis and crisis impacts to recovering from those impacts. In most cases, this transition involves very different skills, personnel and management.

Two examples can illustrate these transitions. First, take a passenger aircraft. Those undertaking pre-flight safety inspections of the aircraft and training of aircrew in dealing with in-flight situations are unlikely to be involved in managing such a situation. When a crisis situation arises, the flight and cabin crews (along with air traffic controllers in some circumstances) try to regain control over the aircraft in order to avoid significant damage (a crash). When an aircraft does crash, these onset response personnel are unlikely to be involved in dealing with the impacts of that situation, as fire fighters, police, paramedics and associated response personnel manage the site. Once the fires are out, victims are dealt with and the site is made safe, a different set of people take over. Air crash investigators and clean-up personnel examine and remove the debris, and reconstruction crews move in to restore the site.

Second, in most business settings those responsible for establishing response and recovery plans and for providing the training involved in being ready for crisis situations may not be those who have to undertake the response or recovery tasks. When a critical situation emerges, those trying to resolve or contain the situation before significant damage occurs are likely to be a different set of people to those handling the impact damage. In tangible situations, this may mean on-site organiza-tion personnel give way to off-site professional personnel from police, fire fighting and paramedic organizations. In intangible situations on-site personnel may try to contain the crisis until more specialized troubleshooters arrive and take over. In tangible situations, the impact-managing professionals are likely to depart once they believe the site is safe for others to enter. Here, those recovering the site, facilities and personnel for the resident organization are likely to be different from those responding to the situation itself. In intangible situations, the specialized respondents are likely to hand over to other specialized recovery personnel who try to rebuild the intellectual and perceptual (or image) components that were damaged during the crisis.

Effectively, BCM still fits under the CM umbrella. This is especially true for most businesses moving from a BCM approach into a broader contingency management or CM strategy. Given that recovery management usually involves different skills and personnel, BCM activities can be linked to the broader CM design while retaining some independence. Such linked independence can contribute four advantages. These advantages are:

1. Greater ease in dealing with tangible and intangible situations. Intangible situations can be handled by CM-sourced teams, allowing BCM teams to remain focused on their more tangible concerns.
2. The response management component of the CM approach is able to handle non-recovery activities and is able to alert the BCM team on the need to stand by. Moreover, the CM team can provide information to the BCM team on what is happening and thus on what may need to be recovered.
3. The use of CM and BCM approaches means that both operations can activate at the same time. While the crisis response personnel are dealing with the emerging situation and the impacts arising from that situation, BCM personnel can alert service providers to possible need, call in specialized personnel (from insurance loss adjusters to engineers), and even transfer the operations of the organization to a pre-selected recovery site. This saves wasted time and loss of business function.
4. The CM structure can coordinate and support the various pre-crisis, response and BCM teams so that transitions between these activities are smooth and resources are efficiently managed. By providing 'host' support when BCM is needed, the CM management can remove obstructions and delays that may arise when BCM activities interact with non-BCM activities within an organization.

As a consequence, BCM and CM efforts can be complementary.

Most BCM activities are triggered by some crisis situation. As CM activities involve dealing with the crisis before recovery management becomes involved, a clearer picture of what constitutes a crisis and what is involved in CM helps delineate the similarities, differences and links between BCM and CM.

So what is a crisis?

Crisis situations appear to happen suddenly. Four key elements indicate the presence of a crisis situation. These four elements are:

- Missing or uncertain (unreliable) information
- Little time in which to act (or respond)
- A threat to people or resources valuable to people
- The resources required to resolve the situation exceed the available resources.

These four factors illustrate the difference between problem situations, critical problem situations and crisis situations. A problem may have missing or uncertain information, and may have a specified period of time in which the problem has to be solved. A critical problem has missing or uncertain information, appears to have very limited time in which to solve the problem and poses a threat to people or to resources valuable to people. A critical problem can appear to be a crisis to those involved in managing the situation. A real crisis situation, however, has a fourth factor added – the situation seems likely to overwhelm those involved. Put specifically, a crisis is a critical problem that has a demand for resources that exceeds the resources available.

This sense of information uncertainty, very limited time, threat and of being seemingly overwhelmed can be seen in most definitions of what constitutes a crisis situation and thus what is involved in crisis management. Note that most definitions use different terminology to describe the same aspects – emergencies, disasters or crises.

- Foster (1980, p. 217) finds that 'emergencies are characterized by four distinguishing features, an urgent need for rapid decisions, accompanied by acute shortages of the necessary trained personnel, materials and time to carry them out effectively'. As a working definition of a crisis, the ideas of 'an urgent need for decisions', 'acute shortages of personnel', 'acute shortages of material' and 'acute shortages of time' point to fundamental aspects of a crisis situation.
- Rosenthal and Pijnenburg (1991, p. 3) outline a broader concept of crisis wherein 'the concept of crisis relates to situations featuring severe threat, uncertainty and sense of urgency'. Crises can be threatening situations that stress urgency in response and which are uncertain in the nature and impact of the crisis.
- Barton (1993, p. 2) finds a crisis to be 'a major, unpredictable event that has potentially negative results. The event and its aftermath may significantly damage an organization and its employees, products, services, financial condition and reputation.' In this statement, Barton points out that there can be tangible and intangible effects from the impacts of a crisis situation.

A crisis can cause other crisis situations (or critical problems) to emerge. This knock-on effect of a crisis situation is termed a 'ripple effect' because these crises seem to fan outward like ripples after a stone is thrown into a pool of water. Mitroff and Pearson (1993) note this ripple effect as a chain reaction that may be caused by poor management of the original crisis situation.

Crisis situations can cause ripple effects in organizations and communities. A physical accident drains money from an organization, puts people out of work and may cause further damage to the surrounding community system through loss of resources or pollution. In Seveso (Italy, 1971), the accidental release of dangerous chemicals from a factory led to long-term pollution of surrounding farming land and communities. This necessitated the relocation of those living in the area. Similarly, the meltdown of the nuclear reactor at the Chernobyl nuclear power station (USSR/Ukraine, 1986) made large areas of land uninhabitable through radioactive fallout.

Some ripple effects may cause crisis situations larger than the initiating crisis. In the first 10 months of 2006, there were 85 120 fires in the United States destroying 9 312 334 acres. The fires in Indonesia in 2003 and 2004 affected the air quality in Kuala Lumpur, Malaysia and Singapore. Once wild fires ignited among communities in Oakland (California, 1982) or Victoria (Australia, 1989), crisis impact management sought to prevent greater loss of resources and life until the fires were brought under control. Once the fires were out, a crisis ripple effect emerged – families disintegrated and communities found recovery difficult. In Oakland, half the residents and businesses did not return to the community, which caused a critical impact on the ability of Oakland to repair and recover its infrastructure through its local taxes. In major community crisis situations such as fire, flood, catastrophic windstorms (tornadoes and hurricanes) and earthquakes, just over one in four small businesses (around 29%) will exist within two years (Stuart, 1993) following the disaster.

So what is involved in CM?

CM covers all aspects of what may precipitate a crisis situation through to recovery from that situation. This means assessing, reducing and managing the risks, threats and hazards that can promote crisis situations, as well as planning and preparing to respond to – and recover from – crisis situations.

Effective CM means seeking to:

- Mitigate or reduce the sources, size and impacts of a crisis situation
- Improve crisis onset management
- Improve crisis impact management when responding to a crisis
- Enhance the recovery from a crisis situation through effective and rapid recovery management action.

As a result, effective CM means acquiring skills and task management capabilities across a number of dimensions – from dealing with processes and structures to managing (and communicating with) people.

In many ways, communication is a central and essential set of tasks for crisis managers. Without reliable information exchange within the CM (and particularly within the crisis response management processes) and effective image management with stakeholders, media representatives and the outside public, CM activities are likely to fail and be seen to fail. Communication tasks include:

- Developing secured communications within the crisis situation
- Acquiring good communication skills – from developing and using patterned communication protocols to dealing with emotionally upset outsiders
- Media management – including the Internet and websites
- Debriefing skills for gaining information from witnesses and respondents
- Image management.

Such tasks are covered in some form in books on crisis management. *Crisis Management for Managers and Executives* (Robert Heath, 1998, Pitman) has three chapters entirely focused on these areas, along with other chapters presenting information on effective communication of risks and warnings. *Crisis in Organizations: Managing and Communicating in the Heat of Chaos* (Lawrence Barton, 1993, South-Western) presents a chapter on crisis communications along with a number related issues throughout the book. *Crisis Management. What to do when the unthinkable happens* (Michael Regester, 1989, Business Books) also considers crisis communications, referring to the author's experience in dealing with some petrochemical crisis situations in the United Kingdom.

Crisis management involves five core activity clusters:

1. Crisis managers work to *prevent crisis situations from arising and to minimize crisis impacts.*
2. Before crisis situations arise, crisis managers *plan response and recovery activities and rehearse organizational members in doing those activities* so that organizations and communities are prepared in some way to deal with future crisis situations and crisis impacts.
3. When a crisis situation arises, crisis managers *deal with the crisis onset* in the available time.
4. When the crisis threat or threats begin to affect the situation, crisis *managers deal with any crisis impacts.* This may mean using different resources, personnel and management approaches from those used in dealing with the crisis onset period.
5. After a crisis, crisis managers can be involved in managing *recovery and restoration* programmes. This may mean using different resources, personnel and management approaches from those used in dealing with the crisis onset and crisis impact periods.

Again note that the recovery core cluster may equally be managed by any existing BCM arrangement. The key point is to link such efforts into the surrounding CM structure so that both BCM and CM operate effectively and efficiently.

Managing in crisis settings

Managing crisis situations generates feelings of pressure. These feelings of pressure can be eased by using stimulus-response 'breakers' (called 'stoppers' in psychology). One technique is the PBR (Pause-Breathe-Relax) method (Heath, 1994). Managers need to find ways in which they can systematically get more time and more information and to efficiently use resources. One way is *CrisisThink* (Heath, 1995) which involves mentally recycling three key questions while operating in a crisis situation:

- *How can I (or we) gain more time?*
- *How can I (or we) gain more information?*
- *How can I (or we) reduce the loss or cost of resources?*

These questions help managers focus on the means to reduce the feelings of pressure and resolve the crisis situation. The focus on preserving or reducing the costs and losses in resources also helps in presenting a positive image.

Developing the CM team

Most people involved in crisis management have some ideas on building a crisis management team. Key features usually include:

- A desire that the crisis manager is as senior as possible
- A need for the crisis manager to be able to manage the crisis
- The need for the team to have fixed membership so that the team's roles are known by all
- The need for the team to be flexible or adaptable because of the different requirements of different crisis situations
- A need to centralize command and control structures
- A need to coordinate and delegate responsibility to different groups who often have specialized knowledge and skills.

Unhappily, these features are often in conflict with each other. Seniority, for example, does not necessarily mean ability to manage crises. Likewise, flexibility and adaptability may be lost if the team membership is fixed (or the 'wheel has to be reinvented' if team members have to be assigned roles each time a crisis situation arises). Many managers with command and control backgrounds – military, law enforcement, fire fighting, paramedic – can be weak coordinators and tend to command and control the response. In most community and business organizations, management by command and control alone is likely to fail. Too many independent and loosely structured groups are involved.

CM often demands quick and decisive action. Such action rarely occurs when consensus and cooperative management are used. This is a core problem as fast decision-making usually needs single decision-makers working in centralized structures. This suggests that a senior manager using a command and control structure provides the best crisis management.

Most crisis situations, however, cannot be managed by a single person. Many crisis situations need responses from different groups of specialists who are likely to resent command and control from someone outside their group. These groups are often more motivated when they provide input into the decisions that involve their actions. This suggests that a crisis manager using decentralized and consultative decision-making and coordination will promote a more motivated effort and thus provide the best crisis management.

In reality, crisis management needs highly motivated respondents operating in a decision structure that uses both authoritarian and participative processes. Crisis managers have to find a balance between speed of decision and involvement in the decision by all involved. We can achieve this by using participative management in the reduction and readiness stages of the RRRR CM model – the pre-crisis components of crisis management. By involving response personnel in planning and training for crisis management, the response and recovery activities become coordinated clusters of pre-selected and agreed tasks that accept the direction and support of command and control teams.

Crisis management and humans

Early crisis situations were either caused by people or by natural disasters within the surrounding environment. Solutions to these crises were very simple until the last two centuries. People *fought* other people or *ran away* and either fought wild animals or ran away. Natural hazards such as quicksand and falling rock were *avoided*. Fighting or fleeing were two basic human responses to sudden events that we still display. These responses are called the *fight or flight* response. These responses can reduce the effectiveness of CM and BCM activities, and may incapacitate victims, bystanders and respondents within a crisis situation should such actions lead to inappropriate behaviours.

Natural weather and geological disruptions (such as volcanic eruptions and earthquakes) were seen as beyond human control and understanding, and thus were caused by some 'godlike' beings. Volcanic activity, earthquakes, floods, droughts and huge storms were seen as caused by some specific god who became displeased with the humans in her or his domain. Crisis management actions were thus quite simple – placate the specific god with some form of ritual offering (worship, gift giving and sacrifice of living animals or humans).

Many of us still react superstitiously to crisis situations. We feel guilty at having survived or express beliefs about our sins catching up with us because of some negative impact. Feelings of discomfort and guilt lead us to find ways to settle our disquiet. Most crisis situations feel threatening, and often leave us feeling powerless. The feelings of being powerless can often lead us to try to identify guilty people so that we can blame them for exposing us to the feelings of threat, guilt and being endangered.

People are core to crisis management and business recovery. Without people (and their valued resources) there would be no crisis situations. Without staff, shareholders, suppliers and customers there would be no exchanges of labour and resources that generate business and wealth for organizations. We thus need to look after people who are involved with our organizations. We call those involved with an organization its stakeholders (as they each hold a 'stake' in that organization). This term covers all of those people who have a direct or indirect investment in an organization and may include customers, creditors, staff, suppliers, product users, shareholders, owners and government regulatory agencies. Each of these groupings needs careful management during response and recovery periods should we wish to accomplish a positive and effective crisis management.

Crisis management can thus be seen as having four faces or 'sides'. These sides are:

- Managing the processes involved in developing and preparing for crisis management
- Dealing with the crisis situation
- Looking after the stakeholders of an organization
- Managing the communication processes involved (particularly those with the outside world through enquiries from the general public, media interactions and the protection of community or business images).

On looking at these sides, a similar structure is apparent for BCM – manage the BCM process, undertake actual BCM, look after the stakeholders and manage appropriate communication and public relations programmes.

BCM and CM management

Good CM and BCM work toward removing any sources of crisis situations and business disruption that can be eliminated, transformed or avoided. The remaining sources are then managed in some way – regulation and careful containment actions; developing plans for responding to an emerging situation and dealing with the impacts of that situation (crisis response management) and recovering from the damage caused by that situation (business continuity or recovery management). All of these elements can be efficiently managed under an organization-wide CM approach. These plans are then regularly rehearsed and tested so that those involved in a response or recovery activity gain the necessary skills and understanding to be able to perform their task effectively and quickly. These common areas of interest link the broad area of managing crisis situations with the more specific skills and actions involved in recovering from crisis situations that is the central goal of business continuity management.

References

Barton, L. (1993). *Crisis in Organizations: Managing and Communicating in the Heat of Chaos*. Cincinnati, Ohio: South-Western.

Foster, H. D. (1980). *Disaster Planning: The Preservation of Life and Property*. New York: Springer-Verlag.

Heath, R. J. (1994). Integrating crisis management: some principles and practices. *Abstracts from the First International Congress of Local Authorities Confronting Disasters and Emergencies*. Tel Aviv: IULA, pp. 45–53.

Heath, R. J. (1995). The Kobe earthquake: some realities of strategic management of crises and disasters. *Disaster Prevention and Management*, 4(5), 11–24.

Mitroff, I. I. and Pearson, C. N. (1993). *Crisis Management*. San Francisco, CA: Jossey Bass.

Rosenthal, U. and Pijnenburg, B. (1991). Simulation-oriented scenarios. In U. Rosenthal and B. Pijnenburg (eds), *Crisis Management and Decision Making: Simulation Oriented Scenarios*. Dordrecht, Holland: Kluwer, pp. 1–6.

Stuart, H. (1993). The Newcastle earthquake: local government response. *The Macedon Digest*, 7(4), 17–21.

Multilateral continuity planning

4

Dennis C. Hamilton – Canada

Dennis is CEO of Toronto-based Crisis Response Planning Corporation and is an internationally recognized expert in crisis management and business continuity planning.

The case for multilateral continuity planning

For many years now the most progressive of organizations have been addressing the need for business continuity planning (BCP). For the most part they have done an adequate job of dealing with all the known issues and problems that could arise from a disaster situation affecting their technologies or their organization as a whole.

For many organizations their business continuity plans were based on a worse-case scenario, meaning the loss or inaccessibility of their primary location for an extended period of time. While this approach is fundamentally sound, it does not go far enough. When executive management and stakeholders directed the implementation of a disaster recovery capability for the business, they did not expect the planning process to stop midway through the exercise.

A few simple questions may bring some perspective to what is without question one of the most important, yet commonly disregarded, issues in BCP:

- What happens if one of your key customers has a disaster? What is the impact on you? What must or should you do to support their recovery efforts? What can you do to ensure a minimal disruption to your organization?
- What happens if one of your major suppliers of product, raw materials or information has a disaster? What is the impact on you? What must or should you do to support their recovery efforts? What can you do to ensure a minimal disruption to your organization?
- What happens if your outsourced contact centre, your web service provider or your application service provider fails you?

The Definitive Handbook of Business Continuity Management, Second Edition.
Edited by Andrew Hiles FBCI. © 2007 John Wiley & Sons Ltd.

- What happens if one of your business partners, distributors or resellers has a disaster? What is the impact on you? What must or should you do to support their recovery efforts? What can you do to ensure minimal disruption to your organization?
- What is the impact on your customers, suppliers and business partners if you have a disaster? What would you want them to do to support your recovery efforts?

The answers to these questions are remarkably similar to those that were first used to justify most business continuity planning, including:

- Customers cannot take delivery of your products
- Customers cannot pay invoices
- Contracts could be postponed or terminated
- Suppliers cannot deliver critical products and services
- Sales projections cannot be achieved because business partners, distributors or resellers cannot meet their commitments.

These are just a few of the reasons why continuity planning must go beyond the corporate borders; why a full operational recovery capability will not exist until the recovery issues surrounding key customers, primary suppliers and principal partners have been addressed.

The need is growing . . .

The business community is not only internally dependent on technology, all external communication is being performed electronically as well. This growing level of technological interdependence further increases the bilateral and multi-lateral affect of technology failure. In today's business environment, the concept of 'just-in-time' affects absolutely every one of us, not just the manufacturing sector, who are normally associated with 'just-in-time' inventory management techniques. In fact, the first and currently the largest application of 'just-in-time' principles is for the provision of information, a delay or absence of which could be devastating.

In the name of 'productivity', 'partnerships', 'cost sharing', 'outsourcing' and 'cooperation', business-to-business integration has grown and will continue to grow to meet these operationally and politically sponsored relationships. Interdependence among organizations has in many situations ensured that when one has a crisis, others who are not affected physically will suffer to the same extent or more as the organization having the disaster.

We must not only view crisis management and business continuity planning inwardly. We must be proactive and embrace multilateral continuity planning as a mandatory component of crisis management. We must extend our planning endeavours to our partners, suppliers and customers.

Obviously, you start by understanding the impact on your organization if one of your key customers, primary suppliers or principal business partners has a disaster and conversely what the impact could be on them if you have a disaster.

A high-level understanding of this impact will probably determine the extent that multilateral continuity planning (MCP) is required. Most of the impact (tangible and intangible) will be relatively evident from discussions with senior and middle management throughout the organization.

Once you have determined that there is sufficient concern to further your investigations, consider a controlled and proven approach. Articulate your concerns and the issues facing your organization to your customers, suppliers and business partners. If they don't share your concerns or if they have not effectively addressed business continuity planning internally, you (or they) may just be out of luck. In order to find solutions you must first have cooperation, understanding and a willingness to participate. If you have been able to achieve this somewhat daunting task, further identification of problem areas and impact is required. Discussions will result in multiple alternatives that all organizations must consider. As is often the case, the final solutions may be totally dependent on cost. In fact, they may be rejected based on cost or the perceived effort required on the part of the participants. If no action is taken, you can at least know that an attempt was made and that the company is fully aware of the consequences.

Contingencies, alternatives and interim solutions during a crisis will ultimately impact all areas within your organization as well as vital operations within your customers, suppliers and business partners. Consideration will need to be given to a large number of operating functions in order to ensure coherence within all affected organizations. These will include:

- Extended payment terms
- Direct assistance through MCP support teams
- Interim or emergency policies, standards and guidelines
- Interim line of credit support/receivables financing support
- Collective bargaining unit emergency agreements
- Alternative transaction processing methods
- Alternative forms of communications to customers/end-users
- Cooperative competitor programmes
- Alternative sourcing of supplies/raw materials/finished goods
- Alternative finished goods production/manufacturing
- Standard inventory level adjustments
- Alternative warehousing of materials and products
- Shared cost on technology backup/recovery solutions
- Mutual personnel support programmes.

MCP approach

Multilateral continuity planning can be a time-consuming and costly process without a well-defined and orchestrated plan. The actual project steps and time required to complete the process will of course be dependent on the availability of internal resources, the scope of the project to be defined by the participants and the priority established within each organization.

The following steps are based on the CRPC methodology for multilateral continuity planning (MCP):

1. **Conduct awareness presentation(s).** The first step is to ensure company management are aware of and appreciate the need for continuity planning with customers, suppliers and business partners. Through a presentation, the management team, representing all business units (functions), should gain a sufficient level of understanding as to the need, objectives, approach, benefits and deliverables of multilateral continuity plans. The primary objective is to receive approval to proceed with this critical project.

2. **Establish an internal MCP project coordination team(s).** An MCP project coordination team will be required from the onset of the project. It is necessary to determine who will be the project director; whether or not there will be an external project facilitator and which business units will be represented on the project team. While this is only a part-time role, it is paramount that the representatives are relatively senior and very knowledgeable in terms of their business unit's operation.

   The project director should be your senior BCP practitioner, crisis manager, technology recovery planner or a business manager having significant knowledge of all major operations within the company. If the project director does not represent the information technology division of the company, a senior IT person is to be appointed to the Project Coordination Team.

   It may be necessary to establish an MCP project coordination team for each of the three major impact groups, key customers, primary suppliers and principal business partners. This will be dependent upon the size of your organization and the probable number of external participants.

   In addition, the overall MCP project coordination team will have a general responsibility to address issues not covered by the three major groups, including: interaction with regulatory bodies, environmental agencies and government departments.

3. **Conduct an internal MCP think tank.** Multilateral continuity planning is a relatively new discipline and as such may require explanation and promotion within the organization. An 'MCP think tank' should be conducted and include senior representation from all major business functions having a direct interface with customers, suppliers and/or business partners. The 'MCP think tank' would consider a number of the 'what-if' disaster scenarios previously discussed. Through interactive discussions, the participants would identify every major issue that must be addressed within multilateral continuity planning. The process is based on an analysis of a disaster scenario; concluding with identification and agreement as to the bilateral and multilateral issues to be subsequently discussed with the respective external

participants. This key step provides not only the identification of the organization's main issues and concerns, but establishes a framework on which to initiate similar discussions with suppliers, customers and business partners.

This internal process is key to identifying all potential problems that could arise from any one of the disaster scenarios. Representation is required from all business functions in the discussion of each business area. Inter-relationships between business functions will have a bearing on subsequent strategy development.

4. **Prepare an MCP strategy statement.** Based on the conclusions established through the internal MCP think tank, an MCP Strategy Statement should be prepared identifying each potential problem area (for all disaster scenarios); a strategy (or options) of how to address those problems caused by a disaster within the organization; and a strategy (or options) of how to address problems created as a result of a disaster at a customer, supplier or business partner location. As an example, if your organization has a crisis that prevents processing of customer orders electronically, your choice would be to process orders manually. However, the advanced systems of your customers may not provide for one-off manual order processing. Alternatives would be required. Additionally, your own internal systems may not be able to support a manual transaction.

The MCP strategy statement, to be prepared by members of the MCP project team, should consist of summary documentation only and consist of as many workable options as can be determined. It is important to remember that the alternatives or options devised by your MCP project team may not be acceptable to your customers, suppliers or business partners, respectively.

5. **Obtain MCP strategy approval.** The MCP Strategy will be the basis for all external discussions in order to complete the subsequent multilateral continuity plans. It is imperative that organizational management understand and support the strategies and alternatives that will be presented to your customers, suppliers and business partners. A formal review and approval is required of the MCP strategy statement prior to disclosure of proprietary information external to the organization.

6. **Prepare an MCP 'participant discussion paper'.** Although the MCP strategy was developed to provide alternatives of business-to-business processes in the aftermath of a crisis, the MCP strategy document itself would not necessarily be provided to all or any external organizations. As an example, it is reasonable that only those issues relating to supplier interaction would be provided to your suppliers. As well, there may be unique alternatives that will be made available to a specific supplier, while other, more general solutions will be provided to the balance of the suppliers identified. This process would also apply to customers and business partners.

Therefore, it will be necessary to prepare a 'participant discussion paper' for distribution to the respective organizations. The discussion paper should provide an overview of the need for multilateral continuity planning, your suggestions as to how the issues should be addressed and your recommendations for collaboration on finding workable solutions.

The discussion paper would suggest conducting an MCP think tank, similar to the internal think tank previously used to identify the potential problem areas and resolutions (alternatives) available. These documents would be presented to individual organizations where a private MCP think tank is required or to a number of organizations where a collective MCP think tank is appropriate.

7. **Identify external participants.** Careful consideration must be given to the selection of customers, suppliers and business partners that will be asked to participate in the multilateral continuity planning process. Every business function within the organization is to be asked to identify external organizations that:

(i)   would be detrimentally impacted should your organization experience a major crisis or disaster impacting its ability to carry on normal operations (a worse-case scenario should be applied) or,

(ii) would detrimentally impact your organization should they experience a major crisis or disaster impacting their ability to carry on normal operations (a worse-case scenario should be applied).

A clear and precise analysis should be provided for each organization or groups of organizations in terms of the impact considered. A standard list of quantifiable and intangible impacts should be created and applied to the analysis. Impacts will vary with each organization and should minimally include:

(i)   loss of sales/market share,
(ii)   inability to provide products or services,
(iii) significant effort required to alternative source supply,
(iv)   detrimental impact to organization's image/reputation,
(v)   loss of customers to competition.

8. **Conduct MCP think tanks for key customers, primary suppliers and principal business partners.** Multilateral continuity planning may be a new discipline for many of your customers, suppliers and business partners. As such, it will be necessary to conduct an MCP think tank with each group or individual think tanks for specific organizations. The MCP think tanks conducted at this stage are similar in approach, scope and objectives to the internal MCP think tank conducted earlier.

The primary purpose of the MCP think tanks is to generate interest in dealing with the joint issues of multilateral continuity planning. It is not likely that every organization asked to participate will attend; nor is it likely that every organization which attends will continue through the entire process.

However, the majority of organizations will understand the issues and potential problems and support the need to address all joint concerns through formal multilateral continuity planning.

9. **Determine project participants.** While each organization will determine whether or not they will cooperate in subsequent multilateral continuity planning activities, it is in your best interest to ensure those organizations most important to your operations become active participants. Ensure that you have pre-qualified those customers, suppliers and business partners who will provide the greatest value to you through their participation. Unique multilateral continuity plans may be required with specific external organizations, depending on the impact that would result from a disaster on your or their operations.

10. **Establish MCP project teams.** Each of the participating customers, suppliers and business partners needs to determine who, from their respective organizations, will be their representative(s) on the MCP project teams to be established. Understandably, there needs to be a limit established as to how many representatives are assigned to the overall MCP project team.

    In those unique situations where multilateral continuity planning will be conducted exclusively with specific organizations, the number of participants may be inconsequential. However, where the MCP project team is to be made up of many organizations (i.e. suppliers), a limit of one representative from each supplier is not unreasonable.

    In theory, you should have no more than one MCP project team for each of key customers, primary suppliers and your principal business partners. The exceptions would be where your organization found it advisable to create an MCP project team with a specific customer, supplier or business partner, or where the number of organizations participating warrant multiple teams.

11. **Conduct interdependency review.** Although your organization has a complete understanding as to the bilateral impact of a disaster, the other participants (your customers, suppliers and business partners) may not. It is necessary for each of them to obtain a clear understanding of the impact of a disaster from their perspective.

    Using your internal think tank, strategy statement and participant discussion paper as guidelines, provide a framework on which you suggest each participant conducts their own internal impact assessment from all of the disaster scenarios presented. Clearly, your suppliers would only be in receipt of your analysis for suppliers: customers for customers, and so on. You are not encouraging them to conduct a complete multilateral continuity planning project, such as yours, but rather to participate in your process, learning from that experience and applying the new-found knowledge internally at a later date.

    Although their conclusions will differ from yours in terms of impact, there should be a correlation between what problem areas must be addressed by both of your organizations. This step is necessary if their management are expected to accept and adopt the recommendations made through the overall Multilateral Continuity Planning process.

12. **Conduct MCP resolutions workshops.** Resolution workshops will provide the informal and interactive process required effectively to analyse and determine which alternatives will be acceptable to all participants. In many cases, it will only be a single organization or related group that decides, while in other cases the ramification could be in multiple organizations therefore requiring a collective decision. Each potential problem area must be dealt with independently, alternative resolutions/options discussed and selection made of the most effective and acceptable solution to all participants.

It is likely that separate workshops will be conducted with customers, suppliers and business partners. Rarely will they have the same issues as the other groups. Further, it may be necessary to conduct private workshops with specific organizations due to the unique relationships that exist.

The project manager or project facilitator has the primary role of ensuring that the appropriate amount of time is applied to each issue that a common solution is adopted where possible and that the workshop concludes with all problem areas resolved.

13. **Prepare multilateral continuity planning implementation plan**. All resolutions agreed to in the MCP resolutions workshops are to be scheduled for implementation concurrently at each of the affected organizations. In some cases it may be necessary to establish joint implementation teams to ensure a timely and accurate completion of the tasks.

14. **Conduct presentation to management for review and approval.** Each participating organization will be required to approve the implementation of the recommendations being made by the MCP project team(s). A summary presentation should be provided to ensure senior organizational management have a sound understanding as to the importance and implications of this cooperative effort. Management must recognize that there must be an ongoing commitment to support these endeavours through general maintenance of the strategies developed and for testing appropriate resolutions.

15. **Implement, install and/or document multilateral continuity plans.** Implementation of the multilateral continuity Planning resolutions may very well be the easiest step in the overall process. It is not likely that the accepted resolutions will be complex, costly or disruptive to day-to-day operations. However, it is most important that all participants adopt a common implementation schedule; conduct regular reviews through the implementation step and keep their own management informed as to the project's status.

Complete and thorough documentation must be prepared for all implemented resolutions. The documentation among all participants should be common in structure and content. This will provide for an easier change transition within each organization and subsequent MCP reviews.

16. **Perform test and/or verification on all strategies implemented.** Although most of the implemented resolutions will be on a contingency basis only, testing and verification of applicability is mandatory if any reassurance is required in terms of their workability.

   All procedural strategies should be reviewed at least on an annual basis and preferably twice a year. Technological resolutions should be tested twice yearly or on the same frequency as the organization's technology recovery plan tests.

   As with all contingency and recovery plans, testing is critical to ensure the plans reflect the organization's current requirements. Multilateral continuity plans are even more vulnerable to change due to the multiple sources of change.

   Although the tasks presented above are shown and numbered consecutively, it is reasonable to conduct several activities concurrently, particularly once the external organizations are on-side with the MCP process. The actual tasks performed will be dependent on the size of the organization, number of key customers, primary suppliers and principal business partners.

Project success factors

Multilateral continuity planning can be extremely rewarding to the organization or it can be a frustrating, counterproductive process. The level of success achieved will be dependent on a number of major 'success factors'.

These are:

1. While the solutions to multilateral continuity planning will be implemented by various business units within the organization, it is necessary to maintain participation on the part of executive management. The fact that multiple independent organizations will be jointly developing continuity and contingency plans in case of a crisis or disaster, dictates the understanding and approval of the organization's senior executive officer. It may be necessary to obtain board of director and/or shareholder approval under the organization's by-laws. It can be a political decision based on the relationship between the organizations for other, non-public, reasons. The most compelling reason to maintain executive participation is the value that can be derived by having the support and participation (reviews and approval of plans) at the highest level.

2. The scope of multilateral continuity planning can easily be drawn into a number of operational issues, and yes, it will take forever to find solutions that meet the approval of a number of parties. A degree of focus is initially

required. It is likely that the technology-based interfaces between any two organizations represent the most critical of interface activity. This is the most appropriate place to begin. Not only is it likely to be the most important, it is probably the most defined and manageable. Once multilateral continuity planning has been established in and around the technologies being employed, other interface processes can be evaluated in a like fashion.

3. We all know how difficult it can sometimes be to get the productive participation of a number of people in the same organization. The complexity is 10-fold when attempting to conduct multilateral continuity planning. Not only are you dealing with different corporate cultures, you are working with a wide-ranging group of personalities who may be unknown to you. The primary success factor here is basically to maintain a mindset of cooperation and compromise. While somewhat obvious and simply stated, its lack is nonetheless the main reason why the process will fail.

4. Depending on the number of key customers, primary suppliers and principal business partners it may be advisable to prepare multilateral continuity plans with a single organization from each external group. The option is to develop the one plan from each group as a working model that can be applied to all other participants within the same group. This approach is strictly dependent on the number of participants within the respective groups.

5. The end result of multilateral continuity planning will be a series of agreements on procedures, cooperative activities, contingency steps, bilateral support and emergency policy interpretations to be applied at time of crisis to all parties to the agreements. All participants are stand-alone entities and, other than through multilateral continuity planning, may have little or nothing to do with each other on a day-to-day basis. As such, each participant will continue to go through change within their organization and will be under no obligation to inform signatories to multilateral continuity planning agreements. Changes in personnel, organization structures, physical locations and internal systems and procedures can all impact on the multilateral continuity planning that has been established. Therefore, it is necessary that multilateral continuity planning be completed and documented at a high level only. The probability of maintaining the agreements decreases proportionally with the level of detail within the agreements themselves.

6. While general cooperation will superficially be maintained by all participants, the overall priority of the multilateral continuity planning project will fluctuate on a daily basis. Maintaining a common priority within all organizations on a consistent basis is impossible at best. The operative word in multilateral continuity planning is patience.

7. In order to achieve the many benefits that will result from multilateral continuity planning, it will be necessary to test and review the resulting plans on a scheduled, but periodic, basis. Not dissimilar to business continuity plans and technology recovery plans within your own organization, multilateral continuity plans must be tested to ensure they perform as and when expected.

The obvious difference will be the degree of testing necessary to the level of planning performed, or even possible, given the organizational autonomy of the participants. Testing of technology-based processes is unquestionably possible and necessary on at least an annual basis. Twice-per-year testing should be acceptable to most organizations. Procedural-based continuity plans should be reviewed once or preferably twice per year. Any new personnel should participate to ensure they are aware of the content and expectations of the multilateral continuity plans.

8. In order to maintain an objective and unbiased acceptance of the project plan, project activities and the conclusions/plans to be implemented, it may be prudent to recruit a project facilitator. This person would ensure all participants are treated equally and that the conclusions drawn do not necessarily favour one over another. The project facilitator would also function as the overall project manager, providing a higher likelihood that project assignments are completed as planned and that status reports are prepared and distributed on a regular basis. Fees of the project facilitator would be shared among all participants, making the costs relatively minor to each organization.

9. Keeping expectations in perspective can be difficult in dealing with such diverse and sometimes, what seem to be, opposite requirements. It is very important for every participating organization to remember that each and every one of you is also a customer of someone, a supplier to someone and probably a partner of sorts to someone else as well!

As with any multilateral project, there will be those who are interested and even excited about the prospect of multilateral continuity planning and those who just can't place its importance as a priority to solving today's problem. Multilateral continuity plans will not be developed with everyone on your wish list. Start with those most enthused, the probability of success increasing proportionately to their level of concern and commitment.

Benefits of multilateral continuity planning

Multilateral continuity planning may very well make the difference between recovery and bankruptcy as a result of a disaster. Regardless of your internal state of preparedness, much of your recovery success will be based on the actions initiated at the time of crisis with your key customers, primary suppliers and principal business partners.

Multilateral continuity planning has a number of benefits that have a far-reaching impact not only in your organization, but equally with all participants. The benefits of multilateral continuity planning are many, including:

- An advanced level of preparedness with critical external stakeholders will significantly increase the probability of a fully successful recovery effort. Integration of emergency response and recovery efforts with key customers will promote an interdependent relationship; thereby protecting those customers from competitor advances.
- Multilateral continuity planning will enhance the functioning relationship with the organization's key suppliers, creating stronger assurances of continuous supply of information, material product and services.
- The promotion and provision of multilateral continuity planning services to prospective customers will provide a measurable competitive advantage.
- Cooperative planning with business partners, distributors or resellers will establish a stronger foundation on which to enhance business relationships.
- Extended influence and support external to the organization will provide an immeasurable level of goodwill value, significantly bettering the organization's image and reputation.
- Interaction with customers, suppliers and business partners by many management and staff will provide a much improved understanding of their operations, priorities and the issues that are most important to them. This provides an opportunity to enhance the operational interface between organizations.

You may also find that you or your customers and suppliers may find marketing opportunities or a competitive advantage through your multilateral contingency planning efforts. Your success will be dependent on a number of factors, not the least of which will be intracompany politics and everyone's willingness to cooperate.

Conclusion

Multilateral continuity planning is not an exact science nor can the methodology presented here apply to every organization. Individual organizational needs, and the needs of their customers, suppliers and business partners, vary depending on a number of factors, including: their industry, business type, business size and the level of technology employed throughout their organization. However, the approach presented does provide a proven road map of how to address what can be a complex and difficult problem to address. Apply the methodology, as you would utilize any procedural approach, learn from it and customize it to fit your needs and method of operation.

The primary consideration in what has been presented is recognizing the critical importance of your continuity planning to a variety of external organizations. Virtually every organization has suppliers and customers of some type. Many of them will have business partners, resellers, distributors, representatives, agents, brokers, regulatory agencies or other types of organizations requiring regular communications and the exchange of information or the physical transfer of assets.

It is necessary to understand the impact your organization has on another and how they may impact on you in a disaster situation. Until multilateral continuity planning is addressed, full restoration may not be attainable – at least not without severe consequences to your own organization and to the detriment of those you rely on.

Marketing protection: a justification for funding of total asset protection programmes?

Andrew Hiles FBCI – UK

5

Andrew is a director of Kingswell International, global consultants in enterprise risk management.

Total asset protection: the concepts

Two concepts could ensure the survival of your organization.

The first is Total Asset Protection. What is total asset protection and why should we fund it? Protecting the enterprise has previously been a piecemeal activity. Disaster recovery planning ensures the recovery of IT systems and telecommunications capability. Business continuity planning is designed to ensure the continued viability and operation of an organization in the event of a disaster resulting in the major loss of product or denial of access to mission-critical facilities. Crisis management planning goes one stage further, and covers contingencies like product recall, kidnap and hostage or branch hold-up – it includes issues like adverse publicity. Other related issues include health and safety, environmental protection, security and insurance. Often there is no coherent escalation process from customer complaint, operational incident or quality defect through to invocation of disaster recovery, business continuity or crisis management procedures and to the declaration of an emergency or a disaster. These piecemeal elements are increasingly converging into a coherent whole under a single umbrella, which we call total asset protection. Without a total asset protection plan, the organization is in peril. There is an 80% mortality rate for organizations that are without contingency plans and that experience a disaster.

An information technology disaster recovery plan alone is not a substitute for total asset protection, since the computers, although fully functional, will be useless if the production system they control has just disappeared in flames. A total asset protection plan will therefore cover all key facilities, such as office buildings, computers, communications, production capability and warehouses.

The Definitive Handbook of Business Continuity Management, Second Edition.
Edited by Andrew Hiles FBCI. © 2007 John Wiley & Sons Ltd.

But, according to a UK Department of Trade and Industry report, the proportion of companies' intangible assets (essentially goodwill) to tangible assets has grown to represent, on average, 70% of their balance sheets during mergers and acquisitions.[1] A total asset protection plan therefore needs to cover all other situations from which an organization can lose its goodwill, image and reputation.

According to disaster recovery company SunGard:

- Every two years, nine out of 10 businesses suffer a serious security breach.
- Every five years, one in five companies experiences a major disaster.
- This year, more than half of all email systems will fail at least once.
- The average cost of downtime is £52 000 per hour.

When businesses without adequate continuity and availability provisions in place experience major disruption a mere 8% survive. News source Datamation claims that, in 2005, any one business had a 70% chance of being hit by disaster.

An example of a business disaster will illustrate the point. Ronson, the lighters and pens group, has international brand recognition. A fire destroyed their Newcastle, UK, warehouse. Their insurance claim was $15 million. A year later, only 60% was being settled. The company faced additional costs from reorganization following the blaze. The result of the fire meant an overall pretax loss for the year of $1.5 million, a dramatic fall in Ronson's share price and severe long-term costs in re-establishing its business.[2]

Marketing protection

The second concept, marketing protection, delivers the justification for total asset protection. To justify the extent of funding for any of the elements of total asset protection (TAP) for any organization, Business impact analysis is undertaken to identify the impact on an enterprise, in cash and non-cash terms, of a disaster. Typically it examines loss of market share, loss of product, cost of restoration (including extra cost of working), cost of fines or other penalties. In addition it will weight 'non-cash' losses like loss of image, regulatory non-compliance or political impact. Using this standard approach, it is frequently difficult to justify spend on consultancy, services and products for business continuity, crisis management or other activities within the total asset protection programme. This is because:

[1] Tim Sutton, CEO of Charles Barker plc, in *Finance Director Europe*, March 1998, p. 34.
[2] *Daily Mail*, Thursday 6 May 1997.

- Some of these costs may be covered by insurance (although in practice insurance usually only covers some 40–60% of the real loss following a disaster).[3]
- The cost of the project usually has to be covered from the budget of an administrative department which has been pared to the bone by downsizing and which is seen as a target for further cost reduction.

The traditional business impact analysis tends to look at short-term costs and too frequently fails to quantify longer-term costs (e.g. lifetime value of customers; cost to regain market share and image). The concept of marketing protection takes the argument into a different dimension. It looks at the whole value of the business at stake from a marketing perspective and looks at the techniques of the worlds of advertising and brand management to demonstrate loss potential and justification for spend on BCP.

Brand value

Seven out of the top 10 brands in the UK in the 1930s remained in the top 10 brands in 1998.[4] Most of these still figure in today's list of top 10 brands. Brands and companies have outlived nations. Smirnoff, the Diageo vodka brand, has survived the reigns of the tsars, Marx, Lenin, Stalin, Gorbachov and Yeltsin. The US beer Budweiser is some 150 years old.

The brand has value outside of any single product: Persil, originally a soap powder, was relaunched as a detergent, followed by an automatic version, followed by a low temperature product, followed by Persil liquid and by washing-up liquid.

Keith Holloway of Diageo[5] says: 'We know from recent experience, particularly the Nestlé episode, that the richest companies are prepared to buy other companies for brands that they own for a multiple of 20 or 30 times their annual earnings (perhaps 40 to 50 times their annual marketing costs). The episode Holloway refers to was Nestlé's purchase of Rowntree in 1988 for $3.9 billion. Tangibles on the balance sheet were worth only $620 million. Even if you added up 10 times Rowntrees' profits the total only comes to about half what Nestlé paid. Since Nestlé was capable of manufacturing anything that Rowntrees could, it meant that they paid $2.3 billion for the brands and the strategic value that went with them.[6]

---

[3] Kingswell International.

[4] Tim Sutton, CEO of Charles Barker plc, in *Finance Director Europe*, March 1998, p. 34.

[5] *A view on the financial valuation of brands – 2* in *The longer and broader effects of advertising*, IPA March 1990.

[6] *A view on the financial valuation of brands – 1* by Stephen King, WPP Group, in *The longer and broader effects of advertising*, IPA March 1990.

Table 5.1—The world's top 10 brands

No	Brand	Country	Industry	Brand value $m
1.	Coca-Cola	US	Beverages	67 000
2.	Microsoft	US	Software	56 926
3.	IBM	US	Computers	56 201
4.	General Electric	US	Diversified	48 907
5.	Intel	US	Computer hardware	32 319
6.	Nokia	Finland	Telecom equipment	30 131
7.	Toyota	Japan	Automotive	27 941
8.	Disney	US	Media Entertainment	27 848
9.	McDonald's	US	Food	27 501
10.	Mercedes	Germany	Automotive	21 795

It is no coincidence that, as soon as Grand Metropolitan proposed the merger with Guinness on 22 May 1997 – a merger which would put the new $36 billion operation sixth among the world's food and drink companies, just behind Nestlé and Unilever – they announced the proposed new name: GMG Brands (subsequently changed to Diageo). Grand Met's price immediately rose 13% and Guinness's climbed 14% to the highest value for both since 1992.[7] GMG was expected to capitalize its brands, which include Johnnie Walker and Gordon's Gin: the brands' stated value could rise from $8.5 billion to $18 billion.[8]

Since 1988, there has been continued debate about brand valuation and whether or not brand valuations should appear on companies' balance sheets. Reckitt and Coleman and Diageo (previously Grand Metropolitan) have both put acquired brands as assets on the balance sheet since 1988. Rank Hovis McDougal declared, in the same year, that the development of Mr Kipling, Hovis and Mother's Pride brands was worth £678 million.[9]

Table 5.1 shows the world's top 10 brands and their brand value from a survey by Interbrand in 2006.

The brand value of Coca-Cola has shrunk by some $15 billion within about five years (mainly because of increased competition and lack of successful innovation). Ford has dropped from the no. 5 to the no. 30 spot – down 16% from 2005 (from safety concerns and competition). Disney's brand value has dropped some $5 billion over the same period. Winners have been Google (no. 24, brand value $12.4 billion, up 40% in a year) and Starbucks (no. 91, brand value $3.1 billion, up 16% and e-Bay (no. 47, brand value $6.8 billion, up 18%).

So brands and the goodwill associated with a company name have a real value – capable of being destroyed by a disaster and resulting adverse publicity. That

---

[7] Nils Pratley and Kate Rankine, *Daily Telegraph Business News*, 13 May 1997, p. 23.
[8] *Daily Telegraph, City Checklist*, 19 May 1997, quoting *Sunday Business*.
[9] *How advertising affects brands – an overview* by Simon Broadbent and Leo Burnett in *The longer and broader effects of advertising*, IPA March 1990.

Table 5.2—Top three business risks

2002/03	2003/04	2004/05	2005/06
1. Legal	Brand and image	Brand and image	Corporate governance
2. Brand and image	Physical assets/ systems	Corporate governance	Systems
3. External dependency	–	Regulatory	Brand and image

value is created by many years of advertising and good experience by the consumers of the product or service and it can be quickly eroded. When contamination of Coca-Cola was alleged in France and Belgium a few years ago, the brand value of Coca-Cola was reported to have sunk by $8 billion.

According to a recent survey conducted for insurer Aon,[10] brand and image have consistently been seen by business leaders as key risks facing business every year since 1997:

- 85% of organizations have established either full or partial risk oversight policies.
- The median total cost of insurable risk was €8.69 per €1000 of revenue, a decrease of 8.5% from 2005.
- All industry sectors have increased the amount of overall spend on risk management, rising from 14% in 2002/03 to 20% in 2005/06.

However, there is still a significant number of organizations that have not assessed the value of their reputation and brands.

There are formulae for spend on advertising, market share or sales volume and product profitability and highly sophisticated ways of analysing the effect of advertising after a campaign has finished.[11] Fundamentally, the more that is spent on effective advertising, the more volume that is shipped and (assuming product pricing is correct) the more profit that makes. The more profit that is made and the bigger the turnover, the more the company is worth and the higher the share price. It follows, therefore, that any disaster which adversely affects the attractiveness of the brand or good will be associated with a company's name, regardless of its impact on production capability, will impact turnover, will impact profit and will impact the value of the company and hence its share price.

Reputation value can apply to government and public organizations as well as to the private sector. The Harris Poll 2006 showed decreasing confidence in the White House (dropping 6% to 25%) and Congress (also dropping 6% to 10%). In

[10] http//www.aon.com/au/pdf/risk_survey_06.
[11] *Accountable Advertising* by Simon Broadbent, published by IPA.

the past four years, overall confidence in the White House has fallen sharply from 50% in 2002 to the current 25%. Others with notable decreases include organized labour (from 17% to 12%) and public schools (from 26% to 22%). In the UK, a survey showed that brands score higher than the police (62%), the judiciary (43%), local government (24%) and multinational companies (13%).

Advertising campaigns and the return on them

Generally, the bigger the brand the bigger the payback of advertising it. Weight tests have been introduced to test the impact of advertising. These are usually evaluated by comparing the cost of more or less advertising with the estimated change in sales volume times the marginal revenue per case. There is new evidence that successful weight tests can show more sales in the years after the test finished than during the test – that is advertising impact has its own momentum after advertising spend has stopped.[12] In one case, sales volume was up against its neighbours 28% in the second year after the campaign and 8% in the third year. In a summary of 44 BehaviorScan tests, it was found an average increase of 22% in year one was followed by year two sales 14% above average and year three sales up 7%.[13] And these effects may spin off onto other 'sister' brands.

So, what sort of money is invested in creating brands? An examination of some of the best recent campaigns will illustrate the large sums of money involved:

- Orange, as a newcomer in 'wire-free' telephony, invested $40 million directly in advertising for its launch alone: it generated $450 million of sales.[14]
- Daewoo's launch in the UK cost $33 million in advertising and generated $275 million in revenue.
- Over a six-year period, $26 million spent on advertising increased the sales of Felix cat food by $162 million.
- Reebok spent $4.5 million on advertising in the UK alone to generate a $3.3 million–£4.2 million incremental gross profit.
- UK telco BT regularly spends over $9 million a month on advertising. BT's 'It's Good to Talk' campaign cost $66 million in some 12 months, with a payback of six times that. One campaign, 'Working Smart Not Just Harder', achieved a 67% return on media spend.

[12] *Are our ways of evaluating advertising too restrictive?* by Simon Broadbent and Leo Burnett in *The longer and broader effects of advertising*, IPA March 1990.
[13] *Are our ways of evaluating advertising too restrictive?* by Simon Broadbent and Leo Burnett in *The longer and broader effects of advertising*, IPA March 1990.
[14] This and subsequent examples are taken from *Advertising Works 9*, edited by Gary Duckworth, IPA.

- Nescafé Gold Blend advertising runs at $7.5 million a year and delivers $75 million a year in sales.
- De Beers' global diamond advertising campaign was designed to maintain sales during recession. De Beers spends around 0.4% of the value of world diamond jewel sales on marketing (4% of rough diamond sales). In just one year, diamond jewel sales worldwide increased by 5%.
- Luxury goods advertisers spend 1% to 15% of revenue on marketing, while perfumers spend up to 25%.[15]
- Barclaycard's Visa advertising campaign featuring Rowan Atkinson as a bungling secret agent cost $60 million, stimulating 3% extra card usage and increasing its share of new card users from 15% to 25%.
- Renault Clio's 'Papa, Nicole' advertising campaign took Renault UK sales from an all-time low to almost double in five years and has sustained the Clio's success at a higher level and for longer than could reasonably have been expected, as well as creating a 'halo' effect on other Renault models.
- Stella Artois invested $21.3 million in advertising to deliver incremental net returns on that investment over a decade of $105 million.

'Traditional' advertising is increasingly being supported by – or replaced by – interactive television advertising and Internet advertising. The UK insurance company Norwich Union introduced a multimedia competition to show the benefits of life insurance. Participants had to complete the line 'Before my next birthday I'd love to . . .' for prizes ranging from piloting an airplane to cutting a single. The campaign involved the *Daily Mail* physical and online newspaper. Fifty per cent of competition entries stemmed from the *Daily Mail* online and the press campaign generated a significant number of searches for the online promotion for Norwich Union.

Internet advertising is becomingly increasingly important. Following the launch of the highly successful *X-Men* film, Fox España turned to MSN to drive awareness of the sequel *X-Men 2*, among a technologically enabled, communications savvy 13–35-year-old audience. Due to a change in première date at short notice, the campaign launch plan was revised. Fox needed an immediate means of advertising the details to their target audience. The results:

- In three days MSN Messenger generated more than 17 million hits to the *X-Men 2* website.
- MSN Today achieved a 2.7% click-through rate to the *X-Men 2* website.

In September 2003, MSN conducted a research study in collaboration with the Dynamic Logic Research Institute to demonstrate the effectiveness of the online advertising campaign for the Volvo S40, which ran exclusively on MSN Italy. The

---

[15] *Economist*, January 1993.

Internet was the only means of communication for the launch of this new car. After the campaign, all brand metrics considered recorded an increase among the respondents, especially after two to three exposures to the campaign, specifically among respondents with income levels exceeding €40 000 per year. The campaign led to significant increase in online advertising awareness and message association.

The 'halo' effect of the reputation of one brand can be passed onto another: Virgin, which started as a record company, opened music mega stores; moved into airline, cola, insurance and pensions and banking. In just 18 months, over $1.5 billion was invested in Virgin Direct's savings and pension products. UK-based Sainsbury's and Tesco stores have both moved to banking. Virgin has since moved into health care. One of the most important factors in this is that 'As popular trust in institutions declines and individuals feel they are faced with ever more choices and even less time to make them, consumers are seeking new partners to help them confront, share and manage the risks they face in their everyday life. In this situation, brands are ideally positioned to fill the vacuum.'[16] Researchers discovered that, over a three-year period, confidence in Sainsbury's grew from 'a great deal' or 'quite a lot' score of 59% to 74%; in Marks & Spencer from 73% to 83%, in Tesco from 52% to 71% and Boots from 78% to 83%. Other scores include Kelloggs (83%) and Heinz (81%).

Impact of disaster

Advertising agencies always consider the upside of the advertising message, rarely the downside. If the company fails to deliver against the expectations set by that advertising message, the message will work just as powerfully against the company. For instance, advertising for banks, which stresses warmth, compassion and humanity, is largely counterproductive because it does not match with customers' experiences and consequently they feel such advertising is an attempt at cynical manipulation.

The corollary of advertising success is that, in the event of loss of image or reputation through a disaster, market share losses from 'negative advertising' could be equally as dramatic and these sums of money would have to be spent *in addition* to the normal ongoing advertising that has to continue merely in order to *preserve* market share. These days, volume is often the key to viability: lose volume and viability is lost. The loss of a brand could mean the extinction of a company. Moreover, the 'halo' effect could work in reverse: like guilt by association. Using the argument of marketing protection, the justification for spend on

---

[16] Henley Centre, *Planning for Social Change*, May 1997.

BCP becomes immediately obvious and immensely strengthened. When the Mer-
cedes A Class small car proved unstable in 1997, it cost some $900 million and
2000 cancelled orders to recover the position.

How much worse the situation could be in a disaster. Insurer Commercial
Union's slogan 'We don't make a Drama out of a Crisis' was replayed to brilliant
effect when their offices were devastated in April 1992 by the Irish Republican
Army's bomb at St Mary Axe in the City of London, UK. Their Business Continuity
Plans worked – but what if they had not? What if they had made a drama out of
a crisis? A software company has the slogan 'The Integration Company'. What if,
in a disaster, they failed to deliver – and the message became 'The Dis-Integration
Company'?

An example of such an impact can be seen from the Perrier water benzene
contamination incident in 1990. In 1989, Perrier was the market leader in bottled
mineral water, its name synonymous with purity and quality. Perrier water was
on the tables of virtually every high class restaurant around the world. Sales peaked
at 1.2 billion bottles a year. The plant at Vergèzem, near Nîmes, was tooled up
for 1.5 billion, with capital investment and personnel to match. After recalling 160
million contaminated bottles and mishandling the publicity, Nestlé took advantage
of the drop in share price, fought off Giovanni Agnelli's Fiat-based group and in
1992 paid $2.5 billion to buy Perrier, giving Nestlé 40% of the French mineral
water market. In 1991, Perrier production plunged to 761 million bottles a year,
heading downwards: the plant was uneconomic, making heavy losses. Perrier was
effectively dead in the USA and in Europe; the French mineral water market,
having grown by 10% a year up to 1990, stagnated for over three years.[17] A lifetime
investment in promoting the images of purity and quality was effectively written
off: all had to be started from scratch.

Third party impact

Moreover, this sort of damage could be inflicted by a third party.

Firestone, the tyre manufacture, is owned by Bridgestone. When Firestone
instituted a major recall programme of allegedly dangerous tyres in August 2000,
Bridgestone's profits sank 50% and shares dropped by over 30%. Ford, who had
fitted the tyres to its Explorer vehicles, suffered a knock-on drop of 15% in share
value.[18]

Rolls-Royce has a name synonymous with engineering quality – an almost price-
less reputation. However, this 100-year image was threatened in May 1997 when

[17] *After the Perrier bubble burst*, by Anthony Peregrine, *Weekend Telegraph*, 23 January
1993.
[18] *Post Magazine*, 25 October 2001, p. 25.

Airbus A330-300s powered by Rolls-Royce Trent engines suffered from inadequate lubrication of gearboxes allegedly by defective parts supplied by a French subcontractor. It cost one airline alone, Cathay Pacific, between US$15.5 million and $19.4 million in withdrawn flights.[19]

Conclusions

When viewed against an advertising budget rather than against the budget of a single administrative department, the sums involved in crisis management planning and BCP seem almost trivial. Product recall plans are readily justifiable to protect reputation and brands and are in place among all major companies. Why should any of the elements of Total Asset Protection be any different?

Since this report was first published in 1997, brand protection insurance has been developed. 'Just as brand building is a long-term exercise, so is brand protection. This must be supported by insurance that considers the value of the brand over the whole life cycle, as well as the potential risks and long-term damage', argues Kate Hinsley.[20]

When considering advertising campaigns, how many agencies consider the downside of the advertising slogan? How could a ruthless journalist turn the slogan against the company? Should not that be part of a risk analysis of the campaign? Before the disaster and during each advertising campaign, should not some creative thought go into how that campaign would be developed to mitigate the results of a disaster?

The marketing protection approach brings a new dimension, a new urgency and a new justification for a coherent programme of total asset protection. Every finance director, every marketing manager, every advertising agency should be aware of the twin concepts of Marketing Protection and total asset protection. Every security manager, risk manager, disaster recovery planner, business continuity planner and crisis manager should be aware of these concepts and apply them to their own (or their client's) organization.

[19] *Financial Times*, 2 June 1997.
[20] *Post Magazine*, 25 October 2001, p. 25.

Operational risk management

6 | Peter Viner – UK

Peter is a director of Scenaris Ltd, Europe's first full-service risk, continuity and business communications consulting group.

The objective of operational risk management

The objective of operational risk management is to identify, assess and control risks such that the business will, as far as is reasonably possible, not be prevented from achieving its business and regulatory objectives.

There is a confusing plethora of standards and regulatory requirements covering many types of business and industry sectors. By way of a regulatory requirement that serves the financial services and insurance sectors, the following is a representative extract from relevant regulatory requirements as stipulated by the Financial Services Authority.

Senior management arrangements, systems and controls

SYSC 3.2.19G states:
'A *firm* should have in place appropriate arrangements, having regard to the nature, scale and complexity of its business, to ensure that it can continue to function and meet its regulatory obligations in the event of an unforeseen interruption. These arrangements should be regularly updated and tested to ensure their effectiveness.'

This increasing emphasis on regulatory requirements for risk management is not only affecting its primary intended audience of the regulated companies, but as a result of risk assessments which have to be carried out as part of the operational

---

The Definitive Handbook of Business Continuity Management, Second Edition.
Edited by Andrew Hiles FBCI. © 2007 Scenaris Ltd.

risk process, it is also affecting the supply chain of those regulated firms. As any risk assessment has to address key supply chain issues, companies are now making demands to audit their suppliers' business continuity arrangements to ensure that any disruption to those suppliers will not prevent companies from being able to achieve their business and regulatory objectives.

So if you are the supplier to a regulated company and you have not yet been asked about your contingency arrangements, be prepared and ensure you have your business continuity plans up to date, tested and in a fit enough state to be audited.

Operational risk management

Risk management is an often used term, but has so many different connotations to different people that invariably the message of its meaning gets confused. Traditionally, for example, for the financial sector if risk management was mentioned it would mean market and credit risk which has been the main area of concern. For many smaller organizations the only real exposure to risk management is health and safety and even then in most cases this is limited.

There are so many definitions of risk management and operational risk management that for many the whole topic appears to be a jumble of conflicting definitions that impede many from even starting to develop the appropriate processes and practices. This is further exacerbated by the existence of the inordinate number of standards and regulatory requirements. However, risk can easily be separated out into three main areas within a business, within which all other subdisciplines can be incorporated.

Strategic risks

Strategic risks are the risks associated with an organization's business plans, strategies and decisions. This area of risk may include plans for entering new business areas and developing new products, expanding existing services through mergers and acquisitions, and enhancing infrastructure. An example drawn from real life is the swift demise of Marconi.

Marconi. The high-flyer that fell to earth[1]

1999   Marconi starts the transformation from defence electronics group to hi-tech telecom equipment maker, buying US companies Fore Systems and Reltec for £4.6 billion. It also sells its defence electronics arm to BAE for £7 billion.

[1] *The Scotsman*, Friday 17 May 2002.

2000   During August, Marconi's share price reaches an all-time high of £12.76 on expectations for huge sales rises for the group.
2001   Sales collapse, Marconi lays off thousands of staff, most of the board are forced to resign.
2002   Talks start on restructuring the £4.3 billion debt mountain.

Financial risks

Financial risks result from business decisions that are influenced by changes in markets, liquidity changes and credit risks.

Operational risks

Operational risks may result from internal processes, people, systems and assets or from external events. An example is the catastrophe that was the Buncefield disaster where processes were in place but not operating.

In the UK the Financial Services Authority (FSA) has probably the greatest influence in the development of operational risk management and risk management practice due to the far-reaching regulatory requirements across the full range of financial business sectors and businesses listed on the London Stock Exchange (LSE).

For example, the advent of 'The Turnbull Report' or to give it its correct name, 'Guidance for Directors on the Combined Code of Corporate Governance', provides guidance to all listed companies on the implementation of internal controls to manage risk and affects every LSE listed company.

The recent absorption of the regulation of insurance and mortgage broking firms under the FSA's remit produced a raft of regulatory requirements (e.g. Consultation Paper 174); again included within this regulation is the requirement for risk management practice and business continuity measures.

However, the most far reaching in terms of global impact is the Basel II Accord which deals with European banking regulation for which the FSA carries full UK responsibility for the regulation of its implementation. While it is European legislation, the Basel II Accord affects all the banks licensed to operate in Europe and thus, due to the huge number of non-EU banks that have licensed offices and trading activities in Europe, it naturally follows that the effects of the Basel II Accord have global reach.

To give an illustration of why the financial sector and its regulators are now taking operational risk as seriously as the traditionally addressed financial risks, below are some statistics[2] concerning hedge fund failures.

[2] Source: Capco Research and Working Paper, 'Understanding and Mitigating Operational Risk in Hedge Fund Investments', 2002.

Percentage causes of hedge fund failures

Investment risk only	38%
Business risk only	6%
Operational risk only	**50%**
Multiple risks only	6%

With an average of 15 fund collapses per year[3] out of a spread of a few thousand funds open to investment, it becomes clear that the risks related to the Operational Risk issues of hedge funds significantly outweigh the levels of financial risk, which are normally the main focus of the managers' attention and investors' concerns.

While the FSA is arguably the single biggest influence in the UK with regard to the adoption and shaping of risk management and operational risk management practice, there is a plethora of standards and regulation from many organizations covering this topic, with varying definitions and requirements as well as practice and process. This is inherently confusing.

Thus it is important to begin with a clear understanding of the specific definition of what is considered to be operational risk as defined by the terminology in a given standard. However, there are several standards that do not necessarily have common definitions and there are variances from standard to standard. So as not to offer all definitions, and thereby confuse matters, we examine one of the key industry definitions of operational risk selected from the Basel II Accord, set out below:

A. Definition of operational risk
644. Operational Risk is defined as the risk of loss resulting from inadequate or failed internal processes, people and systems or from external events. This definition includes Legal Risk, below, but excludes Strategic Risk and Reputation Risk.

Legal Risk includes, but is not limited to, exposure to fines, penalties, or punitive damages resulting from supervisory actions, as well as private settlements.

When looking at this particular definition of operational risk, there are several issues to consider. First is that the definition itself makes no mention of credit or market risk as these specific issues are dealt with as separate risk management disciplines and, within Basel II, they are dealt with as distinct and separate issues from operational risk. This is the norm, not just for banking, but also when dealing with general risk management topics.

This leads directly to the second issue of note within this definition that only mentions 'loss' resulting from issues: thus it is dealing with pure risks rather than opportunity risks:

1. Pure risks are risks that present only a potential loss with no opportunity for gain, e.g. fire, flood, etc.

---

[3] Source: Edhec Risk and Asset Management Research Centre, based on publicly available information only.

2. Opportunity risks are those that present both potential for loss and also potential for gain, e.g. placing a bet.

Third are the specific exclusions of strategic and reputation risks from the definition. When considering these exclusions it is important to examine the purpose of the Accord itself, which is to ensure that the capital adequacy requirement of a banking organization is at a suitable level that is determined by the calculation of potential risk exposures.

Examples of strategic risk include areas such as:

*   Merger and acquisition activity
*   Changes among customers or in demand
*   Industry changes, i.e. keeping pace with market trends
*   Research and development
*   Business development and growth management.

The calculation of potential risk exposures relies heavily upon quantification of such exposures and as can be seen from above such strategic issues are generally neither pure risk nor easily quantifiable and therefore strategic risk provides an obvious reason for exclusion from the definitions of operational risk as set out by the Basel II Accord.

However, the reasons for the exclusion of reputation risk are less obvious as the proximate cause of a significant amount of reputation damaging events can be traced back to the occurrence of an operational risk event. It is, however, a difficult task to quantify the extent of reputation damage both in the immediate and longer term. There are many examples of operational risk events which have caused reputation damage, one of the most notable being the Perrier water contamination incident, a brief summary is of which is as follows.

Perrier's contaminated water incident occurred in 1990 at a time when Perrier enjoyed the position of being the largest supplier of bottled mineral water in the world. However, following a worldwide product recall and catastrophic public relations management Perrier unwittingly sacrificed its reputation and lost approximately 90% of the market share; and to this day, the brand has never recovered. The principal issue was originally reported as being due to the incorrect use of a cleaning fluid, benzene, (process failure) and was then put down to the failure to replace a filter (process failure). Whichever of these was correct the entire incident was made into a public relations failure of global proportions which almost destroyed the Perrier brand completely and has done such damage that it will never recover. The proximate cause of the reputation disaster was one or more process failures.

However, having made the argument for the inclusion of reputation risk within the operational risk model the argument can also be made that reputation risk can lie within both the financial and strategic risk areas as well, because reputation issues can occur as easily from losses or failures resultant from financial and strategic risks as they can from operational risk. The key issue, however, is that reputation risks rarely, if ever, occur without there being an underlying risk which may create the situation that eventually precipitates damage to the reputation. Thus excluding it from the definition could ultimately result in a failure to achieve the objective of the Basel II Accord which is to ensure the capital adequacy of a bank. As with any business, the sustained confidence of customers, investors and other stakeholders is key to maintaining a viable business.

The confirmation of the above assertions with regard to the Basel II Committee's uncertainty of how to deal with both strategic and reputational risk issues is found in the Supervisory Review section of the Basel II Accord in which the following statement is made.

> 742. *Other risks.* Although the Basel II Accord Committee recognises that 'other' risks, such as Reputation and Strategic Risk, are not easily measurable, it expects industry to further develop techniques for managing all aspects of these risks.

Such a statement shows that as the issue of quantification could not be easily addressed, the above regulation from the Basel II Committee and *not* the FSA, to all intents and purposes, washes its hands of the matter. This is the proverbial 'head in the sand' approach that is adopted when an easy solution is not readily available and is unreservedly not an approach the writer of this chapter endorses.

The fourth and final issue to consider is the failure to mention assets within the definition of operational risk. The fundamental reason that this is important is the recognition that assets themselves contain inherent risks to a business and do not have to be influenced by 'external events' to create serious issues for a business. For example, investment in IT solutions upon which a business becomes increasingly reliant, may well be an asset, but IT systems could fail due to an inherent defect without any external influence, in which case the asset becomes a liability until the failure is fixed.

The purpose of this examination of the definition of operational risk is to show that whichever regulation or standard that is under review has its own inherent flaws, which can be exposed and become the subject of lengthy debate. Thus when dealing with operational risk the key to successful development and implementation of a process is reverting back to the common framework of the risk management process that flows through nearly all the standards and regulations. From this framework each organization can then develop its own process and practice such that it not only meets the objectives of the regulators, but further returns significant value back to the business, thus helping the business ensure it meets its own objectives.

The key elements of a common framework are distilled from the majority of regulatory and risk standards and set out briefly below.

Appropriate board level ownership and sponsorship for development of an appropriate operational risk management strategy level processes

Without the appropriate senior board level support and commitment the ability to establish an appropriate operational risk management process is undermined from the start. The process needs to be perceived by all members of staff and management as an important issue for the organization with the board reflecting this in its communications to the organization and staff as a whole and supporting the agreed strategy for implementation by making certain the necessary resources are provided in order to ensure its success.

Understanding the organization's business and regulatory objectives

It is essential to ensure that all people involved in the development and implementation of the operational risk management strategy of an organization are fully aware of the organization's business and regulatory objectives.

This awareness should form the basic approach to developing a workable and embedded operational risk management practice within the organization. Without a full understanding of what is required any processes developed may be fundamentally flawed.

Development of an appropriate and agreed operational risk management strategy that meets both the organization's regulatory and business objectives

It is important that once the development and implementation strategy has been developed that it becomes agreed and signed off by the board of directors. This is to further make certain the board continues to fully support and maintain the strategy, and to make sure that suitable and appropriate resources are made available such that successful development and implementation may be achieved.

Developing policies, practices and procedural documentation to support the implementation of the risk management strategy

One of the key steps so often omitted by organizations is the development of an internal documented policy and procedure to cover the implementation and correct application of the operational risk management process. The main reason for the development of such documents is that they act as a regular reference point for those expected to implement and manage the process; and against which individuals responsible for maintaining the processes and practices can be judged. This documentation further provides the base knowledge upon which the individuals who have to implement the day-to-day management of the process can be suitably trained.

Training is another common omission in the process whereby individuals, who are unskilled or untrained in the processes, are expected to manage and operate them, simply because they have been given the responsibility. Lack of training is a recipe for potential failure, thus training of appropriate managers and staff is therefore an essential element of embedding the process effectively.

Development of the appropriate management and reporting structures that support the effective management of the operational risk management process

A majority of the key regulations and standards determine that the operational risk management process should be embedded in the culture of an organization. The process should be distributed to business lines or areas and, in turn, these areas should report into a central management function which controls the operational risk process. When developing this management structure the organization must take into account ownership of each level of the risk management process, together with the various activities contained within it; and these should be clearly documented. For example, it is important to identify who owns:

- Policy setting and development
- Setting the organization's appetite for risk
- The management of risk process at the different levels
- The tasks for different elements of the management of risk process, such as identifying threats, through to producing risk responses and reporting on decisions
- Implementation of the risk mitigation processes that are used in response to the risks.

Thus, suitable management and control structures should be established to make sure that the process is effectively implemented and continuously managed and monitored.

Defining the organization's risk appetite and determining appropriate process and policies for its maintenance and review

An organization's risk appetite is a definition of each level of risk which it is prepared, or able, to accept. This set of level definitions should be reviewed regularly to make certain that it keeps pace with the organization's changing business objectives and risk tolerance levels as these may change frequently depending on the liquidity and other factors that affect business changes. Once any alterations are made to the risk appetite, they should be applied to the risk profile (discussed later) and all the risks that have been identified and assessed should be reviewed against all revisions, and appropriate actions taken.

Defining, maintaining and reviewing a detailed documented understanding of an organization's processes, structures and the assets, people information and other resources that support them

This element, together with the following element, of the process, which refers to dependency modelling, is critical to produce accurate and appropriate risk identification and assessment processes. This allows critical processes and time lines to be established, single points of failure to be found and appropriate risk identification and assessment activities to be undertaken. Without understanding and mapping an organization in such a way, the identification of key risks may be missed and the true level of impact of a risk to the organization may not be accurately assessed.

Development and continual review of internal and external dependency models that define the key assets, people and other resources in support of the key processes which allow the business to achieve its business and regulatory objectives

Refer to previous point above.

Development of a risk register which records and assists with the processes

The purpose of a risk register is to maintain information on all the identified risks relating to an organization. There must be sufficient information to make it worthwhile collating the information, but each organization will need to decide its own content requirements for each entry. It should be noted here that the various regulatory requirements and standards set out the need for specific data to be collected in specific ways. For example, the Basel II Accord requires that the categorization of risk be undertaken. It therefore follows that this must be done to make sure that all such requirements are met when developing the layout of risk registers.

Continual risk identification and review for the key processes, assets, etc. identified that support the business

Before risks can be assessed they have to be identified and the organization must have a documented and continual process for risk identification as part of its process. This process must be included in any decision-making processes that will materially affect or change the organization's operating processes and anything upon which that process is dependent or supported, i.e. people, assets, processes, etc.

Some methods for risk identification that are widely used include checklists and prompt lists, workshops, questionnaires and brainstorming. Workshops present significant opportunities for the identification of risks through the use of prompt lists, questionnaires and interviews. They can also be adapted to become a platform where risks may be validated and their severity agreed, together with identifying ways of addressing them. The output of risk identification should be documented by use of a risk register and the way in which this is done should be common throughout, thereby assuring consistency.

Determining risk issue ownership and responsibility within the organization

Risk ownership must be clearly set out, documented and agreed with the individual owners at all levels of the operational risk management process. This is to ensure that each understands his or her various risk management roles, responsibilities and fundamental accountability within the organization.

It is perfectly possible that the owner of a risk may not be the person tasked with the assessment or management of that risk, but that the individual in question is responsible for ensuring the management of the risk process is applied, and that the identified risk owners actually deal with the risks. For example, the most common reason for this to occur within an organization is where the Risk Manager does not have sufficient in-depth working knowledge of a specific technical area of the business. It is therefore more appropriate that a suitably qualified departmental manager who has the required depth of technical knowledge is nominated as the owner of that specific risk. However, the risk manager remains responsible for assisting and ensuring that the departmental manager carries out the risk processes.

Continual assessment of identified risks utilizing the organization's risk appetite definition as the indicator for risk control activities

There are many risk assessment methodologies available, but risk assessment is primarily the process of assessing probability and impact of individual risks, taking into account any interdependencies or other internal or external factors that may affect the probability, or severity, of impact should the risk materialize and become a serious and unwanted incident. Probability is the assessed likelihood of a particular threat or event actually happening, including a consideration of the frequency with which it may occur. Impact is the assessed effect or result of a particular risk actually occurring, typically expressed, but not confined to, a financial cost or downtime.

As an example of the use of these two criteria in tandem, there is only a relatively low risk of major damage to a building, but the potential impact to a business of the loss of that building could be disastrous.

There are many issues that affect the level of severity of any given event, such as the time of year or even time of day, depending on the criticality of the processes within the organization which are affected. If, for example, a financial institution is disrupted through an IT failure at a critical trading or regulatory reporting time, the impact of the incident suffered by the organization could be high, but if the same interruption to systems happens at a weekend or bank holiday, when no trading or reporting activity is due, there would likely be little or no impact on the business provided the failure is fixed before trading recommences.

Another example of issues which affect the impact of a risk is the effectiveness of existing contingency measures such system backups, backup power generators, the use of disaster recovery services providers, etc. Each such contingency measure must be noted against the risk being assessed as an influencing factor in the impact assessment. This is key because any change in the contingency measure provision, or the process which that contingency measure is protecting, will need to be reassessed in terms of the change to the level of probability or impact that may occur as a result of the alteration and, if appropriate, further contingency measures may be required to be implemented or existing measures changed. Typically, when an organization applies IT upgrades, it tends not to upgrade the configuration of its disaster recovery services contract; this is a common failure.

Thus it is important when undertaking a risk assessment to take into account and document the key influencing factors of that assessment. The organization's processes and procedures for managing operational risk should take into account changes within the organization, its processes or the infrastructure that supports those processes and ensuring that those changes are continually risk assessed and reviewed as they occur. Once the assessment of risk has occurred the risk appetite of the organization should be applied to the assessment in order to determine if the level of risk to which the organization is exposed is acceptable and determine if risk mitigation activities should be developed and implemented.

A final note on this topic is to ensure that whichever methodology is chosen, in respect of risk assessment, it meets the requirement of the regulatory standard. As a case in point, the Basel II Accord[4] adopts a highly quantitative approach to risk with the statistical analysis of historic loss events forming a key part of the assessment process of risk under this standard, with the capture of relevant historical data being of vital importance. It also places emphasis on the use of external loss event data from the industry as a whole, to further assist with projections of probability through the use of frequency data and impact through the use of severity/loss data.

Determining and recording existing risk control measures and developing additional risk control measures, as appropriate, based upon the risk appetite of the business and its regulatory requirements

Risk control is the process by which an organization reduces the likelihood of a risk event occurring or mitigates the effects should it occur. Arguably the best and simplest described methodology for this comes from the management of risk guidance produced by the Office of Government Commerce of which a brief synopsis is as follows.

The four Ts process
Transfer
Tolerate
Treat
Terminate

Transferring risk can be achieved through the use of various forms of insurance, or the payment of third parties who are prepared to take the risk on behalf of the organization; an example of which is credit financing arrangements.

Tolerating risk is where no action is taken to mitigate or reduce a risk. It may be because the cost of instigating risk reduction or mitigation activity is uneconomic for the business or where simply the risks are at such a low level of impact, or have such a minimal level of probability, that they are acceptable to the business. Even when risks are tolerated they should be monitored because future changes to the business may make the risk no longer tolerable or developments in risk control techniques may precipitate the organization to taking action. For example, a retailer may accept a degree of wastage through theft since to never

---

[4] The Basel II Accord has three levels of approach to the assessment of operational risk.

have anything stolen would increase the cost of security or make shopping conditions intolerable for customers. However, if the retailer subsequently decides to sell items of a significantly higher value than the norm, then the instance of theft may become more costly and therefore less tolerable.

Treating risk is the method of controlling the risk through the actions that reduce the likelihood of the risk occurring or minimize its impact prior to its occurrence. Alternatively there are contingency measures that can be developed to lessen the impact of an event once it has occurred, thus the development of Business Continuity Plans and the associated contingency arrangements.

Terminating risk is the simplest and most often ignored methods of dealing with risk. It is the approach that should be most favoured where possible and simply involves risk elimination. This can be done by altering an inherently risky process or practice, by removing the risk. The same can be used when reviewing practices and process and all elements of the business. If an item presents a risk and can be changed or removed without it materially affecting the business then removing the risk should be the first option considered; rather than attempting to treat, tolerate or transfer it.

No action or inaction should be lightly decided upon and suitable research should be undertaken to ensure that the most appropriate course of action is taken, taking into account the organization's objectives, regulatory requirement, economic circumstances and appetite for risk.

All existing risk control measures need to be fully documented and any new measures implemented following the risk assessments as previously discussed. These measures need to be reassessed and reviewed whenever a change to the organization occurs that may affect the level of risk or the part of the organization or infrastructure upon which the risk has been assessed, to ensure that control measures remain effective and appropriate.

Utilization of the risk register and the risk appetite of an organization to determine and produce a risk profile of the organization that can be clearly reported to the board and/or senior management of the organization

Reporting on the status and exposure of the organization to the board is a key element of all the regulatory and risk management standards so that the board can make the appropriate statements and reports to stakeholders and regulators alike, about the risk profile of the organization. To do this a combination of the 'risk register' and 'risk appetite' needs to be developed to produce a 'risk profile' showing the organization's risk exposures against its appetite for accepting risk following the implementation of the risk control activities.

Ensure that the operational risk strategy developed allows for the long-term embedding of operational risk management within the culture of the organization, ensuring that all staff members are aware of the process and its reporting lines and that those staff expected to maintain and deliver the process are suitable and trained for the purpose

The above is a summary of a generic operational risk process framework, which would need to be adapted to ensure it meets the necessary regulatory requirements and objectives of the organization concerned.

Conclusion

When it comes to operational risk management as discussed above, a key factor is the set of controls that are put in place to manage risks and/or their consequences. It is clear from all the standards and regulatory requirements, as well as our own common sense, that organizations cannot be expected to remove all risk. As such it is both prudent and, as far as the FSA is concerned, a regulatory obligation for all firms under its control to develop and maintain suitable risk and business continuity management measures, including business continuity plans, and to make certain that they are kept up to date and tested.

Business strategy and business continuity planning

Ranjit Kovilinkal Ramakrishnan – India
Satish Viswanathan – UAE

7

Ranjit is a freelance consultant; Satish is the Practice Head for Strategic Planning within the Business Excellence Centre, Dubai World.

What is business continuity?

The new standard, BSI 25999, defines business continuity as a:

> strategic and tactical capability of the organization to plan for and respond to incidents and business disruptions in order to continue business operations at an acceptable pre-defined level.

This definition is more restrictive than the earlier definition supported by the Business Continuity Institute and British Standards Institution in Publicly Available Specification 56 (PAS 56), as a:

> holistic management process that identifies potential impacts that threaten an organization and provides a framework for building resilience and the capability for an effective response that safeguards the interests of its key stakeholders, reputation, brand and value-creating activities.

We believe the PAS 56 definition more accurately describes the strategic value of business continuity.

Disaster impact

The US Bureau of Labor states that 43% of companies never reopen after a disaster and 29% more close within three years. A study undertaken by Gartner found the

The Definitive Handbook of Business Continuity Management, Second Edition.
Edited by Andrew Hiles FBCI. © 2007 John Wiley & Sons Ltd.

average cost of an outage is US$42000 per hour for mission critical applications and for companies that rely 100% on technology such as online brokers, e-commerce companies and traders, hourly downtime risks can be $1000000 or more (www.strohl.com). This only needs to be compounded by the number of hours of downtime in a year to visualize the huge risks to an enterprise.

Most executives are of the view that disasters will never occur to them. While natural disasters are few and far between, technological and manmade disasters and disruptions constitute almost 90% of business continuity issues. As can be seen above, every hour lost per week or per month would lead to huge risks to the earnings of an enterprise.

The historic context for business continuity planning

Business continuity sprung out of disaster recovery and hence the field still tends to focus on managing and mitigating risks with respect to IT (IT forms a major portion of a business continuity project since most of the business operations today depend on IT to a large extent) and operations. While most organizations today have an IT disaster recovery plan, many of them still do not have a plan to cover all the strategic business planning processes. Many still do not treat business continuity as a corporate issue that needs the direct involvement of the CEO and the executive team. BCP as it is practised today focuses primarily on operational risks: the long-term strategic planning aspects are not factored in. Consequently organizations lose sight of the big picture and the associated strategic risks.

It can be concluded that the need for continuity of operations exists today more than ever before. However, does the field of business continuity restrict itself to a narrow approach? Today, as indicated above, a business continuity plan captures only the operational and IT component and does not cover strategic issues.

This chapter looks into some of the examples on how strategic business continuity can help management in taking strategic decisions.

Business continuity planning within a business strategic context

In the 1970s, during the production-based economy the risks were more tangible in nature and were associated with plant, machinery and labour and were national or local. In today's knowledge-based economy, the risks are getting to be more intangible like knowledge/IP, reputation/brand equity, management competence and image. Any effect on these would have an immediate reflection on earning drivers and thereby shareholder confidence and the price of the share. Nothing bolsters this fact more than the EFQM (European Foundation for Quality Management) model, which is a globally accepted excellence model adopted by the best corporations worldwide. The EFQM scoring mechanism places more weight on perception measures (the intangibles) than the earlier mentioned tangibles. Further, failure to meet with increasing regulations and best practices like Sarbanes-Oxley, Basel II, Corporate Social Responsibility and Corporate Governance means that the impacts can cause a potentially debilitating disruption to the business.

Organizations large and small most importantly take strategic decisions that have an impact on long-term profitability and growth. Business continuity planning needs to take all these factors into account.

Most risk assessment exercises fail to capture the imagination of the top management since they talk only of risk mitigation strategies. Management is generally unable to see a direct ROI and frequently does not consider that these activities add value and enhance earnings. This approach spreads to the BCP programme, which also fails to engage the top management, who are critical of the investment in BCP. This is due to the fact that most of the articles and papers on the subject try to focus on business continuity mainly from a controls perspective and thereby do not focus on its value creation aspects. It would be a surprise for most enterprises to learn that there can be significant value creation and increase in earnings potential from a quantifiable and measurable strategic BCP approach.

Let's look at a few examples of how strategic risk and business continuity have a direct impact on earnings and thereby ROI, thus providing management with a strong basis for business decision-making.

Weighing business opportunity and accounting for the opportunity cost of capital and management

Novo Nordisk, the DKr 29 billion Danish firm, had invested around US$50 million of cash on an insulin product. If the future investment was uncertain, progress on the project would need to stop. By performing a strategic risk profiling exercise the Danish firm was able better to control the outcome and invested more funds in the product. As a result they did not miss out on the opportunity to become the market leader and thereby gained substantial competitive leverage.

A company that is part of a well-diversified group and a manufacturer of marine vessels is faced with a dilemma as to whether it needs to spend management time and effort in planning to develop a product rather than haphazardly developing products based on unresearched needs. A business continuity approach, taking into account the above opportunity cost of management and capital, provided substantive information to take a decision on the way forward. The parent company was able to control the losses by identifying the business risks associated with the products being developed in keeping with the market needs and charted a new long-term strategic plan to address these risks.

Stakeholders involved in the decision-making need to have a clear understanding of the business

The same organization also faced a situation wherein its financing arm did not understand the nuances of the segments within the marine vessels manufacturing industry. This had led to delayed decision-making which affected operations thereby delaying the launch of its products resulting in risk of market timing delay.

Evaluate strategic risk mitigation and business continuity strategies not only from a controls perspective but also from a strategic viewpoint

A local company in the Middle East, which is a reseller for Mothercare products, was faced with a situation on whether to shut its shop in Lebanon during the recent war with Hezbollah. In contrast to other companies that were removing stock to other countries as a risk mitigation strategy, this company started stocking more products in its warehouses and stores. When the war ended after a short time, sales boomed. They were not only able to meet the demands of their existing customers but also got many new customers who could not buy these products from elsewhere.

Identify areas for investment/disinvestment

MOL, a €8 billion Hungarian integrated oil production, refining and marketing group, tried to assess the impact of hybrid cars on the bio-fuels market, such as corn-based ethanol. Ducommun, the Chief Strategy Officer, states that: 'By pushing the analysis on hybrid cars, what we discovered were the limits of this phenomenon, because there is not enough land to grow the raw material of ethanol. But it is good to map those extreme scenarios to decide if we should be in those markets, or if our product is oil, or do we sell "mobility", and if it's mobility then ask: Should we be in bio-fuels?' This made the company decide not to enter into this market.

Conclusion

This chapter has sought to emphasize the importance of a business continuity approach extending into business strategy. While the identification of mission critical activities and risk reduction is crucial, business continuity disciplines might also be brought to bear on broader business strategy.

Section Two

Planning for business continuity:
a 'how-to' guide

The business continuity planning methodology

8

Malcolm Cornish, FBCI – UK

Malcolm is a widely experienced and highly regarded consultant employed by Marsh in the United Kingdom.

Introduction

In this chapter we provide an overview and introduction to a methodology that will enable an organization to establish business continuity management in line with BS 25999-1: 2006, and 25999-2: 2007 the new British Standards for business continuity management.

The methodology outlined in this chapter and enlarged on in the ensuing chapters has been proven to provide the required information and result in the successful establishment of business continuity management. However, many organizations that follow the methodology are not successful. This chapter also identifies some of the reasons for their failure and suggests ways around them.

What is business continuity management?

The formal definition by BS 25999-1 of business continuity management (BCM) is as follows:

> A holistic management process that identifies potential threats to an organization and the impacts to business operations that those threats, if realized, might cause, and which provides a framework for building organizational resilience with the capability for an effective response that safeguards the interests of its key stakeholders, reputation, brand and value-creating activities.

This definition recognizes that business continuity management is more than just writing a business continuity plan. Simply producing a plan will not achieve any

The Definitive Handbook of Business Continuity Management, Second Edition.
Edited by Andrew Hiles FBCI. © 2007 John Wiley & Sons Ltd.

benefit to the organization. To benefit fully from business continuity management requires organization, planning, assessment, training, rehearsal and more.

I prefer to describe business continuity management more simply as 'A management system that enables an organization to improve its security and resilience and make sure that it can respond immediately and effectively to a major incident'.

A structured management system

Just like any other management system, business continuity management needs to be planned, implemented and improved on an ongoing basis.

During planning you will set out what you hope to achieve in terms of implementing BCM and how you will go about it. It is vital that BCM supports the aims and objectives of the organization and the needs of its stakeholders, otherwise there is no point in doing it.

You must then implement the key elements of business continuity management identified in the British Standard's business continuity lifecycle. These are described in more detail below. The work must include checks and controls to make sure that each element is implemented effectively.

Ongoing exercising, maintenance, review and audit will provide the basis for management to ensure that BCM improves over time.

Part 2 of the British Standard is the specification against which organizations may be certified. It recognizes that BCM is a structured management system and requires management systems to be implemented in order to obtain certification.

The business continuity management lifecycle

BS 25999:1 includes a diagram that describes the BCM lifecycle (see Figure 8.1).

The BCM lifecycle comprises a number of elements, all of which need to be undertaken in order to implement business continuity management effectively. Apart from BCM programme management, it is not necessary to undertake the elements in a particular order, although there is clearly linkage between some of the elements. For example, many business continuity experts advocate starting with an exercise that raises awareness and emphasizes the need for BCM. Other experts advocate starting with 'understanding the organization' which leads naturally on to 'determining BCM strategy'. BCM programme management is like the axis of a wheel that drives the other elements, so should always be considered as a first step.

The new British Standard describes the elements as follows:

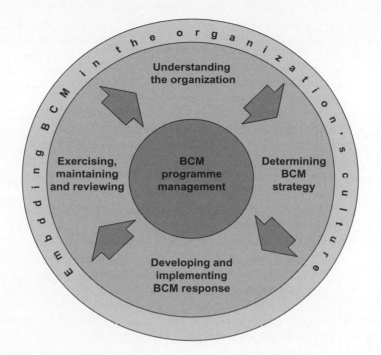

Figure 8.1—BCM lifecycle

BCM programme management

Programme management enables the business continuity capability to be both established (if necessary) and maintained in a manner appropriate to the size and complexity of the organization.

In essence the requirement is to:

- Assign responsibilities
- Implement business continuity, including:

    - Communication with stakeholders
    - Providing training
    - Conducting exercises

- Provide ongoing management in the form of:

    - Maintenance to ensure the plan is up to date
    - Control documentation and sign-off.

Project initiation and management is covered at Chapter 9.

Understanding the organization

The activities associated with 'understanding the organization' provide information that enables prioritization of an organization's products and services and the urgency of the activities that are required to deliver them. This sets the requirements that will determine the selection of appropriate BCM strategies.

The key steps are to:

- Identify:
    - Objectives
    - Stakeholder obligations
    - Activities
    - Assets and resources
- Assess impacts of stopping activities
- Evaluate threats to critical activities
- Consider internal and external dependencies.

These aspects are covered at Chapters 10 and 11.

Determining business continuity strategies

Determining business continuity strategies enables a range of strategies to be evaluated. This allows an appropriate response to be chosen for each product or service, such that the organization can continue to deliver those products and services:

- at an acceptable level of operation; and
- within an acceptable timeframe

during and following a disruption. The choice made will take account of the resilience and countermeasure options already present within the organization.

Business Continuity strategies are explored at Chapters 12 to 18.

Developing and implementing a BCM response

Developing and implementing a BCM response results in the creation of a management framework and a structure of incident management, business continuity and business recovery plans that detail the steps to be taken during and after an incident to maintain or restore operations.

Chapters 19, 20 and 24 address the planning and implementation processes.

BCM exercising, maintaining and reviewing BCM arrangements

BCM exercising, maintenance, review and audit leads to the organization being able to:

- Demonstrate the extent to which its strategies and plans are complete, current and accurate; and
- Identify opportunities for improvement.

These aspects are covered in Chapters 21 and 22.

Embedding BCM in the organization's culture

Embedding BCM in the organization's culture enables BCM to become part of the organization's core values and instils confidence in all stakeholders in the ability of the organization to cope with disruptions.

Section 1 and Chapter 22 are relevant here.

Coordination and management of the process

If an organization is to be successful in developing and then maintaining a business continuity capability, it is essential that there is clear management commitment and support for the process. To ensure that the plans and procedures that are implemented will be effective, there must be overall as well as individual ownership. There must be a BCM programme manager with overall responsibility for managing and coordinating the BCM implementation. The BCM programme manager must have the visible support of top management and the necessary authority to make things happen. To spread the workload, individual plan administrators should be appointed to manage the development and maintenance of individual plans.

So what's the catch?

Many organizations have adopted the BS 25999 lifecycle and been successful in implementing a true business continuity capability. Of those, many have met with disaster and emerged intact. Extensive research by Oxford Metrica has demonstrated that organizations that manage a major incident effectively emerge stronger than they were before the incident happened. There are, however, too many companies that have tried to follow the lifecycle but have failed miserably to complete the first element.

The most common reason for failure is undoubtedly lack of true management commitment. However, there is a way of making real progress and securing the management commitment needed for success.

A major problem is the time it takes to produce the written plan. If you follow the lifecycle in strict sequence and have dedicated resources, you might get a plan out after many months. What usually happens is that failure by key managers to support the first element causes excessive delays. By this time, senior management, who expected you to produce a plan in a matter of weeks, have become disillusioned – and business managers still don't understand what is required of them. No one has any idea what they are meant to produce and the likelihood of getting a plan out in the next decade looks very remote.

The solution is simple. Produce your first business continuity plan as quickly as you can, preferably within a month. It does not have to be perfect and only needs to contain basic contact information and resource data. You will then have something that you can use to show management and business managers. This education should involve walk-through tests using the business continuity plan. This will enable business managers to begin to understand the issues involved and their role in the process.

A practical approach

For the majority of organizations seeking to implement BCM for the first time, a practical approach is to create a business continuity plan for a single location and use that as a springboard for all the other work that needs to be undertaken.

The main elements of a business continuity plan can be developed relatively quickly within a few weeks. Using generally available templates, it should be fairly straightforward to design command and control structures; procedures for notification, invocation and escalation; and clear guidance on how to respond to an incident, including contact lists, forms and checklists. What takes longer is:

- Conducting a business impact analysis
- Determining effective BCM strategies
- Drafting detailed recovery procedures for business-critical activities
- The ongoing work involved in:
    - Plan exercising
    - Plan maintenance

- Audits
- Reviewing business criticalities as the organization changes and develops

- Embedding BCM in the culture of your organization which will involve:
  - Educating all staff
  - Raising awareness of staff, suppliers and customers.

All of the above needs to be set out in a BCM programme that sets out the work that needs to be undertaken, typically over a two- to three-year period.

Key stages are as follows:

- Programme initiation
- Awareness workshop
- Business impact analysis
- Risk assessment
- Strategy development
- Plan writing
- Plan walkthrough
- BCM programme completion.

Programme initiation

From the outset, you must be clear on the scope, objectives, method, timing and schedule of work that you are about to embark on. As the BCM programme manager, you should therefore draw up project documentation that sets out:

- Key activities to be performed and the persons responsible
- Agreed milestones and deliverables.

To ensure that you implement BCM in the correct manner and to the correct level for your organization, there are some key questions that management needs to address. For example, how should BCM link into the organization's aims and objectives? What criteria should be used to determine the criticality of each business activity? What are the most likely causes of a major incident and what types of impact are likely to arise? Who are the stakeholders most likely to be affected by business disruption? How will BCM be managed on an ongoing basis? The answers need to be documented and relevant details published in a BCM policy that:

- Defines the scope of BCM to be established within the organization
- Identifies BCM resourcing requirements

- Sets out the BCM principles, guidelines and minimum standards for the organization
- References any relevant standards, regulations or policies that have to be included or can be used as a benchmark.

Awareness workshop

It is also advisable to get everyone to be involved in developing the business continuity plan to a minimum level of understanding of BCM concepts. A half-day workshop should suffice. The workshop should explain the background, including the needs and drivers, and the methodology, approach, requirements and timescales. Participants to be involved in the business impact analysis should also be introduced to the questionnaire to be used and be given clear guidance on how to complete it.

Business impact analysis

One of the key stages that BS 25999 identifies is the business impact analysis (BIA). This is undertaken as part of 'understanding the organization'.

The standard states that the organization should for each activity:

- Assess over time the impacts that would occur if an activity were to be disrupted
- Establish the '**maximum tolerable period of disruption**'[1] of each activity by identifying:

    - The maximum time period after the start of a disruption within which the activity needs to be resumed
    - The minimum level at which the activity needs to be performed on its resumption
    - The length of time within which normal levels of operation need to be resumed

- Identify any interdependent activities, assets, supporting infrastructure or resources that have also to be maintained continuously or recovered over time.

It may be helpful to examine more closely what the standard means by 'maximum tolerable period of disruption', since this provides the key to the information that needs to be captured in a BIA questionnaire: this is illustrated at Figure 8.2.

---

[1] The maximum tolerable period of disruption is used to determine the recovery time objective of the activity and any support activities and resources that they require.

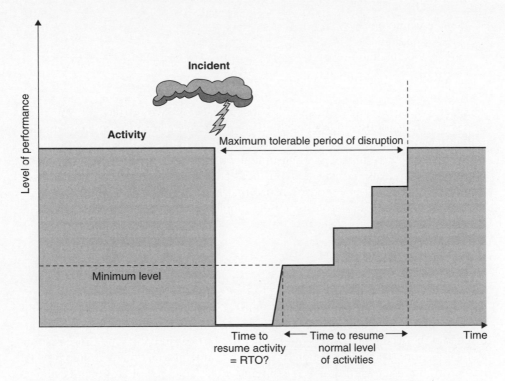

Figure 8.2—Maximum tolerable period of disruption

It is possible to create a simple BIA questionnaire that fits on two sides of a sheet of paper in order to capture:

● Basic information about each activity, for example:

  - Name
  - Department
  - Location
  - Person responsible
  - Description
  - Comments

● The effect of stopping each activity in terms of:

  - Financial impact
  - Operational impact (e.g. customer service, reputation, regulatory)

● Each activity's resource requirements

  - Staffing (normal, minimum on resumption, time before back to normal)

- Technology
- Equipment
- Documentation

● Dependencies on other activities.

Treat as business critical those activities whose loss would have the greatest impact in the shortest time and which therefore need to be recovered quickly following an incident. There may be some other activities, for example manufacturing processes that rely on specialist plant which has a long lead time for replacement, you should also consider as 'business critical'. In essence, any activity that requires pre-planning in order to ensure that it can be fully recovered within its maximum tolerable period of disruption should be termed 'business critical'.

Risk assessment

Threats to business-critical activities should also be evaluated. This requires a risk assessment that identifies threats and vulnerabilities and the impacts that might result from their exploitation. This can be done quite simply by holding a two-hour discussion between the owners of the business-critical activities and those responsible for support activities, such as facilities and information technology (IT). Based on the results of the risk assessment, you should be able to identify mitigation and risk treatment measures that:

● Reduce the likelihood of a disruption
● Shorten the period of disruption
● Limit the impact of a disruption.

Strategy development

Following the BIA, you will need to come up with strategies for recovering the business-critical activities and the support services (IT and communications infrastructure, logistics, legal services, buildings, etc.) that they will need.

A good approach is to have a workshop that identifies options for establishing a working environment in which to recover business-critical activities following a major incident. Workshops should involve managers and operations staff from departments with business-critical activities and representatives from the support services that they will require. The interaction between the two groups promotes real understanding of the issues on both sides and provides an environment in which imaginative and effective solutions can be identified. Options identified during the workshops can then be investigated to determine their feasibility and cost.

Plan writing

The business continuity plan is made up of three components best illustrated in Figure 8.3.

Emergency response identifies the steps required to respond immediately to an incident in order to safeguard life and, if it is safe to do so, limit damage to the site.

Incident management sets out the action needed to mitigate or reduce the sources, size and effect of a crisis, manage the impacts, aid recovery and exploit opportunities. It must include communications with all stakeholders and dealing effectively with the press and media.

Business recovery provides the capability to recover business activities before the impact of their loss causes irrevocable damage and to restore an acceptable level of service to clients, customers and other business partners.

Your plan should include flowcharts and other supporting graphics that explain the steps that need to be followed for each component of the plan. They should set out clearly who is involved, what they are required to do and in what time-frame. This enables the leaders of each team to see clearly at any point in time, the progress made, other actions that should be happening at the same time and the next steps that need to be taken.

The plans should also include forms, logs, checklists, contact lists and call trees that will be needed at 'time of incident'.

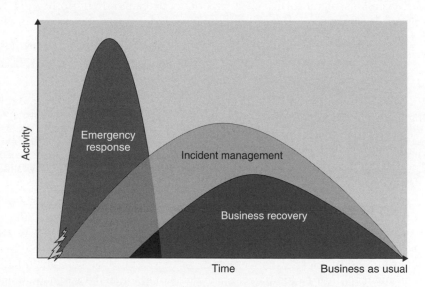

Figure 8.3—Phases of recovery

Plan walkthrough

As soon as you can, conduct a plan walkthrough to validate the business continuity plan and provide training for the teams that will use it. This can be done using a tabletop approach.

BCM programme completion

During the plan walkthough, it will quickly become apparent that the plan is not complete and will require more work to make it comprehensive and effective. There must therefore be an ongoing programme of development, exercising and maintenance. You should also plan the rollout to other locations and parts of the business.

Embedding BCM within the culture of the organization must also be planned. It is essential to provide training so that everyone knows what BCM is and their role in the event of a major incident. This training should be supplemented by relevant support material that promotes awareness and understanding: for example, brochures, newsletters and intranet pages.

Plan exercising

There are many types of plan exercise. Some are simpler to run and are suitable for early versions of the plan and inexperienced teams. At the other extreme, exercising can be complex and should only be contemplated when plans have been exercised extensively and teams are very experienced and confident. Each exercise builds on the results of previous exercises.

Typically there are five levels of exercising that you can undertake:

- **Plan walkthrough** – A walkthrough of a plan is an excellent way of explaining its format and content. A plan walkthrough is a low pressure exercise that uses presentation techniques including videos, slides and handouts, so that participants fully understand their plans.
- **Facilitated discussion** – Facilitated discussions can be delivered in a number of ways, but usually begin with the presentation of a hypothetical scenario. Potential issues and problems are then extracted from the scenario and given to the participants to solve using brainstorming and group discussion.
- **Single team simulation** – This simple form of simulation brings participants together in order to examine both the plan and how the team works together under limited pressure. The team will be expected to manage a fictional incident, manage information flows, make decisions, log activities, handle dilemmas and work together as an effective team.

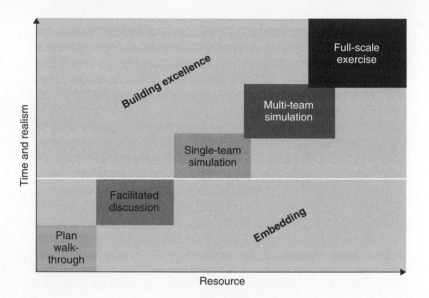

Figure 8.4—Exercising

- **Multi-team simulation** – The multi-team simulation extends the single team version by providing the added dynamic of team interaction. The focus is on coordination, communication and control. Such exercises often highlight elements of the overall plan that have either not been assigned or have been given to more than one team.
- **Full-scale exercise** – Full-scale exercises involve all teams. They should not be considered until other forms of exercise have been conducted and all teams have a high degree of experience, competence and confidence.

Plan maintenance

BCM arrangements and documentation will become of no value if they are not reviewed, maintained and updated as changes occur. Inbuilt mechanisms must be established to ensure that changes affecting BCM are recognized and accommodated. A plan maintenance programme that allocates roles and responsibilities must also be set up.

Auditing

Auditing of the entire BCM process is needed to ensure that it complies with generally accepted industry standards, such as BS 25999, and should ideally be undertaken by an external third party to ensure that they are objective and independent.

Summary

Business continuity is a very wide-ranging and interesting topic. However, like a snowball that grows and grows as you push it along, you will encounter many diversions, challenges and issues that need to be considered. By adopting the approach described in this section, you will be able to tackle them in a logical and focused manner that will enable you to stay on track and achieve your objectives.

Project initiation and management

9 Jayne Howe FBCI, MRP, CBRM – Canada

Jayne is managing partner of The Howe Partnership, a consultant with wide experience in business continuity management within Canada and the USA.

Project initiation

Business continuity planning projects, as well as projects for disaster recovery capability, are initiated, or 'born', from many different sources. The most common scenarios seem to be when a corporation is told that possessing a demonstrable business continuity capability has become a requirement because:

- Of an outside auditor's report
- The regulatory bodies which govern their industry have deemed it to be a requirement for ongoing membership or compliance
- The company's 'stakeholders' (those with vested interest in the company, such as shareholders, owners, insurers, employees and investors) are demanding it
- The company (or a competitor) has in fact experienced an 'event' which opened their eyes to their own vulnerability by not having a continuity capability in place.

But whatever the reason that upper management is now talking about business continuity within an organization, it is still a long way from having them commit funds, resources and time to activating a business continuity project and understanding the ongoing corporate cultural change that will become an integral part of their long-term day-to-day business.

One of the most effective methods used to 'sell' business continuity to upper management is to approach it with the appropriate corporate 'hot button'. Corporate hot buttons can be any one, or a combination, of several different critical mandates. It is, therefore, important to find out what upper management really

The Definitive Handbook of Business Continuity Management, Second Edition.
Edited by Andrew Hiles FBCI. © 2007 John Wiley & Sons Ltd.

cares about in running the business and which elements are vital, in their minds, to keeping the business doors open even in the face of a disaster. Some examples of corporate 'hot buttons' are listed below.

- Protect revenues
    - Ensuring profits
    - Minimizing losses

- Retain market share
- Protect corporate image and reputation
- Customer service
- Satisfy stakeholders
- Auditors
- Product delivery
- Brand protection.

Although a company may sell a product or service as their business, their immediate concern may in fact be continued customer service capability or protecting their corporate image rather than ensuring production. It's important to know which 'angle' to use when approaching management for business continuity project approval and support. Therefore, if building a business continuity capability can ensure protection and continued availability of the true critical mandate, from management's point of view, there is a better chance of success in obtaining appropriate funding and resources.

Timing can also become a critical factor when the reason for initiating a business continuity planning project comes from regulatory bodies, which have compliance deadlines, or from an auditor's report which will have an annual review. Projects that have critical time factors are usually more expensive to execute and involve more internal resource effort.

Once the appropriate hot buttons have been identified, a cost/benefit analysis should be prepared which demonstrates the benefits to the company of ensuring the protection and ongoing availability of those critical mandates. A cost/benefit analysis isn't always just about hard cost.

Project costs – start-up and ongoing

There should be fairly accurate costs associated with the resources, time, effort and third party contracts to be created in the business continuity planning project phase. But be sure to add in ongoing annual costs for plan maintenance/administration, training/awareness, testing and plan updates. (These figures should be a very small fraction of the projected rebuild cost figures.)

Projected rebuild costs

It should be possible to create a scenario of rebuild (with projected costs) if the company does not develop a business continuity capability. Although these costs are estimates, the majority of them would be one-time costs with a smaller component of ongoing costs. Be sure to include new, concentrated marketing efforts, potential employee recruitment and new hire costs, technology replacement and potential moving costs. (As an aside, it is often said that it takes 11 times the marketing effort/costs to regain a lost customer than the cost of acquiring new customers.) Some of these figures can be obtained from past records.

Projected potential savings

Fortunately, developing a business continuity capability doesn't necessarily always just cost money. There are opportunities for corporate savings as well. In some countries and in some industries, there are discounted insurance premiums available to corporations that possess demonstrable business continuity capabilities. Depending on the technology recovery strategies that are developed, there can be opportunities to outsource technology maintenance, support and/or upgrades, which can be more cost effective than providing those services in-house. Off-site vaulting can also be more cost effective than providing the appropriate environmentals and structure in-house. These estimates can also be included in the cost/benefit analysis.

Too often well-intentioned business continuity initiatives are not 'sold' effectively to upper management and only receive funding to perform a disaster recovery planning project or, more commonly, just a technology recovery planning project.

Often a half-day senior executive workshop is useful to build business continuity awareness and generally educate management on the various components of business continuity planning and the overall size of the undertaking. It is also true, unfortunately, that 'scare tactics' sometimes work to drive the message home. There are all kinds of smoke and rubble videos available as well as worldwide statistics on companies without proper continuity plans in place, which experienced some form of physical disaster (or even bad press) and did not survive.

Once the corporate decision has been made to pursue business continuity planning as an initial project, and hopefully as an ongoing corporate process, it is critical and beneficial to disseminate this information throughout the organization. Every employee as well as appropriate third party suppliers and support organizations should be informed that developing business continuity capabilities has become a priority mandate to the organization. Building employee awareness and keeping them informed throughout the process is key to building corporate support for the efforts. Everyone is already busy performing their daily job functions – if upper management is not clear on helping to 'sell' the business continuity planning project as a priority mandate, then resources throughout the firm will eventually just add it to the never-ending list of 'other' things to do when they have time. Management must be seen as visibly supporting and endorsing the continuity efforts of the project throughout the entire process.

Project management

Creating comprehensive continuity plans and ongoing processes for an entire organization is a large and daunting undertaking. Trying to grasp all components of the project and plan development process at the same time can become quite intimidating when trying to figure where to begin. Business continuity planning is managed much more successfully if it is broken into sections with go-forward decisions acting as milestones at the end of each section.

Generally, a business continuity planning project can be broken down into manageable thirds or phases. The *first* phase is *information gathering* and is comprised of risk evaluation and control, beginning to establish appropriate corporate support recovery teams, conducting a business impact analysis and using the information learned from the business impact analysis to develop appropriate continuity strategies. The *second* phase is *plan development* which includes developing emergency responses and procedures to ensure the life and safety of employees and visitors, as well as controlling the initial corporate response or reaction to an 'event'. This phase also includes development of the plan itself, as well as implementation and documentation of the plan. The *third* phase is a true transformation when a business continuity planning project becomes an ongoing corporate-wide process, where internal training and awareness programmes are developed, plan testing/exercising is scheduled and ongoing administration/maintenance of the plans begin.

In order to successfully manage each and every phase of business continuity planning, it is critical to create and install appropriate project-reporting relationships throughout the life of the project and on an ongoing basis as an integrated, corporate process. Overall, the project should report to a small executive committee where the members are the most senior executives in the organization. (Ideally, these would be the same executives who approved the project budget and sent the corporate message to all employees in the first place.) These could include the chief financial officer or senior vice-president of finance, the chief executive officer or president, and the chief information officer or senior vice-president of technology. Although it is not always necessary to utilize their time throughout the project, a reporting structure should be set up which makes it mandatory to give the executive committee some kind of project status update at least every two weeks.

Members of the working committees will change as the project advances through its phases; however, the onus should rest with the project manager to ensure that project status reports are timely and complete for every reporting period.

Phase One – Information gathering

Structure

For the first phase of business continuity planning, the project team should consist of:

- A project manager who coordinates the activities of the team, manages time-lines and budget, and reports to the executive committee
- Enough resources who understand the 'business' of the company and what information is needed to be acquired through the business impact analysis process
- One or two key resources from technology who understand the underlying technical issues as business units prioritize their recovery requirements
- A project liaison officer who will be responsible for gathering together all the required company documentation such as:
  - Any third party contracts
  - Insurance policies
  - Technology topology schematics
  - Employee organizational charts
  - Corporate phone lists, fax and modem numbers
  - End-user workstation configurations
  - Computer inventory lists
  - Asset inventory lists
  - LAN server configurations
  - Building cabling and electrical drawings, etc.

Comprehensive business continuity planning projects should include not only gathering information for the technology systems and business functions of a corporation, but also reviews of:

- Current insurance policies
- Technology maintenance/support contracts
- Physical premises review

- Surrounding geographic review
- Corporate conformity and liability concerns
- Voice recovery requirements
- Paper-based vital records review
- Third party contract review for suppliers, off-site storage providers, etc.
- Human resource recovery requirements and hiring practice policies
- Premises (office workspace) recovery requirements
- Incoming feeds/deliveries review (electronic incoming feeds, mail/courier delivery, etc.).

Budget

The one-time costs incurred here should have been the closest to 'true' costs that were included in the cost/benefit analysis. This phase of the project should have a definite start and end date with, at least, an upper limit on cost. Since it is always better to be seen as coming in under budget, rather than over budget, be sure to add in a 5–15% buffer into the timelines and costs before they are submitted for approval, in order to accommodate unforeseen delays and expenses. Adding in a small overrun buffer should apply to every phase in project management.

Timelines

This phase of the project is the time to maximize on the employees' new awareness and management support which has freshly made its way throughout the organization. This phase involves the most effort that will be required from the general employee population and it's important to meet with them and acquire the needed information while they are still aware and supportive of the initiative. If resources are available, several information gathering methods should be going on at the same time since it is not always necessary to finish interviewing or getting recovery information from one department or business function before another one is started.

Milestones

There are many opportunities within the first phase of a business continuity planning project to identify milestones or successes to show to management. It's always helpful in assisting ongoing project awareness throughout the organization if the project team does a bit of 'flag waving' now and then. Milestones during Phase One can include:

- Publishing the establishment of the corporate support teams by sharing with employees the names of the teams' members and their team responsibilities
- Finishing the risk assessment and analysis and internally publishing the results to management
- Establishing the critical corporate support recovery teams (see section 'Continuing visible support')
- Completion of the business impact analysis and reporting appropriate continuity strategy alternatives to management
- The last milestone in this phase occurs when management decides which continuity strategy will best suit the recovery requirements, budget and disaster recovery time objective of the corporation.

Phase Two – Plan development

Structure

Once management has approved an appropriate continuity strategy, the project team members will change somewhat. In addition to a project manager, the team will also require the services of:

- Corporate legal counsel and/or the procurement function to complete third party contract negotiations
- Senior management with signing authority for third party contracts
- Plan writers to assist with detailed documentation
- Internal/external assistance from human resources, property management and the local emergency authorities to document emergency response procedures
- A corporate communications representative with media training to develop corporate first response scripts
- Lots of resources from technical support to assist in the technology recovery plan development.

This group will be working in isolation from most other company employees until some of the contracts are signed and some of the documentation is completed.

Budget

Budget approval may be necessary if any of the project team members in Phase Two are outside consultant or contract resources. There may also be expenses incurred if media management and communications courses are required for those executives who have been appointed as spokespersons for the corporation. Additional expenses may include recovery plan documentation software and training. The largest budget item in this phase (besides the resource time utilized during plan development) will be the costs of activating any third party contracts for off-site recovery capabilities and/or off-site storage requirements. (Initiation or contract costs to third party recovery providers are included in this budget. However, monthly subscription fees to the providers should become a line item within the company's appropriate department or division.)

Timelines

It is a unique decision to each corporate environment and business continuity planning project, whether the proposal evaluations from third party recovery providers are included as tasks at the end of Phase One or set up as the opening step within Phase Two. Once a strategy has been decided upon, an RFI (request for information), an RFQ (request for quote) or an RFP (request for proposal) must be written and submitted to those third party providers who have been deemed as being most appropriate to have the correct 'fit' of recovery capabilities for the corporation. Then, time must be allocated in order to allow these companies to respond (two to three weeks is usually acceptable). They may wish to give presentations and/or site tours of their facilities to company management and technical support staff in order to properly explain and demonstrate the configurations and capabilities of their facilities.

Plan development, implementation and documentation always take longer than can be originally estimated. Be sure to allow enough time for plan documentation. Documentation should include a draft version that is reviewed not only by the employees who have to work from the plan during recovery, but also reviewed with 'fresh eyes' by someone who would only have to use the documentation if the allocated resources were not available for recovery. It is important to remember that the procedures and language used within the plan documentation must also make sense to someone who didn't write it, or doesn't do these activities as their day-to-day job.

Milestones

This phase of the project seems to hum along in isolation within the project team and the outside support providers, without much involvement from other members of the organization. It's important, therefore, to continue to make every effort to keep corporate management and employees informed of small successes and completed targets within this phase. In addition to regular status reports to management (even if management is currently involved 'hands on' with third party contract negotiations), the project team should publish, or at least make public, certain milestones as they occur within each phase. Some of these milestones can include:

- Completion of third party recovery provider contracts
- Announcing the completion of each business unit's plan
- Completion of each technical component recovery implementation
- Completion of the establishment of all corporate support recovery teams (see 'Continuing visible support' section).

Phase Three – Business continuity process

Structure

Activities during this last phase, as well as those on an ongoing basis, will again shift around to involve more internal staff. It is also this third phase where there will in fact be several different project teams and ongoing process tasks assigned to permanent employees and embedded into daily and annual business functions. Initially, the project team, under the direction of the project manager, needs to stay focused on two main components:

- Developing initial awareness and recovery training programmes for all employees
- Coordinating and scheduling the first recovery 'test' for the organization.

While the project team should still be forwarding status reports to the executive committee on a regular basis, the frequency of those reports may drop down to once per month while training programmes are developed internally (or purchased from recovery training organizations and modified). It also takes many weeks, or in some cases a few months, to schedule and properly prepare for technical or relocation recovery tests. The project team for employee training should consist of:

- The project manager who coordinates the activities of the team(s), manages timelines and budget, and reports to the executive committee
- Representation from human resources or the internal training department
- Representation from one or two key business units to review the appropriateness of training materials
- Outside resources (if necessary) which specialize in employee awareness and training for business continuity issues.

The other set of activities that will be happening at the same time is for a team to develop a test plan, script and schedule for an initial restoration/recovery.

Although some organizations try to test system recovery as well as resource relocation and voice restoration at a recovery site, it is advisable not to try all these
recovery components at the same time, especially for an initial test. It is still critical to have demonstrable successes, especially at this stage when the organization
has now invested large sums of money and effort into building plans. So try an
initial test that is not too big to manage and has the greatest chance of success.
A single system restore test is often a good starting point. Or, redirect only a percentage of incoming calls to a recovery call centre. To accomplish this, a project
team needs to be assembled which includes:

- A project manager (probably the same one) who coordinates the activities
  of the team, manages timelines and budget and reports to the executive
  committee
- Representation from technology support who will be involved in the test
- Representation from a business unit which will be involved in the test
- Representation from the recovery site provider.

Budget

Estimating costs for internal training and awareness programmes is dependent on
whether the programmes will be developed in-house or purchased from outside
training organizations and modified. Be sure to include the costs of software
and/or training materials, internal resource effort, workshop costs, consultancy
fees (if applicable), printing materials, and so forth, into the budget.

Creating a budget for recovery testing is more difficult. There may be hard costs
associated with using 'test time' at a third party recovery facility. However, the
internal (and sometimes external) resource to:

- Prepare, plan and script for a test
- Conduct the test itself
- Produce the post-test audit

is *always* underestimated. Be sure to allow lots of time to prepare for a successful
test, as well as the time that will be spent afterward performing a post-test
audit.

Timelines

Since this phase of the project melds over into an ongoing corporate process, the
timelines are, ultimately, never-ending. However, an end date or milestone could
be determined to, for example, complete a first session of recovery training to all
employees. After that, the process of training each new employee or each employee
transfer takes over.

A target date, or end date, can also be established to set up a test schedule. And it is true that if a third party recovery facility is to be involved, a test date and time will have to be scheduled and reserved with them. This is most often at least two months in advance. Add into the timeline a completion date for the post-test audit work as well. Then the ongoing process will take over for plan updates, maintenance and redistribution to affected business units. In the meantime, activities for the next test and test date should be underway.

Milestones

This phase of business continuity planning has the most visible milestones of all phases. The obvious first milestone will be the general announcement after all employees of the organization have completed their first series of recovery training.

The second milestone will be the general announcement of the first successful recovery test. After that, the company needs to focus on testing and exercising successes every year, as business continuity becomes an integrated, corporate process.

Continuing visible support

Corporate recovery teams

During recovery from a disaster or event, the business units within an organization will need to concentrate on restoring their own environment and becoming productive again. The technology support staff within an organization will be focused on providing a restored technical environment so that the business units can access their systems and data and become productive again. Therefore, it will be necessary to create overall corporate recovery support teams that are activated during recovery procedures. These teams are comprised of the company's decision-makers who have the authority to declare a disaster status on behalf of the organization, as well as the authority to release funds from the organization, deal with insurance companies, the press and process any employee personal claim or pay issues. For organizations which have the internal resources available to create separate support teams, the following suggestions are made.

Crisis management team

The crisis management team consists of selected senior management personnel who will be responsible for making all significant decisions regarding the response to a crisis situation. Only specified members of this team are authorized to declare a disaster (after analysis of the preliminary damage assessment) when they determine the appropriate course of action. All significant notifications will disseminate from this group. This group will be responsible for addressing the longer-term recovery issues once the immediate emergency response strategy has been activated, and as more detailed damage assessment information becomes available.

Key responsibilities include:

- Activating the contingency plan
- Initial notification of recovery team leaders
- Analysing the preliminary damage assessment reports to determine whether a disaster declaration will be necessary
- Determining appropriate emergency response strategy, identifying which components of the recovery arrangements are to be activated under the circumstances
- Determining corporate level communications strategy, including external and internal actions to be undertaken by the corporate communications team (external communications) and the administrative support team (internal communications)
- Initiating the disaster notification (alert/declaration) procedures if required.

Administrative support team

The administrative support team consists of representatives from distribution services, corporate purchasing, facilities, human resources, as well as administrative support staff. Their main responsibility is to provide ongoing support to meet the needs of the crisis management team and other teams if a recovery process has been initiated. They are to set up the alternative office strategy and provide all necessary forms for insurance and expense claims.

Key responsibilities include:

- Establishing the emergency control centre (command centre) and ensuring that ongoing supplies and requirements of the crisis management team are addressed
- Ensuring that key administrative support activities have been addressed (e.g. mail, couriers, etc.)
- Coordinating all internal disaster notification of technical and user personnel, including preliminary notification and ongoing status updates
- Procuring forms and supplies required for disaster recovery processing as detailed by the recovery teams and business units
- May also be required to act as scribes and keep action board updated during support team meetings.

Damage assessment team

The damage assessment team consists of representatives from business units, technical support and property management. Depending on the physical location of the damage or disaster, these team members are best qualified to perform a preliminary assessment based on the usability of the premises and equipment. They are responsible for preliminary damage assessment activities to determine the extent of damage to the affected premises, and whether worker health and safety would be at risk in using all or part of the existing premises. This team should also be able to make a 'first guess' on how long the site will have to remain uninhabited.

Key responsibilities include:

- Conducting a preliminary assessment of damage to the following entities:
    - Structures (e.g. buildings, rooms, offices, furniture)
    - Environmental support equipment (e.g. air conditioning, chillers, power supply)
    - Environmental protection and security equipment (e.g. access control devices, fire/smoke detectors, alarm systems)
    - Computer hardware, software, data communication capability and other specialized equipment
- Estimating the usability and time to recover critical resources
- Reporting assessment and recommendations to the crisis management team for evaluation and selection of the appropriate recovery and restoration action plan.

Recovery coordination team

The recovery coordination team consists of those members of the company who are most familiar with the disaster recovery plans, having assisted with the development and maintenance of them, and who are able to advise staff of their roles and responsibilities in a disaster recovery situation. Once a disaster has been declared, this group will access the plan and issue internal notifications, then ensure that steps in the plan are being followed.

Key responsibilities include:

- Coordinating all activities and communication between the technical areas and the user areas
- Coordinating the activities of the recovery teams and monitoring all planning, backup, recovery, restoration/construction and support department activities
- Conflict resolution at time of disaster

- Assisting the crisis management team with details of the plan or in formulating alternative actions if needed
- Timely updates of recovery plan progress, conflicts/issues that the recovery team cannot resolve
- Receipt and updating of disaster recovery logs from corporate team leaders.

Corporate communications team

The corporate communications team consists of marketing and human resources representatives who have had formal media training and are best suited to script and disseminate all media management, and all internal and external communications issues. They will act as a central dissemination point for all media management, external communications out to shareholders, stakeholders and the press, as well as monitoring/controlling corporate policy statement and status announcements to key customers, suppliers, employees and their families.

Key responsibilities include:

- Assisting crisis management team in finalizing corporate communications strategy
- Initial public/shareholder/stakeholder/market communication
- Key customer contact notification
- Executing competitor response if required
- Activation of internal call trees
- Set-up of internal status notification process.

Human resources support team

The human resources support team consists of representatives from human resources and legal counsel who are trained, knowledgeable and have approval authority for dealing with employee insurance claims, payroll continuance and coordination of temporary staff requirements. This team provides support and direction of employee/family trauma counselling, sick leave claims, payroll at times of crisis, personal injury and loss claims, extended family care and day care, shift work for employees, coordination of temporary staff requirements and family enquiries.

Key responsibilities include:

- Dealing with all employee-related issues on a timely basis
- Scheduling personnel during recovery activities
- Acquiring additional temporary staff as defined by authorized team leaders/resources
- Activating family care centre plans
- Dealing with situations as they arise
- Coordinating with corporate insurance and/or legal representatives.

Site restoration team

The site restoration team consists of representatives from facilities and purchasing, as well as representatives from physical security. Some of the members on this team may be carried over from the initial damage assessment team. This team in fact follows the damage assessment team to ascertain whether salvage operations are possible, and to coordinate efforts to return business units and/or technology groups/operations to the primary or alternative permanent site.

Key responsibilities include:

- Conducting a comprehensive assessment of damage to structure(s), environmental support equipment and supplies that results from a disaster
- Coordinating salvage efforts related to structure(s), environmental support equipment and supplies
- Providing comprehensive damage assessment information to the crisis management team to support longer-term recovery/restoration strategies
- Upon direction of the crisis management team, obtaining new facilities (temporary or permanent) in the event the primary facility is beyond repair
- Coordinating the repair/replacement of environmental equipment, security devices, alarm systems, furniture, etc.
- Ensuring security at damaged facility and at alternative processing facilities
- Working with technology recovery teams to ensure proper environmentals and power are in place to accommodate incoming replacement equipment.

Transportation support team

The transportation support team coordinates travel arrangements/accommodation for personnel as well as for delivery of equipment and supplies, as well as printouts where necessary, at the alternative site. This group will also facilitate the delivery of meals to the alternative site if necessary.

Key responsibilities include:

- Coordinating travel arrangements for all personnel, including activating corporate accounts with several taxi companies, bus rentals, etc., if necessary
- Coordinating with customs brokers if necessary
- Coordinating arrangements for delivery of equipment, computer tapes, supplies and communicating modified instructions to suppliers
- Coordinating meals for personnel
- Accepting travel requests from the crisis management team and all team leaders.

System restoration team

This team is primarily responsible for re-establishing key information resource systems operations. The recovery site provider will largely perform the steps to initially condition the hardware. The systems restoration team will perform all subsequent tasks related to the installation of the operating system, the database and application program within the recovery time and recovery point objectives. Members of this team will also assess the damage and coordinate any salvage effort, as well as complete insurance forms and provide equipment specifications to the vendor.

Key responsibilities include:

- Assisting in the recovery and maintenance of operating system software application software and databases at the alternative processing site(s)
- Establishing and monitoring production operations at the alternative site(s) and the restored/reconstructed primary site
- Coordinating salvage efforts related to computer hardware
- Coordinating the acquisition, delivery, installation, testing, and turnover of the equipment at any alternative processing site(s) and the primary data centre.

Voice recovery team and end-user technical support team

These two sets of responsibilities are often combined into one team. The end-user technical support component of this team is responsible for the restoration of all data communications such as modems and routers for external communication. It is also the responsibility of this team to recover the network operating system(s), applications, and configuration of desktop computers and network servers.

The voice recovery component of this team is responsible for the re-establishment of all telephone services; these would include the redirection of call centre calls, recorded messages on major advertised numbers where necessary, workstations for the processing teams and providing all technical support for them. All tasks related to voice communications, from cabling and equipment installation, to ensuring the proper functioning of telephone services through testing and monitoring, are performed by this group.

Key responsibilities include:

- Activation of interim voice message intercept and assistance in starting up the call centre, if necessary
- Assisting in the recovery and maintenance of network operating system software, application software and databases at the alternative processing site(s)
- Establishing and monitoring network processing operations at the alternative site(s) and the restored/reconstructed primary site

- Coordinating salvage efforts related to telephony, PC and data communication equipment
- Coordinating the acquisition, delivery, installation, testing and turnover of the telephony, PC and data communication equipment at the alternative site(s) and the primary site.

Ongoing support from upper management

As the business continuity planning project winds down, the corporate business continuity processes take over. Part of the changes in corporate culture will include ongoing support from management in continuing to build and reinforce employee awareness and training, and actively participating in recovery simulations, exercises and tests through their corporate recovery support teams. In addition to ensuring that all members of the various corporate teams understand their roles and responsibilities during disaster recovery, it is critical that key backup personnel as well as secondary backup personnel be trained to cover off-staff availability during a disaster and general staff turnover as time passes. Budget dollars should be allocated at the beginning of each to enable the company to continue with ongoing training and awareness programmes and allocate the necessary funds for annual testing/exercising.

Employee BCP awareness

The human resources/personnel/training departments of an organization must play key roles in installing appropriate training programmes for employees of an organization. Initial awareness workshops or seminars should be incorporated into part of all new hire and employee transfer processes as well as assisting with the ongoing maintenance of up-to-date employee notification lists.

Risk evaluation and control: practical guidelines for risk assessment

Ian Charters FBCI – UK

Ian is a consultant with Continuity Systems Ltd in the UK.

Introduction

We spend most of our lives making risk decisions and becoming so adept at it that we rarely analyse how we came to a decision. For example, deciding what time to leave for work will involve many implicit decisions about the chances of delay at various points, applied experience of past journeys and an assessment of the consequences of being late. It is just as well that we do make these decisions intuitively otherwise we would spend all the time trying to assess the risks and never setting off.

However, when we are charged with evaluating risks to our business we must be more explicit in assessment, both because we will need to convince others to take action through our reasoning and because the consequences of getting it wrong may be more serious for ourselves and our colleagues.

There are some fundamental problems when you assess business risks:

- You are responsible to others for managing these risks yet the factors that can affect them are numerous and few may be directly under your control.
- Statistics on catastrophic events are difficult to apply to a single location and type of business.
- We rarely let unlikely events affect our decisions – yet these could have a disastrous effect on our business.

Risk control in many businesses consists of a knee-jerk reaction to near misses and press scare stories. This chapter offers some techniques and strategies to assess risk in a more systematic fashion.

The Definitive Handbook of Business Continuity Management, Second Edition.
Edited by Andrew Hiles FBCI. © 2007 John Wiley & Sons Ltd.

Objective of risk evaluation and control

The Business Continuity Institute states that the objective of risk evaluation and control, within the context of business continuity management, is to determine the events that can adversely affect an organization, the damage that such events can cause, the timescale needed to restore normal operations and the controls that can be implemented to reduce the probability of impact.

Five stages are identified in reaching this objective:

- Understand the loss potentials and vulnerability to such losses
- Evaluate risk analysis tools and techniques
- Define a risk evaluation strategy
- Select a process to evaluate risk
- Establish risk avoidance measures to prevent or minimize the effect.

Threats and vulnerabilities

Some of the many threats to which a business is exposed are fire, flood, power failure, air conditioning failure, lightning strike, industrial action, terrorist activity, malicious damage, contamination, legal action, fraud, theft, software virus, Legionnaires' disease, etc. The specific nature of the threat could be one of an almost infinite list of potential causes and may come from the most unexpected source.

Consider perils:

- From natural and manmade sources
- Having accidental or intentional causes
- That are internal or external to the organization
- Causing material damage, financial loss or damage to reputation
- Resulting from a combination of unlikely circumstances.

Assessing the risk

How do we assess the probability of being struck by a disaster as a consequence of an almost infinite list of threats? There are many surveys and lists but the majority focus on a particular region or industry and will be of little direct relevance to the international readership of this book. You should therefore seek advice from your insurers, local trade associations or business continuity user forums to assess the likelihood of specific threats in your particular location.

Object of risk evaluation and control

The following points illustrate the difficulty of assessing specific threats:

- Certain perils are more prevalent in certain geographic/climatic regions – e.g. tornadoes are more likely in the southern states of the USA but even in the UK we occasionally experience severe storms.
- Earthquakes can occur in any part of the world though they are concentrated on tectonic plate boundaries. Their effects can be felt thousands of miles away – Hawaii was struck by a tsunami caused by an earthquake in Japan.
- Prevalence in the news would lead you to believe that the risk of terrorism in the City of London outweighs the risk of fire. However, statistics show this is not the case.
- Most computer software failures are caused by inexperienced users – they are rarely intentional.
- Employees know how to hit a company – Ernst & Young found 84% of the worst frauds were perpetrated by company employees.
- Most computer fires start outside computer rooms.
- Air conditioning can duct toxic chemicals way beyond their source.
- Floods can occur at almost any height – most high-rise blocks have large water storage facilities on their upper floors.
- Police forces in many parts of the world have considerable powers to declare an area a 'scene of crime' which enables them to deny access and may also prompt a media invasion which can raise security and reputation issues.
- Security companies market their products on saleability and profitability, not on a balanced assessment of the individual company's risk profile. Many of the most crucial security issues cannot be solved by a purchase but are best addressed through staff training, awareness and job satisfaction.

Why undertake risk analysis?

In some industries, risk assessment is mandatory. Increasingly it is required as a key element of corporate governance (e.g. under International Accounting Standards; the UK Combined Code, which has to be complied with for companies listing on the London Stock Exchange; and the UK Financial Services Authority requirements). In other cases, it is being implemented as a result of legislation such as the Sarbanes-Oxley Act (which has an impact far outside the United States, where it originated).

Guidelines for banking and financial services exist in countries worldwide, from the United States to Europe and from India to Canada. Across the globe, Basel II requirements for banking require risk assessment as part of operational risk management.

The UK Financial Services Act 1986 set up a self-regulatory structure to administer non-banking financial markets in the UK under the umbrella of the Securities and Investment Board (SIB). The Act itself allows member institutions to claim force majeure (very loosely translated as act of God) if, and only if, they can clearly demonstrate that the cause of failure was beyond their control and that all reasonable efforts were made to alleviate the effect of failure.

In other words, a securities firm must have examined the effect of disruption to dealing and either have taken all adequate measures to minimize such disruption or be able to show that failure would not materially affect the business. Alternatively, the institution needs to demonstrate that it was beyond its powers to make backup arrangements. Given the existence of commercial DR services and the greater acceptance of the need for BC, this is becoming ever more difficult to prove.

There are increasing pressures for risk assessment for health and safety and for corporate governance across all companies and specifically in a number of other industries, for instance in the food industry and in companies handling hazardous materials. Moreover, there are other pressures that encourage organizations to practise risk evaluation and control:

- Quality standards required of suppliers by their major customers
- The desire of businesses to adopt best practice
- Companies seeking ISO 27001 certification
- Personal liability of directors shown to have been negligent (by not controlling risks)
- Appreciation of the cost to business of disasters and near-misses.

The last point should be the most effective spur for businesses to manage risks. In a competitive environment the loss of reputation or a major customer could be business threatening.

Risk evaluation

A structured approach to risk evaluation involves four steps:

1. Asset and threat identification
2. Quantification of potential losses
3. Assessment of vulnerabilities
4. Evaluation of solutions.

Some pointers to the scope of these steps follow.

1. Asset and threat identification
    Assets:

    (i)   List and categorize your corporate assets
    (ii)   Consider both tangible, intangible (e.g. reputation) and transient (e.g. technological lead) assets
    (iii)   Ensure you have identified all of them

    Look at areas of risk:

    (i)   Policies and procedures
    (ii)   Manufacturing processes
    (iii)   Physical access security
    (iv)   Personnel issues – recruitment, induction and discipline
    (v)   Computer systems and networks
    (vi)   Communications
    (vii)   Marketing and customer interface

    Assess the risks identified:

    (i)   Through interviews and observations
    (ii)   Through structured walk-throughs and 'what-if' scenarios
    (iii)   Then relate these back to your key assets

2. Quantify your potential losses

    (i)   Use company accounts
    (ii)   Let marketing assess the cost of finding new customers or restoring a tarnished reputation
    (iii)   Explore the effects on stock market valuation
    (iv)   Look at recent events in your company and others in your sector
    (v)   Seek outside opinions from insurers, lawyers and consultants

3. Assess vulnerabilities

    (i)   Use appropriate historical data
    (ii)   Apply formulae commonly used in your industry
    (iii)   Make subjective estimates
    (iv)   Agree and apply a risk weighting system (there are many of these which you can adapt or develop your own)
    (v)   Conduct simulation or scenario analysis . . .
    (vi)   . . . then calculate:
            Risk = Impact × Probability
            which should enable you to rank risks from the most serious to the most trivial in terms of their overall impact on the business

Impact Probability	LOW	HIGH
HIGH	Manage	Reduce
LOW	Accept	BC Plan

Figure 10.1—Risk and impact assessment matrix

4. Evaluation of solutions
    Risk control measures fall into one of four categories:

    (i)   Accept
    (ii)   Manage
    (iii) Reduce
    (iv)   Plan

    The types of risk to which each is an appropriate reaction are shown in Figure 10.1.

    (i)   Accept the risk: if the impact of a rare event is low it may be reasonable to accept the risk, such as the occasional theft of company property, which is unlikely to jeopardize the business. Some risks fall outside your control, such as government policy, and so must be accepted by default.
    (ii)   Manage the risk: for frequent low impact risks the most sensible strategy is to monitor and seek to reduce the risk. An example is the development of procedures to reduce operator error.
    (iii) Reduce the risk: a frequent potentially damaging event is a target for risk reduction measures. The hazardous procedure should be re-engineered or carefully monitored to reduce risk. An example in manufacturing could be changing from solvent-based to water-based paints. Alternatively you might outsource the risk – giving it to someone else better equipped to manage it. Insurance can be viewed as an example of outsourced risk.
    (iv)   Business continuity planning addresses risks that are of low probability, such as fire and flood, but whose potential impact is business failure.

It is unlikely that you can remove all risk entirely – any enterprise must involve risk almost by definition. However, by concentrating on their core business many enterprises fall victim to damaging impacts from risks that they had not identified or sought to control.

Is risk control worth doing?

A risk control programme is not a substitute for a business continuity plan. This is because there are serious weaknesses in the various risk analysis methods. They were developed to address wide portfolios of risk, to analyse accidents after the event or to apply quantifiable failure rates in simple engineering systems. When applied to a complex organization at a single location at a particular time they fail because:

- The probability of occurrence for rare events is always a guess.
- Mathematical analysis methods may give a pseudo-scientific exactitude to the results, which are only based on guesswork.
- The least expected can happen – and it is no comfort or assistance to the business that it failed due to a rare event.
- Many disasters happen due to a complex sequence of circumstances that cannot be modelled in advance.
- The reduction of one risk may increase another – a retaining wall can prevent a flood but it can also cause a flood if there is a water leak within the building. Outsourcing risks in particular tends to create other, less obvious, risks elsewhere in the organization.
- The analysis of risk is a means to an end not an end in itself – without action it is pointless.

However, risk control plays an important part in business continuity planning because:

- There is a statutory need for controlling specific risks – especially in the chemicals and financial sectors.
- The control of obvious risks raises awareness and can prevent disasters.
- A risk analysis can support the business case for business continuity at a board presentation.

To finish . . . some ideas to make a success of risk control

- Many problems happen because 'everyone thought that someone else would do it' so make named individuals responsible for each specific risk.
- Make measures appropriate and realistic.
- Use external help from outside (much of it free), from brokers, consultants, fire officers and the police.
- Involve everyone in the evaluation process – education and raising awareness are as important as implementing procedures.

Business impact analysis

Peter Barnes FBCI – UK

11

Peter is an independent consultant with extensive multinational experience in BCM across a number of industries.

Introduction

The business impact analysis (BIA) is arguably the most fundamental and important product of the business continuity lifecycle. It is through, and arguably only through, the conduct of a BIA that the organization's requirements in response to a disaster may be properly assessed and prioritized.

The data produced through the BIA will be used, *inter alia*:

- As a statement of how financial and non-financial losses occur over time, which provides a justification for appropriate spend on continuity and provides a benchmark against which the company's management may assess the risk of underprovision of effective continuity measures or contingency plans and establish their appetite for risk
- As a foundation from which the company's continuity and recovery strategy may be elaborated
- As a method of identifying mission critical activities; the timeframe within which they must be recovered (the maximum tolerable outage or recovery time objective) and the timestamp to which information needs to be recovered (the recovery point objective)
- As a means to establish dependencies and relationships between business processes and, to some extent, the supporting systems or communications infrastructures.

While, depending on the size and complexity of an individual organization or organizational unit, it may sometimes be possible to derive a broad picture of likely requirements using a high-level/'top-down' view of operations, a formal and

The Definitive Handbook of Business Continuity Management, Second Edition.
Edited by Andrew Hiles FBCI. © 2007 John Wiley & Sons Ltd.

well-structured BIA may be almost guaranteed to identify or consider requirements that will not be spotted by any other method. Invariably the benefits of such discoveries far outweigh the apparent costs in undertaking the BIA activity.

This chapter considers the key steps in a BIA, the purpose of each step and the value that it adds to the final outcome. Along the way some of the potential pitfalls and hurdles will be considered together with methods and techniques to overcome them.

Fundamentals – when to undertake the BIA for the first time

A common, though misleading, approach taken by many consultants is to propose to an organization that a BIA be undertaken as a basis from which to develop a business case to commit to development of a business continuity plan. Such an approach assumes that the case for BCP will evolve as a result of the 'shocks and surprises' that emerge from the BIA. This assumption is flawed, not because there might not be surprises along the way, but because it devalues the BIA itself, which will, initially at least, be a significant undertaking that requires a high level of commitment and dedicated resources (all of which we will return to later). Second, and even at this early stage of engagement with business continuity, there is little purpose in undertaking a BIA unless management anticipate a need and will be prepared to act on its findings. The point is that for the BIA itself to be undertaken successfully its purpose must be fully appreciated and supported by senior management in advance of the activity commencing. The precursors to initiating a BIA should therefore be:

- A clearly stated commitment to the wider goals and objectives of business continuity management – ideally driven from the highest levels of the organization
- An indication that the organization has an appetite to invest in the business continuity solutions that will evolve following use of a BIA to help define the requirement
- Prior consideration and, ideally, declaration of policy with respect to the scope of the disaster for which the organization expects to plan.

We will return to the question of when to review or update the BIA in the closing section of this chapter.

Fundamentals – understanding the purpose and goals of the BIA

Business impact analysis (BIA) is defined as 'the management level analysis by which an organization assesses the quantitative (financial) and qualitative (non-financial) impacts, effects and loss that might result if the organization were to suffer a Business Continuity emergency, incident or crisis. The findings from a BIA are used to make decisions concerning Business Continuity Management strategy and solutions'.[1]

In other words a BIA helps to identify what will be lost if business is interrupted, what that loss might cost in profits, loss of revenue, damaged relationships with clients, loss of reputation and so forth. It will also help the reviewer to understand how much of an interruption each process or task can tolerate before the damage or pain becomes real and on what resources (people, machines, documents, other processes, etc.) the business depends. An ideal outcome will have been achieved if the BIA identifies how much resource is needed to protect or recover – and how quickly – in order for the damage to be maintained at a tolerable level such that the business will survive.

The definition above is useful in that it points towards the focus on addressing the 'impacts' of an event – not the cause. Many organizations get deeply involved at the outset of a BIA in defining scenarios but that is not the purpose – in fact overemphasis on scenarios at this stage will only serve to confuse participants and delay the process. It is of no importance in assessing the impact of, say, a denial of access to the organization's head office building, to know whether that denial was caused by a fire, a toxic chemical cloud, or a gas explosion – the underlying result of any of these scenarios is that staff cannot reach their place of work. The consequence, which must be analysed and understood, is that staff being unable to work will impact the viability of the business – the BIA will determine to what extent and how quickly.

In communicating the purpose and definition to colleagues who are not expert in business continuity, a context may be helpful. Experience suggests that the simplest approach is to define three or four high-level scenarios to help your colleagues in the business units that are to be the subject of your BIA, to understand the kind of thinking that should support their input. The simplest scenarios tend to be:

- That the organization's building is out of use
- That the company's ICT is partially or wholly unavailable
- That the company's manufacturing plant has been disabled for an indefinite period of time
- Or any combination of the above (or similar scenarios).

A walk through a comprehensive BIA

The following paragraphs will take you through a step-by-step approach to a BIA. That is not to say that all steps will be needed for all organizations – or that these

---

[1] Business Continuity Institute – Glossary.

steps will be sufficient or satisfy the cultural/organizational working practices of all companies – however, it is hoped that it will offer a useful benchmark.

Step one – define the scope

The first step is to address the scope of the BIA. This may be subdivided into a number of questions.

First, is it intended to conduct the BIA for the whole enterprise or simply for a part – such as a single site or a specific division/profit centre? A number of factors will influence your decision – including the size and complexity of the business, the diversity of the processes to be found within the company and the resources (people) available to undertake the process.

As a general rule it is recommended that, in large enterprises, the BIA process should initially be run as a pilot – preferably with a part of the business that is motivated to participate. This approach ensures that the process to be used is clearly communicated and understood – and that, consequently, the outputs of the process (primarily the questions you need to have answered or addressed by the business) are consistent and in a form that may be used for further analysis and in producing summaries.

In small organizations it may be possible to address the entire requirement without the need for a pilot.

Second, before we can ask the business what will be critical in a disaster we must ensure that there is clarity regarding the definition of a disaster/its scope within the company that is the subject of the BIA. Some thought, and ideally a policy, should also be elaborated with respect to a definition of the period of potential interruption that must be addressed by the BIA. This might be described as the 'planning horizon' and it is clarified or determined by a number of possible factors:

- BIAs developed by subsidiary companies within a group, or departments within an enterprise, should consider the impact their disaster may have on the rest of the companies (or departments) within the enterprise and the impact on the 'corporate' entity or on other brands.
- Some organizations determine that, following a disaster, their goal is to elaborate a detailed strategy, together with associated resources and plans that allow resumption of all business processes within a predetermined time-frame. Such a goal may seem reasonable for a small organization that depends on a relatively generic, easily replaced infrastructure – one with basic office requirements, standard desktop computer and communications require-ments and so forth. Such companies are in the minority – but they exist nonetheless.
- In the majority of organizations it is necessary to start with some high-level questions to come up with a realistic framework or planning horizon. For

example, in a manufacturing concern, the timeframe required to replace a production facility that is destroyed – perhaps by a fire – may be many months or even years. In the service sector the key criteria defining the planning horizon may be determined by the speed with which it is estimated that alternative office space and infrastructure may be sourced and made available – arguably a relatively short time or 'planning horizon'.

- In one example, and where IT recovery capability existed at a secure backup data centre, the decision assumed that, in the worst case, it would be possible to source alternative office space in the same town, and to equip that space with suitable furniture and standard IT and telephone equipment within two weeks; it would also be possible, in that particular location, to route the necessary voice and data communications to such a site within the same timeframe so that staff could commence occupation progressively from that point forward. It was therefore necessary to use the BIA to address the detailed requirements falling critical within the first two weeks (and for which a disaster recovery site would be used). In parallel, recovery of remaining operations could be assessed with a view to commencing the road to full recovery in a newly acquired alternate site, within a couple of weeks.

Step two – data collection – scope

Often the hardest part of the BIA is defining, and communicating to the business under investigation, what you really need to know. Unless you work in an unusually relaxed organization it is unlikely that there is any task or process performed that does not have the potential to become 'important' and potentially 'critical' in due course. However, if you have previously defined and secured agreement to a 'planning horizon' (as proposed in the previous section) your interest is in finding out, and subsequently analysing the requirements of, those processes or tasks that become critical within that horizon. This naturally adds more weight to the argument in favour of defining such a horizon as it sets a clear boundary on the data collection process and, probably, what it is that the business must report into the process. That said, the key issues to be addressed in this section are:

1. What should be within the scope of the BIA (and consequently subject to deeper analysis)?
2. What may be parked – either because it is outside the scope or because its suspension will not have a damaging impact within the 'planning horizon'?
3. Having addressed the previous points, how should we address the 'human' condition that leads us all to assume that everything we do is important – and to differentiate that which is genuinely critical?

Addressing 1 and 2 generally requires an understanding of the business and at least an initial top-down view of the impact of an interruption to part or all of that business. This will generally result in a series of high-level decisions along the lines of:

- 'We must not breach any statutory or regulatory obligation in the event of a disaster but we are not unduly concerned about our other activities'; or
- 'Our core business must be protected at any cost but we can afford to suspend other, non-core activities provided we have a robust method to communicate with our customers and explain why we cannot service them to our normal standards'; or
- 'We cannot afford to be out of the market for any measurable period of time and must seek full contingency of all operations', etc.

Generally, a frank, commonsense discussion with the major stakeholders will arrive at the high-level position that 'fits' your organization.

Some cautionary words about the category 2 issues:

- An important part of the analysis is to identify where a task or process thought to meet the context of category 1 above is found to be dependent upon a task, process or resource that we had initially 'parked' as outside the scope. That such dependencies will be identified is almost inevitable – certainly when conducting a BIA for the first time. A good rule of thumb is that if your BIA fails to identify at least one such 'surprise' you should question the rigour of the application of your BIA procedures.
- In considering what fits in the category 1 processes or tasks that fall critical within the 'planning horizon', consider also the cumulative buildup of a backlog in processing that, if not considered, might result in an unexpectedly damaging or difficult recovery phase. The so-called 'backlog trap' is addressed elsewhere in this book and may lead to affirming a requirement for, say, the accounts department to get back to work rather more quickly than an initial view might suggest is required.

Differentiating 'importance' from 'criticality', to address the third item, is often the toughest challenge to be faced in the data collection phase of the BIA. Typically the way this question is approached is by developing some kind of scoring matrix that measures the interruption to a specified process in terms of factors such as: loss of profits, damage to reputation, damage to customer or stakeholder relations, actual cost to the organization, breach of statutory obligations and so on. The challenge that arises with almost every attempt to score processes using such a method is in the fact that some measurements are 'hard' – they cannot be disputed and the impact will be beyond challenge. However, in many cases the majority will be 'soft' measures – in other words one stakeholder will consider the reputation impact, for example, to be severe and another stakeholder may disagree. Ultimately the decision rests with the organization's executive or senior management to take a view on where they would draw the line between 'importance' and 'criticality'. In this case a useful technique is to apply a process of 'peer review'. To illustrate the way in which this is used, consider the following scenario.

The marketing department have reported that the publication of the monthly customer newsletter should be addressed as a critical process within the firm's planning horizon as failure to publish or delay publication will have a damaging effect on client relationships. Such a statement may well be considered somewhat 'speculative'. This would not be the case, however, in the unlikely event that there is a contractual/legally binding obligation to deliver a newsletter to your customers on a designated day each month. Through a process of 'peer review' the matter may be presented to a small group, perhaps three or four, of stakeholders who are asked to offer their opinion of the position taken by the marketing department. Through such a process it may be proposed and agreed that the newsletter has become such a reliable 'standard' that defines the relationship of the firm with its customers that indeed a delay would have an unsettling effect on that relationship. In this way it might be concluded that the newsletter is regarded as a statement of confidence on the part of the company that must be protected in the same way that maintaining the firm's Internet website presence is increasingly regarded as one of the highest priorities in a disaster.

Step two – data collection – methods

There are a number of ways in which data may be collected for a BIA. These include:

- Questionnaires – to be distributed and completed by responsible staff in the business areas being assessed
- Questionnaires – to be completed bi-laterally in the context of an interview or meeting
- Use of workshops/roundtable discussions. (Such an approach may be useful in achieving a 'balanced' view of the criticality of certain processes and, provided an appropriate cross-section of the business participates in such a workshop, may act as a valid alternative to the peer review recommended in the previous section. However, there is a danger that a senior dominant individual will enforce their views on the group.)

Inevitably there are also a number of software tools available in the market that will facilitate or even automate the collection and analysis of the data.

In any but the simplest of organizations one useful approach born out of experience is to undertake what is fundamentally a three-phase approach to the data collection process although, as will be elaborated below, there may be a number of iterative steps within each phase.

In the first step, approach the whole business (or subunit that is the subject of your BIA). Aim at a reasonably high level of management and invite them to a presentation at which the purpose and scope of the BIA are to be presented. Make it clear that all parts of the business must attend – accept delegated alternatcs if the targeted manager is unable to attend; offer a choice of dates if necessary (according to the size of the potential audience) and be prepared to follow up unilaterally with those who still fail to attend the group discussion. Group presentations are best as the format enables the review team to receive feedback about the BIA procedures that they have presented – to sense the extent to which the messages have been understood and to field questions from the floor with answers that are, hopefully, consistently received and understood by all participants.

Follow up the 'kick-off' presentation with an initial 'filter' questionnaire. At its simplest level this does no more than to ask whether the business unit performs any tasks or processes that, if interrupted or stopped as a result of a disaster event, would lead to a critically damaging impact to the organization. The questionnaire goes on to list those processes considered 'critical'. This approach will clearly only work if the previous step of defining the 'criticality measurement' and the period of the 'planning horizon' has been concluded and communicated. At this stage, the BIA is dependent upon the fact that management in the business understands their processes and tasks best and may be relied upon to identify those processes that meet the criteria for assessment. Some organizations may benefit from having undertaken a comprehensive programme of process mapping. In organizations where this has been performed it potentially simplifies the BIA in that management in a business area may simply be presented with a complete list of their processes for use as a checklist for consideration. A significant added benefit in such cases may be that interdependencies between processes have also been defined by the mapping programme – significantly reducing both the effort in identifying the dependencies and the risk that a significant dependency may simply be overlooked.

There are a number of benefits in the use of the 'initial questionnaire' as a filter in that:

- Inconsistencies in the assessment of criticality will be evident at this stage and may be subject to further discussion/moderation with the owning business unit – or subjected to the 'peer review' approach as previously described.
- The initial input may be compared to the output of the scope discussion, with which we started this chapter, and anomalies or inconsistencies requiring further discussion or clarification may be addressed before the detailed work is undertaken.
- By eliminating processes or tasks that are confirmed as non-critical within the 'planning horizon' you save the business unit what may, in some circumstances, be an extensive amount of time in addressing the more detailed requirements of the BIA's data collection stage.

So up to this point we have:

- Determined the scope of our BIA
- Considered a 'planning horizon' that seems appropriate for the kind of business under investigation

- Established benchmark criteria for assessment of criticality
- Established, and possibly made use of, moderation techniques such as 'peer review'
- Confirmed a list of processes that (subject to further findings) will be subject to more detailed analysis leading to a statement of operational requirements in a disaster.

Now is the time to move forward to the third step of the BIA data collection. In this step we need to collect considerably more data from the business – requiring a more sophisticated questionnaire, or interview process. At this stage the level of detail required no longer lends itself to collection via a workshop – and we become more dependent than ever on input from those who fully understand the processes under evaluation.

The steps in this phase (or the areas for investigation) are:

1. The timing requirement (recovery time objective) – how quickly must the process be recovered?
2. The calendar – is the process continuous or does it follow a cycle or calendar that might be reflected in our later analysis?
3. The recovery point (recovery point objective). Is it essential that business is resumed from the same point at which it was interrupted, i.e. if loss of IT systems and data is an integral part of your disaster event, is it essential to your recovery that when you regain access to your systems that they are in the same position as immediately prior to the interruption or could you revert to an earlier position (and rebuild the missing data) or is data integrity not a prerequisite to continuity of your business?
4. Dependencies (prerequisites) – on what does the process depend (e.g. completion of an earlier process or subprocess by another internal business area or external stakeholder)? What other process(es) depend on this process being completed?
5. Resource requirements – what is the minimum team (staff) requirement – numbers, skills, etc.?
6. What equipment/office facilities, telephones, etc. does the team require and in what quantities to what timeframes?
7. What special facilities does the team need? (This may encompass anything from bespoke equipment to fireproof safes, special pre-printed stationary, etc.)
8. What ICT resources are required (including detailed IT system and application needs)?
9. To what extent does the business already maintain contingency plans/workarounds and what value would these plans be in a disaster?

The emphasis in addressing these questions should normally be on assessing the minimum resources required to sustain the critical process and how the picture might change over time. (Example: You may wish to report a process that usually depends upon a team of 10 people with access to a specific database via a PC client linked to a central server. This process may be able to survive for up to a day provided five people have access to a desk with a telephone within four hours of the disaster occurring – but would need to restore a 'normal' level of operation supported by all the 'normal' resources by the second day.)

1. The time requirement

Increasingly the standard measure for addressing the time requirements of business continuity is the concept of 'maximum tolerable outage' (MTO). This has largely replaced the concept of 'recovery time objective' (RTO) – the difference being that an MTO is considered absolute and is measured from the time the interruption occurred or disaster struck whereas the RTO was often measured from the point at which a disaster was formally declared and could be subject to significant variance if there should be a delay between the point of disaster and the time when a disaster declaration was made.

In assessing the MTO for each process it is important that the business providing the response considers and justifies their response. A broad assumption from the outset is that the faster you need to recover the greater the amount of money that will need to be invested in continuity or recovery strategies. Consider also, in the high speed 'immediacy' of the world in which many of us live today, that if your business continuity or recovery strategy requires staff to move to a second location, there will be a practical difficulty in achieving MTOs that are faster than the time it will take to evacuate your site and travel to the recovery site. It is not uncommon to interview a business manager who insists that his process is critical for recovery within 30 minutes – who has then been quick to concede that the process may survive for at least two hours if the alternative is to permanently split his team across two sites in order to protect a 30-minute MTO. Others, however, have welcomed the two-site operation concept.

2. The calendar

This is a highly significant factor in some organizations and less so in others. It becomes significant in summarizing the resources needed to meet the operational requirement where there is a significant and relatively easily mapped cyclical element to the way in which the business works – particularly in scaling any potential work area recovery site requirement.

3. The recovery point

The recovery point objective (RPO) is another variable that will arise in some kinds of business and not in others. Generally speaking, in businesses that depend upon accuracy of data – banks being an obvious example – that recovery of systems without loss of data may be genuinely essential (in other words, recovering from the point of interruption or even finding ways to avoid interruption in the first place). In other organizations or for other processes it may be perfectly reasonable to expect that business will be resumed from the point of a previous backup and that the missing time can be recovered through re-entering data or by recommencing a production sequence.

4. Dependencies

Identification of dependencies between processes and subprocesses is an essential task for the BIA. The consequences of failure to get this right are prospectively to invest in a continuity or recovery strategy for a key business process only to find that no provision has been made to protect a key prerequisite thereby undermining the entire investment (not to mention leaving the business exposed to significant risk of failure following a disaster).

5. Resource requirements

There is often a tendency for those assessing resource requirements to assume that business continuity assumes the creation of an environment for continuation of business as usual. While this may indeed be the intention in a small minority of businesses, in the majority of cases what is sought, at least for the initial 'planning horizon', is a 'lean mean machine' that can continue what is critical using a minimalist approach pending the stabilization of the disaster and a planned, often phased, resumption of normal levels of business. Treat responses to data collection questionnaires that state that it is an immediate requirement for all staff to resume work with a good deal of scepticism. That is not to say they will not arise – in many cases there will be sound arguments supporting such a case. There may also be a justification in certain cases to increase the number of staff required to support a key process following a disaster – requiring additional staff to be drafted in from other less critical areas. This is a requirement, for example, in a warehouse and distribution facility that was addressing its needs in the face of a loss of IT systems – where the management concluded that a certain level of operation could be maintained by drafting in significant numbers of people to activate somewhat complex manual procedures. Nonetheless emphasis should be placed firmly on the concept of 'minimum resources'.

In this area it is also important to avoid double counting of staff resources. The concept of incremental requirement may be useful here – to ensure that if Process B will require 25 staff but 15 of those had already been identified as essential to resumption of Process A it is only the increment of 10 that is carried forward into the later data analysis phase.

6-8. Equipment, facilities and ICT requirements

The same rules applied to people should be applied to equipment and facilities – that is to say to emphasize the minimum needs – not simply to aim to replicate the normal environment. Bear in mind that, in some cases, the minimum may be higher than normal operations – e.g. to handle call deluge and backlog.

9. Existing contingency plans

Collecting such information can be helpful at this stage as it might influence or at least inform the follow-up strategy formulation. However, you will be well advised not to hold your expectations too high in this area. Experience shows that, in many businesses, a business unit will maintain a contingency plan or a workaround to address the loss of a component of their process (e.g. the temporary loss of access to a communications tool such as email might be protected by falling back to fax or telephone as an alternative). However, such contingency plans will rarely be adequate to provide for the disastrous loss of a significant part of the company's IT infrastructure or the denial of access to a building.

Step three – 'moderation'

It is never sufficient simply to collect data required for a BIA and simply to accept the findings on face value. Some kind of 'sanity check' and moderation process is required to ensure that the findings (from which the organization is expecting to formulate far-reaching strategy decisions that will usually involve significant investment) are sound and reasonable. Experience shows that this step is inescapably a manual task. Even the most sophisticated data collection software/tool can only report on the basis of the data entered into the system and here the old adage of 'garbage in garbage out' should be conscientiously respected.

Moderation is, in some respects, a two-stage process in its own right. First, it is important to assess the validity of the operational requirements that may be elaborated from the data collected. In a second, slightly later, stage, it will be necessary to address the implications of your findings. In other words to address the gaps between the proposed operational requirement and the company's actual continuity and recovery capabilities – or its appetite to address the gaps – so that reasonable recommendations may be proposed. (This emphasizes the earlier observation in this chapter that the output of the BIA is, at best, a 'wish list' to be used by the business as a basis for strategic decisions that will additionally factor in considerations to do with risk and appetite for risk.)

Methods to moderate the BIA data include:

- Comparison of output with the findings of earlier BIA reviews. Is there a sound basis for arrival at different conclusions? Has there been a substantial change to the business such as growth, changes in product or market profile, for example? Or does the change simply reflect a different bias or opinion – perhaps a different person or team has applied different assessment criteria to the criticality or resource demands of a given process. Such issues must be addressed by the BIA team – if doubt still persists as to whether a concrete justification exists for the final position reached, such doubts, if significant, should be presented for guidance to the company's executive (who will ultimately be requested to accept and be bound by the BIA findings or to take and document a different position).
- Comparison of findings across divisions or business units that undertake broadly similar processes – to assess whether they appear consistent and balanced. If they do not, it will be necessary to discuss the findings to balance the output – or to underline why such a variance exists.
- Comparison of findings with initial expectations (which are usually based on experience of the business or of the conduct of BIAs or similar exercises in organizations sharing similar characteristics). The role of the consultant should not be underestimated in this context.
- The use of peer reviews – discussed at length earlier in this chapter.
- Use of a senior figure or panel (perhaps a subset of the company's business continuity steering group or management oversight team) to assess your initial findings and ask questions that will inevitably be asked once your data makes its way to a higher authority.

Step four – the BIA report

The BIA report should present a statement of the operational requirements. It is important to emphasize that it should be limited to this goal – it is not the purpose of the BIA report to propose or recommend the strategy that must be implemented or amended in order to fulfil the requirements. (This can only be done when an assessment of risk, of the organization's appetite for risk and of its ability to invest in continuity and recovery strategies has been taken into account – in other words what the company can and cannot afford to do both financially and to safeguard its reputation.)

The BIA report will usually be structured according to the style and conventions generally used by the organization being evaluated. An additional consideration is that the BIA should be drafted in such a way that it provides sufficient 'evidence' of the process to satisfy a later audit (either an internal audit or one conducted by a third party, for example a regulatory body or other stakeholder with whom you have an extensive disclosure agreement). Consequently the core components would normally include:

- A statement of the purpose of the BIA and its context (i.e. why this BIA now?)
- A statement of, or reference to, the underlying policy or assumptions that form the background to the BIA
- A description of the methods used to conduct the BIA
- An explanation of the steps taken to validate and moderate the data
- A clear statement of any inconclusive output – where a bottom-up analysis failed to convincingly produce a concrete result or recommendation and a higher authority is asked to offer guidance/decide what level of continuity or recovery they require
- A statement of the ramifications of acceptance or non-acceptance of the findings of the BIA. Again this is not an opportunity to develop a strategy recommendation. It is perhaps best illustrated by the spirit, if not the tone, of the following statements:

    - 'Acceptance of the findings of the BIA should lead to evaluation of the current ability of the firm to meet the stated operational requirements following a disaster and implementation of appropriate measures to close any gaps that might be identified.'
    - 'If the [decision-making body/higher authority] chooses not to accept the findings of the BIA or to implement an appropriate programme of work in response to those findings then it must specifically accept the risks associated with such inaction. Such risks include [here follows an illustrative list of the impacts of inaction that may reasonably be extrapolated from the data that has been gathered and analysed].'
    - Finally the report should include specific findings of the analysis – these will usually be in summary form together with directions to the whereabouts of the detailed supporting data.

When to review or update the BIA

This is a topic of much debate and regular pronouncements of so-called 'good practice' which can often be misleading. The most commonly predicated view is that the BIA should be reviewed or updated annually or following a major change to the organization (*change* in this context may be interpreted as anything from the introduction of a new or modified business process, a restructuring of the organization, launch of a new product, etc.).

To assess what really happens in today's businesses one must first address a number of factors that influence the answer.

Depending on the size and complexity of the organization a comprehensive BIA may engage several staff for many months or might be undertaken by one or two personnel in just a few days. In the more complex organization, to follow a literal translation of 'good practice' would mean that the company was in a constant cycle of review of the BIA – which for most companies is unsustainable. What is needed in such organizations is a process to capture and address the impacts of significant change within the organization with, perhaps, a thorough review every second or third year. This implies strong change control, linking BIA to new project or product initiation, HR changes, M&A activity, organizational change, etc.

In the smaller, less complex organization an annual review may well be practical. In some cases it is possible to assign the responsibility directly to the business units to assess only what has changed since the last BIA and analyse the effects of those changes on the findings of the original, comprehensive assessment. Once again it is important to ensure that a thorough bottom-up analysis takes place every second or third year to ensure that the compound effects of 'minor' changes are not allowed to invisibly undermine the basis of the company's recovery strategies.

Experience of BIAs has generally been characterized by the following examples:

- The company that discovered, after failing to undertake a formal update of its BIA for six years, that the company's clients and stakeholders would no longer tolerate a delay in re-establishing communications following a disaster. (Recent years have seen a growing expectation in the immediacy of communications with the growing dependence on the Internet and email and reflecting this acceleration has had the effect of reducing MTOs in many businesses across all sectors.)
- Another company conducted a BIA, implemented a viable recovery strategy based on the IT systems and platforms in use at the time but failed to review the requirements (or the recovery service provision) when, two years later, the company went through a complete overhaul of its ICT infrastructure. The result was that when they suffered a fire in their central IT department their backup tapes were totally incompatible with the systems contracted under a disaster recovery contract (which had never been tested).

Conclusion

The BIA is the basis for decision-making and strategic planning upon which the whole of the business continuity management framework resides. The conduct of a BIA is inescapable if the investment in contingency plans, continuity plans, recovery strategies, etc. is to be properly justified and understood.

I have encountered many scenarios where it has been argued that a BIA is unnecessary. These range from the company that had deployed fast-track planning techniques that claimed to avoid the need for a detailed BIA – however, the later conduct of a BIA identified significant gaps and enhancement needs that were not delivered by the accelerated plan production techniques. (That is not to say they were wrong to fast-track the development in the first place as it could be strongly advocated that any plan is better than none – but it provides a cautionary note for those who believe a BIA will never be required.)

A global leading manufacturer decided that a BIA was unnecessary – only to design an IT and production recovery strategy that failed to consider significant operational or stakeholder needs that, if left undiscovered until a disaster were to occur, would have proved hugely and potentially fatally damaging to the reputation or financial viability of the business. When convinced to undertake a BIA of part of their organization as a pilot, their illusion that they were broadly covered under the '80–20' rule was shattered to the extent that they immediately instituted a global, hugely expensive, bottom-up BIA in order to assess just how vulnerable and precarious their business really was.

However, as with all the steps in the business continuity lifecycle, the BIA should be a 'measured' process. If resources and/or funding are subject to tight constraints then direct them towards a complete evaluation of your most critical business unit rather than a half-hearted and probably inconclusive attempt to skim the surface of the wider organization. Experience proves beyond doubt that a job done properly in one part of the business will invariably generate 'buy-in' to expand the programme progressively throughout the organization – the budget and resources will be found when they are demonstrably needed.

Developing business continuity strategies for the business or work areas

Neal Courtney FBCI – UK

12

Neal is an active writer, speaker and commentator on business continuity management issues and is Market Development Director – International Sales Europe – for BELFOR Europe GmbH.

Introduction

When a business or organization chooses their business continuity strategy it should best reflect the required recovery requirements within the corporate policies of that organization. Ideally it should be the most cost-effective solution, although this may not always be possible within the practicalities of day-to-day business. In order to arrive at this preferred strategy several alternatives, which provide a range of times and certainty of recovery at different costs, should be presented for consideration by the board or senior management. It is recommended that there should be at least three options, each providing relevant solutions to the recovery requirements.

The chosen strategy must be complete and homogeneous in itself. That is, it must meet all the recovery requirements to management's satisfaction without any gaps or weaknesses, such as reliance on a non-contracted verbal assurance of an outside supplier. Any strategy for recovery will always be a balance between acceptable expenditure to the organization versus the peace of mind it provides for those who are charged with running and progressing the organization. It is therefore appropriate to conduct a risk analysis of each alternative strategy and present the logical conclusions of these findings in summary form so that senior management has a real understanding for his or her key decision-making. This will then ensure that if the chosen strategy is not the preferred strategy senior management are aware of the shortcomings and can address these through other means – that is, risk transfer.

The rule of thumb for business continuity is that the less it costs then potentially the greater the risks and the less the speed and certainty of recovery, and vice

The Definitive Handbook of Business Continuity Management, Second Edition.
Edited by Andrew Hiles FBCI. © 2007 John Wiley & Sons Ltd.

versa. It is essential that the organization's senior management take on board the full cost implications of their preferred strategy choice. It is not appropriate or indeed a viable approach to select the recovery results of a strategy without accepting and then implementing the full resourcing requirements with the supporting financial budget. Usually a chosen strategy will lie somewhere between the cheapest and the most expensive alternatives, with perhaps some modifications structured by senior management to reflect the corporate policy for recovery. Such modifications must be examined, however, to ensure that any changes in resource requirements and implied costs are picked up.

Any strategy should demonstrate a clear understanding of the recovery planning objectives and truly reflect what the business needs to be able to continue trading profitably, or, however, it is judged in terms of its viability. It is therefore essential that there is utmost confidence in the business impact analysis which will have been completed to identify the critical functions that must be recovered, the minimum levels of activity that they must be recovered to and the maximum acceptable outage time for each function. These are the targets that the strategy must meet in order to be certain that the organization stands the best chance of survival following a disaster. It is important that the board or senior management also takes into account the strategic direction and initiatives of the organization in their final strategy decision, as only they are likely to be aware of these. Should these not be taken into consideration then it could well be that the organization's recovery is jeopardized, or at best confused and therefore delayed, when the disaster strikes and the continuity plan is activated.

An essential aspect of the business continuity strategy is to ensure that appropriate and timely contingencies and other resources are provided or available, such that the critical functions can be promptly and successfully restarted under the guidance of the business continuity plan. Contingencies refer to planned replacements for any resources, which may become unavailable in an unexpected way or at an unexpected time. These resources would normally be those required to support the organization's critical functions. For instance, a resource could be a service such as the telecommunications infrastructure or a facility such as fully equipped and ready to occupy office space. Any contingency should be suitable for the required purposes. Furthermore, it should be available at a cost that is reasonable for the circumstances and maintainable by the business.

If existing contingency arrangements have been entered into, or contingency plans have been prepared, these should be reviewed for their suitability or content. If their functionality is relevant then they should be included in the appropriate strategic recovery option for consideration. The mere availability of non-strategic options should not be allowed to compromize strategic recovery options. Such a policy could seriously undermine the process of selecting the best recovery solution for the organization. It must also be said, however, that pragmatism may be necessary. For instance, if an in-house mirrored mainframe computer facility has been invested in it would be inappropriate to suggest that this should not underpin any recovery strategy! However, usually existing contingencies and contingency plans are for specific, local situations whereas what is now required is a location-wide or company-wide approach.

There is obviously a risk that any existing contingencies may be unsatisfactory for the new approaches. For instance, if there is a computer facility of a specific type at one of the company's locations it may already have its own contingency in place. This contingency arrangement should be checked to see that it meets the recovery needs of each of the critical functions at that location, but equally should be considered in relation to the other locations of the organization where this is appropriate. It is, after all, quite possible that another location could provide a contingency service for this first location without continuing with the third party arrangement, thus saving costs that could then be reinvested in other aspects of the preferred recovery strategy.

Additionally, where an outside supplier provides computing or other services then that supplier's contingency arrangements need to be examined to see if they meet the organization's needs. Where the strategy determines that moving location is necessary in the event of a disaster, then it is also important to establish whether this supplier's services can be provided at the contingent location within the recovery time limits.

Business/work area recovery

It is a reasonable assumption that in many instances the major contingency likely to be required is for the place of work. This type of contingency is usually referred to as 'work area recovery'. Its specifications need to be decided before the method of contingency provision can be selected.

Requirements for work area recovery

In conjunction with the recovery requirements for the critical functions, which have already been established, it is also necessary to consider the following.

Time

There are two aspects in relation to time. The business impact analysis will have established the time by which work must be restarted. However, it must be borne in mind that there is a time required to get the work area recovery facility operational and then a time, which is required by the business activity, such that they are operational at the predetermined level at that facility. This overall time should obviously not exceed the original time determined by the critical function to re-establish operations to avoid business losses.

Period of occupancy

A further consideration is the period of time over which the recovery area will be required for occupation. This is obviously dependent on the nature of the event and the extent of damage to the normal place of work, and can range from a few days to many weeks. It is wise to plan for a stay of 60–90 days at the very least, as this will provide the required time to procure any alternative contingent arrangements, should they be necessary, before returning to the normal place of work. As a further contingency it is also perhaps diligent to have reviewed what internal arrangements may be necessary in the event that the original premises is too seriously affected to return to at all.

Geography

It is important to consider if there are any business or social reasons, which necessitate the locating of the work area recovery in a specific locale. For instance, if the business customer base is within a specific catchment from the existing location then it is most likely that the business will need to remain in that locality. Second, it is of paramount importance to consider how employees, and perhaps customers, would get to, or access, any contingent recovery area. If this is not reasonably near the normal location of the business then transport or hotel accommodation may be required for employees and communications will need to be made effectively to customers so that you continue to receive their custom.

Size

The size of the work area facility is obviously largely dependent on the numbers of employees requiring accommodation immediately. This number will in turn be dependent on the recovery requirements determined by the critical business functions, as well as the management's policy. Although some very large work area recovery sites are available (some over 2000 seats), it is less common to expect the recovery area to accommodate all employees and more reasonable that only a proportion of them (typically between 20 and 30%) are immediately accommodated.

Where the numbers of employees are initially small and the stay in the recovery area becomes extended, management may wish to increase their numbers and thus return to a more normal work output, using the contingent site. If this could be a requirement of the contingent facility then consideration should be given to this aspect beforehand so that the necessary preparations can be completed.

Assets/facilities

The work area recovery site will need to contain all the assets/facilities, in the required quantities, to enable the work of the critical functions to be restarted and continued within the specified timescales. Such facilities are likely to include the following at the very least:

- Desks and chairs
- Telephones, photocopiers, fax machines, etc.
- Storage for working papers and reference items, i.e. filing cabinets, etc.
- Employee welfare facilities
- Toilet facilities.

Depending on the nature of the critical functions to be recovered, other resources, for example PC network systems or information feeds such as Bloomberg and Reuters, may need to be made available.

Computing and other activities

Many organizations rely on computing services provided by in-house facilities. Some organizations have manufacturing, assembly, warehousing or other activities that are, or have, critical functions for recovery. These are covered in the next sections of this chapter. The point to be made here is that it may be desirable, for reasons of economy or convenience, to include these other activities within the same recovery area as the clerical business functions. In such a case, all the recovery requirements will need to be taken together.

From the above considerations the list of requirements, and therefore selection criteria, for the recovery area can be made. If the organization has an individual responsible for the premises, it could be advantageous to draw on their expertise and involve them in the selection process for the recovery area.

Types of contingencies

In brief, selection of any contingency is a balance between the cost the business can afford to sustain and the degree of risk it is comfortable to incur. Access to a contingency, such as a mainframe computer facility or a work recovery area, can only be guaranteed when it is owned. If any other alternatives are selected then it is essential that wherever possible written contracts or SLAs (service level agreements) be entered into to guarantee provision of the facility. Anything less than this will introduce a degree of risk and while this uncertainty may be acceptable where the impact of the threat is low, it could make the difference between surviving or failing if the impact is clearly of a substantial magnitude.

There are principally four contingency types that can be used by a business continuity strategy.

In-house

The least risk option, and invariably the most expensive, is to acquire or set up an in-house contingency. Such a facility could be put in situ for almost anything from offices to warehouse or production facilities. The limiting factor is the cost of these facilities and the additional assets that are then depreciating and will require maintenance and update. The main advantage is that these facilities are to the exact specification required by the business, potentially without compromizes, and additionally these facilities can be accessed at any time without time constraints on occupation. Furthermore, the organization is able to test the contingency at any time or at any level of activation. It may be possible to offset some of the costs by arranging for a commercial recovery site provider to market subscriptions to the facility to non-competitive organizations.

In view of these advantages and disadvantages such an approach is only usually adopted where facilities must be on stand-by for immediate use or where equipment is unique or difficult to obtain within acceptable business timeframes. A perfect example is a financial securities trading floor where seconds or minutes lost may amount to substantial financial losses if positions remain open. In certain circumstances a business will make use of a contingent site as an overflow facility or as a research and development facility to absorb some of the extra costs. The problem with this is that, more often than not, as business increases the requirement to maintain this facility as a true contingency becomes less of a priority as cost savings accrue through not having to create new facilities to accommodate the increase in trading activity.

Third party contracts

Where the contingency is secured through an outside supplier, this is known as a third party contract arrangement. Usually this facility is sold several times to different organizations to cover the supplier's start-up and maintenance costs. The advantage of this over an in-house facility is primarily one of cost as any owned facility is likely to be far more expensive to set up at the outset, with a considerable outlay for ongoing maintenance. Various different types of contingency are available from third party suppliers, most commonly IT related. For instance:

1. Mainframe and server computing facilities – these could be of a 'warm start' type, i.e. capable of being up and running typically within 24 hours, or of a 'cold start' type where temporary 'Portakabin'-type units are transported to the recovery location and equipment is installed to be running typically within 7–14 days after invocation. Usually such suppliers address any planning permission requirements as part of setting up the contract.
2. PC networks – a number of companies now specialize in providing considerable quantities of preconfigured PCs such that a company's computer networks can be replicated within 24 hours.
3. Telecommunications – contingencies range here from delivering a replacement PABX through to providing complete operational call centres. Times for delivery can range from virtually instantaneous for the latter to most typically within 24 hours for the former.
4. Work area recovery – time from invocation to achieving a working environment can vary considerably, depending on client requirements. A subdivision of this is dealing room workstation recovery centres that are very often available on a 'hot start' basis to meet the financial loss implications of being unable to trade for even a matter of minutes.
5. Web services – some 'hot' recovery sites also provide recovery for web servers. An alternative is a hosting arrangement.
6. Contact centre recovery – this may be catered for by hot sites and can be provided by very large contact centres that have excess capacity.

The overriding advantage of any third party arrangements is the redundancy factor. If a company owns its facilities then it has to maintain the currency of the equipment. With the acceleration of development on computing and the inherent redundancy of equipment, within months now not years, this can become a considerable extra financial burden for a company. Conversely, any external arrangements by their very nature are more risky than an in-house controlled solution. Other potential disadvantages are the time allowance on or using these facilities before they must be vacated or high rental penalties are applied, which may not be covered by increased cost of working insurance.

With most of the suppliers a degree of testing is factored into the annual contract fee to ensure the facility will operate to client expectations if it is invoked in anger. The supplier should be able to integrate the contingency activation details into the BCP and the contract should state categorically what are the exact deliverables upon invocation. It is, however, essential that the client then confirms that all items and facilities do exist and can operate as required.

Reciprocal arrangements

If an organization enters into an agreement to assist another part of the organization or a totally separate organization then this is termed a reciprocal arrangement.

Such agreements for reciprocal recovery should ensure that should one site be affected, the facilities of the other become available to the agreeing party. However, when one business relocates to another the impact of the disaster is invariably exported to that second business. Reciprocal arrangements are often feasible and cost effective in theory; however, unless there is existing compatible spare capacity in the receiving premises which matches the requirements of the displaced personnel, then further disruption will ensue in trying to accommodate them, especially if employees then have to share equipment and other necessary facilities. One resolution to this problem is to utilize parts of the premises or indeed alternative premises where the space is not currently in use as workspace. Examples of this would be an in-house restaurant facility or an off-site training centre. Changes in work patterns could also be used to accommodate two streams of employees during partly extended working hours.

Although reciprocal arrangements incur minimal cost they require considerable thought to ensure the recovery of the affected organization is not compromised. For this reason, wherever possible, such agreements should be written and not left as verbal 'gentlemen's agreements' but should be contractual. This is especially the case where the reciprocal organization may have competitive aspects of the other party's business.

Additionally, it is important to recognize that where the reciprocal arrangements include use of computing equipment, what may start as two similar organizations when the agreement is initiated, can rapidly diverge as the technology requirements of the individual organizations develop.

Reactive

There are numerous examples where a business will secure a replacement at the time of a disaster and this is frequently done for minor events which occur, such as hiring a piece of presentation equipment if the in-house one fails. However, specialist items, say a video conferencing facility, may not be readily available. Normal office equipment is usually available off the shelf but larger quantities of electronic items such as laptops and desktop PCs may take days to obtain, particularly if they must have particular specifications. Also it is important to be aware that, since product design and specification usually change over time, it may not be possible to replace the existing equipment with identical items. In many instances this may not be a problem, but if it is perceived this could be an issue, then periodic checks with the suppliers may be advisable to understand what exactly can be supplied at short notice.

For replacement premises this approach assumes that a suitable property can be obtained and made ready within the predetermined restart time constraint. A list of property agents, or even a list of suitable properties, could be maintained for immediate use. With the exception of maintaining the list, the cost of this option is low, but it has the inherent risk that no suitable properties will be available when needed. Issues which may delay finding utilizable premises include, for example, cabling infrastructure requirements, air conditioning, location, lease/ occupancy contract arrangements and intended usage versus permitted use.

If a reactive approach is chosen, consider the use of furnished, serviced office facilities, available in many large towns. These may include office computer systems, meeting rooms and possibly video conferencing facilities.

Organization, administration and support issues

Any business continuity strategy requires a distinct infrastructure to ensure that the recovery is effectively managed. The recovery organization need not be the same as that in daily use: in fact it is more often preferable to select a unique and specific structure consisting of suitable individuals who are capable of implementing the BCP. Such individuals will need to be organized into teams with specific responsibilities for certain actions of response and recovery. Throughout the recovery the organization would operate under this structure, thereby ensuring that only individuals required for the organization's timely recovery are present and organizing the relevant actions and activities. At the end of the recovery period the organization can then return to its normal management infrastructure.

It is important to recognize that there is usually a requirement for two recovery teams or two tracks of recovery activity. First, the recovery at the contingent site, which obviously takes first priority if business is to be resumed as quickly as possible. Second, the activity which must occur to address the potential damage at the original site to understand the extent and ramifications of the damage such that plans can start to be assembled to return to pre-incident levels of activity. Each of these teams would have differing concentrations of expertise reflecting the main actions and issues that need to be addressed.

For instance, at the contingent site it will be necessary for an 'administration team' to oversee that everything required for the office functions is in place and working – that is, desks, chairs, telephones, stationery and so forth, and that employees can reach the site without undue inconvenience and that rest and eating facilities are available to them as necessary. Additionally an 'IT recovery team' would ensure that the hardware was operational and that individuals were able to access their relevant software applications and data when required.

Vital records and paper documentation issues

Even in our present technological era we are all still heavily dependent on hard copies of information and data. There are moves in many larger organizations towards the paperless office via the use of microfiche, scanning and increasingly document imaging systems. However, for a large number of companies the need for paper records of work in progress is still a reality. Such paper documentation is particularly susceptible to damage from fire, flood and other physical disasters. Clear-desk policies are commendable in principle but notoriously difficult to enforce or maintain. It is better to encourage employees to safely store essential documentation in closed drawers or filing cabinets and archive records off-site or in fireproof cabinets if they are of a critical nature. Comprehensive duplication is not practicable in many instances but for some essential records may be a viable alternative. Where possible, review how essential documentation could be replicated if it became necessary to do so. If this process then highlights which documents are more difficult to obtain this will provide guidance on what to keep protected.

Computerized data and software should have a program for frequent, automatic, backing up with the backups being taken immediately off-site for safekeeping. Any such system should be designed so that the backup procedures are not onerous on the business and consequently recovery is simple to either the existing or contingent sites.

The business continuity strategy should have helped to determine which assets, including documents, are essential for recovery and therefore require protection. It is then relatively straightforward for the recovery team using the BCP to collect these and deliver them to the contingent site. (If any backed-up data is recalled from off-site storage for the computer recovery, remember to return this to the off-site storage as soon as possible.)

If there are any items for which availability cannot be guaranteed, but which are essential to the continuation of the business, then these must be detailed beforehand and 'workarounds' considered to negate the effects of such unavailabilities.

Restoration

Restoration should be an essential aspect of any recovery strategy, although many aspects of the restoration programme can only be determined once damage occurs and the effects are assessed. There are nevertheless a considerable number of preparative measures, which can be planned beforehand. These will ensure focused and effective actions are taken in the very early stages of a recovery, which can dramatically reduce the impact of a disaster and the overall time it takes to get back to pre-incident status.

Such preparations include bringing together the right skills base to accurately assess the damage to the premises and assets so that the options for recovery can be rapidly and objectively assessed. With this reliable and substantive information available, decisions on short-, medium- or long-term displacement can be reviewed and any requirements to escalate procedures can be taken in good time to reduce any additional disruption, which might otherwise result. Conversely, it is also possible that, by knowing quite soon after the event that a return to the existing premises may be possible, this could prevent the second wave of employees needing to go to a contingent location, with all the associated disruption.

Furthermore, just as with data, the strategy should record which assets are essential to support the critical activities and their location as this will assist in the damage assessment and recovery process. If such assets, as is often the case within manufacturing environments, are on long lead times or are unique and no longer manufactured, then restoration may be the only assured strategy for recovering the business operations. In such circumstances a business may find it necessary to outsource aspects of their production process while the equipment is restored. Any such strategy should be preceded by investigating and planning how this could be fulfilled.

Salvage considerations

Salvage and restoration may be the quickest way of replacing damaged equipment. Although the companies operating in the salvage and restoration industry can often achieve wonders with what at first may appear irrecoverable it is still preferable to ensure that critical items receive adequate protection. In the immediate aftermath of a physical disaster there are two major activities:

- How serious is the damage?
- How can we stop the damage getting worse?

In all instances, therefore, part of the recovery strategy should address the coordination of skilled personnel to ensure the damage is quickly quantified and qualified so that time for recovery and the extent of remedial activity can be determined. Second, there needs to be coordination of the activities to stabilize the damage so that the initial losses do not escalate further and cause unnecessary additional activities which could divert other essential resources. An example of this is the rapid freezing of water-saturated documents to prevent further deterioration, or the reduction of humidity to reduce the corrosive action of the products of combustion of PVC cabling combined with water.

There are firms offering salvage and restoration assistance with priority site attendance for a small annual retainer. The business continuity strategy should include a salvage and restoration contract as part of the overall risk management of the business. Selection of a provider for such services should take into consideration:

- Your location(s) relative to the supplier's operational centres
- The level of resources both human and equipment that can be rapidly deployed
- What guarantees are offered on site attendance: the skills and experience relevant to your business
- The insurance cover that the supplier has in force.

Understanding these criteria will ensure that should a fire, flood our other physical disaster affect your business then you will receive the maximum relevant support to effect a timely recovery.

The BCP should then detail when and how to call out these contractors and ensure that liaison with them, insurers and loss adjusters is integrated within the actions of an appropriate recovery team.

Business continuity strategies for financial services

Jillian Simms FBCI – UK

13

Jillian Simms, FBCI, is a director of Cornwood Risk Management, a consultancy specializing in business continuity management in the financial services sector. Jillian is recognized as the only business continuity management professional in the UK with extensive front office trading experience. As European Marketing Director of the Chicago Board of Trade, the world's largest financial futures exchange, she was responsible for managing communication with European members following the Chicago flood. She was previously a stockbroker and bond arbitrage trader.

The financial services sector has traditionally led the way in the development and improvement of business continuity practices and can be expected to do so for many more years to come. This is due to a number of factors including:

- The time horizons under which financial services operate
- The nature of many of the employees
- The complexity of the technology
- The influence of regulators and regulation.

To better understand the financial services sector and how it affects business continuity practices, it is necessary to divide the organizations operating in this sector into two groups: those that service the retail customer (the private individual) and those that operate in the institutional or professional marketplace. It is appreciated that most of the large financial institutions operate in both these areas but they will do this through two different divisions. These two divisions will have very distinct managements, infrastructures and operating models and can best be thought of as two separate organizations under a single corporate umbrella.

Retail sector

Financial services to the retail customer have in the past been provided via a nearby branch of a bank or a local insurance broker, with these individual units

The Definitive Handbook of Business Continuity Management, Second Edition.
Edited by Andrew Hiles FBCI. © 2007 John Wiley & Sons Ltd.

supported by a central or head office structure. The business continuity requirements for this arrangement would need to have in place a method for redirecting customers to another of the bank's branches or insurance company's brokers at the time of a local disruption, together with the means to re-establish the support and head office services within a reasonable time horizon if there was a disruption at the central location. Customers would be expected to be tolerant of being told by the teller in the branch that they could not have the balance on their account or by their local insurance broker that the quote for their car insurance would not be calculated until the following day. This tolerance was assumed because the customer was talking to someone they knew and trusted who could reassure them that waiting a day or two for the service would not be too much or a problem. The customer in having a relationship with this local individual had a relationship with the financial services provider and was unlikely to take their business elsewhere due to a short disruption once in a while.

Today, many of us, at least in the UK, only go into a branch of our local bank in special circumstances, conducting most of our banking over the Internet. Our salaries get paid directly into our bank accounts; we view our accounts online at any time of the day or night at our convenience; and we pay our bills by direct debit or via a few clicks of our home computer mouse buttons. If we need to talk to someone at our bank, we do this over the telephone, not to an individual at a local branch, but to a call centre where our query is answered by an operator who understands our request – if we are lucky – only once he or she has consulted the necessary databases of information about us. Similarly, insurance is obtained by comparing quotes from different web-based providers before selecting the preferred price and conditions. The customer is likely to speak to someone at the insurance company only if they need to make a claim. Once again, the contact will not be to a particular individual but to a call centre where the operator will need to refer to databases of information before responding to the customer's needs.

Customers are encouraged by advertising to consult a variety of organizations for the provision of any new financial product or service they require. Organizations offering these products and services are forced to compete on price and ease of access as well as quality of the product or service. Once an account is opened, or a policy purchased, the customer tends to remain with the provider only if they are completely satisfied with the services they receive. It is no longer considered too much trouble to make a change as all organizations have processes in place to make it easy for the customer to move. Customers have no direct relationship with the provider and so have no loyalty when they perceive there to be more reliable alternatives elsewhere.

This new style of financial services has created a significant challenge to business continuity practitioners. Although the importance of the local service has diminished in day-to-day management of an individual's financial product requirements, this lack of local relationship has eroded the customer's tolerance for any disruption of the centrally provided services. At the time of purchasing a new product such as car insurance, the customer will disregard any supplier where the website is unavailable or too slow to download. An online bank account that is unavailable, even for a short period of time, tends to be viewed as unreliable whatever the message that appears on the site. A person in a call centre that cannot provide the information required because of an unavailable database tends to be dismissed as unhelpful regardless of how charming he or she is and the reasons they give. More and more financial organizations are realizing that this new demanding customer base expects true continuity of service. The organization is then faced with the cost of ensuring there are no single points of failure in their infrastructure, at a time when the market is becoming more competitive and profit margins are being eroded. This means that the business continuity practitioner has to be ever more inventive in ensuring critical services are provided at an adequate level at all times, while keeping the cost of providing these services to a minimum.

It would require minimal analysis, but be extremely costly, just to replicate the entire infrastructure of an organization including people, technology and data. The idea of building an additional call centre and employing additional staff just so that there are services available when there is disruption at another call centre is against the ethos of the current lean working environment. Even if an organization chooses to do this, it would be faced with issues of additional training and motivation. Too often an organization only considers the single points of failure of its technology, rather than its people. To develop viable, cost-effective, business continuity it is necessary for the business continuity manager to understand the way the business is conducted normally, the expectations of the customers, the aspirations of the management and the effect of disruptions. It is only then that BCM can be incorporated appropriately into the organization.

Wholesale or institutional sector

Financial services for the wholesale sector are centred on the dealing room. This tends to be a large open-plan room with row upon row of desks each equipped with multiple screens, systems and communication tools. From this room, highly paid traders, salespeople, structurers and analysts make prices, create financial products and provide advice to professional investors. It is a fast and furious environment where millions of pounds, euros, dollars or yen of investments change hands at the click of a button or the word of a trader on the telephone. Here, even more than in the retail sector, advances in technology have made it possible for traders to execute business across the globe at any time of day or night. Prices in financial instruments are displayed on screens, transmitted via various information providers to numerous offices, and can be traded by the click of a button. In the past, prices on screens were for information only requiring a conversation with the trader before a deal could be completed. Today, with advances in technology that ensure that the image on the screen is consistent everywhere, it has become possible to ensure the information displayed is current and so transactions can be executed directly via the system. Furthermore, if an investor requires a special financial instrument, structurers using advanced technology can price and manage financial instruments with any characteristic the investor desires. It has often been said that the most advanced technological tools either drive rockets or price esoteric financial instruments. These sophisticated pricing techniques require extensive historical data and complex mathematical modelling, all of which would be impossible to achieve without technology and a consistent flow of information.

Ensuring that there is adequate, workable business continuity for a dealing room continues to be a considerable challenge for most of the major investment banks. The markets operate continuously and are highly unlikely to stop due to a disruption in a single location. There are professionals, known as arbitragers, who spend their days scanning the markets looking for mismatches in prices from which to profit, so any unmanaged information on an automated trading screen can be very costly. There is also strict regulation requiring all trading to be done within a 'controlled environment', often within a particular jurisdiction, so relocation of traders is something that needs to be carefully managed.

Outside the dealing room, all investment banks have the additional challenges associated with ensuring adequate, workable, business continuity for the Operations and support areas. The area of the organization that handles the processing and settlement of all the products traded in the dealing room is known as Operations. Here, all the transactions are matched, confirmed, reconciled and settled. Each type of product, in each currency, will have its own operations process, with designated deadlines and methodologies. This means that an Operations department will have numerous tasks throughout the day where a specific process will have to be conducted or the requirements associated with processing a product would be breached. Increasingly, products have very short turnaround times between trading and settlement, such as same day or T + 1 (today + one day). In this type of market, the Operations department often has only a few hours for information to be received from the dealing room, matched with information from the operations department of the organization on the other side of the transaction (the counterparty), confirmed as correct and settled.

In the past, these processes would have been done manually with paper deal tickets being passed from team to team as each stage is completed. However, today the volumes are too large and the turnaround times too short for this manual processing. Much of the Operations process is now completed automatically using technology and this is known as straight through processing (STP). The people employed within an Operations department tend to deal only with errors (mismatches) or special instruments that cannot go through STP. This change in the function of Operations teams means that the individuals no longer have the knowledge to conduct the processes without the technology and so cannot revert to manual processing at the time of disruption even if the volumes would permit this. Furthermore, to speed up this process, various industry-wide bodies, such as Crest for the UK equity market, have been set up to act as a central repository for the processing, so that the technology from each institution does not need to link to all other institutions; instead it needs to link to the industry-wide body.

To ensure market confidence in the use of these industry-wide bodies, these bodies have had to demonstrate evidence of business continuity so that the industry is confident of their availability at all times. Similarly, one of the key features of the wholesale market is that all the major banks are each other's counterparty. So, although it is a highly competitive market, they all appreciate that a failure by one of them could disrupt the settlement of all of them. This feature is known as systemic risk and is one of the main issues facing business continuity in the financial sector.

To properly appreciate the set-up of a participant in the wholesale financial services sector it is necessary to consider the 'middle office'. The dealing room is known as the 'front office', Operations as the 'back office' and all the control functions as the 'middle office'. These control functions usually include market risk management, credit risk management, operational risk management and financial control. These areas are responsible for ensuring and demonstrating that there is adequate risk management and control for the business that is being conducted. They set limits, for example on how much stock an individual trader can hold or how much of a particular currency the organization can hold, and then take data from the other parts of the organization to assess whether these limits have been breached. All of this presents yet a further challenge to business continuity as an organization is not permitted to conduct business until it can demonstrate that it is being conducted in a controlled manner; in other words, until it can demonstrate that it has its systems available to manage the middle office.

Putting in place the business continuity arrangements for an organization involved in trading financial products in the wholesale market is like a jigsaw puzzle as it cannot be regarded as complete without all the necessary pieces being put in place. Each piece needs to be given the right level of priority and connectivity for the whole thing to work.

Finally, although the dealing room, operations and the middle office can be considered as the heart of the wholesale market, there are numerous other functions in the wholesale sector: investment management, where professional managers manage pension funds and other pooled investment vehicles; corporate finance, where professional advisors provide advice to companies on how best to raise money to finance their businesses; and corporate banking, which provides banking services for companies. The inclusion of any these areas adds further complication to the business continuity arrangements as there is the requirement to retain 'Chinese walls'. These are barriers to the flow of information between one department and another to prevent any suggestion of a conflict of interest. For a business continuity practitioner, they mean physically segregated areas in a work area recovery (WAR) centre.

Time horizons

As can be seen from the descriptions above, the financial services industry operates with very short time horizons. A business continuity practitioner working within another industry may find it acceptable to assess the impact of disruption across a time horizon of days whereas in the financial services sector the assessment has to be done across minutes or hours.

When considering the possibility of lost data, most organizations are now appreciating that even the loss of data over a few minutes is unlikely to be acceptable. Consider your own bank account, how would you feel if the few minutes' lost data included your salary payment? Consider the complex pricing model which is continuously gathering data and would be flawed if there is a gap in the data. Consider the multimillion pound transaction where the execution details (price, size, counterparty) are lost. For most financial organizations the challenge is compounded as data in one system may or may not have flown through to another. Reconciling this flow between front, middle and back office systems and identifying and re-entering any missing data is increasingly impossible due to volumes and the delay it would cause to the resumption of money-making and customer-facing activities. As a consequence, the financial services sector is increasingly coming to the conclusion that the only acceptable level of data management is the removal of the risk of any data being lost. An RPO (recovery point objective) of no data loss has become the target for many areas, and so data replication and data management has become a huge investment in money and effort for the financial services sector. Improvements in technology to support this effort are being conducted by numerous technological institutions across the globe.

RTO (recovery time objective) – how quickly an area has to be operational – is even more challenging for business continuity. Even though the analysis may indicate that minimal downtime is acceptable, the challenge to get operational again at the time of disruption may need more than sophisticated technology. Few financial services organizations maintain duplicate teams in two or more locations conducting the same activities. A sales force may be spread across the globe but each location will specialize and have relationships in that location. A trading team may pass a trading book around the globe to cover the different time zones but can they cover each other's time zone? Even if there are duplicate teams, is there enough capacity to cope with one team not being available? We have seen cases where the team in one continent theoretically had the skills and the capacity but not the experience to take over from a team in another time zone. An organization may have more than one call centre but can they cope with the volume of calls if one of the call centres is not operational or does it result in all calls having unacceptable waiting times?

Financial services organizations are in most cases faced with the need to transfer staff from a disrupted location to an alternative location or WAR (work area recovery) site. A major limitation on the RTO is the time it takes to get the people to the alternative location. This on its own would encourage organizations to locate their WAR sites relatively near to the primary working location. However, in the wake of the attack on the World Trade Center and the bombings in London on 7 July 2005, organizations and regulators have become increasing concerned about region-wide disruptions. This has resulted in the locating of WAR sites on the very edge of the City of London, or further afield. The organization has to balance the need for quick recovery times with confidence of availability at the time of wide-scale disruption. For some of the largest organizations, it has been impossible to make this choice and they have implemented both near and far WAR sites.

This pressure of having very short RTO has invariably affected the whole structure and set-up of an organization. Very few major investment banks now have both people and the technology based in a single location. It is now regarded as impossible to cope with both the recovery of the people and the reestablishment of the technology within the required time horizons, regardless of how well an organization is resourced. Increasingly, the dealing room is in one location and the primary and secondary data centres are elsewhere. Waiting for syndicated WAR site space to be made available is also not regarded as acceptable. A dedicated WAR site is now standard for any major participant in financial services, with syndicated space only used to provide additional space for an extended outage.

Nature of the employees

Financial services, in particular the wholesale sector, tend to attract a demanding and focused type of individual who is dedicated to the generation of revenue both for the organization and for themselves. These individuals are resistant to having their time wasted and are not tolerant of being asked questions for which they can see no purpose. Many organizations now employ a layer of 'business management' who are essentially administrators who handle all aspects of running the organization except the conducting of the actual business. Business continuity practitioners who do not have a good understanding of the business and often do not have the confidence to conduct their analysis with the revenue generators tend to conduct it with the business managers. However, this usually results in an overvaluation of the importance of the work done by the revenue generators and a lack of full appreciation of the technology they use and how they use it. It is better to conduct the analysis by tailoring the questions so that information gathered is what is needed, rather than that which populates a standardized template. It is better to conduct the analysis with the people generating the revenue as they are going to end up paying for the solution and they will only pay for what they understand they need. These revenue generators must be informed of what has been implemented so that they can make the best use of it at a time of disruption.

Traders are a particularly challenging type of individual to handle for a business continuity practitioner. They are not willing to be told what to do, preferring to make their own assessment of any situation. In many cases, traders will refuse to participate in evacuations, regardless of whether it is a genuine situation or a practice. Many trading books cannot be left unattended for the period of an evacuation exercise and so most organizations have now implemented a system of 'non-evacuation' permits. These permits are provided to the individuals that are deemed necessary to remain in the dealing room at the time of an evacuation to give them exemption from the evacuation and ensure that the trading books are adequately managed. The intention is to rotate the permits so that everyone participates in some of the evacuations if not all. However, this reluctance to leave the dealing room has resulted in traders becoming threatening or hiding under the desk if they are being asked to evacuate during a genuine situation. Even on 9/11, numerous traders could still be found working in the dealing room at the top of the Canary Wharf Tower late in the London day, long after the planes hit the World Trade Center towers in New York. However, when asked why they did this, they invariably responded that having assessed the situation they felt no more at risk on that day than any other day: with the flight restrictions that had been implemented around tall buildings, they considered themselves to be safer than normal. At one bank, two traders made enough profit that afternoon to cover the losses of the whole of the rest of their organization for the whole year.

The understanding of the way that a trader may behave at the time of a disruption has caused numerous financial organizations to reassess their business continuity and crisis management arrangements. In the past, the management of a financial services organization assumed that business volumes would be reduced at the time of disruption, indicating that they would look to close their holdings and limit the services offered to customers. However, financial markets tend to move around at the time of uncertainty and it is this movement that creates money-making opportunities for traders and sales people. The purpose of a trader is to generate revenue and sales people to generate customer business, and, therefore, it is essentially impossible to stop them conducting business at the time of disruption. Restricting them would require personal compensation for the money they could have made, as well as them questioning the whole reason why they have been employed by the organization. The more realistic organizations have now reached the conclusion that business is going to be conducted at the time of a disruption and so arrangements need to be in place to enable business to be conducted and processed in a controlled and timely manner. Similarly, the more astute have realized that crisis management plans that assume the traders will do as they are told in a crisis are liable to failure.

Complexity of technology

When walking across a dealing room, one of the most immediate impressions is of the quantity and sophistication of the technological hardware. A trading desk often looks very similar to the cockpit of an aeroplane but, perhaps, the greatest difference is that, in a dealing room, there is row after row of these desks whereas in a cockpit there is just one. The technology department would say that the hardware that is visible is only a very small aspect of the complexity of the technology that is required. Each individual sits surrounded by multiple screens and communication tools giving them the ability to scan numerous sources of information, use numerous means of communication and satisfy numerous order management requirements without leaving the desk. Additionally, the trader has connections to various exchanges and trading mechanisms, the structurer has numerous modelling and pricing tools and the sales person numerous direct communication links to their prime customers at the push of single button.

Internally, a dealing room needs to be linked to the operations areas, so transactions can be processed, and to the middle office so that the organization can ensure adequate controls are in place. However, it is all the connections to the outside world that bring information in, distribute information out and ensure the organization can compete effectively in the marketplace that provides the true complexity to the technology. Being a split second behind the competition can mean the difference between making a profit and making a loss, so the quality of the technology is key to ensuring the organization is profitable.

It is often in the operations area where the greatest number of distinct systems meets. Each market, product and exchange tends to have its own processing standards that require the operations department to connect to its specific technology. Gone are the days when a payment is made or received for each individual transaction; now there tends to be a netting process whereby the organization pays or receives the net amount across all the transactions on a particular exchange or in a particular product.

This complexity provides yet another challenge to the business continuity practitioner: how much of this technology needs to be present in a WAR environment and in the second data centre? Unfortunately, it is very hard to find an individual with a full appreciation of the entire set-up. The business people tend only to have a view on the front level of the technology rather than the layers behind that make this front level work. The technology people will know everything that is supplied to the dealing room but are unlikely to know whether a system is truly critical or just 'nice to have'. Following the completion of a business impact analysis, where a business unit is found to be critical, a business continuity practitioner, partnered by a technology specialist, usually has to do a second stage of analysis to ascertain the technology required by the critical business unit to make it operational in the WAR site. For this 'technology needs analysis' to be meaningful, it has to be conducted with both the business person, who knows what they use, and the business unit's technology support, who know how to make what they use work.

The infrastructure of the organization has to be planned with business continuity in mind. As an example, consider one of the major banks in London that found that the only way that its telephony could be transferred to the WAR site was if it was transferred for all three of its local buildings. If, let's say, a water pipe burst in one building, the bank would have been faced with either the people from that building working at the WAR site without being able to receive incoming calls or transferring the calls away from people in the two unaffected buildings.

The cost of equipping a WAR site and a second data centre is expensive. This is why the management has to be given a full appreciation of the risks and benefits associated with the contingency arrangements that are proposed. Workable business continuity cannot be implemented without the full support of an organization's management and so the challenge of getting it on the management agenda needs to be tackled with confidence.

Finally, as any business continuity practitioner knows, it is essential to demonstrate that the contingency arrangements will work when they are needed. However, the complexity of technology within a financial services organization means that there must be a programme of testing which addresses realistic scenarios and provides confidence that it will work when needed without placing undue risks on the operability of normal business.

Where an organization separates the people from the technology as is increasingly happening, it is less risky to test the technology in the second data centre connected to the normal working location or the business people connecting from the WAR site to the primary technology. This is still too challenging for many organizations at the moment, leaving them with only the ability to test segments of the arrangements rather than the full set-up. The need to involve third party suppliers, exchange connections and data information flow means that the full set-up is too great a logistical challenge for all but the most business continuity mature organizations.

Regulators and regulation

The financial services industry is highly regulated but there are two very different philosophies in play. In the UK, for example, the Financial Services Authority (FSA) is principle based. It requires financial organizations to have business continuity arrangements in place which are appropriate to 'the scale, nature and complexity of the firm' and to have, as in business as usual, adequate risk management and control for the business that it is conducting. This non-prescriptive stance, although the most effective way of having the appropriate contingency arrangements as it means that the organization has to be demonstrably well managed, provides a considerable challenge. An organization must develop the ability to continually assess the adequacy of the contingency arrangements given the changes and developments in the business that is being conducted.

The opposite philosophy to the FSA, based on rules rather than principles, is espoused by many other regulators, including the Securities and Exchange Commission (SEC), the US securities market regulator.

Increasingly, business continuity bodies in the financial services sector in the UK have asked for guidance as to what the regulator regards as adequate business continuity. This then results in the development of quasi-regulation where the results of a benchmarking exercise – the majority of critical organizations can recover 80% of their payments within four hours – become an assumed standard with no regard as to whether this is a desirable or necessary outcome.

At one point, the SEC stated it would introduce a rule to require that critical organizations had primary and secondary data centres at least 200 miles apart. Those implementing the rule would have guaranteed that the two data centres were most unlikely to have been affected by the same disruption but, as the major technology vendors contended at the time, would have had huge problems with data consistency due to the near impossibility of replicating data in real-time over such distances cost effectively, if at all. As a consequence, many organizations now have a local data hop to ensure data is replicated in real time and a distant third data centre able to process against a consistent data snapshot although the cost effectiveness of such an arrangement is far from proven.

Business continuity practitioners in the financial services sector tend to divide into two groups. The first group are those that endeavour to ensure the organization has appropriate business continuity arrangements that the organization has demonstrated should work when they are needed. This then satisfies the non-prescription regulatory stance, described earlier, as a matter of course. The second group are those who regard the main focus of their work as ensuring that the organization complies with the business continuity requirements of regulators. This latter group want prescriptive rules so that they can tick the box when they assess the rule has been satisfied. However, this latter group needs to appreciate that the aspirations of the regulator in regard to business continuity are different from that of an individual organization. The main concern of the regulator is that a disruption of a single organization does not disrupt the market as a whole thereby creating systemic risk whereas the main concern of most astute financial organizations is to continue to meet the needs of its customers and stakeholders. The regulator does not care about the shareholder's return on investment or the reputation of the individual organization but the organization and its shareholders do.

The regulators' concern with systemic risk – the stability of the financial system – provides another challenge to the business continuity practitioner. Small-scale disruptions such as floods, fires or localized power failures have been proven to be far more likely to occur than wide-scale disasters and to cost more in aggregate than major disasters and so should be the source of considerable attention. However, the regulators are becoming more and more concerned by widespread disruption due to the fact that many organizations are located within a small area, such as the UK financial industry concentrated in the City and Docklands. The regulators are thereby forcing the industry to look at 'major operational disruptions' rather than true business continuity across the broad range of possible disruptions.

Conclusion

The financial services industry has now accepted that business continuity management is an essential factor in the running of a financial services organization. The debate continues between those who think the effort should be protecting their own organizations and the regulatory-driven approach that seeks to protect the stability of the financial system at the possible expense of the individual firm. There is a second, equally important, debate between those who recognize that BCM is primarily a people and business issue and those who take an essentially technology-driven approach. The supporters of the latter still need to prove that their solutions would work and that they meet the business requirement.

All business continuity professionals working within financial services – whatever their favoured approach – still face the need to fully embed BCM into the organization rather than provide it as an optional add-on at a subsequent date.

Too many of the business continuity practitioners in the financial services sector have a technology, rather than a business, background and as a consequence have insufficient understanding of the concerns of the management. If the financial services sector is to continue to lead the way in the improvement and development of business continuity, the business continuity practitioner needs to have good business knowledge and be able to address the business professional as an equal rather than as a subordinate.

Business continuity strategies for manufacturing and logistics

14   Melvyn Musson FBCI – USA

Melvyn Musson is the Business Continuity Planning Manager at Edward Jones, a major financial services company headquartered in St Louis, MO. He was previously the President of the Musson Consulting Group of St Louis, MO, and a principal of the Recovery Facilitation Network and provided consulting services to manufacturing organizations.

Introduction

Recovery planning in a manufacturing environment encompasses many different issues and different types of planning than those found in work area and data processing recovery planning.

Manufacturing can involve business, information technology, production and distribution functions, so the question is often: 'Where should we put the emphasis for recovery planning?' The emphasis is frequently put on the business and information technology utilizing specific recovery strategies. However, if the production/distribution is unavailable, the company will be unable to provide the product it is selling after recovering its business functions. The other question often raised is: 'If the business and data processing functions are not available, can you still provide product?' The company may be able to, but with difficulty. The increasing link between all these functions means that manufacturing recovery plans should cover all of them, but possibly as separate sections involving different methodologies and strategies. Now, challenges similar to some of these are being found in the general business environment with the continuing increase in globalization, business process outsourcing and increased supply chain dependency. Business firms facing such challenges can learn from what has been done in the manufacturing environment.

Manufacturing recovery also provides challenges often not found in other areas. These range from the increasing globalization, including component manufacture in third world countries, to just-in-time (JIT) inventory systems, the use of EDI

The Definitive Handbook of Business Continuity Management, Second Edition.
Edited by Andrew Hiles FBCI. © 2007 John Wiley & Sons Ltd.

and e-commerce to determine actual production needs and scheduling or the unavailability/delays in equipment availability. Government regulations or recertification requirements are another factor.

As a result, recovery planning and recovery strategies for the manufacturing environment must consider and accommodate:

- A plan that will cover differing areas and functions ranging from office/work area, to data centre, to manufacturing and the related supply chain and logistics functions
- The links between manufacturing and business/data processing functions, e.g. CAD/CAM or CIM, ERP and CRM
- The greater impact that changes in a company's business environment have on the manufacturing operations. This will affect the determination of the actual recovery strategy to be used at the time of the disaster.
- Multiple strategies to be considered at the time of the disaster
- Lack of actual fixed recovery locations
- Recovery strategies that are more business related than technologically related
- Impact of circumstances at locations in other parts of the country or the world
- Impacts of incidents affecting the community infrastructure (e.g. transportation, utilities)
- Dependency on outside sources or services (e.g. raw material or component supplies, partial assembly).

One other factor that has to be considered and allowed for is what one might call the 'manufacturing approach'. First, it should be realized that manufacturing facilities handle emergencies on a daily basis (e.g. equipment breakdown, the quality of components not up to standard). The facilities handle such emergencies as a part of their daily work. Second, the approach for handling problems is often 'put enough engineers in the room and they will take care of it'. While a recovery plan should never be based on a strategy utilizing such attitudes, the plan should accommodate them to help determine whether the situation is an emergency or a disaster, and to help deal with problems that occur in a disaster and which were not considered or planned for during the plan development.

Another consideration is whether the company manufactures final products or components. With component manufacture, the need for and extent of recovery planning and determination of recovery strategies should be agreed between the companies. However, the final product producer does have the opportunity to work with alternative suppliers, although that may be affected by business-related decisions. Another consideration will be whether both companies can be affected by the same hazard (e.g. flooding, earthquake, hurricane).

Developing strategies

The key is to know the hazard, exposure and the potential impact. This includes consideration of:

- Primary hazards and their impact
- Secondary/collateral hazards and their impact.

This can be achieved by completion of a risk and business impact analysis (RBIA). This must be an in-depth analysis and must determine:

- What can happen (risk exposure analysis)
- What will be affected (damage potential analysis)
- What will be the impact (impact analysis).

The RBIA should cover:

- The main facility
- Other company-owned facilities producing products/services for the main facility
- Suppliers and other non-owned facilities providing products/services
- Site/community infrastructure (utilities, etc.)
- Logistics involved with moving materials in and product out of the facility.

The RBIA provides details of:

- The maximum allowable downtime of individual product lines
- The criticality of product lines and their priority for reinstatement
- Key equipment and supplies and their anticipated replacement times
- Critical utilities and other resources
- Suppliers and vendors
- Interdependencies between individual manufacturing operations and possibly individual facilities/locations
- Logistical needs.

An important consideration is that while this information is current at the time of the analysis, product changes can render it obsolete very quickly. It is therefore important that the information be reviewed both periodically and whenever product changes are being considered.

The RBIA should also detail the extent of the damage that an event can cause to the facility, the employees, the locality and the region. For this reason, the use of scenario-based analysis can assist companies in evaluating the potential damage from each type of event. In addition, scenario-based analysis can assist in determining possible actions that could reduce the impact and form the basis of recovery strategies.

Irrespective of whether a standard RBIA or a scenario-based analysis is used, the overall result should be to provide information that forms the foundation of the recovery plan and the development of the recovery strategies.

Types of recovery strategies

Unlike work area and data processing recovery plans, hot and cold sites for manufacturing operations are not available as separate commercial operations. It is possible that there may be some internal arrangements that can be made relating to spare capacity or changing marginal product lines, but companies cannot maintain production facilities sitting idle, waiting to be used in a disaster situation.

There are two types of recovery strategies:

- Pre-incident
- Post-incident

and three main categories:

- Specific
- Mitigation
- Procedural.

All three can be either pre- or post-incident or a combination of both. The use of two types and three categories emphasizes that:

- Consideration should be given not only to the future actions at the time of the event, but also to what can be done now to reduce the impact.
- It is necessary to consider a broad range of strategies and customize these to a company's individual needs.

Pre-incident strategies are those implemented before any disaster situation to mitigate the likelihood or impact of an incident or minimize the downtime. These strategies include risk control/loss control actions, vital record procedures, backup arrangements for utilities and other services, special contractual arrangements and so on.

Examples of pre-incident strategies include:

- Mitigation recommendations
- Spare equipment availability lists from internal and/or external sources
- Buildings and equipment drawings and specifications maintained off-site

- Tool and die drawings off-site
- Contractual arrangements for backup boilers, generators, compressors, etc.
- Arrangements (possibly contractual) with alternative fuel suppliers, rental unit suppliers and potential subcontractors
- Contractual arrangements with specialist salvage/restoration companies
- Load-shedding procedures for potential electrical outage situations
- Special arrangements with specialist contractors for building services
- Alternative operating procedures for key production lines
- Buffer stocks of raw materials and finished product.

Post-incident strategies (whether developed pre- or post-incident) are implemented after the disaster to maintain partial or total product supply. They can include:

- Use of spare capacity within the organizations
- Shutdown of marginal product lines and transfer of key products to those production facilities
- Assistance from competition
- Outsourcing to subcontractors, job shops, etc.
- Relabelling of competitors' products (after consideration of all legal implications)
- Establishment of temporary facilities when production capabilities can be established with 'off-the-shelf' or second-hand equipment.

A company may incorporate several potential recovery strategies in its plan. This results from the continually changing nature of products. The timeframe between major changes of products is often 12 months or less. New products often supersede existing products within similar timeframes. This means that major damage to a production facility may result in recovery of the facility for production of a new product or a new version, rather than recovery of the existing product. For such situations, the decision recovery priorities and tasks will be made at the time of the disaster.

This emphasizes the need for the plan to include procedures for a detailed situation analysis immediately after the disaster. Such an analysis will include not only a damage assessment but also a review of the business environment for the products involved.

Companies may also utilize periodic scenario analysis prior to the disaster utilizing 'what-if' situations to consider what they would do should certain events occur during various business environments. The results of such analysis are then incorporated in the recovery strategies section of the plan.

Within the pre- and post-incident classification, there are three main categories of strategies specific, mitigation and procedural. It should be noted that differentiation between the categories might be a grey area, with certain strategies being considered combinations.

Specific strategies are those which are determined before the event and which are detailed in the plan. These can include:

- Use of specific hot/cold sites for work area and data processing functions
- Use of specific spare production capacity elsewhere
- Mutual aid arrangements
- Use of specific contractors, job shops, etc.
- Discontinuance of specific marginal product lines and transfer of key products to those production facilities
- Closure of the facility and transfer to a new or alternative facility (access to this strategy information should obviously be tightly controlled)
- Use of buffer or reserve stocks.

Although most specific strategies will relate to the reinstatement of a production capability, they can also relate to the utilization of a different course of action. An example of this would be to specify that there would be increased marketing/advertising of similar alternative products rather than attempts to reinstate some form of temporary production capability. This strategy may also be linked to procedural strategies to reduce the time needed for reconstruction or repair of the facility.

Mitigation strategies are actions taken beforehand to eliminate or reduce the likelihood and/or mitigate the impact and downtime. Many mitigation strategies can also be considered as risk or loss control actions. The strategies may be specific actions taken or contractual arrangements made and maintained before the events.

Mitigation strategies include:

- Seismic design/retrofitting of buildings where appropriate
- Installation of sprinkler systems
- Compartmentation of buildings to prevent fire spread
- Anchoring of equipment to prevent damage in an earthquake
- Employee disaster preparedness education and training
- Contractual arrangements for backup generator, boilers, air compressors, etc.

Procedural strategies are procedures developed and incorporated in the plan to:

- Provide limited operational capability at the damaged facility or another location
- Facilitate reconstruction, repair and/or reoccupancy of the facility
- Maintain credibility with employees, the public, customers, regulators and the investment community.

Procedural strategies can include:

- Alternative means of operating. This may involve additional manual handling or use of simpler equipment.
- Use of equipment on a more continuous basis (e.g. three shifts over seven days instead of one or two shifts over five days)
- Accelerated building inspection procedures
- Coordination with local authorities regarding building access, building inspections, construction permits, etc.
- Use of special construction techniques to facilitate reconstruction/repair.

Development of a crisis communications plan may also be considered a procedural strategy.

Conclusions

Recovery strategies for manufacturing operations can be multiple and varied. In addition, unlike those for work area and data processing functions, they may not be as clear-cut and are often dependent upon the circumstances at the time of the event. This means that the recovery plans that are developed must be flexible to accommodate the actual circumstances and changes that are needed and which result from such new circumstances. Therefore a manufacturing recovery plan format should place emphasis on the recovery organization, responsibilities and information database together with recovery support documentation such as checklists, action plans and so on, rather than describing specific detailed procedures based upon a single recovery strategy.

In developing both the recovery strategies and the recovery plan, the planners should follow several basic rules:

- Don't confine yourself to traditional ways.
- Consider whether workarounds used for operational incidents can be adapted to disaster situations.
- Be adventurous in your thinking – use creativity and common sense.
- Use group thinking to develop and review strategies.
- Infrastructure, support functions and interdependencies are major considerations.
- Know the hazard exposures and their potential impact.
- Mitigation is an important recovery strategy.
- Strategize but don't become committed to any one recovery strategy.
- In a recovery mode, you can't do anything until you know the type and extent of the damage and the business environment.
- Educate, train, exercise, educate, train, exercise.

Business continuity for telecommunications

15 Paul F. Kirvan FBCI, CBCP, CISSP – USA

Paul Kirvan is a highly respected writer, practitioner and presenter with over 35 years' experience in telecommunications and 18 years in business continuity. He is currently Senior Manager, Business Continuity Advisory Services, with Prevalent Networks LLC in Warren, New Jersey.

Introduction

Communications and information technology managers in the 21st century are responsible for providing a broad range of facilities and support systems to keep their operations – and their companies – in business. Their responsibilities extend beyond simply providing communications services; they are directly linked to the firm's ability to compete effectively in its chosen markets.

Numerous trends can be identified in communications today that are critical to business success. These include, but are certainly not limited to, the following:

- Continually higher transmission speeds beyond 1.544 Mbps (T1) and 2.048 Mbps (E1); and 34 Mbps (E3) and 45 Mbps (T3); advances in Ethernet technology produce multi-gigabit speeds
- Ethernet-based local area networks (100 Mbps to 1 Gbps and faster)
- Increased use of fibre optic-based transmission services, e.g. optical Ethernet, carrier Ethernet
- Dramatic increase in use of the Internet, and new technologies spinning off from it, such as virtual private networks (VPNs)
- Rapid growth and acceptance of voice over IP (VoIP) technology as the next generation of premises-based voice communications systems
- Continued focus on network management and control
- Increased balance between centralized and decentralized business functions.

Strategic use of these and other communications technologies is a significant factor in business success in the 21st century. For example, the push for higher

The Definitive Handbook of Business Continuity Management, Second Edition.
Edited by Andrew Hiles FBCI. © 2007 John Wiley & Sons Ltd.

transmission speeds that can support data, voice and video in a converged environment continues to grow steadily. While this is important for business and government, it also has a downside. Specifically, the demand for very high capacity network services means that IT managers must place a significant percentage of their information processing needs into a smaller number of high bandwidth facilities. This of course increases the potential for single points of failure that could result in network failures, with potentially disastrous consequences to the company.

The use of fibre optic-based facilities, for example, is easily justified from cost and business perspectives. However, increases in the risk of network failure also exist if:

1.   The facility fails
2.   The network infrastructure associated with it fails, or
3.   The site where the facilities are connected fails.

IT departments have long recognized the importance of contingency planning and disaster recovery for their computers and related subsystems. This typically includes activities such as:

● Backing up data files
● Off-site storage of critical company records
● Duplication and redundancy of critical processing elements
● Creation of corporate disaster recovery teams
● Establishing system security practices
● System/network diagnostic and troubleshooting procedures
● Use of emergency computer operation sites during emergencies.

Today, IT professionals are increasingly concerned about contingency planning and disaster recovery activities for telecommunications. Considering the bandwidth requirements created by the convergence of voice, data and video communications, the need for rapid communications system/network recovery and restoration has taken on new significance. Events of this decade have spurred continuing interest in protection of corporate communications and network facilities. Further, senior management acknowledgement of the importance of communications to business success continues to spur corporate interest.

Protecting a company's investment in information systems is costly – and essential – to survival. As companies have become increasingly dependent on information systems not only to conduct business, but also to remain competitive, the stakes involved in a communications system outage have risen.

New technology initiatives like IP telephony and convergence introduce risks, including exposure to new security issues, unplanned downtime and network performance issues. Mitigating risk requires an agile network architecture that can ensure low latency and high availability for real-time applications, while maintaining security and providing sufficient access control. All these elements are needed to ensure reliable and timely delivery of critical applications and data. Intelligent 'real-time' networks must adjust to application specific requirements, and possess the flexibility to respond to changing business requirements. At the same time, network implementation and management must be flexible enough to leverage existing network investments while delivering the latest capabilities and functionality.

Business continuity strategies

Communications are increasingly recognized as a key element in business success. Many users now think of their PBXs, small phone systems and transmission circuits as corporate assets. Internet access is a strategic part of business as well. The principal strategy regarding this position results from the recognition of two points:

- Communications is essential for the company to remain in business.
- Loss of communications could put the company out of business.

Perhaps the most important user strategy for dealing with disasters is common sense. Users must think carefully about the role their communications infrastructure – which includes communications system and network service – plays in their company, and what would happen if those assets were disrupted. This assessment should be done before anything is designed, planned, ordered or installed.

The following are several broad-based user strategies:

- Determine the true value the corporate network infrastructure provides for the firm, from operational, competitive and strategic perspectives
- Determine potential losses the company could sustain with the loss of the corporate network infrastructure
- Establish plans and strategies for dealing with the issue of contingency planning
- Create decision guidelines to decide whether a contingency plan or business continuity plan is appropriate for a company
- Develop hardware strategies for getting the best recovery arrangement for communications systems
- Develop software strategies to protect an extremely important part of a communications operation
- Define transmission facility strategies to ensure the network components that link applications to users are maintained
- Provide off-site storage facilities to ensure that critical data are properly protected

- Identify supplies of spares and other 'trusted components' that can be used following the failure of similar components
- Develop strategies for reducing personal liability, assuming communications managers are corporate officers and, as such, are potentially liable for lost or damaged network resources
- Encourage use of commonsense strategies to make sure very little falls 'through the cracks'.

Financial institutions, more than most other organizations, depend heavily on network infrastructures to protect their business and to ensure compliance with regulatory agencies. They must protect their networks, applications and data from a wide range of security threats, in addition to technology failures or disruptions. Viruses, worms, malware, denial of service attacks and increasingly sophisticated application-layer intrusions of all kinds can damage financial institutions through lost assets and expensive downtime. These intrusions and attacks originate within and outside network perimeters. In addition, financial institutions typically provide secure and encrypted access to critical resources for internal and external users, while segregating these resources from unauthorized access. Real-time networks let financial services firms ensure that internal applications are only accessed by authorized personnel from trusted networks, and that attacks are mitigated so that dangerous traffic is removed from authorized traffic. Examples of pervasive security include:

- Firewalls and routers placed throughout the network that prevent IP spoofing
- SSL VPN rules that allow conditional network access to specific users at an application level and rules that incorporate device state, such as verifying the installation of up-to-date virus protection, before allowing network access
- Access control that combines identity-based policy and endpoint intelligence to give real-time visibility and policy control throughout distributed and local networks
- Intrusion detection and prevention system signatures (updated daily) that remove known worms from the network, while ensuring the availability of applications to legitimate traffic
- Network-based anti-virus, deep inspection and URL filtering to ensure that no unauthorized software runs on the network.

Financial institutions use real-time networks to provide operational stability, pervasive security and high performance. They manage risk mitigation costs by consolidating resources and introducing operational efficiencies. For example, security devices are available that combine firewall, VPN, anti-virus, intrusion detection and prevention. When these specialized devices are deployed throughout the network, financial institutions can control security capacity and cost while consolidating resources to improve operational control. Specialized application acceleration solutions, using unique algorithms that greatly improve the overall data communication process, help financial institutions achieve greater performance and efficiencies from existing application and database servers, while centralizing data and backup systems. But while all these devices are certainly very sophisticated, if they are damaged or compromized, the networks they support could be rendered useless.

Importance of common sense

While a technology thrust for contingency planning is assumed, one cannot forget simple common sense as a key strategy. Suppose common sense, for example, suggests something as simple – and obvious – as relocating a PBX away from an overhead water pipe. The answer is simple: *move the switch*. However, in a crowded equipment room with minimal extra space that may not be possible. Again, common sense suggests installing something that shields the PBX from water leaks. Options could be plastic covers or even a trough suspended under the pipe to catch drips, routing them to a drain.

Common sense dictates that unauthorized people should not be permitted in an equipment room. So identification badges are required; visitors are signed in at a reception area; entry control systems are installed; and audit trails are periodically analyzed.

Connections between servers and remote terminals are often based on virtual private networks (VPN), which use the Internet as the communications infrastructure. It wasn't too long ago that same connection used dedicated private circuits or a dial-up connection. Common sense suggests a backup of some kind, such as some kind of dial-up service, in case the VPN is unavailable or compromized.

Most of the recommendations found throughout this book are based on experience and common sense. Networking professionals already use many of these techniques in daily operations. What is unfortunate is that most users still do not identify these practices with management as part of business continuity and contingency planning. This approach needs to change.

General strategies

Users can develop contingency plans for networks and communications based on the following primary guidelines:

- Obtain continuing senior management support
- Make sure the plan reflects the importance of communications to the business

- Define hardware, software and facility requirements for business applications needs
- Identify the amount of time the business can survive without communications
- Make sure primary servers and related systems have backups (e.g. redundant CPUs, spare parts) both on-site and at alternate locations
- Test the spare components regularly to ensure they will work when needed
- Make sure primary facilities and network systems have backups available if primary network paths are disabled
- Test contingency plan elements regularly; test the entire plan at least once a year
- Document plan elements; establish plan updating procedures and follow them regularly
- Train and retrain contingency plan members
- Never assume a network is 100% safe and secure.

Hardware strategies

The following hardware strategies are recommended for IT and networking professionals:

- Use products from known manufacturers that offer warranties and emergency recovery options
- Contact other users of the same products for their experience
- Insist on service level agreements (SLAs) to ensure an acceptable level of vendor performance, especially in case of a network disruption or system failure
- Use installation and maintenance sources whose skills and performance are well known, professional and dependable
- Install duplicate, or redundant, processing elements where appropriate, to ensure uninterrupted processing
- Install backup power supplies, diversified and non-overlapping cable routes
- Use quality parts and supplies, cables, connectors, etc.
- Install and test equipment according to manufacturer specifications
- Provide proper environment for equipment, e.g. raised floors, proper temperature/humidity range, and sufficient power
- Provide proper equipment security to prevent damage, theft or vandalism
- Follow building and construction codes
- Follow electric codes for wiring and electrical systems
- Invest in spare components, terminals, circuit boards; store these in protected areas both on- and off-site

- Regularly install spare component in production systems to ensure they work correctly; record the date the component was last used
- Conduct regular tests of system performance, following manufacturer's recommended test and maintenance procedures.

Software strategies

The following software strategies are recommended for communications professionals:

- Maintain backup copies of all critical software: operating systems, applications, utility programs, databases
- Have multiple backup storage resources available, both on-site and off-site
- Keep special databases as current as possible; make sure backup copies are no more than one to three days old, unless more recent updates are available
- Use proven software products for major systems, rather than untested items
- Get references on vendor and product performance from customers
- Insist on service level agreements (SLAs) to ensure an acceptable level of vendor performance, especially in case of software failure
- Analyse software performance regularly; coordinate this with vendor and/or distributor support
- Update software documentation regularly as changes come online; update contingency plans as well
- Install software patches as soon as they are received; implement a patch management capability
- Make sure backup copies of primary applications are the same release level, or generic, as operating versions
- Make sure vendors have emergency backup copies of system software and special programs available
- Make sure software can be used by the technical staff as well as vendors.

Network service strategies

The following network service strategies are recommended for communications professionals:

- Identify and pursue (if appropriate) local access alternative routing options
- Identify and pursue alternative routing options from customer site to long-distance operators

- Use multiple long-distance carriers if cost effective
- Use multiple local access providers and Internet service providers (ISPs) if cost effective
- Identify carrier network routing paths; look for possible overlapping transmission paths across multiple carriers that could represent disaster risk points or single points of failure
- Mix transmission facilities, e.g. T1/E1 with SSL/VPN, to obtain best overall price/performance
- Mix switched access and Internet-based services with dedicated circuits to obtain hybrid configurations, spreading risk more evenly
- Use alternative transmission services, e.g. cellular, radio paging, two-way radio; microwave, satellite where needed
- Deal with carriers who are committed to supporting customer contingency plans; check with other users for their experiences and input
- Insist on service level agreements (SLAs) to ensure an acceptable level of carrier performance, especially in case of a network disruption
- Deal with carriers who have circuit assurance plans, a demonstrated commitment to network survivability, and who have demonstrated a desire to work with users

Off-Site storage and facility strategies

The following strategies are recommended for communications professionals whose business continuity plans include off-site storage and electronic vaulting and for their own facilities:

- Make sure physical layout of facility is conducive to rapid movement of materials
- Make sure the facility uses fire-resistant construction
- Facility should have fire detection, suppression and alarm connections to the local fire department and/or other suitable incident response firms
- Facility should have moisture detection where appropriate
- Facility should have proper temperature/humidity monitoring and control
- Cables should be raised off true floor to avoid damage from minor leaks
- Facility should have regular cleaning of roof and floor voids
- Security and access control systems should be available and linked to local police department or other appropriate organization
- Ensure availability of backup power for user systems, security, fire and environmental systems
- Ensure convenient and rapid access to records within required recovery time frames, e.g. storage facility is open on weekends, holidays, etc.

- Ensure the facility is not located in hazardous geographic or infrastructure areas, e.g. those prone to periodic flooding, earthquakes, power fluctuations, etc.
- Ensure availability of bonded transportation services
- Ensure storage firm flexibility to support various media types in addition to magnetic media, such as printed matter, CDs and DVDs.

Call centre strategies

If your company has a call centre or similar inbound call handling facility, the following strategies will help ensure its continued availability:

- Use incoming routing service arrangements from local and long-distance operators
- Ensure that call centre systems, e.g. automatic call distributors (ACDs) and interactive voice response (IVR), have redundant components, backup power and backup copies of the system database
- If your firm has more than one call centre, configure network services to easily route incoming calls from a disabled system to working call centres
- Ensure availability of alternate call centre staff (e.g. using temporary placement firms) in an emergency
- Arrange for call centre staff to work at home if access to call centre is denied
- Investigate carrier-based ACD call routing services that can supplement premises-based ACD systems; these can be configured to match existing call routing vectors, skills-based call routing and other call centre parameters
- Arrange for rerouting of incoming calls to call centre staff working at home
- If using computer telephony integration (CTI) as part of the call centre, ensure that CTI hardware and software are backed up, and emergency copies are stored in a secure location

Additional strategies

In addition to the operational strategies being discussed, some further strategies for building a robust communication environment are recommended:

- Protect *all* aspects of your communications infrastructure, not just the network or hardware/software elements; be sure to include security, HVAC, lighting, alarms and environmental control

- Build your infrastructure according to industry standards, such as those from the US EIA/TIA or UK Office of Communications (OFCOM)
- Consider mutual aid arrangements in which you can utilize network resources from other companies in emergencies
- Establish emergency arrangements with all equipment vendors, network service providers and other key suppliers.

Strategies for communications products and services

Networking and communications contingency planning and disaster recovery products are generally designed to provide the following:

- Alternative sources of power
- Alternative communications paths
- Fire and smoke suppression
- Backup for critical computer/communications applications
- Testing and diagnostics of critical network elements
- Recovery of phone systems by redirecting service to secure alternate locations
- Rapid replacement of failed or damaged hardware components
- Rapid repair or replacement of damaged transmission circuits.

Equipment vendors, such as PBX and server manufacturers, often market backup and restoration services. The same is true for most network infrastructure providers, including wireless carriers and ISPs. These options are currently available to users, and are worth the investment of time and financial resources.

New alternatives for protecting and recovering voice communications systems are available. Based on hosted technology or Internet-supported platforms, several offerings are available to help companies recover voice services either to an alternate customer facility or to a fully configured vendor site that can virtually duplicate a client's voice service configurations. Successful use of these services depends on access to call redirecting services available from local exchange carriers. In these situations incoming calls, such as calls to a firm's main number or direct inward dial (DID) calls to individual users, can be pointed to an alternate facility for completion. Alternate call routing arrangements must be set up in advance with carriers. There is usually a monthly fixed charge for the service, plus a small charge (often on a per-line basis) when the service is activated or deactivated. In an emergency that damages a voice communications system or prevents access to phones in an office, a single phone call can activate the carrier-based call redirection service. A second call to the voice recovery provider will ensure that calls being redirected will terminate in preconfigured phones at an alternate location.

When the incident has passed, and assuming the main voice system is operational, a call to the carrier will direct incoming calls back to their original destinations. The following firms offer voice recovery systems (VRS) in North America.

- Gema-Tech: www.gematech.com
- TeleContinuity, Inc.: www.telecontinuity.com
- VoiceGard: www.voicegard.com
- Voice Response Systems: www.voiceserv.net

Conclusion

Instituting a communications contingency plan will help ensure the availability of communications hardware and services. It will help minimize the chances of a network disaster occurring. And it will minimize the impact on the company if a disaster occurs. The good news is that plenty of options are available to protect networking assets, so long as they are mixed with a good continuity plan and lots of common sense. A checklist is provided below.

Checklist of developing telecommunications continuity plans

1. Identify current and potential risks to your network infrastructure, addressing voice/data/video, security, operations, administration and maintenance
2. Determine how large a risk your company can take
3. Determine business impact (e.g. loss of revenue) of a network infrastructure loss
4. Obtain support from senior management as well as other departments
5. Define a formal incident response/recovery team
6. Team up with IT and business units in developing the programme; coordinate with existing business continuity programme
7. Develop financial and operational model, with appropriate justifications
8. Review/update/redefine network and data centre architectures
9. Determine recovery strategies, e.g. network diversity, redundant servers
10. Identify and secure technologies and services that satisfy recovery strategies
11. Investigate vendors and suppliers of critical infrastructure assets
12. Design new/updated network infrastructure based on current/future needs
13. Develop and document response/recovery/restoration action steps; organize into a formal action plan to deal with unplanned network incidents

14. Ensure that technical staff are trained in existing and new technologies as well as emergency procedures
15. Based on telecom continuity programme outcomes, update policies and procedures for network management, network security, change management, patch management and other activities
16. Promote awareness of the recovery programme to staff
17. Organize and conduct exercise of new/updated emergency plan; update plan content accordingly
18. Update documentation associated with network infrastructure emergency plan, as well as all appropriate technical documentation
19. Schedule exercises of telecom continuity programme periodically
20. Maintain plan documentation, contact lists, escalation lists, databases and operational steps.

Strategies for IT and communications

Michael Smith and Piper-Anna Shields, SunGard Availability Services – UK

16

Michael is Senior Product Development Manager – Communications and Piper-Anna is Head of Public Relations and Communications with SunGard Availability Services (UK) Limited.

Introduction

Over the last decade technology has been the driver behind the increasing pace and sophistication of modern enterprises. Today, with more people requiring more access to more information more of the time – in or out of the workplace – the definition of 'disaster' has necessarily become far broader and tolerance to it much reduced (see Annex A, Table 16.3). The myriad of potential problems has increased as systems have become more distributed and complex, the associated risks of failure have multiplied further and time pressures for recovery have become ever more extreme to the point of zero downtime.

In addition, the climate in which business operates is changing – literally and figuratively – but regardless of these changes, organizations must be prepared to absorb the impact of any incident or event, with minimal impact upon their business and upon the information and systems upon which they so depend.

For example, the emergence of the Internet and 'always on' living gives companies simultaneously both a local and a global presence. Meanwhile, these same forces of globalization have, in their turn, brought new challenges. Natural disasters, terrorist attacks and other calamities – whether at home or abroad – inevitably impact organizations and the people who work for them. Tightening rules on finance and accounting have placed heightened emphasis on readily available and accurate information.

Organizations exist in an age where strategies are changing to accommodate rapid technological developments. The business landscape has always been dynamic, but technology is making it more so. Information – be that data or intellectual – is the main competitive advantage for businesses today. They need

The Definitive Handbook of Business Continuity Management, Second Edition.
Edited by Andrew Hiles FBCI. © 2007 John Wiley & Sons Ltd.

and expect continuous access to it. The challenge now goes beyond recovering information to keeping everybody in the organization connected with it at all times – no matter what happens. We have progressed from IT-centric disaster recovery, through the process of business continuity planning, to the age of information availability, where an organization's key people and critical information must remain connected at all times.

Information availability encompasses business continuity, disaster recovery and managed IT solutions to ensure a holistic approach, whatever the sector or size of operation or the budget available.

In a 24/7 world, all organizations are keen to leverage their technology investments for maximum return and from a continuity and availability perspective the need to deliver solutions that are both cost and operationally effective is no different.

This chapter will consider how to attain information availability for IT and communications infrastructure by considering:

- Moving towards holistic information availability
- Understanding the business information flow
- How to determine business criticality and conduct risk assessments
- Determining the right strategy for information availability
- Recovery and availability options for IT and communications
- Leveraging communications at time of test, disaster and within production environments
- Future trends within information availability

and will refer to relevant standards and drivers as appropriate.

Assessing information availability needs

Getting a right understanding of your organization's requirements and finding the correct solutions to satisfy your recovery time objective (RTO – the required restore time by system or function) and recovery point objective (RPO – how recent the information restored needs to be) need a strategic approach which feeds into all aspects of the business and connects all former recovery or continuity approaches.

The British Standard for BCM, BS 25999, encourages organizations to take an enterprise-wide view of risks and business resumption priorities so they can improve overall resilience to interruption as well as having appropriate strategies for continuance of your business functions when the worst happens.

Attaining information availability therefore is a three-step process:

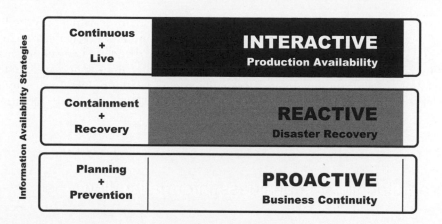

Figure 16.1—Moving towards information availability

- **Proactive** – This first stage involves the analysis and decision-making that will feed into planning and strategy to ensure overall business continuity for the organization as well as to understand which approaches are needed throughout the organization in order to deliver a workable information availability strategy. Often this process will involve some form of external consultant and/or one or more individuals in the organization in order to understand the chains of dependency and the relationships – both internal and external – which underpin the business and IT operations. By prioritizing their importance and time criticality companies can begin to determine the directions the information availability strategy will lead as well as which individuals within the company should run it. Once plans have been formulated, keeping them apace with the organization is vital to ongoing success and relevance, hence the need for business continuity provision to incorporate ongoing plan maintenance and testing, which will highlight any changes required as the business moves.
- **Reactive** – The reactive elements of information availability are usually termed 'disaster recovery' and generally come into operation – or are invoked – when downtime occurs. It is here that the traditional elements of continuity provision are to be found, such as fixed hot site and mobile/cold site solutions which deliver alternative accommodation for people and technology. The spectrum of response varies to suit business need – from fixed site solutions which typically deliver a 2–4 hour response to mobile units that are be deployed within 8–48 hours of invocation. Should premises be damaged (or unavailable for longer than the contractual period of invocation) there are even long-term workplace and data centres available which provide up to two years of alternative premises.

- **Interactive** – Some aspects of the business, usually those which are the life-blood of the organization, require ongoing or continuous availability. These systems and processes need to be permanently live and as such require a far higher degree of information availability service. This is where interactive solutions come into their own, designed to deliver 24/7 production availability via real-time high availability recovery through to fully managed IT solutions – all governed by SLAs for additional peace of mind.

Understanding the business information flow

According to the British Standards Institution's (BSI) Publicly Available Specification (PAS) 77:2006 for IT Service Continuity Management, there is a relationship between IT strategy, IT service continuity strategy, IT architecture and IT service continuity plans as per Figure 16.2. And business continuity (BC) and information availability (IA) are also clearly defined elements within the information technology infrastructure library (ITIL) framework. Once the business impact analysis is complete and you have a good understanding of the applications that are critical to protect in order not to suffer significant financial loss or loss of reputation and to be compliant with regulations, the next step is to bring together those with technical skills and business sponsors in order to work through the information flow model.

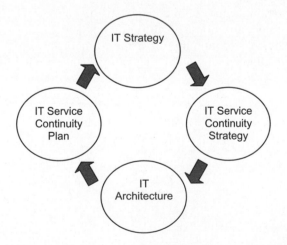

Figure 16.2—The relationship between the IT strategy, ITSC strategy, IT architecture and ITSC plan (source: PAS 77)

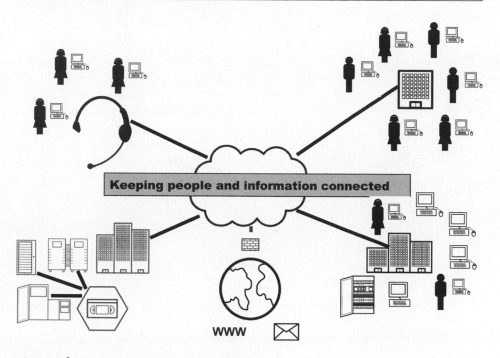

Figure 16.3—Understanding your business information flow

For example, an insurance company would lose significant reputation if it didn't settle claims, so for this function you would see a process similar to that depicted in Figure 16.3.

A call arrives from a customer wishing to make a claim on a dedicated claim phone number, the Automated Call Distribution (ACD) system locates the next available agent. The agent answers the phone and obtains the policy number and the nature of the claim, which is entered into a terminal/PC which in turn is connected to a distributed server. The distributed server prints the appropriate claim form for dispatch to the customer.

The customer returns the claim form, which is then batched for processing with all the claims being made, typically on a larger enterprise server which assesses the risk of future policies and sets future insurance pricing correspondingly.

The above is a simplified process for following an insurance claim transaction. The same process should be followed for all critical transactions: e.g. quotations, renewals, breakdown services, for example.

Building an information flow model gives a company an overview of the technologies and topology deployed, depicting the communications speeds and feeds. A simple diagram is a great visual aid for technical and business sponsors alike to work through various availability scenarios – such as traditional tape-based recovery, shipping of servers, fixed site recovery, electronic vaulting, storage, highly available geographically dispersed multi-site solutions (clustering, mirroring and load balancing) – for an always-on operation.

When looking at the solutions that protect the information flow of a company, it must be done in conjunction with what is financially prudent and address the RTO and RPO needs of the organization.

Another critical factor is the synchronization of information between systems; in the above example, if the enterprise server is still available but the distributed branch server is recovered to the last backup, the claim forms batched for processing may be re-created from journals and the price of policies inflated and/or customer claims settled twice as it is resent to the enterprise server, or if the batch file had not been sent before the outage, then the claims may be missed entirely and the customer's claim not settled and the price of the future policies not adjusted to reflect the loss.

Protecting critical information

- **Why?** – Risk, health and safety, regulation and compliance, drive down RTO, ensure the correct RPO and SLAs for solutions taken. Control costs, protect organizational reputation, enhance security, loss of trade.
- **What to consider:**

  - Buildings – power, fibre, copper, location, space
  - People and process – information flow
  - Servers – mainframes, midrange, Unix, Intel
  - Subsystems – SANs, NAS
  - Networks topology – replication, LAN, WAN, customer, EDI, banks/suppliers and VOICE/dealer rooms
  - Networks hardware – PBXs, switches, routers, firewalls
  - Tools – Fault or health monitoring and management, virtualization
  - Vital records – including backups
  - Hosting/web hosting.

- **How/where do we use it?** – Voice, email, web, mobile and home workforce, call centre, distributed processing and globally.

Business analysis

Having an appreciation of the flow of information through the business means that the organization is well placed to conduct a thorough business impact analysis, which may also include vulnerability assessments and risk analyses. A proper approach to BIA will not only consider business function, but from an IT service continuity perspective should also consider profiling areas of specific technological risk, the main areas being:

- Infrastructure
- Storage
- Security and
- Networking.

Business impact analysis (BIA)

This provides an extensive analysis of an organization's business functions. The BIA helps to identify the following:

- The critical processes, priorities and single points of failure
- The key dependencies, both internal and external
- The inherent risks and vulnerabilities that may exist.

Vulnerability assessment

To be conducted in parallel with impact analysis – the specific vulnerabilities associated with IT service delivery ought to be determined. The IT infrastructure's exposure should be reviewed in terms of:

- System resilience and availability
- Key suppliers and agreements
- Documents
- Hardware and software assets
- Storage
- Backup regimes
- Staff exposure
- Staff training
- Location of buildings and facilities
- IT security
- Systems monitoring
- Power
- Data communications
- Archiving

- IT environment and monitoring
    - Telephony
    - Any other relevant exposure.

The above is taken from PAS 77, Section 6.2; however, the last point could as easily be read as any exposure highlighted as part of the BIA and RA processes.

Risk assessment (RA)

The RA provides a review of the business's risks and threats, looking at physical, logical and procedural risks. It allows the business to act on recommendations to reduce their exposure to risks and vulnerabilities.

RA process – IT service continuity plan (PAS 77 Annex A)

- Process and risk identification
- Response selection
- Response planning
- Assign responsibility and implementation
- Rehearse/exercise and learn lessons.

As a result of both BIA and RA, the organization will have a better understanding of the impacts and risks facing it and will therefore be better positioned to determine priorities and timescales for continuity and be able to establish a risk mitigation process. This will form the basis for putting in place a viable continuity strategy.

In conjunction with BIA and RA, the organization must factor in the following as they pertain to it:

Challenges for the head of IT

- Budget
- Power
- Connectivity
- Systems – platforms, integration, change control?
- Monitoring
- Resources – skills and focus on core business, as opposed to BCM

- Follow the sun
- Technology trends
- Internet
- Legislation and compliance
- Cyber crime and security – OS weaknesses, viruses, industrial espionage, script kiddiez, worms, Trojan, etc.

In addition, there are various factors that are driving current and future IA investment. At any one time, several of these will be influencing the overall strategic direction of the organization's technology spend and its priorities for continuity and availability. They fall under three broad categories:

1. Business
2. Infrastructure and
3. Marketplace.

Business challenges

- Costs in managing complexity:

    - The complexity and associated costs in providing a BC solution increases as the RTO and RPOs decrease
    - Complexity of distributed processing
    - Synchronization between disparate systems
    - Security issues
    - Vital records off-site
    - Skills
    - Technology
    - Site resiliency, diverse power and multivendor diverse communications
    - Management information to meet internal and external SLAs

- Meeting regulations – according to the sector in which you operate, you may be subject to one or more of the following – and your BCM programmes may help you achieve/demonstrate compliance:

    - Turnbull Report – listed on the London Stock Exchange
    - Higgs Report – all UK PLCs to manage risk effectively
    - BS 25999
    - BS 7799 or ISO 17799
    - Financial Services Authority – CP142
    - Basel II – international Banks

- Civil Contingencies Act – councils, public services, health, utilities
- Sarbanes-Oxley (SOX)
- Audit pressure

● Increasing end-user productivity:

     - Always on workforce:

         ○ Home working
         ○ Mobile devices

     - Call centres
     - Workflow systems and processes

● Focusing on core competencies:

     - Business systems available to customers via web tools:

         ○ Ability to order
         ○ Track progress
         ○ Logistics systems

     - Business partners providing non-core competencies – outsourcing or select sourcing agreements

● Developing comprehensive roadmaps for optimal sourcing and/or leveraging global sourcing:

     - Companies will benefit from taking the most cost-effective routes to finance their IA programmes, and these may involve in-house or third party solutions or a combination of the two.
     - Consider that recovery and availability for IT and communications requires significant investment in infrastructure, as well as skilled personnel.

(See Annex A Table 16.1—To insource, outsource or select source—that is the question for more.)

Infrastructure challenges

● Maximizing utilization and performance of infrastructure:

     - Monitoring the environment – using virtualization tools such as VMWare to consolidate servers into virtual servers and allocated a shared resource based on requirement as opposed to dedicating the entire server

- Need to reduce staffing levels:

    - Deployment software
    - Scheduling systems
    - Select and outsourcing
    - Cross-training

- Getting access to a reliable, always-on infrastructure:

    - Handheld devices
    - 3G cards for laptops
    - Internet facing systems clustered across multiple sites

- Ensuring a secure infrastructure:

    - Layered approach:

        ○ Building security
        ○ Physical security
        ○ Logical security
        ○ Penetration testing
        ○ Virus protection
        ○ Intrusion detection and prevention
        ○ System patching policies
        ○ Security agents
        ○ Equipment security
        ○ Document security.

Marketplace trends

- Driving down costs to meet lower budgets and to maximize ROI. This often entails adopting alternative service delivery models and technologies/innovations, for example:

    - Using alternate vendors
    - Outsourcing/select sourcing
    - Off-shoring

- Centralizing IT infrastructures:

    - Managing systems (security and system patches)
    - Security layering
    - Removing single points of failure – multiple paths, building Tier-IV data centre environments
    - Ensuring backups completed and synchronization points are known

  - 24/7 support
  - Monitoring – faults, health, database, networks and trending
- Leveraging infrastructure to support business processes
- Maximizing utilization rates of IT infrastructure
- Streamlining service delivery across IT and business processes and integrating same
- Shifting to leverage utility computing and on-demand services:

  - Virtual servers
  - Speed of deployment
- Rationalizing and managing applications portfolios
- Procuring services from a broader array of providers:

  - Removing single supplier reliance
  - Providing healthy competition for cost savings
  - Providing a greater service resilience
- and the need for ROI.[1]

Development of a programme

The launch of BS 25999 means that a standard now exists as a framework for implementation of an IA programme, but there are other current good practices available for reference and these include: SAS 70, ITIL and PAS 77 for BCM, data centres and IT recovery.

But you may be subject to other forms of guidance/compliance/legislation as discussed under the heading 'Meeting regulations' above and these should be considered as the IA is created because it may actually enable compliance with these requirements in whole or in part. Examples include: Basel II, Civil Contingencies Act, Higgs, MiFID, Sarbanes-Oxley, Turnbull and more.

Proactive (prevention)

Prevention is all about risk mitigation, removing single points of failure, having paper-based recovery plans and performing 'what-if' exercises in order to harden the environments from conceivable eventualities.

For example, a circuit failure is fairly commonplace, this could be prevented by utilizing diverse and separate serving exchanges, or by using multiple providers with separate building entries, or triangulation via a recovery/hosting facility.

---

[1] Sources: Drawn from SunGard Availability Services' own experience and also three reports by IDC 2003, 2005, 2006, see further reading for details.

Diverse exchanges should be fine, but carrier brownouts happen, such as the BT Manchester Tunnel fire in the UK in 2004. Multiple providers are also good, but it is difficult to determine the actual fibre/copper routes in the ground, and writing a contract with multiple providers is awkward. Circuit triangulation via a third party provider of hosting/business continuity would be more expensive than straightforward circuit protection, but will facilitate site protection into the design.

This may all look too expensive, so another alternative is local loop backup, backing up leased lines with PSTN/ISDN or xDSL services.

If you are fully to protect the circuit from outage, multiple routers and switches need to be deployed to reduce equipment failure, taking the circuit out of service, and you can look at protecting the equipment better with redundant logic, interface cards and power supplies.

Another often missed form of prevention is to eliminate human errors, having common equipment in the network, good documentation/change control and processes. Having a policy so that changes are only made out of hours by a restricted number of people.

Tools can give an early warning to circuit degrading or network congestion, by monitoring error thresholds and utilization as part of a preventative maintenance programme.

It is always a balance of costs versus risk, which solution is right, how much prevention is affordable or sensible? The options are to create such resilience that there will always be a service or to accept the possibility of an interruption to service and plan for the recovery time objective and recovery point objective.

Reactive (containment)

These are policies, processes or services that serve to avert and/or prevent incidents escalating into disasters. For example, by monitoring systems and/ or environmental conditions in critical areas, such as data centres, for critical servers – including email – and networks, a disaster can be contained or even prevented, and a stable environment can be maintained.

Reactive (recovery)

One of the advantages of conducting the BIA and ascertaining RPO and RTO is that the organization identifies what really matters in terms of protecting operations and ensuring the continuance of key business functions in the event of any disruptive incident. This then enables any response to focus on needs, not luxuries – in other words, what is fundamental to keeping going in a crisis, as opposed to the wider organizational infrastructure and activities that happen during 'normality'.

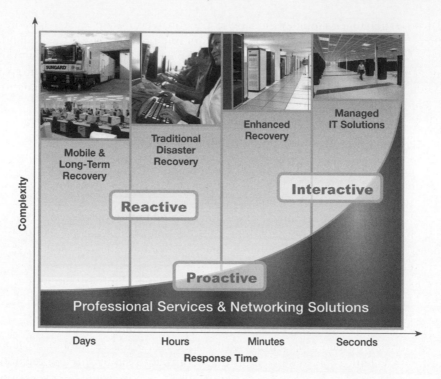

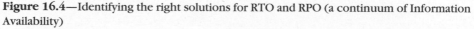

Figure 16.4—Identifying the right solutions for RTO and RPO (a continuum of Information Availability)

From a technology recovery perspective, many options exist according to the RTO/RPO identified and the available budget and resources of the organization. This range of services may be regarded as a continuum of availability options, in accordance with Figure 16.4.

Below is a list of technology recovery options – listed in order of descending RTO and ascending RPO (i.e. travelling along the continuum from left to the right).

- **Mobile and long-term recovery** – Mobile offerings comprise solutions which are shipped to a designated site – either the organization's own or to a third party provider – these tend to be technology-centric or trailer-based solutions which can also offer alternative work space for staff:

    - **Ship-to-site PC** – PCs, screens, keyboards, etc.
    - **Ship-to-site server** – Servers including processors, disk and tape to cover such platforms as Wintel, iSeries, pSeries, SUN, HP and more
    - **Ship-to-site PBX** – Fully configured PBX and handsets

- **Mobile technology recovery** – Truck-based computer environment delivered to site for local recovery of customer environment
- **Emergency response package** – mechanical and electrical (M&E) recovery services to provide emergency replacement of failing infrastructure – generators, UPS and air conditioning
- **Mobile workplace recovery** – Trailer-based office/workplace building for housing a percentage of staff

With long-term recovery offerings, a set of prefabricated building units is delivered to the organization's site and constructed to create a permanent building, which can be configured as an alternative office, data centre or both – available as single and double-storey buildings.

- **Long-term recovery (workplace)** – Fully functional workplace recovery environment for tens up to hundreds of people, with desk, chairs, power and LAN infrastructure
- **Long-term recovery (data centre)** – Fully configured data centre environment providing up to several thousand square feet with generator, UPS and cooling infrastructure.

- **Traditional disaster recovery:**

  - **IT recovery** – BC providers should be able to offer fixed, fast recovery of all major (i.e. Wintel, IBM, SUN, HP) and also older technology platforms within predefined timescales on a shared or dedicated basis. It is worth ensuring that you select a vendor agnostic provider if taking a third party solution. IT recovery should be available on a shared, syndicated or dedicated basis – and this should hold true for recovery services in general.
  - **Dealing room recovery** – Recovery of full function dealer positions including dealer voice turrets, market data, direct and matching systems and settlement
  - **Computer equipment room** – Purpose designed secured computer rooms for housing IT hardware within secure dedicated cabinets, facilitated with network access, power and cooling provision

- **Enhanced or advanced recovery options** – Facilitate an improved RTO and RPO but at more affordable price points than adopting a fully managed IT solution, and make an attractive proposition for companies seeking higher availability but for whom zero downtime is either too costly or not necessary. Enhanced/advanced recovery services are a welcome addition to the continuum of recovery solutions and bridge the gap between both traditional disaster recovery and managed/hosted offerings as well as offering additional choice for those devising IA programmes:

  - **Enhanced recovery services** – These deliver improved recovery time and server preparation from stored OS backups, recovery profiling and rapid OS builds for platforms such as HP, Sun, IBM pSeries and iSeries, and Wintel.

- **Testing services** – These can augment a customer's recovery team by offering a full range of services, from simple test assistance through complete turnkey testing.
- **Remote access service** – A single remote access gateway solution to enable customers to test and potentially recover from home sites or local recovery site.

Workplace recovery

There is no doubt that recovering data and systems efficiently and effectively is important. But it is equally imperative to get essential work functions up and running in line with RTO/RPO without delay. Organizations will need to address the logistics of planning for the people and place aspects of recovery with a thorough BCP for the workplace. Having evaluated through the BIA key worker and workplace requirements in the event of a major incident, one of the first things to do is identify alternate locations where employees can go in the event a primary work location is unavailable (typically, plans are based upon 25–30% of staff being deployed to the alternate workplace). These end-user locations must be equipped with technology and business resources – ranging from desktop computers and telephony to desks and chairs – that allow for recovering systems and resuming business as usual. Key points to cover for the physical space and related technological components for end-users to function in the event of a major incident include:

- Physical office space
- Workplace amenities (desks, chairs, conference, post and meeting rooms)
- Desktop technology (PCs)
- PC system builds (operating system, applications software, data)
- Intel-based local server technology
- Telephony services for inbound, outbound and call diversion (see 'Voice protection and recovery' below)
- LAN and WAN connectivity to IT systems
- Office systems (printers, photocopiers, fax machines).

Deployment plans must be developed and tested for the rollout of end-user PC desktop requirements to an alternate location through PC imaging. Technology can be utilized to build telephony recovery plans for call volume handling at an alternate location, number redirection in conjunction with telecom providers and end-user profiling. For some businesses, such as call centres or financial services organizations, managers and other staff may require manual processes in place to keep operations running until the recovery is complete. The workplace recovery planning must include an incident escalation and notification communication strategy and process. The physical safety and psychological well-being of employees must also be planned for. Finally the recovery plans must be well communicated and exercised throughout the organization so that everyone knows how to respond in a disaster situation.

Interactive (managed IT solutions)

When business critical applications cannot be allowed to fail, managed IT solutions offer IT resources and skills to ensure availability, reliability, security and cost efficiency. Offerings in today's marketplace are many and varied, but include:

- **Secure hosting** – A secure co-location, or hosting, environment that includes a cabinet, operational support, and device monitoring for multiple devices in the cabinet
- **Continuous web presence** – DNS-based redirection services and web servers to provide immediate cost-effective always available web presence
- **Email availability services** – Immediate access to alternative email for receiving and sending mails using customer user email addresses (for more detail, see email availability options below)
- **Platform and device monitoring** – Covering secure server, device, IT platforms, website and equipment management
- **Install services for both hardware and software**
- **O/S and database management**
- **Security and network management** – Covering DNS administration, managed Internet access, managed firewalls, managed load balancer, managed customer-provided equipment and managed intrusion detection services
- **Vaulting and backup** – Including options such as managed electronic vaulting services and managed tape backup.

External facing applications

Any systems that are outward facing – such as the corporate website, telephony and email – need to be managed and protected in the event of an incident in order to contain it. The issues and alternatives are considered below.

Websites

The Internet global accessibility of websites, email and file transfer servers means that any loss of availability of these services could damage a business financially and affect a company's reputation. One solution is to provide highly available geographically dispersed Internet sites, hosted at the organization's own data centre or outsourced to a co-location facility. This can be costly and complex but will ensure that the business can continue as usual following an incident.

An alternative is to use dynamic DNS located with a recovery provider. These servers ensure that even in the event of disaster at the hosting location, a company's presence on the Internet is maintained. As the Internet is an environment that has instantaneous exposure to failure, the switchover to a standby server(s) has to happen within a few minutes.

Most Internet server environments comprise many components, all of these elements need to be recovered in the event of an unplanned outage:

- Web servers, application servers, database servers, mail servers and FTP services
- Domain name servers
- Firewalls
- Routers and switches
- Access to an Internet service provider's network.

Without careful design, the Internet does not easily support shutting down Internet presence and bringing it back online elsewhere on the web. Because a number of systems have been designed to reduce Internet congestion and speed up the end-user's experience, these systems can work against a company when trying to recover an Internet presence after a disaster. Some of the issues are: DNS caching, DNS time-to-live and ISP change management procedures.

Technical overview

Website visitors first connect to web servers through the domain name resolution service that converts www.mysite.com into an IP address that is accessible across the Internet.

The dynamic DNS checks the availability of all web servers for a domain. In the event of loss of connectivity to these web servers, for whatever reason, the dynamic DNS system can redirect new visitors to an alternate site, or a standby server at the recovery centre. The server could hold 'brochure ware' (all branding, static information, etc. but no access to back-end databases) or a web page informing of a system maintenance window. Either is far better than the standard Internet message '404 site not found', where visitors are confused and sceptical as to why you are no longer trading.

If there is an interruption to delivery of pages from the main web servers, then the DNS servers will automatically redirect visitors to an alternative site on the standby servers. This ensures that, regardless of the variety of reasons for loss of service from the primary web server, visitors will still be able to connect to the alternate (standby) site.

Voice protection and recovery

- **Protection** – Voice is arguably the single most critical application; being able to communicate with suppliers, customers and colleagues is essential normally, but even more so following an unplanned outage. Dual parenting lines – from diverse and separate exchanges – offers a high level of resilience, by running clustered PBXs and dual parenting the chance of failure is further eliminated. PBXs are generally considered highly reliable and therefore for less important sites that can operate for some hours without service, could balance the risk of equipment loss with a ship-to-site PBX, as a cost-effective alternative.
- **Site loss – voice recovery** – There are three main strategies for recovering voice:

    1. To have multiple call centres in a network with intelligent number (IN) plans for automatic voice redirection, should a site be unreachable or busy. This is a deployment for a very large organization that has multiple sites across a geographic spread.
    2. VoIP systems are usually built with multiple PBXs in a cluster. The cluster is split between the primary site and the recovery location, both sides of the cluster being able to work as one cluster, or independently and always on, so protecting system loss and site loss. The incoming lines need either to be connected to both sites or switched upon failure from the primary to the backup site.
    3. Where companies have an onsite PBX or a Centrex solution (hosted PBX solution) – and they don't want to run a split-site live/live solution depicted in option 2 – then the provision needing to be made is to switch calls through to an alternate site. If the choice has been made not to make the investment of purchasing additional PBXs this will most probably be a BC provided solution. It is essential that the backup site is planned with all the essential services needed to support the users being relocated.

For each of these options it is really important to test, to refine the recovery configuration, to get users familiar with the recovery site, to set up 'business as usual' operations, abbreviated dial plans, class of service, call barring, etc. For staff to be effective at the backup site, the goal must be end-user transparency. The phones may look different but they have all the same buttons and features. Organizations running at their own secondary site may have the luxury of permanently having space and desks dedicated to recovery. If using a third party provider, however, PBX tenant partitioning is desirable, to keep the organization's configuration independent of whoever else is testing or invoking the site, so it is important to define the specific number plan and extension number range, and when pressing 0 or when multiple customers are testing or invoking the site, to ensure that a dedicated operator is available.

On top of the day-to-day PBX features taken for granted, others can be adopted at time of disaster. Generally most PBXs support 'hot-desking' features which should be exploited at time of test or disaster – often companies plan to shift work to allow less space or fewer desks to be utilized in an effort to reduce costs. 'Voice announcements' are another feature, which allow a hot-line for pushing a message to callers, for example: 'We are working from our backup site, our systems will be back in 8 hours, call back on this line for an update'. Automatic Call Distribution (ACD) can be used with voice announcements and call classification to say: 'press 1 for sales, 2 for finance, 3 for support, 4 for billing', etc. This is particularly useful when extension number information is lost (as in the standard voice redirection from most carriers).

- **DDI** – The lines themselves make a difference to what can be done, DDI lines can be redirected by the carriers and some have formal products such as BT's Site Assure Options 1 and 2, Colt's Colt Voice Line DR Service and THUS' Emergency Divert Feature. If the provider does not want to offer voice redirection or offer a service that has individual DDI redirection, there is always the option of number porting to another carrier that does DDI redirection.

Most carriers will offer as standard to push all your calls to a lead number at the recovery site, this will have an additional redirect cost, and lose extension number information. This is the most common practice in the BC marketplace today, and companies choose to handle a massive influx of calls to a backup site in a number of ways, e.g.:

1. Operator(s) manually forwarding the calls
2. The caller is asked to re-enter typically the last four digits of the number they have just dialled
3. ACD asking the dialler to select a department.

- **IN** – Intelligent numbers/intelligent network services (e.g. 0800, 0500, 0845, 0870, etc.) have predefined call plans both for normal operation and recovery. These are by far the easiest to administer in terms of a recovery plan, and they are quick to invoke. They can work on varying conditions, based on the area of the country the caller dials from, whether a site is busy or engaged to follow a path to an alternate site – there is so much flexibility here! It is essential these services are used for support calls (e.g. enquiry lines, customer services, help desks) and that the voice recovery plans for these lines are established up front to effect a speedy voice recovery.

Voice recovery is of paramount importance to any business suffering an unplanned outage. With voice, take a consultative approach, call in the PBX vendors, carriers, support staff and BC providers to ascertain the best solution for your budget.

Email availability options

Every day, more and more businesses are concluding that email is one of the top mission-critical applications and an essential part of an information availability programme. Email addresses are stored in address books, so when the response, 'Email Recipient Unknown' appears, and is not due to inputting the wrong email address, failure is highly visible to the business community.

A number of options do exist within the marketplace to provide additional protection for email systems, these include:

- Traditional tape backup
- Replication and clustering
- Email continuity services.

1. **Tape backup**
   - **Advantages of tape:**

       - Low cost
       - Simple and widely deployed
       - With database corruption, can return to the last good backup

   - **Disadvantages of tape:**

       - 24–72 hour recovery time
       - Harder to recover:

           o Media failure
           o MS Exchange specific – brick level (single mailbox) recovery
           o MS Exchange recovery in conjunction with Active Directory

       - Substantial data loss window (RPO of 24 hours for nightly tape backups)

2. **Replication and clustering**
   - **Advantages of replication:**

       - Email service can usually be restored in less than 1 hour
       - Planned system maintenance can be performed without downtime

   - **Disadvantages of replication:**

       - Expensive
       - Database corruption and viruses can impact the secondary backup just as they impact the primary

– Administration, failover, and failback require highly skilled staff
– Local pairs (clustering) provide minimal protection while remote pairs are expensive and can easily get out of synchronization

3. **Email continuity**

- ● **Advantages of email continuity:**

   – Low cost
   – Email outages are never visible to the outside world
   – Email functionality can be restored in less than one minute
   – Only solution to work through all types of outages including database corruption, viruses and 'malware', hardware failures and connectivity outages
   – Simple, rapid deployment

- ● **Disadvantages of email continuity:**

   – Continuity only – does not recover the primary environment
   – Not all email capabilities/features supported in email client
   – Limited historical data.

	Tape Backup	Replication/Clustering	Email Continuity Services
Cost	$	$$$$$	$
Recovery Time	24-72 hours	1-3 hours	1 minute
Designed for Continuity	No	Yes	Yes
Designed for Recovery	Medium	High	High
Continuity During			
Hardware Outage	✘	✔	✔
Most Disasters	✘	✔	✔
Database Corruption	✘	✘	✔
Directory Corruption	✘	✘	✔
Viruses	✘	✘	✔
Connectivity Loss	✘	✔	✔
Planned Outages	✘	✔	✔

Figure 16.5—Comparison of email availability options

Networking and communications

The need for effective recovery and/or production networking

Networking is this 'Golden Thread' that ties together recovery and live production systems, data storage, workplace environment(s) and the Internet. Today downtime is clearly not an option and smart communications are an essential aspect of achieving workable IA solutions. Smart communications work to resolve a range of issues, including:

- Reducing RTO
- Reducing RPO
- Reducing costs
- Providing resilience
- Business protection
- Demonstrable risk management and compliance
- Providing additional resources and/or skills.

Best practice when putting a recovery network in place

- Build a recovery network that closely resembles the production network. The network is then predictable, the support and documentation is easier to produce. If the recovery network feeds and speeds correspond with the live network it will be effective when used in anger or load tested.
- Consider BC testing: How can the network be tested? Does the production network have to be shut down when testing? What changes need to be made to bring the recovery network into being? In user acceptance testing (UAT), which users are allowed to access the BC test systems? An often used technique is where companies use the production IP addresses for BC testing and network address translate (NAT) to a new IP addressing scheme. This provides a network which appears invisible to all, except those that have been given access at time of test; at time of invocation the NAT is removed and the live subnet advertised. All systems appear available as before, and any hard-coded IP addresses between systems remain intact.
- Full duplication of network equipment and circuitry can be prohibitively expensive, so consider using a BC provider with shared equipment, i.e. routers, switches, firewalls and bandwidth-on-demand alternatives. Bandwidth-on-demand is available in many ways: dial-up (PSTN and ISDN); shadow VLANs; switched circuits; shadow PVCs and ATM. Private circuits often have a backup provision via ISDN or ADSL – these backup mechanisms can also be used to switch the neces-

sary connectivity to the backup site. Once again, by using existing technologies the network connectivity is predictable and has sufficient capacity.

- Larger networks may have additional network hubs, which if triangulated via the recovery centre would provide bandwidth for replication in normal operation and also extend the wide area network back to the recovery centre upon invocation.

- Remember BACS, EDI, business master and voice services: these applications are critical but often don't appear on core network diagrams, which generally focus on the corporate data network.

- Carefully plan any communications that are externally facing – especially to customers, suppliers, stakeholders, etc. Obvious candidates are: VPN access, voice communications, corporate websites and email. Create standby web servers with maintenance pages and voice systems with pre-recorded messages to inform that business as usual will resume in n hours or 'call back on this line for an update'. Establish a mail relay provision to store and forward emails to an alternate location.

There is a raft of options when devising a BC network strategy, and for the recovery solution to be effective it is vital to get it right. Use subject matter experts within your own organizations, business sponsors, BC professionals and suppliers. It is very much a collaborative approach and as it will represent a substantial investment, do consider any anticipated future needs and/or trends and how they will affect the BC network to be adopted.

Rollback – delivering voice and data to users via third party network resilience

When putting an availability solution together third party BC providers are an attractive option to reducing costs. The providers communications solutions should include; connectivity to all the major carriers with the benefits of diverse and separate communications for resilience, affordability – with so many companies to choose from and choice - and the ability to work with existing network providers.

As communications is an essential part of any total site loss plan, when choosing a 3rd party provider, look at the investment they have made in their own support infrastructure, do they have a dedicated rollback network, and network alternatives for reaching your key suppliers and for extending the hosted or recovered systems close to home.

BC providers must manage the risks of multiple invocations which could impair the effectiveness of the solution: for example, allowing customers to rollback to an alternative site in the case of a multiple invocation, considerably reducing the customer's risk. When choosing a supplier, a key factor is knowing that when an incident occurs that affects the organization, the supplier will have adequate resources to support that invocation. Bear in mind that while having multiple sites is all well and good, if they are dissimilar then the ability to recover is compromized: a common infrastructure and an intersite network capability help ensure that recovery to an alternate site is possible even in the most complex situations.

It is, therefore, essential that you understand the risks and mitigation. These standard questions may help:

- How does my solution work when my provider supports multiple invocations?
- Have you handled multiple invocations?

  - What is your experience?
  - Can I talk to any of the customers?

- Can I test an alternative recovery site scenario?

  - Are the PCs/servers the same?
  - Is the telephony transparent?
  - How do I extend my network provision to the alternative site?
  - Do you have a rollback network, how would it work with my recovery scenario?
  - What multiple invocations have you supported upon disaster?
  - Do you emulate multiple invocations by concurrent testing?

Harnessing the power of the network for holistic IA and maximum ROI

Organizations wishing to reduce their RTOs and RPOs further move naturally beyond reactive IT-centric DR, through proactive BC measures (such as automated data backup or systems monitoring), to interactive IA solutions that deliver a range of options which capture mission-critical information electronically off-site and deliver such benefits as:

- Further reduction of RTOs for optimum business availability
- Achieving RPOs that deliver zero or near-zero data loss
- Overcoming recovery challenges, for example duplication of servers that are difficult to restore.

These are some of the ways in which organizations can leverage networks as a means towards improved and cost-effective continuity and availability:

- **Multiple recovery scenarios** – If the BC supplier has a national network, connecting to the hub of that network offers the ability to recover office staff to any of the workplace recovery sites.

- **Network triangulation** – Improved resilience for ease of recovery and/or replication for active failover.
- **Live/live** – Some organizations are running active/active configurations between a primary and a secondary recovery or data centre location.
- **Email support** – Some companies have their mail servers sitting upon third party BC providers' networks, evidence of the growing criticality of email applications.
- **Secondary domain controllers** – The general purpose is to hold the user account information (logon) profiles and policies (security/file access rules), often also incorporating DNS (domain name system) and DHCP (dynamic host configuration protocol – providing network address administration and resolution).
- **Vital records off-site** – Customers place business continuity plans, key documentation and recovery information off-site, whilst still having them accessible via the network.
- **Protecting vital transaction history** – Journals and log files may be copied off-site as a means of improving the RPO.
- **Backup server catalogue replication** – Vital systems are typically backed up over a network to a backup server, which needs recovering before any application servers can be recovered. Many customers choose to replicate backup servers and their corresponding tape catalogue in order to speed up this process. The most frequently used examples of this being TSM Tivoli Storage Manager, Veritas Netbackup, CA BrightStor and Legato Networker.
- **Electronic vaulting** – Immediate, automated transfer of file and system backups to a secure remote data vault.
- **Managed hosting:**
    - Geographic load balancing of multi-site website solutions
    - Continuous web presence – hosted hot-standby web server(s)
    - Email relay
    - Internet backup service
    - Managed firewalls
    - Data replication and disk mirroring
    - Multi-site clustering
    - Tools for network and systems health monitoring and reporting.

Embedding the culture

In line with best practice guidelines, ensuring the success of any information availability implementation – whether business continuity, disaster recovery or managed IT solutions – depends upon creating an environment in which plans and programmes are verified, exercised, maintained and reviewed in line with business and technology change (including changes of key personnel or operating environments) and their impact upon the RTO/RPO requirements of the organization.

Of course, such a programme must be endorsed – if not led – from the board and will include additional personnel drawn from relevant areas of the business (often being involved as key members and/or team leaders of appointed crisis management and emergency response teams). The teams will be responsible for such areas as:

- BCM policy:
    - BCM scope statement
    - BCM terms of reference:
        - Business impact analysis (BIA)
        - Risk and threat assessment
        - BCM strategy/strategies
        - Awareness programme
        - Training programme
        - Incident management plans
        - Business continuity plans
        - Exercise schedule and reports
        - Service level agreements and contracts
- Their associated documentation (as outlined by BS 25999, section 5.5).

As this chapter considers IT and communications continuity especially, then a crawl/walk/run approach towards achieving the above is recommended. So, for example, the business may initially conduct tests on a single platform basis, progressing to multi-platform and/or multi-location tests. Once assured of the recovery processes for systems and communications, they will logically progress to tests that relocate users to test workplace recovery solutions and also involve senior and board-level management for the ultimate in scenario planning. (See Annex A, Table 16.2—Hints for testing IT recovery plans for more.)

Other issues

There is plenty to consider when developing an IA programme that is contiguous with the organization's needs. Whenever putting together such a strategy, in addition to the wealth of material contained above, do consider the industry and/or sector developments and technology futures, in order to make adequate provision.

For example, in the next 3–5 years the impact of such technologies and issues as: Next Generation Networking; green computing and its associations to both power consumption and climate change concerns; Virtualisation; Multi-channel Messaging (voicemail, instant messaging, email, wifi, GSM, VoIP, video, text and location sourcing); RFID; collaboration and presence awareness applications; ITIL adoption; in-, out- and select-sourcing and homeworking upon Information Availability strategies will come to bear.

But whatever approach is taken one thing is certain: Information is the number one key asset for every organisation: it is central to every process and cannot be restored, repaired, reconstructed or replaced. Information cannot be bought, only earned and, whether it sits as data in IT systems, as paper in filing cabinets or as knowledge within the brains of employees, it must be protected and, even more importantly, available at all times.

In summary, Information Availability is all about keeping people and information connected. It protects the flow of information so vital to organisational survival. It helps protect profits, operations, customer-base and reputation. It is not a cost of running technology – but an investment for the business.

Annex A

Table 16.1—Sourcing

To insource, outsource or select source – that is the question!

Reasons for choosing to insource:
- Justifiable cost, especially true for the financial sector
- Overcapacity from consolidations and mergers
- Campus environments as in the public sector
- Flexibility for organizations requiring the highest levels of availability
- Dislike of the shared model
- Market pressure from hardware suppliers
- Empire building
- Response to third party provider pricing.

Issues associated with insourcing that can be overlooked:
- Change
- High availability (HA) does not equal disaster recovery
- Technology does not equal business continuity
- Integrity of the alternative site
- Core business and resource management
- Production creep
- Cost cutting.

Costs:
- Tin accounts for only 20–25% of overall service cost
- Capital versus maintenance, upgrades, environment
- Asset(s) on the books
- If it's sitting idle, it'll be utilized within two years
- If it's part of an HA solution, expect running costs.

Table 16.1—*Continued*

To insource, outsource or select source – that is the question!

Ramifications*:
- Revenue loss per incident 3.6 times greater for the internal solution. Or about $1.1 million versus $4.0 million
- Share of IT budget spent on internal BC solution 84% greater than external solution
- Share of total budget spent on technology 21% greater for internal solution
- Number of end-users supported by IT department 37% greater with external BC solution.

Staffing:
- Can the organization hire someone with the wealth of knowledge that a third party specialist has?
- Will that person be flexible in line with any future change in direction/technology?
- Third party personnel are dedicated to their function so cannot be hijacked
- Has the organization considered shift requirements and cover for absence?
- Salary is only 50% of the cost of an employee.

Challenges to insourcing:
- Is a second site being considered?
- How close is the alternative site?
- How are the sites connected and at what cost?
- What is the integrity of the second site?
- Has the business accounted for maintaining two data centres?
- Is older technology being used for recovery?
- Have maintenance costs been included?
- Has the business budgeted for twice the continual investment?
- What are the procedures in the event of a disaster?
- What are the testing procedures?
- Where will end-users go in a disaster?
- What provisions are in place for end-users?
- Is the business confident the second site won't be subject to cost-cutting measures or hijacked for other uses?

* Source: IDC White Paper 'Outsourcing Business Continuity Needs: Ensuring Information Availability While Ensuring ROI', David Tapper, June 2003.
Source: SunGard Availability Services 2007.

Table 16.2—Testing

Hints for testing IT recovery plans

- Attempt to schedule at least one 'surprise' test every year
- Set objectives, build written plan and follow it
- Set objectives, and stretch objectives – crawl, walk, run
- Schedule testing after major system upgrades
- Careful to record timings, problems, etc.
- Regular component testing
- Remember supplies; tapes, manuals, vital records, pre-printed stationery
- Contact software suppliers to obtain licence keys
- Business continuity as part of change control
- Skills matrix of staff
- Create regular system images and use imaging tools
- Check procedures for control of security system passwords.

Source: SunGard Availability Services 2007.

Strategies for IT and communications

Table 16.3—Causes of business interruption

Annex A: An A–Z of Business Interruption

Acts of God – air conditioning failure – arson – blackouts – blizzards – boiler explosion – bomb threats – bridge collapse – brownouts – chemical accidents – civil disobedience – communications failure – computer crime – corrosive materials – disgruntled employees – denial of service – earthquakes – embezzlement – explosions – extortion – falling objects – fires – floods – hardware crash – high winds – heat or cooling failure – hostage situations – human error – hurricanes – ice storms – interruption of public-infrastructure services – kidnapping – lightning strikes – malicious destruction – military operations – mismanagement – mud-slides – personnel-non-availability – plane crashes – phishing – public demonstrations – quirky software – radiology accidents – railroad accidents – sabotage – sewage backups – snow storms – software failure – sprinkler breakdown – strikes – telephone problems – theft of data or computer time – thunderstorms – tornados – transportation problems – unexpected vandalism – viruses – water damage – worms – xenon gas leaks – yellow fever outbreak – zombie, attack of the (yes, that really is a hacker attack).

Source: SunGard Availability Services 2007.

Further reading

Basel II: International Convergence of Capital Measurement and Capital Standards: A Revised Framework, Basel. Bank for International Settlements Press and Communications, 2005.

BSI PAS 77:2006 'IT Service Continuity Management'.

BSI BS 25999 'Business Continuity Management' Part 1: Code of practice.

The Civil Contingencies Act 2004. Cabinet Office: The Stationery Office (UK).

The Data Protection Act 1998. British Parliament: The Stationery Office.

Emergency Preparedness: Guidance on Part 1 of the Civil Contingencies Act 2004, its associated Regulations and non-statutory arrangements. Home Office: The Stationery Office (UK).

The Higgs Report on the Role of Non-Executive Directors: Department of Trade and Industry: The Stationery Office (UK), 2001.

IDC White Paper 'Outsourcing Business Continuity Needs: Ensuring Information Availability While Ensuring ROI', David Tapper, June 2003.

IDC White Paper 'Ensuring Information Availability: Aligning Customer Needs with an Optimal Investment Strategy', David Tapper, October 2004.

IDC White Paper 'Optimizing Business Performance Requires Optimizing Information Availability Investments', July 2006.

The Sarbanes-Oxley Act, 107th Congress of the United States of America, 2002.

TR 19:2005, Technical Reference for Business Continuity Management (Bt GM). Spring Singapore.

The Turnbull Report on Corporate Governance: Department of Trade and Industry: The Stationery Office, 1998.

The Orange Book Management of Risk – Principles and Concepts: HM Treasury, 2004 (UK).

BroadGroup Managed Services Europe, April 2006.

'Generally Accepted Practices for Business Continuity Practitioners'. *Disaster Recovery Journal and DRI International*, 2005.

Business Continuity. CBI with Computacenter, 2002.

'A Risk Management Standard'. The Institute of Risk Management, The Association of Insurance and Risk Managers and The National Forum for Risk Management in the Public Sector, 2002.

Microsoft Operations Framework, a pocket guide, Van Haren Publishing, ISBN 9077212108.

Management of Risk: Guidance for Practitioners. Office of Government and Commerce: The Stationery Office (UK).

Andrew Hiles, *Business Continuity Management: Best Practice*. 2nd Edition 2003, ISBN 1-931332-22-3 2003, 3rd Edition Rothstein Associates Inc., 2007.

Andrew Hiles, *Enterprise Risk Assessment and Business Impact Analysis – Best Practices*. ISBN 1-931332-12-6 Rothstein Associates Inc., 2001.

Jon William Toigo, *Disaster Recovery Planning*. Prentice Hall. ISBN 0-13-046282-9.

Andrew Hiles and Peter Barnes, *The Definitive Handbook of Business Continuity Management*, 1st Edition. ISBN 0-471-48559-4. John Wiley & Sons Ltd, 1999.

Brahim Herbane, *Business Continuity Management – A Crisis Management Approach*. ISBN 0-415-20492-5, 2007.

Planning to recover your data

17 Thomas Carroll MBCS – UK

Thomas is Principal Consultant with Kingswell International, a global consultancy specializing in business risk management and continuity.

Introduction

All organizations would agree that effective data recovery is mandatory and not optional. How and what we choose to implement as a data recovery and data protection solution depends on several factors but most important is the mindset.

The protection of the business comes from the ability to effectively recover from a disaster with as little data loss and downtime as possible. Hence, the mindset needs to be 'How do we recover our data?' and not just 'How do we back up our data?' It is about recovery management and not just backup management. Recovery management is a wide-ranging strategy and approach to data protection that starts with the end goal in mind – effective recovery. This mindset also needs to include how we increase the availability of our data and systems, as the most common disaster is the unavailability of our data to users and customers.

The most common recovery strategy is data backup. So why do we back up our data:

- To restore our data in the event of a disaster
- To retrieve a file in case of deletion or corruption
- To store historical data to ensure compliance with industry regulators.

The method or methods we utilize to back up our data will mostly depend on the reason we are backing up our data. Whatever the individual reason, backing up is simply preparing to restore at some point in the future. With a data recovery focused mindset, the data protection methods we may wish to implement are governed by the following factors:

The Definitive Handbook of Business Continuity Management, Second Edition.
Edited by Andrew Hiles FBCI. © 2007 John Wiley & Sons Ltd.

- RPO – recovery point objective
- RTO – recovery time objective
- Availability
- Budget.

Recovery point and recovery time objectives

A recovery point objective (RPO) defines how much data you are willing to lose in the event of a disaster or other data failure. It refers to the previous point in time to which you wish to recover the data following a disaster. This figure will differ from organization to organization and system to system. For example, an organization utilizing overnight tape backup may have an RPO in the region of 24 hours. This is assuming the tape was unaffected by the disaster. In which case the RPO will have been overshot by another 24 hours assuming the tape stored off-site is readable. Achieving an RPO of zero or near zero data loss requires a more comprehensive solution than mere tape backup. We will review some possible solutions to achieving differing RPOs below.

The RPO for each data set or system should be determined by your organization's recovery needs. This should be determined by the business during the business impact analysis (BIA) phase of the business continuity planning project and reviewed on a regular basis.

Recovery time objective (RTO) refers to how much downtime an organization is willing to tolerate. Again, this figure needs to be set by the business during the business impact analysis (BIA) phase of the business continuity planning project and also reviewed on a regular basis. This figure may vary by system and data set. Organizations that utilize traditional tape backup recovery techniques would have an RTO measured in hours and even days. An RTO of minutes or even seconds is possible, but it involves an investment in technologies, processes and procedures that go far beyond the tape backup. The implementation of these technologies will, in most cases, also have a beneficial effect on the RPO.

This raises the question, what is your organization doing to ensure that it can set and meet your RTOs/RPOs over time?

Availability

Research has shown that 31% of the organizations today would experience significant revenue loss or other adverse business impact within one hour or less of application downtime and 58% within four hours or less of application downtime.[1]

Increasingly, to many organizations the availability of critical systems and data is as important as the ability to recover. Increased availability of applications and data is about reducing downtime whether planned or unplanned. It is not just about increased reliability but also requires greater resilience and removal of single points of failure.

Just because a system is reliable does not mean it is available. About 20% of unplanned downtime happens for a wide variety of unpredictable events from increasingly rare hardware failures to human error (which accounts for 40% of unplanned downtime), power failures, environmental issues, attacks by hackers and increasingly software failure (which accounts for another 40% of unplanned downtime).[2]

The other 80% of unavailability can be attributed to planned downtime. Systems and applications may be unavailable due to a variety of activities such as data backups (which accounts for almost 60% of planned downtime),[3] application and database maintenance and software and hardware upgrades. Planned downtime will be scheduled to occur when it will have a reduced impact on the business but it will still have an impact. Users and customers will still be unable to access the systems and information. Today, with remote access and e-business applications, there is a greater requirement for 24/7 availability. Consequently, the business starts losing money from the very first minute of downtime, regardless of whether it was planned or unplanned.

Dunn & Bradstreet reports that 59% of Fortune 500 companies have at least 1.6 hours of downtime per week. This includes both planned and unplanned downtime resulting from software failures, system reboots and normal maintenance. This equates to at least 83.2 hours of downtime in a 52-week year. What is the cost of this downtime? Well, it depends on your business type. But don't forget some of the more intangible costs such as the impact on reputation, erosion of customer goodwill, strangling of new business, cost of backlog recovery and the cost of recovery itself.

There are many high availability solutions in the market at the moment and choosing the right solution for your budget and business is not always straightforward. One of the common mistakes is to implement a solution in isolation to other factors affecting downtime and unavailability. For example, implementing an application high availability solution without planning for hardware or operating system high availability. Other factors which contribute to downtime need to be reviewed as to their impact on availability, i.e. power, software patch failure, etc.

Depending on the high availability solution implemented, it will also reduce the number of times you may need to recover your systems.

---

[1] *Thinking Outside the Tape Box* by The Enterprise Strategy Group, Inc.
[2] *Understanding Downtime* by Vision Solutions, Inc.
[3] *Understanding Downtime* by Vision Solutions, Inc.

Budget

Along with currently available technology, budget will nearly always be a limiting factor as to the solution we implement to protect and recover our data. If we understand the value of the data to the business, we can justify the cost of the data protection and recovery solution. The value of the data to the business should be established during the business impact analysis (BIA) phase of the business continuity planning project.

It does not make sense to implement an expensive recovery solution to prevent a potential loss of data that may have little value to the business. It may also not make sense to implement a recovery solution that enables an RTO of days if the business requires minutes. Any solution chosen should be justified on a cost/benefit basis.

That said, there is continued concern at board level over the effectiveness of their business continuity plans including continued availability of critical systems and their recover strategies. A well-justified and reasoned proposal may well get board approval even if the cost/benefit is unbalanced.

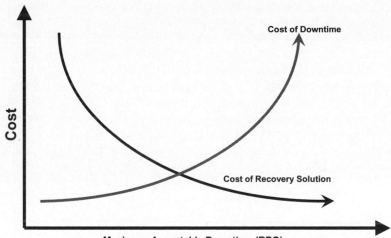

Figure 17.1—Cost vs benefit

Backup strategies

With production data volumes expected to grow by 30% year on year for at least the next five years[4] (some research organizations are even predicting rates of 60%

[4] *Disk-Based Data Protection Forecast: 2006 to 2011* by Forrester Research, Inc.

growth or more), conventional tape technologies are struggling to keep pace. Additional requirements for retention and availability of data for compliance purposes have been heaped upon companies of all sizes. In some industries, compliance rules stipulate retention of data for up to seven years. In the health care industry, patient data may demand retention for 20 years. For major infrastructure, construction or engineering projects, data may need to be kept for decades (in the nuclear industry, maybe for centuries).

There is no single backup or data protection strategy; each organization must formulate a strategy that meets its unique backup, compliance or disaster recovery needs.

Tape backup

Tape has been with us for many years and over that time its strengths and weaknesses have become clear.

Strengths

- Inexpensive medium to store data
- Portable format that can easily be moved off-site
- Familiar for administrators, who know and understand tape backups.

It is also a widely adopted data protection solution, over 71%[5] of organizations currently back up to tape, which should ensure some longevity in the technology.

Weaknesses

As beneficial as tape backups can be, there are three key challenges with tape. First is reliability. Industry reports indicate that tape can fail up to 40%[6] of the time. This does not include incomplete backups due to open file errors. The second is complexity. Tape lacks the flexibility and simplicity that many organizations require today in a data protection solution. Last is speed. As data volumes continue to escalate, tape backups are taking longer and longer. A few other notable drawbacks to tape backups include:

- High impact on production server (backups must occur during off-peak hours)

[5] *Disk-Based Data Protection Forecast: 2006 to 2011* by Forrester Research, Inc.
[6] *The Benefits of Continuous Data Protection* by Symantec Software Corporation.

- Compatibility issues for long-term storage due to software and hardware changes
- Once-a-day backups only capture a single point of recovery
- Increasingly complex management (incrementals, differentials, multi-vendor solutions, etc.)
- Reliability.

Inadequate or unreliable data protection is a silent killer and most businesses don't realize their tape-based data protection presents some critical vulnerabilities until disaster strikes. Only 37% of businesses actually test their backups regularly, and of those that do, an alarming 77% are unable to fully recover data from those tapes, meaning that the data they get back could be many days old.[7] This may be due to a variety of reasons, including human error, bad tapes, software bugs, hardware/ software compatibility issues, loss of tapes by third party storage companies and more.

The unpleasant reality is backup and recovery from tape can be a time-consuming and tedious chore with an element of risk as to the end result. Considering the time it takes fully to restore from tape, this is not a viable recovery option if your organization has a short RPO and/or RTO.

However, tape-based backups should not be considered an outdated technology: a complete tape backup could still mean the survival of your business. Tape should still be considered as a viable data protection and recovery management strategy in conjunction with other techniques and technologies.

Putting the reliability and recovery issues to one side, the main issue is the time it takes to back up to tape – it's slow! Given the rate of data growth, and the same infrastructure being shared across multiple systems, the key benefit of storage area networks (SAN), situations are arising where existing tape library infrastructure cannot back up all the data in the time available.

Given the ever-increasing time to back up the data to tape, organizations have to reassess what data is backed up and when. Storage administrators are quickly realizing that not all corporate data is alike and different data must be handled in ways that benefit the business. They must sometimes perform data triage, allocating backup resources for only the most critical data. Data classification tools are growing in importance, allowing administrators to categorize the data for more effective backups.

Online backup

Online backup can offer, particularly smaller organizations, the opportunity to get their data off-site utilizing existing or upgraded Internet bandwidth. Depending

[7] *Top 10 Reasons Why Online Backup is Replacing Tape* by LiveVault Corporation.

on the technology utilized by the online backup vendor, many utilize incremental backups that only back up the files that have changed since the last incremental backup. This does have a downside, if you make a small change to a very large file or database it will have to backup the entire file or database which may take some time over existing upstream broadband bandwidths. Even if you only backup once at night to avoid slowing your Internet connection, it is a better solution than the office manager or IT manager taking the tape home each day.

Another advantage in online backup is that most vendors offer an easy-to-use web-based restore application. You can restore mistakenly deleted files and some vendors even offer the capability to restore previous versions of the file, thus offering a form of document version archiving. By keeping backup data online the management headaches and administration costs associated with tape and traditional 'tapes on trucks' scenarios are completely eliminated.

Some vendors even offer on-site disk-to-disk (D2D) hardware to enable continuous or frequent on-site backups. The changes are then replicated off-site; see details on asynchronous replication below.

Data deduplication

If your backup window is still too long the only other option is to reduce the quantity of data. Data deduplication, also known as data reduction or commonality factoring, is a technology enabling the reduction of data volumes. Data conditioning, data cleansing and deduplication software can consolidate disparate databases delivering duplicate-free data.

Data deduplication technology takes backup data volume reduction to the next level by ensuring that multiple occurrences of the same data do not get stored. Instead of storing everything only unique data segments are stored and tiny 'pointers' replace the storage of redundant data. These pointers serve as reference marks for the reassembly of data. Then, once deduplication has occurred, compression can be applied to further reduce data volume. Often a reduction factor of 20× or more of the data volume is achieved. Data deduplication is still in its early stages but with this level of data reduction it is bound to develop into a mainstream method of data volume management.

Disk-to-disk

Time-proven backup methods like tape continue to work adequately in some situations, but analysts agree that disk-based technologies are systematically displacing tape-based systems for primary backup tasks. Sixty per cent of backup will be on disk by 2011.[8] Disk-to-disk platforms are expected to remain more expensive than tape on a cost per gigabyte basis, but they offer better backup, and restore performance and eliminate some of the common problems of failed backups and tape management. Analysts currently estimate that 29% of backups are to disk and 71% to tape. In two years, they estimate this to shift to 43% disk and 57% tape.[9] As the cost differential between tape and disk continues to decline and it becomes more cost effective due to advanced capabilities such as data deduplication, enterprises will shift more and more of their data protection to disk and increase the time that data is stored on disk before it is ultimately vaulted to tape.

Virtual tape libraries (VTL), content-addressed storage (CAS) and continuous data protection (CDP) are three principal disk-based storage systems that can address specific backup needs.

A VTL is a backup solution that combines traditional tape backup methodology with low cost disk technology. It is an intelligent disk-based library that emulates traditional tape devices and tape formats. Acting like a tape library with the performance of disk drives, data is deposited onto disk drives just as it would onto a tape library (sequentially), only faster.

A VTL platform can directly replace a tape library while utilizing existing backup software and policies. VTLs are far less disruptive to introduce, have performance and flexibility advantages over conventional disk, and maximize existing investments in tape. However, they still require the intervention of a backup administrator to restore individual files as the VTL emulates tape backup and stores the files sequentially.

Archiving data to CAS can move data off primary storage, reducing the amount of data that has to be backed up in the first place and snapshots allow for more frequent restore points for entire systems or individual files. CDP can protect mission critical data in real time with essentially no backup window and a restore point up to the moment. Organizations are utilizing disk storage systems for faster backups, which also allow more frequent backups, offering them far more granularity in their RPO.

Analysts estimate that 30% of enterprises have already adopted a VTL. They also estimate the adoption of VTLs to increase by as much as 20% in five years.[10] For those enterprises that continue to use a mix of disk and tape in their backup environment, a VTL is the preferred backup target for its non-disruptiveness, flexibility, manageability and ability to facilitate physical tape creation, i.e. disk-to-disk-to-tape (D2D2T). The majority of enterprises express a desire to continue to use both disk and tape in their backup environments. VTL adoption is poised for growth!

[8] *Disk-Based Data Protection Forecast: 2006 to 2011* by Forrester Research, Inc.
[9] *Disk-Based Data Protection Forecast: 2006 to 2011* by Forrester Research, Inc.
[10] *Disk-Based Data Protection Forecast: 2006 to 2011* by Forrester Research, Inc.

Content-addressed storage (CAS) is one emerging disk-based storage technology that promises to improve the storage of long-term fixed content while lowering primary storage requirements. CAS systems are designed to store fixed data that rarely, if ever, changes and is only called for infrequently like patient medical images or legal documents. However, CAS is not an appropriate solution for high performance transactional storage tasks and should be seen as only part of the solution to your data protection strategy.

Organizations that demand more recovery points are often incorporating snapshot products, such as Microsoft Volume Shadow Copy Service (VSS™) and CDP technology into their backup strategies. A CDP product is one that will continuously monitor an object for changes and will preserve copies of all prior versions of the object. The user will have the ability to view and access these prior versions as required. The time to perform recovery of specific files changes from hours to seconds or minutes from implementing these technologies.

Snapshots have come a long way since the days when they integrated with databases and backup applications via scripts. Snapshots can be full clones or space-efficient snaps and can be used in rapid succession to offer multiple recovery points. While snapshots do not provide the literal 'any point in time recovery' of CDP, they are space efficient and provide recovery at multiple, consistent points in time. Enterprises will select snapshots as the protection and recovery method for databases, as well as messaging and collaboration applications. Analysts estimate adoption of snapshot technology at 37% today, and expect this to increase to almost 60% by 2011.[11]

'Near-CDP' is similar to snapshots. There are vendors that market near continuous data protection (CDP) solutions that do not technically meet the Storage Networking Industry Association's (SNIA) definition of providing any point in time recovery. SNIA defines CDP as 'a methodology that continuously captures or tracks data modifications and stores changes independent of the primary data, enabling recovery from any point in the past'. However, near-CDP products do offer recovery from multiple points in time by using successive snapshots and/or replication. This approach reduces processing overhead on production servers, will meet most enterprise RTO and RPO requirements, and is increasingly a feature of mainstream backup applications. Thus, while it is not CDP as defined by SNIA, this is still an advantageous approach to recovery.

CDP will be used to protect the most mission-critical data. There are several different types of CDP products that provide any point in time recovery from disk. They differ in the methods they use to track continuously; their awareness and integration with applications, databases, and file systems; and their recovery object granularity. CDP products may track data changes at several different levels: block, file or through application-specific integration. Similarly, the most granular objects they recover can range from individual files, mailboxes or even messages.

---

[11] *Disk-Based Data Protection Forecast: 2006 to 2011* by Forrester Research, Inc.

As a rule of thumb, because CDP continuously tracks all changes to data, the additional storage requirements can be quite significant. For example, if you assume a 10% rate of change to a given data set and you want to recover to any point in time in the last two weeks, you will need as much as 1.5 times additional storage capacity as the amount of data you are trying to protect. For this reason, most enterprises will probably use CDP to protect just their most mission-critical databases and messaging applications. Analysts estimate that current CDP adoption is at approximately 20% and will increase to 35% by 2011.[12]

High availability

The goal of availability is to maximize the access to and uptime of the designated systems and applications – in essence, to make them fault tolerant.

The primary difference between availability and high availability is that the latter is designed to tolerate virtually no downtime making them completely fault tolerant.

That elusive goal of 100% availability, the ultimate goal of high availability, is virtually impossible to achieve when you consider some of the wider negative influences on such an achievement which could include budget, human error, wide area disasters, software coding errors, market changes affecting the business such as mergers, civil unrest and political changes. These factors are all outside the sphere of total control and will impact that elusive goal.

In order to maximize availability a holistic approach to the design of the overall system architecture needs to be taken. The overall design should be resilient and capable of withstanding individual failures. This should include areas such as power, environment, network infrastructure, system hardware and software.

To achieve high availability there are several key factors that will require particular attention.

Redundancy

Single points of failure should be removed from all areas of the system's infrastructure to provide fault tolerance. For example, the design may include items such as dual power supplies, hot standby hard drives, dual network cards and even hot standby servers.

---

[12] *Disk-Based Data Protection Forecast: 2006 to 2011* by Forrester Research, Inc.

Reliability

Best of breed products should be installed or at least products with long MTBF (mean time between failures) figures. Without reliability and redundancy your system's availability will be governed by the weakest link.

Recoverability

This refers to the ability of these systems to failover to a hot standby. This may be automatic or manual failover but the process needs to be simple and well documented. This documentation should also include the failback process to the normal production systems.

Serviceability

Items need to be either quickly repairable or easily swapped out otherwise you may now have a single point of failure in your system.

Training

Your IT and infrastructure staff should be well trained and exercised on their responsibilities and actions following a failure. The same should be said for your key suppliers.

Monitoring

There should be some means of monitoring the ongoing performance of the entire network. Changes in normal performance may indicate a potential failure. Preventive action may just save the day.

When it comes to application and data resilience and availability one of the common approaches is replication. Replication creates a copy of the live data on another server or storage system in real or near real time depending on the type of replication implemented. This enables the ability to failover to the standby system with no data loss and little downtime. Replication is one of the key recovery management technologies, because it offers distance and immediacy to data protection. There are two main types of replication, synchronous and asynchronous, which can ensure zero or near-zero data loss in the event of a primary system failure.

In synchronous replication or synchronous mirroring, such as Microsoft Cluster™, all data is sent to both storage systems at the same time in a data write instruction. The instruction will not be considered completed by the application until it has receiver a data acknowledgement from both systems. Depending on the distance and capacity of the connection between both systems it can take a relatively long time to write data to the secondary storage. Since the application has to wait for both systems to confirm the write this can lead to very slow storage access speeds.

Synchronous replication is not normally considered suitable for remote or off-site replication due to the bandwidth and latency issues. There can also be a problem that occurs when one of the sets of storage becomes disconnected. Recovery from these events can take extended amounts of time before the data is fully synchronized. The applications and operating systems also need to be 'cluster aware' which will add considerable expense to the solution. However, it does offer continuous data protection (CDP) with zero data loss.

In asynchronous replication, such as Double Take™, data is written to the primary storage system as normal and a copy of the write instruction may be sent to the secondary storage system in real time or buffered until suitable bandwidth is available. This means that the application can be informed that the data has been written before the data has been passed to secondary, potentially slow, off-site storage system. The downside of this is that there is a possibility of data loss if a fault occurs before the data has been written to the secondary device. Hence, depending on the configuration this solution could be considered as continuous data protection (CDP) solution with 'near'-zero data loss. Which solution is best for your system's data depends on your organization's RPO and of course your budget.

If your organization can tolerate a near-zero RPO, asynchronous replication can provide some tangible additional benefits. The secondary storage device can be located anywhere with no distance limitations. The amount of bandwidth required is minimal in comparison to synchronous replication and there are no latency issues. The applications and operation systems do not need to be 'cluster or replication aware', hence the existing licences do not need to be upgraded. However, one of the really tangible additional benefits is that the secondary storage device has no open files as on the primary server. By moving your backup device to the secondary device, you can run regular incremental or even continuous backups on your data without any effect on application or network performance and with no open file issues, effectively D2D2T.

Another advantage of asynchronous replication is that your data can be off-site in real or near-real time negating the risk to the data of a site-wide disaster and depending on the location of the secondary system, negating the risk of a wide area disaster such as Hurricane Katrina.

In addition, you do not need to worry about your courier losing last night's tapes or the time delay in having them couriered back. An example of this was when in May 2005 Time Warner Inc., in New York, reported that data on 600 000 current and former employees stored on 40 backup tapes was lost in transit by Iron Mountain. Also, following the London bombings on 7 July 2005, some organizations invoked their business continuity plans and started preparing to occupy their DR sites. Those who had DR sites in London had severe delays in receiving their last backup tapes from the storage companies due to the fact that traffic in London was gridlocked. One company waited for over 24 hours for their tapes, their RTO was eight hours.

Of course, the main advantage of both forms of replication identified above is their ability to failover. In asynchronous replication, the DNS address and server name are transferred from the primary server to the secondary server. The secondary server then becomes the production server with potentially no data loss and may be accessed by users via the WAN. This recovery process can take only a few minutes enabling a high availability of the data and an RTO of minutes rather than hours or days as with tape.

Another reward is greatly reduced planned downtime, thus greatly improving availability. If you need to upgrade or perform maintenance on your production server, you can failover to the secondary server while the upgrade and testing takes place. On completion of the work, the two servers will synchronize and your primary server will come back online.

However, one of the issues with replication is that it will replicate data corruptions from the primary to the secondary. Therefore, it is recommended that some form of snapshot of the primary system is taken on a regular basis.

In real terms, true data protection will come from a combination of snapshots, replication preferably off-site, and backups. Tape backup on its own is now increasingly insufficient due to its inherent risks, data volume sizes and slow speed.

WAN availability

Comprehensive strategies for business continuity planning should not only focus on data protection and availability of IT systems, as above, but also consider solutions for WAN and Internet resilience. ISP outages are a reality and they can directly affect the organization's ability to function and its reputation, considering around 20% of all unplanned downtime for email systems is caused due to connectivity loss.

Access to the wide area network (WAN) is vital to most organizations' systems and users. It is used for communication with customers via email, for replication and high availability solutions, and for remote access to centralized databases, virtual private networks (VPNs) and voice over IP (VoIP), to name a few. Many organizations rely solely on a standard service level agreement (SLA) from the Internet service provider (ISP) to provide a guarantee of availability to the WAN links. However, an SLA may only guarantee minimal damages (typically a refund of fees) in the event of a prolonged failure, not availability. Proactive measures need to be taken to ensure resilience and fault tolerance of the WAN connections.

There are many solutions and technologies on the market at the moment to assist in improving our WAN and Internet resilience. Multi-homing or multi-WAN switching provides one such solution. A multi-homed WAN uses more than one link and/or service provider to connect to the outside world. These links run in parallel to connect to the Internet or between offices, etc. Multi-homing can provide continuity of service for WAN-based applications ensuring continued customer satisfaction, regulatory compliance and protection of reputation.

Multi-homed solutions can offer immediate detection of link failures with automatic failover to another available link. It can utilize multiple link types and even simultaneously utilize all available links to provide a form of load balancing for bandwidth requirements.

Other WAN issues involved in moving operations to a DR site include DNS and HTTP redirection. This can be a time consuming and frustrating operation. This refers to redirecting your Internet address to another location enabling access to Internet traffic such as email from the new location. Propagating this address change across the Internet can take 24 hours but there are services such as NeuStar's Ultra-DNS™ and Radware's Global Redirection™ that enable seamless and near immediate redirection via a web-based client.

Virtualization

Virtualization will have a considerable impact on the way we plan and develop IT business continuity and availability strategies for years to come. Its main impacts will be reducing operational costs and improving overall operational efficiency. Of course, virtualization is not new: IBM, for example, have been utilizing this technology for years in its mainframe environments.

Virtualization can be defined as a methodology of dividing the resources of a computer into multiple environments, by applying technologies such as hardware and software partitioning, machine simulation and/or emulation. When you consider most servers are running at less than 15% utilization most of the time it makes sense to use this untapped resource. This technology can also dramatically decrease capital and operating costs.

There are many forms of virtualization – hardware or server and operating system virtualization to name but two. The former involves the loading of a proprietary operating system called a hypervisor, such as VMware® ESX Server or Microsoft® Virtual Server. This virtualization layer then emulates and shares processor, memory, storage and networking resources to multiple virtual machines enabling greater hardware utilization. That is to say, you can run different operating systems in isolation, side by side on the same physical machine. Hardware virtualization has many advantages:

- Server consolidation, as many as 5 to 10 production servers to one
- Supports operating systems, including Windows, Linux, Novell NetWare and Solaris all on one server
- Can support multiple virtual workstation environments
- Consolidation greatly reduces environmental footprint, i.e. requires less space, less power, less cooling in your data centre or equipment room
- Can provide multiple virtual test and development machines. VMware supports encapsulation in which the state of a virtual server can be saved to disk and restarted at another time.
- Can provide fault tolerance.

Operating system virtualization involves an operating system, such as Windows Server 2003, and an application, such as SWsoft Virtuozzo™, which emulates the kernel of the operating system. This enables multiple virtual environments running from the same operating system. As with hardware virtualization, there are similar advantages to operating system virtualization; other advantages include:

- Server consolidation, operating system virtualization has a far higher potential for virtual environment density – as many as 10 to 15 production servers to one.
- Lower performance overhead than hardware virtualization
- I/O intensive applications such as Exchange and high end transactional databases may perform better in this environment.
- Live virtual server migration without the requirement for a SAN (IP based).

Do not throw out your old servers. Utilizing virtualization, these servers can be configured with multiple server configurations reflecting your production servers and used in the event of a production server failure (with reduced capacity, of course). However, with multiple physical servers configured as a shared processing environment you remove the performance limitations of using any one server.

The following is one example of using virtualization to provide a fault tolerant, high availability solution including remote replication.

Let us say we have several physical servers connected to a storage area network (SAN). These servers have all been configured with the latest offerings from Vmware® and configured as a shared resource. The virtual servers all exist as files on the SAN. Assuming physical server number one needs to be taken offline for maintenance the virtual servers currently running on physical server number one can be moved to any of the other servers where there is spare capacity without any downtime. This could also be the case if physical server number one crashed due to a hardware failure. Dynamically the virtual servers would be migrated to utilize the resources of the remaining servers. This configuration greatly enhances fault tolerance and availability.

Taking this a step further, one can create a point-in-time copy of virtual machines data that can be used for backup and recovery operations. If we require protection from a site-wide disaster, we could install a replication product, such as Double Take™, and replicate the data from the virtual servers in real time to a DR site. At the DR site, we can have a reduced number of physical servers, as they will only be utilized during a disaster presumably with a reduced capacity requirement. Should failover be required, it can happen in a few minutes due to the rapid boot time of a virtual server. This solution provides us with a near-zero RPO and near-zero RTO with very high availability.

Due to virtualization, this data protection and system recovery solution was achieved using a greatly reduced number of servers and enables a lower dependency on the reliability of any one server. The overall cost would be greatly reduced from the typical physical installation.

Virtualization, in whichever form, will have a considerable impact on the ability of organizations to recover from a disaster, with the added advantage of a reduced price point.

Summary

The objective in this chapter was to highlight the need for organizations to have a multifaceted approach to data management and availability with the primary focus on recovery management. With a recovery management mindset the organization, once it has set its RPOs and RTOs, will be able to justify the implementation of an improved data management and availability solution to achieve its recovery targets.

Highlighting the weakness of tape does not mean it is obsolete; it does, however, require the support of other technologies, such as D2D and snapshots, to achieve the end result we require – effective reliable recovery.

Organizations with shorter RPOs and RTOs need to leverage technologies such as replication and virtualization to increase availability and recoverability.

If your organization understands the mindset of recovery management, it needs to plan for recovery – which includes the need for training and exercising to ensure personnel have the ability and documented procedures to enable efficient recovery.

If your organization is still solely relying on tape for recovery ensure the integrity of the tape is tested on a regular basis. This can be achieved by rebuilding the data to a test environment. Don't be one of the 40–50% of organizations who fail to fully recover their data following a disaster! You have been warned!

Strategies for funding recovery

Danny Rowland – UK

18

Danny is head of Dispute Resolution Ltd, UK specialising in post loss insurance claims and commercial disputes.

Introduction

Writing in an article for the UK *Financial Times* in late 2006, Lord Levene, chairman of Lloyd's of London, said: 'Every business takes risks, and in today's world those risks simply must be well managed to ensure success. Everyone involved, from the coal face to the board room, has to understand the risks they face, know their limits, and be prepared in case things go wrong.'

Risk takes many forms assessed through the business impact analysis. The decisions reached enable organizations to accept, reduce, avoid or transfer the risk of loss.

Insurance is simply one mechanism by which loss flowing from the occurrence of an unforeseen event transfers from the business to an insurer. The whole process is governed by a contract – the insurance policy. Each policy is unique and although based on insurers' standard wording there are often specific warranties that apply. For example, the stock section may include wording requiring all stock to be stored above a certain height to avoid flood damage.

The range of events which triggers a claim is listed within the contract of insurance. All risks headings are followed by a list of exclusions. The contract consideration is the policy premium in exchange for which, subject to the terms and conditions of the policy, indemnity is provided, so reducing the cost of loss to the business.

Policy payment rarely amounts to a complete indemnity and thus insurance needs to be looked upon merely as a fund of money. Properly claimed for, however, the money received can be used not only to cover post-loss remedial expenditure but where not spent it is available towards the opportunities presented by the incident.

The insurance policy can be a flexible instrument and it is for the disaster manager to understand how the mechanisms can be unlocked to access the policy

The Definitive Handbook of Business Continuity Management, Second Edition.
Edited by Andrew Hiles FBCI. © 2007 John Wiley & Sons Ltd.

fund. Alternatively, within the continuity plan, there should be identified the expert assistance required both pre-loss and at invocation to achieve this aim.

Leaving the insurance issue to others, such as insurance brokers or corporate accounts managers, results in loss of control and loss of focus on remedial works. This delays consideration of options during the critical immediate post-loss period. Time is money and the delay ultimately requires either detailed justification to insurers for actions taken or reduces the expected claim payment. Perhaps it is salutary to remember that following serious loss, the board of directors will be looking for more than just explanations when faced with an unexpected call for significant funding.

What is usually covered?

Traditional property insurance replaces loss of capital assets including buildings, plant, machinery, vehicles, stock and assists, in a formulated way, towards loss of business gross profit and post-loss increased cost of working. The modern concept of risk to a business though goes beyond this.

Corporate liability portfolios cover legal liability to employees, the public and for supply of defective products or professional negligence. Good corporate governance has recognized the liability of the board of directors and senior management and thus there has been an expansion in demand for directors and officers' liability insurance.

Stricter government-driven compliance standards exemplify the focus on enterprise risk management. The need to widen the financial cover to protect intellectual property and web-based trading represent significant changes when only a decade ago bad debt insurance was the perceived limit.

There is also the burden of increasing legislation, for instance with the development of concepts such as corporate manslaughter in the UK and increased expectations of a developing blame culture within Western society.

ICT cover requires understanding of the integration into and control over business processes various systems have. Cover for hardware is relatively easy to understand and value, but so often it is not the technically aware who arrange cover or brokers who understand the client's rather than the insurer's definitions of technology. Clear, unambiguous terms are essential: definitions are vital to avoid false confidence in the extent of cover.

There is much ambiguity and misunderstanding but it is the data which is mission critical to the business plus the ability to communicate this throughout the organization. Data recovery is more difficult to underwrite and cover will not exist to recreate data from a zero base rather as restoration from existing backup.

There are many limitations, in particular time excess, virus attack or cyber theft and need for backup is a precondition. Reference back to the fear of the millennium bug serves to illustrate this when many systems were thought to be in danger of crashing as the year 2000 ticked over.

The policy

An insurance policy is a contract and like any other contract is underpinned by the law where the contract is issued or where the risk exists. For a multinational company this is fundamental to understand not only from legal, cultural and political viewpoints, but also from commercial and currency understanding as well as the timescale for the release of funds.

In many common law jurisdictions there are established common law principles but whatever the jurisdiction, it ought to be remembered that the policy is produced as a standard by an industry relying heavily on lawyers. This is not a negative indictment as in particular in North America and the UK insurance is a well-regulated industry. Institutional protection exists through regulatory bodies although this is aimed mainly at the non-corporate or domestic insured.

An understanding of the dispute resolution clause, in particular referral of disputes to arbitration, enables the disaster manager to structure the insurance claim and control the level of investigation required. One insured, rather than rely on a promise by insurers to share a forensic fire report, put in hand a private investigation. Ultimately this was needed to defeat the propositions insurers chose to rely on following receipt of their forensic scientist's report.

Definitions within the cover are important particularly with regard to specialist assets such as computers. The words 'data carrying materials' include disk arrays, CDs, memory sticks and the like but do they extend to laptops, fibre-optic cabling or satellite dishes? Do they cover mobile telephones and the microchips that now appear in a wide range of consumer-related products from vehicles to microwave ovens? It is important not to be misled by headings such as 'all risks' or 'comprehensive' – there is no policy covering every risk!

The pre-loss

Too often the insurance aspect is left to other areas of the business. It may fall under the remit of finance, accounts, and company secretary or even be left to 'the broker' – as though he knows more about the business than the people who run it!

It is thus essential for the disaster manager to know what risks are being transferred and the level at which this occurs. There needs to be harmony with whoever controls the insurance portfolio. In the Caribbean, hurricane cover is expensive and it carries a 2% deductible of the sum insured. If the sum insured is of a blanket cover, such as a range of buildings on a particular site then the threshold which needs to be reached before a claim is payable can significantly outweigh the effect of even a Category 4 hurricane. This is the case for many international hotel and resort chains.

Value is the basis for insurance and undervaluing will result in reduced claims payout. Calculating value is not straightforward. Value differs to satisfy differing objectives. Guidance may come, for instance, from the plant register but is the value assigned to an asset its reinstatement or indemnity value (actual cash value)? Pure value may also ignore the actual costs involved in satisfying current design and legislative requirements; obtaining delivery, installation and testing; and, in particular, inflation.

There are wider accounting questions to be asked such as determining how depreciation is dealt with in the company's accounts. How is the valuation of stock and work in progress dealt with? Is there an accrued fund for renewals and what currency considerations should be taken into account?

The policy will be written setting out contract conditions to be met for replacement of asset and deductibles which apply. Consideration needs also to be given to increased costs that may fall under other policy sections, in particular business interruption. Fees to professionals such as lawyers, surveyors and accountants also need to be considered although there is generally no cover for the cost incurred in making a claim.

Post-disaster it is also important to know the threshold for the cover. Policy excesses or deductibles reflect extent of premium discounting and can be surprisingly high. Awareness of investigation for liability cover is also essential, particularly where employees or the general public are harmed.

Thinking wider?

The business impact analysis will have considered technology and people not only within the business process but in relation to customers and suppliers. This should have expanded to consider contractual as well as trading obligations and relationships. Insurance for financial loss within the business interruption cover is possible to cover loss at third party premises as is failure of public utilities and importantly denial of access.

There continues to be difficult areas for insurers. Long-term risk, as posed by asbestos, macro risks, as posed by flood plain development, and pandemics such as avian flu, pollution, terrorism or radioactive leakage illustrate the margins where Insurers are calling for government responsibility.

Changing weather patterns have resulted in major losses. Islands and economies dependent on tourism are at greatest risk.

In 1995 Category 4 Hurricane Luis (the highest being 5 on the Saffir–Simpson scale) devastated Antigua in the Caribbean. For months thereafter the inflow of insurance funds to the island was the major contributor to gross domestic product. Tourism revenue, particularly from cruise liner passengers, instantly ceased. Tour operators cancelled programmes and airlines reduced flight schedules. This scenario played out again during 2004 on Grenada and Grand Cayman. Coastlines as well as islands are at risk. Hurricane Katrina in August 2005 took out of production a large percentage of US oil extraction and inflicted, even as a Category 3, extensive damage and loss of life in and around New Orleans.

Inevitably the threat of terrorism remains and permeates through society. The passing of the Civil Contingencies Act in the UK highlights this and suggests that this will continue for generations. Considering its impact has to both reflect a local assessment of area and target risk set against full corporate resilience.

Retained insurance – captive or accepted risk?

Larger organizations will have a wider range of options to traditional insurance. Alternative risk transfer reflects the convergence of the insurance and capital money markets.

Retention of risk, whether by a policy deductible or non-insurance of a particular peril such as 'impact by vehicles' or the creation of a self-insurance pool, can have important effects on the speed of post-loss recovery, cash flow and capital funding.

Insurers control the extent to which they are prepared to accept risk by cover limitation, premium pricing and the contract wording of the insurance policy. A retained fund can streamline procedures but may well be less able to respond to large loss.

Management of the fund is a specialist task but again it is essential to understand the parameters set and interdepartment issues to access the money. In one instance money, placed on the money market for best return, based on a three-month call was needed for post-loss recovery expense. The fund incurred significant penalties to release immediate post-loss finance for rebuilding fire damaged property.

As with any fund there will be a reinsurance provision and this can lead the disaster manager back to a stage one position where enquiries by reinsurers are necessary.

Insurance has an essential role

Lord Levene, Chairman of Lloyd's, has called for all businesses to make risk management a key priority:

Effective risk management ensures that a good understanding of risk is backed up by the right appetite, capacity, and controls. In today's increasingly risky world, and particularly in the insurance industry, I just don't see how any business can survive without it. It separates those who are educated, careful risk takers, from those who are simply gamblers.

Delivery of the promise

No business continuity plan is complete without consideration of the post-disaster question:

- Who pays?

From this follow two subsidiary questions:

- Which source(s) do monies come from?
- How quickly can these funds be accessed?

What is of equal importance to the existence of insurance is ensuring delivery of the inherent promise purchased from insurers, and that is to pay. There is a strange comfort in believing that because 'we are insured' all is well. From the outset it would be a mistake to believe that insurers' systems and processes have been designed just with the particular loss to the insured entity in mind. Far from it! There will be a chain of people and outsourced companies involved, all with their own agendas. These can range from those supplying dehumidifiers or replacement carpets to forensic scientists, loss adjusters, accountants and lawyers. Generally, insurers are willing to part with their money but only after they have undertaken proper investigation and are satisfied that the contract terms and conditions are complied with.

There is thus an important and essential duty on the business continuity manager to be aware of the need to accommodate the necessary post-loss enquiries which in the longer run may well be just as important to the survival of the business as actions taken based only on speed of response as provided for by the plan. This will certainly involve dealing with loss adjusters and also the clamour of loss assessors willing to prepare claims. It is at this time that the role of a disaster manager with insurance experience is invaluable. At least access to one within a plan can answer the core issues that often arise and remove the sense of uncertainty and loss of control.

This position may be better understood by considering a cause of loss arising from third party action. In Avonmouth, Bristol, UK, a road tanker was making a routine delivery of a bulk chemical. Mislabelling on the tanker and failure of correct paperwork resulted in a delivery pipe being connected to the wrong storage silo. Police, health and safety and forensic scientists for insurers investigated the resulting explosion.

The insured was well served by loss adjusters but there was an uninsured loss. Through diligent investigation policy monies were accessed swiftly leaving insurers to recover later through litigation. To that claim was added the uninsured value. This aspect of the loss required funding and was paid later yet the immediate rebuild cost had to be funded by reserves from the company.

Legal awareness is an essential necessity just as much as knowing the demands and constraints of existing business contracts. Early statements are often invaluable as are eye witness accounts. Although the continuity plan focuses on the business recovery, proper facility should be built into the post-loss period to investigate cause and have regard to any dispute resolution requirement.

This will assist lawyers but inevitably will be demanded by statutory bodies such as the Health and Safety Executive. On a lower level, investigation may be wanted as a business activity tool, for instance to improve processes or training. The commonest demand, however, is from insurers.

Control over this *essential* financial link often falls between job descriptions where finance is seen as a separate operation, distinct from the scope of material repairs or even the disaster management process. It is the disaster management process that needs to capture the expense and apportion it to the differing directions. Different people may be required to sign off a claim and internal processes may not operate at necessary speed; disaster funding cannot be treated as an expenses claim!

Added value of a disaster manager

The first objective is to apply the plan to the loss. This requires an understanding of what the plan is seeking to achieve? In some cases this is simply recovery of systems. The larger the incident the more interaction occurs and the more people feel under threat.

In truth the commercial objective is to minimize the impact of the incident on business gross profit. For larger losses this has an added time dimension. A typical approach for a disaster manager is to test decisions against the overriding objective of minimizing the loss of gross profit.

Second, the focus is on who pays? As far as the insurance, including self-insurance, is concerned, the prime role is to capture information under full breadth of policy cover and speed interim payments wherever possible. This will involve dealing with a range of professionals, investigating cause, and considering policy liability and recovery position against others.

Thus it is the insurance claim where initial funding is sought. The disaster manager will liaise with brokers and adjusters and create an interface for speeding funds or identifying difficult problems.

Insurance though is simply one source of post-loss funding. And as part of the brief other funding sources will be considered. These include:

● Company's own funds
● Increased shareholders' capital
● Institutional funders
● Third parties against whom legal liability is established.

The disaster manager must understand who the paymaster is and foremost this will be the company. Early information is needed to establish what liquid assets are available to meet the anticipated costs. After a loss, immediate finance comes either from company cash flow or reserves (which may even be the directors' pockets in small concerns), or short-term overdraft.

Raising money from shareholders or new institutional funders will take time and require a far more detailed business offering than a mere call for cash to meet the effects of the disaster. Perversely the disaster itself may be seen as a negative reason to lend and the way in which the problems are addressed become an important persuasive tool. Much rests on the disaster manager's shoulders.

Bankers' and financial institutions' own risk analysis bears no relation to the business loss. In January 2002 one of the oldest public houses in southwest England, The Rising Sun in Somerset, suffered a fire resulting from an electrical fault. The thatched roof of the building readily ignited leaving the property with partial collapse of walls. The company's bankers, an internationally known name, carried out a risk assessment and without consultation sought to foreclose on the business, calling in the outstanding loans and thereafter disposed of the site to recover their mortgage interest. There was no discussion with the local branch manager, the matter being dealt with by a remote regional office.

With effective disaster management temporary funding was acquired, insurance claim issues resolved in six weeks and 12 months later the premises had been rebuilt and business remodelled with turnover increasing 235%. The insured changed banks.

Third party recovery requires increased investigation to prove loss and will require careful record keeping.

Turning to the secondary question:

● Which source(s) do monies come from?

Monies can come from several sources such as insurance, loans, even grants. Of equal importance is ascertaining the ultimate funder. For instance, a third party company may have insurance that does not fully cover the liability. Who will be paying the difference – is the liable company solvent?

Another example arises in small jurisdictions that suffer catastrophe such as Caribbean islands. Local insurance will soon exhaust and funds will come from offshore reinsurance (if it has been effected at all). Where is this placed?

A government may step in such as in New Orleans post-Katrina or in tornado alley in the Mid West of America. Flood assistance in Florida is common from local authorities as well as charities. The benefit is more personal but business relies on its employees.

Having identified funding sources an assessment can be made as to how quickly these funds can be accessed. The disaster manager must know the paymaster's requirements. Essentially, this will be an understanding of insurers' processes and procedures. Pre-loss knowledge is critical so that all stakeholders in the loss can be quickly contacted. For legal recovery full investigation is critical to capture information and consider the best route towards resolution of the matter.

Conclusion

The role of insurance is as one provider of funds. Although it is the most usual it is not the only option. The use of a disaster manager can focus the plan into minimizing the loss of gross profit and take a wider holistic view at business development. A good disaster manager also turns a disaster into an opportunity for longer-term business development.

Emergency response and operations

19 Gregg C. Beatty – USA

Gregg is Senior Vice-President of The Darien Group Ltd of Glenn Mills, PA.

Identify potential types of emergencies and the responses needed

Emergency response is that period of time during which your adrenaline is flowing. Some events seem to be happening in slow motion while others are going at the speed of light, and you keep having the nagging feeling that something is being overlooked. Decisions come more quickly for some people and others freeze when having to make a quick decision. The future of organizations, structures and people is hanging in the balance. How confident are you in your ability to recognize the situation and make the correct decisions? In another day or another week you will be able to provide an accurate evaluation of how well you performed but you need an answer now. Preparation is the key.

If this chapter were organized like a Hollywood movie, the opening scene would focus on you in the midst of an emergency (fire, flood, building collapse, physical violence, hurricane, etc.) giving orders and wondering if you are making the correct decisions. The future of people and your company is at stake. Then the camera would fade and in a series of flashbacks we would all have the opportunity to see how you, and your company, prepared for the emergency. We would see you and your planning group trying to identify just what is an emergency. After hours of conversation, citing examples to support various positions, stories of known emergencies, and the retelling of actual experiences, you would have reached the conclusion that an emergency isn't just one single type of event but that it is wide reaching and a composite of many different elements. You decide to use the definition of an emergency that is used by the Federal Emergency Management Agency in its publication *Emergency Management Guide for Business and Industry* which states that:

The Definitive Handbook of Business Continuity Management, Second Edition.
Edited by Andrew Hiles FBCI. © 2007 John Wilcy & Sons Ltd.

An emergency is any unplanned event that can cause deaths or significant injuries to employees, customers or the public; or that can shut down your business, disrupt operations, cause physical or environmental damage, or threaten the facility's financial standing or public image.

This definition opens the door to considering many different types of events that could have a negative impact on your people and your business. And the question it raises is: 'How do we identify the types of emergencies that we are most likely to experience and what will be the impact on us?' This two-part question then leads you to design a simple, effective matrix system for identifying, estimating the probability, anticipating the potential impact and recognizing existing internal and external resources to respond to the emergency.

Such a matrix is shown in Figure 19.1 and is referred to as a Vulnerability Analysis. One of its strengths is that it is simple to use and simple to understand. The key to the use of the Vulnerability Analysis is the recognition of the many types of emergencies that could affect you, the projected impact of the emergency, and the resources that are available to respond to the emergency. From this beginning you are now in a position to begin the process of allocating resources to minimize or even prevent some emergencies, determine what elements of your organization and facilities are at greatest risk and how you want to spend your limited resources to prepare for the various emergencies. The Vulnerability Analysis becomes a very valuable planning tool to help you prepare, respond and recover from an emergency.

When you start the process of completing the Vulnerability Analysis, one of the questions you will raise will be, 'Where do I find information about past emergencies and potential emergencies?' so you can complete the first column. The knowledge of long-term employees will be a rich resource of emergencies, and near emergencies, that have occurred in the past.

The actual emergency experiences at other locations of members of your planning group will also assist you. Local newspaper and magazine records are a source of information about previous emergencies. And then there are the community emergency response organizations.

The community emergency response organizations include fire, law enforcement, medical response, rescue, Red Cross, emergency management (civil defence) and others. They know what types of emergencies are most common, which ones they are prepared to respond to and what potential emergencies worry them the most. Establishing a rapport with these organizations before any emergency occurs is extremely valuable in ensuring an effective response on their part to your emergency. Having these organizations work with you as you develop, test and maintain your emergency response capabilities is a win–win situation for everyone.

Many local governments, probably under the auspices of the local emergency management agency, have developed a hazard analysis or risk assessments for their jurisdiction. In the United States the Army Corps of Engineers have developed 'Dam Failure' Studies for many of the dams and these studies are very useful. In

Type of emergency	Probability	Human Impact	Property Impact	Business Impact	Internal Resources	External Resources	Total
	High Low 5 ←→ 1	High Impact 5 ←→ 1		Low Impact	Weak 5 Resources ←→	1 Strong Resources	

Figure 19.1—Vulnerability analysis chart

New Zealand, for instance, the local emergency authorities have modelled the effect of an offshore volcanic eruption. Similar types of study have been carried out in many countries.

Within your corporation you want to examine the experience of various emergencies, including the size and impact of the emergency, at locations throughout the company. Events that occur in other industries, states or countries may possibly happen at your location and you will want to gain from the experience of others. One of the most difficult aspects of emergency planning is examining emergencies at other locations within the same company and learning the lessons. Most organizations tend to remain isolated within the various locations and not only are the lessons of previous emergencies not shared but the sharing of resources in responding to a future emergency is ignored or minimized.

For a business continuity scenario, make sure you look carefully at the issues of vital records, computer operations, hot sites, continued supplier operations, continued customer operations, death of the CEO/founder of the company and the negative news media reports based upon either fact or fiction. All of these events can have a very significant impact on your company and its very survival. The loss of electric power, telephone service or other utilities can create a real-time emergency that doesn't involve the loss of life or structural damage to the facilities. But it can have a very significant negative impact on your business operations.

Identify the existence of appropriate emergency response procedures

Once you have determined what can constitute an emergency and established a framework for determining the impact of the various emergencies on your company, you can begin the task of determining what emergency plans and/or procedures are currently in place. This may seem to be a futile task as you either find that there are no plans/procedures which specifically address the various potential emergencies; determine that the plans/procedures were written 10 years ago and won't work in today's environment; or find that there are too many separate plans/procedures that are very redundant. In some ways it is easier to start with nothing rather than to try to bring order out of the chaos of a dozen or more incident-specific emergency plans/procedures.

However, the collection of the numerous plans and procedures will provide you with an opportunity to create several matrices. On the first one, list the names of the various plans/procedures across one side of the matrix and on the other side list responsibilities, communication channels, notification systems, operational areas, equipment and so forth. Each of these may be subdivided to permit you to list all of the information. For example, communications may have telephone (office, cellular, pager, power failure), radio (different frequencies), email,

Internet, commercial radio stations and commercial television stations. Then in each box of the matrix identify the specific information from each plan/procedure. Usually you will see that a number of the plans/procedures use the same operational area, or the same position has the same responsibilities no matter what the emergency. A pattern will quickly develop along with empty boxes. This matrix will permit you to see how you can consolidate much of the common information into a single plan.

We will use the information from the first matrix to begin to develop a second matrix that will provide us with a clear picture of responsibilities. This will be a simple primary and support matrix that will clearly outline the emergency response functions and the organizations or individuals who are responsible for carrying out those functions. Along one matrix, list the organizations/department that might be involved in response and recovery to an emergency (management, human resources, maintenance, information systems, environmental, safety, production, public relations, communications, engineering, etc.). On the other matrix list the functions that need to be performed (notification, direction and control, public information, hazardous materials response, medical response, employee notification, notification of next-of-kin, etc.). Then for each function place a P (for primary) in the box by the organization/department that has the primary responsibility and an S (for support) for those organizations/departments who will have support responsibilities. When this matrix is finished not every box will be completed. This matrix will identify for you, and your entire organization, who is going to be responsible for each function.

These two matrices will next lead you to determining what is missing. Is it a lack of communication systems, a central location for directing the response to the emergency, training for hazardous materials incidents, not having an organization identified to handle the news media, or whatever? Now you can begin to make assignments and allocate the necessary resources to ensure that the organizations and individuals are prepared to respond to an emergency.

As you continue the process of consolidating the existing documents into a single, effective emergency management plan, you want to determine how effective the current plans/procedures have been in past emergencies. This is best accomplished by talking with the individuals who have used the procedures. Ask questions such as:

- Did you use the procedure in response to the emergency?
- How effective was the procedure?
- What needs to be changed in the procedure to make it more effective?
- Did you have sufficient training on the procedure prior to the emergency?
- Does existing equipment or facilities need to be upgraded to make the procedure more effective?

If the procedure has never been used in an actual emergency, you can ask the same questions about the use of the procedure in a drill or exercise. Be very careful to identify the type of drill or exercise that was conducted and whether it really provided an opportunity to test the procedure in a situation very close to an emergency condition.

At the same time you are asking questions about existing plans/procedures also interview the key participants in your emergency response organization. They will be the individuals identified in the primary and support matrix. You should interview them with the idea of picking their brains to identify good ideas and learn at first hand what each individual believes is the best way to respond to an emergency. You need to ask them about their perceived role and responsibilities in an emergency, and:

- What type of procedure they would most likely use/follow
- What experiences they have had in actual emergencies (either at this location or at another company)
- What they think would be the worst emergency for their department and the company
- What they think can be done to make the emergency management programme better.

Recommend the development of emergency procedures where none exist

When the emergency occurs we anticipate, and hope, that every employee will respond as they have been trained to. And for those individuals who have response functions to perform, that they will follow their training and their procedures. In the heat of battle, people won't turn to an extensive plan but will rely on a simple, concise procedure. And if one doesn't exist then they will respond by the seat of their pants. Thus every emergency response function must have a procedure detailing the activities that must be considered and/or taken in response to an emergency.

For the members of the emergency management group (the individuals responsible for the overall response to an emergency) their procedures may be included in their position notebook (see below). Ideally, their individual procedures will be a checklist of actions to be performed and considerations that must be evaluated. For example, items such as determining the exact location of the emergency along with the number of injured and killed are recorded. And considerations for evacuating other areas of the facility, notifying customers of possible delays in product delivery and determining the message to be given to stockholders are also included.

For members of the emergency response group (the individuals responsible for the immediate response and termination of the emergency – fire, medical, hazardous materials, etc.), the procedures will clearly identify actions for establishing triage areas, conducting hazardous materials response, and for conducting search and rescue. These procedures will help to ensure a safe response as well as to protect both the victims and the responders.

The format of the procedures is dependent upon company policy and usability. Whether the format is one with each sentence being numbered or merely a simple checklist, the users of the procedures have to be comfortable with the format. The format must encourage the use of the procedure, not restrict its use.

A good test of the usability and effectiveness of a procedure (short of use in an actual emergency) is how easily employees who are being trained on the function for the first time can understand and follow the procedure. If it takes hours and hours of training to be able to understand and follow the procedure then it is probably too complicated or confusing. You can test the readability and understanding of a procedure by asking someone who has never seen the procedure to read it and tell you what they would have to do if they were asked to follow it.

Like the emergency plan, the procedures will go through a sequence of steps before being implemented. A standard sequence or cycle is a first draft followed by a review by a number of potential users. Then comes a consolidation of the comments and development of a second version. The second version should then be tested in a limited drill or tabletop exercise. This testing will highlight additional changes and permit the issuance of the final version. Of course, over time the procedure will be updated and revised, based upon actual emergencies, new equipment and changes in personnel.

Integrate disaster recovery/business continuity procedures with emergency response procedures

The transfer of emergency operations into recovery operations begins as soon as you know the location of the emergency and initial estimates, or perceptions, of damage. Knowing that a fire occurred in the main warehouse will have you thinking about the loss of product, delays in shipping, impact on customers, lost profits and other business concerns.

Therefore the emergency procedures must logically lead you into recovery and business continuity procedures and activities. One way to facilitate the transfer is to have representatives for business recovery operations as members of the emergency management group. Some of these positions are naturally occurring, such as the risk manager, production manager, maintenance, public relations and engineering. They are present to respond to the emergency and their knowledge about the emergency will permit them to initiate recovery and business continuity activities very quickly.

One of the major concerns for any business will be the actual and perceived impact of the emergency on customers and suppliers. This concern is initially addressed during the emergency when the decisions are made about the content of press releases, the contact with customers by customer service or sales, and what the sales department is told to tell customers when they call. Those first statements will have a dramatic impact on business continuity.

This is not to imply, or state, that you give false statements and mislead customers about the seriousness of the emergency – or about the impact of the emergency on the customer. But it is the opportunity to put into place the backup systems, operations and options that will allow you to continue to meet the needs of your suppliers and customers. In some cases the most immediate option available to you may be to supply your customer with products from one of your competitors. But you should plan that in advance.

Early in the emergency response phase you may be considering how to shift production to another facility or to use contract manufacturers. Or you may have to use backup shippers to deliver products. But at the very least, you want to contact every customer who is affected by the emergency and inform them of how you are going to meet their needs. And then you want to contact your other customers and give them a status report. Customer service is still paramount.

The business continuity procedures should identify the backup operational facilities, contract manufacturers, testing laboratories, shippers and suppliers. Have contracts in place immediately to activate their services. And include in the procedure the names, telephone numbers (24 hours a day), fax numbers, email addresses and so on for each backup organization.

Before any emergency strikes, have a very candid conversation with your insurance carrier. Be very precise in determining what types of emergencies are covered, the amount of deductible, the percentage of loss covered, the amount of business loss covered and for how long, and if the loss of potential new business is included.

At this point you will also want to develop a list of contractors who can be called upon to help restore, repair or rebuild your buildings. You can lock in rates and know in advance the type of work they can perform and the number of people they can provide.

Identify the command and control requirements of managing an emergency

Who is in control of the emergency response and recovery? What are their responsibilities? Where do they operate from? Who reports to them? Who do they report to? How do they function? These are all essential questions and ones that will help to shape your emergency response organization.

There are two different organizations, or groups, who may be involved within your company. The first one, the emergency management group, should be present in every company. The second one, the emergency response group, may or may not be present in every company. Let's look at both groups, their roles, their composition and how they interact with one another.

The emergency management group (EMG) is responsible for the overall big picture of the emergency and its impact on the company. They are responsible not only for identifying the location and source of the emergency but also for determining the emergency's impact on the rest of the facility, employees, visitors, contractors, surrounding community, stockholders, customers and suppliers. They will be responsible for coordinating with regulatory agencies, contacting family members of victims, interfacing with the news media, working with insurance companies, providing additional resources to resolve the emergency, and keeping control over the entire situation. They must be able to look at the big picture and make decisions that will have the potential for long-term ramifications.

So who makes up the EMG? For the most part it is senior management representing functions such as production, engineering, safety, environmental, human resources, public relations, risk management, accounting, information services, legal, records management and management. They are supported by administrative staff who are absolutely essential to the successful operation of the group. The number of members of the EMG will vary depending upon the type of emergency, its location and consequences, but all members should be assembled at the beginning of the response so all the potential aspects of the emergency are addressed and the best allocation of resources is accomplished.

The EMG is directed by an individual referred to as the emergency director. In some organizations the individual maintains his/her usual title, but for our discussion we will use the title emergency director. He/she is responsible for the EMG and for assuring that it has the information it needs to make informed decisions. He/she authorizes the individual members of the EMG to perform their responsibilities while creating teamwork among the members by having information shared, decisions arrived at jointly (where appropriate) and using all the necessary resources within the organization to limit and terminate the emergency and undertake the recovery process. He/she has the authority to authorize the expenditure of funds and to commit the organization to specific actions.

While the emergency director is normally the highest ranking company official, in some organizations this individual may want to play a different role. He/she may want to be free to go to the scene of the emergency, to be interviewed by the news media, to visit victims at the hospital, and to go where he/she believes he/she can have the greatest positive impact. If this is the case in your company, then the individual needs to be equipped with a radio/cellular telephone so you have constant communications with him/her (to keep him/her informed of changing situations and information) and someone else has to assume the role of emergency director.

The second group, the emergency response group (ERG), consist of individuals who have been specifically trained to deal with one or more unique emergency conditions. They are prepared by training, organization, equipment and authorization to respond to fires, hazardous materials spills, medical emergencies and/or search and rescue operations. They are probably organized under the 'incident command' system and are led by an incident commander. They have a very specific mission which is to report to the scene of the emergency and resolve the immediate issue. They are not concerned with notification of regulatory agencies, meeting with the news media, contacting family members or other actions being performed by the emergency management group. The ERG has tunnel vision in terms of recognizing, responding and resolving the immediate emergency.

The ERG will have their own equipment, training programme, organization and communications. They should be highly trained individuals who have the necessary physical and mental requirements to meet the immediate challenge. They will be organized under the concepts of incident command and understand the roles of incident commander, safety officer, logistics officer, operations officer and scribes. The incident commander must have a secure means of communication with the emergency management group since he/she will be required to keep the EMG informed about the situation and the progress that is being made. The EMG will also actively promote procuring additional resources that the ERG needs. These may range from additional personnel to drinking water. But it is essential that the two groups work together.

An additional key element in the command and control of the emergency response is the community emergency response agencies. Those companies that do not have their own emergency response group will be totally dependent upon the community to provide fire, law enforcement, hazardous material, medical and rescue services. This will require the company to know the capabilities and individuals of these organizations and to actively promote the exchange of information between the two organizations. Tours of the company's facilities, joint training sessions and joint exercises will be the best way to build confidence in each other.

When an emergency occurs, the company should automatically provide the responding community emergency response agency with:

- Personnel to direct the response organization to the scene of the emergency
- Personnel to serve as a liaison between the company and the response organization
- Technical support personnel to identify chemicals, shut-off valves for chemical process and/or electrical lines, the location of natural gas lines, the location of water and sewer lines, and other vital pieces of information.

The company will also have to provide the number, names and last known location of missing personnel to the response organization.

So where do the EMG and the ERG operate from? The ERG will operate from a command post at the scene of the emergency. The command post may range from the front seat of a response vehicle to a mobile command post. The incident commander will operate from this location and will have his/her communication resources at this point. This is the location to which the company must send representatives to provide communication between the incident commander and the emergency management group and to answer basic questions from the incident commander. If the incident commander needs technical advisors from the company, the command post is where they will report.

The emergency management group will operate from an emergency operations centre (EOC). The EOC is a predetermined location that will be equipped to permit the EMG to operate 24 hours a day for as long as necessary. It should be equipped with tables, chairs, telephones, radios, television, commercial radio, clock, flip charts/white boards, computers, display boards, copies of plans/procedures, maps/diagrams of the facility, telephone directories (community and company) and other pieces of equipment that will permit the EMG to do their job. The facility should be tested at least twice a year through exercises and should not take more than 10 minutes to be made fully operational. There should also be an alternative location outside of the facility.

The EOC can be a conference room, training room or some other location within the facility. It may also be a fully dedicated facility that is only used for this purpose. It should have nearby restroom facilities, eating area, sleeping area, duplication facility and small rooms that can be used for private meetings.

You will also want to identify both a primary and an alternative media briefing centre (MBC) for meeting with the news media. In today's society, you can never assume that the news media won't make an appearance when you have an emergency. Part of your planning process is to recognize the needs of the news media and how you can provide them with the information they need to assist you to transmit important information to your employees, customers, stockholders and the general public. One of your planning tools is the development of the media briefing centre, where you can conduct press conferences.

The MBC will most likely be a multipurpose room such as a conference room, auditorium or cafeteria. It should be able to accommodate 20–30 members of the news media and provide them with seats, electrical outlets for their equipment and refreshments. You will also need to equip it with a podium, television, DVD/VCR players, clock and audio visual equipment that you might need to use in detailing the emergency, its location and its consequences. The briefing and press conferences that are conducted in the MBC will reflect the decisions made by the emergency management group. Any news conference/briefing should be written to DVD/CD or videotaped and played for the members of the EOC. Remember to include the Internet and website in your media plans. To be effective, you will need to know the deadlines for local and national TV, radio, newspapers, trade magazines, etc. and arrange your briefings in time to meet them.

The last command and control component you will want to examine is dependent upon the size of your company and whether it operates from more than one location. If you do have multiple locations then you will carefully examine how the location directly experiencing the emergency can be supported by one or more other locations. From the perspective of a large corporation, you will probably want to create a corporate crisis response team (CCRT) who will be able to provide very specific support to an individual facility for a limited amount of time.

The CCRT usually provides unique skills/experience that the location experiencing the emergency either does not have or has expended. For example, the local facility may have one individual who can meet with the news media, but because of the duration of the emergency (or other reasons) this one individual cannot meet all of their demands. In this case the public relations member of the CCRT can be dispatched to the local facility to work with the local organization in responding to the news media.

The CCRT is not to take over or assume control from the local organization, unless that is the request of the local organization. The CCRT is there to provide support and fill in missing elements. Members of the CCRT may represent risk management, legal, engineering, environmental, safety, production, public relations, information systems, human resources and management. Each company needs to examine its organization and determine who should be a member of the CCRT.

To be effective the CCRT must be capable of being activated and on the road to the location of the emergency within 90 minutes. It will take with it its own equipment such as: palmtop or laptop computer(s), credit cards/purchase orders, cellular telephone(s), maps, plans/procedures, safety equipment (hard hats, safety glasses, hearing protection, steel tip shoes), paper, pens, portable printer, clothing and so on. If the emergency involves the entire community (hurricane, tornado), the CCRT will want to take extra clothing and perhaps bottled water and/or canned food.

Avoid over-reliance on cellular phones: there could be network overload or prioritization that means you could be unable to access the cellular network.

Recommend the development of command and control procedures to define roles, authority and communication processes for managing an emergency

The members of the emergency management group, emergency response group and the corporate crisis response team will all have their own procedures. The ones for the emergency response group will mostly likely be a series of checklists to ensure they respond safely and effectively to the specific emergency. They will be based upon the incident command system and be very specific for the response to the specific emergency. These checklists may be laminated so they can easily be used and marked on with china pencils and then be cleaned and used again and again.

The corporate crisis response team will have procedures that are more general in nature but will give them a checklist of issues and activities that must be examined to ensure that the local facility is effectively responding to the emergency. They will also have a site description for each of the company locations they may have to support. These site descriptions will include: brief description of the facility; local government officials; local news media contacts; directions from the airport to the facility; local hotels; and other information that will permit the CCRT to begin working immediately upon their arrival.

The emergency management group will have simple checklists that will be a part of their position notebooks. Each position in the EMG will have its own customized notebook (probably a 1/4 inch three-ring binder) detailing the activities they must execute or examine, resources that are available to them and any unique information that they want to have available to them. Each notebook may have a section of common information (emergency action levels, organization table, communication directory, etc.) but each will have its own unique checklists and support materials. A copy of each position notebook is always kept in the emergency operations centre and each member of the EMG should also have their own second copy that they will keep in their office and/or briefcase. The notebook could be in electronic format, but hard copy is usually necessary at some stage.

The position notebook will permit each member of the EMG quickly and effectively to perform their responsibilities in an emergency. In those instances where a primary member of the EMG is not present, the position notebook will permit the replacement to easily determine what actions need to be considered or completed and to become an effective member of the EMG with a minimum of downtime.

The checklists within the position notebooks should be just that: a checklist of actions that should be considered, reviewed and/or implemented for each emergency. Not every action will be completed for every emergency, but each action should be considered. This approach will permit each member of the EMG to work both independently and jointly to achieve a quick resolution of the emergency. It eliminates having some individuals just going off to do their own thing (and perhaps working in a counterproductive manner) or relying on individuals to use their best judgement and the seat of their pants to respond to the emergency.

The basic section of the comprehensive emergency management plan will detail the roles, authorities, organization, operational areas and responsibilities of the emergency management group and the emergency response group. This basic section is not long (usually between four and 15 pages depending upon the size of the organization) but gives a very precise overview of how the organization is structured and how it will respond to an emergency.

The roles and responsibilities identified in the primary and support matrix earlier are detailed in the basic section. A brief listing of the responsibilities for each member of the EMG is given and an organization table clearly identifies both membership and organization. The location, layout and equipment needs for both the emergency operations centre and the media briefing centre are included. The basic section will also identify any emergency action levels (EALs) that the organization will use to initiate automatic actions.

EALs are brief descriptions of trigger points that call for automatic actions to be implemented by the emergency management group, the emergency response group and general employees. They are usually based upon a combination of weather conditions, type of emergency, size of the emergency, number of injuries/deaths, off-site consequences or regulatory requirements.

Communications in any emergency is always the one topic that everyone afterwards agrees could be improved. Identification of existing systems is one of the primary functions to be accomplished when developing your emergency management programme. How many radio frequencies currently exist? Who can talk to whom on which frequencies? How many telephone systems exist? Are any of the telephone lines able to function when the basic telephone system is non-functional? Who has cellular telephones? What kind of information can be sent out over email? Do we have an internal television network? If so, who has access to it? Are our fax machines on separate telephone lines?

The members of the EMG need to be able to talk to:

● Each other (usually face to face in the EOC)
● Members of their staff (telephone, radio)
● The incident commander (radio or cellular telephone)
● The news media (face to face, telephone, company website)
● Customers/suppliers (telephone and news media)
● The general public (news media, company website, Internet)
● Employees (telephone, radio, email, news media)
● Other company locations (telephone, cellular telephone, email, Internet, intranet, satellite television broadcast)
● The board of directors (telephone, news media, email, Internet).

The communication channels need to be identified and their reliability established. Backup systems must be established and the limitations of the current systems understood. The types of information that can be transmitted over the various types of communication systems must be recognized. For example, you never want to transmit the names of fatalities or injured personnel over a non-secure radio frequency.

You also want to recognize that the news media can be a very valuable channel for informing employees, families, general public, customers, competitors and regulators about your situation and what is being done to relieve it. Knowing all of this in advance will permit you to develop sample press releases, determine the types of messages that need to be prepared for the individual audiences and be prepared to keep everyone informed about the situation.

At the same time, you need to be aware of the rumour and innuendo that may be being spread through gossip, the news media and/or the Internet. The emergency management group needs to anticipate that this will happen and be prepared to respond to these false reports in a very positive manner. Facts and the method in which they are presented are essential.

Ensure emergency response procedures are integrated with requirements of public authorities

While most emergency management programmes are developed to ensure the proper preparation, response and recovery to an emergency, some programmes are only developed because of a legal requirement. The occurrence of various emergencies (chemical releases, Three Mile Island, explosions, etc.) over the years has resulted in a wave of regulations from local, state and federal agencies. They are intended to protect workers and the general public but they place unique planning requirements on the specific industries or companies.

In addition, in the United States, homeland security agencies including the Federal Emergency Management Agency (FEMA) have widespread powers that need to be considered in writing your crisis plans. Similar emergency and anti-terrorist legislation has been enacted in many other countries (e.g. the Civil Contingencies Act of 2006 in the UK).

The emergency services may also constrain your actions. Most fires are deliberate – arson. If the fire services and police consider this a possibility, you may be denied access to the premises until forensic searches have taken place. A similar situation arises in the event of a bomb incident.

If your premises are leased or rented, the owner of the premises may impose constraints. Insurance companies' requirements may also inhibit your actions.

Equally there may be legal, compliance, regulatory or liability considerations that should be reflected in your crisis plan.

You need to identify the specific regulations or constraints that apply directly to you and determine how you are going to meet them. In some instances it may seem expeditious to merely write a plan that will follow the outline of the regulation and thus, one hopes, permit you to comply with the regulation. However, while this approach might get you an approval rating from the regulatory agency, will the plan permit you effectively to prepare for the emergency and, more importantly, effectively respond to the emergency? The plan and procedures need first to permit you and your organization effectively to respond to the emergency and then to address each of the elements of the regulation. This may require you to actually create another section at the end of your plan, identifying where in the plan you meet the regulation and/or address the remaining regulatory requirements.

You may also have to create a matrix to show where your one overall plan meets the requirements of several regulations. Creating a separate plan for each regulation is asking for a disaster. A multitude of plans will not only contain a great deal of repetitive information but will also confuse your people when they are trying to figure out which plan they should be following to meet an emergency.

You may also find yourself trying to meet the standards from some international organizations. Again, the key element is how usable the document is for your employees in an emergency. Required, standardized formats tend to create 'cookie cutter' plans that look great on paper but are less than effective in an emergency. Discuss these issues with the regulators and try to find an approach that will satisfy both needs.

Finally, it is vital that all of your emergency planning efforts are coordinated with the organizations that you are relying on to help you respond to an emergency. As was stated earlier, share your needs, requests and resources with the local community emergency response organizations. Joint training and exercising will permit both organizations to develop a working relationship and test equipment, procedure and organizational coordination.

If they know your facility and your capabilities then they can respond more effectively. If you know their capabilities and limitations then you can plan accordingly. In either event, both you and the community response organizations are winners in this type of arrangement.

Developing and implementing the written plan

20 Andrew Hiles FBCI – UK

Andrew Hiles is a director of Kingswell International, a global consultancy specializing in business continuity, risk management and service delivery.

Developing the plan: scoping

Where do you start?

What is the scope of the plan? Will it cover all sites? Will it assume skilled people remain available after the disaster? How far will it go into the customer chain and the supply chain? Will it cater for multiple disasters – perhaps simultaneously at different sites? Will it cover just information technology disaster recovery, or all functions? Will it cover industrial relations issues? Will it cover a wide area disaster or just loss of company facilities? These initial scoping decisions are important and the decisions and assumptions made should be exposed.

The next step is to define what your recovery capability is going to be. Is it to be 'business as usual' or simply operation in survival mode? Can you get by simply by supporting the 20% of customers who give you 80% of your profit – or the 20% of branches that provide 80% of your turnover? How long can you get by without serving your customers? Your business impact analysis should have considered these issues and your recovery strategy should balance the potential losses against ongoing costs for business continuity and business recovery services. However, there are many ways of achieving your objectives, and a sound plan is usually a judicious mix of the strategic recovery options outlined below.

Business continuity strategy: options

The best business continuity plans tend to take the worst possible case, on the basis that such plans are likely to cater for lesser events. They also split the orga-

The Definitive Handbook of Business Continuity Management, Second Edition.
Edited by Andrew Hiles FBCI. © 2007 John Wiley & Sons Ltd.

nization into two teams: one to manage the ongoing business activities, the other to handle disaster response and recovery.

The restart strategy is an important determinant of the costs. The options that follow are not necessarily mutually exclusive; they may be complementary. Options are as follows.

Do nothing

The 'do nothing' option is to wait until a disaster happens and hope to acquire equipment and facilities at the time. This may be appropriate where an organization has a recovery time objective permitting restoration of services, without prejudice to the business, which can be met by the normal equipment and facility acquisition lead time. In this case the BC plan should also factor in the possibility of acquisition from PC supermarkets (normally open six and a half days a week, frequently keeping a stock of up to 20 of each of their top selling lines). Another source could be equipment brokers.

Bunker

A bunker or fortress approach will seek to limit risk to a level where management decides any further disaster recovery plan is unnecessary. A fortress can only protect what is inside it: the operation may still be vulnerable (for instance, through loss of external data or telecommunications or denial of access to the site). Moreover, in some cases buildings may be open to the public and in other cases may not be suitable for a fortress approach. In all cases, however, a degree of 'hardening' will be possible.

Continuous processing

Continuous operation will provide continuous 'shadowing' or 'mirroring' of the production operation at an alternative site with adequate capacity and communications links to permit the production operation to be switched to the alternative site at minimal notice. This can apply to non-IT production or IT operations, but is normally prohibitively expensive for manufacturing. One major bank, for instance, has a four-minute recovery window. They triplicate equipment in each of three different locations, with triangulated communications (replicated from different vendors). Each communication link and each of the three configurations at each of the three sites has sufficient spare capacity to take the whole of the workload. In addition, they have capacity on demand and storage on demand at each location. If one CPU or one site fails, the work is automatically switched to another. Data is collected at each location from identical but independent sources. The cost of this option is high: it implies high levels of redundancy and resilience with standby, installed and operating equipment and telecommunications waiting for a disaster.

Distributed processing

Distributed processing spreads the risk around different locations so that not all the corporate eggs are in one basket. Some production or operations may reside on dedicated equipment so that the loss of this equipment leaves other production unharmed and available. Alternatively, operations may be replicated at different sites in order to gain even more resilience. Distributed processing may be designed with disaster recovery capability in mind, so that there is excess capacity on which to rebuild the lost application. Recovery is facilitated by standardization of equipment.

Alternative site

During the Buncefield oil terminal fire in the UK in 2005, two logistics companies were denied access to their sites within the Buncefield complex. Their customers did not notice the difference, because both had business continuity plans that involved operating from an alternative site. For technology, an alternative site may be selected either from a commercial disaster recovery service supplier or from spare in-company accommodation. Standby workspace needs to be considered as well as standby equipment. Depending on the required recovery timeframe, the alternative site may be:

- **Cold** – A 'cold' site will provide an environment in which a new facility can be built from scratch.
- **Warm** – A 'warm' site will provide an environment and basic infrastructure to enable the facility to be reinstated before its absence becomes critical to business survival. It may have most of the equipment required except, perhaps, for items that can be supplied quickly from stock.
- **Hot** – A 'hot' site will effectively provide a duplicate facility in another location, with capacity to absorb the additional workload before its absence becomes critical to business survival. A hot site will have all the equipment and facilities required operationally and will simply require installation of systems, applications and data.

Cold, hot and warm facilities may be mobile (delivered in trailers with independent environment), portable (delivered in prefabricated form, with independent environment) or static (preinstalled at the supplier's or in-company premises). Most commercial DR service providers will offer the option of dropship of equipment. This can be useful, for instance, where there has been an equipment failure but the site remains intact: it saves the disruption and risks associated with moving to the alternative site.

Where an organization has more than one site, relocation from the stricken site to another site or sites may offer relief. While these might offer short-term havens for a few people, they may not offer a reliable site for relocation of all the essential work unless it was agreed that these premises would be evacuated in a disaster.

Increasingly we are seeing big multinationals create alternative sites in-state, out-of-state and out-of-continent. This is a practice followed, for instance, by some of the big Indian business process outsourcing companies. The major commercial disaster recovery service vendors are also able to offer this option.

Commercial disaster recovery service vendors normally limit the period for which a warm or hot site can be used. This is typically six weeks – so in the event of a major disaster such as a fire or explosion, it may be necessary to move from the warm or hot site to a cold site and then back to the original premises.

Many plans rely on use of a hotel as a recovery site; however, if the hotel is booked for say Christmas, Eid, a wedding or other function it may not be available. It can, however, work. The author was in Islamabad the day following the earthquake in Kashmir on 1 October 2005, for a meeting with the CEO of a major telecommunications company. The meeting took place in the ballroom of the J.W. Marriott, where 150 staff were working with laptops following damage to the company's head office. To quote the CEO: 'We didn't miss a beat.'

A little lateral thinking may help. The author had presented a workshop in Auckland, New Zealand, and asked the delegates what standby sites they had arranged. One replied: 'We have a contract to charter a ferry. It has its own power and communications, catering facilities, restaurants that can be used as office space and sleeping accommodation.' A few months later, the main umbilical power line in North Island failed: it took five weeks to restore power. That delegate got it right!

'Budge up'

This is a variation on the alternative site option: it simply means optimizing the use of your own existing facilities. This may mean working weekends or shifts in office or production facilities where this is not normal practice – or it could mean sending non-essential staff home to make space for staff undertaking higher priority work.

Staff training facilities, restaurants or leisure facilities may be used as alternative sites. Setting up a wireless network is quick and relatively simple: but security aspects need to be addressed.

Quick resupply

This approach depends on acquiring equipment, software and communications facilities when the disaster occurs. Equipment vendors or disaster recovery service suppliers may guarantee resupply within a specified timeframe in return for a retainer.

Off-site storage

Commercial services are available for off-site storage of materials vital to recovery. These can range from storage of buffer stock, equipment, documents, tools, plant, samples, as well as computer tapes and discs. Computer data can be transmitted to online backup to tapes stored in tape libraries or silos or to disc arrays, replicated network attached storage or storage area network. increasingly, smaller companies are using the Internet or intranet for backup.

Off-site backup should aim to supply secure storage, with contents retrievable 24 hours per day, 365 days per year.

Working from home

Using PCs with modems, working from home may be practicable for some staff. PCs may be:

- Drawn from a quick resupply contract; redistributed portable PCs
- Salvaged
- Obtained from PC superstores, some of which are open six and a half days a week.

Access can quickly be gained to the Internet for email – subject to security constraints.

Reciprocal arrangements

Reciprocal arrangements tend not to work in practice. Frequently they are not adequately documented and supported by a contract or service level agreement – this leads to conflicts of priorities, dispute and sometimes refusal to honour the commitment in a disaster situation.

Stockholding

In some circumstances, especially where there is a long lead time on resupply of production equipment and where the product has a low unit cost, it may be practicable to maintain a buffer stock to allow customer supply in the interim. The extra cost of inventory needs to be balanced against potential loss of market share.

Outsourcing business continuity planning: plan management and maintenance

Disaster recovery planning may be managed in-house or outsourced. However, the development, ongoing maintenance and testing of any business continuity or disaster recovery plan requires the active support and commitment of in-house specialist staff to provide detailed information on requirements and configurations and to supply appropriate technical procedures.

In-house staff need to take 'ownership' of the developed plan, and their ongoing commitment to training, plan testing and maintenance is essential if the plan is to be effective when implemented.

Staffing of recovery teams could be outsourced to some extent, although the substantial involvement of internal staff will be essential in the event of disaster.

The effect of weekends, public holidays and transport disruptions on equipment delivery needs to be considered as well as the basic resupply timeframe.

Lateral thinking

By focusing on the deliverable of the operation, rather than on its existing processes, it may be possible to identify alternative ways of servicing customers. For instance:

- Could you outsource or subcontract the service to a competitor, or buy product from a competitor to maintain supply?
- Instead of calculating, could you estimate, negotiate or arbitrate?
- Could you agree a procedural solution (e.g. for a government funding operation, could you simply agree 'same as before' with the paymasters)?

Insurance

Insurance is a critical part of the recovery plan. However, insurance in itself simply provides money if defined risks occur. It does not necessarily pay out immediately – in some cases payment can take years. Stating the obvious, it only pays for what it covers – which is why one financial institution received only half what it would cost them to restore a historic building to its former glory. Insurance by itself will not supply customers, nor will it guarantee recovery of market share. Moreover, the recovery plan should take into account that the insurer will have a major say after a disaster in decisions to replace or salvage equipment and in any actions that involve extra cost of working or which are intended to alleviate loss of profits. Issues of salvage and purchase of new equipment will need to be cleared with the insurers.

If the insurers do not like what you are doing, their payout may be reduced. Insurance of loss of profits and for extra cost of working only covers a specific time period – typically six or 12 months after a disaster. After that, you are on your own. And while self-insurance sounds like a good idea, in many cases any self-insured loss eventually comes back (in one way or another) to hit the bottom line.

To make an effective claim, you need to prove loss. This usually involves production of records and inventories of equipment, stock, software and data. A claim for loss of service at say $100000 an hour is difficult to sustain – it has to be proved that such a loss has occurred. Insurers may claim, for instance, that it is not really a loss, merely a deferred sale. If a disaster happens just as a new product or service is about to be launched, it may be difficult or impossible to prove what the profit from it would have been. Insurers may look back at history rather than forward at plans.

However, appropriate insurance of assets, working costs and profits does provide a lifeline and should be considered as part of the continuity strategy.

Options and strategy recommendations

The cost of the recovery option has to be weighed against the impact of loss of service on the business. Cost is usually related to speed of recovery.

The effect of weekends, public holidays and transport disruptions on equipment delivery needs to be considered as well as the basic resupply timeframe. Typically the strategic options outlined above are not mutually exclusive – the optimum solution may 'pick and mix' from these strategies for individual business functions or combine several elements to form a comprehensive solution. A business unit may, for example, decide that it needs 100 workplaces available within eight hours followed by quick resupply of equipment for 25 people working from home within 48 hours and a cold site to house another 100 people within five working days.

Option evaluation

Basically, the 'hotter', bigger and more comprehensive the restart capability, the more expensive it is likely to be. It is therefore important to be realistic about the timeframe within which recovery can physically be achieved, bearing in mind the specific nature of each organization's operations, and to keep the numbers of staff involved during recovery to the minimum required to maintain operations.

How the plan builds up

Figure 20.1 shows how the plan is developed as the business continuity project progresses. Existing procedures, asset registers, inventories and similar information can provide a starting point. The business impact analysis helps to justify the

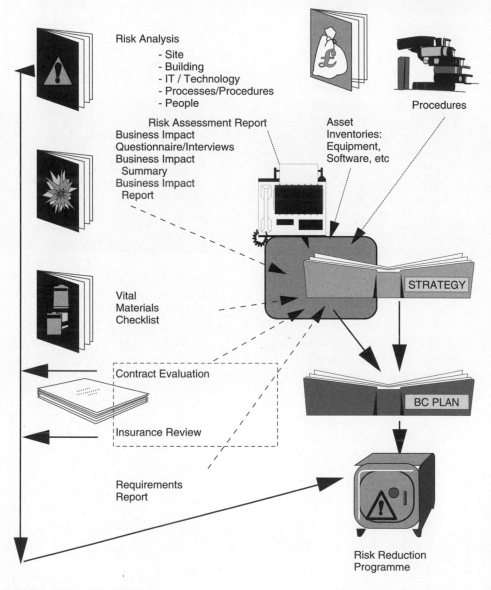

Figure 20.1—Plan build-up

business continuity strategy. Often the business impact analysis overstates the timeframe for recovery – few departments will admit to being unnecessary for days or weeks! It may also be used to:

- Identify materials vital to recovery, which should be kept off-site
- Establish equipment and resource requirements over time
- Establish capacity requirements.

A 'sanity check' should be run on equipment and resource requirements – again, these may be overstated. Capacity requirements, however, are often understated. If there is a backlog of orders following a disaster, greater capacity than normal may be required to avoid an irretrievable backlog situation.

An evaluation of contracts and service level agreements may also identify exposure to vendors or customers: this needs to be reflected in recovery strategy. Once the strategy has been defined, the requirements can be firmed up and arrangements made for their provision following a disaster.

Service contracts

Depending on the strategy selected, contracts may need to be negotiated with vendors – for instance, for standby facilities and equipment or quick resupply of equipment. These contractual arrangements will need to be reflected in the business continuity plan – they are not, by themselves, a business continuity plan.

Business continuity organization and roles

An effective plan needs an organizational infrastructure. Classic business continuity plans divide the operational activities into two: one arm dealing with the ongoing operations unaffected by the disaster, and the other arm dealing with the consequences of the disaster and recovery from it. Typically an emergency management team will be established, comprising key senior managers, public relations and marketing, and the business continuity manager or coordinator. This management team will have their own top-level business continuity plans which are integrated with subordinate departmental or business unit recovery action plans (see Figure 20.2).

The role of the emergency management team (EMT) is to take business decisions, assess and make judgements on business priorities and to facilitate and support the business continuity manager. It also has an important role in marketing, public relations and media management issucs.

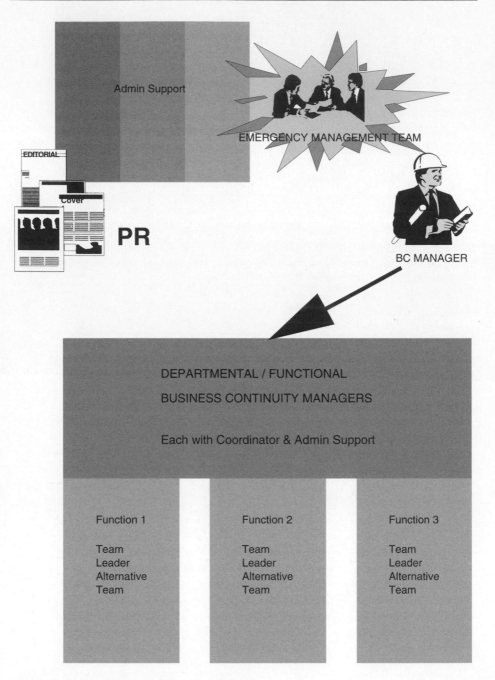

Admin Support

EDITORIAL

Cover

PR

EMERGENCY MANAGEMENT TEAM

BC MANAGER

DEPARTMENTAL / FUNCTIONAL

BUSINESS CONTINUITY MANAGERS

Each with Coordinator & Admin Support

Function 1	Function 2	Function 3
Team Leader Alternative Team	Team Leader Alternative Team	Team Leader Alternative Team

Figure 20.2—Business continuity organization

Normally an emergency control centre (ECC) has been established: this is a 'war room' that contains all of the technical infrastructure and documentation necessary to oversee the recovery effort. The loss of premises will have been considered as part of the planning and arrangements for an off-site ECC will have been made.

The business continuity manager (BCM) is usually a member of the EMT and is effectively the project manager for the recovery operations, reconciling priorities and coordinating recovery efforts of the departmental or business unit recovery managers. The BCM ensures communication between teams and public relations, marketing and the EMT.

In their turn, the departmental and business unit recovery managers manage the recovery in their own areas and ensure communication with other affected teams and with the BCM.

The plan will have considered what staff are needed for the recovery effort and non-essential staff will have been sent home or found alternative accommodation. The roles of departments will change fundamentally, for instance:

- Human resources will not be involved so much in annual appraisals and training as in providing welfare and logistical support, particularly for members of the recovery teams, and possibly in arranging trauma counselling.
- Internal audit will be involved in policing ad hoc financial and procurement activity and may provide spare resource for the recovery teams.
- The legal department may be involved in litigation rather than in contractual issues.
- Sales may be trying to restrain customers from buying while maintaining customer confidence and market position.

The premises management plan is crucial to effective and speedy damage limitation and restoration of the facility.

The plan

The business continuity plan will have an incident escalation procedure that allows the incident to be compared to a definition of disaster. If the incident is, or may be, a disaster, a decision is then made as to whether to alert teams or to mobilize the plan. A notification procedure will be established to alert and mobilize management and members of business continuity teams. This is often a documented calling tree or 'cascade' or 'calling tree' arrangement whereby one person calls several others, who then call others, until all key personnel have been notified. If contact centre-type technology is available, this may be automated.

The plan will cater for all phases of the disaster. The initial emergency phase covers evacuation, incident escalation, damage assessment and limitation, disaster declaration, invocation of standby arrangements, recovery of off-site materials to the standby site(s) and staff redeployment. The recovery phase covers the re-establishment of operations under standby arrangements in parallel with restoration of longer-term facilities. The plan should also consider the move back from standby facilities to a permanent base. In the recovery phase, different procedures, practices, equipment and software may be involved. Change management and the audit trail of change is therefore crucial – otherwise the move back to permanent base may become a disaster.

The plan should also cater for logging of actions to begin as soon as possible: this will be essential to provide evidence for insurance claims, for possible legal actions, and to keep track of spend (using predefined disaster account codes). If available, it may be possible to use existing help desk tools or to design a simple database for this purpose.

Plan documentation

The plan should be an action-oriented document. It needs to include:

- Title, document control, date and version number, confidentiality marking
- Table of contents
- Assumptions and known weaknesses of the plan
- Alert, invocation, notification and briefing instructions (sometimes issued on a credit card-sized document or on the employee identity card)
- Contact lists for internal and external contacts including business continuity team members
- Information on staff redeployment, standby locations and how to gain access to them
- Prioritized action plans and the timeline for actions to be initiated and completed
- Lists of vital materials and instruction on how to obtain them
- Equipment and resource requirements necessary for recovery, the timeframe in which they will be provided and how to obtain them
- Communication, reporting and logging requirements
- Instructions on media and reputation management
- All supporting detailed technical, operational and administrative procedures, plans, drawings maps, etc. (or references to where they may be obtained).

The plans should not include details of business impact analysis, risk assessments, tests, audit report, methodologies, detailed testing and maintenance instructions and other information not essential to the recovery effort. These should be kept separately to avoid cluttering the plan.

Plan format

The plan should be simple, clear, unambiguous and comprehensive. Plans based on different risk scenarios (e.g. fire, mechanical breakdown, etc.) are usually not effective: it is not usually the cause of the disaster that matters – it is the result. Whatever the cause, the result is usually damage to or loss of use of facilities. That becomes the starting point for planning. However, there may be different actions in the event of loss of facilities for say one day, three days or longer.

There are many different ways of designing the plan, including the use of:

- Specialist business continuity software tools (see Chapter 23)
- Project management software
- Database software
- Standard word processing, spreadsheet and presentation tools.

Selection of the right tool depends in part on who is going to become responsible for the plan. If it is to become a line management responsibility, it is probably best to use tools with which the line manager is familiar – otherwise buy-in and maintenance of the plan may be problematic.

The plan itself may be in hard copy, on USB data sticks, CD/DVD, handheld devices or laptops. Whatever the format, version control is crucial and the balance must be maintained between security and availability. Some organizations issue credit card-sized documents to BC team members telling them of the immediate actions required.

In a multi-site environment, where departmental or operational functions span several sites, the structure of the plan is extremely important. It may be preferable to have two views of the plan: a site-based recovery plan and also an overall view of all recovery plans for the multi-site department, process or operation. This can be done provided:

- A standard plan template is developed
- Terminology is absolutely consistent throughout each plan
- Each site plan has a section for each multi-site department or operation that is structured so it can be collated into an overall plan for that department, process or operation.

We recommend that the plan include:

- List of assumptions on which the plan is based (so that they can be challenged and so that, in the event of a disaster, they can be compared to the real situation)
- Scope of the plan

- Known weaknesses of the plan, together with a contact list of those people responsible for their rectification
- Guidance on how to use the plan
- Table of contents
- Action plan for the relevant BC team, including:

  - Names of team members and alternates with contact details
  - List of priorities for recovery
  - Recovery time objectives
  - Recovery point objectives
  - Reporting requirements
  - List of vital documents and materials and how to obtain them (include password, combination numbers, etc.)
  - Resource requirements and timeframe for their provision
  - Contacts, both internal and external
  - All necessary supporting procedures, plans, maps, etc.

- Document control and configuration management.

Annex 20.1 provides an example of a table of contents for one organization. Annex 20.2 contains an example of a simple plan for media management.

The end – or the beginning?

A business continuity plan is never completed. The more detailed the accompanying procedures, the more effective the plan is likely to be. It is normal that, on handover, the plan will contain less detail than is ideal and that further detail will be added during the life of the plan. A schedule for plan enhancement is therefore a normal part of business continuity planning.

One of the objectives of plan audit and review and of both initial and regular testing of the plan is to find areas for improvement that can be included in the plan enhancement schedule. Equally the plan needs to be kept up to date. Clearly major organization, staff or equipment change will require revisions to the plan. Plan maintenance therefore needs to be linked to change control procedures.

Annex 20.1 Example of contents pages from a business continuity plan

Note

'TBD' identifies areas for completion (omitted to preserve client confidentiality).

BUSINESS CONTINUITY PLAN CONTENTS

Commercial in Confidence

Commercial in Confidence

BCPlan.doc   *BUSINESS CONTINUITY PLAN*

BUSINESS CONTINUITY PLAN APPENDICES: CONTENTS

Annex 20.2 Example of a working draft media and public relations team business continuity plan

Originators: TBD
Creation Date: 21 February 20xx
Reference: BCPMedia
Version: Working Draft Version 1.0
Classification: Commercial in Confidence when completed

Section 9:   Media & Public Relations Team Plan

9. **Media & Public Relations Team**

9.1 Media & Public Relations Team Role

The role of the Media and Public Relations Team is to:

- Be the sole source of information to the media (directly or indirectly) from within TBD concerning the Emergency or disaster and progress of recovery
- Ensure that, under *Emergency or disaster* conditions, positive media messages portray TBD as being:
  - Compassionate of their employees and any third parties affected by the *Emergency or Disaster.*
  - In confident control of the situation.
  - Able to service their customers as their customers expect.
  - Able to retain market share.
  - Uninterruptedly profitable.
  - Able to meet their financial, legal and contractual commitments.
- Check and approve any message to the public (through Marketing, Legal or other relevant expert) and to staff, suppliers, contractors, landlords, tenants or others which may get in to the public domain.
- Establish Media and Public Relations functions at the Standby site or under Emergency conditions at *Base Site.*
- Implement *Standby Procedures.*
- Liaise with TBD Managers and Managers on Business Continuity arrangements.
- Keep the EMT and BCM informed of actions and progress.
- Maintain day-to-day contacts with TBD Managers and Managers.
- Ensure timely and appropriate information is provided to stakeholders.
- Maintain corporate reputation, image and credibility so as to preserve market share and managership value.

9.2 Staffing

Team staffing is at 9.7.1 and Appendix A.

9.3 **Standby Locations**
Standby Locations are detailed at Appendices A and N.

9.4 **Statement Template**

The team should be briefed on question evasion methods as appropriate. The statement should cover the following areas:

9.4.1 Concern for staff, stakeholders over death/injury and other disaster impact on them

9.4.2 Impact in perspective

9.4.3 Implementation of effective BCP

9.4.4 Confidence in ability to continue to meet client requirements/impact on customers

9.4.5 Recovery timescale

9.4.6 Impact on environment – reassure local population

9.4.7 The future – confidence

9.4.8 Next update – when and where.

9.5 Media & PR Team Action Plan

Commercial in Confidence

BCPMedia   *BUSINESS CONTINUITY PLAN*

No.	Reference	Action	0	3	6	24	36	1	>1	Contact	Y
			Timescale Hours					**Weeks**			
001	TBD	Receive notification of Emergency from EMTL	X							TBD	
002	TBD	Contact other team members	X							TBD	
003	TBD	Arrange to meet at Control Center	X							TBD	
004	TBD	Get a Communications (i.e. Media and PR) Team member to Incident asap	X							TBD	
005	TBD	Meet at Control Center	X							TBD	
006	TBD	Spokesperson to receive briefing from BCM Covering: – Extent of loss or damage – Anticipated duration of loss – Anticipated recovery timescale – Emergency contacts and telephone numbers etc.	X							TBD	
007	TBD	Brief telephonists and security guards	X...........X							TBD	
008	TBD	Ensure emergency web site activated	X........X							TBD	
009	TBD	Liaise with Marketing, HR, Procurement and EMT as necessary to ensure consistent positive message is delivered in all communications to stakeholders (other TBD offices, managers, employees, suppliers, customers, financiers etc.)	X...............X					X	X	TBD	

No.	Reference	Action	Timescale Hours 0	3	6	24	36	Weeks 1	>1	Contact	Y
010	TBD	Prepare statement from pre-defined template. Cover concern for people and stakeholders, nature of incident and steps for recovery; impact on business, customers and profit; time/plans for next briefing.	X							TBD	
011	TBD	Obtain EMT approval for statement.	X							TBD	
012	TBD	If possible issue statement on website with additional information (e.g. people profiles, company/site profiles, product profiles, annual accounts summary, corporate videos if relevant).	X							TBD	
013	TBD	Release statement to media and list of stakeholders. Consider using fax bureau/call center for contacting stakeholders and media.	X							TBD	
014	TBD	Arrange time and place for press conference.	X							TBD	
015	TBD	Contact TBD Directors and Managers and brief accordingly.	X							TBD	

Commercial in Confidence

BCPMedia   *BUSINESS CONTINUITY PLAN*

No.	Reference	Action	Timescale Hours 0	3	6	24	36	Weeks 1	>1	Contact	Y
016	TBD	Prepare staff and Customer communications, in liaison with Marketing, Human Resources and Finance, Facilities and Administration and IT.	X			X		X	X	TBD	
017	TBD	Handle media enquiries	X..............X					X	X	TBD	
018	TBD	Update statement prior to press conference and obtain EMT approval for revised statement.				X..............X		X	X	TBD	
019	TBD	Identify spokesperson				X				TBD	
020	TBD	Arrange time and venue or channel for partner and staff briefing.				X				TBD	
021	TBD	Prepare enhanced statement for staff briefing – cover: – pay – expenses – relocation – job security – as well as issues above.	X..............X					X	X	TBD	

No.	Reference	Action	Timescale Hours 0 3 6 24 36	Weeks 1	>1	Contact	Y
022	TBD	Hold press and manager/employee conferences.	X..........X		X	TBD	
023	TBD	Contact key suppliers etc. in liaison with Marketing, Finance, Facilities and Administration and Production & IT.	X-X			TBD	
024	TBD	Ensure media handling procedures are in-place.	X-X			TBD	
025	TBD	Create pro-active PR campaign.	X X			TBD	
026	TBD	When time permits, read the Business Continuity Plan. Be well informed about the current status of restoration work and client/public impact.	X..........X		X	TBD	
027	TBD	Contact all TBD Managers, Managers as appropriate and other contacts according to Appendix TBD or other lists. Inform them about: *Your recovery situation: what services are available* *What services are not available* *When services will become available* *What this will mean for them (alternate methods for supply and other deviations from normal procedures).*	X..............X		X	TBD	

9.6   Key Tasks

Departments/Areas
TBD

Secondary Department/Areas

9.7   Contact Lists

9.7.1   Internal

The key internal interfaces and contacts for the department are provided in the following tables

Media & PR Team	Members	Work Tel.	Home Tel.	Mobile Tel.	Pager
Leader	TBD				
Alternate					
Marketing					
Member					
Member					
Member					
Admin Support					

9.7.2   External

The key external interfaces and contacts for the department are provided in the following table

Company/Org.	Name	Telephone/e-mail	Position
TBD			
Journalists			
Trade Press			
PR Companies			

BCPMedia   *BUSINESS CONTINUITY PLAN*

9.8   Vital Materials List

On activation of the department's Business Continuity Plan, one of the first activities will be to retrieve the Vital Materials from the salvage teams and/or the archive store and transfer them to the Business Continuity Site.

The Vital Materials required for the recovery of the department are stored at the following location(s):

Vital Materials	Desk (specify)	Filling Cabinet/Firesafe (specify)	Archive Site	Network Backup
TBD				
BRAD				
Stationery blank with TBD Logo only				
Avery Labels pre-addressed to Corporate and customers				
Pre-prepared faxes to other offices and customers				
List of contacts (home and office) of managers				
List of contacts (home and office) of customers				

Business Continuity Plan

9.9 Equipment & Software & Timescale for Provisioning

Equipment/ software	8 hrs	16 hrs	24 hrs	32 hrs	40 hrs	48 hrs	3 days	5 days	7 days	10 days	14 days	>14 days	lead time to acquire
Server (specify)													
PCs (specify configuration)													
Office Systems Server													
Printers													
Other (specify)													
WP software (specify)													
Spreadsheet (specify)													
Database (specify)													
Other software (specify)													
Telephones													
Telephones (mobile)													
Fax													
Photocopier													
Desks/chairs													
Other (specify)													
Photocopier-fast													
Dictaphone/ playback													
Special Stationery: Avery labels													
Other													

Notes:

1. Specify the quantity of each item required and timescale by which that quantity is required under the appropriate timescale column(s)
2. For PC equipment specify memory, hard disk and modem requirements and operating system
3. For software specify make and version
4. Summarize all functions/departmental requirements for use in resupply

Commercial in Confidence

BCPMedia   *BUSINESS CONTINUITY PLAN*

9.10   Media & PR Business Continuity Activity Log: _____ **TEAM**

Sheet No: .... **Completed by**......................... **Date:** .... **Time:** ....

Name of Requester: ....**Tel:** ....

Contact Point: ....

Name of Supplier/Service Provider: .... **Tel:** ....

Delivery to: ....

Reason for request:

Details of Requirements:

Response:

Expected Delivery   To: .... **Date/Time** ....

Cost £ ....   **Account Code** ....

Progress Chasing – Time of calls/result:

Delivery Confirmed/Service Completed:................. . **Date/Time**...................

Delivered/Completed: ....

APPENDIX A: DOCUMENT CONFIGURATION MANAGEMENT

A.1   Document Approval

Approver	Sections Approved	Signature

A.2   Document Configuration

Title:	Business Continuity Plan: Working Draft
Reference:	BCPMedia
Author:	Andrew Hiles
Issue and Date:	Working Draft v 1.0 2 April 20_____
Location of Electronic Copy:	TBD
Location of Paper Copy:	Project File
Owner:	TBD
Change Authority:	RBD

Distribution: TBD*   Copy No._____of_____copies

A.3   Change Log

Issue	Date	Details of change	Author

Awareness and training

Andrew Hiles FBCI – UK

21

Introduction

The objective of awareness and training programmes is well defined in the BCI/DRII common body of knowledge. It is to create corporate awareness and enhance the skills required to develop, implement, maintain and execute the business continuity plan.

This includes:

- Establishing objectives and components of the programme
- Identifying functional training requirements
- Developing the training methodology
- Acquiring or developing training aids
- Identifying external training opportunities
- Identifying vehicles for corporate awareness.

BSI 25999-1 Business Continuity Management Code of Practice requires that:

> The organization should have a process for identifying and delivering the BCM awareness requirements of the organization and evaluating the effectiveness of its delivery.
>
> BCM staff should make themselves aware of external BCM information. This may be done in conjunction with seeking guidance from emergency services, local authorities and regulators.

The Definitive Handbook of Business Continuity Management, Second Edition.
Edited by Andrew Hiles FBCI. © 2007 John Wiley & Sons Ltd.

Awareness: benefits of business continuity planning

Awareness can be raised by threats of the 'big stick' – the doomsday scenario and loss of the enterprise. However, this can backfire. People are more likely to be enduringly supportive by being persuaded rather than by being threatened. It is helpful to get a statement of support from the CEO or from a senior board member, stressing the importance of the BC project. It is equally important to stress the benefits that can accrue. These benefits include:

- If risks are identified, exposure can be reduced
- Improved understanding of the business (by identifying its criticalities and dependencies)
- Improved operational resilience (by implementing risk reduction measures)
- Reduced downtime (by creating alternative processes and quick fix capabilities)
- Compliance with:

    - Regulatory requirements (e.g. in finance, food, utilities and pharmaceutical industries, Sarbanes-Oxley, Basel II, etc.)
    - Legal requirements (general and industry-specific laws)
    - Companies legislation requiring records to be maintained and protected
    - Public records legislation requiring records to be maintained and protected
    - Health and safety legislation, requiring risk assessment
    - Duties of care ('stewardship duties') identified in Cadbury, Greenbury, Hampel, Turnbull, Sharman and Higgs reports

- Improved operational effectiveness (since many BC projects result in business process improvement)
- Improved organizational resilience (by designating and training alternate people to support key processes and by proceduralizing recovery processes)
- Protection of assets (by risk management)
- Protection of markets (by ensuring continuity of supply and brand and reputation protection)
- Cross-discipline business training and proceduralizing knowledge (important to cover rare skills or experience)
- Improved security and peace of mind
- Avoidance of liability actions
- Demonstrable continuity capability, providing competitive edge and marketing advantage.

It is vital to the success of the BC project to communicate these benefits to senior management and all those involved with the BC project and subsequent programme. This may be done by a mix of email, newsletters, posters, presentations, meetings or videos/DVDs. The presence of the BC manager at all relevant meetings may help – any major project initiation, quality meetings, etc. – to ensure the BC perspective is considered.

Establish BC policy

The board should establish business continuity policy. This demonstrates high-level approval for the BC project and helps to empower the BC manager by providing a reference authority. An example of a BC policy follows:

> The organization is committed to the effective support of its stakeholders and requires that robust and processes and procedures are adopted. These will apply to all aspects of the operation of the organization. All processes will be administered according to documented procedures, which ensure consistent operation under normal conditions and rapid recovery from abnormal circumstances.
>
> It is the responsibility of the manager of each support department and each business unit to develop, maintain, review and test plans for business continuity in the event of loss of any mission-critical facility and to train staff in the use of these plans. It is equally the responsibility of the manager of each support department and each business unit to assess and manage risk on a day-to-day basis and to consider business continuity and risk issues when considering the development of any new product, service or project.

This policy can be reinforced by the development and promulgation of BC mission and vision statements.

The establishment of a high-level business continuity steering group will also help to raise the profile of BCM. Such a group is necessary, in any event, to:

- Set business recovery priorities and objectives
- Sign off BC deliverables
- Agree maximum acceptable outage, recovery time and recovery point and the organization's appetite for risk
- Reconcile any conflicts of priority
- Make recommendations, including budget recommendations, for board approval.

Its existence again demonstrates board commitment to BC, empowers the BCM and helps to raise the profile and awareness of BCM.

Establishing objectives and components of the programme

The awareness programme can be divided into two parts:

1. Training of individuals who will have a BC role ('the players'). Training individuals who will have a BC role includes:

    –   Identifying initial team leaders and team members, together with their alternates
    –   Conducting skills gap analysis to establish what additional skills are required
    –   Identifying suitable internal and external training opportunities

2. General awareness, raising awareness of:

    –   Those whose commitment is required to make the BC project a success, but who are not part of a BC team
    –   All others within the enterprise.

Functional awareness and training requirements for 'the players'

'The players' include the board. It is well worthwhile getting time at board meetings to raise awareness of BC issues – but try to ensure the item is not at the end of the agenda, otherwise it will be either cut or hurried over. A few minutes may be all that is needed. One particularly brave BC manager, whose organization did not have a BCP, simply showed a picture of a similar building in flames and said: 'If that happened here, now, what would you do?' The board meeting overran . . .

If BC deliverables form part of departmental and team objectives and of an individual's job description, general job standards and individuals' targets and objectives – and if they are appraised and preferably remunerated on their achievement – motivation and awareness will spread and BC will become embedded in the organization.

Skills gaps in BC team members may be identified in the BCI/DRII Common Body of Knowledge, notably:

●   BC project initiation and management
●   Risk evaluation and control
●   Business impact analysis

- Developing business continuity strategies
- Emergency response and operations (including incident management)
- Developing and implementing BCPs
- Maintaining and exercising BCPs
- Public relations, media and crisis communication
- Coordination with public authorities.

'Soft skills' training may also be required, covering:

- Consulting and interpersonal skills
- Leadership skills
- Assertiveness skills
- Project management
- Communication skills
- Presentation skills
- Analytical skills
- Business processes and process flow.

Do not forget the training requirement when roles change, or when organization structures, technology or locations change.

Developing the training methodology

The general policy on training is to train the team leaders and alternates first ('train the trainers'). Focus on individuals and individual skills first, then build up to team training. The training should be conducted in logical sequence so that individuals are trained in the relevant skills required before the start of each part of the BC project. Team training may then be undertaken through exercising the plan.

Acquiring or developing training aids

Most BC consultants will readily design and develop courses for their clients, ranging from 20-minute executive briefings through to three-day workshops. They usually also have standard workshops they have developed. Training courses and workshops may be presented as standard in-company courses or tailored to individual organizations' requirements.

Identifying external training opportunities

Many commercial organizations and professional associations provide some relevant training (e.g. DRII, accounting, audit, insurance risk, information security and other institutions). Equally, conferencing companies from time to time provide events that may be of interest and value.

Commercial training companies and BC consultants will be pleased to present in-company briefings and develop in-company BC training programmes.

General awareness

A BC general education and awareness programme could include:

- The BC manager attending key meetings – e.g. project meetings, progress meetings, quality meetings, service management meetings, etc. – to ensure BC considerations are input to the activity or project specification.
- Getting BCM as a standard item on meeting agendas
- General briefings and presentations on BC
- Induction training for new hires
- A BC consultation process involving all departments
- Articles, news and letters in corporate newsletters
- Use of internal web pages, blogs and intranet
- Use of suggestions schemes
- Circulating news items, DVDs, photographs and articles and disaster or incident reports of BC relevance
- Promoting attendance at BC-oriented conferences and exhibitions
- Organizing visits to the recovery site(s)
- Conducting tests and exercises, with observers.

A search within each organization will reveal operational incidents, failures of service level achievement, quality defects, help desk issues, product defects and other problems which have been – or which could have become – disasters. Awareness may be raised by referencing such incidents to make the point.

An enthusiastic business continuity manager will also find his or her way into all relevant meetings – meetings concerning quality, new projects, etc. – to raise the profile of business continuity and to ensure that it is considered at an early stage as part of the specification for new products or projects.

Sources of information to circulate include television and radio stations and their websites; newspaper and journals and their websites; international, national, federal, state, local and professional crisis, continuity and disaster organizations' publications and websites; insurance, fire and other publications and websites; BC service vendors and other sources at Appendix 4. A 'Google' naming your industry and 'disaster' will yield a mass of useful information.

Publication of the results (always positive!) of BCP audits, reviews and tests will also raise awareness.

Every contact with those you wish to influence is a chance to raise BC awareness. Throughout the whole BC project there will be interviews, meetings and correspondence: take every opportunity to promote the principles and benefits of BCM. In the words of the salesmen: 'Never miss a selling opportunity!' Use the business impact analysis to demonstrate the real cost of disaster, remembering to include the lifetime value of customers. Seek help from internal audit and finance – when you have a case they can support.

Getting buy-in needs persuasion, enthusiasm, logic and emotion. It starts from the board. The message has to be broadcast that protecting the business is everybody's responsibility and is part of each line manager's job.

Senior management is often reluctant to invest time and money in business recovery. However, they are more likely to accept an argument based on the need for 'prudent management' than to the threats of catastrophic natural or manmade disasters that are unlikely to materialize. Waving a stick may work – but enduring commitment is more readily built up by patient persuasion – leading, not driving, management to your side. Use the BC organization structure and benefits discussed and the techniques of business impact analysis to bring powerful business arguments to support the need for BC management.

Brainstorming what the organization would do in a disaster may help to illustrate the need for planning. Try using fire drills and emergency response drills, providing workshops and seminars, and discussing the personal impact of disasters on employees and their families. Protection of the family can be a powerful motivator. Emphasize the people side of disaster and of disaster recovery at least as much as the technical. And above all, be enthusiastic – it is hard even for a cynic to withstand enthusiasm.

Awareness through maintenance, review, audit and testing

Maintenance, plan review or audit and testing all present opportunities to raise awareness of BCM. Try to ensure responsibility for BCP maintenance is pushed down to the lowest BC team level and get people actively involved in it. Testing is also possibly the most effective way of training BC team members, so take every opportunity to get as many people to participate in the tests suggested in Chapter 22 – including deputies and alternates.

Summary

Aim to:

- Raise awareness and commitment from influencers of the BC project
- Train individuals who will have a BC role
- Identify BC team leaders and team members, together with their alternates
- Conduct skills gap analysis
- Identify suitable internal and external training opportunities
- Develop the training methodology
- Acquire or develop training aids
- Identify external training courses and conferences
- Identify vehicles for corporate awareness – reference the business impact analysis, use websites, DVDs, press cuttings, and the sources at Appendix 4 and treat existing meetings as vehicles to promote BCM.

BC plan testing

22 Tim Armit – UK

Tim is Principal of Clifton Risk Management, UK.

Introduction

One of the oldest axioms within the field of disaster recovery or business continuity planning is that a plan that is not tested or maintained is of little value, or in some cases worse than no plan at all. The objective of this chapter is to introduce a variety of methods of testing and maintaining your plans, procedures and strategies.

As many organizations have matured in the field of business continuity planning a new concept arose, that of business continuity management. Business continuity is no longer a project but an integral feature of 'business as usual' across the organization, as such it ceases to be planning and becomes management. Maintaining and testing plans is unique within business continuity as all organizations, be they large, small or multinational in whatever sector – finance, utilities, manufacturing, retail or any other – can adopt a similar approach.

As a part of the business continuity plan development project there is a continual need to prove plans and strategies by testing. Tests will be executed for a variety of technologies and for business areas involved in the planning process to date. The aim will be to raise awareness and give the organization confidence that the approach and strategies adopted could be used in the event of a genuine incident. As planning advances and includes a wider spectrum of business areas and supporting technology, the required tests become more complex and need more detailed planning. To ensure that all parties are aware of tests and appreciate the importance of other ongoing business and technology projects a test schedule needs to be prepared. This chapter will help to identify which areas require testing and what form these tests should take.

Maintaining plans inevitably falls behind established schedules as business units view it as an overhead that is rarely of the highest priority. However, plans must

The Definitive Handbook of Business Continuity Management, Second Edition.
Edited by Andrew Hiles FBCI. © 2007 John Wiley & Sons Ltd.

be maintained to hold credibility and to encourage ownership across the organization. Methods of maintaining plans will be discussed later, especially focusing on how testing improves plans and helps to keep them current. Testing will ensure that projects, change management and operational enhancements address business continuity management as part of their ongoing working method. To assist in this, tests for each year must reflect changes in operation and improvements in recovery planning. The tests selected for each year should build on the organization's past experience and introduce new technological solutions or new business functions to the testing process.

Testing can be used for many reasons and this chapter aims to explain a few of these including:

- Training personnel in the use of BC plans
- Gaining buy-in across business areas
- Proving completed plans and strategies
- Proving the adequacy, completeness and accuracy of the current recovery plans
- Component testing of technical elements
- Improving technical or business recovery procedures
- Ensuring that plans incorporate all aspects of the business
- Ensuring that the plans reflect current business priorities
- Building interdepartmental teamwork and relationships
- Working through realistic scenarios – 'role playing'.

Overview

There is no limit to the imagination of the business continuity manager when it comes to testing. As a simple rule, if it has not been tested it does not work. There are few that would argue about the importance of testing and yet so few organizations test regularly, thoroughly or realistically enough. There are many reasons (or excuses) for this but they will not be discussed in this review. At a basic level the following list covers some tests every company should be running annually:

- Scenario tests and walkthroughs
- Components tests
- Business areas tests
- ICT tests
- Cascade tests
- Media testing
- Invocation testing
- Full ICT recovery testing

- Full business continuity testing
- Board level testing.

In 2005 the most thorough analysis of business continuity in place was undertaken in the UK[1] and two key findings came from this:

- Testing was being undertaken with a silo mentality.
- A form of designer disaster was being assumed in the testing.

The silo testing demonstrates how few companies involve their working environment in testing. If you are in a multi-tenanted building or are not sole tenants of your building how can you have a physical disaster that does not impact the others? You cannot. As such your strategies must merge with theirs, and so must your tests. What about suppliers, key infrastructure providers, the emergency services, local authorities and utilities? If you don't know what their plans are how will yours work? How can you test in isolation without these support areas? The future must be multiple-company and support area tests. Integrated large-scale testing will introduce reality. Some business sectors are now running large-scale exercises but for a single sector only – how can there be a single sector disaster? These are a good basic level start but need to become more realistic and all encompassing.

The designer disaster showed how many companies' scenarios ensure only they are impacted, all staff are not shocked or upset by the events, the weather is fine, all information is presented in a timely manner and is accurate. This is quite fanciful and delivers a false level of confidence to all involved. Realism must be brought to bear to challenge plans and strategies.

In addition to this, recent reviews have found two other major weaknesses in companies' tests:

- In many areas testing is undertaken in such a contrived, preplanned, rehearsed manner, especially ICT recovery testing, that it has little value at all in assuring management strategies will work.
- Testing rarely, if ever, looks at the future business after initial recovery. Can you run the end of day processing? Can you bring positions up to work tomorrow? How will you operate in the next week in a reduced manner? What will the company look like in two weeks' time? In most cases these questions have not been addressed and thus are not tested, once again leading to a false level of confidence for management. Longer, more realistic tests must be introduced to ensure companies are protected.

---

[1] UK tripartite (Bank of England, FSA and HM Treasury) benchmarking of the financial sector's recovery and resilience capability.

Testing

Before continuity plans can be signed off as operational, an understanding of their use and value has to be proven. This can only be achieved through structured testing. A business impact analysis will identify critical processes, and the current plans will, in the major part, reflect these. However, over time organizational reviews will be undertaken and current plans are likely to become out of date. To ensure that solutions are implemented across all business areas it is necessary to implement a series of tests as the first step in enhancing the continuity plans.

Overview of the testing process

The testing process should be defined so that all parties involved understand the methodology. Certain organizations have introduced a form of test contract to enable the business and IT areas to define their own test objectives, scope and approach. An example of this is provided later. This means that when a test is being planned all those involved will know what to expect and what is expected of them. The following items are a suggested process for planning a test. These are not all encompassing but present an overview of a successful operational approach:

- The scope of the test is agreed and all parties to be involved are informed.
- The objectives of the test are agreed and published.
- A change management request is raised to book time and personnel.
- Contracts are raised with external suppliers for any support or equipment that is required.
- Agreements are gained from any impacted bodies (internal or external) such as public bodies (e.g. town councils), utilities or regulatory bodies.
- Briefings of all personnel are held on a number of occasions. These briefings are held with individual recovery teams and with the entire test team. The objective of these is to ensure that all aspects of the test are covered and that all potential risks and failures are identified. They also help the teams to build up their task lists for the tests and to document what they will actually be doing. The combined briefings ensure that all parties understand how they will relate to each other and identify any dependencies between teams. The briefings are key in building the team for the test.
- Independent observers are selected to be present at the test and to log events above and beyond the logs kept by each team. These may come from internal audit or an external organization.
- Preparation and support for staff is put in place such as catering, accommodation and transport.

- Business areas are briefed about the test and the potential impact on those not involved.
- A memo is drafted and distributed informing all areas of the test.
- The test is executed to a strict project plan with a clear cut-off time to ensure operations are available post-test.
- A post-test review meeting is held to discuss what took place.
- A test report is written collating all team's logs and any key findings and observations.
- Plans are amended and strategies altered to reflect findings.

The template in Figure 22.1 is an example of the internal testing contract described above. It is to be completed by the business area proposing to test its business continuity planning status. Each area containing a note in italics is to be replaced by relevant text.

Title: Replace this line with the title of the proposed test				
Objectives				
People	*IT*	*Vital Records*	*Facilities*	*Dependencies*
Enter the objectives for the test. You are not limited to two: this is displayed for demonstration purposes only. Tick the boxes above which will be proven. 1 2				
Exclusions				
Enter specific processes or areas of technology being excluded from the test.				
Method				
Enter the method the test will take.				
Justification				
Enter an explanation as to why this is the best approach to the test and how this will achieve the objectives set. Also explain any exclusions and justify why they have been omitted.				
Requirements				
Enter the requirements for the test at an initial high level. This list should include any dependencies on IT, facilities or other business areas. It should relate to the method selected and outline what specific requirements are needed to execute the test.				
Sign-off				
Business	IT	Facilities	Management	
Signed off by the business that the test will satisfy their objectives.	*Signed off by IT that the test is feasible and support will be made available.*	*Signed off by facilities that support will be made available.*	*Signed off by management that the test is sufficient to meet periodic testing requirements.*	

Figure 22.1—Testing template

Planning your test

So when should plans be tested? In almost all instances organizations will follow a structured approach to continuity planning and having completed a lengthy project will then attempt to prove the deliverables through testing. This is the standard practice and works excellently, if somewhat time consuming, expensive and old fashioned; however, certain organizations take an alternative approach. Historically plans were initially developed from within the information technology departments and later rolled out into the business areas. This has often led to reluctance within the business areas to becoming involved or to owning the responsibility for determining strategies. A successful approach to helping the business understand their exposures and responsibilities is to test them before they have been through the structured methodology. This immediately shows the business managers how bad their situation really is and quickly focuses them on their need to plan in detail. This is an unusual approach but is mentioned since it was successfully used in, among others, a multinational investment bank to encourage the trading floors to take ownership.

There is always a drive towards large-scale multi-platform, multi-user tests but in most cases this is inappropriate in the early stages of the planning cycle. In fact best practice has shown that to improve plans and work towards successful testing a three-year cycle should be adopted. Tests in the early years are probably mis-named and can lead to trepidation, the word test conjures up exams and success or failure criteria, and this is not the aim. A better name may be a training exercise or workshop. The aims in the first two years of the programme are to prove the procedures and plans and train those involved in their roles and responsibilities. To assist in this, exercises should build up in a structured manner. It may be a cliché, but don't run before you can walk.

Stage One – Plan audit

The first test to be considered should be to carry out an audit. While it could be argued that an audit is not a test, any process that challenges what is in place and demands proof is testing the credibility of the plans. This approach will ensure that a structured methodology to business continuity has been adopted within plans. The audit should cover the following areas:

- A review of the business continuity management process, including an assessment of the following:
    - The scope of the plans. This will reveal areas of the business or technology not included in the plans, which could lead to services and functions not being recovered.

- Whether an appropriate level of business impact analysis has been carried out. This is to prove the reasoning behind the strategies selected and to understand if the plans will mitigate the impacts discovered.
- Whether an appropriate level of risk analysis has been carried out. This determines if risk reduction measures have been implemented and potential risks identified and agreed.
- Whether the recovery strategy has been clearly defined. If the strategy has not been clearly defined and agreed, the planning will not reflect the actions to be carried out.

- A document review, including an assessment of whether:

  - The document is logically sequenced. Plans should be simple to follow and navigate, continual references to other chapters or moving from page to page will cause confusion and lead to errors.
  - Document version control has been applied. Change management of plans and the ability to easily correlate many plans through version control is essential to ensure all parties are working from the same copy.
  - The document is sufficiently comprehensive and complete
  - The document is accurate

- A review of the plan implementation, including an assessment of whether:

  - The recovery strategies have been successfully implemented
  - Management involved in the recovery understand and are familiar with their roles and responsibilities
  - Tests have been undertaken
  - There is an ongoing plan maintenance and change management strategy.

Stage Two – Walkthroughs

An integral part of any planning process is to provide an understanding of the plan and its strategies to all key management. A walkthrough of the plan should be undertaken and measured against an agreed scenario. The walkthrough will bring together all key management for a tabletop exercise using the plan as a baseline to measure events against.

The walkthrough will identify whether:

- All managers with roles in the plan understand what is expected of them
- Board level management understand their roles and responsibilities within the plan
- The disparate business and support areas have equal expectations
- The assumptions made within the plan are accurate
- The plan flows logically to meet the recovery requirements.

The walkthrough is a highly visible exercise across all of the business. This will provide a tremendous opportunity to emphasize the importance of planning and ensure 'buy-in' from management, and should be used as such. On completion of the walkthrough, any findings should be presented in a report and plans should be amended.

It should always be emphasized that any testing, including the walkthrough type, is not aimed at testing individuals. The main objective of this test is to prove the value and completeness of plans and to validate that the correct infrastructure is in place to facilitate those plans, while improving and completing plans and educating the users. Future tests can be created to put individuals under examination.

Example one: Walkthrough

To ensure walkthroughs are successful, management must be able to commit their uninterrupted time to them. As such running them out of working hours, in the evenings or at weekends is sometimes the best approach. As an example a walkthrough that requires seven hours and involves over 20 managers immediately demonstrates that the organization takes business continuity management seriously. Walkthroughs allow scenarios to be introduced and discussed which allows plans to be tried and proven in alternate ways.

One particular walkthrough dealt with a slowly creeping incident that took hours to manifest but resulted in all systems down for three days. As no immediate crisis occurred and no major event happened the organization's plans did not initially cope with the problem. Most plans are based upon incident, crisis, impact, containment and recovery. Where an alternate scenario was presented, it led to confusion and disagreement. Walkthroughs allow this approach to be used and allow the coordinator to have a variety of scenarios into which they can move as the day progresses. In this instance, no information was given out beforehand and only regular update briefings were passed out, this simulated the confusion and lack of information, which could be expected.

The walkthroughs also brought many disparate parties to the table and in many cases opinions and assumptions held by ICT, facilities and the business areas were very contradictory. These issues were resolved at the tabletop before any physical testing was carried out. The walkthrough completed led to plans being updated to reflect the findings. This was a very 'simple to organize', cost-effective way to raise awareness and involve management from all areas in a planning exercise.

Stage Three – Component testing

The most effective means of identifying that the plans are complete is through a full test. However, this costs time and money that could be wasted if components of the plan fail. Experience shows that there are significant benefits in carrying out tests on individual key components of the plan to avoid this. A series of tests should be identified to assess the effectiveness of the various components of the plan. Once completed, amendments can be made to the plans and a complete plan test can be aimed for with confidence. Examples of component tests are:

- An out-of-hours telephone test to prove the capability of the cascades in place and ensure all key team members can be contacted in a timely manner
- An audit of off-site data with random testing to prove the currency and validity of the data to the business
- Recovery of individual specific technologies to prove in isolation that technological procedures are accurate
- Execution of identified business 'workarounds' to prove the business can operate without technology or in a reduced capacity
- An invocation of recovery contracts to ensure the contracts in place are adequate to requirements.

On completion of each test a report should be produced in an audit format to highlight all findings. This will be used to ensure plans are updated and complete.

It is recommended that each of the stages is exercised to ensure that a gradual build-up to a future complete test is undertaken. By following this approach organizations will be assured that all personnel and subcomponent areas are aware of their roles and responsibilities before a full test is undertaken.

Example two: Call-out communication test

Recently in two organizations exercising has started with proving the callout communication cascades. These are simple tests to organize, very cost effective and are the perfect vehicle for raising awareness of business continuity and how it affects individuals. A key part of any plan is communication. This can be the initial callout or the ongoing liaison with staff. To ensure this can be done effectively, callout cascades are a key feature of all plans and generally look as shown in Figure 22.2.

This test aimed to prove that within three hours of an incident being identified out of hours, key messages could be passed to every member of staff. The primary organization used in this example employed 1500 staff within the scope of the test.

The test specified that every member of staff contacted would complete a log, pass on and record a specific message and answer four questions. The log keeping is essential in any incident for many reasons and encouraging staff to maintain logs in simple exercises ensures that more complex, stressful events will be logged adequately. The message passing was considered important to help to ensure that

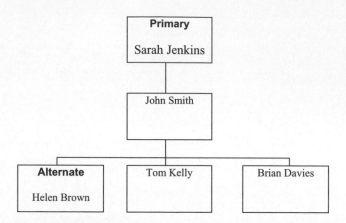

Figure 22.2—Example callout cascade

staff logged key events accurately and could transmit this information to others. The questions were:

- Do you have your plan at home?
- What version is it?
- Do you have a company laptop?
- If yes, is the laptop at home?

The first two are standard questions that allow the control team to understand how effective their distribution of plans has been and to identify if staff have them to hand. The last two questions were specific to this organization. Many business areas had insisted that they had company laptops and as such planning was not essential as they would have the information on their laptop and would not be impacted.

A single call was made to the initial 'out-of-hours' contact. He was then responsible for contacting the initial crisis management team and subsequently triggering cascades across the organization. Each member of staff contacted was instructed to call into a central area to allow the flow of the test to be monitored by the BCP management team. This element had been introduced after an earlier exercise which, having been left to run alone, had missed out significant large areas of the business. As at this stage we are still trying to educate not test, there was more value to the organization to trigger these areas independently and log the event than there was in leaving them to fail. After three hours the exercise finished.

The results showed 672 people, or 45% of the workforce, were contacted directly within three hours, and that over 90% of staff who had company laptops had left them at work. While the contact figure does not look significantly high no single area of the business had not been contacted and for a first event this was deemed a success. When retested 12 months later over 1000 people were contacted.

The benefits from this exercise were many. As people across the business were contacted in their homes this brought business continuity out of the project phase and into their lives. The next day at work had over 45% of employees talking about business continuity and challenging their management as to what it all meant, there could be no quicker or more efficient way to raise the awareness of business continuity other than a real incident. Business managers now took a real interest in their cascades and ensured that everyone was included. Cascades were revised as people recognized that making over five calls was impractical. Ownership for maintenance was accepted and taken away from the central area into the units affected and plans were amended to show that reliance upon laptops was fatally flawed. The exercise also showed that, while key management had been issued with pagers, many did not know how to use them properly – which led to another minor exercise.

Example three: Pager exercise for the crisis management team

As mentioned earlier about 'not running before walking' the callout exercise had proved that we should not make assumptions. This exercise was required to prove that all holders of pagers within the critical crisis management team understood how to operate them and how to respond to them.

Both of these tests are incredibly simple, very inexpensive to run and are very high profile. They can be run on a number of occasions per year with no impact on operations. They prove the most important part of planning, that of communication, and quickly give senior management a level of comfort in the business continuity programme.

Example four: Specific technology tests

An organization had changed its baseline desktop services infrastructure and in upgrading machines had also changed it primary choice of operating system. Plans had been written and proven on a number of occasions for the previous technology. A large-scale test was planned but, before this, an exercise was run to demonstrate that the procedures and understanding were in place to rebuild the new machines. This very small test impacted nobody in the business as it was run offline but did demonstrate a need to alter recovery timescales: while the improved technology simplified the recovery it did take longer. IT had instigated the change in technology and change management had not addressed the impact to the business. A certain level of explanation and rethinking therefore had to be undertaken following the tests.

Example five: Telephony recovery

Voice recovery is essential to any planning and the rebuilding of a telephone exchange in the shortest possible time will allow for the minimum interruption to operations. Many organizations implement commercial contracts to recover these services but rarely test them, and tests that are conducted often do not test to an appropriate scale. For example, if a telephone exchange handles 20 000 calls a day, one should question the value of recovering the system and proving that it can receive a single call. A test was undertaken to prove that a mobile telephone exchange could be delivered to the recovery site, installed and handle all incoming and outgoing services. Included within this were voice, fax, modems for remote access, Internet services and automatic call distribution. Given the number of exchanges available in the market very few service providers will guarantee to match like for like. This in itself caused the first issue: if a different machine was delivered would the installed software work? The answer was no. With the exchange delivered, the problem of how to run services out to extensions arose. Frames running internal services can hold thousands of pairs of wires and can be extremely complicated and time consuming to rebuild. In fact we learnt that while the system could be rebuilt in six hours it was estimated that to reconnect all 800 extensions could take up to a week. A test like this to prove the assumptions meant that once again scale of recovery and timescales had to be revisited.

Example six: New technologies

As organizations modernize their technologies, very often this can improve normal operational services to the business; however, it does not always simplify the recovery process. The example of the change in desktop technologies was mentioned before. In this case, an organization was moving forward its mainframe-based services towards 'state of the art' disk farm technology. The organization had previously relied upon recovery services delivered to its alternative site on the back of lorries. This had meant, with a 24-hour invocation period, that the recovery time for the mainframes was up to 52 hours. The new disk farm technology would bring this down to less than 10 hours. Initially this looked ideal and the business areas were obviously relieved. However, the new technology implemented in one area (the mainframes) was not being matched in others, in particular the local area network (LAN) servers. During a test to prove the ability to recover the new systems and understand timescales it was observed that the LAN servers and desktop were already in place. As they were beyond the remit of the mainframe team they had not been recovered. However, the recovery of the servers, including invocation, needed 32 hours which meant that delivery of mainframe services were not available until 22 hours after the services themselves were restored. As such, any points of consistency of recovered data were also impacted. Initially this may look like an obvious flaw, but, as business continuity is not considered in change management or project planning in many organizations, this is a common finding.

Stage Four – Large-scale testing

As confidence in the business continuity management process grows and as the strategic infrastructure is proven and known to be in place the ability to run larger-scale tests improves. Tests of both technical support and business areas will prove that plans and strategies in place are accurate, maintained and can operate across the business. This scale of test moves from the rehearsal, practice-type exercise to an actual test of assets in place.

The test itself must be planned in detail, it will be expensive to undertake, bring its own risk to the business and draw on a great deal of operational time and effort. Management must clearly understand why the test is being undertaken and the scope and objectives should be clearly defined. It is important that business areas own these tests and look to IT and facilities as service providers.

The checklist detailed earlier in this chapter is ideal for the large-scale test. The following example will assist in explaining the set-up and execution of such a test.

Example seven: Business recovery test

An organization had plans in place for over 40 business functions and the 12 components of the IT department. The organization was divided equally into two buildings and its strategy was for mutual support between the two sites. The test was to prove the ability to recover eight diverse business functions with associated technology services into the alternative site. To do this, six mainframe computers, eight LAN servers and 40 PCs would have to be recovered, in addition to telephony services and an appropriate business environment. In total over 80 personnel from 24 different areas within the business were involved in the test. To bring this number of people together into a test team and to ensure that the dependencies and requirements of all were understood and taken on board by the team involved detailed project planning.

The test itself started at 19.00 hours on a Friday night and had to finish by 13.00 hours on the Sunday to leave enough time to return the environment to normal operations for the Monday. A note here, be careful when picking the date, in recent time tests have run on Valentine's Day, Mother's Day and the day of the changeover between British Summer Time and Greenwich Mean Time, all of which caused problems! The test discovered many issues that had not been considered. For example, PCs are delivered in three boxes, as such 40 PCs means 120 boxes. Simply storing and handling this number must be planned for, as they have to be repacked and returned at the end of the test.

Many organizations note that they cannot re-create the stress and anxiety of a real event, which is generally true. This can be an issue when testing on commercial sites, many of which will not allow 24-hour operations for testing – this is unacceptable. In a real event, to ensure the quickest level of recovery, personnel will work around the clock; in this particular test some key personnel worked for up to 38 hours, at which stage they were making mistakes and showing signs of tiredness. However, this is what would happen in reality and as such must be addressed through testing.

The business areas were closely involved at all stages and this led to a much closer relationship with IT and a much clearer understanding of how services were delivered to them. It also helped them to realize why it took so many hours to restore information and the need for business workarounds for periods without them. These workarounds subsequently were implemented and included procedures for manual operations and agreement with counterparties for alternative methods of work.

In most organizations no matter how often it is explained, business managers rarely understand the issues of lost data and how you rebuild it. A test of this scale shows the business what they will get and asks them to function with it. In the post-review meetings it was clear the situation had now been taken on board and solutions would be sought. The test was a success in achieving the aims set and many staff are now involved in the BCM process. However, the administration and control of a test of this size should never be underestimated.

Maintenance

Plans and strategies, once implemented, reflect the requirements of the business at that time. These requirements and recovery timescales are not constant and as such both components must be maintained. A business continuity change management process covering maintenance and review changes is required. Maintenance changes keep plans up to date but do not change the underlying objectives or strategies and can include staff changes, contact detail changes or the correction of errors. Review changes may affect the strategies in place or may alter the plan's objectives and can include business reorganization or the introduction of new business processes or systems.

Testing is an excellent process to maintain plans, but in itself is not enough. A regular testing schedule will ensure that plans are current, proven and maintained by the people needing to use them. However, in addition to this, maintenance schedules need to be produced but experience has shown that implementing these and policing them is time consuming and rarely successful.

Clear ownership of the change management process is essential to ensure the process is accepted and implemented. The overall strategy, standards and methodologies to be implemented and maintained across an organization should be owned by a central business continuity coordinator. A business continuity management steering group should be established with responsibility for implementing, testing and ensuring that plans are maintained. This group must be empowered to resolve disputes, instruct management of their responsibilities and prioritize projects. The group should meet at least bi-monthly and should be presented with the current status of plans: this will assist in policing plan maintenance.

The ownership of plans must reside with the management teams that require them and they must take responsibility for their maintenance changes. The plan owners will issue new pages to replace those requiring minor changes, at the same time they will inform the central business continuity coordinator to ensure central copies are consistent. To assist in this, basic document rules should be applied. An agreed schedule for reprints should be determined for example, a full reprint will occur annually, updated quarterly with key pages replaced on demand. Each page should be version control numbered and show a date of issue. The version numbers should increment by 0.1 for each update or page replacement and by a full integer (1.0) on each annual republication. This number and the date will ensure that plan holders are operating to the most current issue.

Plan owners must also take responsibility for identifying review changes. These should then be actioned centrally by the business continuity coordinator in conjunction with the affected plan owners. These parties should assess any changes required in the recovery strategies and timescales, plans and business impacts and ensure, if necessary, relevant changes are implemented. These types of changes can negate the entire planning capability and as such may need to be acted on either during the development cycle of the change or very soon after its implementation.

It is always difficult to maintain plans and it is unrealistic to expect a plan owner to give business continuity a continually high priority. As such a proactive approach will often achieve better results and will gain support from the business and IT management involved. This can involve regular questionnaires distributed by the central business continuity coordinator or a proven method to ensure continual ownership and sign-off, and this can be achieved by distributing a monthly memo to all plan owners requesting sign-off that plans are current and accurate. As many organizations use electronic mail this can be set up as an automatic distribution list and thus reduce the effort required. While this does not guarantee plans are maintained it does put responsibility on the plan owners and the sign-off gives a level of confidence.

Testing itself will lead to plans being maintained as the observers will make amendments and the plan holders will see improvements and changes that are required.

Links should be established with personnel systems to ensure that leavers and joiners to an organization are recognized and that these are reflected in plans. If a specialist software tool has been selected then this can, in some instances, assist in the maintenance process; conversely it can lead to information being stored and maintained in two places. Some software tools show dates and audit trails against the last time areas were maintained; this can help in policing plans and allowing the central controller to pursue plan owners not updating plans. The tools can also assist in identifying links across plans and thus simplify identifying areas requiring updates following a change. Consideration should be given to the method and cost of maintaining plans while in the initial planning stage.

Many organizations have established mature change management systems that allow for flags to be incorporated to prompt specific questions. Ideally, a flag should be placed on the system asking the change raiser to state 'yes' or 'no' if the change affects business continuity plans or strategies. This will then ensure that any technical or production alterations consider the impacts on plans and are amended if necessary before changes are signed off. This can be taken a step further so that project plans and methodologies recognize business continuity requirements during the development and initiation phase, thus allowing strategies to be developed and tested as an integral part of the project.

Conclusion

This chapter has outlined an approach to testing which is supported by many examples used in successful implementation of business continuity management programmes. The chapter also outlined an approach to maintaining plans, which although notoriously difficult, is essential if plans are to retain credibility and support. Until all aspects of plans are realistically tested they cannot be said to work. In many cases business continuity strategies and managers are presenting false levels of confidence to their senior managers, as tests have not been run. Testing is the most interesting, realistic and fun part of business continuity and the future will see larger, more holistic, more realistic tests, which will bring business continuity to life.

BC audit

23 Rolf von Rössing FBCI – Germany

Rolf is a partner, advisory, in KPMG Deutsche Treuhand-Gesellschaft AG.

Introduction

BCM is a complex field. It covers business issues and technology with a perspective on the entire enterprise. The business continuity manager and the auditor require a diversified set of skills and extensive knowledge to assess business continuity as a question of business survival. There has been a lot of confusion about the terms 'business continuity', 'disaster recovery', 'IT security' and many other words attempting to describe the continuation of critical business processes under adverse circumstances. However, for the auditor these terms refer to one and the same notion: businesses should take adequate precautions to ensure that no going concern issues arise from crises or disasters.

Auditing and assessing a business continuity management process includes all phases of the life cycle, from the underlying business assumptions to testing and exercising. Throughout the 1990s, many auditors restricted their activities to simply asking for the existence of 'a business continuity plan' or a 'disaster recovery plan', without performing any further tests or audit procedures. It was no surprise that organizations being reviewed provided exactly what they were being asked for: written plans with or without any reference to reality. In many cases, this fundamental misunderstanding persists until today, for instance where IT disaster recovery plans are taken to be the BCM concept of an organization, or where BC exercises are restricted to reading through the plans once a year without changing them. It is obvious that a diligent auditor would like to do more, while an equally diligent auditee organization would like to be compliant with any BCM regulations that are known and recognized. It is still quite difficult to document what it is that a BCM auditor should know, and what a full-scale BCM audit should encompass. Defining the basics may be straightforward, but as the world changes, so does the specific audit programme to be developed for an organization. Older audit methodologies[1] may be applicable in principle, but there is certainly room for improvement.

Audit as a function applied to BCM is therefore still very much about removing some of the uncertainty around the subject. What are the applicable standards or regulations? How is full compliance recognized? What needs to be done first to achieve compliance? What does acceptable risk mean? These and many more issues must be addressed even before actual audit planning can commence. For both sides, it is important to discuss a set of simple questions that will set the scene for all subsequent activities:

- What is the overall objective of the audit – compliance, due diligence, forensic, other?
- What is the maturity level of the auditee organization – novice, intermediate, advanced?
- What is the strategic approach taken by the auditee organization – standards based, individual, IT based, other?

The answers will determine the framework of the overall audit, including time and budget.

Audit objective

From the perspective of the board of directors, or that of the supervisory body tasked with appointing the auditors, there is no immediate need to understand more than the high-level, strategic objectives, and to convey this message to the internal or external auditors. An experienced auditor will use this opportunity to provide a clear and unambiguous audit programme that addresses the need of the auditee organization. The often one-dimensional approach seen in the past – compliance with a given set of standards in the context of year-end financial accounts – is unsuitable for management purposes. Rarely will business continuity become the decisive factor in compliance failures or other risks threatening the accuracy of the financial accounts. In these rare instances, the very existence of the firm will have to be threatened[2] by a lack of business continuity management, or disaster recovery activity (not planning). In reality, the motivators behind a business continuity audit are diverse and very much different from the traditional going concern issues:

---

[1] Rössing, Rolf von, *Auditing Business Continuity – Global Best Practices*. Rothstein Associates, 2002.
[2] Known as 'going concern' issues which denote events, acts or omissions that might put the firm out of business.

- Compliance
- Preparatory/pre-implementation
- Post-implementation
- Due diligence
- Benchmark
- Forensic.

In recent years, the primary focus on compliance with applicable laws and regulations has rapidly expanded to include pre-implementation and post-implementation audits. As organizations commission large BCM projects, the internal audit function or external consultants are utilized to deliver an impartial and independent opinion on the success or failure of the project. In many cases, even the initial project plan and budget are subject to scrutiny by an independent organizational unit. It is indicative of these developments that 'risk assessment', 'risk evaluation' and other audit-related terms are used more frequently than 10 years ago.

The due diligence audit approach recognizes the need for a thorough analysis of technical infrastructure and IT assets prior to committing to a corporate transaction. Continuity of business operations, or the ability to conduct business under adverse circumstances, reflects the growing need for a robust organization. Hence, the due diligence audit of business continuity should not be restricted to information technology, or any other infrastructural element of the business being reviewed. The concept of 'applying due diligence' in preparing a transaction and pricing in any risks that may exist in the target organization is much wider than that of a compliance or project-related audit.

Since business continuity management has been accepted as a managerial discipline, many sectors have established good practices that are measured against known standards and guidelines.[3] However, these standards provide no more than an indication of what constitutes 'good' business continuity management. The specifics of certain sectors of industry, for instance in banking and finance, often require a different approach to analysing the efficiency and effectiveness of the BCM programme. This is where benchmark audits are used as a tool to positioning the BCM programme being reviewed against a broader set of companies or organizations. While some benchmark audit programmes address BCM in an informal manner, others may encompass a large set of detailed audit procedures aligned to multiple standards.

Forensic audits – in contrast to the other types of audit discussed here – address business continuity in a retrospective manner. Once an organization has experienced the impact of a critical or disastrous event, a large number of questions will have to be resolved. These often include an ex post analysis of events, activities and perhaps errors. Liability and responsibility for certain outcomes may have to

---

[3] E.g. *The BCI Good Practice Guidelines* (2005) or BS 25999-1 (2006) as well as several other national standards.

be ascertained, based upon 'what really happened'. In these situations, auditing BCM will be the prerequisite to enabling decisions as well as legal work.

Determining the maturity level of the organization

In a typical organization, BCM forms part of risk management, security or even information technology. The contributing departments and individuals are often organized as project groups, using their skills and experience to initially set up a BC project which subsequently becomes some form of a repeatable exercise. In organizations that have reached a higher maturity level, business continuity is an annual cycle following a lifecycle model. In a more formal definition, BCM as a subset of all corporate processes and controls requires a well-defined set of criteria for measuring success or failure, and for establishing good corporate governance. Standards such as BS 25999 require that a formal audit of BCM includes several components and management subprocesses. In general, the maturity level of an organization in terms of its business continuity capability may be categorized as follows:

- **N/A** – Business continuity has neither been discussed nor addressed in a managerial sense. No documentation exists. Some isolated initiatives for managing specific risks (fire, flooding, etc.) may have been completed following past events or incidents. However, the organization as a whole would not classify these as 'disaster recovery' or 'business continuity'. Typically, the specialist solutions implemented for some specific risks and threats are not coordinated. Management and staff are not aware of the risk management steps taken, and only a few individuals such as facilities managers or IT staff have any knowledge of the 'hidden' precautions taken.
- **Novice** – The entity under review is vaguely aware of business continuity, perhaps indirectly in the sense of IT disaster recovery. No attempts have been made to categorize business processes or extend the paradigm of IT recovery to core business activities. Typically, some middle managers within the organization will have recognized the need for mitigating risks and threats, without calling it 'business continuity'. Some departments may have tried to implement initial steps, but it is not uncommon to find that such initiatives have been discouraged by higher levels of management due to the burden they might place on departmental budgets.
- **Intermediate** – Technical recovery has been initiated and partially implemented. Core business processes are not covered by the methodology applied. Management uneasiness is evident, but no steps have been taken. Organizations at this stage of maturity often display a comprehensive documentation on IT disaster recovery, decentralized backups, contracts for alternative data

centre sites, and elaborate technical protection concepts. Typically, these solutions have been implemented to mitigate 'security' risks. IT recovery, security and other terms are used synonymously with business continuity, but it is often found that these expensive technical precautions are seen as sufficient to protect core business. When the organization is close to reaching the 'advanced' level of maturity, it is likely that there will be quite a few managers acknowledging that more comprehensive plans are needed.

- **Advanced** – Business continuity has been addressed in one or more projects. Some plans exist, and they may be comprehensive. Business continuity, as a notion, is integrated by means of a part-time or full-time position within the organization. This stage is often characterized by a 'top-heavy' BCM process: headquarters and some large subsidiaries may have had a head start, perhaps assisted by local or regional regulations. At HQ, the teams and BC managers are experienced individuals with a clear sense of direction and a willingness to expand BCM to other parts of the corporate network. Other subsidiaries and recently acquired entities are far less developed in their BCM efforts. There may have been cultural, budgetary or other difficulties that have prevented standardization and international rollout. When discussing BCM, the majority of managers and departments will have adopted continuity-based thinking, and the reasons for not having implemented this throughout the organization will be found in other areas such as finance or even language.

- **Mature** – Business continuity management exists as an ongoing process. Plans, concepts and documentation are well developed and up to date. Insular weaknesses in BC may exist. Typically, senior managers have demonstrated their 'buy-in' to BCM by placing responsibility for it with an officer or senior vice president. The dynamic nature of the continuity process within the organization is clearly visible, and frequent testing and maintenance activity can be observed. Another indicator may be the ongoing and active involvement of managers in BCM-related institutions and working groups. Characteristically, a standardized set of documents will exist which is distributed or even published beyond the borders of the organization.

It is obvious that the maturity stage will determine audit scope to a large extent. For instance, a company displaying signs of being 'untouched' need not be audited in detail. The mere statement of non-existence of business continuity will suffice to escalate the matter. Conversely, a company in the 'mature' stage will benefit only if the auditor can provide a meaningful, targeted contribution by identifying insular weaknesses or potential improvements at a detailed level.

Depending on the national and regional situation, maturity and expectations may change considerably. In some countries, business continuity may be a highly regulated professional discipline, whereas in others the situation requires day-to-day survival rather than elaborate planning and continuity management. 'Maturity' is therefore a relative term that cannot be assessed without the cultural and regulatory system of reference. While an auditor may make assumptions with regard to the overall understanding of BCM in any given country, comprehensive background research is needed prior to attributing a maturity level to an organization in its cultural and economic context. Many standards and guidelines implicitly assume a certain set of beliefs and values relating to business continuity. Even in organizations that share this set of overall assumptions, auditing subsidiaries internationally may present challenges and difficulties. The perceived 'maturity' in one place may not match the expectations at corporate headquarters, and subsequent audit reports may be misunderstood.

Individual audit approach

In contrast to traditional (financial) audit, BCM reviews are inevitably based upon a 'what-if' scenario. Rarely will the auditor actually witness a critical event, or the management of a real crisis. At best, there will be an opportunity to be present as an observer when full-scale exercises are being conducted. It is therefore difficult to decide whether the audit opinion is accurate and complete. In financial audit, the retrospective analysis of numbers is comparatively straightforward – in business continuity audit, there is no certainty as to the actual BCM capability of the organization being reviewed. Hence, the overall audit approach should be adapted to the target organization. The auditor should take into account the managerial objectives as well as the overall perception of risk, particularly where the maturity level observed is between 0 and 2. In many cases, experienced auditors will be able to serve as a sounding board for senior management. The strategic view on risk, and any detailed risk management activities in the target organization, is likely to be discussed from a compliance and governance perspective. It is up to the auditor to set the scene for BCM thinking and concepts. Likewise, mature organizations often show a strong culture that has incorporated business continuity as a corporate value. In these cases, audit vocabulary and the overall approach may have to be adjusted to adequately reflect the organization's 'translation' of generic BCM thoughts into the local management structure. In an environment where the term 'disaster recovery' denotes an otherwise mature BCM lifecycle, there is no need to insist upon the broader 'business continuity' unless mandated by law or regulation. As long as the practical level of resilience is high, the audit approach should be individual in the sense of recognizing valid BCM components and strategies.

Auditors should resist the temptation of falling into the compliance trap. As outlined above, the audit objective may be different to start with, and the focus of activities may not be on identifying weaknesses or formal errors. The 'true and fair view' to be delivered by the auditor requires an individual view on the target organization. In many cases, a proactive approach may be more helpful to the auditee organization's management. Senior managers, i.e. the recipients of audit reports, will usually ask three questions that should have been covered by an individual audit approach:

- What's wrong? How bad is it?
- Do I need to do anything at this point, and if yes, what are the exact things I should do?
- How much is this going to cost me, and how do I maximize return on investment?

The answers to these questions – after applying an agreed-upon audit programme – should be concise, easily understood and factually accurate. Formal weaknesses identified during the audit are less important than providing a clear picture of overall risk, dangerous weaknesses and points for immediate action. The auditor is well advised to calibrate the approach towards senior management expectations and even fears. In a corporate governance framework of thinking, experienced managers expect their auditors to deliver meaningful guidance rather than a long list of minor findings.

Practical knowledge and experience in conducting business continuity audits are prerequisites to formulating and presenting the optimum approach for any target organization. It is extremely helpful and reassuring for senior management if an auditor can point to comparable organizations or previous audits, depending on the maturity level and the audit objective agreed beforehand. The planned review should adequately address the need for information (facts about the current BCM capability) as well as the need for improvement (guidance about the future BCM capability). The future state depends on many factors influencing the target organization. Where IT is strong, improvements may include broadening the corporate programme to other business functions. Where risk control and risk assessment are strong, potential improvements may focus on emphasizing the 'hands-on' crisis management throughout the organization. As an analogy, an in-depth and competent diagnosis is as important as the subsequent therapy. Both must be individual and adequate to the patient, in order to avoid costly and painful errors.

Defining the audit programme

Once the audit objective and the maturity level have been clearly defined, the audit programme specifies the global scope and the assumptions for planning, deployment and reporting. It is recommended that the programme be structured according to the BCM lifecycle as shown below. This will enable both the auditor and the organization being reviewed to ensure completeness and adequate level of detail for all aspects of BCM. The lifecycle in this context should be seen as an overall framework reflecting organizational tasks and requirements rather than personal skills and experience.[4] The term 'audit programme' may span multiple parts of the organization, and more than one year. As a result, more comprehensive programmes should take into account the transition from one maturity level to the next, particularly where the organization has implemented audit recommendations relating to business continuity.

Some areas within the lifecycle (more fully described in Chapters 8 and 16), specifically 'Understanding the organization' and 'Determining BCM options' usually require a wider view on business processes and financials. The central function of BCM programme management is a convenient starting point for the auditor in terms of identifying timelines, budgets and milestones as identified by the auditee organization. It is likely that at least part of the audit programme will follow the internal programme management cycle, for instance where larger components of a full BCM have been completed.

While other standards and regulations may influence the scoping and definition of the audit programme, these will normally address specific aspects, such as information security[5] or financial audit risk.[6] The decision not to review the full BCM, and to restrict audit activity to a subset of items, is equivalent to a different audit objective. Such restricted audits may still be termed 'business continuity audit' in some cases, although they address different objectives such as information security or internal controls over financial reporting.

Audit planning

Business continuity planning and management incorporates elements from multiple disciplines and the corresponding skill sets required to perform an assessment. Rarely will the auditor be able to personally evaluate all areas of a complex corporate environment. Even when relying on accepted standards, 'connecting the dots' may be very difficult indeed at an in-depth level. Consider, for instance, the specific knowledge needed to review either the acceptability of escape and evacuation routes from a building, or the adequacy of post-trauma counselling arrangements made by the HR department. It is therefore recommended that the audit be subdivided in a modular fashion. One or more of the modules may have to be covered at a certain level of granularity, allowing the definition of a simple matrix (see Table 23.1).

---

[4] These are defined in the 10 certification standards published by the BCI – see Appendix 3.
[5] ISO 27001 as a typical framework for information security addresses aspects of business continuity.
[6] The COSO framework, as applied in the context of audits governed by the Sarbanes-Oxley Act 2002 and PCAOB Standard No. 2.

Table 23.1—Audit areas

Audit area/ module	Auditor	Expert assistance/3rd party
Area 1 (Understanding the organization)	Core business analysis, completeness, adherence to standards, framework, stakeholder management, process management . . .	possibly: verify the business structure in overseas subsidiaries possibly: verify the business structure for auditee's business partners
Area 2 (Determining BCM options – risk analysis)	existence, methodologies used, recent documentation, risk quantification, insurance, etc.	possibly: actuarial opinion on insurance policies, external data on risks and events, government or institutional historic data . . .
Area n	. . .	. . .

If the auditor is not an integral part of a very large organization, it is unlikely that the variety of data and external skills required will be readily available. The sample matrix clearly shows how networking and subcontracting considerations ought to precede the actual audit. In the homogeneous environment of financial audit or specialized consultancy, this will rarely be an issue, but it is certainly worth mentioning in a field as complex as business continuity management.

In a practical sense, the usefulness of third parties or external experts is often questioned. There may be budget constraints, or the auditor may perceive an external resource as a competitor. The commercial aspects of audit are certainly worth considering, although the ultimate goal should be to assemble a well-balanced and sufficiently skilled audit team. In some cases, maximizing audit revenue, or instrumentalizing the project to insert relatively unskilled junior audit staff, have been put forward as reasons for not using an appropriate (perhaps expensive) external consultant. While 'training on the job' is an acceptable practice, the distribution of tasks and work packages will show if and to what extent the internal skills of the audit team can satisfy the requirements. Without an adequate and well-rounded set of skills and experience, the auditor may run the risk of having their professionalism questioned by the auditee organization.

Once the overall requirement for expert or third party assistance has been analysed and defined, all areas should be planned in more detail to allow for appropriate initial audit coverage and subsequent procedures. Instead of covering as much of an implausibly broad audit programme as possible in the limited timeframe envisaged, the objective should be to select the right areas for 'drilling down' and producing meaningful results. High priority items may merit closer examination, whereas some areas (as agreed with management) may not require more than a high-level review. The audit itself can now be mapped and qualified in terms of time and cost involved. Table 23.2 illustrates an extended matrix, which may serve as an outline for estimating.

Table 23.2—Extended audit matrix

Area/module	Detailed step	Auditor's effort	3rd party effort	Auditee effort
Understanding the organization	Business process model	2 days	nil	3 days
	Process criticality	5 days	nil	3 days
	History of incidents	4 hours	nil	2 days
	. . .	. . .	. . .	. . .

The detailed matrix for estimating should reflect the issues and questions of the audit programme used. Table 23.2 shows that internal (auditee) effort is not to be neglected. While the auditor may not be limited in spending time and effort on individual steps, the organization being reviewed will often be much more constrained, due to the requirements of day-to-day operations. Actual effort is usually determined by a number of factors, such as previous audit experience on the part of the auditee, maturity level, organizational structure, etc.

Audit deployment

Having planned the overall audit framework, scope and individual modules – perhaps multiplied by a number of audit targets – the execution phase of the BCM audit requires additional planning. In contrast to the initial setting of constraints and logical boundaries, conducting on-site activities is largely based upon previous experience, an individual auditor's perception of the situation encountered, and effort estimates gathered from similar projects. For a less experienced audit team, these considerations may pose unexpected problems. For instance, estimating durations of interviews, administrative overhead or average times allotted to compiling a documentation folder are rarely taken into account when planning for on-site presence. There may be other reasons that lead to a 'compressed' timeframe: overly ambitious project goals set by the auditor to win a competitive bid, increased pressure by the auditee management or audit committee, and even scope creep introduced in the early stages of the audit project. The end result is almost always identical – audit quality is compromised due to unforeseen pressure and the need to meet tough deadlines. This is particularly important when it comes to BCM, which extensively relies upon human interaction rather than the study of documented materials. The validity of representations made by the auditee organization may not be as clear-cut as a set of financial accounts, and the notion of accuracy is replaced with the much wider idea of adequacy.

Fieldwork

As a rule of thumb, the information gathering part of the BCM audit may be sub-divided as follows:

- Interviews and requests for information – 50%
- Filing, perusal – 10%
- Analysis and interpretation of information obtained – 40%.

If the overall audit objective – as stated in the scope document – is to verify compliance with standards or regulations, the analysis phase may take longer, while forensic activities might require an emphasis on obtaining data rather than interpreting the material. The above listing should nevertheless be indicative of the additional effort for administrative and analytical purposes. An additional overhead for administrative purposes should be included as a buffer or safety margin, particularly when conducting international audits. Unexpected delays may occur as a result of numerous factors, irrespective of the budget and timeframe agreed. Practical experience has shown that the organization being reviewed may be under pressure to perform day-to-day tasks, and senior management intervention often serves as a means to reprioritize or delay business continuity activities.

Given the general nature of an audit, interview often creates an atmosphere of investigation, or even interrogation. As issues of business continuity are almost inevitably linked to notions of 'faults', 'failures' or 'disruptions', an adversarial situation easily sets in. Questions highlighting areas where problems or weaknesses exist will often lead to attempts on the part of the organization to disguise or misrepresent the facts. In many countries, expenditures for business continuity management are minimized, and staff responsible may be working under enormous pressure. If such a corporate culture is in evidence, the audit is more than likely to provoke resistance and defensive reactions. Conversely, the auditor may be viewed as an external source of credibility, tempting the interviewee to instrumentalize the – technically inexperienced – auditor as a witness to claim additional funding or project sponsorship. In any event, the auditor should go to extreme lengths to avoid 'taking sides' or even adopting the intra-organizational thinking of 'us and them' that is often found between technical (even BC) and senior managerial circles of the firm.

Depending on the timeframe and budget agreed for the audit, the question of prefabricated questionnaires or individual interviews will often arise. Business continuity management, as a multidisciplinary field, does not often lend itself to the questionnaire approach. While standardization and uniform questions may be desirable in terms of a general comparison between entities and units under review, the multiple aspects of BCM – particularly in technology-biased departments or business functions – are rarely grasped by finite questionnaires which might easily miss the nuances and 'between the lines' statements providing additional value to the auditor. BCM, given its diversity and broad coverage of most business functions, has an even higher potential for errors or misunderstandings. The initial time savings seemingly realized by distributing a standardized questionnaire are inevitably offset by ambiguous or misguided responses that cannot be used for further analysis. Despite these shortcomings, large-scale BCM audits may rule out the face-to-face approach and the individual processing of results. The analytical scope of the audit, as explained below, will often sacrifice information density and precision in favour of standardized patterns applicable to many corporate entities or countries. Hence, the auditor should balance this legitimate concern with the need to obtain information in as detailed a manner as possible. It is advisable to refer to the scope (as discussed above) to determine whether standardized response format or exhaustive information have the highest priority.

When conducting the audit, the challenge of extending the auditor's skills to adequately cover all areas will inevitably arise at some point. Various strategies have been suggested to overcome this latent difficulty:

- Assign corporate personnel to support the audit, including travel to the audit location to support special tasks
- Assign local staff where available to provide specialist expertise
- Assign local third party experts to special tasks.

While these steps usually improve the overall skill set, the reliability and validity of expert judgement and opinions may vary, and the assessment of results thus obtained is a double-edged sword. There may be a trade-off between efficiency of specialist resources and their adherence to the objectives of the audit. The auditor cannot always judge the quality of work provided by specialists (otherwise there would be no need for them in the first place). Corporate personnel specializing in BCM may prove ineffective in remote countries where they have had no experience. Local staff may not have the necessary skills that the auditor requires. Third parties may follow their own agenda rather than pursue the audit objective. There are many caveats that the auditor will have to consider prior to enlisting experts. In the great majority of cases, the seemingly trivial question of language emerges as the single most important criteria for selecting experts.

Table 23.3 shows some typical difficulties encountered when enlisting expert help on an international basis. While the 'recommended solutions' can only be indicative of the choices the auditor may have, they nevertheless point to the fact that a rigid approach towards pushing a uniform agenda may sometimes not be

Table 23.3—Audit challenges

	Recommended solutions
Specialist (external) entertains different ideas on BCM audit	Prior agreement on audit scope and planning, sign-off by external specialist.
Specialist (external) extends involvement to maximize profit	Limit timeframe and budget prior to commencing on-site audit, include limit clauses in service contract. Agree on milestones and deliverables on a pay-per-milestone basis.
Specialist (internal) has difficulty in adjusting to local culture and conditions	Appoint local 'counterpart' and regroup teams where appropriate.
Local staff do not have required skills or experience	Bring in corporate specialist staff as necessary. Support local training and awareness measures.
Specialists (internal or external) have difficulty in adjusting to audit requirements	Provide knowledge transfer on audit, not BCM. Reiterate audit framework and objectives.
Local culture does not support audit (for various reasons)	Shift focus from audit to consulting aspects of the project. Research background and reasons for adversity or lack of support. Readjust audit objectives if mitigating circumstances exist, after consulting with audit sponsor.

enough to accommodate unforeseen circumstances and difficulties. It is suggested that the auditor should remain reasonably flexible in terms of reacting to cultural, political and third party issues. Where in doubt, it may be advisable to discuss the points in question with the audit sponsor, the audit committee or local management, depending on the nature of the problem.

Analysis

Structuring, analysing and interpreting data from a business continuity audit is, arguably, the most challenging phase of the audit. In contrast to other activities, the analytical process directly reflects the auditor's BCM knowledge and requires professional judgement as well as consideration of dependencies. Collectively, the data represents the basis of subsequent reporting, but appropriate analytical methods must be applied to make sense of it all. In comparison with financial audit and the well-established tools for data analysis used in conjunction with its subdisciplines, the BCM framework is somewhat less developed.

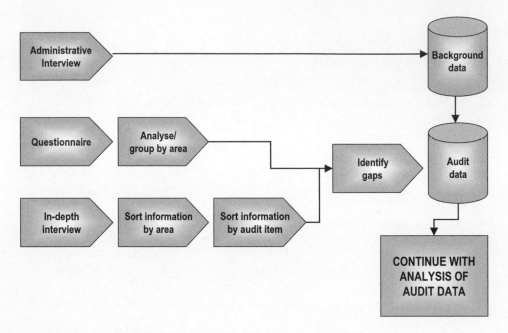

Figure 23. 1—Analytical steps in the BCM audit[7]

After conducting the planned interviews, supported by questionnaires and other data gathering instruments, the information obtained requires sorting, grouping and condensing. Depending on the total size of the audit programme, this process of streamlining data will be more or less formalized. Given a limited audit scope, there is no immediate need for applying a formal process to elicit comparable information from a large number of interview notes. At the other end of the scale, in a multinational audit with several auditors, it is evident that some form of calibration is needed to ensure clear and unbiased interpretation of what data and information the auditee entities have provided.

As a first step, interview results should be visualized in order to gather a detailed understanding of the actual information transmitted. Any undue emphasis or other elements introducing bias should be eliminated at this stage. Initial, 'raw' results are likely to be fairly unstructured, as many interviewees will return to an item of discussion or voice changing opinions and incidental information. The second step in summarizing interview results is to group the interviewee's narrative into the areas of the lifecycle (see below). Any direct statement made by the inter-

[7] Rössing, Rolf von, *Auditing Business Continuity - Global Best Practices*. Rothstein Associates, 2002.

viewee, while perhaps not directly related to what the auditor had in mind, usually fits into one or another area within the BCM lifecycle. The auditor should note how the interviewee arrived at the mental connection between a question and a seemingly unrelated topic, as this may indicate both organizational habit and prevalent thinking within the organization being reviewed.

The next step is to consolidate interview results by area and identify any further interview or clarification requirements. These 'gaps' in information gathered will require additional audit steps. It is suggested that a tabular representation in three successive steps be used to visualize what is to be done next:

- **Step 1** – Draw a matrix of departments against audit areas and indicate which department made any statements in which area(s). Identify 'blanks'. Verify if these blanks are justified, for instance where a department has no apparent link to the audit area concerned. Decide on further interviews or other audit activities for those cells in the matrix that should not be blank.
- **Step 2** – Highlight department/area statements that indicate risks or possible audit findings. Decide on further audit steps or clarification requests for these.
- **Step 3** – Prepare a follow-up matrix that subdivides further action and interviews by department. The result should be a list of planned activities to be presented to the department manager(s) respectively.

Depending upon the scope and magnitude of the audit, the level of documentation on both sides (auditor and auditee) is likely to be extensive. It is recommended that a systematic approach be taken that incorporates the audit areas covered, proper cross-referencing and clear guidelines that define the degree of detail. Storing and classifying a vast amount of documents may prove counterproductive if the scope and detailed plan for the audit have a different objective. Any documents or working papers included should have a direct bearing on the overall question to be answered by the audit. This is specifically important when dealing with an audit environment that is highly technical in nature, for instance information technology or facilities management.

The choice of analytical methods for both interview notes and additional documentation will usually vary in line with the audit plan, the budget and the timeframe for completing the different audit stages. The material collected rarely lends itself to direct quantification. It is therefore recommended to categorize the findings using a predetermined rating. While this will not necessarily provide any information as to the absolute meaning or severity of a finding, it can serve as a ranking for comparative analysis. It is the auditor's choice whether a verbal or numeric scale is used to denote the opinion on each item. However, oversimplification in terms of categories and ratings should be avoided at this stage – results may be simplified later in the course of reporting.

Reporting

An essential component of any BCM audit is the way in which results are communicated to the organization under review or other interested parties. The design and contents of reports should represent a coherent framework within which the auditor may express their opinions and place the necessary emphasis upon certain findings or circumstances. The decisive factor in determining the success or failure of a reporting system is the degree of detail provided to the individual, the business process owner, and the audited entity as a whole. By definition, the reports distributed as a result of prior audit activities are the only means of conveying the auditor's opinion. The amount of knowledge that the auditor will inevitably have accumulated over a period of days, weeks or even months may cause difficulties in reporting, quite simply because the wealth of data appears overwhelmingly comprehensive, and condensing the facts into adequate reports for different management levels is a seemingly hopeless task. Within the constraints of deadlines, budgets and limited resources, the auditor is nevertheless expected to submit a complete set of reports, outlining both factual findings and an answer to the overall issue addressed by the audit. The difficulties increase with the amount of data to be categorized, documented and properly cross-referenced.

Report structure

It is recommended that a formal structure be defined for different types of reports and other working papers. The auditor should adopt a 'top-down' approach where possible, allowing targeted reporting towards different audiences, and standardization of report contents in more complex audit assignments. Conversely, writing the report papers is sometimes easier using the reverse 'bottom-up' direction, as this allows compiling single findings and analytical results into clusters which are easier to summarize at the more strategic reporting levels.

Contents broadly fit into one of three categories: descriptive, analytical or normative. The descriptive part of a report simply states facts and figures as determined by the preceding audit steps. While this may be stating the obvious, it should be noted that not all auditee personnel may be as familiar with the facts as the auditor, and due to the many areas of work covered, the compilation of an overview of factual statements is often the first step to ensure that all parties involved can find a common basis for discussion. The report should clearly indicate how facts and findings relate to predetermined benchmarks or to an 'ideal world' which is usually difficult to achieve but nevertheless demanded by standards and regulations. For the organization being reviewed, it is more important to know about audit findings and the overall audit opinion on their significance than to study lengthy analytical treatments of questionnaires. The normative part

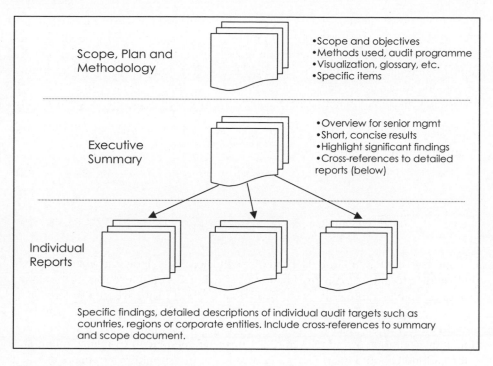

Figure 23.2—Report structure

of a report, based upon both the facts and their validation, should indicate clear recommendations and practical steps to be taken within the auditee organization. Recommendations are often translated into projects at the organizational level, and it is not uncommon for organizations to initiate major changes following audit findings.

In order to adequately address the needs of the auditee organization structure, the audit findings and recommendations should be both general and specific, to distinguish between different areas of work, different business units, and findings relating to parts of the auditee entity or entities. The framework for these categories of findings is set by the audit plan, suggesting a simple system of visualization. This 'matrix' approach ensures transparency and reiterates the scope of the audit as well as the audit plan. Moreover, it supports the toolbox approach towards reporting suggested here, in that it allows the auditor to build up individual reports to a whole, in a coherent and clear manner. Matrices should not be overly complex, depending on the set of organizational entities to be reviewed. In most cases, it is recommended that the matrix approach be adapted to the existing organizational structure and terminology.

A 'unifying document' in the shape of a summary report should always be provided. This report docs not contain any findings or detailed audit opinions. It is designed to give an overview of the structure and summary findings that the auditor wishes to bring to the attention of senior management. Any details should be cross-referenced, such that the interested reader is able to peruse a detailed report where necessary. For the summary report, the audit scope and plan should be included – at least as an outline – to introduce the reader to the BCM work areas and the overall objectives. Methodology, approach, analytical tools used and the reporting structure itself should be explained in a concise manner. The auditor may wish to include some important findings that require senior management attention, or a brief summary of countries, regions, etc.

Technical references

In contrast to other audit fields, particularly finance, it is likely that many findings will require footnotes to provide additional evidence or references to books or articles. A bibliography is therefore recommended for an overview of relevant publications. While it may be argued that the managerial reader is unlikely to read such technical references, they are nevertheless important for the more operational levels of the corporate hierarchy, for instance in facilities management and information technology. Hence, technical findings should be explained at an appropriate level of details, using attachments and appendices where necessary. When referring to published or unpublished material in this way, the auditor might wish to include copies of articles and papers with the audit report. Unlike an academic publication, the audit report should not require further research on the part of the reader, although copyright restrictions may limit the amount of material that the auditor can copy and provide as a matter of courtesy.

Management presentations

Many audit engagements require final presentations to management which should be based upon the audit findings and reports. In most cases, these presentations will be given to senior management or the board of directors. Consequently, they differ significantly from the detailed reporting schedule outlined above. Presentations should be short and to the point. Auditors should avoid trying to compress a full report into a set of slides. Huge presentations containing numerous slides may be counterproductive. Most of the target audience is likely to have less of an interest and less experience than the auditor. As a result, the general attention span is likely to be shorter than in workshops among members of the BCM community.

The auditor, in presenting to management groups, should acknowledge that BCM may be an unfamiliar topic to the majority of the audience. While some knowledgeable individuals are always present, others will be confronting the issues of business continuity for the first time. It is therefore very important that all participants are comfortable with the subject, and that there is enough time for discussion. Ideally, senior managers should themselves formulate the conclusions and action points arising from the presentation, rather than being told what to do. Despite the fact that the auditor is presenting findings and recommendations, the latter should be formulated in a manner that invites managerial reactions and decisions, rather than pre-empting these decisions.

BCM audit areas

The BCM lifecycle encompasses six global work areas representing a continuous business continuity process.[8] These areas should form the foundation for standardized or individual audit programmes. In order adequately to reflect the maturity level of the organization being reviewed, it is recommended that a decimal hierarchy be used to subdivide each area into manageable audit items. This will enable both the auditor and the auditee to adjust the audit depth and the planned effort on an item by item basis. In line with overall audit planning, the relative maturity level observed for each area should be used as a basis for applying a predetermined set of audit items. The following sections give a high-level overview of typical audit items to be considered for each of the lifecycle areas. However, these should not be seen as a full-scale standardized audit programme. It is recommended that an experienced BCM auditor be consulted to define the more detailed levels of audit items and related questions.[9]

Understanding the organization

In order to comprehensively and adequately address the BCM needs of an organization, its processes and dependencies must be fully understood by management and continuity managers. This includes, but is not limited to, core business processes, support processes and infrastructure. 'Understanding' in the sense of BCM

---

[8] BS 25999-1.
[9] The definition and listing of a generic (detailed) audit programme, taking into account existing methods and standards, would require more space than there is available in a high-level, overview book chapter.

is equivalent to a thorough knowledge of mission-critical activities and their relationship to the organization as a going concern. In order to obtain the required information, process analysis, business impact analysis (BIA) and risk assessment are important tools. The BCM-related activities leading to an understanding of the organization are a prerequisite to formulating and executing a BCM strategy.

In auditing this area of the lifecycle, the auditor should place particular emphasis on the fact finding and documentation done by the organization being reviewed. Any errors or omissions on the part of the management may lead to flawed assumptions that may influence the BCM strategy. Where process models are undergoing frequent change, the overall understanding of the business may have to be reviewed on an annual basis and after major changes.

Determining BCM options and strategy

Once an organization has determined the state of BCM readiness and process robustness, risks and potential impacts may be mitigated in an appropriate manner. The BCM strategy allocates limited funding to specific BCM options in order to maximize the level of protection and robustness. The strategy should address defined areas such as processes, people and technology. Substrategies may be developed to individually optimize the cost benefit expectation in each category. These strategies subsequently form the framework for the development of detailed BCM solutions.

All strategic concepts and documentation reviewed should form a coherent framework that gives a sense of direction to the organization. The auditor should consider all components of BCM strategies in the larger context of what the auditee organization has defined as overall goals and objectives. External links and relationships – particularly those in force during a declared civil emergency situation – should be given particular attention, as these often impose restrictions and additional duties on the organization being reviewed. While most strategies in BCM may be adapted to the organization itself and its culture, the components mandated by external legislation require compliance and adherence to locally prescribed practices and rules.

Developing and implementing a BCM response

Following the initial formulation of a comprehensive BCM strategy, the development phase addresses what has been termed the 'disaster timeline'[10] following an adverse event. Detailed plans should cover incident management, resumption to

---

[10] The concept of a linear progression from initial event to full recovery is called incident timeline as per BS 25999-1.

Table 23.4—Audit subareas

Subarea	Audit Items	Procedures/evidence
Business environment	• Core business activity/ies • Markets and sectors • Competitive environment • Vulnerabilities	• Market overview/surveys • Benchmarks and sector analysis • Competitive analysis • History of sector-specific vulnerabilities • Internal documentation of environmental analysis
Business entities	• Legal entity structure • Stakeholder structure • International activities	• BCM-related map of entities • Cross-referencing to risk assessment • Business strategy documentation
Process model	• Organizational structure • Dependency analysis • Outsourced components	• Organization and process charts • Process documentation tools • Outsourcing contracts • Service level agreements
Business impact analysis	• Impact models • Quantitative impact assessment • Qualitative impact assessment • Maximum tolerable period of disruption • Maximum tolerable period in alternative operations • Going concern and related boundaries	• Quantitative basis for assessing impact, e.g. accounting, controlling • Qualitative basis for assessing impact, e.g. regulations, statutes • Plausibility of critical time periods • Plausibility of going concern threshold and boundary values
Critical activity definition	• Impact-based classification • Criticality ratings • Criticality as a function of time	• Rating tables and impact ranges • Time/impact charts • Financial data
Resource requirements	• Internal resource requirements • External resource requirements • Service requirements	• Standard resource listings • Plausibility of reduction in resource requirements • Standard vs BCM-related services
Risk assessment[a]	• Risk listings (internal and external) • Risk relevance analysis (process based) • Risk treatment • Single points of failure	• Risk map • Risk to process mappings • Treatment decisions and sign-offs • SPOF listings

[a] BS 25999-1 suggests the use of ISO 27001 for risk assessment purposes. In future, this standard will be extended by adding 27005 and 27006 which specifically address risk. Where the BCM risk assessment is business centric, additional standards should be used by the auditor.

Table 23.5—Audit subareas (2)

Subarea	Audit items	Procedures/evidence
High-level strategy	• Strategic options and adequacy/plausibility • Impact/investment equilibrium • Choice of preferred option(s)	• Documentation for each option, including financials • Investment calculation and impact calculation • Risk acceptance and sign-off
People strategy	• Skillset definitions • Additional attributes • Knowledge dissemination • Protection • Third parties	• Job descriptions and BCM tasks • Generic and individual skillsets/definition • Succession plans, job rotation, training • Standard third party contracts, BCM contracts • Specialist (rare) attributes required • Statutory attributes required[a]
Premises strategy	• Spatial requirements (standard) • BCM requirements, plausibility • Availability/contracting • Alternative options (telework, etc.)	• Floor plans and related documentation • Fixtures and fittings maps, specific requirements • Lease contracts (standard and BCM) • Special requirements planning for BCM • Plans for alternative options
Technology strategy	• Basic infrastructure • Productive technologies (e.g. manufacturing) • Information technology (ITDR) • Outsourced technology	• Strategy documents for facilities, HPVAC, basic services • Productive technology plans[b] • ITDR concepts and strategy documentation • Third party strategic arrangements, incl. contracts
Information strategies	• Non-IT information strategy • Vital records • Single or multiple retention/document management	• Document retention policies • Location maps for original documents (vital records management) • Document management systems

Table 23.5—*Continued*

Subarea	Audit items	Procedures/evidence
Supplies strategy	• Core supply chain • Secondary supply chain • Office supplies and materials • Services	• Supplier selection and backup • Supplies classification scheme and criticality • Service classification scheme and criticality
Stakeholder strategy	• Key stakeholders (business) • Key stakeholders (BCM/crisis) • Health and safety considerations	• Listings of stakeholders • Definition of stakeholder attributes and special needs • Cross-referencing to health and safety issues
Civil emergencies strategy[c]	• Corporate/public network • Emergency requirements (external) and restrictions • Communications • Responder duties	• Listing of bodies and authorities identified (external agencies) • Communications plans and matrices • Responder documentation

[a] E.g. first aiders, qualified accountants, etc.
[b] Depending on the technology being reviewed, it is highly recommended that the auditor seek appropriate expert advice.
[c] In BS 25999-1, the term 'civil emergency' and related strategies are subject to the Civil Contingencies Act 2004. However, other civil emergency laws and regulations may apply outside the UK.

a defined state and recovery to full capacity. In contrast to the full BCM lifecycle, the detailed planning and implementation phase represents the former 'BCP' paradigm, i.e. writing and documenting individual business continuity solutions.

The structure and contents of incident management and business continuity plans invariably change over time and in line with strategic requirements. In reviewing the plans themselves, it is important for the auditor to assess adequacy as well as completeness. Any practical use of the plans (test or real invocation) should be utilized to evaluate feasibility and practicality of individual plans. In contrast to the BCM framework, individual plans (whether incident management or business continuity) do require an in-depth audit approach.[11] The auditor should take note of the improvement process, for instance where evidently 'strong' plans are used to improve 'weaker' plans, based on practical experience and test results. When reviewed together with the state of testing and exercising (see below), the quality of planning is an important indicator for the overall maturity level of the organization.

[11] Cf. Rössing, Rolf von, *Auditing Business Continuity – Global Best Practices*. Rothstein Associates, 2002, for an example of detailed audit items for incident management and business continuity plans.

Table 23.6—Audit subareas (3)

Subarea	Audit items	Procedures/evidence
Incident response	• Incident teams[a] and organization • Links to other organizational units • Skillsets and tasks	• Organizational charts • Required skills and attributes • Individual skills
Plan structure and contents	• Planning hierarchy for incident management • Planning system and hierarchy for business continuity • Generic table of contents (completeness) • Cross-referencing system • Organization-specific elements in plans	• Planning guidelines and templates • Planning/documentation software and BCM tools • Mappings of planning systems against standards and policies • Mappings of plans to incident management and business continuity organization
Incident management plan	• Scope and relevance[b] • Adequacy of contents[c] • Senior management links • Containment activities • Links to business continuity plans	• Sample incident management plans • Test results and change history (where available) • Documentation of known (unmanaged/managed) incidents • Improvement process
Business continuity plans	• Scope and applicability • Adequacy of contents[d] • Granularity and feasibility • Links to incident management planning • Senior management links • External links	• Sample business continuity plans • Test results and change history (where available) • Documentation of known (unmanaged/managed) invocations or business continuity events • Improvement process

[a] The terminology used here is equivalent to crisis management, related teams and crisis-related planning.
[b] IMPs should be easily understood, short and to the point. The auditor should distinguish between the immediate actions following an event, and the subsequent invocation of business continuity plans (see below) that address specific processes or resources.
[c] Categories suggested in BS 25999-1 include tasks and action lists, emergency contacts, people-related activities, media response, stakeholder management and incident location.
[d] The auditor should note that in the UK, plans must comply with a minimum requirement in terms of contents, as per the Civil Contingencies Act 2004. Similar requirements may apply in other countries.

Exercising, maintaining and reviewing

Exercising (including testing), maintenance and review form the nucleus of an ongoing lifecycle, i.e. the business continuity process within an organization. Tests and exercises should be part of an overall programme that may cover a period of several years. For the auditor, testing and exercising will provide an important indication with regard to the overall BCM capability of the organization and its current maturity level. In conjunction with maintenance of plans and business continuity solutions, tests and exercises are a central element in improving BCM arrangements throughout the organization.

Auditing this area of the lifecycle is a direct function of the actual maturity level found in the organization being reviewed. Where the level is between 0 and 2, it is unlikely that the auditor will find extensive testing and maintenance. Internal or external reviews should be utilized to develop an opinion on management attention as well as the current state of business continuity. The test–maintenance–review cycle within the overall BCM lifecycle is similar to the PDCA model[12] that is often applied to BCM in an organization.

Embedding the BCM culture

The auditor should place particular emphasis on identifying the overall culture with regard to business continuity. While this area does not strictly follow any specific activities in the BCM lifecycle, it is nevertheless present in all phases. Both BCM awareness and the culture that develops over time should be taken into account when determining BCM capability and maturity for the organization being reviewed. A strong cultural 'tradition' of business continuity thinking will usually be expressed by strong management support (at board level) and visible investments in maintaining a high level of resilience. Where cultural influence is weak or non-existent, both financial and other indicators are likely to be absent.

Awareness and culture require strong support by BCM and non-BCM staff in order to maintain an adequate level of resilience. The auditor should review the level of skills as well as the acquisition of skills through formal and informal training mechanisms. While the former is visible in the shape of BCM certifications, the latter is often present in internal communications and informal workgroups.

[12] The PDCA model is used as a fundamental element in many standards, e.g. BS 25999-1, ISO 27000 series, ISO 14000 series, ISO 9000 series. For the auditor, it is useful as a generic model describing improvement processes in the context of general change management.

Table 23.7—Audit subareas (4)

Subarea	Audit items	Procedures/evidence
Test and exercise programme	• Scoping and planning (test calendar) • Life cycle/maturity alignment • General BCM capability • Maturity level	• Test calendar documentation • Progression of individual tests and exercises, including objectives • Improvement process
Testing	• Objectives and contents • Links to other test/exercise events • Scope and timing, underlying scenarios • Results and activities	• Test plan templates • Individual test plans • Test documentation, logs, results • Interview results (test participants)
Exercising	• Objectives and contents • Links to other test/exercise events • Scope and timing, underlying scenarios • Results and activities • Re-runs	• Exercise plan templates • Individual exercise plans • Exercise documentation, logs, results • Interview results (exercise participants) • Exercise re-run documentation, logs, results
Maintenance	• Maintenance programme (maintenance calendar) • Maintenance events • Outcomes and improvement process (including financing) • Links to test and exercise programme	• Maintenance plans and change management documents • Maintenance logs and sign-offs • Investment and finance strategy for maintenance • Recommendations from testing/exercising • Feedback to tests and exercises
Review/audit programme[a]	• Internal reviews (scope/frequency) • External reviews (scope/frequency) • Review programme adequacy and completeness • Audit and review results	• Self-assessment report and tools • Audit documentation and history • Policy/standards compliance statements • Audit findings and recommendations (including implementation/closure)

[a] This does not imply that auditors should review their own work. However, in many instances it will be useful to include results from existing audits and reviews to avoid duplication of work. The degree of reliance placed on such review results will depend on the auditor's professional judgement.

Table 23.8—Audit subareas (5)

Subarea	Audit items	Procedures/evidence
BCM culture	• Senior management support • Terminology and use of BCM standards • Test and exercise activity (high level) • Investments and financing for BCM	• Policies and standards • Prescribed and actual use of terminology and standards (mail, correspondence, general wording) • BCM investment planning • BCM controlling
BCM awareness	• Size and positioning of BCM organization • BCM staff awareness • Non-BCM staff awareness • Internal information distribution • External information distribution	• Organizational charts • Awareness documentation, e.g. intranet or written • Standard BCM brochures or leaflets • Supplier/3rd party communications for BCM
Individual and organizational skills	• Certification levels • Internal training (BCM/non-BCM staff) • External training (BCM/non-BCM staff • Use of consultants	• Number of certified individuals • Extent and frequency of training courses including analysis of participants • Consultant-driven projects and programme components

BCM programme management

The BCM programme represents the backbone of the BCM lifecycle in an organization. At low maturity levels, project management is likely to be the predominant element in delivering 'version 1.0' of the business continuity strategy, plans and other components. At higher maturity levels, programme management covers individual BCM-related projects and work packages to be performed by the organization. Depending on the maturity level identified prior to the start of the audit, high-level and detailed elements of programme management should be reviewed. This specifically includes the financial framework defined for business continuity, as this will usually indicate how the organization intends to develop BCM over time. It should be noted that the programme management review does not address the organizational capability to manage projects as such. The auditor should restrict review activities to those projects and programme components that are BCM related.

Table 23.9—Audit subareas (6)

Subarea	Audit items	Procedures/evidence
BCM policy	• Scope and contents • Link to internal control system • Links to risk management systems • Context sensitivity of policy (business, geography, etc.) • Improvement process	• Policy documents • Version history and sign-off documentation • Risk management system and documents/tools • Business understanding[a] • Policy support given by senior management
BCM standards	• Scope and contents • Effectiveness of standards • Improvement process	• Standards templates • Standards developed • Change management history and sign-offs • Business understanding
Corporate governance	• Inclusion of BCM in corporate governance • Internal resources and financing • External resources/outsourcing arrangements • Use of consultants	• Corporate governance documentation and statements • Financial details for BCM (comprehensive) • Outsourced BCM services and activities, including financials • Consultancy contracts
Project management	• Project management methods and frameworks • BCM as a business process • Embedded BCM resources/staff in line organization	• Project breakdown structure • Statements of work for BCM • Budgeting and controlling • Staff listings and job descriptions • Milestone planning and sign-offs

[a] See above.

References

British Standards Institution. *BS 25999-1; Business Continuity Management, Part 1: Code of Practice.* London: BSI, 2006 and BS 25999-2: 2007 Business Continuity Management – Part 2: Specification.

Business Continuity Institute, The. *Business Continuity Management – Good Practice Guidelines.* Caversham: The BCI, 2007.

Committee of the Sponsoring Organizations of the Treadway Commission. *Enterprise Risk Management Framework.* COSO, 2004.

Civil Contingencies Act. UK HMSO, 2004.

International Organization for Standardization. ISO 27001; *Information technology – Security techniques – Information security management systems – Requirements.* Geneva: ISO, 2005.

Rössing, Rolf von. *Auditing Business Continuity – Global Best Practices.* Rothstein Associates, 2002.

Selecting the tools to support the process

24 Lyndon Bird FBCI – UK

Lyndon is Technical Services Director of the Business Continuity Institute and Managing Director of UK-based business continuity software and consultancy service provider CPA Ltd.

Introduction

Since the mid-1980s much effort, enthusiasm and originality has gone into developing a wide range of software support tools to assist the business continuity planner. Despite some success stories, it is fair to say that the overall business acceptance of such tools has often been disappointing. This disappointment has been experienced both by the developers (for whom sales have regularly fallen short of predictions) and by end-users who have found the tools less valuable than they had expected. Possible causes are discussed later in this chapter but at this stage it is sufficient to suggest that a prime reason has been inconsistency between the business continuity management process in a particular organization and the ability of the BCM software to support it.

This is not, however, a negative observation – it is simply a common problem of any emerging business discipline and supporting technology. While the rules, standards and definitions about what constituted business continuity planning were vague and open to wide interpretation, the software tools available were likely to be equally disparate. Developers either had to produce products that required the end-user to conform entirely to their philosophy and approach, or else produce products that were so generic and flexible that they fitted no organization particularly well.

Now that business continuity is better understood, new software tools are beginning to emerge which are supportive of the process rather than being at odds with it. In addition, there is a much wider appreciation that software tools are purely to assist with developing and maintaining business continuity programmes. They do not replace the BCM analysis phase, the BC planner, the selected methodology or the ongoing management commitment to the process.

The Definitive Handbook of Business Continuity Management, Second Edition.
Edited by Andrew Hiles FBCI. © 2007 John Wiley & Sons Ltd.

What are BCM tools?

Originally, most BCM specialists concentrated on the tools that supported the actual development and documentation of business continuity plans. It was in this area that the majority of products were targeted and still forms a high percentage of the market for BCM tools.

It is important, however, to recognize that of the 10 areas of business continuity competence jointly defined by the Business Continuity Institute (BCI) and the Disaster Recovery Institute International (DRII) only two are directly assisted by this type of software. These are:

● Unit Six: Developing and Implementing BCP.
● Unit Eight: Maintaining and Exercising BCP.

Other software tools do exist, however, which are valuable additions to the wider BCM armoury. Specifically discussed in this chapter will be tools that support the following certification standards:

● Unit Two: Risk Evaluation and Control.
● Unit Three: Business Impact Analysis.
● Unit Five: Emergency Response and Operations.

The remaining standards might well make use of technology and software tools for project management, awareness training and process mapping (among others) but these are not discussed in this chapter because the tools used are likely to be general purpose proprietary products not specifically designed for BCM use.

Enabling technologies such as the corporate intranets, multimedia training, automated call diversion and the like will only be referenced within the context of the BCM tools they may support.

A brief history

It is difficult to understand why we are where we are today unless the history of BCM tools is fully appreciated. First, it is necessary to reflect on the early days of disaster recovery, even before BCM was conceived.

Disaster recovery was almost exclusively a data processing function, solely concerned with the technical recovery of mainframe computer systems. The earliest plans concentrated on technical recovery procedures, backup methods and the logistics of moving tapes and operations staff to a remote backup facility. They were often documented on the system with printed copies kept off-site. Most were word processed (or even typed) and kept mainly for reference purposes.

There was little or no input from the system users and certainly no overall link to the business strategies of the organization.

Once it was realized that disaster recovery was a complex and costly business, financial controllers became involved. Naturally they questioned if disaster recovery contracts were necessary and whether or not the risk to the business justified the expenditure. Inevitably therefore the earliest tools to emerge (around 1982) were the risk assessment products; so-called 'expert systems' used to justify items of IT expenditure by balancing risks, impacts and vulnerabilities to formulate appropriate countermeasures. An almost universal countermeasure was the need to have a properly written, tested and maintained computer disaster recovery plan (DRP). The plans to be written were always very similar in structure because they only related to the IT (EDP) department and so the idea of template plans became popular. It was then but a small step before this template concept was automated and software aimed at quickly generating a DRP hit the market. By 1987 there were around 40 such products available in the US, some of which had started to arrive in other English-speaking parts of the world. Today's mainstream BCM planning tools are often the descendants of these early DRP products.

As disaster recovery planning gradually evolved towards full business continuity planning in the early 1990s more and more emphasis was placed upon the business impact analysis (BIA) phase. This led to three developments in the support tool arena:

1. The traditional risk assessment tools were extended to identify impacts and incorporate them into an overall risk management model.
2. Some of the BCM planning tools started to include a BIA module within their standard packaged software.
3. Specific software tools were introduced to assist with the process of conducting a BIA study and to give a wide range of presentation options for the results.

The most fundamental advance made by developers in this field came with the widespread acceptance of Windows as the de facto operating system for corporate PCs. Those developers who realized the implications quickly moved their products from DOS to Windows and almost overnight generated a wider new base of business user. Those that remained longer with DOS products, lost market share and product credibility and often did not survive. A similar shift and product/supplier consolidation occurred in the mid-1990s with multi-user LAN versions and more recently with fully web-enabled products. Conversely, however, the standardization of integrated office programs and the universal availability of the Internet made the building of in-house bespoke planning tools (combining elements of word processing, spreadsheets, contact databases and communications) a more attractive option for many organizations.

One of the problems faced by potential purchasers of the main proprietary products has been the price, which has always appeared disproportionately high for PC software. The developers have always argued that the price represents a fair return for their investment in a limited and specialist marketplace. Nevertheless the high price did deter all but the largest organizations, while simultaneously attracting many small-scale developers into the market with cheaper (and often simpler) products. In the United States the trend has been market consolidation from around 40 suppliers/products in 1990, to only one major supplier and a handful of niche products in 2005. In Europe (mainly the UK and the Netherlands) the reverse has happened with most of the newcomers being small developers with some BCM consultancy background launching products at around 20–30% of the price of their US rival.

Since the millennium other types of BCM products have emerged. One example with growing popularity is the use of computerized telephony to automate the whole callout and emergency response phase of the plan. To some extent these tools are most useful for those organizations that regularly need to activate and notify people quickly. Some product suppliers have extended this capability using Internet hosting, chat window technology and virtual battle boxes to become full incident management tools.

Many large corporations are already using intranets to maintain and distribute BCPs around their organizations.

In such a varied market there are no commodity products and as yet no 'killer application' has emerged to persuade everyone to buy BCM software tools. I have therefore divided the range into the following generic groupings:

1. Business continuity planning software:

    (i)   Templates (WP)
    (ii)   Questionnaire
    (iii)   Relational databases
    (iv)   Integrated DB/WP
    (v)   Enhanced feature products

2. Risk assessment tools:

    (i)   Methodology products
    (ii)   Audit products

3. Business impact analysis tools

    (i)   Analysis and presentation products
    (ii)   Integrated risk assessment products
    (iii)   Integrated BCM products

4. Incident management tools

    (i)   Computerized telephony
    (ii)   Command centre (EOC) products.

Business continuity planning software

This group of products is the traditional perception of a BCM software tool. To an outsider, they may appear perplexing in the sense that all claim to be unique in some way or other. This can be explained by reference to the underlying conflict within the BCM industry about what really constitutes a documented plan. From the beginning, two fundamentally different points of view have existed. These are:

1. A written plan is simply a document; like a manual, a book or a detailed business report.
2. A plan is a collection of critical elements of data that might need to be referenced once a disaster has occurred.

The difficulty early developers had to resolve was whether their product should be primarily based upon text processing, or be driven by the need for powerful data management capabilities.

For those who selected the textual route the reasons put forward were:

- People feel comfortable with a well-presented text document that they can easily understand.
- Much of the updating can be done by standard WP functions (find and replace, etc.) and such concepts are well known by a wide range of business users.
- DBMS are more complex to handle than word processing and the volume of really volatile data needed to be included in a place is often exaggerated.
- The output quality in terms of presentation is much better from WP than any proprietary database can offer.

The counterarguments as presented by the developers who favoured the database route were:

- Recovery planning is about knowing in precise terms what needs to be done. This can mean generating detailed checklists for teams or individuals, and linking these lists to specific resources.
- There are vast amounts of data that can be needed rapidly post-disaster. The only way to ensure this data is accurate, consistent and current is to use proprietary database technology.
- Maintenance is even more important than the original plan development. Once you get multilevel plans for multiple locations only a DBMS can hope to handle the maintenance workload.
- Although presentation is important – the most crucial aspect is to ensure plans are used in a disaster situation. Large well-written text manuals will simply be ignored in a real disaster.

This argument has not been fully resolved even today although most products now try to incorporate elements of both in their capabilities.

The simplest form is naturally a word processor-based set of templates. This provides the novice planner with an easy start-set of basic documents, tasks, procedures and resource requirements which he or she can modify to suit a specific organization.

A more sophisticated form of this is the questionnaire-generated template. The user answers questions in an interactive session that automatically triggers appropriate sections of text to form the basis of a documented plan. Further customization is normally possible as for basic templates.

The basic problem with both of these approaches is that the software designer, rather than the BCM planner, specifies the design and framework of the ultimate plan. It tends to lead to a very generic looking format with no (or very limited) buy-in from the organization.

Pure relational database products, on the other hand, give users much more control over the way their plans are formulated and collated. They are, however, more complicated to learn and the final output is often not as attractive as those generated purely from word processors.

Some combined WP/DB products insert selected data variables into predefined text (almost like mail/merge does in basic office software programs). These can be difficult to master for infrequent users, and it is almost impossible to incorporate more than a very limited amount of data in this manner.

Other combined DB/WP products try to manage text within a database text editor or provide their own add-on text editor to facilitate the process. This is rarely as satisfactory as using proper word processor software. Linking and embedding documents from proprietary software like MS Word is usually a more attractive route to combining database and text processing needs.

For purposes of competitive edge, vendors have increasingly added new functionality to their basic core-planning product. Typically these are project management, integral BIA modules and sometimes threat/impact assessment models. In recent times integration of BCM planning tools with incident management real-time tools have become popular although the different demands of planning from activation tools make this a challenging concept.

In many ways the choice of software depends largely upon the methodology you intend to use for plan development and ongoing maintenance. It is recommended that before purchasing any of the available tools, serious thought should be given to how you are actually going to embed BCM into your organization. There are numerous examples of clients purchasing extremely expensive database BCM products and not using them because their organization decided not to manage the detailed data in its BCM software. Managers often believe that a BCM is akin to a procedure manual and do not see any reason why they needed to learn a complex data management tool simply to maintain it. Although their understanding of BCM may be limited, given the prevailing company culture it might be pointless to purchase a sophisticated piece of BCM software.

The same often applies to the emphasis at the selection stage placed upon the need for compatibility with particular in-house software standards, rules usually imposed by in-house ICT departments. Often clients pay for technical design features they will never need, given the way they intend to manage the BCM process on a regular basis. If you have a centralized approach to plan maintenance, audit and review you will need different tools to a company taking a very distributed view. Remember the software is a tool to help you achieve your objectives, not a replacement for management judgement and decision-making. The criteria list in the following section is useful as a guide but simply because particular software does not support a particular point does not mean it should be excluded from consideration. The bottom line on your decision is not whether the software has every conceivable feature but rather whether it will fit with your method of working and meet your business objectives.

Suggested criteria for evaluating BCM planning software

System performance

1. Is the product written in a compiled, executable programming language?
2. When using the product in a multi-user network environment, with many users accessing the product simultaneously, will the system continue to perform as well as it does when just a few users or one user are accessing it?
3. Can the product code and data be separated?

Designing the plan

4. Does the system provide the capability of defining multiple databases to segregate sets of plans and data for training, change control implementation, planning for separate subsidiaries/divisions, etc.?
5. Does the system include an advanced call list module with a graphic hierarchical format (similar to Windows Explorer)?
6. Is a data file navigator included to assist new users of the system?
7. Will the software 'roll up' to create a master, enterprise-wide plan, which includes summarized information by location, building, floor, business unit or department plans?
8. In the event that a building is inaccessible, can users print the plan at a facility or building level where all the plans in that building are printed automatically, instead of selecting and printing each subplan individually?

9. In the event that a disruption affects a particular business unit across various locations, can that plan be printed individually, regardless of what building or location it is in?

10. Does the software provide a built-in facility to organize and design all the business continuity planning phases including crisis management, emergency response, business resumption and full restoration?

11. Does the software include a proven step-by-step methodology addressing areas of prevention, response, resumption, recovery and restoration as part of the overall business continuity plan?

12. Using this software, can users develop data centre plans, network plans, telecommunication plans, business unit plans, facilities plans, power system recovery plans and specific scenario plans if needed?

Customizing software

13. Does the software include a utility that allows users to change the terminology in all the data entry screens to reflect the vocabulary of a particular industry and company?

14. Does the software include a utility to let users resize data entry fields, to fit unique requirements? Will the system automatically perform the change and display the adjusted screens?

15. Does the software include a utility to eliminate information from the system that does not pertain to a particular industry or company and then automatically display the adjusted screens?

16. When the product is customized, will these changes automatically carry through to the included reports?

17. When the product is customized, will these changes automatically carry forward with all software upgrades?

18. Does the software include a textual 'baseline plan' addressing issues such as the purpose of the plans, scope, objectives, assumptions and missions?

19. Does the software let users customize the textual word processing documents using any word processor?

20. Does the software include a tool for creating private look-up fields in the entry screens to simplify data entry and ensure data standardization?

21. Can users design and control the output of their plans (what comes out and the order in which it comes out) based upon own unique needs?

22. Can users insert pictures, telecom diagrams, floor charts, maps, etc. into the database so that when plans are executed they are automatically printed?

23. Does the software include a utility to customize the standard reports that come with the system?

24. Does the software include a utility to let users create totally new reports?

Security

25. Does the security in the software permit users the right to view specific plan information, even when they cannot build or maintain that information?
26. Does the security in the software restrict users from unauthorized customizing and the use of all administrative functions?
27. Does the security in the software decide which pieces of plan information can be accessed and by whom, by 'hiding' that information on any screen?
28. Does the system administrator have the option of installing the software on a file server as a single or multi-user product?

Developing the plan

29. Does the system allow identification of recovery time objectives, recovery point objectives, mission critical activities and appetite for risk?
30. Is the system Internet/intranet enabled?
31. Does the system include integrated recovery task scheduling?
32. Are features included to assist new users of the system and novice planners?
33. Does the software include hypertext help?
34. Does the software include context-sensitive help?
35. Does the software include wizards where users simply answer questions to perform various functions?
36. Does the software provide a direct and seamless interface to the 'text' portion of a plan using any word processor?
37. Does the software provide a direct and seamless interface to standard office spreadsheets (e.g. MS Excel®)?
38. Does the software provide a direct and seamless interface to standard office database tools (e.g. MS Access®)?
39. Does the software provide a direct and seamless interface to drawing and presentation tools (e.g. Visio®, MS PowerPoint®)?
40. Does the software include an import utility for loading information and from other computer systems, such as purchasing (vendors), and human resources (employees)?
41. Does the software include a mapping utility to help specify how other database files are laid out?
42. Does the software include a data-gathering tool to send out questionnaires and entry screens to users, via disk, network files, or email?
43. Can users enter data 'on the fly' as they build plans instead of having to wait for information to be loaded into dictionaries before a plan can be built?
44. As users develop multiple plans, can the software display those plans in a graphical hierarchical format, so they can expand and collapse the view, and drag and drop selected plan data?

45. Does the software provide for 'drag and drop' functions to move and copy data from plan to plan?
46. As users build plans, can they view and edit data in a 'datasheet' format (spreadsheet-like)?
47. Can users view and edit multiple screens simultaneously as in other Windows products?

Printing the plan

48. Can enterprise-wide plans be printed as a cohesive document integrating word processor and database information?
49. Can enterprise-wide plans be printed as a two-part document consisting of individual business unit packets and a textual plan overview?
50. Can the standard reports that come with the software be sent to screen, printer or file?
51. Will the software send reports to a specified file (Excel®, Lotus 1-2-3®, MS Word®, etc.) placing it in the correct format?
52. Can plan output include any word processing document and project management schedule whose associated application uses DDE (Dynamic Data Exchange)?
53. Will the software directly send standard and custom reports to users via a compliant email system?
54. Does software come with standard reports that include summarized lists of items that need to be ordered?

Maintaining the plan

55. Is the plan data stored in an industry standard relational database?
56. Does the software comply with the standard MS Windows® conventions?
57. Can users view and edit information in a 'datasheet' format (spreadsheet-like) for easy plan maintenance?
58. Can users define templates (where data columns begin and what type of data is in each column) to import information from other computer systems on a regular basis?
59. When changes need to be made, such as people moving from one plan to another, does software have a drag and drop function to quickly and easily move information around?
60. Does the software contain a search and replace facility throughout the database portion of the plan?
61. Does the software contain a replacement facility, so that when a person or piece of equipment is replaced, it can be replaced at the click of a button?

62. Can users maintain plans on a LAN file server, where multiple users can maintain their plans simultaneously?
63. Does the software provide an automated data-gathering tool, where users can gather and maintain plan information electronically from non-LAN or remote users?
64. Will all plan updates be reflected in the software's audit/history subsystem, from which auditors can print reports on demand?

Using the plan

65. Does the system date and resource stamp each update individually, so auditors can track exactly what part of each plan is updated, when and by whom?
66. Does the software contain a query utility, which allows users to turn data entry screens into query, or search forms to quickly and easily find information?
67. Does the software provide an interface to a project management tool, so team tasks checklists, business processes, and their required resources and durations, can be managed in a disaster mode or a test through PERT and Gantt charts?
68. Does the software include post-exercise or post-disruption assessment forms?

Vendor

69. Does the vendor provide technical assistance 24 hours a day, seven days a week?
70. To help with promotions, re-engineering, new hires and corporate-wide planning, does the vendor provide ongoing training?
71. Is initial training required to use the software?
72. Is the vendor a specialist in business continuity management, supporting the latest in technology and industry trends?
73. Does the vendor provide updates and enhancements as part of the maintenance contract?
74. Does the vendor provide a bulletin board service to quickly get updates, fast answers and exchange information with other users?
75. Does the vendor publish newsletters to keep abreast of new developments among the user community and industry?
76. Is there an organized open forum or user group for user information exchange and education?
77. Does the vendor provide consulting assistance?

78. Does the vendor have a global network of subsidiaries or distributors to support multinational organizations?
79. Does the vendor provide support in your country?

Risk assessment tools

In the past decade there has been a major expansion in the types of risk management software available. Once the unfashionable end of the BCM software market it has risen in importance almost directly in line with the rapid growth of operational risk and corporate governance as top-level management issues.

Prior to this much of the pioneer work in this field came out of the UK, driven by the adoption of the UK government back in the late 1980s of a risk management methodology called CRAMM (Computer Risk Assessment and Management Methodology). During the 1980s and 1990s most US risk managers were still concentrating on insurance procurement. Although this was also still common in Europe, there was also a movement to view risk management as a wider management discipline, where it inevitably came into direct contact (or even conflict) with business continuity concepts.

Lack of clarity about the role of risk management in a BCM context has hindered the development of software that has any real value to a BCM professional. To many it has been seen as still synonymous with insurance, which is largely about actuarial data and spreading risk over a range of clients. Consequently, BCM specialists often assume that risk analysis software has something to do with the likelihood of threats being realized based upon statistical data and actuarial calculations. A number of quantitative risk analysis tools entered the market in the 1980s. None of them were very successful and few of them remain available today. In the United States, a standard formula was generated to calculate ALE (annualized loss exposure), which became incorporated into all quantitative products. This turned these products into little more than specialized spreadsheets useful to calculate average annual losses from small exposures (e.g. pilferage), but of no credibility in assessing the risk and consequences of an unlikely but potentially catastrophic large disaster.

It soon became obvious that risk management in the business continuity sense was different. Since the late 1980s the software support tools that have emerged have been what are generally called 'qualitative risks analysis' products. The main advantage of the qualitative approach is that no probability database is required and that risk levels are expressed in relative rather than absolute terms.

Unlike BCM planning tools, software in this area is far from generic. Most tools cannot be separated from the conceptual methodology involved or the industry to which they apply. A full and proper understanding of both the terminology being used and the algorithms by which scores are generated is essential.

Since the emergence of Basel II requirements for financial institutions and compliance legislation like the Sarbanes-Oxley Act, a number of specialized tools have been developed for the assessment of financial risk. These, however, have little to do with mainstream BCM.

Benefits claimed for risk assessment tools include:

- Better targeting of security and cost-justified security
- Increased security awareness
- Consistency between different parts of an organization
- Better application of policy and base standards
- Improved business communication of risk
- Greater productivity and audit savings.

Critics of use of automated tools argue that all of the above benefits can be obtained by manual paper-based methods and that software support tools are complicated to learn and provide no real advantages:

- **Speed** – Any normal audit inspection or review takes considerable time to plan, undertake, report, discuss and conclude. It becomes a showpiece event. It is not undertaken regularly, it is only a snapshot. With risk analysis software a survey can be so easy that perpetual review, improvement and self-audit are the norm.
- **Consistency** – If an organization has hundreds of locations, how can you guarantee consistency in standards between branches and different types of site? Imagine having 100 different inspectors visiting 500 locations around the world. Would the results be accepted as fair or consistent, without a common method of measurement?
- **Participation** – If the review is non-disruptive and fair, people do buy into it. The best results come from each individual making those small day-to-day decisions that cannot easily be enforced by policy or policing.

Finally, of course, the question comes down to which tool you should select. The following tips will help you decide:

1. Ensure that you understand the benefits you wish to achieve before you start looking. As with any other software requirement, draw up a specification of requirements and review software against this.
2. Ensure that you know how your method and software tool will contribute to those benefits. The software should *improve* your productivity – *not* tie you to a difficult and inappropriate methodology. Ideally, the software will make your job much easier.
3. The knowledge base of the system must be able to be tailored to you. Check that the software allows this.

4. Ensure that you are comfortable with it, it is easy to use and it makes instinctive sense.
5. Check that the reports are meaningful and that it does not leave you with the task of interpreting difficult computer output.
6. Check that it links *risk* and *impact*. In other words, the reports not only detail the risks, but also explain what the implications of these might be. This is critical in selling risk concepts to business managers.
7. Make sure that you are not tied to external consultants for support in operating the tool or conducting the risk analysis exercise. The software should give you all the assistance you need.
8. Ensure it is flexible. It must dynamically customize its approach/question base to suit your environment.
9. Ensure that you can use the software for one-off security reviews or health checks to make your life easier on a day-to-day basis.
10. Ensure that you can experiment on the basis of 'what-if . . .' scenarios.

In recent years, the complex methodology-based products have been augmented by a few simpler audit-type products. In particular the BS 7799/ISO 27001 information security standards prompted several developers to produce automated tool versions of the standard. With such products, end-users can easily audit themselves against BS 7799/ISO 27001 requirements – to determine the degree of compliance and highlight the areas to be addressed further.

Business impact analysis tools

Conceptually business impact analysis (BIA) products are really only a subset of the functionality that should be provided within a good risk assessment product. Unfortunately most risk assessment products do not really concentrate upon business impact – they tend to be more concerned with threats and the probability of them being realized, rather than the consequences so resulting. Some risk assessment tools have attempted to bridge the risk/impact gap and this is an important factor in evaluating such a product. Nevertheless in recent years the importance of the BIA phase has led developers to produce tools that specialize solely in that element of the process.

Some developers have produced a BIA module as a front end to their full BCM product. This has the advantage of allowing 'minimum resource requirements' defined in the BIA to be automatically incorporated into the planning process. The disadvantage of this approach is that a user would be committing to an expensive BCM product, purely to get access to the small BIA module. Separation of the BIA and BCM tools has become the norm, although when developed by the same company they do usually provide some level of integration.

The stand-alone tools have been produced mainly for presentation purposes. They allow a series of results generated by interviews or questionnaires to be analysed and presented in a variety of formats. This is very useful in terms of cost justifying a particular recovery strategy. Senior executives need to see a professional business presentation that focuses on the salient points. Products that are modules within a BCM or RA framework often lack sufficiently high quality output. The main concern with stand-alone tools is not in their design, but in their interpretation. The results they provide are only as good as the quality of the data collected. If the user of the software does not validate the answers provided properly, then the analysis produced by the BIA module may be totally erroneous. A good rule when shown the output from such tools is to ask 'Does it fit with common sense?' If not, then usually the fault lies in a misunderstanding of a question or an incorrect answer given by an inexperienced person. BIA software does not help an experienced business continuity practitioner to get the right answers, but it does help him or her present them more effectively.

Such products may, however, be useful for an inexperienced planner who is not sure about the questions to ask when conducting a business impact analysis study. Of all the types of software support tools, this is the most dangerous if not correctly implemented because the results from the BIA provide the entire conceptual basis for the remainder of the BCM product. As such some developers have taken on board ideas from other management processes such as process mapping and dependency modelling to undertake BIAs.

It is clearly theoretically possible to define an organization in such detail as to identify all linkages and dependencies. If this is done accurately, then any interruption to any process can result in an automatic recalculation of impact across the entire model. It sounds a perfect solution to the often time-consuming and repetitive process of undertaking a BIA. However, the model design process can be complex, the buy-in from the organization is often weak and it moves BCM further away from the business manager and towards the technical expert. Depending models for BCM are not new and although conceptually attractive have yet failed to find a significant level of support from the BCM community.

Incident management tools

The most critical part of a recovery is in the early stages. Failure to properly notify key people and services not only loses time and money – it can cost lives as well. Consequently the use of automated computerized telephony has become increasingly popular in supporting incident management plans.

In general these consist of preprogrammed instruction sets so that against individual scenarios telephone numbers can be automatically dialled, customized messages given and responses monitored by use of the telephone keypad. Some products link a fairly simple auto-dial facility to a list of disaster recovery vendors – to speed up the acquisition of a locksmith, glazier or the like. Others are much more sophisticated and can be tailored to provide callout scenarios in a wide range of situations. Usually such products are a combination of hardware, software and telephone network services. Because they are so time critical, users will normally have dedicated equipment to support such products. The cost of ownership of such products is often, therefore, much higher than would appear initially from the vendor software price alone. Technical support for such products is also more complicated than for other types of BCM software.

The key things to look for if selecting such a tool are:

- Speed of notification achieved
- Confirmation and feedback of the message delivery service
- Flexibility in type of telecoms utilized
- Ability to modify scenario and callout lists easily
- Ability to activate the callout process remotely.

Most vendors have realized that the limited usage and technical complexity of purchasing such software is a major disincentive for potential clients. They have generally only sold the actual software to very large corporates and now tend to concentrate their efforts at smaller clients on fully hosted services where the vendor does all the product and operational maintenance. The customer simply activates the service via a security code at the time of an incident. A fully hosted or ASP route does seem to be the most likely future for such products if they are to make a major impact.

The limited functionality of these products has led to a number of developers trying to extend call notification tools into full command centre (or emergency operations centre) communication tools. Such products are designed to give full management control of all the information resources and communications needed immediately following an incident. They also allow virtual command centres to be set up, thus saving time and travel. In such products all essential data can be made available via secured Internet access to all members of an incident management team, public and private chat room facilities can be utilized, virtual battle boxes of charts, maps, contracts, etc. can be accessed and recovery status monitored and made available for later analysis and audit. These tools can be very powerful but they do require some rethinking about the conventional views of how a crisis or incident should be managed. Many organizations are not ready to do that yet but it does seem to be a direction that many BCM software providers are now targeting.

Conclusion

Software support tools are now widely used in many major organizations for one or more of the processes described in this chapter. They have not eliminated the need for the experienced BCM professional and are unlikely ever to do so. When selecting a tool it is important to consider carefully what you need it for and how you intend to utilize it. There is little point in buying a tool because the sales demonstration was slick and it looked functionally sophisticated. Concentrate on the benefits it can give. If there are none or they can be achieved in more cost-effective ways – do not buy it.

Despite this health warning, there is no doubt that there has been a tremendous advance in the variety and flexibility of such tools and they can be useful in a wide range of situations. Remember a good plane or chisel will not make you a good carpenter. Neither will a good BCM tool make you a good business continuity manager – but it might help!

Coping with people in recovery

25 Allen Johnson – UK

Allen Johnson is co-Founder and Director of Scenaris Limited, Europe's first full-service risk, continuity and business communications group.

Objectives

The objective of this chapter is to set out before the reader the non-trivial people-orientated issues that come with serious and disturbing incidents. Business continuity management (BCM) inside any organization is incomplete if it does not deal with the issues in this chapter. If the focus on the needs of people coping *in extremis* changes the approach and considerations of the BCM practitioner, then the author has also achieved his second objective. Advice at Appendix A2G is also relevant.

Qualification

The author was a victim of terrorist violence in West London in the early 1980s, when the offices in which he worked as a technician for a US-based computer manufacturer were bombed. Returning to the office the next day he saw desks, chairs and cabinets contaminated with embedded glass; shattered computer screens and paperwork littering the floor of the open plan office. The building had lost approximately 90% of its glass, front and back. He was not physically injured, but for several years afterwards he carried the troublesome burden of how he felt without the realization of what it meant. Within two years of this incident, 38 of the 41 people in the department where he worked had resigned and left, him included. The cost to the employer was a massive sum in terms of lost expertise and cost of replacement, and none of it recoverable from any

The Definitive Handbook of Business Continuity Management, Second Edition.
Edited by Andrew Hiles FBCI. © 2007 Scenaris Ltd.

insurance claim. A serendipitous career change placed the author in the disaster recovery industry and it was in here he encountered Michael Stewart, a clinical psychologist and partner of the Centre for Crisis Psychology. Through his contact with Michael Stewart, the author discovered the meaningfulness of both psychology and trauma and trauma management and later learned how to deal with the issues he had slowly come to realize he had. The lesson was invaluable and one worth sharing.

This was also at a time when post-trauma stress disorder was not as readily recognized or accepted as it is today.

The catalysts

Major terrorist outrages occur regularly but when they ignite in the western world, they take on the aura of greater significance and the stark need for the establishment of contingency issues for a business takes closer order. Unfortunately, it is high profile incidents that promote the thoughts of precipitating resilience measures, despite them being primarily seeded by commonsense.

The effects of shocking circumstances upon people has always been an issue understood by too few but it is these effects that play a significant role in determining the welfare of those to whom it means so much. It is not confined to having impacts upon those directly affected, but also to those to whom they are close, either in work or socially or domestically; who may feel the gusts of the backlashes from a myriad of reactions.

The journey begins with the ambush of the event. Even if it is expected, when it happens it comes not so much as a surprise, as a shock and even though it may be predictable, the timing usually is a sharp and sudden tug of the rug upon which one stands.

Proximity to an incident influences reaction

When a serious incident strikes, our closeness to events will largely determine what it means to us and how we react. If watching it on television, we may become fixated with the story and events as they are broadcast. It is our fascination of the unusual that draws us in; and the more extreme it is, the more our interests are aroused. If it happens right in front of us, the natural instinct is to quickly get away. The immediate response is for personal safety. The scale and extremeness of an incident are parts of the process that also deliver shock and reaction. Physical proximity will establish personal response to self-preservation and decisions taken in dangerous situations determine the outcome, in certain cases, of life or death. It is as if the physical proximity to an extreme event is relatively proportional to the fear it generates in an individual. Referring to the bombing incident in the 'Qualification' section above, the author was next door to the affected building in a basement wine bar with a colleague, John Foster. They heard a noise that sounded like the explosion that it was. The author motioned to go outside to investigate and Foster, an ex-military man, simply said, 'Stay here. Here is safe, and there may be another explosion.' He was right on both counts, and a second and much bigger explosion happened approximately two minutes later. You may rest assured that events like this stimulate the senses in ways that will surprise in terms of speed and intensity.

The King's Cross Station fire

On 18 November 1987, an escalator fire at King's Cross Station in London killed 31 people and physically injured more than 60. The fire was from the ignition of accumulated debris around an escalator machine room. In the early stages, the fire appeared insignificant but it was rapidly exacerbated when escalator routes acted like chimney flues and the thin fumes from the combusting wooden escalator steps changed to thick, acrid, black smoke as the oil-based paint on walls and ceilings caught fire. But for those that survived this tragedy, not all was resolved, and traumatized people, some 20 years on, still struggle to understand their own behaviours when faced with a reminder of what it was like. Take Jeff (not his real name), for example; he was a duty policeman summoned to the underground railway station to assist with rescuing the afflicted and to help control the situation. Nobody there, Jeff included, had ever seen such an incident, or dealt with anything like it, let alone being expected to take lead responsibilities in actions that quite clearly looked more likely to cost lives than to save them. In order to save lives, many rescuers, some completely unequipped, had to endanger their own by reaching into an inferno to get to those that were closer to fatality. In response to the audible cries of one victim, Station Officer Colin Townsley from A24 Soho, entered what a BBC reporter described as 'an efficient furnace'; Colin Townsley did not survive. It was an emotional and physical experience of effort and despair, of bravery and horror, of fear and risk, and one from which Jeff has never recovered. It does not haunt all of his wakened moments, but take him towards the gateway of any underground station entrance, and he turns away; visibly disturbed at the prospect of descending into a subway station and all conversation with him stops and he visibly perspires; instead he will take bus or taxi. Since 1987, Jeff has not taken any London Underground train nor any subterranean railway journey.

How do people deal with difficult events that change their lives?

Reading this from the comfort of your seat, you may think this sort of thing never happens. But it does. And the effects upon people will change how they behave in the short term, and potentially the medium and long term, depending on the circumstances and their effects.

Disasters are the ultimate catalyst in change management. You do not want them, and yet they arrive. And when they arrive, you have to deal with them: it is not an option. People who experience serious and unwanted incidents have found themselves catapulted down a path of dramatic and rapid change. And the daunting task of maintaining control, in what is often a runaway process, is the testing examination that such unfortunate people must face. But because most who face the incident are meeting it for the first time, it is reasonable to assume that in the challenge between the people and the disaster, the smart money is on the disaster. The last statement is not intended to be flippant, merely to indicate that a serious incident may cause suffering because those affected have neither knowledge nor experience of how to cope or deal with it.

How do people deal with difficult events that change their lives? There is no single recipe because we are all different and our responses, reactions and feelings will be expressed to levels of varying control.

The trauma of Mary Edwards

Mary Edwards is a striking, petite, smartly dressed, American businesswoman. Posted to the London office of her employer, she was one of a group of people in her department to undergo an 'awareness session' in business continuity management. These sessions are informative, but benign, descriptions of the contingency measures an organization has adopted so it may respond to serious incidents; the sort of 30-minute lesson that all employees should sit through so they may understand the seriousness with which their senior management treats such matters. Mary was the last one in through the door before the session began and slipping into the room she went to the back and 'hid' behind 40 or so of her colleagues. When the session had ended, she was the last to leave: a deliberate ploy on her behalf as the presenter later discovered. In leaving, she approached and said in her American way, 'Thank you for helping me through this half hour.' Her facial expression was a forced smile that was cracking beneath the increasing shiver of an emotional chin. That had never been said to the presenter before nor has it since, but at once he knew he was in a situation that required delicacy, integrity and sympathy. Choosing his language carefully, he continued, 'You're welcome; but it will help me better understand what you mean if you would care to share with me the reasons why you said it.' Mary explained that prior to the session and because of pressing business matters, she was reluctant to attend; that is until her immediate manager made a polite insistence by telling her that the 30-minute session was to inform her of contingency measures adopted by their organization. 'This is London,' he said, 'and in terrorist terms, you *could* say we are in a war zone.'

One may think this description as being a tad overstated, but for reasons that she could neither fathom nor account for, they were the words that made her strangely overcome with fear. Mary then went on to recount the tale that six months earlier, she was working in her New York office on an ordinary trading day when an announcement was broadcast over the public address system which informed the building's occupants that there was a threat of a terrorist bomb and that the building should be evacuated via the normal evacuation routes. All escalators and elevators were not to be used and evacuation was down the stairwells as indicated by signage and fire marshals and security would be on hand to help. She made her way to the stairwell and joined the descending throng of over 9000 people. Her shoes were fashion statements and not the trainers she now needed. In the accelerating evacuation, there was public cocktail of panic, shouting, anxiety and wailing. Mary was buffeted, she was pushed, the heal of her shoe broke off and what saturated her imagination was the fearful realization that she had no knowledge of whether she was getting further away from the bomb or closer to it. Nobody knew. She described her descent from the 38th floor of this 70-storey block in graphic detail with a deal of taut emotion. When she got to the ground floor, she was shaken, her tights were torn and she was frightened and very alone. Familiar faces were no comfort for how scared she felt, and she ran. As awful as she felt, there was no bleeding, no wound, no scar, no bruise and no outer evidence that here was a troubled soul in need of help. So instead of dealing with her concerns, she coped by boxing them up in her own mind to hide them forever. And six months later, in a foreign land, her manager's words describing London as a terrorist zone unleashed the very feelings that she had experienced on that fateful day. The genie in the box had been unwittingly released. The fact that the New York terrorist bomb was a hoax caller counted for nothing. Until our meeting, Mary had coped with the issue: she had not dealt with it. Subsequent to our exchange she sought help from a clinical psychologist and received the support she needed.

To the reader, two further points are worth making about this story. The first is that as Mary started the telling of her story, it became instantly obvious to the listener that some of her descriptions were as if they were happening to her there and then. She spoke quickly and with passion and there were no brakes to this runaway account until the journey of its telling had come to a natural halt. That tearful halt was determined by Mary. The second point is that the events of Mary's story occurred before 9/11; thus her reactions were not influenced by any other high profile incident to which she had previously been exposed.

Psychological reactions to an incident

When an accident or other traumatic incident happens in the workplace, the board of the organization has both a legal duty of care and a moral duty to provide help to its employees. Such an event can result in two sorts of trauma:

1. Post-traumatic reactions directly related to the event
2. Negative reactions to how the business or its managers handled the situation and its ensuing aftermath.

The latter is longer lasting, and is more damaging in terms of anger and resentment towards the company and its management. While such anger may lead to the bitterness of litigation, and the monetary value of that action, it may almost certainly lead to decreased morale, and diminished or lost productivity and in some cases resignation.

The bank and its rejected employees

To illustrate the erosion of morale by way of example, the following case study is of private Bank RB, a victim of the terrorist bombing of Bishopsgate in London's then principal financial district on the morning of Saturday 24 April 1993. In this particular serious incident, the Bishopsgate Bomb, staff that lived within easy commuting distance arrived to site to help and were met by three senior management representatives, already present because they occupied local bank-supplied apartments and who had responded immediately. Non-senior employees were unceremoniously turned away as being both surplus to requirement and a hindrance. The nature of this unequivocal employee rejection was emotionally and intellectually unacceptable to those dismissed and instantly fostered a rancour that lasted in excess of five years, the point at which they, individually, and without reference to one another, recounted their story to the author. In this instance, management decisions taken on site served more to divide than unite, and at a time when striving for common goals demanded unification. Furthermore, the language used to tell these people where to go was brusque and expletive ridden. And after the disaster had struck and recovery was achieved and the business was put back together, then what happened? The bewildered 'rejects' returned to a company awash with heroes, heroines and champions. The champions had worked long hours; they had done unusual deeds; they had met demanding challenges in difficult circumstances; and despite being held and shaken in the teeth of adversity, they had come through it all, victorious and euphoric. An example was the IT contractor who was serving the penultimate week of his contract for setting up systems. Post-recovery, he was made a permanent employee and immediately promoted to IT director, a freakish and hastily taken decision. This was his reward for rebuilding the systems that only he knew how to do. In reality, the company's employee population has also gone through a significant cultural change. And the 'rejects' who still belonged to the pre-disaster age did not understand this, which had the effect of further isolating them. The combined effects of this isolation, the initial rejection and the violent nature of this particular incident meant that over the following few months, over 25% of the staff resigned and left the company. Resulting staff resignation from a traumatic event is not unique, since there is an understandable, normally fear-related, reluctance to return to an environment that has been physically devastated.

To provide an effective response to a traumatic incident, senior management should expect to deal proactively with post-traumatic reactions and this requires training and education. Management should also react positively to personnel in order to make them feel valued, and much of this is to do with management style. Acting out of character by a manager who expresses a different style to his typical behaviour is a sham which may be seen in a flash and the affected employee will likely as not compensate by carrying the burden of the inadequacies of the manager(s) in question. A significant issue about which management types are commonly ignorant is that trauma is a powerful foe and that investment in trauma management is not a bottom-line decision.

The following are a selection of questions to some of the issues raised by senior officers and managers from a range of organizations:

1. Why does management need to respond to the human side of traumatic incidents?
2. What's the benefit to my company?
3. Do you honestly think a critical incident is likely to happen to my business?
4. Why should I invest money in this?
5. If such an event did happen, wouldn't our HR department be able to handle it?
6. What if I already have a business continuity plan in place?
7. I have an employee assistance programme – surely this will help?
8. Is a trauma care programme different to counselling?

Why does management need to respond to the human side of traumatic incidents?

Senior management has a duty of care and also a moral duty to show that the company cares. You may be able to affect the course of legal action by responding, and protect company reputation and brand image. But, most important of all, it is in the interests of the company to have staff members functioning normally as soon as is possible, with positive views of the organization as a caring employer. The most valuable and volatile asset of a company is its people; without people, there is no company.

What's the benefit to my company?

Proactive management of the people side of a traumatic incident will bring your business back quicker than if you treat staff as being further down the food chain than business issues. At some stage, the issue of people's needs will bob up to the surface, so dealing with them sooner rather than later will enable those that have business management responsibilities to do so with the personnel resources required to run the business. It is commonsense.

Do you honestly think a critical incident is likely to happen to my business?

It is not a question of how I think; it is a matter of how you think. It is accepted that it is part of our nature to believe 'this only happens to other people'. But when it does happen, if dealing with the human side has not been properly thought through, then be prepared to deal with business recovery and people recovery. But understand that they will come as a couple with linked arms and not in Indian file. While one may reach for New York's 9/11 and London's 7/7 as high profile examples, UK disaster recovery services providers rescue, on average, at least three subscribing client companies every week. Such events are not good for the image or reputation of the afflicted company, so they are less likely to be today's news and far more likely to be today's well-kept secret.

Why should I invest money in this?

First, investment in the right preparation may save money that could be lost through making incorrect and costly management decisions that are thereby an exclusion from extra cost of working insurance cover. Second, its employees are the very people the company hired to help it progress, so the question is sufficiently poignant that if it is decided that such investment was considered by the board and then declined, then the board should be able to articulate the basis upon which the decision was reached, not least to its investors and shareholders. If you value your employees but times are tight, then invest in this and cancel the Christmas party and tell staff what you have done and why.

If such an event did happen, wouldn't our HR department be able to handle it?

While HR may respond following a critical incident, it is commonly found that the usual procedures are not attuned to working with trauma. In the absence of any preparation they may understandably decide to do nothing at all. Conversely they may try to do too much. HR is not endowed with expertise of dealing with people needs *in extremis*, simply because it is an HR function. An effective expert response does just enough, and does it exactly when it is needed.

What if I already have a business continuity plan in place?

Business recovery plans typically focus on restoration of IT technologies, voice and data communications and an emergency site from which to reboot operations as necessary. However, it is of little use having systems 'up' if people are 'down'. If, on the other hand, HR and related entities have inclusion in their plans for such matters, they should be trained to know what to do rather than allow it to be a subject for which they have responsibility but neither knowledge nor confidence in their own abilities to respond appropriately. Most BCPs focus on business requirements and completely miss the people issues.

If I have an employee assistance programme (EAP), surely this will help?

The typical EAP individual counselling model does not meet the post-incident needs of a group of staff. The wrong time to discover this is when an incident has struck and the EAP is found wanting. Our experience is that EAPs do not want to embrace the issues of their responses even in a desktop exercise, if only because it may expose their frailties. So in the grip of a real event you are dealing with an EAP support service that is an unknown entity. Many organizations subscribing to EAP support have found this out and as a result have identified the need to employ a fully practised clinical psychologist to work alongside an EAP.

Is a trauma care programme different to counselling?

Yes. Trauma care is a specialist activity. Whereas counselling is targeted to the needs of an individual, the trauma care programme is initiated for all affected staff. The programme is driven by the overall needs of the situation, whereas counselling is driven by the individual's personal preoccupations.

How to respond?

Since 1990, a clearer picture has emerged as to what is genuinely helpful in early intervention following traumatic events.

A holistic approach is unquestionably the right approach and 'one-off' interventions are without context and are now known to be of little value and in certain circumstances can prove counterproductive. Best practice is a balanced and sustained intervention with distinct phases over time on the principles of:

- Not too much
- Not too little
- Not too soon
- Not too late.

An understandable response to the immediate aftermath of a traumatic event, when an organization feels overwhelmed, is to flood the affected location with 'counsellors'.

This is not helpful because affected people cannot make use of 'counselling' or any other formal psychological intervention at this point. It is simply too early. What they require is attention to practical needs, containing and calming of their initial reactions, a message of care and concern, and information about what has happened and what is going to happen. There is no absolute reason for this to be provided solely by outside professionals, and indeed they may not be best placed to do so. Suitably trained members of the organization itself, working within a framework of available advice may be better situated to achieve this as they know and understand the organization. This is the task known as 'defusing'.

It is the focused, purposeful, judiciously timed intervention which counts, rather than the misguided belief that by throwing increased numbers of 'counsellors' at the issue in order to manage the process. It is a matter of quality and timing that will make the telling differences for a positive outcome; not the volume of helpers. Post 9/11, there are examples aplenty where hundreds, if not thousands, who were qualified in virtually any discipline related to mental or psychological remedial interventions or counselling were hired by organizations and individuals alike, to help the affected cope with the trauma. Five and a half years on and the scars of this error still tread the streets of New York.

Once the initial crisis has passed and things are calmer, the organization looks to its normal priorities, but another factor lurks in the shadows. As commitment to longer-term support dilutes over time and business as usual is the order of the day, those affected feel forgotten, because they become forgotten: not forgotten that they are the people that they are, but forgotten as those that still need help. Evidence of the lack of support may manifest itself only when the organization recognizes something is wrong, e.g. lower productivity, increased instances of sickness, increased absences, lateness to work or appointments, mood swings, etc. And when problems become deeply entrenched, any future intervention is more difficult.

Thus, rather than waiting for problems to emerge the organization must proactively initiate a programme of interventions which ensures that everyone who needs help has access to it.

The format of help is crucial. The workplace is the context for recovery, and colleagues are potentially a major resource for each other. Interventions are often best conducted in work groups where it is possible to mobilize group resources and group dynamics.

Policy

Many organizations may have business continuity plans, but precious few plans are derived from a wider policy that includes the human aspects of recovery. All organizations need a policy element for dealing with the human aftermath of traumatic events in the workplace.

Widespread incidents

While much of the above may be appropriate to businesses and corporate organizations, the same issues cannot necessarily be handled in the same way when the event is geographically widespread and catastrophic. This is illustrated with the example below.

In August 2005, the exceptional ravages of Hurricane Katrina throughout Louisiana, Mississippi and Florida caused $81.2 billion in damage, shattered communities and accounted for in excess of 1800 lives. For some, the physical devastation was paramount, for others the disintegration of the social infrastructure and the instant infusion of lawlessness was most salient. Five days after the storm made landfall in excess of 500 police officers in New Orleans went absent without leave. While condemnation was vociferous, this situation arose because of normal human reaction or frailty, call it what you will. If people have to choose between their job or their own welfare or that of their loved ones, then it is understandable that the job is considered as the lower priority. The poor response from the authorities amply demonstrated the failure to account for the needs of people in disaster response planning. To further confirm this point, a subsequent benchmarking study conducted by *Continuity Insights* magazine and KPMG showed that 35% of respondents indicated that the weakest link in their continuity plans and associated strategies was people-related risks. Only 19% considered technology risk to be the weakest link and for 27% it was process risk.

However, it is not always thus, as it is the combination of the nature and the extent of the incident that will be the prime driver in determining how people will react to recovering a business, and, more importantly, themselves and each other.

The significance of personal territory

Where there has been a violent invasion of one's workspace, such as through criminal act, fire, explosion, etc., then problems of a different ilk visit those personally and directly affected. And those problems tend, in the main, to be emotionally charged. So why is this the case, and what can be done about it?

Begin by understanding how one's own workspace is treated. The majority of employees tend to have something at or about their desk or workstation that tells others that this is where they work. These may be photographs, a sports trophy, a photocopy of an amusing cartoon, a small soft toy, a child's early painting, etc. Whatever it may be, it is a 'thumbprint' that expresses a message to the world and says, 'This territory is mine.' Although this declaration is made indirectly and implicitly, it is, nonetheless, a very strong statement. Others may enter and move around this territory, but usually only with the licence of the territory owner. But this area can be invaded by unwanted intrusion. For example, think how you would feel if you return from lunch one day to find a person, you do not know who they are, sitting on *your* chair at *your* desk. They are using *your* telephone and writing on *your* notepad with a pen that was given to *you*, by a loved one, last Christmas. Answer yourself honestly; how would you feel about that? Now the only thing that is genuinely and legally yours is the pen. The desk, the chair, the telephone and the pad all belong to the company. But that is not the issue. The issue is, *how do you feel about the intrusion?* Mostly the feeling is one of negative reaction because you want that person out of your space. So the relationship between ourselves and the territory we are required to operate within is very important; and there would likely be an understandable attempt to defend it. Take it away, even temporarily, and there is potential for a problem. So why is this an issue?

When a violent invasion of that territory by criminal act, fire, explosion, etc. occurs, then there is a case for emotional response that may well require managed intervention for trauma.

By personalizing ownership of one's territory, emotional links become established and any invasion, particularly from a devastating event, will solicit an emotional response. It is this response that requires careful management and it will differ from person to person.

Soft and hard incidents

In the world of BCM and disaster recovery, companies and individuals may encounter soft or hard incidents from which they will be required and expected to recover. Soft incidents are those that range from irritating to business threatening and may be IT failure, communications failure, critical power loss, theft, minor flood, denial of access, reputation loss, etc. Hard incidents are those that carry elements of serious violence that are a threat to life or safety and they tend to reveal that humans have a natural predisposition to post-traumatic stress disorder or PTSD.

Post-traumatic stress disorder (PTSD)

PTSD occurs when a person has experienced or witnessed an incident that involved actual or threatened death or serious injury, where the response involved fear or helplessness. It includes a traumatic incident persistently re-experienced through distressing recollections and incident-related dreams and showing response to cues of how the senses were triggered during the incident, e.g. Joanna was a 36-year-old woman who, from time to time since childhood, would find herself overcome with inexplicable melancholy, to the point, in later years, where she became potentially suicidal. After much research, the reason was eventually traced to a tune that she would hear from time to time on radio, television, in a store, etc. It was the very tune that was playing on the radio when, at the age of four, she discovered her mother on the kitchen floor, dead from a stroke.

There are more clinically correct descriptions of how PTSD shows itself in an individual, but in essence, if somebody who has been exposed to a hard incident, and changes in their behaviours become sufficient that they are noticeable, then it is likely that they are suffering from PTSD.

Pastoral issues

Having considered the psychological aspects of recovery from a serious incident, we must not forget the practical day-to-day issues that staff may be expected to deal with.

An Italian bank based close to Threadneedle Street, in the heart of London's financial district, was displaced from site by the efforts of a disgruntled employee who plugged up all the sinks in the male toilets on Friday evening and left the premises with all taps turned full on. The ensuing flood had all weekend to run and successfully wrecked the five floors below as well as the basement. The bank's staff were relocated to a recovery centre in West London and 99% of their staff mostly commuted in from Essex and elsewhere east. Within two weeks, staff became disenchanted with the extra journey time and two key traders resigned, defecting to a competitor who had been previously wooing them. The bank stayed in the recovery centre for another three months and lost almost 30% of staff through resignation.

The same was true of an insurance company whose Manchester, UK, offices were destroyed by a weekend fire. It had business continuity plans but they were untested and so the initial recovery took place in a local hotel, irrespective of what the plans contained. The author of the BCPs was so far down the pecking order that senior management simply ignored her. However, towards the end of the weekend, the plans were opened and the recovery strategy had the organization in question decant its Manchester office functions to lesser regional offices. The Manchester office was significantly bigger than any of the regional entities so each office got 'invaded' by their Mancunian cousins. This had the effect of speading the disaster to those parts of the business that were hitherto unaffected, and this stroke of dubious wisdom made sure everybody had a piece of Manchester's miserable misfortunes. Offices quickly became cramped, there was insufficient documentation, insufficient desks, insufficient telephones, insufficient IT networked screens, insufficient support infrastructure and insufficient coffee cups; as literal as that. On paper, the strategy appeared sound enough, but when the human element was applied to the strategy, it did not work. While the BCPs addressed the needs of the business, they patently excluded the needs of the people expected to implement recovery measures. As a final and painful lesson for this company, towards the end of the first week in recovery, they managed to get in touch with their IT manager who was enjoying his annual leave so far up some distant foreign mountain that cell phones were irrelevant. He informed his company that he had signed a disaster recovery services agreement with a proven provider immediately before he went on holiday. It was his well-intentioned action to avoid catastophic IT failure in his absence, but he had not told anybody else.

By simply having a solution in place does not endow it with success. Over a few days, the irritation of working from an alternative address is bearable. When business recovery extends into the longer term then other issues begin to materialize. The matter of loyalty shows its face and individual responses to rally around the flag have variable reactions based upon a longer history of how each has managed their term of employment and what it has meant to them.

Testing plans is essential in ensuring that they amount to something, but they only matter if you account for the people issues. People represent the key to business and to business recovery. By thinking through what is required of them and how they are expected to undertake their tasks and what it means to them personally, you may end up with measures that are worthwhile and an appreciation of how we humans deal with difficult circumstances.

Leadership

Make no mistake, deliverance from a disaster depends upon a wide range of skills but at the head of the pack is leadership. The leadership of people has no equal and in the teeth of adversity, folk want to identify the back of the person who is moving with purpose and they will follow. In times of uncertainty, people want direction, not options.

Most organizations are run by consensual management but delivery from a disaster requires leadership. While it does not necessarily follow that a leader is always right, it is leadership that wins the day. The following four examples are cases to support the point.

Example one: Confectionery manufacturer

The culture of this particular company is one of extreme consensual management. Have a good idea on 1 January and decisions are forthcoming on 30 September after everybody affected has been consulted, right down to the last operative on the shop floor. The management team was presented with a fictitious disaster in a desktop exercise. Before long, the management team had grown to in excess of 70 members. Towards the end of the exercise, the team was advised that it had

45 minutes left and that it had nothing on the board. The chairman immediately stood up and, with pointed finger gesticulations and barked instructions, divided the group into discrete teams each with specific tasks to do and times by which they must be done. This behaviour cut across the culture of the organization but it was effective and it achieved the end objective of recovery. It was leadership that made the difference between doing and dithering.

Example two: International bank

In August 2005, the London arm of one of the world's biggest financial institutions had to deal with a power outage that was so severe it stopped the organization from trading, although it was able to pass its positions to its Asian office. The UK-based incident management team that was endowed with the responsibility of managing the situation, congregated in order to make its decisions. Not a single person in that team had a clue what to do and it settled into a committee and the collective safety of its inadequacies with nobody taking a leadership role. Nine hours later, and when power had been restored, the situation righted itself but the stain of incompetence was borne by all in that group. The word 'group' is used in this context because team dynamics were never present. It was not a team other than by title – a common misnomer. To the credit of this group, there was a collective realization that their performance was woeful and a need to address the issue became a driving force that precipitated the changes that were obviously required.

In this particular case study it was the lack of leadership that prevented any successful attempt to recovering from the situation. In truth, the problem largely fixed itself and it was only when the situation was restored did any worthwhile analysis reveal the obvious – that their recovery performance rudderless.

Example three: Leasing company

When the CEO of a leasing company found himself as leader of the internal crisis management team in a crisis management training session, he resigned after about 15 minutes. He had realized that nobody was doing anything without his sanction and in one statement he made his position perfectly clear. 'You will not decide on anything with me in here. This is not in my comfort zone when I am the only one taking any initiative. So you can do what you decide to do with my blessing. I'm leaving this room. You may call me but only if you cannot proceed without me. David (he pointed to his operations director), you're in charge.' And with that he left the room, and the team with a leader. The outcome was successful and the team realized that leadership does not necessarily rest with one person.

Example four: Newspaper

A UK national newspaper encountered major difficulties via a major power failure and in turning to its facilities manager expected guidance. He did not disappoint and his decisions were excellent. However, he was not mentioned in the business continuity plan and the BCP was rendered useless when it was discovered that the technology support personnel listed in the document had all left the company. Recovery can be achieved without a BCP, but if you have a leader, then you have a chance. Without both BCP and leadership then you have a more significant problem.

The cases above are living examples of where leadership has made a telling difference. To illustrate further one could compare the actions of President George W. Bush with those of Mayor Rudolph W. Giuliani in the aftermath of 9/11 as well as the air crash on 1 November 2001 in the Rockaway area of Queens in New York. In both instances Rudy Giuliani led.

Coping without people

As a final twist, let us take a brief look at not so much coping with people under duress, as coping without people.

History is a great teacher and experience shows that epidemics are significantly more likely than pandemics. The greatest cause of epidemics is influenza of one strain or another, and they occur with a regularity that is almost forgotten when the warmer seasons begin. Around the Chrismas period in 1992, staff members of a big retail store in London's Oxford Street became victims of a highly contageous type of flu, so much so that their shop floor was devastated. Store management hired in temporary staff, who not surprisingly also succumbed to the same flu. The following year, and every year since, staff are treated to an annual flu jab. It is perhaps not the best idea for a Christmas present, but avoiding the problem before it begins is as sound a strategy as you are likely to encounter.

As odd as it may appear, an epidemic is the risk that is most likely to strike an organization with a comprehensive effect on its people; so plan for it.

Research results

The results of the seventh survey undertaken by the Chartered Management Institute on business continuity management were published in May 2006. The research was a collaborative effort between with the Cabinet Office and the Continuity Forum and one of the key conclusions identified the need for greater focus on the risks posed by the loss of people and their associated skills. A common shortfall was that, in general, business continuity plans showed a relentless focus on the technological aspects of IT and voice and data communications; failing completely to address a wider range of potential exposures. While 16% of respondents believed that their BCP would be sufficiently robust in the event of an influenza epidemic, 43% confessed to having no plans for this risk despite acknowledgement that they could predict serious disruption. Mass absences may not necessarily manifest themselves through the H5N1 strain of avian flu, but more localized epidemics are a genuine and seasonal threat.

Conclusion

We can make businesses more resilient. To do so we must include measures for people to cope and deal with their recovery needs. To do this, the expertise of the clinical psychologist is, without question, the most valuable and appropriate resource. At the beating heart of every organization lies its most volatile and valuable resource, people. No business can fully recover from disastrous circumstances without its staff, and this means *all of them*.

The missing elements

26 Andrew Hiles FBCI – UK

Andrew is a director of Kingswell International, consultants in enterprise risk management and business continuity.

Where next?

What are the trends in business continuity planning and where is it heading? We may get a better glimpse of the future by first looking at the past.

About 15 to 20 years ago, leading edge organizations were coming to grips with their dependency on computers. The Fortune 1000 corporations, led by the finance sector, began to implement disaster recovery plans for computers and vendors responded with standby services. This example slowly filtered to the smaller, dynamic and entrepreneurial companies and through the public sector. As it was doing so, the Fortune 1000 companies began to realize that, while computers were important, so were communications and telephony, production facilities, equipment and offices. Business continuity planning was born – again filtering from the biggest to the smallest. A few years ago, a German delegate at a business continuity workshop looked confused. 'Am I making myself clear?' asked the presenter. 'Yes, you are perfectly clear,' replied the delegate. 'It's just that in Germany we are not allowed to have a disaster!' It seemed amusing at the time, but actually he was right. We have moved from a situation of disaster and recovery from it, to a situation where increased resilience and redundancy means that business goes on, no matter what facilities or assets are lost. Many organizations that survived 9/11 did not survive because they did not lose people and facilities. They survived because of the resilience of their people and the diversity, robustness and resilience of their infrastructure.

Blue chip corporations have long held contingency plans for specific situations, such as hostage, kidnap, armed robbery. Now, these are being absorbed into full enterprise risk management functions that incorporate crisis management, with IT and telecommunications disaster recovery planning, business continuity

The Definitive Handbook of Business Continuity Management, Second Edition.
Edited by Andrew Hiles FBCI. © 2007 John Wiley & Sons Ltd.

planning, operational risk management, compliance issues, insurance, product recall, health and safety risk management, etc. Every aspect of risk, brought under one coherent management structure. And all this is being underpinned by reputation management with an emphasis on managing media. Other contributors to this book have endorsed, from different perspectives, the need for business continuity and operational risk management approaches across all business strategies and activities.

But, more important, is the underlying reason for this: the message is getting through. More and more chief executives are realizing that they simply cannot stick their heads in the sand and pretend a disaster will not happen to their organization. More and more pressure for effective contingency planning and risk reduction is being applied by legislation; by regulation; by governance requirements; by auditors; by class actions against negligent directors; by government inspectors; and by insurers.

Yet another pressure is the interdependency of corporations through just-in-time supply and electronic trading. The big customers are demanding that their suppliers have business continuity plans in place: they do not want their supplier's disaster to become their own disaster.

Over the last few years, we really are beginning to see a critical mass on the side in support of aggressive risk prevention and business continuity planning, so that it is rapidly becoming the norm rather than the exception. And as that happens, everybody benefits – the business, the shareholder, staff and the innocent passer-by.

The business continuity industry

The business continuity market is growing at around 25% a year in most developed countries. Of course, this is good news for suppliers: as long as they provide the services the customer needs at the right quality and the right price, suppliers have a rosy future.

Increasingly customers are looking at a one-stop shop for all their business continuity services. At the same time, customers have an increasingly diverse range of technical platforms to support, taxing the skills and resources of their service vendors. The result has been a series of acquisitions, mergers and partnership arrangements by vendors – a trend that will continue.

This trend has been boosted by the globalization of the industry: global customers want global vendors. Apart from computer manufacturers, there were few truly global players in business continuity say five years ago: now there is a positive stampede to acquire global capability.

Profitability can be high among vendors, some of which are showing upwards of 20% profit and 30% annual growth. Once the cost of a standby facility has been covered by subscriptions, every additional sale goes straight to the bottom line. Since the cost of such additional sales is marginal, the astute customer may drive a hard bargain: in one recent case, facilities initially offered at $200 000 were eventually signed up for $60 000. This also means that the earlier subscribers on three- or five-year contracts may not be getting the best deal.

The more subscriptions a facility has, the more profitable it can be. It is incumbent on the customer, therefore, to verify that the vendor does not have so many subscribers that there is a strong possibility of the standby site being occupied by somebody else at the time of invocation. Even a few customers could cause this situation if they are geographically close together.

Service vendors are still primarily focused on providing recovery for the computing and communications technology – albeit with workspace attached. Quick resupply services have developed. Dealing room recovery facilities abound. From 25-seat recovery facilities we have seen growth to 250, 2500 and even 4000 seat facilities. Co-lo (co-location) facilities and hosting services are available for web services. Call centre overflow and standby services are available in several countries.

General office space is now readily available in most countries, with or without office systems. Document protection vaults are also becoming more widely available. However, there remains little in the way of formalized recovery services for manufacturing production, logistics and distribution. In these areas, the business continuity planner remains very much on their own.

However, we have yet to see the development of commercial factory or warehouse recovery sites suitable for manufacturing or logistics.

Laws and standards

One of the most noticeable changes impacting business continuity over the last few years has been the growth in laws and standards pertinent to emergency planning, continuity management and disaster recovery.

These are explored in Appendix 4. Suffice to state here that, pre-9/11, there were probably fewer than 10: now there are over 35.

Business continuity professionals

Over the last few years there has been an emphasis within almost every organization on downsizing, right-sizing, outsourcing, offshoring, 'flat pyramids' and various other initiatives for headcount and cost reduction. Mergers and subsequent efficiencies of scale have added to the problem. The tendency for greater centralization means the big manufacturing plant, logistics depot or head office represents a single point of vulnerability. This has resulted in a number of outcomes impacting the business continuity professional:

1. In business continuity planning, it means that in many corporations skills are just one deep: there are no alternative people to stand in during a disaster. This situation is aggravated by the need to have teams at the damaged site, and at a recovery site, probably working extended hours at each site. Pressure on headcount has become a major challenge for recovery planners.
2. In times of economic stringency, business continuity professionals have sometimes been seen as a soft target for cutbacks. Alert professionals have therefore moved from a technical orientation towards a business orientation. They have been seeking to demonstrate their professionalism by professional qualification and certification. The Business Continuity Institute (BCI) and the Disaster Recovery Institute International (DRII) both have a rapidly growing number of certified professionals. The business continuity professional has come of age.
3. Reorganization has led to a reappraisal of different roles with responsibilities for various aspects of risk. These include physical security, insurance, health and safety and business continuity. We are increasingly seeing these roles consolidated.

Corporate resilience

If we have done our risk assessment and business impact analysis effectively, we will already have put in place alternative accommodation, personnel, production capability equipment, logistics and other facilities. These will enable reputation to be protected, operations to continue and customers to be served despite the disaster. You will have rehearsed recovery procedures and you will know they work. So at that stage, has business continuity been effected? Is the business continuity planner still necessary?

Take a few examples:

1. A bank has its proven and tested in-company, dedicated recovery facility with workspace, equipment and telecommunications capabilities. Its main IT centre suffers major hardware problems causing an immediate and prolonged service outage. Is this a disaster? No – it is an operational decision by IT management to relocate operations to the standby facility.
2. A head office has arranged for standby recovery facilities with a commercial hot site vendor. It is planning a major hardware upgrade and agrees with its recovery service vendor that it can conduct equipment operations from the

standby site during the upgrade. Is that a disaster? No. And if the cause of the operational relocation was not a planned move but was a relocation forced by fire in the head office, why should the fire be a disaster?

3. A gale causes major damage to a manufacturer's production plant: it will take several days to re-establish production. The manufacturer supplies just-in-time components to a major customer. However, its continuity plan involves maintaining one week of buffer stock. Is the gale a disaster? No.

What we have been witnessing over the last few years of business continuity planning is the downgrading of disasters to operational incidents. In many cases, business continuity planning has become simply another (important) element of operational risk reduction. In these cases, we do not necessarily invoke the full business continuity plan, but handle it as an operational incident. Why involve the business continuity planner – it's an operational decision. So are business continuity professionals actually doing themselves out of a job?

There are trends both for and against corporate resilience. Developments supporting resilience include:

● The growth of expert systems and artificial intelligence, reducing reliance on individuals
● Increasing resilience and fault tolerance in equipment (in part to save field service and maintenance engineering costs)
● Improved reliability of software
● Improved resilience of suppliers, including power and telecommunications providers
● More and more corporations and cities are introducing video surveillance which will reduce business loss through theft, hooliganism and arson.
● Mergers leading to mega-corporations with international multi-sites – a pain-tolerant situation. An organization worth a trillion dollars can afford to lose a few million!

Trends tending against corporate resilience include:

● Increasing integration of technology across the whole range of operations – for instance, manufacturing control and integrated financial, sales and logistics systems. This complicates recovery and can cause delay. In recovery, modularity rules!
● Time pressures on computer backups may prevent interdependent systems from being backed up in a synchronized fashion, causing integrity and reconciliation problems.

We have seen resilience, redundancy and alternative capability increasingly built into equipment and processes to the point where disaster avoidance and mitigation is simply the way we work. But, as always, there is the opposite side of the coin. Again, examples may illustrate this.

1. A retail chain has a central distribution centre and an integrated point-of-sale, logistics, distribution and financial system. The company supplying the software implements a new version without a fallback position in the event the upgrade fails. The upgrade fails. Point of sale tills cannot be polled to feed the logistics chain. The tills' memory fills up: the option is either to stop selling (and preserve system integrity) or to resupply manually (and potentially lose the integrity of the stock control system). Is this a disaster? How many business continuity plans cater for software problems like this?
2. An international courier is prevented from landing its plane through bad weather. Is that an operational incident or a disaster? Is it a disaster if its competitors have been able to land their aircraft?
3. An aerospace company loses its office systems at 10:30 on a Friday morning. There is no indication as to when they will become available. The company is responding to an invitation to tender for a billion dollar contract. Is this a disaster?
4. It is late December. The New York offices of an international law firm are handling a high profile case of sexual harassment. It involves a senior politician and his personal assistant. The law firm is representing the personal assistant, to considerable media interest. News breaks that, in the London office in the UK, a Christmas party got a bit out of hand. A senior partner got overamorous with his young attractive lady clerk. She is claiming that 'he kept pouring me drinks and forced himself on me'. Could this start an Arthur Andersen-type meltdown?

Many organizations are fixated on big, physical disasters – the Godzilla scenario. But they have recovery plans to cover these. Companies can die just as easily from being nibbled to death by rats. Does the continuity plan cover this, too?

In summary, probably both corporate resilience and corporate vulnerability are increasing. Despite the growth (in number and scope) of commercial BC services and the increased professionalism of BC practitioners, we cannot afford to be complacent about our resilience: we must be vigilant to a potential disaster situation. Defining 'disaster' is fundamental to business continuity planning. Too loose a definition can cause a disaster – either by invoking an unproven and deficient plan unnecessarily, or by failing to recognize that a potential disaster condition exists until irreparable damage has been caused. The lesson is straightforward. Disasters are not always self-evident. There has to be a clear definition of disaster – and escalation procedure from customer complaints, help desks and contact centres, quality defects, service level failures and production incidents so that decisions can be made about each incident against established disaster criteria.

Appendix 1
Case studies

Compiled by Peter Barnes FBCI and/or
Andrew Hiles FBCI

The Definitive Handbook of Business Continuity Management, Second Edition.
Edited by Andrew Hiles FBCI. © 2007 John Wiley & Sons Ltd.

AN INTRODUCTION TO THE CASE STUDY SECTION

Statistics

How likely is a disaster? Statistics show that one in five businesses suffers a major disruption to their business activity every year. According to Dell, a third of all companies with a disaster recovery plan have had to invoke it. Some other relevant statistics from European surveys:

- 57% of business disasters are IT related (London Business School).
- 35% of firms suffering a computer disaster lost over £250000 ($435000), (survey by PricewaterhouseCoopers).
- 30% of disasters are caused by fraud, malice and misuse.
- 30% are caused by software and hardware failure.
- 20% are caused by fire, flood or tempest.
- Terrorism accounts for 2 to 5% of disasters (SunGard).

Natural catastrophes

Table A1.1 identifies the 10 most costly world insurance losses from natural catastrophes, 1970 to 2005. The uninsured losses could be up to five times the value of the insured losses. Loss estimates vary widely: Bermuda-based Aspen Insurance Holdings Limited estimated industry insured losses for Hurricane Katrina and the subsequent New Orleans floods to be in the region of $40 billion; Risk Management Solutions, a leading insurance industry analyst, estimated $40–60 billion with total economic losses of $125 billion; Jonathan Rauch, in D.C. Dispatch, raised the figure to $200 billion for direct and indirect economic losses.

The United States has sustained 67 weather-related disasters during the 1980–2005 period, in which overall damages and costs reached or exceeded $1 billion at the time of the event.

Other sources offer further cases – notably because some of the biggest catastrophes were not insured. The Disaster Center cites several catastrophes not included in the Swiss Re figures. These include the earthquakes around Kobe, Japan, on 20 January 1995, which cost some $131.5 billion and 6433 lives. On 27 April 1991, floods in the Russian Federation cost $60 billion. On 7 December 1988, earthquakes in the Soviet Union caused losses of $20.5 billion.

Terrorism

Terrorist bomb attacks have taken place around the world, in most capital cities and softer tourist targets.

Table A1.1—The 10 most costly world insurance losses from natural catastrophes, 1970 to 2005

Rank	Date	Country	Event	Insured loss in 2005 $ millions
1	24 Aug, 2005	US, Gulf of Mexico, Bahamas, N. Atlantic	Hurricane Katrina (aka Katrine); floods, damage to oil rigs and levees	45 000
2	23 Aug, 1992	US, Bahamas	Hurricane Andrew	22 274
3	11 Sep, 2001	US	Terrorist attacks on WTC, Pentagon, other buildings	20 716
4	17 Jan, 1994	US	Northridge earthquake (magnitude 6.6)	18 450
5	2 Sep, 2004	US, Caribbean	Hurricane Ivan; damage to oil rigs	11 684
6	20 Sep, 2005	Gulf of Mexico, Cuba	Hurricane Rita; floods, damage to oil rigs	10 000
7	15 Oct, 2005	US, Mexico, Jamaica, Haiti, etc.	Hurricane Wilma; torrential rain and floods	10 000
8	11 Aug, 2004	US, Caribbean	Hurricane Charley	8 272
9	27 Sep, 1991	Japan	Typhoon Mireille/No. 19	8 097
10	25 Jan, 1990	France, UK, Belgium, Netherlands, etc.	Winterstorm Daria	6 864

(1) Property and business interruption losses, excluding life and liability losses.
(2) Adjusted to 2005 US dollars by Swiss Re.
Note: Loss data shown here may differ from figures elsewhere for the same event due to differences in the date of publication, the geographical area covered and other criteria used by organizations collecting the data.
Source: Swiss Re, sigma, No. 2/2006.

In October 2005, 23 people died, including three bombers, in attacks in Jimbaran and Kuta in Bali, Indonesia.

On 12 October 2002 terrorists used a suicide bomber and a car bomb in the nightclub area of the holiday resort of Kuta; 202 people died and a further 209 were injured. Most of the dead were tourists, mainly Australians. A third, smaller bomb attack on the American embassy did relatively little damage.

A total of 2976 people perished in the 11 September 2001 terrorist attacks in New York, Washington and Pennsylvania, excluding the 19 hijackers. Insured losses from the World Trade Center attacks in New York City and the Pentagon are expected to total about $36 billion (in 2005 US dollars), including property, life and liability insurance claims.[1] These barbaric acts are not covered further in this book: they deserve more comprehensive coverage than we have space for.

On 7 August 1998, terrorists deployed two truck-bombs in Nairobi, Kenya, to destroy the United States embassy there. There were simultaneous attacks on the US embassies in Dar es Salaam, Tanzania, leaving 257 dead and injuring more than 5000 people. Collateral damage affected nearby businesses: in Nairobi, this included the head offices of the Cooperative Bank, one of the countries biggest banks.

On 19 April 1995, in Oklahoma City, terrorists used a Ryder rental truck to conceal a huge bomb together with additional charges inside the building, to destroy half of the nine-storey Murrah Federal Building, killing 168 people and injuring hundreds of others.

Animal-rights terrorism has caused an estimated £150 million ($261 million) in property damage in the UK over the past 25 years. Millions are spent on policing and security every year.

The Animal Liberation Front (ALF), which advocates illegal activism, is responsible for dozens of attacks in North America each year. It took credit for $750 000 in damage to offices and equipment at the University of Minnesota in 1999, where researchers study Alzheimer's disease and work on a vaccine against brain cancer.

A report published in April 2005 by the US National Counterterrorism Center, identified 651 terrorists incidents worldwide, causing 1907 deaths. These included:

- 9 attacks in Africa
- 327 attacks in South Asia
- 24 attacks in Europe and Eurasia (with the highest pro-rata number of fatalities, at 636)
- 8 attacks in East Asia/Pacific
- 270 attacks in the Near East
- 13 attacks in the Western Hemisphere

Ten per cent of these involved United States targets.

Manmade disasters

Except in war, man cannot emulate the scale of disasters caused by nature – but some manmade disasters can come close. The cross-section of examples in Table A1.2 illustrates the range of causes and results.

[1] US Insurance Information Institute.

Table A1.2—Examples of man-made disasters

Date	Place	Event	Deaths
19 Nov, 1984	LPG BLEVE, San Juan, Mexico	Explosion	500
3 Dec, 1984	Bhopal, India	Explosion, dioxin contamination. The world's worst industrial accident	15000
26 Apr, 1986	Chernobyl, Ukraine	Nuclear power plant disaster. 335000 people evacuated	9000
24 Mar, 1989	Prince William Sound	Exxon Valdez oil spill	–
6 Jul, 1988	North Sea, Scotland	Piper Alpha oil platform explosion, Phillips Petroleum Co.	167
23 Oct, 1989	Pasadena, Texas	Isobutane UVCE explosion	23
22 Apr, 1992	Guadalajara, Mexico	Sewer explosions	296
29 Jun, 1995	Seoul, South Korea	Sampoong department store collapse	501
14 Sep, 1997	Visakhapatnam, India	Hindustan LPG UVCE explosion	58
11 Nov, 2000	Kaprun, Austria	Fire in rail tunnel	155
13 May, 2000	Enschede, Netherlands	Fireworks factory explosion	22
27 Jan, 2002	Lagos, Nigeria	Armoury explosion	1100
18 Feb, 2003	Daegu, South Korea	Subway fire	198
21 Feb, 2003	West Warwick, Rhode Island, US	The Station night club fire	100
30 Dec, 2004	Buenos Aires, Argentina	República Cromagnon night club fire	194

Even as this edition was being revised, there was news that a widespread fire in central Dhaka, Bangladesh, on Thursday 12 October 2006 damaged over 100 neighbouring factory premises. The fire was reportedly caused by a short circuit in one of the factories at midday. Eighteen fire-fighting units tackled the fire, which was brought under control at about 5:00pm local time. The cost of the fire was estimated 20 million taka ($300000). Other local businesses were affected by the resulting exclusion zone and the road closures.

Yes, disasters do happen, and the causes can vary from the dramatic to the mundane – such as the dripping tap that led to loss of communications, causing DFDS, a shipping company, to invoke its disaster recovery plan.

The case studies that follow are summarized from presentations at conferences, published articles (with the permission of the authors); from experiences of the contributors to this book; and from cases from Kingswell's disaster database, which was made available to various business continuity user groups.

I am grateful to Peter Barnes FBCI, my co-editor of the first edition of this book, for his authorship of the summary and introduction sections and for his work in collecting, editing and formatting many of these case studies.

A1A   STORM, EARTHQUAKE, EXPLOSION –
A GENERAL OVERVIEW

We are all familiar with storms, the possibility of explosions has been part of everyday life for some, and even the UK has the occasional earthquake. Each type of occurrence requires a different approach if the damage is to be contained and the status quo restored.

Fire and flood are the most common causes of damage to property, but recent years have seen an increasing incidence of storm and explosion damage. Future weather patterns may become even more erratic and violent if we believe the predictions of global warming, and terrorist action is an ever-present threat in many parts of the world. Earthquakes are still not predictable, but the continents continue to move and further activity is inevitable. It is therefore important to be able to apply the knowledge and experience gained from past events to those still to come.

Hurricanes and storm damage

The Caribbean had major hurricanes in 1988 (Gilbert) and 1989 (Hugo), 2004 (Ivan and Charley), the United States in 1992 (Andrew), 2004 (Ivan and Charley) and 2005 (Rita and Katrina). The United Kingdom experienced severe storms in October 1987, January 1990 and June–July 2007, while Japan suffered a major typhoon in September 1991 and Pakistan in June 2007.

Hurricane Gilbert focused the damage management industry's attention on storm damage. On arrival in Jamaica it was found that virtually the entire infrastructure had been not destroyed but certainly put out of action. There were no telephones, no power, no piped water, and immediately after the storm the airport runway had been blocked so that access to the island was difficult.

What do you do first in such circumstances? Communication with head office to arrange supplies – of money, men, materials, methods and machines – is impossible, there is nowhere to stay since the hotels are uninhabitable, there is no cooked food for lack of power and gas.

The airport was soon reopened, and major efforts were devoted to loss mitigation by, for example, oiling machinery to arrest corrosion in the warm, moist and salt-laden conditions. Thus damage management contractors were able to reach Jamaica two days after the hurricane, and were soon busy at dozens of damage sites.

Hurricane Hugo and the damage it caused, principally in Puerto Rico, reinforced the lessons learned. The even bigger financial loss caused by Hurricane Andrew was very largely to domestic premises. But the biggest of all was Hurricane Katrina, perhaps the biggest hurricane of its strength on record. By 29 August 2005 it breached Lake Pontchartrain and the Mississippi River, which flooded most of the city of New Orleans. At least 1823 people perished, some as a result of exposure to carbon monoxide from portable generators. Total damage cost was variously estimated to be from $100 to $200 billion. Over a million people were evacuated. Federal disaster declarations covered 9000 square miles (233000 km²) of the United States. Over five million people were without power, many for months.

But even tragedies can have their lighter side – like a problem encountered in Indonesia over Christmas 1988. A storm had caused a storage dam to burst, flooding a textile factory 14 kilometres downstream with up to three feet of soft mud. A few days later the panels of a drying machine were opened, revealing two large snakes hissing angrily. Damage management procedure No. 237 was quickly instituted: tap loudly and listen before opening!

Earthquake

There was an earthquake in remote terrain in the Philippines some years ago. A hydroelectric dam had been constructed and the reservoir contained quantities of silt due to deforestation. The earthquake caused landslides into the reservoir, stirred up the silt, and flooded muddy water through the power-generating equipment.

Minor seismic faults are even to be found in the UK, and there are industrial installations downstream from storage dams in the fault zones. The companies concerned would be well advised to include the possibilities of earthquake damage and severe flooding by muddy water in their contingency plans.

Explosion

The risk of explosion damage has been recognized as being of major concern among business continuity professionals since the IRA bomb blast in St Mary Axe, London, in April 1992, and even more so since the anniversary blast in Bishopsgate in April 1993 and the New York WTC blast in February the same year. Explosion damage is likely to be restricted to commercial premises, and therefore to include high-rise buildings. One can feel sympathy for those people at the HSB building who, without power and therefore with no lifts, had to climb the stairs as far as the 27th floor.

Apart from the obvious problems, such as lack of power, rainwater ingress through broken windows, glass falling from windows high up in the building, and the need for structural safety to be established, a few of the problems which may not have been anticipated were:

- Security considerations caused the police to prevent any access to the building for some time after the explosion, even by the structural engineers who would necessarily be first in to ascertain the building's safety.
- Emergency contractors brought in to clear debris caused as much damage as the bomb, including attempts to open safes by force, deliberate deposition of waste material, and deliberate or accidental damage to computers by thrown debris.
- There were considerable amounts of money, blank traveller's cheques and other negotiables in the buildings, and their secure removal was difficult and time consuming, and interrupted access to the buildings by all other parties.
- The City did not have sufficient stocks of hard hats, glasses and safety boots for the number of people requiring to enter the building, and it took time to bring them in. The site managers took the view that 140 was the absolute maximum number of people that could be allowed into the not-yet-safe build-ing at any one time. This meant that bookings for access had to be made, and everyone experienced further delays.

For many affected businesses, it was fortunate that there was a recession at the time, since that made it possible to find alternative premises in the City at short notice. Of course, to organizations with contingency plans in place, this was not a problem.

Electronic equipment in the blast-affected area generally survived extremely well, and many computers continued to operate during and after the explosion. In one case, it would have caused considerable business interruption to switch them off, and the priority was to install plastic sheeting at the windows to protect them from the elements.

Several computers were scrapped unnecessarily, mainly from buildings that lost power, so that direct evidence of continuing function was lacking. One major bank with a developed contingency plan, realizing the complexity of the problems involved in the replacement of several electronic items, decided at once on decon-tamination. In this case the contamination was from glass fragments as well as ceiling debris and dust, and the contamination from normal use, which includes skin, paperclips, coffee, sugar, staples and general detritus. The glass fragments came in all shapes and sizes.

There remain two good reasons for thorough removal of the fragments:

1. Until the device has been dismantled and checked it is not known whether any more damaging large pieces of glass are present.

2.   There is a serious risk of cut fingers of operatives or maintenance personnel, with consequent liability claims.

A car bomb also set by the IRA exploded at Brent Cross, North London, in April 1992. It released considerable quantities of dust within the warehouse of a company stocking electrical and electronic components, and destroyed all of the Perspex rooflight panels. Temporary sheeting was installed over the rooflights, but very strong winds associated with heavy weather in the succeeding weeks blew off the sheeting, and large quantities of rainwater cascaded into the warehouse, to the extent that rainbows were visible within it. To add to dust created by the explosion, there was therefore considerable suspected damage from water. Most of the items remained in a fully functional condition, but they had been new, and the problems of warranties and the unacceptability of damaged items as being new meant that the possibilities of mitigation by reinstatement were reduced.

Conclusion

Storms, earthquakes and explosions are all forms of damage, which need to be considered in contingency planning. Their effects on buildings and equipment are often largely the same as those of fire and flood, with additions such as glass fragments. Electronic equipment is much more robust than is normally credited and reinstatement is probably more successful than it is in the more common cases of fire and flood incidents.

Loss mitigation of over 90% can be achieved by professional reinstatement, and all contingency planning should include damage management procedures. The importance of this step is exemplified by the effects of the February 1993 bomb at the World Trade Center in New York, where 150 of 350 companies put out on the street subsequently went out of business.

A1B   LIVING NIGHTMARES – SOME
APOCRYPHAL TALES

And not a drop to drink . . .

Water in the wrong time and place can be a complete washout for computing
and communications equipment, as the management of a bank discovered to their
consternation when a chilled water pipe fractured next to its switchboard and
ruined it.

The bank's voice capability was restored only after the equivalent of a week's
work over a public holiday weekend and at a cost of £175 000 ($305 000). Worse,
customers thought the bank had gone out of business because they could not
reach it by telephone.

The bank could have used several cellular options to get round the problem,
retain customer confidence and plan for recovery of its voice systems at a slower
and more economic rate.

Generators that don't

Many organizations are alive to the problems caused by power failures but can
still be caught out if their own contingency plans are not fully thought through.
During the power breakdown in Manhattan in 1991 one company was counting
on its diesel generator to save the day. They had tested it faithfully for months
and were sure they were adequately prepared. Incredibly, the motor to start the
generator was connected to mains electricity so when that failed the generator
could not be started.

In another instance a consultant called on a customer, asked to see their backup
generators and was introduced to 'Bob' who oversaw them. When the consultant
asked questions about the start-up procedure Bob had all the answers but, when
probed as to whether these were documented, the vagueness of his response indicated they were not. One night a few weeks later a 100-mile-an-hour gale tore down
the power lines. Alas, the customer could not get its generators started because
Bob was on holiday. Written procedures now exist, if a little late in the day.

Litigation and near misses

Whatever the reason, sudden loss of data processing capability can imperil a firm's
very existence, as happened to a US company that suffered a loss of no more than
four hours' processing time. In that relatively short period it was, however, unable

to deliver some contracted-for information. In the subsequent court case it was sued for $600 million but managed to negotiate an out-of-court settlement of $60 million. This problem had not been identified before the computer went down.

I told you so . . .

The computer manager at an overseas office of a Swiss bank felt that they did not have sufficient disk resilience. He put up a case that would have cost $100 000 to implement. It was rejected. Two weeks later, the disk crashed: the cost? Over $2 million.

Oops!

A brand new computer room had just been installed for an insurance company, complete with inert gas for fire suppression. It seemed a good idea to test the system. The gas was dumped. Unfortunately, the specification had used the volume of the empty computer room in its calculations. Now that it was full of equipment, the gas requirements were less. The excess gas pressure blew a wall half an inch out.

A brand new computer room had just been installed, complete with inert gas for fire suppression. It seemed a good idea to test the system. Unfortunately, the workers who had fitted the suppression system had failed to clear swarf from the pipes. The result: hardware failure.

A miss is as good as a mile

All these incidents actually happened. Almost as hair-raising are the near misses – the problems that could have occurred but, mercifully, were spotted or headed-off in time following a business impact analysis.

For example, one particular company factored its receivables. During a business impact analysis it was found that if they could not deliver the receivables to the bank, as contracted for, the bank could assume control of the company.

In another case a firm had inert gas extinguishing in a room housing its processing system but the room was found not to be airtight, thus rendering the gas ineffective. Outside the room the building's staff did their welding. The system's batteries emit highly explosive hydrogen. The welding was moved.

To err is human

The human element is clearly present in all these situations, to a greater or lesser degree. Occasionally the problem is all human in origin. In one company a visiting consultant insisted on visiting the storage location for backup tapes, which was in a vault in a nearby building. Once inside the vault it was found to contain some rubbish . . . but no tapes! A quick search found the tapes in the company van parked outside the computer centre. These were large old reels each weighing more than two and a half pounds, of which the operators had to take as many as 300 a night up a flight of stairs. They had become rather tired of this so had taken to using the van as the off-site storage location.

Solid investment

Minimizing the risk of 'nightmares' is an investment that, in the event of a disaster, will pay for itself in no time. One company has calculated that by using a computer disaster recovery service, all the costs involved with this, including salaries, testing, subscriptions to 'hot' sites and consulting costs, would pay for themselves after saving just 42 minutes during the recovery effort.

A1C WORLD TRADE CENTER EXPLOSION – 26 FEBRUARY 1993

Background

Everyone is familiar with the tragic event of 9/11, but there are also lessons to be learnt from the earlier attempt on the WTC in 1993.

The World Trade Center in New York City was the second tallest building in the world. Its familiar twin towers were each 110 storeys tall, seven floors underground, seven buildings in the complex that covered 16 acres. There were 2000 parking spaces underground. The complex contained more than 1000 businesses and eight retail tenants. Some 50 000 workers were employed in the complex and there were 80 000 visitors daily. The WTC was home to 350 firms including commodity exchanges, two major brokerage firms, banks, law firms, a major hotel and a shopping mall. The twin towers alone contained 70 000 phone and data communications lines.

Problems

Many fire safety systems that are routine in office buildings were exempted by New York: no emergency lights in the stairwells; no pressurized fire stairwells to seal them from the rest of the building. New York sets its own standards for high-rise skyscrapers . . . most of the rest of the nation builds skyscrapers to uniform engineering standards. Pipes were broken, causing flooding in the basement and all generators shorted out.

The explosion

The bomb contained 1200 pounds of explosives and was triggered by nitro-glycerine. It had been smuggled in inside a van and there appeared to be no difficulty in getting the bomb placed in the WTC. Terrorist involvement was indicated although the target of attack was uncertain. There was immediate concern for 'copycat' activities.

The bomb took out all security. The bomb in B-2 in the parking garage created a crater 100 feet wide and down through four floors of concrete. Columns supporting the towers and hotel were damaged. Structural supports had to be reinforced. All emergency lighting and all power were lost. All 250 elevators were inoperative. The underground train station sustained damage. Over 50 000 people had to be evacuated, there were five deaths and more than 1000 injuries.

The explosion was, at the time, the largest single emergency response in United States history:

- 45% of the entire New York Fire Department on-duty staff and over 700 police officers and federal agents were utilized. 170 ambulances responded to the scene.
- 2000 personnel were counselled for stress.
- Reconstruction cost was estimated at $300 million.
- Business interruption costs to Port Authority (the owners) and other business were estimated at an additional $185 million.

Outcome

It was considered that it could take a month just to figure out what needed to be done. At the time 350 businesses were disrupted. Disaster declarations began within one hour of the incident. Many companies were forced to reroute information systems and telecommunications to alternative sites. Most firms did not lose any data and were able to resume operations by Monday morning. Large tenants, such as Dean Witter who employed 5000 personnel, did not have a problem because they had a contingency plan and alternative offices in New York.

Comdisco Disaster Recovery Services (since acquired by SunGard), with bases in Illinois, New Jersey, and elsewhere in the USA, accepted three customers totalling 615 employees – the Bank of California and two large Japanese banks. In addition to the Coffee, Sugar and Cocoa Exchange, SunGard Recovery Services had five customers declare disasters. Tower 2 was still closed 31 days after the incident.

Considerations

Many office workers fled to the stairwells. Some huddled together by windows to await help. Fire fighters arrived two hours after the blast. Some of the workers, after several days, were still coughing black mucous. People believed it could happen anywhere and at anytime. The complex is so huge, it is questionable how a bomb could be prevented. Nevertheless, questions arose:

- Why was it so easy to get the bomb into the car park?
- Why did both WTC power systems fail?
- How well prepared were telecommunication organizations in New York City?
- How well prepared were WTC tenants in the event of a disaster?

Client reactions

It was hard to believe, during the contingency planning process, that the WTC would ever be brought to its knees!

Problem was we didn't acknowledge, in our contingency plan, what was really required to make the problem transparent to our customers.

I was more worried about having a copy of my résumé at home [as opposed to in my desk] ... upon returning from lunch and seeing smoke billowing from the WTC.

Lessons

Harsh lessons were learnt:

- Security in all critical areas of WTC needed to be increased.
- Relocate primary/backup power systems in WTC.
- Install battery-powered lighting in stairwells.

Whether you are trapped in an 11-storey office building in New York or a seven-storey hotel in Omaha, there are basic things that can be done to protect oneself:

- Learn two escape routes, even in the dark.
- Make sure smoke detectors, sprinklers, emergency lights are there and working.
- In an emergency, head for fire exits, closing doors behind you to slow the spread of fire and smoke.
- Before opening a door, feel it with the back of your hand and, if the door is hot, use an alternative exit.
- Crawl low under smoke, clearer air is near the floor.
- Never use an elevator.
- Develop more comprehensive disaster recovery plans that will include the actions to be taken by fire, bomb disposal, police and other public safety organizations.
- Existing disaster recovery plans must be regularly updated and emergency relocation strategies must be developed and tested.

A1D   HURRICANE ANDREW, MIAMI – 24 AUGUST 1992

Background

Grand Metropolitan Information Services managed three data centres providing IT services and facilities to the Grand Metropolitan Group Companies. [Editor's note: Following continued business developments and mergers, this organization is now Diageo.] One data centre was in the UK and the other two were located in Minneapolis and Miami.

Disaster recovery plans had been developed in the UK over the previous two years and fully tested a number of times. Based on this work, similar projects had been implemented in the USA. The last dry test for the Miami data centre had been carried out at the hot site in March 1992 so there was a certain level of preparedness when Hurricane Andrew struck Miami in August.

Preparation

Because there was some advance warning of the hurricane's arrival a planning meeting was initiated on 23 August, the system was backed up, gracefully disabled, and the recovery site was put on notice of disaster declaration. Although they were prepared there were many surprises.

The enormity of the disaster had not been comprehended. It was a personal as well as a physical disaster for employees. Many employees lost their homes and this became their priority rather than the company losses. The scale of personal issues therefore impacted the recovery timescales.

Cellular phones proved very inadequate for communication. Ground transportation problems were enormous. The scale of the disaster caused unreal competition for recovery resources. Vendors and suppliers responded beyond expectations and the staff response was outstanding.

Hurricane Andrew arrived in Miami on Monday morning, 24 August 1992. A disaster was formally declared and a control centre set up at an alternative company site in Minneapolis. Attempts were made to move system backups to the recovery site in Seattle but ground transportation problems made this impossible. They were eventually dispatched on 25 August.

Even the helicopters being used for transportation purposes encountered problems. They were being given directions using landmarks in and around Miami. Many of the 'landmarks' no longer existed in a recognizable form.

BMS-CAT were hired to assess damage and their initial report on 26 August indicated a recovery timescale of 'a few weeks'. On 26 August the National Guard was moved in and a curfew between 07:00 and 19:00 declared, which caused further logistical problems.

All mainframe processing was eventually transferred back to the restored data centre in Miami by 31 October, two months after the incident.

Lessons

Grand Met got a lot right but also learnt a few things:

- Prior investment in DRP is essential to a recovery capability.
- Ability to provide out-of-area resources is essential.
- You can't overprepare – discipline is critical.
- Expect the unexpected – it will happen.
- Good communications are very difficult – but absolutely essential.
- Time zones and status updates pose special problems.
- Although recovery procedures for mainframe systems were well established those for distributed systems (PCs/LANs) were not so secure.
- Be more proactive:

  - Consider hot site as off-site vault for recovery purposes.
  - There will be more cooperation and less resistance to DRP now.
  - The disaster highlighted a critical need for business continuity plans.

Hurricane Andrew's toll

The scale of the disaster is hard to imagine:

- 38 deaths in South Florida.
- 175 000 homeless in South Florida.
- 25 000 homes destroyed; 100 000 homes damaged.
- 1.3 million homes and businesses were without power immediately after the storm.
- 700 000 people were evacuated from the area.
- 80 000 people were housed in temporary shelters.
- 7800 businesses were affected.
- 22 000 federal troops were deployed; it was the largest US military rescue operation ever.
- $20 billion in damages.

- $10 billion in clean-up costs.
- $7.3 billion in insurance claims.
- $1.04 billion loss to agriculture.

When faced with a disaster of this scale, no plan can handle everything – but a good plan will provide a sound basis for recovery and allow flexibility for some improvisation 'on the night'!

A1E   CHICAGO FLOODS – 13 APRIL 1992

Background

One of the features of the Chicago downtown infrastructure is the freight tunnels running beneath the city, constructed in 1904 to enable merchandise, coal and trash to be moved around. They were also designed to reduce the amount of traffic above ground. The tunnels are 60 miles long, seven feet high by six feet wide and 50 feet below ground. They had been unused since 1959, but were later used to house power, phone and TV cables. The tunnels run under the river at several points.

At 05:57 the first reports of building flooding were received, followed by several additional reports by 09:00. It was originally thought to be a water main or sewer break. Then a whirlpool was sighted in the river and sonar confirmed a car-sized hole into the tunnel system. It was thought that the hole was created by construction activities nearby.

Water was rising in subbasements at the rate of two feet an hour. City, Army Corps and contractors worked to try to slow or stop the leak. Some 250 million gallons of flood water were estimated. The leak was still active on the Saturday with a wide variety of reports on status and repair time estimates being received.

Impact

At least 200 buildings were without power; 250000 people were sent home from work; 21 square blocks were affected; $40 million per day was lost in productivity; and the cost impact was estimated at $1.5 billion.

The regional headquarters for computer equipment of a large European bank were based in Chicago. A US leased line network connects the branches. A disaster recovery plan existed for the IT systems. The plan had been tested three times over the previous six months. No plans existed for business recovery at any site.

Events

Morning news gave the first reports of the incident. Disaster alert was declared and building evacuation notification given at 10:30. Operations personnel arrived at the alternative backup processing site by 12:00 and began the system rebuild.

Key staff were routed to a nearby restaurant and an initial strategy meeting was held. An operational area was established by 15:30. Customers were notified of the situation and phone notification was used for funds transfer. By the following Wednesday night all work was up to date. However, the leak in the tunnel system had still not been plugged so it was decided to remain at the recovery site. Systems were eventually reloaded at the home site on 25 April and the disaster situation 'stood down' on 26 April, 13 days after the incident.

Post-mortems were held and a business recovery project was reprioritized. An initial meeting with the insurance carrier was held.

What went right

The existing IT recovery plan held up and was reinforced. An off-site operation was successfully established and business losses minimized. Team play by all units provided excellent experience and corporate politics were avoided.

What went wrong

There was an obvious critical need for a business recovery plan. Communications difficulties with non-key personnel were experienced due to lack of up-to-date information.

Reflections

Business recovery plans quickly became a high priority for all sites. Specific plans were needed for PC system recoveries. A review of the insurance policy was needed. Senior management awareness of potential losses became acute.

A1F THIRTY SECONDS OF TERROR!
THE CALIFORNIA EARTHQUAKE

Background

1993 was a peak year for disasters in Southern California with:

- The Rodney King trial and verdict which ignited into the LA civil disturbances
- The firestorms in the Malibu and Pasadena areas
- The mudslides in Malibu and Ventura Canyons caused by fires.

1994 began with the earthquake on 17 January.

All catastrophes, natural or manmade, can and will destroy people, property and businesses. Earthquakes, of all natural disasters are the most devastating! We do not know when they will happen, how long they will last or how severe they will be and they impact that which is most dear to us – our home, family and security.

Imagine for a moment an event so enormous in its destruction that its damage cost £30 billion. This is what the majority of LA County survived. Anyone can survive a large magnitude disaster if you know what to do before, during and after.

It has been determined that in some places the ground actually leapt 12 feet. The Santa Monica and Santa Susana mountains are now 15 inches higher and 7–9 inches closer to the ocean because of the quake.

A personal view

At 04:30 on Monday 17 January I woke to the radio alarm. At 04:31 I thought our world and our lives had ended. The house moved in every direction possible, finally being slammed down with such a force that it drove me so deep into our water bed that I couldn't rise.

After what seemed like an eternity but what was in reality only 10–30 seconds, the violent shaking quit. After dressing we grabbed the portable radio and flashlight, which we keep on hand for such emergencies, before we left the house. All this took a couple of minutes during which time the first of many strong aftershocks hit.

Staying outside until dawn, I checked the outside of the house for cracks, gas leaks or any other kind of leak and backed the car out of the garage. After a few minutes in which the initial tremours and immediate aftershocks subsided, I re-entered the house and picked some items of importance like household papers, some jewellery, a video of the house contents, food, water, change of clothes and *money*! I put all this into the boot of the car where we also keep an emergency preparedness kit for travel. This was in case we had to evacuate the area.

After dawn I again checked the house and found some water leaks, which I was able to fix. I tried to call family members to let them know we were all right but all out-of-state phone circuits were shut down. We were one of the fortunate ones having water, gas, intermittent telephone service, shelter and food. The only thing we lacked was power.

About now I figured I had better check with work. After several tries I finally got through to the office and got the recorded message. I was able to find out that the office had some minimal damage and the company was requesting if possible for all employees to report to work in casual clothing for clean-up duty the following day.

The damage in the office consisted of a broken water pipe on the third floor which had soaked some non-essential documents. A few personal computers were thrown to the floor, none of which was severely damaged, and what seemed like tons of paper documents were spilled all over the floor. When the quake hit, the backup generators kicked in and the end-users never noticed any problems. Two hours after the quake the system was back on normal power and working as though nothing had ever happened. By Wednesday morning the whole complex was back to business as usual.

The calling tree had been invoked but the vice president in charge of the data processing operation was unavailable because his home was closer to the epicentre and had received considerable interior damage. The data processing manager who lives two blocks from me had little damage but could not get in as our area was cut off because of the freeway damage.

Our power was returned early Tuesday morning and for the first time we could turn on the TV and see the total damage this quake had caused. All the exits from our valley had been damaged and we were physically landlocked.

During work that first week we experienced two severe back-to-back aftershocks. By now the seismology people had calculated over 250 aftershocks, which they were considering normal. They also calculated that we could expect the number of aftershocks to reach in the tens of thousands during the coming year.

Friday of that first week was like a mass exodus from LA. It looked like anybody and everybody who could was packing up all their belongings and leaving the state.

Situation status

The situation was initially chaotic:

- Large portions of major freeways were closed because of severe damage and several of the secondary roads were opening and closing because of the aftershocks.

- Santa Monica freeway at the damaged point was levelled and cleaned up within the first 72 hours.
- A 64-car freight train had derailed, spilling toxic chemicals.
- Four vehicles travelling along the freeway were caught on an island with a 90-foot drop in front and a 60-foot drop behind.
- Utilities were disrupted from day one. Gas and water lines ruptured. Water and gas were temporarily repaired within the first 48 hours but it was estimated to take six months to do the jobs permanently.
- Power stations and lines were destroyed.

Summary

People whose homes were destroyed and who were sleeping in open areas were given food and water, and several shelters were open within the first 24 hours.

Insurance companies had plans in place whereby claims representatives were out and set up for claims aid and assistance within the first two hours after the quake. It was estimated that over 230 000 victims filed insurance claims. It is hard to estimate the number of people who had losses and did not have insurance.

Within the first 72 hours the government and Federal Management Agency approved loans and aid at $6.6 billion.

Several people needed psychological help following their traumatic experiences.

Only 57 deaths were attributed to the quake, while over 400 were injured. These are small numbers when you look at the devastation caused by the quake.

Key issues learnt

You can learn a lot from experience! We found out:

- You can survive a large magnitude catastrophic event if you as individuals prepare.
- Federal and local government must prepare as they did in California.
- Government must mobilize quickly and react quickly to the need of the victims. This saves lives and property and helps people in coping.
- Business must plan and be prepared for catastrophic events.
- Insurance must be on hand to settle claims quickly and equitably.
- Government must spend more on per person protection.

Our greatest enemy may not be Mother Nature, but rather human nature. Will we soon forget our present earthquake concerns? Or will we take the necessary action to properly plan and prepare? If you stay prepared and learn from these events you can and will survive any catastrophic event.

A1G AFTER THE FIRE – FIRST INTERSTATE BANK, LOS ANGELES

Background

On the evening of 4 May 1988 the nightmare began for the tallest building west of the Mississippi river. The 62-storey First Interstate Bank building in Los Angeles, California, was ablaze.

At 22:37 the Los Angeles Fire Department's Operation Communication Dispatch Section (OCD) received three separate 911 calls from persons reporting a fire on the upper floors of the First Interstate building. At 22:38 the initial fire companies were dispatched. While en route the battalion chief observed and reported a large 'loom-up' in the general area of the bank building. On arrival at the scene he requested an additional 15 fire companies and five chief officers. The firemen fought the fire successfully and confined it to five floors of the 62-storey building. Even so, the fire had caused multimillions of dollars damage, the water damage was extensive and the smoke contamination was almost total.

One only has to pause for a moment to realize the catastrophic results that a fire such as this would cause to one of the largest banking corporations in America. In just a matter of hours their corporate headquarters, and one of their main banks, is shut down, totally out of service. All employees, computers and day-to-day operations conducted in this building are terminated for an undetermined period of time. How would your company handle such a situation?

Solutions

In this case the costs were minimized because the First Interstate Bank Corporation had a plan. Within minutes after arriving on the scene, the bank management initiated their disaster plan. Their plan took into account catastrophic events such as earthquakes, fires and other types of disasters that could affect the bank's operations. The main objective was to get the bank back into service as soon as possible.

Blackmon-Mooring-Steamatic Catastrophic Incorporated (BMS-CAT, whose headquarters are located in Fort Worth, Texas) was contacted immediately and had supervisors on the scene by 07:00 the following morning. BMS-CAT had one specific goal – to put the building in a pre-fire condition, and this would be tough. They had a 62-storey building with five storeys totally destroyed by fire and the entire building had major contamination from the products of combustion.

Cleaning up after a disaster is nothing new to BMS-CAT. The first major job for the Catastrophic Division of BMS was the clean-up of the Las Vegas Hilton after a fire in 1981. Since that time they have cleaned up after floods, fires, earthquakes and other types of large disasters in the US and Canada.

Initially the parking garage of the bank building was used as a command post where a taskforce was set up with major logistical responsibilities. One of the many obstacles facing BMS-CAT was the restoration of an estimated 7000 items of electronic data processing equipment. This equipment ranged from small personal computers up to mainframe computers and printers. Priority one equipment was pre-identified in the bank's plans as for immediate restoration. Priority two was equipment that could be restored as they got to it.

A service centre was set up on the 27th floor. Over 200 technicians were hired to clean equipment. Each piece of electronic data processing equipment was taken completely apart and cleaned. After the equipment was reassembled it was given to a representative of the company that serviced that brand for inspection and recertification. There was a less than 5% failure rate for the reassembled equipment. Hundreds of thousands of floppy disks were salvaged by being vacuumed and wiped clean with special materials.

Another obstacle in the cleaning process was the monumental amount of paper materials that had to be sifted through and cleaned. Bank personnel felt sure that the documents in their major vaults would be safe from contamination, but upon opening the vault, they found out differently. It seemed that there was no place safe from the smoke contamination. Thousands and thousands of pieces of paper of all kinds had to be gone through. Each and every shelf, filing cabinet, vault and drawer throughout the building had every paper removed.

After all this was taken care of, the real clean-up effort started. During the reconstruction security consisted of a metal detector and off-duty Los Angeles police officers. All employees were screened daily as they went in and out of the building for the entire 12 weeks that clean-up crews were on site.

On 12 September 1988 the First Interstate Bank was reopened, more than four months after the fire. Due to appropriate planning on the part of the bank the disruption to their operation was kept to a minimum. Why? Because they had a plan.

A1H ONE MERIDIAN PLAZA, PHILADELPHIA

Background

A major high-rise office building fire occurred on Saturday 23 February 1991 in Philadelphia, which resulted in fire extension to nine floors, severe structural damage to the 38-storey building, injuries to 24 and the death of three firefighters. During the $18^1/_2$-hour effort to control the blaze, the firefighting activities were hampered by the loss of electrical power, including emergency power and inadequate firehose pressure to suppress the fire. As a result the fire was able to spread from the 22nd floor to the 29th floor with practically no resistance.

The structure at One Meridian Plaza is a 38-storey modern office building rising 491 feet above the streets of downtown Philadelphia. Located directly across from City Hall, at one of the busiest intersections in the city, the building was constructed in 1972 at a cost of $40 million.

Generally the floors were arranged with enclosed offices along three perimeter walls. Between these private offices and the building's core there was usually a large, open, unobstructed office work area, subdivided with five-foot high dividers between workstations. The roof of the building is equipped with two helicopter landing pads that would become vital during the fire.

The building was equipped with a manual and an automatic fire alarm system. Smoke detectors, heat detectors and manual pull stations were installed on every floor. The activation of the alarm system provided an audible alarm signal throughout the building. An audible and visual alarm signal would also sound at both the security guard station and the annunciator panel on the ground floor. An automatic transmission of the alarm would also be sent to a central monitoring station in the city.

The fire

This fire was a prime example of Murphy's law and would have presented the ultimate challenge to the resources, training, experience and equipment of any major fire department. A total force of over 400 firefighters, 51 engine companies, 11 ladder companies, 21 chief officers, nine medical units and 14 specialized apparatus was deployed on this incident.

The fire started in a perimeter office near a central window on the 22nd floor. It began by spontaneous combustion from rags that were contaminated by linseed oil, left by contractors who were restoring a large section of wooden panelling. Once ignited, the fire quickly spread into the open ceiling area and continued freely along the top of the unprotected open floor plan.

Very early on in the fire the door to the electrical room on the 22nd floor burned completely away. This immediately destroyed the ducts for both the primary and secondary electrical supply for the building. At 20:23 the fire alarm system in the building notified personnel of an apparent problem on the 22nd floor. Simultaneously, a telephone call was received from the central alarm monitoring company to inform One Meridian Plaza personnel of an alarm activation.

Neither the building personnel nor the monitoring company bothered to notify the fire department. Instead a building maintenance worker determined from the alarm annunciator panel the location of the alarm signal and went to investigate. When the elevator doors opened he was confronted with dense smoke and heat. The security guards were able to override the elevator controls and bring the maintenance worker safely down to the ground floor. Even at this time no one notified the fire department but instead notified the central monitoring company, which finally notified the fire department after a considerable delay. At 20:27 dispatch ordered four engine companies, two ladder companies and two battalion chiefs to proceed to One Meridian Plaza. At 20:34 a second alarm was requested, based on initial determinations of the first responding officers. While firefighters were preparing their interior attack the fire had already spread to the 23rd floor.

As the firefighters approached the 22nd floor they were confronted with heavy smoke and heat conditions within the stairwell. Stairwell doors were glowing 'cherry red' from the extreme heat. They reported difficulty in forcing the stairwell door open as it had expanded from the heat and was securely locked from the inside. A serious water problem was faced when the 'wet' standpipe system did not deliver adequate water. Temperature levels on the fire floor of some 2000 degrees precluded any advancement without adequate water supply.

The early failure of the primary and secondary electrical systems and the total failure of the emergency generator to provide any backup power were the most significant inhibiting factors faced by the firefighters. Without elevators, all equipment and manpower had to traverse, vertically, at least 20 floors. All this was in almost total darkness, depending entirely on limited portable lighting. As a result dozens of firefighters spent as much as eight hours in dark, smoke-filled stairwells, repeatedly shuttling hundreds of pounds of equipment up through the entire length of the darkened building.

As the fire spread both horizontally and vertically, by 02:30 a total of 12 alarms and numerous special assistance calls were ordered to assist with this incident. The delayed alarm, severe fire conditions, the failure of the electrical and emergency systems and the critical water pressure problems in the standpipe created what was the ultimate challenge of a high-rise fire into the ultimate nightmare for a fire department.

While these severe logistical problems were affecting the fire-suppression operations, an emergency arose. Two hours into the fire a sector commander ordered that the rooftop doors be opened to 'ventilate the stairwells'. An officer and two firefighters undertook the task to ventilate stairwell number two. For reasons unknown they never reached their objective. They became disorientated and requested permission to enter the office tower and break out a window for some clean air. The following communication from the team indicated that they were 'inside the office tower on the 30th floor'.

While the fire was burning out of control many firefighters risked their lives trying to locate their endangered comrades. Firefighters began a room-by-room search of the 30th floor but found no one. They then moved on to the 31st floor and continued upward to the 38th floor. Simultaneously at 10:53 the Pennstar helicopter was dispatched to pick up a rescue unit of three firefighters and lift them to the roof, to commence another search.

Finally, hours later, a circling helicopter spotted a broken window. The pilot indicated this was on the 28th floor. At 02:30 rescue teams located the fallen fire-fighters and removed them to the medical triage area on the 20th floor. The three missing firefighters had run out of air and suffocated.

Despite these severe and formidable conditions, firefighters continued their valiant attempt to contain the blaze. Finally at 01:30 five hours into the inferno, an employee of the contractor that had installed the standpipe system showed up and located the proper tool to adjust the pressure-reducing valves so that the fire department could start to produce an effective water supply to the firefighters. By this time the fire had engulfed the 23rd, 24th and 25th floors.

The ultimate decision

As dawn broke, the fire was still angry and growing. Concern for the structural integrity of the building increased considerably. This was confirmed by an inde-pendent structural engineer's examination of the damage inflicted on the building. After completing his assessment he informed the incident commanders that there was a very real potential for an internal collapse from the 28th to the 18th floors.

With 280 firefighters inside the building, three dead and 24 injured, at 07:30 Sunday morning, 11 hours into the incident, the fire commissioner ordered all personnel to abandon the building in an orderly evacuation. The fire would free burn for seven hours up through floors 27, 28 and 29 to the 30th where sprinklers would be relied on to stop its spread.

At 03:00 Sunday afternoon, $18\frac{1}{2}$ hours into the incident, the fire was declared 'under control'. Smoke was still rising from the building. No one was allowed to approach or enter it for several days.

Some 12 weeks after the fire, restoration work had still not started. Doubt remained on the integrity of the structure. Immediate and direct losses to the building and its contents were estimated at some $150 million. Litigation was at a staggering $3.2 billion and mounting.

The conclusions

Investigations revealed that the fire originated on the 22nd floor in a private office. Once the fire had ignited it was able to involve other volatile materials contained within the room of origin and soon engulfed its combustible interior furnishings and finish materials.

Although the building was provided with an emergency electrical generator, designed to operate upon main power supply failure, a post-incident investigation determined that this generator did not produce any output voltage. This was the reason for the complete failure of all elevators, lighting, fire alarm, smoke control systems and fire pumps. One of the toughest decisions a fire department incident commander has ever had to make is to order all firefighters to abandon all firefighting and immediately leave the building.

The sprinklers on the 30th floor activated because of heat being transferred to that floor from four principal sources:

- Fire lapped at the outside from the 29th floor and entered the floor through broken windows.
- Fire transmitted through spaces between the floor slab and the glass and granite outer curtain wall.
- There were conduction and heat transfer through the five-inch concrete floor plate.
- Fire and heat also impinged on to the floor through cracks in the floor caused by buckling.

Each of these heat-transfer methods resulted in the ignition of combustibles on the 30th floor. Several ignitions were discovered throughout the floor. All were extinguished by sprinklers.

Significant factors

Some of the key factors influencing the spread of fire and the effect of firefighting efforts were:

- Lack of automatic fire sprinklers on the 22nd floor
- Accelerated growth, development and spread of the fire from the room of origin
- The early loss of the main electrical power supply
- The complete failure of the emergency backup power supply system
- Lack of early warning smoke or heat detection in the area of fire origin

- The effectiveness of fire department-supplied, automatic sprinklers to stop the vertical spread of the fire at the 30th floor
- Building personnel did not call the fire department when the fire alarm system first activated. They decided to investigate first.
- The central control monitoring company did not call the fire department when they received an alarm signal from the building. They instead called the building personnel to verify the alarm.
- No one from inside the building called the fire department. The eventual first call to the fire department was placed by someone outside the building.

The lessons

The facts are outlined above. Take a few minutes to study them carefully and identify lessons that can be applied in your organization.

A1I   THE MERCANTILE FIRE

Background

Churchill Plaza is a 14-storey modern office block in the centre of Basingstoke, Hampshire, UK, housing around 1000 staff with a medium size computer room and large PABX on the ground floor. The basement is used for car parking and a standby generator.

The fire started at 21:40 on Tuesday 16 April 1991 near the eighth floor wiring closet/office equipment area. The fire was detected by smoke sensors, alarms sounded and the fire brigade arrived at 21:46 with three pumps. The fire spread rapidly to the ninth floor and part of the 10th floor by failure of external glazing and strong winds. The number of fire appliances and men engaged increased in several stages, peaking at 30 pumps and 200 men. The fire was fully under control by 04:00 on Wednesday 17 April.

What would you do if you were watching the evening TV news and the reports stated that your office was on fire and it was your responsibility to do something about it?

Major problems

We were faced simultaneously with a number of major problems:

- There was no power, heat or ventilation, and hence no computers.
- Two floors with around 100 PCs were lost. The paper backup documentation was also lost, which meant several departments had no information.
- A lot of equipment was damaged by water from the firefighting activities.
- PC and LAN server backups, kept in desks, were burnt, although a number were retrieved and found to be usable.
- Much of the cabling was damaged.

Initial assessment indicated that the bottom six floors could be made usable within two to three weeks; however, some key functions needed to be working within a few hours. Senior management fatigue began to set in. How could the 900 displaced staff be best employed?

Actions

Here are a few questions to ask yourself as 'contingency' man in the heat of the moment:

- Have you confirmed event and scale? Don't overreact and try to get a second opinion.
- Who has been informed?
- Have the right people been notified?
- The security guard may have told you, as the nearest convenient person, but has he logged the problem, reported it to management, or is he expecting you to do this?
- What action has been taken so far?
- Who will take the decisions?
- Have the fire, police and ambulance been advised?
- Do we have a plan we can use?
- Who has a copy to hand? (It's no good in the vault!)
- Have all staff been evacuated and sent home if necessary? Do not leave hundreds of people milling around, getting in the way.

Actions often have to be based on inadequate information. We have to decide who needs to be involved (as few as possible). The best way of turning a crisis into a disaster is to assemble the full executive team in the foyer for a committee decision! Among the first actions was to establish a chain of command and a command centre.

Selected senior management were able to inspect most of the building at 07:00 on Wednesday morning. The eighth and ninth floors were gutted and the 10th floor partially damaged. On the seventh floor there was serious smoke and water damage and the sixth floor downwards was heavily water damaged (the computer room false floor was floating!), hence there was no power, heat or light, and water was still running down walls. The main structure of the building appeared to have survived in good condition.

Some advice

As we progressed, we found things out that we can share with you:

- Having determined who takes what decisions, make sure there is a cross-checking process. Try to communicate simple messages.
- Beware of Rambos making dynamic decisions, especially if this can risk life and limb. (Some managers feel they must be seen to be dynamic – try to harness this energy by getting them to organize a soup kitchen/mobile canteen!)
- If you have a plan, great! If not, establish a modus operandi.
- Ensure accurate feedback from emergency services re current status, keep up to date with their chain of command. They may also require information from you.
- It is essential to appoint a good PR/press officer to respond to press/TV coverage that is inevitably exaggerated and inaccurate. Harness the help of the local radio station to keep staff/local residents briefed on current status.

- Call staff, using a cascade principle via normal chain of management. To achieve this will need up-to-date home telephone numbers, which must be readily accessible.
- Establish a help desk, maybe two, one for customers and one for staff. If you don't the switchboard will be swamped!
- Start to evaluate the likely impact on the business.
- Do you need to activate third party contingency suppliers (e.g. salvage companies, mobile computer room suppliers)? It may be worth contacting them to put them on notice of potential need.
- Set up project teams and get the key decision-makers to meet regularly.
- Discourage other staff from turning up to help (everyone wants to join in the boys' own adventure, especially the guy who forgot to back up his PC yesterday!).

Positive factors

It was not all gloom. There were some positive factors in our favour:

- The main computer centre in North London was unaffected although switching of data communications was problematic.
- The branch network and Northern Processing Centre in Manchester was unaffected (all Churchill Plaza voice traffic was switched to Manchester from 08:00 on the Wednesday by BT and their call rate increased from 1000 per day to 3000 per day).
- A local office two miles away with communication links was used as a command centre and enabled 40–50 key staff to be working by the Wednesday lunchtime.
- We had plenty of spare office space and computer equipment was available locally in Basingstoke.
- TV and radio coverage ensured there were plenty of offers of help; however, responding to these offers, sorting out the cowboys, does take a lot of management time.
- As the fire occurred at night there were no staff injuries.
- Parts of the ground floor were just about habitable and the PABX worked on standby power.

Assistance from vendors

The timescales set were very ambitious, asking for items, which normally take three months to arrive, to be delivered and installed within four to six days:

- Acceptable, vacant, local office space (although in three locations) was found and signed up within 24 hours.
- BT provided 50 mobile phones and several FAXs within hours. They located and installed a PABX extension in the main temporary building and delivered multiple kilostream links within five days.
- Computer suppliers gave priority with orders for equipment, which started arriving in hours rather than days.
- Local companies installed voice/data mains cabling at breakneck speed (one building for 250 people was completed within 48 hours.

The loss adjuster insisted on a lengthy cleaning process for all the salvaged terminals and PCs. With excellent assistance from the suppliers/maintainers several cleaning 'production lines' were set up at their locations. Despite this several hundred vital terminals and PCs were lost for between one to two weeks, while the dismantling, cleaning, reassembling and test procedures were followed through.

Vendor relationships

We received an excellent response from the key vendors. Some of this may have been motivated by the sudden sales opportunity in the middle of a recession, but most did appear to be a genuine desire to help an 'old friend'. But it is useful to have the home telephone number of your account manager to be able to ring him at 2 am!

You need to have a good level of trust to handle major purchases over the phone and agree free loan of equipment if you will be unable to pay for a few weeks. However, with the pressure of the urgent situation there is insufficient time to negotiate discounts. A number of suppliers' staff were extremely helpful over and above the call of duty. Letters of thanks were obviously forwarded to their senior management.

What went well

The contingency plan was up to date and accessible (probably luck in that they were due to do one of their twice yearly tests the following weekend). Staff enthusiasm, and their willingness to work in difficult conditions, made a huge difference to recovery. We succeeded in reassuring staff that the building was now safe by sending a video to each staff member's home address.

Rapid PR response enabled damage limitation to public image, especially when the competition was mischief making!

Lessons learnt

These are a few lessons we can pass on:

- Don't keep PC backups in the desk drawers or filing cabinets.
- Do have an up-to-date directory of home telephone numbers of key staff readily to hand.
- Avoid day-to-day use of important documents, use photocopies instead.
- Have easily accessible copies of up-to-date site plans, plans of cable runs, power distribution, etc.
- A hot standby computer system is not a lot of use if the end-users have no terminals or telephones (or desks to put them on!).
- Don't underestimate the damage water can cause (much of the cabling started failing two to three weeks after it was back in use due to corrosion). It would have been best to replace it from day one.
- You may need to appoint a loss assessor from day one to negotiate on an equal basis with the loss adjuster.
- Maintain a clear desk policy – large amounts of paperwork left lying around can fuel a fire.
- Beware of overenthusiasm – the same microfilm library duplication was ordered at least twice!
- Develop a modular contingency plan so that the right components can be quickly assembled for a number of different scenarios, as the response will vary depending on the type of incident.

Summary

We hope you never suffer a similar experience. If you do, recovery will be greatly helped by a few basic principles:

- Do have a plan, if only a simple, general purpose one.
- Do determine a simple chain of command.
- Keep a copy of the plan and list of home phone numbers at home/in the car.
- When a fire/disaster happens you don't normally have time to plan, and if you don't determine who does what beforehand, abject chaos will occur very quickly!

A1J   HOW FLOODS CAN RUIN YOUR DAY: LONDON COLLEGE OF PRINTING

Background

The following study tells the story of a disaster and its consequences at the London College of Printing. In addition to the events themselves, several major issues are raised about the role of the manager whose organization is faced with a disaster and how this relates to the role of the disaster management organization.

The London Institute is the largest education organization of its type in Europe, embracing art, design, fashion, distribution and communication. The London Institute was formed in January 1986 when seven colleges, including the London College of Printing, were brought together to form a new major national centre of excellence with the unique feature of providing courses at all levels from apprentice to PhD. The Institute has a major task ahead in improving its range of services to students in the complex inner city environment but work has begun on consolidating and improving upon their building and hostels.

The background to the disaster that occurred at the London College of Printing has to be seen in the transfer of responsibility from the Inner London Education Authority (ILEA) to the London Institute and the College. In spite of the Authority's well-publicized limitations, much of what happened to the College from the early 1980s onwards was out of the Authority's hands. The Authority suffered a severe shortage of funds and this in particular had led to the neglect of the buildings and maintenance under its control, culminating in an enormous backlog of building and maintenance problems for the new college. Even where maintenance was carried out priority was given to schools. Examples of neglect included no window cleaning taking place for five years, long intervals between checks on such things as water, and the building had not been painted for 10 years.

The London Institute began its responsibility for the buildings by taking it on centrally. The management of the College in an education sense was the responsibility of the Head of College but all building matters were handled by the Institute, who in turn handed regular maintenance to a contract company. They also instituted a series of health and safety checks including checking the water system. As a result of such a check in September 1989 the following events unfolded.

The London College of Printing had to close down after Legionella bacteria was found in the water system in October 1989. The closure lasted a week, but major flooding followed on the refilling of the water tanks located on the top of the 14-storey building. There were two header tanks and the water supply was not stopped until both were full (determined by a non-return valve cutting off the water supply). A faulty non-return valve led to both tanks continuing to fill . . . and overflow. The top seven floors were badly damaged. These floors housed courses with very expensive equipment, including film, photography, radio and print journalism. The problem was compounded by the presence of asbestos ceiling tiles, which seriously contaminated the top five floors. These had to be removed by specialists and the floors needed to be extensively refurbished.

Lessons

The best advice that can be given to managers faced with disasters is very clear – 'don't have them'. Unfortunately this is not always possible and it becomes a matter of damage minimization and ensuring the efficient operation of the organization in the meantime. In calling in a disaster management company half of this problem disappeared, leaving the College free to concentrate on reorganizing their internal activities, confident that the other matters were in safe hands.

The initial impact of disasters inevitably provokes the best sort of 'blitz' response from all concerned. When things have settled and the extent of damage and disruption becomes clear, management must be alert to morale problems that may surface among staff and make sure the response is clear, effective and communicated within their organization.

It is essential that management deals quickly and effectively with questions from, and decisions relating to, those dealing with the crisis, from the disaster management company through to builders, equipment specialists and insurance loss adjusters. The early identification of an individual within the organization able to deal with those companies, and make decisions on major issues, is a further essential step in ensuring disruption is minimized.

A1K FLOOD HIGHLIGHTS

Some miscellaneous examples of floods follow.

In Scandinavia, after a prolonged drought, they had 50 cm of rain in two hours. A hillside stream flooded and 200 cubic metres of water entered a company building, lifting a 20 cm-thick concrete floor 50 cm. The torrent broke down two steel doors and wrecked the communications and tape storage areas. In the computer room, a moisture detector went and a steel door caved in, pushing modem racks across the room towards the operators. Power and UPS were lost. There was 1 cm of mud on the floor. The whole incident took under 15 minutes. A damage management company was called and arrived in half an hour.

The Road Research Laboratory had a retaining wall, which had been built to keep rainwater from the computer room. The next time it rained hard a pool of water formed by the retaining wall, which collapsed. The water surged towards the computer room. Unfortunately a delivery was expected and the doors were open. The room was flooded!

In Chicago a data centre had been located on the 15th floor to avoid flooding from the adjacent Hudson river. Freak weather conditions caused water from the Hudson to be siphoned up through the toilets, flooding the building (including the data centre) from the top floor downwards.

In a public sector organization, a sewage pipe ran through the roof void above the false ceiling of the computer room housing a PABX. It blocked. Dynarod was called in to clear it on a Friday and did so, but the pressure had caused an unnoticed fracture to the pipe. Over the weekend sewage seeped into the roof void. Eventually the ceiling collapsed and the sewage fell . . . into the PABX fan!

In Chicago the Household Finance Corporation had fish swimming in the data centre when nine inches of rain fell in eight hours, causing water tables to rise and drains to blow back.

A UK insurance company was holding a party to celebrate the opening of their new disaster recovery standby facility. At the same time flash floods took their main data centre off the air! They fortunately resolved the problem without having to invoke their brand new disaster recovery centre.

In a utility company, following rain after a dry spell the ceiling of the computer room was found leaking in several places, leaks also went into the engineer's and the plant rooms. Equipment was covered in polythene sheets. A temporary tent roof was built over the existing flat roof of the one-storey block while a new roof was built. It took three months to complete the work. There were no contingency plans and during the three months the computer system had to be powered down each time it rained!

At the *East Anglian Daily Times* in Ipswich, UK, a heating engineer was working in the roof on a Sunday afternoon when he damaged a sprinkler pipe which dumped 30 000 gallons of water in 20 minutes, flooding the editorial suite and ruining £250 000 ($435 000) of production systems.

A computer aided design system was giving trouble with workstation screen flicker – a real problem, since a high level of accuracy was required. The problems ceased when the rail company went on strike: the flicker had been caused by power disturbances or bad connections becoming acute when trains were passing.

Some years ago the editor appeared with fellow BC professionals Dave Allen and David Frost on a live TV programme about business continuity planning. As Dave Allen was getting into his stride, reading from autocue, up came . . . garbage. Fortunately the corruption only lasted a sentence! Did we have a contingency plan? Of course – wing it!

A1L   A CAUTIONARY TALE

Lightning can strike twice

On two separate occasions within two rather grey December weeks in 1991 the Union Bank of Finland (UBF) computer facilities were put out of action.

In their city office they employ some 90 people in the provision of wholesale banking activities, involving corporate banking, trade finance, shipping, property and syndication and project finance, some retail and electronic banking activities, and the full range of treasury products, as well as Finnish capital market operations. So, like any other risk management business, they are dependent upon a reliable means of controlling, recording, processing, reporting and monitoring substantial volumes of data, as well as being able to access their database at any moment.

Central to their ability to do this successfully is their AS/400 computer. They had always had backup procedures of some sort. However, on reappraising their recovery plan in late 1991, they came to the conclusion that they needed to do things much better, in order to have an acceptable degree of certainty of being able to recover their computing facilities and database within 24 hours and return to normal operations within 36 hours.

In the autumn of 1991 they developed a full-scale disaster recovery programme. As it was to turn out, their timing was immaculate! On Monday 9 December 1991 at 11:23 the AS/400 system, together with all the peripheral equipment in the computer suite, unexplainably lost power, and simply closed down. It didn't take long to discover what the problem was: the water board had been carrying out maintenance work on the mains in the road outside the building and had accidentally fractured a mains pipe. The escaping water finally worked its way through the foundations of the building, and leaked into the basement directly on top of the uninterruptible power supply (UPS) unit, ruining it in the process.

The recovery centre was placed on standby, and the morning save of the data library, together with the most recent systems saves, were retrieved from the off-site security storage centre. At 14:15 the Fire Service began to pump out the basement, and make the area safe. This process was to take two hours, after which UBF were hoping to receive a visit from their UPS maintenance people to inspect the damage.

At 17:10 the UPS maintenance representative finally confirmed that they would not be able to inspect the equipment and give appropriate advice until the following morning. Since they could see for themselves that the UPS was in any case useless, it was decision time! UBF decided to invoke their recovery plan.

At 17:35 the operations team left for the recovery site taking with them all the necessary tapes and equipment, and began loading the system. Remote links were established between the bank and recovery site. By 04:00 on Tuesday morning the system was completely restored. So within 18 hours they were up and running again. Immediately thereafter they began to input Monday's and Tuesday's daily work and this continued throughout the day. All relevant documentation and reports were transferred by taxi between the bank and the recovery site, but then it was realized that courier bikes moved much more rapidly through the traffic; after that they found that one of their messengers travelling on the tube train (subway) was even quicker, confirming yet again the old adage that money is not the answer to everything!

Some 25 hours after invoking the disaster recovery plan they were almost back to normal. This continued for the rest of the week, while repairs were being undertaken at the bank. During the following weekend a transformer was installed to smooth the power supply at the bank. By the Monday the system was live again at the bank, the links to the recovery site were cut and disaster recovery status removed.

On the Tuesday the MIS supervisor left for the recovery site to remove the system from their machines and disconnect. At 10:15 that morning one of the disk drives on the AS/400 at the bank froze, stopping all input! As a precaution the supervisor at the recovery site was told not to clear down the system, but to restore the morning save of the data library.

The stoppage had nothing to do with any of the previous difficulties. It turned out to be the result of a broken solenoid, which is just about as unlikely an event as the flood that caught them out in the first place. Later that afternoon the drive was fixed, with no loss of data and all users began to input the current day's work. However, as we all know too well, reassurance, if not actual complacency, is often the mother of big trouble, and only minutes later, disaster struck again!

An unexplained drop in power was followed immediately by a huge electricity surge. It subsequently turned out that despite their best efforts to rectify the previous damage, a loose neutral wire in the fuse box had not been repaired. The effect was to completely destroy the power supplies to all racks, two disk drives and the processor. The popping and crackling noises lasted for a full 10 seconds and they knew they were witnessing the complete destruction of their primary facilities. This hardly seemed a fair reward for all their efforts, and confirmed that lightning does strike twice!

On the Wednesday, with a somewhat weary sense of déjà vu they again invoked their disaster recovery process. By first thing that morning the system was ready for input, and all remote links re-established to the recovery site. Everybody by now was getting pretty tired and fed up, but they were enormously encouraged by the fact that they were able to provide to the bank a virtually uninterrupted service, to the extent that a lot of people didn't even realize that there had been a second disaster.

On the following Friday the new UPS was delivered and installed, and the system restored at the bank over the weekend. By the Monday morning they were completely restored and up to date again, and finally stood down from the recovery situation, this time without any further mishaps.

Lessons

You may consider that one disaster is a misfortune, but two in succession is beginning to sound like carelessness! In the comprehensive post-mortem that was carried out to assess how things had gone, one or two conclusions were reached:

- The time and money spent in devising a well-thought-out plan had justified itself many times over. The recovery process had gone very well, since in spite of the complete collapse of the computer facilities, they had remained in business throughout, and continued to be able to manage the financial risks involved.
- They had not intended that the first disaster should be a practice for the second! However, the greater speed and efficiency of the recovery on the second occasion demonstrated only too clearly the absolute importance of rehearsal, for the purpose of confirming the logistics of the exercise and preparing the people involved.
- Since prevention is better than cure, they reappraised the complete system, looking for the situations that were asking for trouble, such as placing the UPS in a basement liable to flooding. (It's now in the computer room, three floors up!)
- After any sort of crisis involving electrical power failure they will not again assume that all they need to do is to replace the defective part, and simply plug in and switch on. Every part of the system will be checked first.
- Where keeping your business operations running is concerned, it's a myth to suggest that lightning doesn't strike twice! It can – and it does (sometimes known as Murphy's law).

A1M   IT HAPPENED TO THEM

Background

This case study shows how a company with a very small plan survived a major disaster and now has very big plans for the future.

In the early hours of Thursday 4 November 1993, thieves broke into the premises of a printing company in Bermondsey, London, UK. After taking items of office equipment, they started a fire on the second floor, 'probably to cover their tracks', according to local police, who told reporters: 'The firm is virtually wiped out.' The fact that the culprits have since been caught and are serving sentences for arson, offers little consolation.

The premises of a working printer will usually contain highly flammable components alongside the expensive and bulky plant and machinery. Although firefighters battled through the night, by 07:00 the following morning there was nothing left but an empty shell. Added to the loss of the 150-year-old building was the hefty archive of essential information and reference material that any business accumulates over 30 years, here combined with all the records, client specifications and plant recently bought.

Disaster recovery and business continuity had not been part of the company's day-to-day vocabulary. They had enough problems keeping the business going without worrying about things that might never happen. In short they had no plans to cope with the situation facing them on the morning of Guy Fawkes' day. Nevertheless, by 08:00 a temporary office had been set up on the street corner. Production staff were making lists of everything they could remember – clients, work in hand, orders, delivery schedules. Sales staff used mobile phones to ring customers to warn them there had been some slight 'technical problems'. Competitors were contacted to arrange transfer of production to fulfil existing commitments.

By 11:00 operations were being directed from an old coach, parked at the side of the road, with a power line running from a nearby confectionery shop, and, by the following Monday, a temporary office had been established two streets away, with organization of subcontracted production well under way.

In early January the printers were able to commence their own production once more; installation in their own premises was finally completed in May and on 29 June the local MP, Simon Hughes, pressed the button on a new printing press at an open day. This heralded the return to full commercial operation and a future that had looked impossible on that dark November morning 'it's true we had no formal disaster recovery plan,' said one of the co-directors, 'beyond the usual precautions taken by any small business operating reactively. What saved us was the fact that individuals had contingency plans of their own, safeguarding their particular areas of operation. Without them we would certainly have gone under.'

The accounts manager, for example, routinely took home a set of backup tapes for the accounts package and, by chance, had also taken home the books to prepare wages – due to be paid on the day of the fire: 'We thought we had done enough but our contingencies were woefully inadequate.'

The fire and burglary alarm systems were in reasonable condition but proved to have a faulty connection to the BT system. This meant that, although the alarm went off, it did not show up at the local police station – a failure that might have been crucial.

Apart from the invaluable safeguards put in place by individuals, the recovery was achieved through the resilience, ingenuity and unflinching support of many of the staff. Employees 'mucked in' magnificently. People more used to planning and running departments offered to do all sorts of jobs from shovelling rubbish, to logging refuse and even plastering. One or two wilted under the pressure, and eventually went their separate ways, while others seemed to thrive under the same pressure, determined not to be beaten. Likewise there were employees who could be relied upon to work uncomplainingly in appalling conditions, while others behaved like spoilt children whining about things that could not be helped.

Initially there was confusion. Staff were used to operating almost robotically, taking few real decisions. Suddenly there was a whole range of new decisions to be taken and there was a period of great frustration with little information available. After the first rush of adrenaline came a phase of very low morale as staff became aware of the very real difficulties the company was facing. It was mid-winter, managers were clearly preoccupied and employees had no way of knowing what the future might hold.

Lessons

A sense of direction was restored by an unprecedented meeting of senior staff at which responsibility for the various aspects of redevelopment was allocated, action defined and a programme planned for short, medium and long term. Being forced to rebuild the company, from the ground up, had created opportunities for fresh concepts and methods that might otherwise never have seen the light of day.

New attitudes to marketing ensured that the company now actively seeks to promote their services with a computerized database of contacts, direct mailing of a colourful newsletter and regular lobbying of the press. Publicity had not previously been a priority and inviting clients to view the presses in action would have been inconceivable in the old environment. Formalizing an existing commitment to adopt a proactive environmental stance is already proving popular, with the company guaranteeing environmentally friendly materials and practices, wherever possible, and a planned environmental audit to reduce waste and improve disposal methods.

Looking back, the company realized that some of the old ingrained habits made the difference between survival and extinction: the attention to detail in negotiating contracts, the most fanatical cost control and the instinct not to spend money on non-essentials. There were also decisive moments where a different decision would have wrecked any hopes of continuing. Obviously the insurance company eventually agreeing the claim was a significant milestone, although the waiting was a particularly anxious time.

Deciding on alternative premises, which took six weeks, was the most vital step. Already in train, due to merger negotiations, the move had been in danger of getting bogged down with various options and conflicting dogmatic positions. The urgency created by their situation 'concentrated people's minds' and a site was chosen on the basis that, while not ideal, it offered the fastest means to get up and running. In fact they moved in before the previous tenants had moved out.

In the wake of the disaster the very best of the old and the new have been forced to find a harmonious path through the flames and have emerged victorious. They have learned much from the experience, not least the realization that their survival was due to the foresight of those individuals who made their own contingency plans, but it has been a tough education. What they need now is the support of existing and potential customers to ensure their efforts have not been in vain.

A1N   FIRE HIGHLIGHTS

A 32-year-old man was arrested after he walked into a bank in Hong Kong carrying two canisters of inflammable liquid which he ignited and threw into the bank. The fireball filled the room with black smoke. Six people, including the bank manager, died and many more were injured after being trapped behind bullet-proof security doors, unable to escape the flames. A customer using the outside cash machine called the emergency services. The 30-year-old building did not have a fire exit, or a sprinkler system, or fire-resistant furniture, although it complied with government standards.

An IBM employee was charged with setting fire to his office in San Jose and the home of his supervisor, in March 1993. Witnesses claim he drove his car through the IBM office foyer and then set it alight with camping stove fuel. He had apparently been aggrieved since 1987 when he persistently phoned and wrote to colleagues about the state of work at IBM. He was put on disability leave. He blamed IBM for the break-up of his marriage and accused his supervisor of forcing him to go on disability leave.

A security guard for a large UK electronics company started two fires to teach another security guard a lesson because he had been abused by him. The first fire was dealt with, but the second, started in a waste bin on another floor, caused fire up to the 15th floor. The ground floor computer centre was untouched, but a message switching centre was destroyed and there was £35 000 ($61 000) worth of damage to terminal equipment. Fire hoses flooded the eighth floor, ruining audit files and security tapes. The culprit was sentenced to four years in jail. He had claimed to be a hero and was expecting the Order of the British Empire for discovering the fire.

At the University of Cambridge, UK, on a Friday evening, a fire started in the Department of Zoology (adjacent to the computer laboratory). To access the fire, the Fire Service had to open fire doors to the lower of two computer rooms, causing entry of smoke, debris and water. Smoke went up a disused lift shaft into the upper computer room and triggered the inert gas system. The lower room contained multi-supplier servers and desktop PCs. None avoided damage; the cleaning and replacement took six months.

A £25 million ($49 million) new data centre for a bank at Bracknell, UK, was equipped with UPS. It suffered a power cut. The UPS and backup diesel generator cut in but at 06:00 the duty shift leader smelt burning. The exhaust pipe of the generator was venting near timber, causing the wood to smoulder. Moreover, there was a leak in the diesel fuel pipe leading to the generator. The system was powered down. Mains power was subsequently restored but, as the systems were being rebuilt, the electricity board brought the power down again for 30 minutes: the UPS had not recharged and the system rebuild was lost.

A major supplier of network products set out to develop new security services and took the decision to be underinsured, bearing half the risk themselves. After several months' research and development in partnership with another organization that provided market intelligence and a potential customer base, they were poised to launch the new service. A fire destroyed most of their equipment and all of their records. Shortly after, key staff were plundered by a rival. It was rumoured that the rival would market a similar offering within a couple of months.

DEC Customer Services HQ in Basingstoke, UK, had a fire that started on the roof, destroying the building, which housed 400 staff. Plastic covers protected computers after being saved by the inert gas suppression system. The fire gutted the building in six minutes. Overnight backups had protected most orders except any hard copy currently being processed, and that day's orders. Two weeks later, according to press reports, customers were blaming late delivery of spares on the incident. The cost of damage to the building was £20 million ($35 million) and the cost to the business was estimated at between £10 million ($1.74 million) and £38 million ($66 million).

At the Bank of England the rule was to store floppy disks in a metal fire safe. However, some staff persisted in storing their floppies in wooden desk drawers. A fire occurred; the fire safe was not up to standard; the metal safe overheated, ruining the floppies stored in it. Although the wooden desks were charred, the disks stored in them survived, and were readable!

In 1990 a fire at the main Scarborough, UK, telephone exchange burned through megastream and kilostream data cables and 23 000 business and residential lines. The cause was believed to be an electrical fault in the computer equipment. It impacted building society and bank ATMs; links between North Sea oil rigs; Scarborough Borough Council; and Marks & Spencer (a multiple retail chain).

A10   WESSEX REGIONAL HEALTH AUTHORITY

Picking up the pieces

The background

Few IT professionals have experience of dealing with the press. Yet disasters frequently provoke great public and media interest. Managing press relations should form part of any disaster training. When Wessex Regional Health Authority was forced to write off a £40 million ($76 million) systems project it took some explaining.

It started in April 1991 with a phone call from the UK magazine *Computer Weekly*. 'Was there any truth in a rumour they had heard concerning two senior staff at [UK] Wessex Regional Health Authority (RHA)?' The rumour was true – they had been suspended for gross misconduct and the Fraud Squad were called in to investigate suspected contract fraud on a fairly major scale. Both members of staff were later sacked.

Despite being well briefed, it was one of those inquiries which sets alarm bells ringing somewhere in the darkest recesses of the mind. On the face of it, it was the kind of inquiry that prompts an intensive but short-lived spell of media attention. The issue was relatively straightforward: they had answers to all the likely questions and were prepared to be open and honest about it all.

The difficulty was that the inquiry actually went straight to the heart of a much bigger issue which most people at the RHA thought was dead and buried. The issue was the RHA's abandoned Regional Information Systems Plan (RISP), which had been scrapped in April 1990, and its mismanagement heavily criticized in a National Audit Office report in November 1990. Both milestones had been marked by minor blazes of media attention – after all, they had been dealing with severe criticism of RISP virtually since its inception in 1984, interspersed with occasional media interest surges. One such was the story about the mainframe computer that stayed unused in its packaging in a Slough warehouse for 18 months.

The staff suspensions and Fraud Squad involvement came about as a result of an intensive internal investigation into RISP. For the first time ever, the RHA was determined to find out how much had been spent, by whom and on what. They wanted to know what went wrong, who was responsible and to make as much information public as possible.

The scenario was one of serious mismanagement and mishandling of public funds, possible serious fraud, possible exploitation of the RHA by sharp contractors, poor project management and an almost total lack of financial, budgetary and audit controls. There were also some remarkable conflicts of interests. For six weeks a former employee fulfilled the roles of both contractor and client. He was effectively writing the specifications, selecting the company (i.e. his own) to do the work, fixing the price and signing the cheques.

Not surprisingly, journalists with a particular interest in RISP began to put the pieces of the jigsaw together for themselves. In fact, some of them seemed able to provide details and information very quickly after the RHA itself had been able to get to information! The picture was further complicated by legal battles with various IT suppliers over aspects closely associated with RISP.

They adopted an open stance from the beginning which reflected credit on the organization in the long run but which created painful, time-consuming headaches as more and more details entered the public domain. The District Audit Service was brought in to produce a comprehensive, definitive account of the RISP affair. When that report became available to the RHA in July 1993 the true extent of the calamity became clear. The bottom line was that, of the £43.6 million ($76 million) spent on RISP between 1984 and 1990, about half of it had been effectively wasted. It was time to go public in a very proactive way.

The response

Since it is impossible to keep a £20 million ($38 million) public money scandal under wraps, together with a genuine commitment from the authority to openness and accountability, a major news conference seemed the best way to handle the release of information. To a degree, this would also manage the way it would be reported. A few frantic weeks of preparation followed before the regional general manager was thrown to the mercy of half the nation's press corps. That press conference was an extraordinary event. Many of the assembled media were staggered by the way in which the Authority was prepared to meet the issue head on, to expose and condemn the waste and mismanagement, which characterized RISP, and to make no excuses. In short they were handed on a plate one of the best public cash squandered stories in recent years – and they were grateful, albeit initially taken aback.

Once the screaming headlines and condemnations, which greeted the revelations, were past, more considered, analytical pieces began to appear which recognized and highlighted the three issues the RHA hoped the journalists would bear in mind in return for the RHA baring its soul.

Factors, which did not receive as much publicity, were:

- All those with principal responsibility for RISP were no longer employed by the RHA.
- The District Auditor praised the RHA for the remedial action taken since 1990 to ensure that such an inexcusable scenario should never happen again.
- It had been the Authority's new administration, which had got to the bottom of RISP and made the painful details spectacularly public.

There then followed endless hours of explaining the whole story to journalists with no prior knowledge of RISP – an average of 30 minutes per telephone enquiry. Then came follow-up stories, developments in the legal aspects of the saga, sackfuls of critical, probing letters to answer, and answers and ministerial briefings to be provided for questions in both Houses of Parliament.

Lessons

There are a number of lessons that can be passed on in handling the public relations aspects of such an incident:

- It pays to take the initiative.
- Openness and honesty are usually the best policies.
- There is no substitute for planning and preparation.
- Be prepared to believe the unbelievable.
- Listen and think carefully before formulating an action plan and/or giving advice.
- Remember you are part of a team – others will need to know what you know and vice versa.
- There is no substitute for good information, straight from the horse's mouth.
- Grow a thick skin and don't take it personally.

One other lesson was the importance of being able to relax and switch off. Luckily RISPs don't come along very often, but when they do they can become all-consuming and encroach into one's personal as well as professional life.

Support was forthcoming from the chairman and regional general manager, and colleagues and others who became involved in sorting out the nasty mess RISP had left on the corporate carpet. Without that support you would probably crumple under the strain and/or go stark staring mad!

A1P   THE BISHOPSGATE BOMB – 25 APRIL 1993

EXPLOSIONS – DO THEY REALLY HAPPEN?

Background

Since 1993 there were major terrorist explosions in New York, Tokyo, Frankfurt, Bombay, Florence, Madrid, Milan, Rome, Cairo, Paris, London, and Oklahoma. Between 1983 and 2007 there were 45 000 bombings in the USA.

Accidental explosion can be as serious: a blast at Sumitomo Chemical, Japan, in April 1993 destroyed 60% of the world's manufacturing capacity for epoxy resin, used to package memory chips and other semiconductor devices. This led to a doubling of the price of computer chips and allegedly delayed computer manufacturers in releasing new models.

The impact of the Bishopsgate bomb

The homemade fertilizer bomb, exploding in Bishopsgate, London, UK, at 22:30, killed one person and forced 91 companies to relocate. In addition:

- 2 buildings were destroyed.
- 25 buildings were heavily damaged.
- 3 buildings suffered moderate damage.
- 100 buildings suffered broken glass – £2 million of glass in one building alone.
- The estimated damage was £400 million (insured loss) and 40 companies were affected.
- The explosion made many companies face up to reality: lightning can strike twice.
- Several companies had suffered from the IRA bombings at both St Mary Axe and Bishopsgate in spite of security measures, which included additional security guards, increased vigilance and CCTV.

Some case studies from Bishopsgate

SIGITO, a public sector service organization, had held a party during the evening to celebrate moving into their new premises. Catering staff were still on-site when the windows blew out. The heating system flooded computer equipment and important paper records. Papers in steel cabinets survived reasonably well, but water, first from the heating system and later from rain, damaged other documents. Access was denied to the building for three days. It took two days to acquire portable telephones, during which time business was conducted from telephone boxes. A serviced office nearby was rented – initially a short-term measure, but one which lasted in practice for almost a year until the damaged site could be reoccupied; meanwhile, service charges were being levied on a property that was uninhabitable! There were access problems with the temporary offices; cranes were needed to get computer equipment into the building.

The insurance company Guardian Royal Exchange had four City offices impacted by the explosion: all four nodes on their network were out of action. Fortuitously at that time they were running trials with a software tool that checks network survivability – and so got a flying start in establishing the best way to restore communications!

A subsidiary of Commercial Union (insurers), Quilter Goodison, was hit by the blast: they decided to continue running the business and clear up later. By 08:00 on the Monday morning, fund managers were up and running in another building.

Rea Brothers Group, a City bank, showed £175 000 ($345 000) in their annual accounts for uninsured losses attributable to the bomb. Sir John Hill, Chairman, said: 'Although the Bishopsgate bomb incident in April necessitated our departure from Alderman's House for some months, there was no dislocation of service to clients.'

The Hong Kong and Shanghai Bank was severely damaged and they transferred operations to the Sheffield data centre of the Midland Bank.

Windows were blown out of the NatWest Tower . . . the day before, the glazier had completed reglazing following the damage from the St Mary Axe explosion and had expressed concern about future business! Two hundred PCs had to be salvaged.

Other companies seriously impacted included Mocatta, Long Term Credit Bank of Japan, Daewoo Securities, Tokai Bank, Mitsubishi Corporate Finance and Oracle. Other dealers accommodated many dealers on an ad hoc basis.

Lessons

The explosion and aftermath showed the need for:

- A broader planning perspective – to cover business, not just IT
- Standby facilities for work areas, dealing rooms, offices, PCs/LANs
- Improved safety measures
- Geographic separation from recovery sites – the police cordon exclusion zone denied access to those who were not affected by the blast

- Bomb-shielded glass; window blinds; entrance canopies to protect people and equipment from flying glass
- Security – nine security guards were charged with theft and cowboy glaziers were breaking windows
- Limiting personal effects left in offices
- A clear-desk policy
- Evacuating the recovery team separately to minimize confusion and speed recovery
- Out-of-hours numbers for contractors
- Staff information – free phone lines
- Keyholders – information about who they are and contacts (in rented multi-occupancy accommodation keyholder bottlenecks can be a real hindrance to gaining access)
- 'Disaster packs' to include hard hats
- Patrolling control points for fast access
- Food and drink for the workers!
- Those with plans recovered twice as quickly as those without plans.

Food for thought

The disaster also provoked thought about things we may take for granted:

- Are suppliers really available 24 hours a day?
- Beware heroes – especially board room heroes! They often confuse motion with progress and frequently wreck the best plans.

A1Q   CITY BOMB BLAST: ST MARY AXE – 10 APRIL 1992

Background

An IRA bomb exploded in St Mary Axe, a side street adjacent to Liverpool Street Station in London, UK. Three people died; two buildings were destroyed; 40 companies were forced to relocate; damage was put at £1.4 billion ($2.44 billion).

The Baltic Exchange was virtually demolished and the Commercial Union Building took the full brunt of the explosion. All 650 Commercial Union employees had to be relocated. The five-storey Chamber of Shipping was reduced to rubble. James Capel's computer room ceiling was severely damaged and staff wearing hard hats were bringing the systems back up. By 09:00 the following Monday about 30 affected firms had been relocated and were open for business. The account that follows is the personal story of one of them.

Mocatta's experience

In the 321-year history of gold and silver bullion dealer Mocatta London, the company has seen many disasters hit the capital, but seldom can a disaster have affected it so closely as the massive bomb explosion which caused so much damage in the City during the weekend just before Easter 1992.

Apart from a few shattered windows, the bomb blast caused little damage to the company's substantial 19th century listed building in Crosby Square (only 100 yards or so from the explosion). However, police security measures restricted access to the area and threatened the operation of the computer system that is so vital to the success of Mocatta's dealer activities.

Fortunately, Mocatta had for the past eight years been a contracted client with a disaster recovery hot site service provider and by the Monday a backup system was fully operational at their recovery centre in Hertfordshire. It transpired that Mocatta was able to operate the computer system after all, but the recovery centre continued to run the backup system for a week as a contingency measure.

Manager of the management information system and telecommunications at Mocatta was Michael Moore. It was he, a year after joining Mocatta in 1983, who decided that any unforeseen incident could have a catastrophic affect on the running of a precious metals trading company. After looking carefully at the disaster recovery field he signed the contract mentioned above in 1985. Subsequently all the New York processing was transferred to Mocatta House in 1990. It was these systems that Michael was concerned about when he was telephoned at home on the Friday evening of the bomb blast by one of his operators. Later that night he established that the building had not suffered extreme damage and that the computer system was capable of running on generator power.

Very early on the Saturday morning he stepped outside Liverpool Street Station – and was faced with a scene of devastation. There were security cordons around the area, but he managed to convince the police of his need to reach Crosby Square and check on the safety of his computer system. He found Mocatta House standing remarkably unscathed in the midst of the incredible devastation, with the neighbouring insurance company high-rise block across the square reduced to a concrete skeleton. Inside the building, a few window frames had been blown in by the blast and one or two pieces of equipment up-ended. The only human casualty was one of the trading staff who had been knocked bodily out of his chair – but otherwise unhurt – by the shock of the explosion.

A tour of his department showed that the computer system had not been damaged and was capable of normal operation. He was, however, aware that security restrictions imposed on that part of the City, coupled with the continuing danger of falling debris, was likely to prevent the company staff being allowed access on the Monday morning. At this point he decided to give formal warning to the recovery centre that it might be necessary to invoke the disaster recovery contract and he made the necessary telephone calls to key personnel.

Michael stayed in London throughout the weekend and – although other tapes were stored off-site – collected all the current output tapes and documentation for despatch to the recovery centre, confident of the outcome, as he had taken part in a successful disaster recovery test at the site only two weeks beforehand.

The prospects of the Mocatta staff being allowed access to their building after the weekend continued to be uncertain, so early on the Monday morning the Mocatta London management decided on invocation. A member of the Mocatta operations staff travelled to the recovery centre and the backup tapes were delivered. By 10:00 the base system had been recovered and by midday the system was fully restored and ready for operation.

Normal computing activities were, however, resumed at Mocatta House on Tuesday morning. As it turned out the bomb blast, though tragic for some, did not bring total disaster to Mocatta, but it might have done, if they had not been prepared.

A1R EXPLOSION ROUNDUP

A one-ton IRA bomb was discovered at Canary Wharf, London, UK, in 1992. Security guards challenged two suspects. They drove off in a van, leaving a lorry abandoned with the fertilizer bomb. The other van, later found abandoned, also contained explosives. Access was denied to offices in the area, including the *Daily Telegraph*, which subsequently issued the paper with a blank front page, being unable to complete it in time. The detonator was subsequently found to have been triggered but a wiring fault prevented it from causing the bomb to explode.

In March 1993 10 car bombs exploded in the financial district of Mumbai, India: 255 people were killed, 1100 were injured. The first explosion, in an underground car park beneath the 28-storey Bombay Stock Exchange, killed several dozen people; two traders were blown through windows and fell to their deaths; others died in the stampede to leave the building.

In 1992 two two-pound bombs exploded in Manchester City Centre, UK. One was in a car parked outside the Inland Revenue and Department of Employment offices and went off at 08:45 (six minutes after a warning was phoned to the Samaritans) and the second at 10:10 at the corner of Cateaton Street near the Arndale Shopping Centre. Some 56 people were injured, one seriously when a two-foot shard of glass went into his back.

In 1994, 600 staff were evacuated from the Croydon, UK, HQ of Direct Line after a letter bomb in a jiffy bag, addressed to the chief executive, exploded at 11:00. His secretary was treated by ambulance crew at the scene for minor burns and shock. The chief executive was away on business at the time. Customer calls were transferred to regional offices as soon as the emergency alarms went off. Business was not 'dented'.

A 28-pound test bomb was aimed at a target being towed by HMS *Ark Royal*, but hit the aircraft carrier, penetrating the mess deck. Five sailors suffered flash burns: one lost fingers and suffered severe abdominal injuries. The pilot of the plane was to aim at the carrier, and a computer program would steer the bomb 7 degrees off to hit the target, which was 600 yards astern. The software was blamed. The aircraft radar locks on to the ship but the onboard computer automatically aims 600 yards astern. The highly experienced RAF flight lieutenant lost radar contact twice with the ship and finally locked on only seconds before firing the bomb, but he was unaware that the computer software was unable to cut in the automatic aim-off so quickly. He received a formal warning. The training system was suspended.

In another incident London clay shifted under the road, fracturing a cable under the victim's office. Heat build-up caused the pavement to explode, sending molten pitch 15 feet into the air, where it was taken in through the air conditioning intake. The mainframe computer room was filled with smoke so thick it was not possible to see if operators were present. All the equipment had to be checked and cleaned before computing services could be resumed.

Two Kurds walked into the seventh floor UK branch of the Turkish Bank, and poured a gallon of petrol on the floor on the customer side of the bank: it was set alight, with a customer getting burnt. The customer fled and was arrested by police as a suspect and interrogated for an hour before they realized he did not speak English. About the same time the Turkish Embassy was fire-bombed (it was next to the Turkish Airlines offices and the terrorists threw the fire-bomb through the wrong window).

A1S STOP THIEF!

The growth and impact of computer and component theft

In 1989 the US National Center for Computer Crime summaries barely mentioned theft of equipment as an issue. Now theft of computer equipment and components in the USA is costing US business around $3.5 billion/year. There is hardly a hi-tech manufacturing company that has not suffered a substantial theft of components. One 'sting', Operation Grey Chip, resulted in 30 arrests and recovery of $2.1 million in cash and $1.5 million in equipment.

All these thefts had huge knock-on effects. Memory supplier Datrontech, having suffered a van hijack, now has the permanent overhead of security guards. Intel changed manufacturing processes to include serial numbers on components to aid tracking. The theft of $5 million (retail value) of chips from Oki Semiconductor in Oregon caused prices of 1 Mb memory to rise by $10 in the USA and £6–10 ($10–17) in the UK.

When it comes to personal computers, servers and minicomputers, theft takes on a new dimension. Nearly all the national and regional newspapers, for example, have suffered major equipment raids. It is initially amusing to read of a UK publisher who had their Apple Macintoshes stolen and carried off in a stolen fruit lorry. It is much less amusing when theft of Apples reaches such proportions that publishers are put out of business and at least one insurer is refusing to provide cover for publishers.

In Hampshire, UK equipment theft has risen 70% in one year. Insurers put losses at over £100 million/year UK-wide – and that is just replacement equipment value, not the cost to business. Much of the stolen equipment heads for technology-hungry Eastern Europe.

Often the thief steals not just the equipment but also any on-site backups lying around. Theft to order is commonplace – with thieves waiting for victims to be re-equipped before striking again . . . and again. In some cases the stolen hardware has been recycled and sold back to the original owners ready for a return visit. A Manchester company's office was robbed 12 times in a year; terrified security guards stood by while armed youths cleared offices during midnight raids.

At the lower level, often a small theft becomes a big, truly personal, disaster. The theft of one PC can destroy a lifetime's work (as several researchers know to their cost). Thefts from doctors' surgeries put health at risk, endanger patient confidentiality and risk sanctions on the victim under data protection legislation. Theft of a computer from the surgery of a doctor in London's Harley Street was said to contain patient details of Princess Diana. The theft of computers from the Institute of Offshore Engineering cost £30 000 ($52 000) – but the research they contained, on clearing oil spills, is priceless.

Precautions

Thieves these days know exactly how long they have to raid premises before police arrive. Alarms don't always frighten thieves – but sometimes they may deter, and anything that slows thieves down, or helps identify equipment, will deter theft. Physical security is the poor relation of business protection planning. Maybe it is time it took the limelight.

According to statistics from a National Home Security Week survey, which runs from 27 August to 2 September 2005:

- 29% of burglars install CCTV in their own homes, compared to just 4% of the rest of us.
- Similarly, 43% of burglars have a home intruder alarm system, compared to just 34% of all households.
- CCTV is a deterrent. Over two-thirds of burglars questioned rated CCTV as an effective security measure; they said that they would probably or definitely not break into property that had CCTV installed. Burglars also feared intruder alarms and security lighting.

Conclusion

The burglar has begun to attack the office complex in greater numbers, and premises that are 'open' for business. Access in these cases is often gained by walking through the front door unchallenged, or via a rear goods entrance left unguarded. This is the most common method of entry – sometimes assisted by use of a boiler suit, warehouse coat and invoices sticking out of the pocket. If challenged at all they have a well-rehearsed story about collections, repairs, maintenance or some other glib reason for being there, which is rarely checked out. Burglaries still happen after hours but many commercial burglaries occur during the working day and much of the 'research' by criminals goes on in the daytime. How many times do you or your security staff pay more than a fleeting attention to the man 'repairing' the photocopier, or the person pushing a trolley along the corridor dressed in that overall with papers sticking out of the pocket; and how about the electrical subcontractor or decorators?

Burglary, like business, is driven by market forces. A balance between customer and supply is all-important. Market research determines just what and how much the supplier can expect to offload. At one scene of computer theft the police found what was thought to be a 'shopping list' of equipment on the office floor.

The right commodity at the right price will ensure a queue of eager customers. At present there is a never-ending and fast expanding marketplace for computer equipment. Following the opening up of Eastern Europe and growth and development in the 'Third World', markets are clamouring for hardware and off-the-shelf software packages. In 2003–2004 in the UK West Midlands area alone the value of property stolen totalled £177 million ($308 million). That is one of just eight police areas.

When one looks at the pressure placed on insurers over the years, payments must be reflected in premiums. These premiums are then offset against profit margins. Inevitably they are passed on to the customer which increases, however insignificantly, the relative cost of products in a very competitive market.

When one looks at the attacks on such premises as colleges, schools, local government buildings and charities, where there is no room to offset loss, the quality of service will suffer. Computer equipment in these premises is often extensive and protection is difficult, with access by the public easy by the nature of their activities.

A computer is not necessarily 'logged off' or switched off before it is stolen, it is just pulled from the socket or connection. The disk may well still be in place so, apart from the loss of hardware, damage is caused in several areas. First, valuable information may be lost in the system; processes, customer records, development projects and a lifetime's work could just disappear. The value of information is only just being realized by all concerned. Additionally, if that information does fall into the hands of a skilled or shrewd operator, it could find its way to a competitor. The mere loss of a process in itself can be damaging enough, but for that information to pass into another's hands can double the blow. No insurance can cover that.

A1T   MISCELLANEOUS HIGHLIGHTS

The distribution depot of a PC distributor was being manned by a security guard who was called out to help a woman who had apparently crashed into a parked lorry. As he opened the door, an armed gang with sawn-off shotguns entered the warehouse and locked the guard in the van backed against the wall. The gang took the keys from the transport manager's office, used them to get a bolt cutter, went to the truck containing 3000 PCs, cut the locks, loaded up two vans with the PCs and drove off. The guard had noted the number plate of the 'crashed' car and described the gang: 56 PCs were recovered.

Following the Iraqi invasion of Kuwait, virtually all data centres were looted with equipment being ripped out by troops and transported by open lorries to Iraq. Most firms are said to have preserved databases outside Kuwait. One example was the National Bank of Kuwait. They 'knocked out' their systems to stop the Iraqis getting into them but had all their records and databases backed up in the UK, so they could easily fly out and get their computer operations going again. The problem was that, once they tried to restore their operating systems, some automated operating software refused to work on the basis that the serial number of the CPU was different to that for which it was licensed. It allegedly cost them £250 000 ($435 000) for permission to run on the CPU at the recovery site.

Mice had nested in the powerhouse of one UK organization. When the backup rotary generators were switched on, the nest was destroyed and the generators rendered unserviceable.

In the US the Nasdaq electronic share trading system was brought down by a squirrel, which had gnawed through the UPS power line.

In a City of London silver dealer, a secretary, Annabel Bird, found that every time she tried to back up her IBM PC to its internal floppy disk drive an error appeared on the screen. She had corrupted boxes of disks. An engineer from the software supplier reformatted disks and ran backup programs successfully. The secretary proved she was implementing the backup procedures correctly. The engineer claimed he had discovered the cause. The secretary cannot wear some watches because they break and every time she picks up a disk she scrambles it. She had natural animal magnetism! He suggests manufacturers who believe their disks are resistant to electrical interference should see if their products pass the 'Annabel test'.

At London Heathrow airport, an office block was on the point of collapse in 1994, following subsidence of a tunnel being built for a new rail link. Roads and car parks around the site were closed, causing traffic congestion on the M4 approach to the airport. Tunnelling work was suspended. Torrential rain may then have weakened earth and clay beneath the office block. The building was tilting towards the hole that was 40 yards wide. Millions of tons of concrete were poured into the hole in an attempt to stabilize foundations. The Express Rail Link was due to open in December 1997. The £300 million ($522 million) Express Link and the £2 billion ($3.5 billion) Jubilee Line Extension both came under question as both use the controversial Austrian Tunnelling Method!

A certain sales manager took a backup tape containing 1700 clients' details from his company which he later used to target potential customers for his own start-up firm. The UK Crown Court gave him a conditional discharge for six months. The company discovered the theft after its own records appeared to be scrambled and one of its customers received a mailshot from the new company. The individual claimed he had taken the tape by accident. The company claimed they lost a substantial amount of business.

In another organization over £100 000 ($174 000) was invested in UPS to ensure continuity of computer and network operation. However, when the power failed during the winter, UPS cut in and computer operation continued uninterrupted, but there was no standby power for the central heating, which stopped. It got so cold that staff had to be sent home and computer operation could not be supported, so it ceased!

At a disaster recovery seminar in Dublin, Ireland, a delegate challenged the speaker about the effectiveness of UPS, saying they had just installed almost 100 for a distributed operation without any problems so far. A lady delegate (from another insurance company) replied that they had installed five and three had blown up! (Leaking batteries release hydrogen with consequent risk of explosion.) They had discontinued use of UPS on the grounds that they felt it represented a greater potential threat than power failure.

At a food processing plant in northern England a computer system was installed without anyone realizing the impact of frequent electrical storms, which were common in the area. Although there were standby generators for the food store, there were none for the computer. Each storm took out power for 1–2 seconds, causing computer failure. After every power failure backup copies of data had to be used to restore processing. Often power failure recurred during this process. As a result backups were taken four times daily and computer operations suspended when a storm looked likely! UPS was eventually installed.

An international European organization, based in Luxembourg, had a recovery site a couple of kilometres away from their main site. All power to Luxembourg comes from Germany. When the power went out, they relocated to the recovery site – which suffered from the same power outage, but which had UPS and generator backup. However, when power came back, it fluttered on and off several times, confusing the UPS, which could not decide whether it should be on or off. It decided it should be off. Wrong call! The same organization had problems during a BC test, when one of the key players took half an hour to find a parking space.

Unidentified insects invaded a factory in Nottingham, UK: employees were breakfast, lunch and dinner. One hundred employees downed tools and walked out.

An aerospace company had a key application program wiped when an employee walked through an area carpeted with nylon carpet and then operated the computer: he discharged a 2000 volt charge of static!

A North Sea petroleum operation almost lost a propeller-driven rig that went walkabout after transmissions from a walkie-talkie interrupted the flow of data from a geostationary satellite.

A1U LESSONS IN RISK MANAGEMENT FROM THE AUCKLAND POWER CRISIS

Introduction

PricewaterhouseCoopers performed a survey of companies located in the Auckland Central Business District affected by the February 1998 power crisis. The purpose of the survey was to gather and share information about how the crisis affected organizations, the lessons learnt, recovery strategies that worked well and those that did not. The survey also aimed to identify how risk management and business continuity planning disciplines helped organizations during the crisis.

The power crisis affected all organizations surveyed. Some had only minor disruption, while for others the crisis was in fact a disaster. As disasters go, this should have been, operationally, easier to cope with than most. There was not the destruction of equipment and records that would have been experienced in a fire. Neither was there any limitation of access to normal premises, such as in disasters, which affect building safety. More than one participant in the survey made the comment that the crisis had the benefit of showing what they are able to achieve in a recovery situation, while allowing them to change strategies, which were not working.

By sharing this information more organizations may be better prepared for the next crisis, whatever that may be.

How long did it take to get started?

As each of the four power cables supplying Auckland's Central Business District (CBD) failed it became increasingly likely that a crisis would develop. Events came to a head late on Friday 20 February 1998, when Mercury Energy stated publicly that there would be little or no power in the Auckland CBD during the following week. It would have been feasible to prepare for this over the weekend, to minimize disruption by Monday morning, but many people did not hear about the crisis, or did not understand its significance for a couple of days, which resulted in recovery times being eroded.

Although more than 90% of the organizations surveyed had heard about the crisis before Monday 23 February, fewer than half took any action. The reasons for this time being lost included:

- News of the crisis was not heard until late in the weekend.
- Where power was on over the weekend it was not clear who would be affected and how badly.

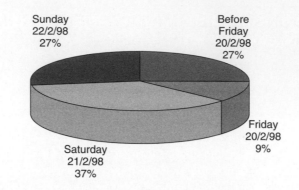

Figure A1U.1(a)—When did you become aware of the crisis

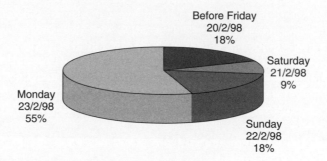

Figure A1U.1(b)—When did you start to take action?

- Contacting colleagues to agree on actions was difficult over the weekend.
- Plans were made over the weekend, to be put in effect on Monday morning.

Lesson one

> **Businesses that had identified their critical business processes and analysed the impact of risks to business continuance appeared to be able to assess the significance of the disaster early and take timely action.**

What strategies were used to continue business?

The main strategies for a power crisis fall naturally into two alternatives:

- Use generator power, or
- Relocate to facilities with power.

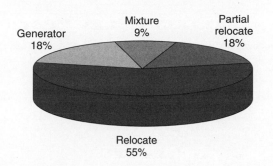

Figure A1U.2—Strategies used

A mixture of these strategies was used, with some organizations relocating part of their staff while the remainder struggled on with or without power. In many cases the strategy used was determined by the nature of the business. Hotels, for example, could not relocate. Other organizations found that their alternatives were limited, usually by a shortage of generators. Generators were arriving in the city, from various parts of the world, for more than a week after the crisis started.

Difficulties encountering information

Not surprisingly the most difficult aspect of the crisis was obtaining reliable information about when power would be available. The uncertainty this caused delayed action being taken by some organizations at the start of the crisis.

Staff

Most organizations were impressed with the way their staff coped with the crisis, particularly where they were working in unfamiliar and far from ideal surroundings. As the crisis dragged on morale became more difficult to sustain. Staff safety was an issue in some cases.

Communications

Communications were frequently difficult, particularly where staff were in different locations. While cell phones were useful, there were periods when the analogue network was overloaded. They should not be relied upon totally. Many

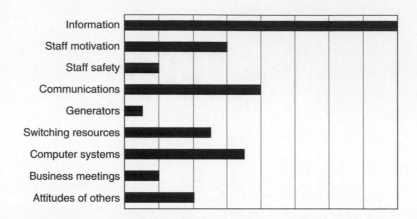

Figure A1U.3—Difficulties encountered

organizations found it useful to have a communications centre, which kept track of where staff were and forwarded messages. In some cases email servers were also moved to somebody's home, so that staff could dial in for their mail.

Generators

Organizations who had or were able to find generators appeared to cope more easily with the crisis, although generator use was not without pitfalls.

Resource relocation

Switching resources to a new location was surprisingly easy, with the telcos being proactive in setting up call diversion where required. Installation of new data circuits was also speeded up, but still took up to three days. Couriers and other services were diverted with only a small amount of confusion and delay.

Computer systems

Computer systems were difficult to move in a few cases, particularly where new data circuits had to be installed and some reconfiguration was required.

Recovery times

The time taken to return to a satisfactory level of operations, given the circumstances, varied greatly.

External attitude

Generally organizations outside the CBD were understanding about the crisis, although a couple of parent companies became impatient about reporting delays. Offshore attitude was of concern to some.

Lesson two

> **Businesses that chose appropriate backup and recovery options based on a business impact analysis appeared to cope well with the disaster.**

How bad was the crisis?

Impacts from a disruption generally fall into the following classifications:

- Financial – loss of revenue and additional costs
- Operational – the effect of not working at normal efficiency, which may result in backlogs, missed deadlines – and delayed projects
- Intangible – such as poor customer service, leading to loss of goodwill, reduced staff motivation and loyalty, etc.

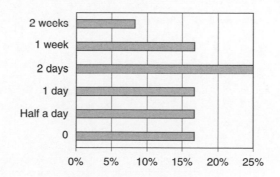

Figure A1U.4—Time to achieve satisfactory recovery

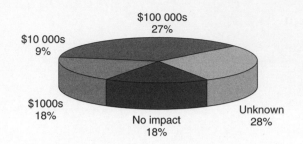

Figure A1U.5—Financial impact of crisis

Financial impacts

The main feature of the financial impacts was the number of organizations who do not know what the crisis has cost them. Nearly 30% of organizations surveyed, however, believed the crisis had cost them over $100 000. The biggest and most difficult to measure impacts were in lost revenue, and it is likely that at least some organizations would suffer for some months after the crisis. Loss of profits insurance, where held, was difficult to assess in many cases.

Operational impacts

Most companies, in the first one to three days of the crisis, were operating well below normal efficiency. However, most improved to about 85–95% over the remainder of the crisis. As a result of this reduction in efficiency a number of projects were delayed, including due diligence exercises, and the backlogs took some time to clear.

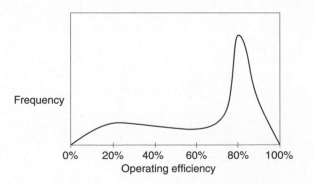

Figure A1U.6—Operational impacts

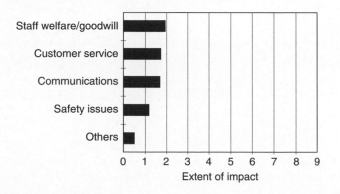

Figure A1U.7—Intangible impacts

Intangible impacts

The intangible impacts considered did not appear to have been greatly felt. Respondents were asked to estimate the intangible impact of the crisis on a scale of 1-9, one being of very little impact. The impact on staff morale and welfare was greatest, followed by customer service and the ability to communicate with business partners. The impact of poor publicity overseas was raised as an additional concern by a number of respondents.

Status of business continuity plans

No organization surveyed had a full business continuity plan. Some had risk management plans and others were in the process of writing plans.

Relating the impact suffered to the state of planning cannot be conclusive in a small sample, where there was a mixture of industries and head office/operational locations. However, the indication is that prior planning helped the recovery by

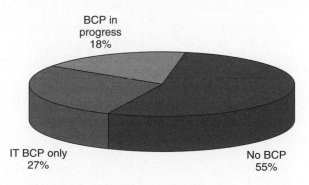

Figure A1U.8—Status of business continuity plans

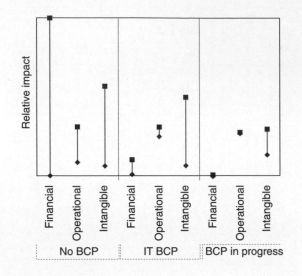

Figure A1U.9—Impact vs BCP status

reducing the impacts. In fact, just thinking about the plan, and going through the first phases of a continuity planning process, seems to have helped, largely because the alternatives had already been identified and considered.

Lesson three

> **Businesses that progressed business continuity to a formal planning stage appeared to cope with financial, operational and intangible aspects of the disaster.**

The pitfalls of generators

A lot of lessons have been learnt about running generators, including the fact that they need fuel and regular maintenance.

Many of the lessons are less obvious, such as the issues relating to the tower blocks around the city. Some have emergency generators, many do not. Emergency generators enable limited lift access, security systems to operate, and keep emergency lighting on after the batteries run down. However, on their own these emergency facilities are not sufficient to make offices habitable for the longer term.

Some buildings have more powerful generators, which are capable of running 70–80% of the building's needs. However, care needs to be taken running computer equipment on these facilities, as it may be difficult to control the load, and hence the supply to equipment. Some uninterruptible power supplies, which provide protection against fluctuations in mains power, were unable to cope with fluctuations in generator power.

The cabling of buildings also influences how generators may be used. Some buildings have individual circuits for each floor or group of floors. This enables a generator to supply a localized area for which it may be easier to control the load.

Lesson four

Operational issues need to be considered in the plan, for example:

- **Build the logistical support for your generator, such as fuel and servicing, into your plan**
- **Know your building and the structure of its cabling**
- **If generator supply is a strategy, check that the uninterruptible power supply will cope.**

Risk management and business continuity planning

Risk management is the process of identifying the organization's risks, their impact and probability, and establishing a plan to manage the risks to an acceptable level. There are many sources of risk to an organization, some representing hazards while others are opportunities.

A high-level review (see Figure A1U.10) of key business risks can reveal much about the organization's risk exposures and profile, and provides senior management with comfort that they are aware of, and understand, the material exposures.

The key to effective risk management is to understand that to be reactive is not enough in today's business environment. A demonstrable and proactive approach is needed if stakeholders are to have faith in the competence of the senior management team.

Business continuity planning is a response to manage identified risks, which involve a disruption to business operations. It is performed in four phases:

1. **Business impact analysis**, to identify the critical functions performed by the organization, the impact of disruptions and the maximum acceptable time to recover

Figure A1U.10—Key business risks

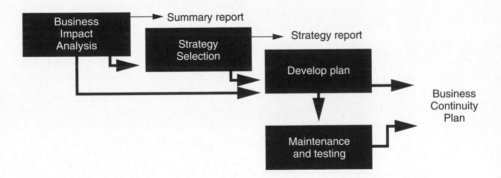

Figure A1U.11—Business continuity planning process

2. **Strategy selection**, to compare and select the most appropriate, cost-effective strategies for risk reduction, continuity of critical functions and recovery

3. **Plan preparation**, involving documentation of the plan, including measures to reduce the risk and impact of disruption

4. **Testing and maintenance**, to ensure that the documented plan works, and that any changes to the business are properly reflected in the continuity plan.

The benefits of this approach are that it:

- Protects the business not just computer systems
- Focuses on critical business processes not disaster scenarios
- Balances the cost of strategies against the impact of disruption
- Reduces the risk and impact of disruption as well as enabling effective recovery.

The aim is to prevent an unfortunate event from becoming a disaster.

A1V FOOT AND MOUTH: A PREVENTABLE DISASTER

The beginning: a disease concealed

A month before foot and mouth disease (FMD) was 'discovered' in England in January 2001, Irish farmers had been warned to improve their biodiversity to prevent FMD being spread. The UK Ministry of Agriculture, Fisheries and Food (MAFF) had contacted timber merchants to ascertain the availability of rail sleepers from which to make funeral pyres. In February 2001 the EU voted to test the potency of emergency vaccine stocks – the EU political process taking weeks, if not months, to arrive at that point.

FMD takes a grip

Since mid-February 2001 foot and mouth disease (FMD) spread across the British Isles and on to Ireland, France and the Netherlands. MAFF said the disease appeared to have spread from a farm at Heddon-on-the Wall in North East England and a possible cause was feeding infected swill to pigs. Virus from this source spread from sheep sent to seven other farms in Tyne and Wear. Sheep from one of these farms were sent to Hexham market on 13 February and from there to markets at Longtown, Cumbria, from whence they were dispersed between 14 and 24 February.

From Longtown market, sheep were sent to Carlisle on 16 February, Welshpool on 19 February and subsequently to dealers at Highampton, Devon; Lockerbie, Dumfries and Galloway; Dearham, Cumbria; Nantwich, Cheshire; and indirectly to markets at Hatherleigh, Hereford, Northampton and Ross on Wye. This spread took place until 23 February before infection was detected and before movement restrictions were imposed. Even then, the attempt was half-hearted and substantive response was not made until after 21 March, when experts publicly stated that the outbreak was out of control.

However, there were persistent rumours that the outbreak started at least a month before. David Owen, of Farmers First, took 400 sheep on his ferry to France on 31 January that subsequently tested positive and he recalls lambs from South Wales being unfit to export in October 2000. Sheep on the Scottish borders showed signs consistent with foot and mouth in early January 2001. There have been suggestions that the epidemic was caused by MAFF inspectors who visited infected farms or markets, spreading the disease, and an even more astonishing claim that a phial of foot and mouth virus went missing from a MAFF laboratory before the epidemic.

FMD was already endemic in the Middle East (one million sheep died), Africa (particularly Kenya and South Africa) and India (said to be threatening the extinction of the white rhino). While countries like the USA, Australia and New Zealand have strict import controls and checks on imported foodstuffs, in the UK such checks were almost totally lacking. According to one report, up to 10 tonnes of illegal meat is brought into Heathrow airport each day, much of it from countries suffering from FMD.[1]

In May, a total of 1522 vets from the State Veterinary Service were deployed in tackling the disease and 1842 soldiers were deployed at the request of the Ministry of Agriculture, Fisheries and Food (MAFF – since changed to the Department for Environment, Food and Rural Affairs – Defra).

On 23 July it was reported that the UK Prime Minister stopped payments of the clean-up and disinfectant operation because of the cost (£100000 – $174000 – average cost of disinfecting a farm in UK compared to £30000 – $52000 – in Scotland). He did not mention that provision of these services is a Defra responsibility, rather than the farmer's.

New licences to allow cattle and pig movements in foot and mouth at-risk and high-risk counties were to be available from Monday 24 September from local trading standards authorities. Farmers experienced severe delays in obtaining them, making the commercial and animal welfare problems thousands were already experiencing worse. The government was accused of gross ineptitude when the new arrangements to allow autumn movements of livestock descended into chaos.

Dr Jonathan Birnie, north-east NFU policy advisor, said he did not know of a single farmer who had a licence by the Monday morning. He said the government's handling of the situation was inept.

By 20 October 2001 there were 2030 confirmed cases in the UK (compared to 1260 cases on 12 April 2001 – despite claims then that the epidemic was under control). There were no new cases between 17:00 Thursday 18 October and 17:00 Friday 19 October (the last case was on Sunday 30 September 2001).

Of these, Defra claim that most extra cases occurred within so-called dangerous contact culls. These figures are understated – to give just one example, a farmer who farms in Bicester and also near Oxford, 20 miles away, had FMD on both farms: it was counted as one incident and no outbreaks were recorded for Oxford at that time.

Official government statistics put the final death toll as 4068000 animals slaughtered. However, the Meat and Livestock Commission claim 10849000 animals were killed.[2] The difference in numbers, over 260%, together with the previous evidence of cover-up, smacks of government distortion of the truth on a massive scale.

---

[1] *Sunday Telegraph*, 17 February 2002, p. 15.
[2] *Sunday Telegraph*, 17 February 2002, p. 14.

Analysis of government statistics indicated that only 2% of cattle killed in the contiguous culls were subsequently diagnosed as having FMD: a failure rate of 98%.[3]

The scale of this unnecessary disaster was epic.

The disease

FMD is caused by a virus and triggers high temperatures and sores, known as vesicules, in the mouths and on the hooves of animals. Symptoms can include lameness and animals going off their feed. It does not usually kill but traditional methods for stopping the spread are to put down infected animals and isolate farms.

FMD is a highly infectious disease of most farm animals except horses. It is spread in three ways:

- Directly, from an infected animal to another animal, by contact, or through the air
- Indirectly, from infected animals by people who have handled them
- Indirectly from infected material such as dung, urine and saliva picked up by people, vehicles, equipment, dogs, scavenging animals and vermin.

An animal can be infectious for some days before it shows signs of FMD and the signs can go undetected, or are much more difficult to see, in sheep than in cattle and pigs. This makes preventing its spread very difficult.

Although foot and mouth disease is extremely unpleasant, causing large blisters on the tongues, lips, hooves and udders of the infected animals, it is not usually fatal. Ninety-five per cent of animals get better within 2–3 weeks although they may be slower growing, less fertile and lame as a result. Only in about 5% cases – generally the very young animals – does the disease cause death, usually in the form of a heart attack.

Impact

Only 10% of farmers had insurance cover against the disease: one of the few insurers still offering to renew cover would pay only 25% of the market value of livestock.

[3] BBC Radio 4, Today, 06:30, 26 March 2002.

Despite £1.723 billion ($2.3 billion) compensation to the farming industry 12 400 farmers and farm workers lost their jobs. The cost to the taxpayer was put at £2.74 billion ($4.77 billion). Cleansing and disinfection cost £701 million ($1.22 billion).

While the government suggested that the crisis may be coming under control, senior scientists said delay in killing and disposing of carcasses was unacceptable and was prolonging the outbreak. An advisor to the US Department of Agriculture pronounced the killings as misguided and claimed vaccination was a better solution. French ministers called Britain 'the weak link' in European agriculture.

Almost a year on, 26 of the 29 mass grave sites at Great Orton were covered. However, these mass graves leak fluid ('leachate'): some 300 000 litres a day had to be specially treated – equivalent to the waste from a village.[4]

Despite propaganda, continued closures and movement restrictions had a 'devastating impact' on agricultural and tourist income. The tourist industry contributes 4% to the UK's gross domestic product, compared with the 1% contributed by agriculture. Tourism was estimated to be worth about £96 billion a year. At that time of the year the countryside tourist industry – worth £12 billion ($20.9 billion) a year in England alone – was losing an estimated £100 million ($174 million) a week, and faced a nightmare Easter season as visitors stayed away.

Almost two-thirds of people planning an Easter trip to the British countryside cancelled their holiday because of the foot and mouth crisis. An internet survey, by an organization linked to the National Farmers' Union, showed many of those questioned were still unsure what was open to the public and stayed away. Official government figures showed British tourism was devastated by the foot and mouth crisis. One hotel in Cumbria saw its bookings fall by 97%. The South-West, one of the worst hit areas, reported income losses of £51 million ($88.7 million) for March, and its tourist board called for additional financial support to help badly affected businesses.

Culture Secretary Chris Smith told cabinet colleagues that income from tourism in parts of Cumbria and Devon was down by as much as 80%, and by 10% overall nationally.

American tourists stayed away from Britain in droves because of the foot and mouth crisis, leading to an estimated £2.3 billion ($3.5 billion loss in trade by Easter.

On 18 October 2001, the government announced a £24 million ($41.8 million) extension to the Business Recovery Fund to help rural economies and small rural businesses damaged by foot and mouth disease.

Tourism Minister Janet Anderson indicated to BBC News Online that cabinet ministers would be spending their holidays in the UK in solidarity with the tourism industry while the disease continued.

[4] *Sunday Telegraph*, 17 February 2002, p. 15.

She accepted that more needed to be done to speed up the slaughter process with only 50 000 of the 1.5 million animals then earmarked for culling on welfare grounds so far processed.

The final loss to the tourist industry was estimated at £4.25 billion ($7.4 billion). In March 2002, the actual loss was put at 'only' £2 billion ($3.48 billion).[5] Although the insurance industry's *Post Magazine* put it at £4.1 billion ($7.1 billion), 0.5% of GDP.[6]

Suffering to animals was intense:

- Cows went painfully unmilked
- Animals gave birth unattended, in sodden fields with lambs drowning as they were born
- Cattle and sheep went unfed and starved
- It was not possible to attend to injured animals, which were left to suffer
- If animals had been kept in their current condition before FMD, the Royal Society for the Prevention of Cruelty to Animals (RSPCA) would have had an open and closed case for prosecution for cruelty leading to fines, imprisonment or both. Yet farmers were banned from moving their animals a few yards to fresh pasture or safety.

In January 2002, Defra formally announced that the FMD epidemic was over.

The medium- and long-term consequences affected everybody in the UK. Some unexpected dependencies have been exposed. Just a few examples:

- The only source of income for some farmers was removed and the average farm income (£57 ($99)/hectare) sank even lower, causing bankruptcies and 60 farmer suicides (to put this into context, this is around twice the number who died in the UK Hungerford and Dunblane massacres, which resulted in a law banning handguns).
- The British Tourist Authority told BBC News Online that it could take years to return overseas visits to pre-outbreak levels.
- Travel agents, airlines, the rail and coach industries were all affected by reduced leisure and business travel. Just one example: Leeds castle, in Kent, axed 200 jobs.
- The postponement of the UK County and General Elections (expected 3 May and, on 4 April, postponed until 7 June) cost up to £10 million ($1.74 million) in early, aborted and protracted political advertising. Cancellation costs on poster advertising can be 90%: the choice was effectively to lose the hoarding advertising budget or let the advertising run a month early. Since farmers represent only 3% of the electorate, their interests came low in the government's election priorities.

---

[5] BBC News 24, 29 March 2002.
[6] Ian Bailey, Royal & SunAlliance, in *Post Magazine* 18 April 2002, p. 23.

- The cost of meat increased and some 30% of the population was said to be considering vegetarianism, having a permanent impact on farm incomes.
- A total of 9000 Chinese takeaways and 1000 Chinese restaurants reported trade down from between 20% to 40% following an unsubstantiated statement that infected swill said to be the cause of FMD outbreak came from a Chinese restaurant. Seventy-five per cent of the 300 000 Chinese living in Britain work in the food trade.
- The betting and leisure industries lost millions – the cancellation of the Cheltenham Gold Cup was said to cost the town of Cheltenham some £2–3 million ($3.48–5.22 million). Badminton horse trials and the Royal Bath and West Show were cancelled with a similar impact. Betting turnover was said to be down by over £100 million ($174 million).
- Dun & Bradstreet reported UK business failures increased by more than 15% in the second quarter of 2001 – 10 804 bankruptcies, with the largest number in the North East.
- Rare breeds have been perfunctorily killed and may be lost forever.
- MAFF stopped farmers using artificial insemination for their cows and banned farmers from buying bulls to service their cows. No calves, no milk. No UK produced milk for the next year, hitting farm incomes and increasing the cost of living as imports compensate.
- Angling, a sport enjoyed by over 2 million, was disrupted since many rivers, streams, lakes and canals are on dairy or sheep farmland. Spending in angling venues was greatly reduced with consequent impact on local incomes.
- Hunting was cancelled for a season. Hunt staff and the 16 000 jobs depending on fox hunting were placed in jeopardy and, regardless of the anti-hunting bill, the demise of hunting may have been hastened.
- Many shoots cancelled the 2001–2002 season. Some breeders of game birds went bankrupt and the pheasant and partridge population diminished. Local hotels suffered from the loss of crucial trade in the winter. The country jobs of 'beating' (driving pheasants towards the guns) and picking up ended – these were not just pin-money jobs, but essential sources of income in some subsistence farming areas of Wales and Scotland.
- Hefted (territorial) sheep were culled. It can take generations for their territory to become imprinted on their offspring. The alternatives are that moors and heath return to nature (impenetrable gorse) or become fenced.
- Consider one typical dairy farmer – his best income over the last three years before FMD was £6000 ($10 400). He had a wife and three children to keep. Farmers like him could not continue. Small farmers were no longer able to service the tourist's countryside: large farming conglomerates took over. On 11 April it was reported that the government expected 50 000 small farmers to go out of business and farms to become consolidated. The face of the countryside was changed forever and with it a permanent loss of tourists.

Lessons not learnt

Almost nothing was learned from the lessons of the 1967/68 outbreak of FMD and the subsequent report. Indeed, a report into the 1923 epidemic found transporting cattle aggravated spread and as long ago as 1714 Thomas Bates presented a paper to the Royal Society highlighting the need to dispose of slaughtered carcases immediately:

- To save £250 000 ($435 000) a year, the government unit that previously impacted the health of sheep being traded was disbanded, which could have detected the rogue sheep trading that is largely the cause of the disaster – did nobody do an impact analysis?
- Contingency plans, drawn up after the 1967/68 outbreak, were initially ignored and, it is said, not made available to the Army until April – two months after the start of the outbreak.
- Animal movements were permitted to continue for one to two weeks after the outbreak – doubling the size of the problem.
- Red tape prevented vets on the spot from backing their diagnosis and promptly killing sick animals.
- Closure of local abattoirs, through overdiligent interpretation of EU red tape, meant animals had to travel further, spreading the disease more quickly and more widely than would otherwise have been the case.
- Delays were caused by environmental legislation and lack of coordination between environmental experts, water companies and farmers so that corpses were left unburied for weeks.
- Delay in calling in the Army led to logistic shambles.
- Although the British Veterinary Association offered the help of 500 vets, MAFF turned them down. Vet students were not drafted in for weeks.
- Conflicting messages – keep out of the countryside, but the countryside is open – led to the worst of both worlds – possibly contributing to the spread of the disease while strangling tourism.
- Protracted timescales between killing animals and disposing of their remains added to the spread of the disease. Roaming foxes (covering wide distances in the mating season) gorged on the carcasses of infected lambs, dragging parts over long distances. High winds and rain carried infection on the air. Infection leached with rain and floodwater.
- Burning of infected carcasses may well have caused the disease to spread on the air.
- Political correctness led the government to ignore the offers of help from over 100 qualified slaughtermen belonging to hunts, leading to further delays in killing infected animals.
- Offers of help from the Countryside Alliance, to provide slaughterers and retired vets, were ignored.
- The government failed to learn any of the lessons from the 1967 outbreak.

On 5 May 2000 the UK *Daily Telegraph* revealed that the European Commission formally instructed MAFF that, to avoid an FMD disaster, it should develop contingency arrangements for a full-scale vaccination programme.[7] It listed 10 criteria for implementation of such a plan: in February 2001 at least seven of these criteria had not been met.

On 22 June 2002 the UK National Audit Office (NAO) produced a report savagely critical of the way the affair had been handled. It revealed that in 1999 a government vet warned ministers that there were no proper contingency plans in place to prevent a multiple FMD outbreak.

The lessons

In July 2002 the Royal Society produced its report on the epidemic. Professor Sir Brian Follet, the inquiry chairman, outlined the key recommendations:

- Strengthen international surveillance of diseases and understanding of their spread
- Set up a national centre for animal disease research and surveillance with a £250 million ($435 000) investment over 10 years
- Improve farmers' recognition of signs of diseases
- Develop quicker diagnosis, including a 'pen-side' test
- Use vaccination as 'the major tool of first resort'

The inquiry also claimed that there was 'no sense' in the countryside closures.
So, what are the lessons for business continuity? They are clear:

- Without an effective contingency plan, dither and delay compound disaster.
- Without prompt, decisive action, losses are compounded.
- Clear communication with a consistent message is vital in disaster.
- One small disaster (a single case of FMD) can affect hundreds and thousands of businesses and apparent onlookers in different industries and even in countries remote from the original victim.

What can we do to prevent a recurrence?

- Reinstate preventive surveillance – an ounce of prevention is worth a ton of cure (and is a great deal cheaper)
- Update the contingency plans, maintain them and make sure everybody relevant knows that they exist and where they are
- Waste no time in tackling the outbreak. Have a proper escalation process to ensure the contingency plans are invoked immediately

[7] *Sunday Telegraph*, 23 June 2002, p. 16.

- Call in resource immediately. Strike quick and hard
- Listen to vets – do not allow ministries to procrastinate and delay
- At the first hint of procrastination, hand over to the Army
- Use *all* the resource that is available – the rural, tourist and leisure economies are too important to allow petty politics to lay the countryside to waste.

Will governments learn? Sadly, the track record is that they do not. The key lesson of the government's enquiry (published March 2002) was that media management needed to be improved.[8]

---

[8] BBC Radio 4, Today, 06:30, 26 March 2002.

A1W THE MADRID RAIL BOMBINGS – 11 MARCH 2004

Background

A country's transport system is a soft target for terrorist attack.

In Mumbai, India, on Tuesday 11 July 2006, eight terrorist explosions devastated packed commuter trains during rush hour in India's commercial capital, killing some 200 people and injuring over 700.

In London, on 7 July 2005, there was a concerted attack on the London transport system (see A1Y below).

The coordinated bomb attacks on the Madrid commuter rail system took place on 11 March 2004. There were 10 explosions on four commuter trains (several in different carriages of the same train). All trains were travelling on the same line from Henares station to Atocha station. The explosions occurred between 07.40 and 07.57, at the height of the rush hour. The locations of the explosions were:

- Atocha station, where three bombs exploded
- Outside Atocha station where four bombs exploded
- El Pozo del Tío Raimundo station where two bombs were detonated
- Santa Eugenia station, where one bomb exploded.

The blasts killed 200 and wounded some 1700. In response, Spanish voters ousted Aznar's pro-Iraq war government for Zapatero, resulting in the immediate withdrawal of Spanish troops from Iraq.

Sarhane Ben Abdelmajid Fakhet, a 35-year-old Tunisian accused of spearheading the attacks, was among those who died in the explosion in Leganes, south of Madrid. Fifteen suspects were already in custody in the Madrid attacks. Six had been charged with mass murder and nine with collaborating with or belonging to a terrorist organization.

In April 2004, as the police closed in, the terrorists detonated explosions in the apartment block in which they had taken cover. The suicide blast that killed the alleged ringleader of the Madrid, Spain, train bombings and four other terror suspects has left the core of the terror group either dead or in jail, Spain's interior minister said.

Lessons

- The bombings demonstrated how effective an attack on public transport can be in terms of death, disruption and devastation. Rail networks have suffered hundreds of attacks over the last 10 years.

- Foresight pays. New York commuters had already been substantially protected from a similar attack: in Westchester, local police departments and the Metropolitan Transit Authority police are responsible for security at commuter rail stations and have put a number of measures in place to improve security since 11 September 2001, including increasing the size of its force by 200 officers – an increase of more than 25%. Roughly two years ago, the MTA launched a $600 million investment programme to make its train, bus and subway system more secure. The MTA board of directors approved an additional $500 million in security projects over the next five years as part of its five-year capital programme.[1]
- In the United States, there have been several plot attempts on rail operator Amtrak.

Outlining efforts that need to be undertaken immediately to prevent an attack from happening in America, the senators noted that there are many simple, effective steps that can be taken to enhance security. For instance, adding more police officers, more dogs to sniff for bombs, additional security cameras, fencing for the yards, and tighter security for the major tunnels along the heavily trafficked Northeast Corridor.

The senators argued that since 9/11, the President has spent $24 billion on the airlines and enhancing aviation security but has invested less than $450 million on passenger rail security. Experts agree that a conservative railway protection programme would cost about $1.1 billion.[2]

- When terrorists only involve local people in an operation, it is quicker, easier to perpetrate and easier to conceal.
- Terrorist activities in one country affect many: following the Madrid bombings, there was a seven-point increase in support in the United States for a timetable for withdrawal from Iraq.
- Don't assume there will only be one attack. In this case, there were several coordinated attacks. Moreover, on 2 April authorities cancelled six bullet trains using the Madrid–Seville line after a railroad inspector found a 26-pound bomb just before mid-day under a track about 40 miles south of Madrid. About 1600 passengers transferred from their trains to charter buses. The same group was blamed for the failed attempt.
- To deflect blame for Spanish involvement in Iraq being the trigger for the bombings, Prime Minister Aznar originally claimed that Basque separatists were responsible. The facts showed him wrong and Spanish voters turned their backs on him in the elections that followed. In public relations, deceit does not pay.

[1] New York Senator Charles Schumer, Press Release, 1 October 2004.
[2] Delaware Senator Joseph R. Biden Jr, Press Release, 10 March 2005.

A1X ISTANBUL BOMBINGS – NOVEMBER 2003

Background

On 20 November 2003, suicide bombers exploded two truck bombs in Istanbul, Turkey, at the British Consulate and the HSBC Bank. The blast killed 32, including the British Consul General, Roger Short, three HSBC personnel and the bombers. The explosions wounded a further 400. The bombs went off as traffic was stopped by nearby traffic lights. Al-Qaeda claimed responsibility. These bombings followed five days after truck bombings of the synagogues at Beth Israel and Neve Shalom.

Impact

HSBC has a 160 branch network in Turkey, supported by its head office building in Levant, Istanbul. This building was severely damaged.

On the day of the bombings, HSBC provided a situation report to 3000 corporate customers. The following working day, HSBC began 'business as usual' at temporary head office premises in Esentepe, Istanbul.

A1Y   LONDON BOMBINGS – 7 JULY 2005 (7/7)

Background

On Thursday 7 July 2005, four suicide bombs were detonated in a coordinated attack on London's transport system. The bombs were timed for maximum death and injury during the morning rush hour, aimed to kill and maim commuters.

At 08.50 three bombs exploded within a few seconds on three London Underground trains. These bombs struck, in chronological order:

- An eastbound Circle Line train in transit between Liverpool Street (also a main line station) and Aldgate stations in the City of London
- A westbound Circle Line train travelling between Edgware Road and Paddington (having picked up passengers from King's Cross main line station)
- A southbound Piccadilly Line train travelling between King's Cross, St Pancras and Russell Square.

The explosions damaged track and adjacent infrastructure. At 09.19, following an amber alert, London Transport closed down their rail network.

At 09.47 a fourth bomb blasted a double-decker bus in Tavistock Square heading from Marble Arch towards Hackney Wick. This explosion happened close to the headquarters of the British Medical Association, from which a number of doctors immediately came to help the injured.

The explosions left 52 dead and some 700 injured. They disrupted London's transport systems for the rest of the day, and had a longer impact until the infrastructure was repaired.

The attacks occurred while the UK was hosting the G8 summit and the day following the announcement of London as the venue for the 2012 Olympic Games.

Two weeks later, on 21 July, there was a second coordinated attack, with four bombs being used against the London Underground and a double-decker bus. Fortunately, although the detonators fired, the main charges failed to explode.

Impact

The attacks had a major impact on mobile telecommunications operators: Vodafone invoked its Access Overload Control Scheme (ACCOLC) and other mobile operators also reported problems. In some cases, key people were denied access to the mobile network since they were not registered or enabled under ACCOLC.

The casualty bureau – emergency phone operators – handled 45 000 calls during the first hour of 7 July.

The attacks led to a sharp but temporary increase in faith hate crimes in the UK. By October, these crime figures had normalized.

The FTSE index fell from a three-year high by about 4% within a few hours, later recovering to finish up a little over 1% down.

The pound fell 89 cents against the dollar – a 19-month low.

The UK terrorist insurer of last resort, Pool Re, had ample reserves to meet claims.

Lessons

Several reports were published following the bombings[1] and an excellent overview of these has been prepared by Link Associates,[2] which draws together the following lessons.

People

- Information must be better shared and practical and emotional support provided to the bereaved and to survivors
- Establish reception and assistance centres quickly
- Identify potential problems in advance and provide for self-help, rather than elaborate plans that might not work
- Select and train response teams in advance and give authority for those responsible to act decisively
- Do not assume HR will take overall responsibility.

Communications

- Older emergency telecommunications systems did not perform very efficiently. Some radio equipment did not work effectively under ground.

---

[1] *These include:*
The report of the 7 July Review Committee (London Assembly) dated June 2006.
The House of Commons Report of the Official Account of the Bombings in London on 7 July, dated 11 May 2006.
The Parliamentary Intelligence and Security Committee Report dated May 2006.
Looking Back, Moving Forward (London Resilience Forum) dated September 2006.
Home Office Report *Addressing Lessons from the Emergency Response to the July 2005 London Bombings.*
[2] *July 7th 2005 – A Business Perspective*, Link Associates, October 2006, from info@lynxassociates.com

- One of the criticisms levelled at 999 services, including the Metropolitan Police, on 7 July was an over-reliance on mobile phones to communicate between sites and Gold commanders.
- Be prepared for website overload if directly impacted by the incident.
- Develop ways of swiftly passing messages to staff, especially in the first hour following the incident. Consider using senior executives/CEO.

Response

- Accurate, detailed records are essential.
- Understand own and local evacuation plans. Do not develop procedures in isolation.
- Consider declaration of a major incident at the earliest possible stage. Adopt the principle of 'precautionary over-reaction'.

Off-site recovery

- Ensure off-site arrangements remain appropriate to the business.
- Understand the limits of recovery site syndication ratios.

Post-incident

- Conduct a formal review once the incident is over.
- Ensure BC plans have a mechanism to facilitate review and improve procedures.
- Incorporate experiences into future exercises.

A1Z BUNCEFIELD (UK) OIL TERMINAL DISASTER – 11 DECEMBER 2005

Background

Buncefield oil storage terminal was originally built in 1960 to supply Heathrow airport, and further developed in the 1980s and 1990s with pipelines to transport fuel from Humber and Merseyside in the north of England. The company that owned Buncefield, Hertfordshire Oil Storage, was a joint venture between Total and Texaco and was operated by Total.

The site, Marylands Industrial Park, attracted other businesses because of its low cost.

Soon after 06:00 on Sunday 11 December 2005, a major explosion and fire took place at Buncefield oil storage terminal in Hemel Hempstead, Hertfordshire, England.

The explosion measured 2.4 on the Richter scale and was heard in France and the Netherlands.

General impact

The Buncefield incident was the biggest explosion and the biggest fire in peace-time Europe.

- Although the explosion caused 43 reported injuries, fortunately there were no fatalities.
- The explosion and fire destroyed some 5% of the UK's petrol stock.
- The north side of the oil storage terminal was largely destroyed, with the blast area covering over half a mile.
- The M1 North–South motorway, the main highway between London and the north of England, was closed.
- Smoke from the blaze could be seen from the neighbouring county of Buckinghamshire and from London.

Impact on businesses

Many businesses were affected by the disaster – some directly, some indirectly through disruption to their suppliers or their logistics operations. Some of their stories follow:

- Supermarket chain Sainsbury's had to temporarily close three stores damaged by the fire.
- Brewers Scottish & Newcastle lost stock valued at about £10 million when fire damaged its warehouse.
- Retailer Marks & Spencer had to close one of its six food depots, causing disruption to deliveries to its retail outlets.
- Fujifilm, 3Com Corporation and Alcom buildings close to the site were all damaged.
- Andromeda Logistics experienced damage to its distribution centre, which was close to the terminal. They evacuated the site but were able to resume operations by 12 December (the day after the explosion) from their alternative distribution centre at Hitchin, Hertfordshire.
- Although not directly involved in the event, British Petroleum took an immediate hit on its share price. Its shares settled back to normal after a few hours.
- ASOS (As Seen On Screen), an online fashion retailer, had opened a new, central warehouse in Hemel Hempstead in November 2005, close to Buncefield. The explosion destroyed ASOS's new warehouse and its entire stock, valued at £5.5 million ($9.6 million). ASOS was unable to fulfil orders. The CEO had to suspend trading of ASOS shares on the Alternative Investment Market (AIM). ASOS shares were suspended at 77.5p ($1.25) on 23 December. Sales and profits anticipated from busy Christmas trading were lost. Instead of selling goods, the corporate website was used to cancel orders and generate refunds. Some 19 000 customers, who had ordered goods for Christmas, had to be refunded. New premises had to be found.
- Buncefield terminal supplied around 30% of London Heathrow airport's fuel via a direct pipeline. British Airports Authority began rationing aviation fuel at Heathrow, causing airlines to divert to other European airports to refuel.
- There was concern that motorists would start panic buying. Garage Watch CEO, Mark Bradshaw, broadcast on BBC radio and television news to try to calm fears. 'This is not a problem of supply but of distribution,' he said. 'Our industry is well prepared for this kind of problem and measures are already in place to deal with the situation . . . UK refining is still at 100% with all nine UK refineries still at full production . . . we can assure the motorist that garage supplies should not be affected.'
- XL Video is a video producer for trade shows, events, television and concerts. Its HQ was 500 metres from the centre of the Buncefield explosion and suffered structural damage. A driver was at their site when the blast occurred, with tour trucks ready to unload. The site was evacuated within an hour: they no longer had access to warehouse or office facilities. They had 12 projects to load on the Monday morning. Their DRP was invoked to divert projects to First Network in Northolt. Staff were able to access the IT systems to establish requirements for each project. All shows were shipped on Monday 12 December.

- IT services company Northgate IS had its HQ near to the terminal. It provides managed services and outsourced applications. Northgate IS found it necessary to issue a statement to the London Stock Exchange to reassure investors and shareholders that it had successfully invoked its disaster recovery plan and had the situation under control. However, it admitted that its backup systems were 'rendered inoperable'. Client data was duplicated at the site and collected for off-site storage at 07:00 daily. But the fire happened at 06:00, before the backups were collected, and destroyed a whole day's client data. It was estimated to take two weeks to recover the data. All records could (over time) be reinstated, as a result:

    - Client Haringey Council was unable to collect any council tax payments.
    - Billing information for utility companies was lost.

Summary

The explosion and subsequent fire resulted in the following:

- Some 5% of UK petrol stocks were destroyed.
- 200 people were injured; 2000 were evacuated; more than 300 houses were damaged.
- 600 businesses and 25 000 staff were impacted.
- Global air traffic schedules suffered disruption.
- Many organizations, directly and indirectly affected, invoked their BC plans.
- Big retailers had to reassess supply chain issues.
- Companies were forced to make public statements to protect their share value.
- 20 fuel tanks were destroyed.
- 25 000 people were unable to get to work.
- Hundreds of schools were closed.
- Local transport was disrupted.
- There was a major environmental impact from millions of gallons of burning oil.
- 12 million litres of contaminated firewater with up to 40 different contaminants needed to be disposed of. It took 500 tankers five weeks to move it to temporary storage before incineration.
- The local Chamber of Commerce warned the cost to businesses and local authorities could reach £1 billion ($1.74 billion).
- 10 buildings were demolished.
- By 10 January 2006, data recovery and communications restoration was still ongoing.

- By 11 January 2006, 75 businesses employing 5000 people were still unable to use their premises.
- Insurance cover was often inadequate to cover losses.

Emergency response

Emergency response was, by general recognition, excellent:

- Hertfordshire County Council's crisis management plan worked: it had been used at the Potters Bar and Hatfield rail incidents and been tested in October 2005. The Council had also implemented a Local Resilience Forum (required by the UK Civil Contingencies Act) including Category 1 responders. These initiatives created a coordinated, multi-agency response, involving people who understood their crisis roles and the roles of others and who actually knew each other and had worked together previously. The Council's 12-person Emergency Planning Team implemented shift working to staff teams at both police HQ and County Hall.
- 25 different fire services were involved in tackling the blaze with 600 firefighters.
- Local education authorities closed most of the schools in the county because of risk from air pollution.
- Local residents who had not been evacuated were advised to stay indoors with windows closed.
- Motorists were advised to keep windows closed and air conditioning off.
- Regional radio and TV companies broadcast advice.

The cost

The cost is still being calculated. The items below cover some of the costs identified to date.

- Initial estimates put the financial impact of some £5 billion ($8.7 billion).
- Council tax and business rates will need to rise to cover the Council's rebuilding costs of around £7 million ($12.8 million).
- Rebuilding/refurbishment costs were put at £100 million ($1.74 million).
- The East of England Development Agency reported:
    - Cost to businesses was £70 million ($121.8 million).
    - 25 businesses were affected.

- 16 companies had to relocate.
- This caused job moves for 1422 people.
- There were 79 redundancies, 21 of those made redundant found new jobs.
- In August 2006, 2700 claimants banded together to sue – claims worth 'hundreds of millions of pounds'.

Lessons

- Communicate: to all key stakeholders
- Keep investors and customers informed
- Communicate: to emergency services and staff. Effective communication protects reputation, brand and share value and market share.
- Have an alternative site to work from and for a control centre
- Read and understand the emergency plans of the local authorities
- Ensure key resources are in place:

    - Information (status, contacts)
    - Accommodation (operations and work area)
    - Reserves (stock, spare equipment, etc.)

- Check insurance cover
- The impact of a major disaster could last for weeks . . . or months.

Appendix 2
General guideline notes

Appendices A2 A to A2 F:
Andrew Hiles, FBCI

The Definitive Handbook of Business Continuity Management, Second Edition.
Edited by Andrew Hiles FBCI. © 2007 John Wiley & Sons Ltd.

A2A RISK: A PROCESS APPROACH

Many countries run national lotteries – the biggest payout I have heard of was the recent US$185 million prize. In the UK, payouts can be over £15 million ($21 million). The Irish National Lottery is popular throughout Europe. And if you win El Grande in Spain you will need a wheelbarrow to cart your cash away. Do you buy lottery tickets? I admit I do. Strange, isn't it? We are prepared to accept odds of tens of millions to one against winning, on the basis that someone has to win and it could just be us. It is even stranger, then, that we dismiss the odds of hundreds to one that a disaster will actually happen to us!

A comprehensive approach to risk starts with an examination of business processes and the facilities, infrastructure and other assets necessary to support them. Ideally this should be done at the inception of a new process, project or product. For existing infrastructure and services, risk assessment needs to be applied retrospectively.

We were impressed by the process approach developed by a parastatal organization responsible for a country's entire infrastructure. They examined risk in planning, development, implementation, operational use and after-use. Geographically, they examined risk associated with the place of use – the area, the line (end to end topography of the infrastructure) and point.

This covered process and technology and process and infrastructure. Management risks were reviewed in terms of strategy, of the production process and operations. In terms of the production activities, risk data was gathered concerning pre-process activity, the core process itself and post-process activities. These risks were related to operational strategy, management and operations. They examined interaction with associated (dependent) processes and parallel processes (e.g. using the same facilities) and any consequential processes.

They developed a geographic warehouse, which literally maps all identified risks and includes navigational information, topographical information, infrastructure information and process information. It is possible to zoom in on a large-scale map; identify their infrastructure; zoom in on specific sites to site plans and photographs and thence on to buildings for building photographs and building plans. Some infrastructure may follow adjacent and parallel routes (e.g. highway, rail, power, telecommunications, water pipes). By looking at the geographic line of infrastructure and assets, it is also possible to identify what assets may also be affected by an incident: for instance, telecommunications or electricity supply ducts might be flooded by damage to adjacent water pipes.

Critical component failure analysis will examine the statistical possibility of the failure of components that represent a single point of failure, and can also identify the lead time to recover. A mathematical model (Monte Carlo analysis) can be run to identify the likelihood of multiple component failures. The theoretical end-to-end availability of infrastructure can then be calculated. When the impact of the loss of the component is identified, the recovery time objective can be set and a cost/benefit case may be made to introduce redundancy, resilience or alternative paths and processes to deliver the required level of availability or recovery time objective.

Some risk assessment methods seek to identify the cash and non-cash cost of the risk happening against the likelihood of the risk occurring (e.g. a fire costing $10 million once every 10 years). The cost of loss can then be averaged out on an annual basis. The spend on preventive measures can then be justified against the annual cost of loss. But we should remember that real life does not usually happen like that: nothing may happen for 20 years, then it all happens at once.

The most common form of risk assessment is to identify risks and the impact if they occur (at its simplest, catastrophic, high, medium, moderate or sustainable – cash values can be used for cash loss, 'points' can be used to weight non-cash loss). Each risk may be identified by a letter or number. An assessment is then made of the likelihood of the risks occurring (inevitable, probable, possible, unlikely – or timescales could be used if they can be estimated). A matrix can then be developed (Figure A2A.1) with the implication that the highest impact, most probable risks should have highest priority in the risk reduction programme. Traffic-light colours can be used to identify priorities.

Software tools may help to take some of the grind out of risk assessment. There are many risk assessment software tools available and some provide a good structure for risk assessment and a sound checklist of risks. Some are too generic and do not adequately relate these risks to the specific situation. Some simply massage subjective risk data and lend it a (perhaps specious) authenticity.

Combining a top-down process approach and a bottom-up assessment of risk will provide not just a powerful tool-set for risk management, but a risk-aware culture which benefits the whole operation. We often find that a risk and impact assessment provides the stimulus for improved control, procedures, resilience or processes – and this benefits the organization every day, not just in disaster!

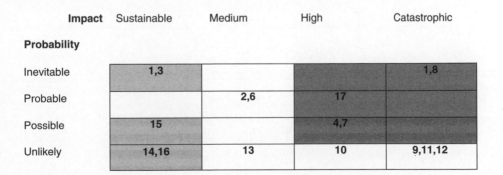

Impact Probability	Sustainable	Medium	High	Catastrophic
Inevitable	1,3			1,8
Probable		2,6	17	
Possible	15		4,7	
Unlikely	14,16	13	10	9,11,12

Figure A2A.1—A simple risk assessment matrix

A2B   DATA LOSS: WHERE DID IT GO?

Lost data: reasons and examples

It sounds self-evident that if data is worth collecting and keeping, it – and access to it – is worth protecting. But all too often it is vulnerable to loss or denied access.

Some survey results are summarized below – the results may differ depending on the sample surveyed.

A survey by SecureIT found that over half of respondents had recently suffered data loss and 75% of them blamed faulty or non-existent backups. It really is amazing how many organizations fail adequately to check that backups really are working – the only real way to prove it is to do a restore (but not to a live system – you might find out backup deficiencies the hard way!) Theft accounted for 8% of the loss. The survey also noted a steady increase in the amount of mission-critical data held on networks – over 80%. The occurrence of a serious network problem at least once a month was reported in 28% of networks. Data loss is costing UK business over £1 billion ($1.74 billion) a year, according to a Prodata survey. In Germany, a survey of national computer centres a few years ago resulted in a call for risk analysis and backup plans.

There are many reasons for loss of data, among them lack of systems integrity or systems inadequacy. A few real examples will prove the point. The British Army computerized supply system 'lost' millions of pounds worth of stores. At one point £6.7 million ($11.7 million) of ammunition could not be accounted for – 500 separate consignments went walkabout and 452 Milan anti-tank missiles were 'lost'.

Operator or user error is another common cause of lost data. In the USA, SunGard has reported a number of invocations over many years because of data loss. Their Carlstadt New Jersey facility came to the rescue of several of these. In one case a user mistakenly deleted a user journal; in another case a production IDMS database was rendered useless.

In a £100 million ($174 million) outsourcing contract, Scottish National Health Service complained of loss of patient records, both digital and paper. Records had been misdirected to other hospitals and in some cases pages had been lost. A British Medical Association spokesman said: 'This is a serious breach of security.'

Malicious damage by unauthorized access can also destroy data. An employee was fired by Digital Technologies Group of Hartford, Connecticut. The next day, all its web pages were deleted. The company lost business and was shut for a week.

Disgruntled employees are often the cause of loss of data – and frequently they destroy or remove backups, too. In another case, a tyre distributor lost nearly $2 million when a credit controller was fired: he kept a spare set of keys, re-entered the building, destroyed all invoice records and planted logic bombs in systems and programs – including the payroll.

A UK company, BAC Computer, discovered its client records were scrambled – later finding that an ex-employee had set up a similar business and was targeting their clients. The cost of damage was put at some £300 000 ($522 000) a month.

Data terrorism and extortion is also a cause for concern. Guylain Olivera de France de Terfant and Michel Bruchon (both French) gained entry to Barclays International Bank at Trafalgar Square, London, and stole computer disks. They were sentenced to four years in prison.

Sometimes data may be erased that protects fraud. In the infamous case of the Bank of Credit and Commerce International (BCCI) investigations were ongoing in the UK, Luxembourg and the USA. An attorney admitted that he had erased parts of a diary kept by Zafar Iqbal, former Chief Executive of the Ubu Fhabi-based bank. The entries were thought to show when the Abu Dhabi authorities first became aware of fraud at the bank. The attorney's defence was that he had erased the entries because they were held in an insecure location.

Malware

There are some 3.5 million virus infections a month, growing each month – many capable of destroying a database.

In 2003, the Blaster virus reportedly cost $15.2 billion worldwide. In February 2006 Commtouch® announced spam and computer virus statistics for the month of January 2006.[1] The data was based on information continuously gathered by the Commtouch Detection Center, which analysed more than 2 billion messages from over 130 countries during the month of January. In summary:

- Four massive virus attacks occurred in January, including a multi-wave attack of seven variants.
- The most aggressive attacks penetrated before the average anti-virus solution could even release a signature.
- There were 19 new email-borne significant virus attacks, of which eight (42%) were graded 'low intensity', seven (37%) 'medium intensity' and four (21%) were massive attacks – a rare phenomenon for a single month.
- One outbreak of specific interest, consisting of seven variants, illustrates how viruses are growing in sophistication: the first variant was launched around 25 December 2005 as a low intensity virus; however, with subsequently released variants the attack's intensity grew into a massive outbreak towards the end of the month.

[1] http://www.commtouch.com/Site/News_Events/pr_content.asp?news_id=602&cat_id=1.

- There is a clear connection between the attack's speed and its intensity – the faster attacks are the biggest ones: while the average distribution time of low intensity attacks is a 'leisurely' 27 hours and medium-intensity attacks can take 17 hours, massive attacks take as little as 5.5 hours to spread in hundreds of millions of emails.

According to the FBI, viruses, spyware, PC theft and other computer-related crimes costs US businesses an amazing $67.2 billion a year. The FBI calculated the cost by extrapolating results from a survey of 2066 organizations. The survey, released in January 2006, found that 1324 respondents, or 64%, suffered a financial loss from computer security incidents over a 12-month period. The average cost per company was more than $24 000, with the total cost reaching $32 million for those surveyed.

Theft

Theft of PCs and no backup are a lethal combination: a UK cosmetics firm, Cosmetics to Go, lost its customer database this way – the £1 million ($1.74 million) company subsequently went bankrupt.

When burglars emptied a fire extinguisher into a server at Clifton Securities, causing severe data loss, the securities authorities closed the firm down.

Motivation may be political as well as commercial: Members of Parliament in the UK complained that computer disks have been stolen from the House of Commons, and party leader Paddy Ashdown discovered his constituency computer had been tampered with. Access was gained to constituency member information. At about the same time private documents were stolen from his London solicitors' offices.

Hardware and software failure

Hardware failure – a disk head crash during a routine backup – hit 17 north London, UK, hospitals causing cancellation of appointments and failure to find patient records. And when a power supply unit in a Scottish bank's main server failed, the result was a lock of all IMS database files.

Software failure can be equally damaging: in 1994, American Express UK cardmember services division systems, serving all of Europe, were down for two and a half hours because a software application bug prevented access to customer history database, stopping files from being updated and causing telephone queries to be unanswered. It took another five hours to bring systems back online.

Data loss can have its lighter side: for two weeks, a UK rail operator business 'lost' a £1 million ($1.74 million) 17 metre long Inter-City 125 train weighing 75 tons. In another case, backups were kept in a fireproof safe. When thieves broke into an office building, all they stole was the safe.

Post-disaster

Are backups accessible in a disaster? Charles Schwab & Co. suffered when trying to recover their backups following the California earthquake: tapes were stuck in gridlock on the highway in transit to the airport and onward flight to the backup site. By the time the highway had cleared, the airport was closed down.

In another sensitive case, thieves stole a PC and backup disks from the UK National Association for the Care and Resettlement of Prisoners: it held data on prisoners. Voters were disenfranchised in a UK election when they were deleted from the electoral role by a data processing firm.

Backups are not always what you think they are. A colleague was inspecting a client's IT operations when he noticed an operator load a tape and key in a few instructions. Almost instantly the tape drive leapt into life – and stopped just as quickly. 'What was that?' my colleague asked. 'Oh,' the operator replied, 'that was the backup. It used to take hours, but it's ever so quick now we've got the new program.' Yes, you have guessed: when checked, the program merely wrote a header to tape. Effective backups had not been taken for weeks. A similar case arose when one organization tried to restore from its backups: it found it had been writing zeros to tape for months.

Yet another problem can arise where the device reads a block from memory, transfers it to tape, verifies the data on tape is the same as was read, then moves along a track repeating the process. A stepping motor then drops down to the next track and the process is repeated. On some devices, if the stepping motor is jammed, the device may simply go back over the same track, overwriting what was previously saved.

Another issue can arise when trying to restore: some devices have such sensitive head alignment that only the device that wrote the cartridge can read it. It pays to check read capability before it's really needed!

The cost of lost data

According to a report on data loss in Europe by Previo (since acquired by Altiris[2]), over 6% of PCs will suffer data loss in any year – a total of 1.7 million incidents. Looking at the issue globally, in Q2 2006 alone, worldwide personal computer

[2] www.altiris.com

sales were almost 55 million units according to Gartner. Both Gartner and IDC agree that International shipments continued to expand at roughly 11% year over year. The two analysts put Q3 numbers at between 57 million and 59 million. Cumulative sales of PCs in use total around 1 billion. That represents a huge amount of data and a vast amount of loss.

At the time of the report, there were approximately 27.2 million PCs in use in Europe – 23.2 million desktops and 4 million laptops. The report identified six main causes of loss of data:

- Hardware failure, including damage by power surge and hard drive failure (42%)
- Human error, including accidental deletion (31%)
- Software corruption (13%)
- Virus (7%)
- Theft, especially laptop theft (5%)
- Hardware destruction (including floods, fires, lightning and power failure) (3%).

Each incident will have one of two outcomes: successful recovery of data or permanent loss. The calculation of the cost of data loss considers each of these possibilities.

Data recovery experts claim that in 80% of cases, lost data can be restored – at a cost. Even if the recovery is by an in-company support engineer, the cost of their salary averages out at around $35/hour. Typically, data recovery takes around six hours – a cost of $210. Using an external data recovery company increases this cost to $420, on average.

However, a more significant cost is the cost of lost productivity by the user, impacting sales and profitability. The salary cost of lost productivity is around $32.50 – an average hiding huge differences. Using this average, the six hour loss of productivity adds another $195.

If we assume that the other 20% of cases result in permanent loss of data, the cost can rocket. It may take hundreds of man-hours to rebuild data – in some cases, if the data is historic or experimental, it may never be possible to reproduce it. Several sources suggest that the value of 100 megabytes of data is worth approximately $1 million. Thus, if the average loss is just one megabyte of data, the loss costs $10 000.

Bringing all these figures together, the average cost of each incident is $2615 (ranging from $615 for retrieved data to $19 615 for permanently lost data). Data loss costs European business $4.5 billion annually – and even this does not take into account potential loss of customers, loss of business, loss of market share, compliance failure or legal breach.

The implications are clear: regular and effective backup is vital. Products are now available that not only save this waste, but also improve IT help desk productivity in problem solving. One such product snapshots the entire hard disk content including operating system, applications, data files, preferences and user settings. The information is automatically compressed at three levels (file, block, data) and stored in a network repository. Standard settings (e.g. for basic set-up and applications for many PCs) are stored only once and cross-referenced for optimum capacity usage and speed of recovery. This means that in many cases it will be more productive for the help desk to roll back the last snapshot than to spend hours in problem diagnostics. And should a user lose data, restoration from individual files or the entire content of an individual PC can be done within minutes rather than hours. Subject to access rights and policy, the more computer-sophisticated users could do this without help desk intervention.

The payback speaks for itself – using such a tool, one organization identified a return on investment of around £3 million ($5.2 million) over two years from savings on data loss and improved IT help desk productivity.

Other vital materials

The importance of backing up non-IT vital records and materials cannot be over-stated. But all too often, the mindset stops at backing up computer data and programs. Vital materials can be almost anything – not just disks and tapes. If you have conducted a critical component failure analysis, you may have found areas within your organization where there is a single point of failure. Applying redundancy or keeping a spare off-site may be the answer. A few examples will illustrate the point:

1. A £35 million ($61 million) installation needed four air conditioner compressors to cool it in summer. There was no redundancy. The manufacturer of the air conditioning had long since gone out of business. There was a 16-week manufacturing lead time to produce a one-off compressor in balance with the others. The compressor cost £15 000 ($26 000). Worthwhile to have one made and keep it in reserve? Or to take out a contract for quick supply of another unit?
2. A retail fashion chain depends on its top selling lines. Some of these are classics and may be regularly reordered from manufacturers. The only way you know if you are getting the same colour, cut and quality is by checking the new batch against sample garments and colour swatches. Therefore among vital materials backed up off-site could be, for instance, samples of the top 20 lines.
3. A manufacturer depends for its unique market position on patented designs produced by special dies and moulds: the dies and moulds are vital materials and should be backed up off-site.

4. A sauce, spice and condiment supplier operation depends on its unique recipes – the recipes are vital materials.
5. A market research operation receives input via audio tapes of interviews around the world. Until the tapes are captured on to a computer system, are these vital materials?
6. Many companies receive vast amounts of paper – orders, invitations to tender, contracts, work in progress. Some of it may be irreplaceable. When thinking about backup, don't forget the paper or the mission-critical work in progress. In many cases the need to recover vital paper documents has been the justification for microfilm, microfiche or document management systems.

Summary

Cases like some of those quoted above may seem like a joke – but not if they happen to you! And data loss isn't even funny for comedians: entertainer Ruby Wax threatened to 'murder' an operator who accidentally wiped her script. The lessons are self-evident:

- Back up frequently and ensure you can restore from back up.
- Keep backup off-site; ensure you are fire-walled against hacking and virus.
- Use automated backup tools.
- Back up all vital records and materials – not just IT.

According to the UK Department of Trade and Industry, 70% of organizations that experience serious data loss go out of business within 18 months: the choice is clear – it could be a case of back up or die.

A2C THE ROLE OF INSURANCE

Is it safe to rely on insurance?

Myths, misconceptions and delusion abound in the customer's perception of insurance. It is comforting to take out a policy and believe the insurer will pay out when the worst happens. But will they?

Insurance companies periodically go through lean times and wish to avoid unnecessary payments: and insurers have a duty to shareholders to return decent dividends. So insurers generally are getting more picky about accepting claims as valid and, when accepting valid claims, about how much will be paid out. Increasingly, negligence on the part of the insured may lead to a reduced payout . . . and the interpretation of negligence is open to debate. For instance, is failure to have a business continuity plan (to limit loss) negligence? Indeed, recent conferences in London, UK, were designed to help insurers interpret insurance policy clauses so as legitimately to avoid paying out on claims.

All too often, the business continuity manager or the line manager does not know what insurance is in force – they just assume the corporate insurance manager or risk manager has it taped.

Beware the small print

So, what is covered? Often, insurers do not understand the detail of the business they are insuring (especially high-tech businesses) and the insurance is negotiated with the insurer by, say, a finance person who again may not fully understand the technology. The result may be an ambiguous insurance policy which misses the point and leaves much inadequately covered. Please, check your policy – and, if in doubt, ask the insurer for an unambiguous definition or clarification. Here are just a few examples of ambiguous words found in insurance policies:

- 'Data carrying materials' – so disk arrays, CDs, DVDs, USB memory sticks and tapes should be covered . . . shouldn't they? But does this include copper or fibre-optic cable? Filing cabinets? Safes? PCs? Laptops? Just the hard or (if we still use them) floppy disks in PCs and laptops? Are hand-held devices covered? Cellular telephones? Anything with a memory? Computer control systems for automobiles? What about microwaves?
- 'Computer' – with chips in virtually all equipment, do we know what a computer is any more?
- 'Test equipment' – if we run diagnostics across the infrastructure, does this make it all 'test equipment'?

- 'Data' – typically insurance will not cover the re-creation of data from a zero base, but only the restoration of data from an existing source.
- 'Maintenance must be in force' – to what level and by whom? If we have not advised the insurer of a third party maintenance contract, does this mean we have withheld 'relevant information'?
- 'Any single loss from any one event' – on 9/11 2001, at 08:45 ETD, a hijacked passenger jet, American Airlines Flight 11 out of Boston, Massachusetts, crashed into the north tower of the World Trade Center, setting it on fire. At 09:03 ETD a second hijacked airliner, United Airlines Flight 175 from Boston, crashed into the south tower of the World Trade Center and exploded. At 10:05 ETD the south tower of the World Trade Center collapsed. At 10:28 ETD the World Trade Center's north tower collapsed. There were two different pilots flying two different aircraft, striking two different buildings (albeit within the same World Trade Center complex) at different times. Each building collapsed at a different time.

  The World Trade Center complex was leased to the partnership of Silverstein Properties and Westfield America. They took out an insurance policy for the complex including a clause that, in the event of a terrorist attack, the full insured value of the property would be paid and obligations under the 99-year lease would be void.

  After the attack, Silverstein Properties claimed twice the value of the insurance policies on the grounds that there had been two separate 'occurrences' entitling them to claim a double payment of $8.9 billion instead of the single payment of $3.6 under the policies.

  The point of law was not so much about whether the 9/11 attacks were two different events: the World Trade Center was destroyed just once. The issue was whether this destruction was caused by one, or two, 'occurrences'. The arguments swayed backwards and forwards until, in December 2004, the leaseholders' claim for double payment was upheld.

Self-insurance

Self-insurance is not necessarily of help. If you are self-insured, does that mean 'corporate' has reinsured loss or are they carrying the risk themselves? All of the risk . . . or do they have an insurance reserve? One public sector enterprise became a government agency as the first step towards privatization. We asked if that meant they needed commercial insurance, instead of being covered by the government contingency fund. Several months later, the reply came back: 'Yes, we need insurance, but we are self-insured.' Our response: 'How?' Another few months elapsed and the reply came: 'We have our own contingency fund.' Another question: 'How much?' Another few months went by until . . . '$4 million'. The installation we were inspecting cost $75 million – and that was only one of many operational assets. Some of the operational plant was valued at hundreds of millions of dollars. If it failed, the potential consequential liabilities could have run into billions.

As a business continuity planner, do you know how to get your hands on the insurance reserve (or at least get authority to commit spend against it in a disaster situation)? If not, you need to find out – or you could get bogged down in multinational conglomerate-style financial politics where 'corporate' expects individual business units to cover themselves and individual business units think 'corporate' has it covered. Do you know how big the insurance reserve is? Is it enough? In any event, one way or the other the insurance reserve has to be funded and eventually it comes back to the bottom line.

Insured value

What value do we place on the asset? Depreciated cost? Depreciated how . . . tax depreciation or book value? Are these the same, or different? Do our corporate depreciation policies really reflect the true cost of acquiring similar equipment? And what if the asset is worth more to the business than its book value?

Are we insured for exact replacement of an asset (like for like) or for the nearest equivalent – and if for the nearest equivalent, what if it is not fully compatible (say with existing software applications or with other parts of a production process)? Who pays for redesign? Is just the equipment cost covered, or the full project cost of reinstatement to the pre-disaster status?

Building insurance, for instance, may be covered for rebuilding costs according to a cost-of-building index (one commonly used is the Baxter index). However, this applies to a standard building. When we reviewed insurance cover for an international law firm, we discovered that the Baxter index had been used. However, the quality of the offices was outstanding: expensive exotic wooden panelling, marble, high quality fittings – the best of everything. When we checked, the offices had cost over 20% more than the Baxter index construction costs for premises of that size. They were substantially underinsured.

What risks are insured? The one thing we can be certain of is that an 'all risks' policy does not cover all risks! In some policies (notably cases concerning malicious damage or fraud) for an effective claim we may have to prove the identity of the perpetrator. Could we?

We can insure for loss of profits, cost of cashflow disruption, interest, extra cost of working and many other things. But to be sure of getting paid, we have to prove the loss beyond reasonable doubt. So do we have pre-agreed formulae with the insurers . . . do we have evidence of the existence and value of our assets? Inventories . . . videos, photographs?

Uninsured losses

Following a disaster we often see in the headlines huge figures for loss and, reading the level of claims or the actual payout in the insurance press, we note a large discrepancy. Sometimes the first figure reflects journalistic sensationalism: but sometimes it also reflects a high element of uninsured loss.

The US Geological Survey Marine and Coastal Geology Program advises that: 'Insurance coverage for losses resulting from natural disasters is typically less than 20 percent of the total loss, because of limited participation in voluntary insurance coverage.' Costs and losses relating to Hurricane Katrina, which struck New Orleans in August 2005, were put at $125 billion – with only one-fifth covered by insurance. This percentage broadly applies for most losses, however caused, around the world.

Although tax relief may be available for uninsured losses in the United States, this is not the case worldwide. In the United States of America, Federal 1 disaster assistance can be provided through the Stafford Act when the President declares a major disaster. In certain cases the United States Small Business Administration (USSBA) can declare a disaster under its own authority. But the end result may not be compensation, but additional debt. In any event, business loans for the repair or replacement of real estate are limited to $1 500 000.

New Orleans City, following the devastation of Hurricane Katrina, advised home owners that:

> Additionally, in most cases with substantial damage (generally defined as an unin-sured loss of 40% or more) we can lend an additional amount up to the uncompen-sated property damage (but not more than $200 000) to refinance a prior recorded mortgage

In terms of personal property, the Washington Military Department Emergency Management Division advised:

> . . . secondary homes and recreational homes are not eligible for disaster assistance of any kind. Detached garages and storage buildings do not count either. So, when you are submitting damage reports, please know that these will not be counted in determining eligibility for disaster assistance.

It adds (with its emboldening):

> To get federal disaster assistance via the Stafford Act (major disaster declaration) for anything less than 100 uninsured/underinsured homes (primary residences) is going to be difficult, **but not necessarily impossible**. More than the numbers of homes sustaining major damage or destroyed, **the supplemental justification will need to paint a picture of a devastating loss for which there are no resources to help with recovery**

If your organization suffers from a wide area disaster, what prospect is there of employees being around to help you recover, when they are homeless and their best prospect may be the crushing burden of additional mortgage debt? Bear in mind that, while personal debt may increase, in Louisiana per capita income reduced by 25% following the disaster.

Following the Los Angeles civil unrest in April and May 1992:[1]

> The report, *The City in Crisis*, by former FBI Director Webster, dated October 1992 (p. 23) states that $1 billion in property was damaged or destroyed. A separate door-to-door survey by Dun & Bradstreet, the credit reporting agency, suggested that the number of businesses damaged or destroyed totalled 2314. Dun & Bradstreet further estimated that as many as 4500 businesses were touched by the riots.
>
> A Dun & Bradstreet study estimated that 40% of the destroyed businesses have closed their doors for good. That survey also found widespread lack of insurance and under-insurance, reporting that only 25% of the businesses had adequate insurance, and one-fifth had no coverage at all. In addition, news reports and information reported the great difficulty in qualifying for Small Business Administration (SBA) loans.

It's not all bad news

Insurance is full of pitfalls, and my view may seem jaundiced: it is not intended to be. Insurance companies have a perfect right to protect themselves and their stakeholders from frivolous, ambitious or fraudulent claims. It isn't all doom and gloom – a client had a claim of almost $1 million agreed for a flood that, in the strict interpretation of the policy, our consultant believed could have been excluded from cover! The damage was caused by construction workers breaking a mains water supply, which flooded our client's basement – home to some computer equipment and the frame room. The insurance policy had a clause, under exclusions: '... escape of a mass of water, whether natural or man-made'. The insurance company paid out. That might have been partly because the insurance company was a mutual organization, answering to its subscribers instead of shareholders, and there to protect them rather than make commercial profits. Or, it might just be that the $1 million was peanuts compared to the annual premiums our client was paying worldwide, and the payout was simply a goodwill gesture. But it is in the interests of both the insurer and the insured to make sure the risks are clearly understood – and covered.

---

[1] www.usc.edu/libraries/archives/cityinstress/newinit/part7.html.

A2D   FIVE NINES: CHASING THE CHIMERA?

Five nines (99.999%) availability: why chase it? 'Because it's there?' Is it actually achievable? Or for a sound business reason? What's the payback? Is it some goal we strive for, like the ultimate truth or perfect beauty, that we know we are unlikely ever to attain? Or should we really be striving for six nines (99.9999%)?

Let us examine the maths of it, first. A definition of availability may help: 'The percentage uptime achieved per year.' Given this definition, the maximum downtime permitted per year may be calculated as reflected in Table A2D.1. Please do not debate with me leap years, lost seconds or even changes to the Gregorian calendar. Equally let us not debate time travel! To quote a Cypriot: 'I am from a village: I know nothing.' The figures in Table A2D.1 are sufficiently accurate to make the points this appendix is trying to get across.

If you really want to throw a spanner in the works, change the definition of availability to: 'The percentage of *scheduled* uptime per year.' But let's not go there. We are talking absolutes.

Table A2D.2 summarizes components (i.e. dependencies) just for an ICT facility, excluding ICT equipment, systems and software.

All this implies alternate power sources: for example, mains power from separate substations; dual UPS; backup generators with automatic cut-in and capacity to cover equipment and, where necessary, end-user environments, elevators, etc.; adequate fuel supplies.

We also need permanent – 24/7/365 – on-site support with appropriate skills, tools, etc. This falls short of the fabled five nines, but it is as high as the Uptime Institute's tier classification goes – and only 10% of organizations achieve this.

Well, let us assume we can engineer the facility (including the personnel involved in running and supporting it) to deliver a 99.999% availability.

The next question is: 'How do we measure the availability within our service?' Now we need to include ICT equipment, operating systems, diagnostic, performance measurement and management software, middleware, applications and anything else used in the delivery of the service. Then we need to calculate the availability of each of these components on which the service depends.

Table A2D.1—Uptime and maximum downtime

Uptime	Uptime	Maximum downtime per year
Six nines	99.9999%	31.5 seconds
Five nines	99.999%	5 minutes 35 seconds
Four nines	99.99%	52 minutes 33 seconds
Three nines	99.9%	8 hours 46 minutes
Two nines	99.0%	87 hours 36 minutes
One nine	90.0%	36 days 12 hours

Table A2D.2—Calculating availability: facility (Source: Uptime Institute)[1]

Specification item	Specification
Number of delivery paths	3 active
Redundant components	2 (N + 1) or S + S
Support space to raised floor ratio	100%
Initial watts/ft^2	50–80
Ultimate watts/ft^2	150+
Raised floor height	30–36″
Floor loading pounds/ft^2	150+
Utility voltage	12–15 kV
Construction \$/ft^2 raised floor[a]	\$1100+
Annual IT downtime due to site	0.4 hours
Site availability	99.995%

[a] This excludes land and abnormal civil costs. Assumes minimum of 15 000 ft^2 of raised floor, architecturally plain one storey building fitted out for initial capacity but with backbone designed for ultimate capacity with installation of additional components. Make adjustments for high cost areas.

It is easy to assume that replicating components halves the downtime: but, in introducing more components, we are also introducing greater complexity and more possible points of failure. A relatively simple service is illustrated at Figure A2D.1. Components have been replicated; however, they also need to be kept in synch and switchable between the two parallel configurations at any point of failure, so switches are introduced. If one configuration is active and the other passive, the switches detect component failure in the primary (active) configuration and switch the load to the secondary (previously passive but now active) matched component in the second configuration, which assumes the role and identity of the primary component. The result is improved resilience – but also more complexity, more components and more than double the cost.

Where there is only a single configuration, and if each component has a 99.999% availability, the theoretical availability of the overall service is calculated by multiplying 99.999% by 99.999% and multiplying the result by the availability (99.99%) for every component in the configuration. If we arbitrarily say there are 10 physical components in the configuration, if my trembling finger has hit the right keys the appropriate number of times, the theoretical availability works out at 'only' 99.988%. Even if we replicate all these components to the extent that we increase the configuration availability overall to 99.999% and if we manage to get the physical infrastructure to deliver 99.999% our overall theoretical capability will still 'only' be 99.997%.

[1] *Data Center Construction Costs*, by Larry Smith, President, ABR Consulting Group, Inc. for the Uptime Institute. The Uptime Institute® http://upsite.com/TUIpages/whitepapers/tuitiers.html has developed a classification approach to site infrastructure that includes measured availability figures ranging from 99.67% to more than 99.99%.

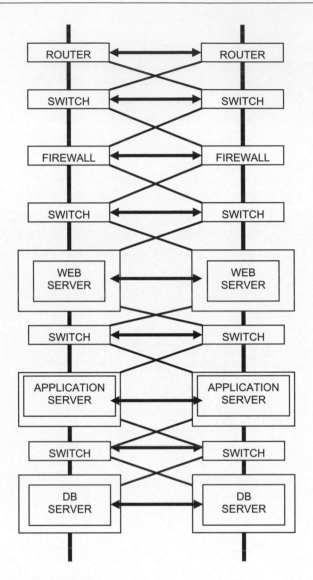

Figure A2D.1—Replicated service

So far this figure represents purely infrastructure and hardware failure: we should also include the possibility of loss of end-to-end tele- and datacommunications, operating systems, middleware, application software, databases and data. Even including these elements, the two systems need to be geographically separated since, if they are in the same data centre, a fire, bomb, geophysical, meteorological or common infrastructure incident or facility or utilities failure could impact both of them. And on top of this is the security level: outage could equally well come from security breach as equipment or software failure. Finally, we have to consider the people issues: operator error or loss of key personnel.

Just one other point: our availability figures typically derive from manufacturers' (or maintenance companies') statistics on mean time between failure (MTBF). MTBF is exactly that: it conceals variations in actual performance and comes up with a 'normalized' performance. That is, every user of a piece of equipment with a 99.999% MTBF does not get 99.999% MTBF: some people get better performance, some worse. Microsoft claimed that its top-end Windows 2000 servers were 'designed to deliver 99.999% server uptime'. This is not the same as delivering it! An Aberdeen study of Windows 2000 customers running production systems reported that, on average, customers were achieving only about 99.964% uptime – about 3.2 hours of downtime per year.[2]

Another consideration is fix time, when the equipment does fail. In the case of a single component, a 99.999% availability implies a time from fail to fix of less than five seconds! OK, you have a redundant component. Have you ever had two flat tyres on a single journey? I have! You could call it Murphy's First Law of Availability.

So is 99.999% achievable? Yes. But over how long a period? A year? Two years? Five years? Seven years? Basically, unless we calculate the numbers, we are effectively walking into a casino and betting against the bank. Sometimes we win. But over time, sooner or later, the bank always wins. Murphy's Second Law of Availability.

But, if you are lucky, the equipment will become obsolete before it fails. Over time, technology upgrades are necessary. Upgrades mean change. Change means danger. How good is your testing and your change and configuration management? How good are your checks and balances, quality processes and management of people? A 2002 survey said that 31% of network downtime was due to human error. Chernobyl was caused by operator error.

Your equipment vendors may claim five nines or better – but can your service suppliers deliver five nines to support you? Even if they offer it, we know of no service vendor that will accept consequential loss for failure, so the vendor's failure is still your risk. There is almost always a weak link in the chain. Murphy's Third Law of availability.

Another issue is: When does availability happen? Even in the most demanding, time-sensitive environments, there are business cycles: some times of the day or days of the year may be more critical than others. The day the markets go mad . . . The end of the year . . . The day the new, mission-critical web or call centre service goes live . . . The day the multimillion dollar advertising campaign hits the media. The billion dollar transaction or deal . . . When availability is most required, that is when it is most likely to fail. Murphy's Fourth Law of Availability.

[2] By Graeme Bennett (posted 11 July 2001; updated 9 July 2002) 'five-nines uptime = 99.999% reliability, or one hour out of service every 11.4 years' – dansdata.com.

So to our next questions:

- Why do we want it?
- What's the payback?

Undoubtedly there are situations where there is a financial case for five nines – or as close to perfection as is possible. We have clients who have successfully operated at that level (so far for over two years) – typically in real-time financial trading situations.

An interesting case study found that, while some telecommunications vendors offered five nines,[3] three nines was adequate for retailing. The study[4] evaluated costs and business benefits of 99.999% of scheduled availability for point-of-sale tills, as opposed to 99.9%, to retail operations. It identified a potential benefit of only $297 of increased revenue and $204 of reduced expense – total $501 – per store.

So, what does downtime cost? Partly it depends on what other channels customers have to access your services. If you have a branch network, a call centre and a web service maybe service outage is less important than if you only have a call centre or just have a website. We hear banks talk of five nines for automated teller machines: Yet they are taken down each night to replenish them with money. As long as there is another nearby, this does not cause a problem. Downtime impact also depends on your customers' loyalty and on the effectiveness of your competition. And, as we have seen earlier, it also depends when the outage happens.

Some industry statistics may help to put a context to potential losses from downtime. The numbers differ, depending on the source, but Table A2D.4 gives some idea of possible impact.

Other surveys fill in similar estimates for other industries and provide a cross-check. A 2004 survey,[5] for instance, put losses on brokerage operations at $4500 000/hour; banking at $2100 000/hour; media at $1150 000/hour and e-commerce at $113 000/hour. Retail trailed at $90 000/hour. There is also a possible hit on share value (e-Bay's outages in 1999 saw shares drop by over 26%, while e*Trade's similar problems saw a 22% drop) – but this may be only temporary.

If your industry is on the list, it is worthwhile trying to work out the relative impact on your business of downtime of, say, 99.5%, 99.9%, 99.95%, 99.99% and 99.999% – and comparing it with the cost of implementing availability at each level. There is probably no additional cost below 99.95%. Does higher availability pay back? Some of the generic costs and losses that can be incurred as a result of service downtime are illustrated at Table A2D.4.

Uptime is important. In high value, high transaction volume operations it can cost big bucks (but so can a wrong business call). In military systems, often the

---

[3] *Business Week*, 2003.
[4] *PDMA Toolbook II, Establishing Quantitative Economic Value for Features and Functionality of New Products and New Services*, by Kevin Otto (Product Genesis Inc.), Victor Tang and Warren Seering (Massachusetts Institute of Technology).
[5] Yankee Group, 2004.

Table A2D.3—Downtime losses

Industry sector	$ks revenue/hour
Energy	2818
Telecom	2066
Manufacturing	1611
Finance	1495
IT	1344
Insurance	1202
Retail	1107

Source: Meta Group.

Table A2D.4—Potential causes of loss – downtime

Cause of costs/loss

Impact on stock price

Cost of fixing/replacing equipment
Cost of fixing/replacing software
Salaries paid to staff unable to undertake productive work
Salaries paid to staff to recover work backlog and maintain deadlines
Cost of re-creation and recovery of lost data
Loss of customers (lifetime value of each) and market share
Loss of product
Product recall costs
Loss of cashflow from debtors
Interest value on deferred billings
Penalty clauses invoked for late delivery and failure to meet service levels
Loss of profits
Additional cost of credit through reduced credit rating
Fines and penalties for non-compliance
Liability claims
Additional cost of advertising, PR and marketing to reassure customers and prospects
to retain maximum share
Additional cost of working; administrative costs; travel and subsistence, etc.

decision time will exceed five minutes. In life safety-related activities five nines may be crucial – but even in air traffic control, we have seen systems down for hours without a disaster. Should we chase six nines? Do the maths. But probably not. There are more dangerous threats that we can address were cheaply. A slow and poorly designed website or an insensitively thought-out interactive voice response system may have far more – and longer lasting – effects on customer loyalty and market share than 10 minutes of downtime a year. It was not downtime that pushed a number of airlines, Enron or WorldCom into Chapter 11. Prolonged outage has caused bankruptcy, certainly. Even outage of a few hours has caused serious loss. But I still await a case of a five-minute outage causing total corporate collapse.

A2E   CONSULTANCY WITHOUT TEARS

A consultant is a person who borrows your watch to tell you the time, charges you for doing so and then sells you back your watch. Consultants have had a bad press – sometimes they have themselves to blame. Once they get into an organization they can infest it like woodworm, creeping through every part of the company – and business consultants have a vested interest in reorganization, since it makes work for them – hence a cycle of centralization and distributed operations, consolidation and diversification. I know one consultancy responsible for a corporate culture change programme who told the client 'you are going to go through three years of chaos, and we will not know the outcome until it's all over' – and charged a $2.2 million fee for doing so. From the consultant's viewpoint, this was neat: if you set off for an unspecified destination without a map, you cannot blame the consultant if you never arrive – alternatively at any convenient point the consultant can say 'hey, we're here'. To my simple mind, one ought to have a good idea of the destination before setting out.

Is business continuity consultancy any different? As a director of a consultancy company, I admit to being embarrassed at times at the quality of work we see from other consultants – large companies as well as small. But, on the whole, business continuity consultancy is different.

Companies serious about business continuity frequently use consultants for some or all of the business continuity project lifecycle: risk analysis, business impact analysis, business continuity strategy, plan design, implementation, testing, plan audit. Where software is used, the consultant may help the client to exploit its full potential and train the client in its use. In some cases, the business continuity planning activity is outsourced to consultants.

Effective use of consultants depends on the client having a good idea of what they are looking for in the consultant. Does the client want a partner in solving problems, a guru, a silent influencer, a technical assistant, skilled resource, or a skills transferrer? In each case, the role of the consultant – and that of the client – may be different.

The problem solver consultant:

- Acts as a facilitator whenever it is appropriate
- Avoids 'quick fixes' and produces solid lasting solutions
- Understands and acts to further the client's mission
- Does not confuse the client by talking in a different language
- Only makes promises when they can be kept
- Keeps a good relationship with others in the company
- Minimizes dependency of the client on the consultant
- Encourages the client's competence, confidence and commitment
- Works with the client on the problem solution

- Focuses on the relationship with the client and technical problems
- Doesn't take on any of the client's responsibilities.

The consultant will concentrate on two-way communication, developing an attack plan, accumulating and analysing data, solution finding and managing his or her side of the project. The client usually defines the problem and subsequently implements the solution, often in concert with the problem solver.

The guru generates the plan, develops the solution, makes technical judgements and organizes data collection while the client's role is typically to define the problem and effect the solution.

The silent influencer is viewed as a leader with potential to change the pattern of events, acts as an objective, detached sounding board and returns feedback to the client. Often their contribution is enormous but, at the end of the contract, those not immediately involved may say 'what did he do?' because the resultant actions have been owned and delivered by client managers. It's a little like the effective manager who goes into his slightly bemused but flattered boss and says 'I've been thinking about what you said the other day – it's a great idea, I've just developed it a little for you.'

The technical support consultant or skilled resource pursues the implementation while the client defines the project plan, constructs requirement specifications, describes the required solution and advises on implementation.

The skills to be transferred are defined by the client, while the skills transferrer consultant passes on expertise in the most appropriate and effective way. In many ways, this is the most effective use of consultants: suck their brains out and throw them away as quickly as possible!

Of course, sometimes the edges between these approaches may be blurred, some assignments involve the consultant acting in more than one of these roles – and one can debate the detail of the roles endlessly. The real point, however, is that the client must know what they want from the consultant and both client and consultant must define and deliver against their roles. Expectations of each have to be set out clearly from the outset, or they will not be met.

How do you pick a good consultant? Asking for references may help, but many consultancy contracts contain confidentiality agreements and the consultant may not be able to divulge appropriate clients' names. Also, with the extent of reorganization and downsizing that has been going on in recent years, it may be difficult to track down the individuals with whom the consultant worked on relevant contracts. So the best way is to make sure the consultant has an appropriate qualification and profile in business continuity – and it would be surprising if I did not put in a plug for the Business Continuity Institute. Why risk your whole business at its most critical time by employing someone whose effectiveness cannot be determined until it is too late? One thing to avoid is accepting a proposal without knowing specifically who the consultant will be: the world is full of disappointed clients thinking they were getting a superman and ending up with an acne-covered newly qualified MBA literally practising on the client and learning at the client's expense. When a consultant has been identified, examine their CV carefully. If it is a reasonable-sized project, they will be pleased to discuss client requirements on-site, which gives the client the opportunity to assess the consultant's interpersonal skills and how relevant their knowledge and experience is to the client's industry, culture and approach.

Please, don't ask every consultant in the book to put in a proposal – it simply wastes everybody's time. Remember that the cost of bid can be up to 10% of the project value: the cost of failed bids ultimately gets passed on to other clients. It also sets the whole project off on the wrong foot, because it usually means price is the key determining factor rather than the quality of the finished project at a fair price. By making consultancy a commodity, you are likely to get a commodity product and the consultant may be looking for ways to cut corners. If you have identified a suitable consultant, there may not be a need to do more than have them provide a detailed breakdown of time and costs: often the best assignments – for both parties – are those which were not competitive. If you intend to get competitive proposals, a shortlist of say three or four consultants should be enough to ensure you are getting a good deal. Finally, you may require the consultant to sign a confidentiality agreement while, at the same time, asking for references. The consultant may have done great jobs for many clients – but if they, like you, have asked him or her to sign a confidentiality agreement they cannot be quoted as references. Consider of the consultant's reputation and standing as well as references.

Business continuity planning is a project like any other project, and a reasonable-sized assignment should be accompanied by a project plan identifying timetables, deliverables and milestones. However, unlike many other projects, business continuity planning often gets downgraded in priority as a result of higher business priorities arising. The consultant depends on interviews being arranged and kept, information being received, reports being read and decisions being made by the client to agreed timetables. If this does not happen, the cost may go up, the timescale may go out or the result will be less effective – sometimes all three.

So, do we consultants deserve a poor image? Well, check your wrist. You're still wearing your watch, the time here is 11.00 am – and there's no invoice overleaf.

A2F FINANCING BUSINESS CONTINUITY: WHY IS IT A PROBLEM?

Why are we so hung up about money? Why is the financial and business case always such a pain?

The creation of a business continuity plan can typically be justified on one or more of the following grounds:

- Marketing
- Financial
- Statutory or regulatory requirement
- Quality.

Marketing

It is crucial to retain customer confidence in the event of a disaster. Seamless integration with the customer is often crucial to retention of market share. Competition is intense and market share, once lost, would be hard to regain.

Often the most powerful corporate advertising can work just as powerfully against an organization in the event of a disaster. Just imagine the effect on the UK's Commercial Union insurance company if, when it was hit by the IRA bombers, it had not lived up to its slogan: 'We don't make a drama out of a crisis'. The marketing image of competence and capability so carefully built up over many years could be destroyed in two cartoons.

How much is your annual advertising budget? What increased market share does it buy you? Typically an organization may spend three or more times its normal annual marketing budget in the aftermath of a disaster to retain customer confidence and to retain and regain market share.

Financial

Many contracts contain liquidated damages or penalty clauses. Increasingly penalty clauses are being expressed as a percentage of contract value per week or month of delay, or provable liquidated damage clauses may be invoked.

Although contracts may include force majeure clauses, increasingly force majeure defence is being contested in the courts on the basis that events should have been foreseen and safeguards should be in place to eliminate them or to limit the damage caused by them. Other sources of loss could include:

- Loss of interest on overnight balances
- Cost of interest on lost cashflow
- Delays in customer accounting, accounts receivable and billing/invoicing
- Loss of control over debtors
- Loss of credit control and increased bad debt
- Delayed achievement of benefits of profits from new projects or products
- Loss of revenue for service contracts from failure to provide service or meet service levels
- Lost ability to respond to contract opportunities
- Penalties from failure to produce annual accounts or produce timely tax payments
- Loss of licence to trade.

Where company share value underpins loan facilities, share prices could drop and loans be called in or be re-rated at higher interest levels

Statutory or compliance requirement

Many organizations may have to meet legal requirements to maintain records or audit trail, or regulatory requirements of industry regulators, health and safety, government agencies, tax authorities, customs requirements and import and export regulations. Loss of capability to comply could lead to severe penalties.

Quality

A BS 5750 organization is subject to QMS and BSI audits and surveillance visits. There is a strong move to include disaster recovery capability as part of the BS 5750/ISO 9000 series requirements. In addition, there are the requirements of ISO 27001 (code of practice for information security management) and British Standards Institution 25999 Business Continuity Management Code of Practice (or, in the USA, NFP 1600).

These guidelines require, away others, that: 'Business continuity plans should be available to protect critical business processes from major failures or disasters' and go on to outline a planning process consistent with the approach recommended in this report. Loss of service, aggravated by lack of disaster recovery plans, could result in non-compliance action and possibly withdrawal of accreditation. This could have a serious impact since customers may require contractors to be BSI/ISO certified.

A quality accreditation – ISO or national – leaves the organization open to audit. A disaster may destroy the capability to document consistency or process, batch tracking or other requirement of the standard. Loss of quality accreditation could have a severe impact on production costs or market share (or else why did you go through the quality accreditation in the first place?).

Summary

So, we have just written your business case for you – all you have to do is fill in the blanks. Easy, isn't it? So now all you have to do is to manage the politics and a few million other minor details. Good luck!

Figure A2F.1 is indicative of the nature of costs that could be incurred.

Some of these costs may be insured but:

1. The risk would fall back on the organization for aspects which are self-insured and thus would still be a real corporate cost.
2. In the event of payout of self-insurance, the insurance reserve fund would need topping up, leaving less capital available for productive investment.
3. Commercial insurers and reinsurers are increasingly limiting their liability, reducing or denying claims if there is any suggestion of negligence (questioning force majeure defence on the basis that the events should have been foreseen and guarded against) and charging punitive subsequent premiums.

Cause of Loss

Cost of replacement of buildings and plant

Cost of replacing equipment and software

Salaries paid to staff unable to undertake billable work

Salaries paid to staff to recover work backlog and maintain deadlines

Cost of re-creation and recovery of lost data

Loss of cashflow

Interest value on deferred billings

Penalty clauses invoked for late delivery and failure to meet Service Levels

Loss of customers and market share

Additional cost of advertising to reassure customers and prospects to retain market share

Additional cost of working; administrative costs; travel and subsistence, etc.

Figure A2F.1—Cost of disaster: causes

A2G   PANDEMIC PLANNING

Malcolm Cornish, FBCI, FCA

Background and considerations

The main emphasis of business continuity management is to understand the impact that the failure of activities would have and making sure that you clearly identify the most critical activities. You can then put arrangements in place and draw up plans that make sure the critical activities can be recovered before the organization becomes permanently damaged. It is recognized that planning for specific scenarios is fraught with difficulties and is unlikely to result in robust plans that are capable of dealing with real-life events. Scenarios are undoubtedly valuable during exercises, when they can be used to test that plans deal with specific events and situations. There are, however, occasions when it is useful to employ scenario planning to assist in the development of plans for dealing with a specific event. One example is pandemic planning.

Many people are convinced that there will be a pandemic within the next five years. After all, there has never been more than 40 years between pandemics. The source and virulence of the pandemic are not so clear. Mutation of the current H5N1 avian flu virus into human form is considered by many to be the most likely source. There is plenty of evidence to suggest that the three pandemics in the 20th century were caused by pandemic flu viruses that originated in birds. The clinical attack rate (the percentage of people that will contract the virus) and the case fatality rate (the percentage of deaths among those who contract the virus) are the real unknowns. For planning purposes, the UK Health Department suggests a case rate of 25% and a case fatality rate of 0.37%. This is in line with the 1957 pandemic, and on current projections would result in an additional 48 400 additional deaths in England and Wales. This compares with around 12 000 deaths per year caused by seasonal flu. If the clinical attack rate were to be 50% and the case fatality rate 2.5% as it was in the 1918 pandemic, deaths in England and Wales could rise to 645 000. Unlike seasonal flu, however, the pandemic virus will strike all ages and therefore have a direct impact on the workforce.

As well as dealing with more deaths in service, businesses need to consider the impact that high levels of absenteeism would have on their ability to continue operations. This should be the major thrust of advance planning.

Influenza pandemic preparedness (IPP) planning

The starting point for any planning should be the business continuity work that has already been undertaken. As with 'pure' business continuity, the focus of

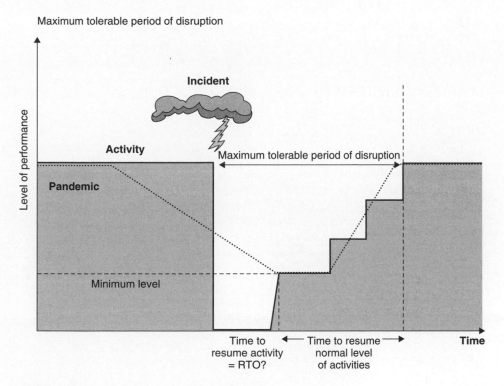

Figure A2G.1—Maximum tolerable disruption

planning must be on the organization's 'critical' activities. Chapter 11 explains how to conduct a business impact analysis (BIA). One of the key objectives of the BIA is to establish for each activity its 'maximum tolerable period of disruption'. This is achieved by considering the impact of stopping the activity for varying periods and measuring the impact of doing so. During a pandemic, there is unlikely to be an immediate cessation of activities. It is more likely that there will be a gradual decline until the point is reached when serious problems arise. Figure 8.2 used in Chapter 8 is adapted here to suggest that the minimum level at which an activity must be performed is the same as the minimum level at which an activity needs to be performed on resumption.

As well as considering the impact on business activities, risk assessment techniques should be used in order to identify what can be done to prevent a particular situation from arising and identifying mitigation strategies. For example, it is highly likely that employees may stay away from work if they believe that they are more likely to contract the disease in the work environment. To prevent this, the organization should educate staff, introduce new cleaning regimes and may even provide medical kits to limit the spread of the disease in the workplace.

The list below provides a checklist of topics that should be considered in the context of IPP and a practical summary of actions is provided at Annex A2G.1:

Business activities

Operational levels and performance:

- Product and service revenue streams
- Identification of business-critical functions and key dependencies
- Continuity strategies
- Pandemic impacts
- Status reports
- Mechanisms for measuring impact
- Impact on critical activities
- Market reaction
- Supply chain
- Pricing
- Business continuity plan implementation.

Legal and regulatory:

- Government directives
- Contractual agreements and liabilities
- Employer liability
- Government and regulatory compliance.

Finance and cashflow:

- Financial impacts
- Analysis and forecasting
- Insurance coverage
- Banking arrangements
- Cashflow
- Taxation
- Treasury
- Salaries and pensions
- Internal audit
- Risks and controls
- Financial reporting.

Alternative working arrangements:

- Workplace practices
- Working hours
- Key staff
- Technology infrastructure.

Staffing:

- Categorization – consider:
    - Required to provide medical and pandemic response
    - Required for continued operation of critical business functions
    - Management and governance of the business
    - Support of general business functions
    - Support of non-essential functions
    - Special needs employees

- Succession planning
- Licensing and certification requirements
- Company support
    - Provision of 'clean' facilities and environment
    - Premium pay
    - Work from home capability
    - Priority for remote access and support
    - Paid leave

- Issues
    - Ethical stance
    - Employee relationships
    - Trade union consent.

Procurement and supply chain:

- Identification of essential supplies and services
- Mechanisms for ensuring continuity of supplies and services
- Contractual terms.

Pandemic specific issues

BCM and crisis management:

- Crisis management structure
- Notification, escalation and activation
- Monitoring media response
- Impact assessment:
    - Speed of spread
    - Virulence of disease and other characteristics
    - Economic and business impact

- Coordination with local bodies
- Decision-making
- Lines of communication
- Triggers and thresholds:

    - WHO phases
    - Local situation
    - Travel ban (international and domestic)
    - Critical absenteeism

- Post-pandemic evaluation of response.

Occupational health:

- Cases identified at work:

    - Policy for employees displaying symptoms or feeling ill
    - Policy for contractors and visitors
    - Preventing spread of disease

- Employees diagnosed at home:

    - Preventing infected employees from coming to work

- Personal hygiene:

    - Guidance – employees, contractors and visitors
    - Coughing and sneezing techniques
    - Hygiene supplies (hands-free bins, tissues, surface cleansing)
    - Distribution channels

- Vaccination
- Local public health issues
- Medical supplies
- Access to medical support and usage of facilities
- Psychological issues
- Identification of personnel who may be more vulnerable to infection
- Identification of those who have had the disease.

Human resources:

- Personal sickness
- Family member illness
- Compassionate leave
- Family leave – children at home
- Annual holiday
- Unpaid leave

- Staff training
- Disability payments and assistance
- Benefits
- Issues
- Ethical stance
- Employee relationships
- Employee categorization
- Trade union consent.

Internal communications:

- Internal pandemic communications plan
- Concerns to be addressed
- Languages
- Frequencies and triggers
- Delivery format
- Different employee categories may require different messages
- Parent company
- Business partners.

External communications:

- External pandemic communications plan
- Link into crisis communications plan
- Policies for release of pandemic information
- Communications strategy
- Pre-written statements.

Travel:

- Reducing risk of transmission
- Locate and contact mechanisms
- Emergency repatriation of staff on business or holiday
- Travel categories
- Mechanisms for monitoring status of disease.

Workplace and infrastructure:

- Security procedures
- Personnel tracking (employees, contractors and visitors)
- Facilities shared with other organizations – movement and control (e.g. restricted access)
- On-site communications (keeping staff informed)
- Disinfection, testing and monitoring

- Cooperation between landlords and tenants
- Outsourcers.

Security:

- Perimeter protection
- Traffic control
- Internal protection
- Civil protection.

It is important to recognize that one case does not fit all and every organization should consider the specific impacts that it faces.

Having considered all the issues, the organization should assess what is already in place to deal with issues, and then draw up an action plan for making sure that it is adequately prepared. One should not go overboard and try to anticipate everything that will need to be done during the pandemic. At the present time, for instance, when considering avian flu, there is too much speculation and not many hard facts. Most practitioners therefore suggest drawing up a plan of action that sets out what needs to be done at each of the World Health Organization's pandemic phases, shown at Figure A2G.2, and when the pandemic does strike (Phase 6). In terms of avian flu, at the time of writing we are at Phase 3.

Further useful information may be downloaded at: http://www.birdflu-manual.com/bird-flu-manual/pandemic-influenza-faq.htm and http://www.birdflu-manual.com/bird-flu-manual/bird-flu-faq.htm

Inter-pandemic period	Phase 1	No new influenza virus detected in humans. If a new influenza virus presents in animals, the risk of human infection is considered to be low.
	Phase 2	No human infections, but a circulating animal influenza virus poses a risk to humans.
Pandemic alert period	**Phase 3**	**Human infection(s) with a new virus, but no (or very infrequent) human-to-human spread.**
	Phase 4	Small cluster(s) with limited human-to-human transmission but spread is highly localized.
	Phase 5	Larger cluster(s) but human-to-human spread still localized.
Pandemic period	Phase 6	Increased and sustained transmission in general population.

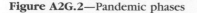

Figure A2G.2—Pandemic phases

Annex A2G.1: A practical summary for pandemic planning

Andrew Hiles FBCI

Planning

- Develop a pandemic crisis management plan (PCMP)
- Unless advised otherwise, assume potential absenteeism of 10–25% (highest in cities)
- Plan cover for sick absence
- Plan employee health assessment and to turn back the sick who report for work
- Plan for subsequent trauma (see Chapter 25)
- Plan for lower level of operations because of lower customer demand, staff absence, disruption of inbound materials, services and utilities
- Consider partnering within your industry to deliver critical services/supplies
- Update BIA, RTO, RPO based on pandemic scenario
- Review/exercise BCP against pandemic scenario: use alternatives
- Update BCP/PCMP with results
- Develop contingency plans for inbound supplies/services and buffer stock.

Policy and plan development

Employees

- Ensure job descriptions/profiles of key staff are up to date
- Arrange with employment agencies for resupply
- Ensure documented procedures are up to date, comprehensive, clear and unambiguous
- Identify and train alternate staff for key positions/rare skills
- Consider issues/opportunities arising from overtime/shift work/part-time work/flexible working hours
- Provide PCMP/pandemic response training and internal communications facilities for staff
- Consider impact on payroll, allowances, etc. Develop policies/procedures
- Since public medical services will be overloaded, prepare to offer internal medical support to staff
- Review insurance coverage for pandemic impact on business, employees' health
- Consider provision of items in short supply (e.g. food, medicine, etc.) to key employees, customers, suppliers

- Consider providing in-house day care facilities
- Get advice from health authorities on avoidance measures: publish to employees
- Avoid handshakes; if handshake, avoid touching face especially near eyes or mouth
- Increase cleaning schedule using medically recommended disinfectants and detergents
- Pay particular attention in disinfecting handrails, door handles, phones, keyboards
- Increase hygiene regime in canteens, restaurants
- Increase hygiene regime in washrooms; provide disinfectant wipes
- Stop travel for training, conferences, etc.
- Stop all non-essential face-to-face meetings
- Consider vaccinating staff
- Consider provision of support to employees who are carers, to free them for work
- Consider/supply personal protective equipment (masks, etc.).

Supply

- Assume shortages will occur
- Ensure there are sufficient buffer stocks of inbound supplies to permit continued operations
- Identify alternative sources of critical inbound services and supplies, including consumables
- Ensure maintenance and repair supplies/spares are in place
- Consider bringing forward maintenance schedules
- Subject to cost of inventory constraints, create sufficient buffer stocks of finished products to permit continued supply of prioritized products to prioritized customers.

Logistics

- Expect and plan for restrictions in the movement of inbound and outbound goods and waste materials
- Expect and plan for fuel shortages
- Ensure, contingency plans provide for this. Consider stockholding or standby supply contracts. Consider reallocation of company diesel vehicles
- Identify alternative transport and logistics services: consider standby contracts
- Plan to provide transport for critical workers to/from work.

Communication

- Prepare and tell stakeholders about the communication channels that you will use to keep them informed during the pandemic
- Develop pre-planned media statements for use when needed
- Prepare contingency statements for delivery to employees
- Communicate early to suppliers/customers to set expectations
- Develop alternative communications channels in case normal communication channels become unreliable or overloaded.

Customers

- Identify/plan for customers' expectations during the pandemic
- Determine extent of impact on products/services
- Prioritize products, services and customers in case supply capability becomes limited
- Identify and communicate to stakeholders any changes to lead times/delivery schedules
- Consider bringing forward deliveries/provision of services.

Technology

Consider:

- Use of tele- or videoconferencing/website promulgation of information/email instead of face-to-face meetings
- Increasing remote access/WiFi capacity
- Increased use of VoIP/cellular/satellite phones for (now) remote staff
- Increasing capacity of telephone systems/use of VoIP to handle increased teleconferencing and telephone loads
- Increasing Internet/intranet connectivity
- Security enhancements necessary as a result of the above.

Appendix 3
Certification standards

The Definitive Handbook of Business Continuity Management, Second Edition.
Edited by Andrew Hiles FBCI. © 2007 John Wiley & Sons Ltd.

CERTIFICATION STANDARDS FOR BUSINESS CONTINUITY PRACTITIONERS

The following certification standards form the basis of the professional certification programme offered by the Business Continuity Institute and have been agreed in collaboration with the Disaster Recovery Institute International. Contact details for both organizations can be found in Appendix A4C.

Business continuity management is defined as a holistic management process that identifies potential impacts that threaten an organization and provides a framework for building resilience with the capability for an effective response that safeguards the interests of its key stakeholders, reputation and value creating activities.

Its primary objective is to allow the executive to continue to manage their business under adverse conditions, by the introduction of appropriate resilience strategies, recovery objectives, business continuity and crisis management plans in collaboration with, or as a key component of, an integrated risk management initiative.

The summary of the Certification Standards is presented below. A full version can be obtained from the BCI website at www.thebci.org. The 10 sections of these standards are not presented in any particular order of importance or sequence.

1. **INITIATION AND MANAGEMENT** – To establish the need for a business continuity management (BCM) process, including resilience strategies, recovery objectives, business continuity and crisis management plans and including obtaining management support and organizing and managing the formulation of the function or process either in collaboration with, or as a key component of, an integrated risk management initiative.

    The professional's role is to:

    a. Lead sponsors in defining objectives, policies, and critical success factors
    b. Coordinate and organize/manage the overall BCM process
    c. Oversee the BCM process through effective control methods and change management
    d. Present (sell) the process to management and staff
    e. Develop budget to initiate the process
    f. Define and recommend BCM structure and management
    g. Develop and implement the BCM process.

2. **BUSINESS IMPACT ANALYSIS** – To identify the impacts resulting from disruptions and disaster scenarios that can affect the organization and techniques that can be used to quantify and qualify such impacts. Establish critical functions, their recovery priorities, and interdependencies so that recovery time objective can be set.

The professional's role is to:

a. Identify knowledgeable and credible functional area representatives
b. Identify organization functions
c. Identify and define criticality criteria
d. Present criteria to management for approval
e. Coordinate analysis
f. Identify interdependencies
g. Define recovery objectives and timeframes, including recovery times, expected losses and priorities
h. Identify information requirements
i. Identify resource requirements
j. Define report format
k. Prepare and present business impact analysis.

3. **RISK EVALUATION AND CONTROL** – To determine the events and environmental surroundings that can adversely affect the organization and its facilities with disruption as well as disaster, the damage such events can cause, and the controls needed to prevent or minimize the effects of potential loss. Provide cost/benefit analysis to justify investment in controls to mitigate risks.

   The professional's role is to:

   a. Understand the function of probabilities and risk reduction/mitigation within the organization
   b. Identify potential risks to the organization
   c. Identify outside expertise required
   d. Identify vulnerabilities/threats/exposures
   e. Identify risk reduction/mitigation alternatives
   f. Identify credible information sources
   g. Interface with management to determine acceptable risk levels
   h. Document and present findings.

4. **DEVELOPING BUSINESS CONTINUITY MANAGEMENT STRATEGIES** – To determine and guide the selection of possible business operating strategies for continuation of business within the recovery time and recovery point objectives, while maintaining the organization's critical functions.

   The professional's role is to:

   a. Understand available alternatives, their advantages, disadvantages and cost ranges, including mitigation as a recovery strategy
   b. Identify viable recovery strategies with business functional areas
   c. Consolidate strategies
   d. Identify off-site storage requirements and alternative facilities
   e. Develop business unit strategies
   f. Obtain commitment from management for developed strategies.

5. **EMERGENCY RESPONSE AND OPERATIONS** – To develop and implement procedures for response and stabilizing the situation following an incident or event, including establishing and managing an emergency operations centre to be used as a command centre during the emergency.
    The professional's role is to:

    a. Identify potential types of emergencies and the responses needed (e.g. fire, hazardous materials leak, medical)
    b. Identify the existence of appropriate emergency response procedures
    c. Recommend the development of emergency procedures where none exist
    d. Integrate disaster recovery/business continuity/crisis management procedures with emergency response and escalation procedures
    e. Identify the command and control requirements of managing an emergency
    f. Recommend the development of command and control procedures to define roles, authority and communications processes for managing an emergency
    g. Ensure emergency response procedures are integrated with requirements of public authorities (refer also to Subject Area 10, Coordination with external agencies)

6. **DEVELOPING AND IMPLEMENTING BUSINESS CONTINUITY AND CRISIS MANAGEMENT PLANS** – To design, develop and implement the business continuity and crisis management plans that provide continuity within the recovery time objective and recovery point objective.
    The professional's role is to:

    a. Identify the components of the planning process
    b. Control the planning process and produce the plans
    c. Implement the plans
    d. Test the plans
    e. Maintain the plans.

7. **AWARENESS AND TRAINING PROGRAMMES** – To prepare a programme to create and maintain corporate awareness and enhance the skills required to develop and implement the business continuity management programme or process and its supporting activities.
    The professional's role is to:

    a. Establish objectives and components of corporate BCM awareness and training programme
    b. Identify functional awareness and training requirements
    c. Develop awareness and training methodology
    d. Acquire or develop awareness and training tools
    e. Identify external awareness and training opportunities
    f. Identify alternative options for corporate awareness and training.

8. **MAINTAINING AND EXERCISING PLANS** – To pre-plan and coordinate plan exercises, and evaluate and document plan exercise results. Develop processes to maintain the currency of continuity capabilities and the plan documents in accordance with the organization's strategic direction. Verify that the plans will prove effective by comparison with a suitable standard, and report results in a clear and concise manner.

    The professional's role is to:

    a. Pre-plan and coordinate the exercises
    b. Facilitate the exercises
    c. Evaluate and document the exercise results
    d. Update the plans
    e. Report results/evaluation to management
    f. Coordinate ongoing maintenance of plans
    g. Assist in establishing audit programme for the business continuity plan.

9. **CRISIS COMMUNICATIONS** – To develop, coordinate, evaluate and exercise plans to communicate with internal stakeholders (employees, corporate management, etc.) external stakeholders (customers, shareholders, vendors, suppliers, etc.) and the media (print, radio, television, Internet, etc.).

    The professional's role is to:

    a. Establish programmes for proactive crisis communications
    b. Establish necessary crisis communication coordination with external agencies (local, state, regional, national, emergency responders, etc.)
    c. Establish essential crisis communications with relevant stakeholder groups
    d. Establish and exercise media handling plans for the organization and its business units.

10. **COORDINATION WITH EXTERNAL AGENCIES** – To establish applicable procedures and policies for coordinating crisis, continuity and restoration activities with external agencies (local, state, regional, national, emergency responders, defence, etc.) while ensuring compliance with applicable statutes or regulations.

    The professional's role is to:

    a. Identify and establish liaison procedures for emergency management
    b. Coordinate emergency management with external agencies
    c. Maintain current knowledge of laws and regulations concerning emergency management as it pertains to the own organization.

The full version of the Certification Standards is displayed on the BCI website at www.thebci.org where they can also be download as a .pdf file.

These standards have been produced in cooperation with the Disaster Recovery Institute International of the USA and are used by both bodies in their certification programmes.

Appendix 4
International perspectives, standards and sources

A4A   THE IMPLICATIONS OF RECENT LEGISLATION AND STANDARDS ON BUSINESS CONTINUITY

Andrew Hiles FBCI

The growth of standards

Pre-9/11, there were probably around 20 standards, worldwide, relating to business continuity planning. Among these were:

- Australia National Audit Office Best Practice Guide (Australia)
- American National Standards Institute/National Fire Protection Association ANSI/NFPA Standard 1600 (USA)
- British Standards Institution BSI 7799 Information Security Standard (UK)
- DRII/BCI Common Body of Knowledge (USA and UK)
- Federal Emergency Management Agency (FEMA) Guidance Document (USA)
- Federal Financial Institutions Examination Council (FFIEC) BCP Handbook (USA)
- Office of Management and Budget (OMB) Circular A-130 (USA)
- Presidential Decision Directive 67 (USA)
- Turnbull Report (UK).

Post-9/11, standards have proliferated. To identify a few:

- Australia/New Zealand ANZ 4360: 2004 Risk Management
- Australia Standards BCM Handbook
- Bank of India BC Guidelines
- Bank of Thailand BC Guidelines
- Bank of Pakistan BC Guidelines
- Basel Capital Accord (International)
- BSI/BCI Standard, PAS 56 (UK)
- BSI 25999 Business Continuity Standard (UK)
- California Senate Bill SB 1386 (USA)
- Civil Contingencies Act (UK)
- Fair Credit Reporting Act (USA)
- Federal and Legislative BC Requirements for Internal Revenue Service (IRS) (USA)
- Federal Energy Regulatory Commission (FERC) Security Standards (USA)
- FFIEC BCP Handbook (USA)
- Board of Governors of the Federal Reserve System; Office of the Comptroller of the Currency; and Securities and Exchange Commission
- (FRB-OCC-SEC) Guidelines for Strengthening the Resilience of US Financial System (USA)

- Financial Services Authority (FSA) Handbook (UK)
- General Accounting Office (GAO) Potential Terrorist Attacks Guideline
- Health Insurance Portability and Accountability Act (HIPAA) Final Security Rule (USA)
- Information Systems Audit and Control Association (ISACA) Guidelines for BCP Audit (International)
- ISO 20000 (BS 15000/BS 15000) IT Service Management Standard (International)
- ISO/TS 16949 – The Harmonized Standard for the Automotive Supply Chain (International)
- Monetary Authority of Singapore (MAS) BCP Guidelines
- North American Industry Classification System NAIC Standard on BCP (USA)
- NASD (National Association of Securities Dealers) Rule 3510 (USA)
- North American Electric Reliability Council (NERC) Security Guidelines (USA)
- National Futures Association (NFA) Compliance Rule 2-38 (USA)
- National Fire Prevention Association (NFPA) 1600 2004 (USA)
- National Institute of Standards and Technology (NIST) Contingency Planning Guide (USA)
- New York Stock Exchange (NYSE) Rule 446 (USA)
- Sarbanes-Oxley Act (USA)
- SS 507: 2004 Singapore Standard for Business Continuity/Disaster Recovery Service Providers
- BSI Publicly Available Specification 77 (PAS 77) IT Disaster Recovery Guidelines.

In addition to the regulations and standards, methodologies such as Information Technology Infrastructure Library (ITIL), Control Objectives for Information and related Technologies (CobIT) and project management practices require business continuity and/or risk assessment.

The impact on BCM

We explore below some of these significant initiatives that will have a profound effect on the way in which business continuity planning and management will be implemented. These are:

- The Civil Contingencies Act 2004 which contains sweeping emergency powers that place new duties and responsibilities on 'responders' to disasters and contain wide-ranging powers over citizens. Both of these aspects require thorough review of existing business continuity plans or development of such plans.

- Business Continuity Institute/British Standards Institution Publicly Available Specification PAS 56 Guide to Business Continuity Management. This specification effectively provides a standard of good practice in risk assessment and business continuity management. It evolved into British Standards Institution BSI 25999 Business Continuity Standard, the methodology for which is covered at Chapter 6.
- Australia/New Zealand Standard ANZS 4360: 2004 – Risk Management, which provides greater emphasis on the importance of embedding a risk management culture into an organization and on the management of potential gains as well as losses.
- Singapore Standard SS 507: 2004 for Business Continuity/Disaster Recovery (BC/DR) Service Providers, which provides a basis for committed BC/DR service vendors to differentiate themselves from other, lesser, players and helps end-user organizations to lower BC/DR outsourcing risks.

UK – Civil Contingencies Act 2004

Introduction and background

The UK Civil Contingencies Act 2004, which came into force from May 2006, was intended to rectify weaknesses in the previous Civil Defense and Emergency Powers legislation, which was primarily built on the precept of attacks by foreign powers. Recent disasters included foot and mouth, the fuel crisis and widespread flooding and terrorist attacks and the new Act was enacted to cover ant-terrorist activity and civil disasters. Part 1 of the Act covers local arrangements for civil protection by 'blue light' services, local authorities and the like. Part 2 covers emergency powers in a wide-scale regional emergency. Part 3 is mainly technical detail.

Part 1 of the Act defines 'emergency' as:

- An event or situation which threatens serious damage to human welfare in a place in the United Kingdom
- An event or situation which threatens serious damage to the environment of a place in the United Kingdom, or
- War, or terrorism, which threatens serious damage to the security of the United Kingdom.

Human welfare covers:

- Loss of human life
- Human illness or injury

- Homelessness
- Damage to property
- Disruption of a supply of money, food, water, energy or fuel
- Disruption of a system of communication
- Disruption of facilities for transport
- Disruption of services relating to health.

Environmental damage is specified as contamination of land, water or air with biological, chemical or radioactive matter, or disruption or destruction of plant life or animal life.

Two categories of responders are identified (see Figure A4A.1).

Emergency powers

A minister only needs to be 'satisfied' that the conditions apply and is able orally to declare an emergency. There is no test of 'reasonableness'. The Act enables the UK Defence Council to authorize the deployment of the armed forces and provides wide-ranging powers for first responders to the emergency including:

- Confiscation or destruction of property with or without compensation
- Travel embargo
- Compulsory evacuation.

This includes the powers to:

- Prohibit, or enable the prohibition of, movement to or from a specified place
- Require, or enable the requirement of, movement to or from a specified place
- Prohibit, or enable the prohibition of, assemblies of specified kinds, at specified places or at specified times
- Prohibit, or enable the prohibition of, travel at specified times
- Prohibit, or enable the prohibition of, other specified activities.

The Act also creates offences of:

- Failing to comply with a provision of the regulations.
- Failing to comply with a direction or order given or made under the regulations
- Obstructing a person in the performance of a function under or by virtue of the regulations.

Category 1 Responders	Category 2 Responders
Emergency Services: Ambulance Services Fire Services Police	Government: Health & Safety Executive
Government Agencies: Environment Agency Maritime & Coastguard Agency Scottish Environmental Protection Agency	Utilities: Electricity Gas Telecommunications Water & sewage
Local Authorities: All local authorities responsible for emergency planning	Health: The Common Services Agency in Scotland
NHS Organizations Health Boards Health Protection Agency Health Trusts Port Health Authorities	Transport: Airports Harbours and ports Highways Agency London Underground Network Rail Train operating companies Transport for London

Figure A4A.1—Responders

New offences can be created allowing for imprisonment for up to three months or a fine.

However, to prevent abuse of emergency powers they must be compatible with the Human Rights Act and may be challenged in court. The UK Parliament has just seven days to approve the invocation of the new powers: if they do not, the powers cease. The powers may be invoked not only nationally, but also on a regional basis. New Regional Nominated Coordinators will coordinate response to a regional emergency.

The Act came into full force in May 2006.

Business continuity aspects

Business continuity aspects are covered in the Contingency Planning section. Responders have to periodically:

- Assess the risk of an emergency occurring
- Assess the risk of an emergency making it necessary to invoke their emergency functions
- Maintain continuity plans
- Maintain contingency plans to:
    - Prevent the emergency
    - Reduce, control or mitigate its effects
    - Take or enable other relevant action
    - Publish plans if necessary to help others to develop or maintain their contingency plans
- Develop and maintain emergency communications with the public.

Local authorities therefore should be able to offer (for a fee):

- Advice on business continuity planning
- Information about their own plans to help others plan
- Help in the development of business continuity plans.

It is the responsibility of Category 2 respondents to give information to Category 1 responders to assist them with their contingency planning and emergency response.

Guidance

The Act is accompanied by two documents. The first, *Emergency Preparedness*, is statutory guidance under Part 1 of the Act. It sets out what the legislation requires and gives good practice to help responders comply with their legal requirements. It covers the following:

- Cooperation
- Information sharing
- Local responder risk assessment duty
- Emergency planning
- Business continuity management
- Communicating with the public
- Advice and assistance to business and voluntary organizations
- London
- Scotland
- Wales
- Northern Ireland
- Monitoring and enforcement
- The role of the voluntary sector
- The role of the minister
- Cooperation at the regional level in England
- Planning at the regional level in England.

Its Annexes contain various useful forms, example plans and checklists together with a glossary and bibliography.

The guide details the main duties and responsibilities of responders and provides performance measurements for responders to establish their compliance with the Act.

The second document, *Emergency Response and Recovery*, is non-statutory guidance that deals with the response and recovery phases of emergencies. It addresses:

- Principles of effective response and recovery
- Responding agencies
- Management and coordination of local operations
- Care and treatment of people
- Information and the media
- The government offices for the regions
- Regional civil contingencies committees
- Response arrangements in Scotland
- Response arrangements in Wales
- Response arrangements in Northern Ireland
- The role of central government in response
- Emergency powers.

This guide provides an explanation of how UK agencies will work together to mitigate and resolve the emergency and also contains a glossary and bibliography.

What does the Civil Contingencies Act mean for business continuity and facilities managers?

All UK facilities managers, business continuity coordinators and managers should obtain copies of the Act and of the companion guidelines *Emergency Preparedness* and *Emergency Response and Recovery* and should establish contact with their local authority emergency planners to understand and assess the impact of the new Act on their business. If you are based outside the UK, check your country's emergency powers: you may find them very similar.

If you are in either Category 1 or Category 2, contingency and business continuity plans need reviewing to ensure the new roles and responsibilities are reflected in them.

All facilities managers should review their business continuity plans to ensure they cover the disruption to mission and business that the imposition of emergency powers would cause.

In particular:

- Travel may be restricted so that business continuity teams may not be able to get to their standby recovery sites: they may be either within an exclusion zone or staff may be restricted from travel or from leaving a building. Salvage teams may be unable to access damaged buildings and start restoration.
- Essential supplies and services may be denied because of imposition of exclusion zones and travel restrictions.
- Suppliers may be effectively blockaded, unable to deliver manufactured stock with consequent implications for space, inventory and failure of just-in-time delivery.
- Exclusion zones may become larger, imposed for longer periods and managed more rigorously.
- Telecommunication services could be denied to normal users and the Internet could be subject to control.
- Other utilities could be denied in favour of higher priority users.
- Staff may be directed to undertake activities in support of the emergency and no longer be available to their employer.
- Insurance companies may not be liable to pay for losses or damage if emergency powers are invoked.
- Although the emergency could be international (e.g. pandemic, or major radiation release) there is no provision for accessing European Union emergency relief funds and compensation could be denied.
- It is unclear what effect a regional declaration of a disaster will have for an organization that has telecommunication or Internet services provided from outside the region affected.

Overall, the Act is open to authoritarian abuse and manipulative interpretation. The Parliament Act has been used for purposes for which it clearly was never designed and the danger is that the Civil Contingencies Act will be similarly misused.

Such draconian legislation exists in many countries – for instance, the powers of FEMA in the USA and other powers under the Patriot Act.

British standards institution PAS 77:2006 IT service continuity management

PAS 77:2006 provides a generic framework and guideline for an IT service continuity programme. It has been developed in partnership with Adam Continuity, Dell Corporation, Unisys and SunGard and is designed for organizations of all sizes whether in the private or public sector. The new code of practice is intended for use by anyone responsible for implementing, delivering and managing IT service continuity within an organization.

PAS 77:2006 provides guidance on the aspects of ITSCM which organizations should consider when investing in this area. It complements other existing and internationally renowned standards such as BSI 25999, BS ISO/IEC 20000, BS ISO/IEC 17799/27001 and ISO 9001 and does not replace or supersede them. Chapter 16 provides a practical guide to PAS 77.

ISBN 0 580 49047 5, BSI order reference PAS 77 is priced at £49. The standard is also available for instant purchase and download from the BSI eShop or www.bsi-global.com/eshop. This, with the output from the business impact analysis, allows an organization to set its appetite for risk.

BS 25999 business continuity code of practice

The methodology behind BS 25999 is described in detail at Chapter 16.

USA NFPA 1600, standard on disaster/emergency management and business continuity programs, 2004 edition

The more succinct US National Fire Protection Association (NFPA) standard 1600 (downloadable at www.nfpa.org) establishes a common set of criteria for disaster, emergency management and business continuity programmes in both the public and private sectors. It outlines the constituent parts of a disaster/emergency management programme. It is meant to be widely applicable, including government agencies or jurisdictions, private companies, non-profit agencies, partnerships and other entities holding emergency management responsibilities. It also contains a useful cross-reference to other standards including those of the BCI.

NFPA 1600 promotes a disaster/emergency management organization with a programme coordinator and a programme committee that embraces all relevant interests. It reflects the 13 programme elements identified by the US Federal Emergency Management Agency in its Capability Assessment for Readiness self-evaluation tool developed to assess state and local emergency management programmes. These elements are:

- Laws and authorities
- Hazard identification and risk assessment
- Hazard management (risk assessment, mitigation strategy, etc.)
- Resource management (performance objectives to include personnel, equipment, training, facilities, funding, expert knowledge, materials)
- Planning (strategic plan, emergency operations plan, mitigation and recovery plans)
- Direction, control and coordination (incident management system)
- Communications and warning
- Operations and procedure
- Logistics and facilities
- Training
- Exercise, evaluation and corrective actions
- Public education and information (including dealing with the media)
- Finance and administration.

Australia and New Zealand Standard AS/NZS 4360:2004 – risk management

This new edition of this risk management standard sets out in detail a seven-step process for managing risk. This edition provides greater emphasis on the importance of embedding a risk management culture into an organization and on the management of potential gains as well as losses.

It provides a generic guide for managing risk and may be applied to a very wide range of activities, decisions or operations of any public, private or community enterprise, group or individual.

AN/NZS 4360:2004 specifies the elements of the risk management process, but it is not the purpose of this standard to enforce uniformity of risk management systems. It is generic and independent of any specific industry or economic sector.

The design and implementation of the risk management system will be influenced by the varying needs of an organization, its particular objectives, its products and services, and the processes and specific practices employed.

AN/NZS 4360:2004 should be applied at all stages in the life of an activity, function, project, product or asset. The maximum benefit is usually obtained by applying the risk management process from the beginning. Often a number of discrete studies are carried out at different times, and from strategic and operational perspectives. The document *HB 436 – Risk Management Guidelines – Companion to AN/NZS 4360:2004* provides detailed advice on how to implement the standard and is intended to be used in conjunction with the standard. This is supplemented by a range of handbooks on how risk management can be applied in different industries and sectors.

Standards Australia website is www.standards.com.au

Singapore Standard SS 507:2004 for business continuity/disaster recovery service providers

Background

Singapore is the first country in the world to introduce a standard and certification programme for BC/DR service providers. Developed by the Infocomm Development Authority of Singapore and the IT Standards Committee (ITSC) with input from leading vendors, the standard specifies stringent requirements for BC/DR service providers. These requirements benchmark against the best practices in the region and stipulate the operating, monitoring and maintenance of BC/DR services offered.

Service providers that have been certified for the full BC/DR Service Provider category under the new standard include Hewlett Packard, IBM, NCS Pte Limited and Singapore Computer Systems; and Equinix, SingTel Expan and StarHub for the Disaster Recovery Facility category.

By engaging a certified BC/DR service provider, assurance is provided to the end-user and frees the customer to focus on its core competencies. This enhances the customer's competitive advantage, as it is able to achieve stringent recovery time objective; minimize business and data loss; and enjoy uninterrupted services. The certification also serves as a quality mark for service providers to upgrade themselves to provide better services.

Structure

The standard's foundation layer explores the infrastructure that supports the service and consists of six 'P's: policies, processes, programmes, performance

Business Continuity / Disaster Recovery Standard						
International Best Practices						BC/DR Industry
Services						Development
Infrastructure						
Policies	Processes	Programs	Performance Measurements	People	Products	

Figure A4A.2—Singapore standard – layers

measurements, people and products. Figure A4A.2 illustrates the layers of the standard. The Services Level reflects the services that can be provided, given the supporting infrastructure. The international Best Practices Level examines the potential value-added above the basic services. The standard specifies the requirements, without prescribing the method of meeting them.

Scope

SS507:2004 contains two main elements:

- Clauses used in certification (clauses 3, 4 and 5)
- Clauses that are not used in certification but which identify DR/BC best practices and the location of recovery sites (clauses 6 and 7).

BC/DR service providers can be certified under two categories:

- Facility provider
- Service provider.

Facility provider certification centres on the physical infrastructure while service provider certification focuses on service capability. Service providers may apply for certification in both categories at the same time.

BC/DR service vendors need to comply with:

Clause 3 – General Requirements (e.g. third party vendor management – required from all service providers)

Clause 4 – Disaster Recovery Facility Certification (physical infrastructure and facility requirements, e.g. physical access control and security, air conditioning, no-fail electrical supplies)

Clause 5 – Service Provider Capability Certification (this includes computing equipment, staff BC/DR training and skill, operational availability and change management).

Conclusion

In developing SS 507:2004 Singapore was seeking to establish itself as a regional centre for BC/DR services. In doing so, it has established a new benchmark for service vendors and new evaluation criteria for their customers.

Summary

The UK Civil Contingencies Act is essential reading for UK facilities managers and others involved with risk management and business continuity. It raises new threats to, and inhibitors on, an organization's ability to control its recovery processes. Despite some safeguards, the Act is wide open to abuse. And unless it is substantially amended, abuse will almost certainly happen. The same could be true of similar legislation in other countries.

British Standards Institution BSI 25999 provides good general guidelines and useful checklists in the form of identified outputs but it is more of a management overview than a practitioner's guide. It is also imprecise in places and illogical in sequence, following the order in which the Business Continuity Institute/Disaster Recovery Institute International professional disciplines are placed rather than the logical sequence of the BC activities. Despite its faults, however, it may well emerge as a fully fledged standard over the next few years. A revised BCI Good Practice Guide has been drafted to support BS 25999.

PAS 77 is based very much on PAS 56, the predecessor to BSI 25999.

Australia/New Zealand Standard ANZS 4360: 2004 – Risk Management provides a holistic approach to embedding a risk management culture and seems likely to become generally accepted outside the region.

The updates to NFP 1600 have not significantly affected the content and it remains a valuable voluntary standard.

Singapore standard SS 570: 2004 provides a way for vendors to stand out from their competition and a new benchmark by which potential customers will evaluate them.

Sources of information

To download the *Emergency Preparedness* guide and *Responding to Emergencies* visit www.ukresilience.info/contingencies/cont_publications. This site also contains other useful reference material.

A4B   BUSINESS CONTINUITY MANAGEMENT: AN INTERNATIONAL PERSPECTIVE FROM THE BCI

Lyndon Bird FBCI

Lyndon is Technical Services Director of the Business Continuity Institute and Managing Director of UK-based business continuity software and consultancy service provider CPA Ltd.

Introduction

My career in business continuity management started back in 1986 in the Netherlands. In those times it was necessary to try to convince business people that disasters and major incidents might actually happen. Today we all know of the increase in catastrophic events (both natural and manmade). The question today is not 'if' but 'what, when and where'. Travelling around the world as Technical Services Director of the Business Continuity Institute (BCI) it is striking that we all recognize the same images. The largest incidents like a terrorist attack, air crash, tsunami, flood or hurricane are broadcast globally on our screens within minutes of them happening. People with mobile phone images take photographs and video clips that are soon in world circulation. Even for more localized events like fires and gas explosions, provided the picture is dramatic enough, it will soon receive wide publicity. Even when there is nothing much to photograph, like after a power outage in the US, we get interviews from affected people telling tales of hardship and difficulty and pointing the finger of blame at someone.

This chapter mainly covers the major activities taking place in Europe, North America and Australia. Asia is covered more exhaustively in Appendix A4C. The BCI is in a unique position to monitor what is happening via the extensive feedback that we receive from our members, who are currently active in over 80 countries. The BCI has a great opportunity to help set the standards and drive the changes that are required to make business continuity a normal management discipline whether you work in a major international financial institution in Tokyo or a small local firm of 100 people in Yorkshire, UK.

The drive towards business continuity

Business continuity evolved from the protection of computers and systems commonly known as IT disaster recovery. The early pioneers of the type of activity were to be found in the United States where large-scale mainframe computing was adopted earlier and more extensively than elsewhere. Apart from technical malfunctions and fire, the major threats to US business operations tended to centre on natural disasters with the consequent wide-scale problems that might present. It was, therefore, natural that in both the US and Canada the connection between emergency planning and business continuity was always very close.

By contrast in the UK, natural disasters on any large scale were rare but the threat of terrorist attack was very real. During the IRA bombing campaign in London in the early 1990s it was clear that systems alone did not keep you in business. Technology, systems and data are essential but people, property and business processes are just as vital. The terrorist threat also meant that the BCM synergy in the UK tended to be with both security and emergency planning during this period.

Despite the valiant efforts of the BCM community in the late 1980s and 1990s, it was not until the perceived threat of the millennium bug (and the subsequent media hype that surrounded it) that many senior executives saw BCM as a wider issue than just technical recovery. The work for Y2K provided many organizations with the first real opportunity to develop plans for failures that did not relate primarily to the loss of IT or office-based facilities.

In the UK, action by truckers led to the fuel crisis of September 2000, which had a nationwide impact on the public, business, customers and suppliers alike. Firms had the opportunity to put business continuity to a real test. For many organizations in retail, distribution or logistics this was the first time that company's wide-scale plans were invoked, as their operations are totally reliant on the availability of fuel for transportation.

Less than six months later the foot and mouth epidemic of February 2001 highlighted many more weaknesses and vulnerabilities of the UK plc's preparation for handling a major incident.

While lessons were being learned on one side of the Atlantic, an event occurred in the US that changed the BCM landscape completely and forever. There is much we could write about the events of 9/11 but it is sufficient to say that in conventional BCM terms it redefined the term 'worst case scenario' – which previously most US companies had considered to be a total loss of a building or data centre.

These have been some of the key events that have moved organizations rapidly along the BCM route. Still for many individuals the threats seem remote until they are personally involved. For many UK people on 7 July 2005 the terrorist attack on the London transport system made the theoretical threat a reality. This shock was the same as it had previously been for residents of Tokyo and Madrid and was later to be so for the citizens of Mumbai. The public transport network is clearly the Achilles' heel of any modern crowded business city.

Despite the horrendous nature of these events, it is important to remember that business continuity is not really about what happened; it is about the business consequences of what happened.

BCM in a global context

Over the last few years and in particular just reflecting on the recent major incidents, there is a growing awareness across the world of what business continuity really is and why it is so important to corporate survival. We have seen a real increase in high profile events that have been broadcast on our televisions and in our newspapers that have highlighted the benefits of good planning and response capabilities. There is consequently a perception of increased threats, some of which we are aware of and some of which come as a surprise if they are realized.

In today's world there is a more global nature to these threats. Businesses have far more economic interdependency between regions than ever before. We invariably rely on longer supply chains for physical production of the goods we consume, and we increasingly rely on offshore, outsourced operations for much of our service delivery and back office administration.

This can be manifested in different ways. For example, a disaster in Asia might mean a break in a key part of a European supply chain. This might mean loss of business and cash, it may mean loss of market share or reputation, and of course one company's disaster can be a competitor's opportunity. Service delivery failure might well be picked up by the media, leading to loss of confidence from your customers, suppliers or investors. In relation to most events there will be key people issues which need managing. You must also remember the need to manage both the incident and how you represent the incident to the media. In the words of the leading US investor Warren Buffet, 'It can take 20 years to build a business and 15 minutes to destroy it.'

An interesting example is what happened to Primark, a large and successful UK fashion retailer. In November 2005, just before the start of Christmas peak trading, they lost 50% of their garment stocks in a fire at one of their two large distribution centres. They were able to continue trading by permanently chartering aircraft to fly to and from China bringing new stocks in every day. In effect they created a virtual distribution centre at 35 000 feet above the ground. The strategy worked but the cost was significant and the risk to the organization enormous.

Another aspect of globalization is the increased outsourcing that companies now undertake for both products and services. In India, business continuity professionals are rising to meet the demands of the business process outsourcing (BPO) sector. Virtually all major European and US corporations have some outsourced activities, mainly in India and South East Asia. It soon became clear that the simplistic approach adopted by some companies towards BCM in their outsourced operations would just not work. Contracts and SLAs are of course important but partnership and strategic cooperation is equally vital in dealing with the outcomes from a major incident.

Probably the most global industry of all is the financial sector, and it is in this field that regulation, legislation and standards have really started to take hold.

Compliance with a myriad of different requirements in different countries is making the role of the compliance professional both extremely challenging and increasingly risky. In this sector at least BCM is now often being seen as a compliance issue rather than a risk, security or emergency planning issue.

The need for international standards

What does appear to be needed is the emergence of common standards for BCM that can be applied across all business sectors and geographical areas. This is a complex task but one that is getting much attention. A few years ago the BCI created a definition of what business continuity management actually is and this definition has provided the foundation on which the Institute developed its approach to standards, education and individual development. The definition states that:

> Business continuity management is a holistic management process that *identifies* potential *impacts* that threaten an organization and provides a framework for *building resilience* and the capability for an *effective response* which *safeguards* the interests of its key stakeholders, reputation, brand and value creating activities.

The BCI also set out to promote good practice around the world. As well as the 10 certification competences, the BCI Good Practice Guidelines have given an excellent framework upon which many internal and external standards and methodologies have been based.

Many people look to ISO for a commonly accepted BCI standard and this is likely to eventually emerge. However, currently we find that various national BCM standards are on the way. The UK may be considered the forerunner with the publication of *BS 25999 – The BCM Code of Practice*. This is built on and replaces the internationally successful publicly available specification PAS 56. Although theoretically only a British Standard, BCM practitioners on a worldwide basis have purchased this in their endeavour to implement a consistently high quality BCM programme.

In the United States the National Fire Protection Association (NFPA) appear to be the leaders in gaining a wider acceptance for a standard in this field. They have been drafting the *Emergency Preparedness Standard* since 2004, and it covers both emergency management and business continuity. However, it lacks the focus on BCM that the UK approach is taking, and concentrates on recovery from physical incidents rather than dealing with consequences of business interruption. It reflects the different philosophies that still exist between North America and much of the rest of the world on the nature of BCM in a modern context.

Another problem in the US is the wide number of different standards and guidelines and good practice books on business continuity for different industries and management interests. None of these specifically link back to NFPA 1600 and they tend to confuse rather than clarify.

There are also other countries actively moving on a standards agenda that differs from both BS 25999 and NFPA 1600. In particular much work has been carried out in Australia and Singapore.

Standards Australia have produced their business continuity handbook HB 221 2003 which although not a formal standard is being informally treated as one in Australasian territories. The Australian Prudential Authority (APRA) has also implemented regulation for the finance sector via their standard APS-232-BCM.

The Singapore directive TR19:2005 on BCM is mainly related to IT recovery standards and has replaced the earlier and somewhat wider SPRING directive of 2003 which was itself based mainly on PAS 56.

ISO is actively working at putting together a standard that involves all of these key national standard bodies. Such a standard is likely to need considerable give and take for an acceptable international consensus to emerge.

Cultural BCM differences

An interesting part of the BCI role is in understanding the different cultural perceptions of BCM in different countries.

Many of the developing BCM countries are still confused about its place in the management hierarchy, and how it meshes with risk management, security, IT recovery and compliance. Many countries judge the value of a topic by the qualifications (and hence marketability) it can provide to individuals. As such quite a lot of professionals have first come across BCM in a different context to that of Europe or North America.

Partly this has been caused by a number of specialist areas incorporating business continuity into their own disciplines. The first to do this was information security, which led to confusion between business continuity and IT backup and recovery. This confusion was formalized to some extent by its inclusion in the BS 7755 Information Security Standard, which eventually became the ISO 27001 standard. As this standard has been widely adopted in such places as India, Japan and Korea, the first references to BCM many people experienced came as part of information security. This misconception then became incorporated into many education and certification programmes such as CISSP, ISACA and ITIL.

This pattern has continued with physical security, emergency planning and risk management, all areas in which professional bodies and certification schemes have tended to include BCM components into their own disciplines. To an extent that often confuses the practitioner and student alike.

There remain considerable gaps in perception about the nature of BCM between Europe and North America. This is not ideal in attempting to achieve a world consensus that allows us to move ahead coherently. For example, in Canada the subject is clearly seen as closely linked to emergency planning and dealing with natural disasters. Pre-9/11 this was mainly the US view, but business continuity is now equally associated with homeland security as well as Federal Emergency Response. The US government is confusing the picture by trying to redefine BCM as relating to commercial recovery and looking at the term Continuity of Operations Planning (COOP) for non-commercial BCM.

The trend in Europe seems to be the reverse. Many of the older EU countries are now turning their attention to BCM in a big way, after many years of relative indifference. The BCI *Good Practice Guide* is the methodology all EU institutions (Commission, Council and Parliament) use for BCM. The interest and desire to move ahead quickly was apparent by the detailed questioning I received at a recent meeting in Brussels and the priority this meeting was given. Representatives of all member states attended both the formal meeting and a later more general presentation.

In the UK the term BCM is fully established to both national and local government levels and given the force of law in the Civil Contingencies Act. Given the success of this model and encouragement from the EU, it is likely that all EU member states will move ahead rapidly with a similar application of BCM principles.

In Japan BCM is not yet widely developed despite enormous theoretical interest in the topic. Many key business leaders still think of it as planning what to do if there is a major natural disaster like an earthquake; they appear to have absolute confidence in their management skills to deal with any manmade incident without formal BCM.

Israel, not unreasonably, largely sees it as a subbranch of security rather than a management discipline in its own right. Australia is very active and has made considerable in-roads in Pacific Rim areas to promote its BCM philosophy, which in many ways are emergency response specific. Singapore has a very technical IT approach and Korea is almost entirely concentrated on IT resilience for its large financial base.

South Africa sees itself as a beacon of knowledge for the rest of Southern Africa, and in the north of the continent Nigeria is starting to move ahead with BCM at a governmental level.[1]

Of the BRIC countries (Brazil, Russia, India and China), India is most active but given its dependence on the international BPO market it is very concerned about

---

[1] A 2006 KPMG UAE survey, *Information Security and Business Continuity*, identified that, in the UAE, most BC programmes are IT focused and may not cover the business issues; there is inadequate separation between primary and secondary (recovery) sites; and that the investment in BC as low, with 66% having an annual budget <US$50 000 while another 16% spend between $50 000 and $100 000. From experience, a similar situation exists generally throughout the Middle East; in Central and Eastern Europe; most of Africa; and Pakistan, with financial institutions and multinationals taking the lead in BC. (Editor)

audit, compliance and standards. Most BCM practitioners in India come from an audit (particularly IT audit) background.

Russia still seems to be at the IT/technology recovery phase with only a limited concept of BCM beyond that basic level. However, this year in Moscow, the first BCM Conference and Exhibition was held with a good level of participation, so the dawning of interest is certainly taking place there as well.

The BCI is starting to get membership applications from China and Brazil and has appointed area representatives in these territories. We are likely to see major BCM growth activities in all of the BRIC countries over the next two to three years.

Regulations and legislation

What this is all leading to is more control on how organizations operate and how they guarantee continuity of business operations. In particular we see much stricter regulatory control in the financial sector. In the UK for example, the FSA (Financial Services Authority) have for some years been moving their regulated firms towards BCM standards, which although not very specific are still required for compliance. In the United States the Federal Reserve have taken a similar but more powerful approach with some mandatory elements. Other powerful if not legally enforced directives have been issued in many areas of the world including Singapore, Korea and Singapore.

There is clear evidence that there is a coming together of BCM thinking among the various financial regulators, which is likely to be a strong driver for more consistency. The Basel Committee on Banking Supervision Joint Forum has issued a document of seven high-level principles for BCM that individual country regulators will look to enforce. The countries represented were USA, UK, Canada, France, Netherlands, Hong Kong and Japan, so although not universal it does represent most of the major players in financial markets.

Governments have also started to become engaged in the BCM debate. The Sarbanes-Oxley Act (SOX) in the US has created a situation in which directors and officers of companies are personally responsible for control failures within their organizations. This Act not only applies to US companies but also to non-US companies operating within US markets, and of course to the foreign subsidiaries of US domiciled corporations. There is now a Japanese version of SOX and talk of a European SOX.

The UK government has linked its support for business continuity as part of its general strategy to upgrade its public protection capability. The Civil Contingencies Act has defined a group of Category 1 responders (police, emergency services, local authorities, hospitals) and Category 2 responders (government agencies and utility providers). All of these organizations must have full BCM capability in place.

From May 2005, the law also put a duty of care on local authorities to promote the concept of BCM to firms in their locality. The effectiveness of this is being closely monitored by other European countries, who are considering similar legislation.

Benefits of international cooperation

This should ultimately lead to improvements in the quality and consistency in the delivery of business continuity globally along with the development and capabilities of the business continuity professional who can operate internationally. It will certainly go a long way towards bridging the gap in business continuity maturity levels between the established BCM countries and those just starting. It will also make the path of moving a BCM programme from the basic stage through intermediate to advanced more attainable when local expertise is limited.

Another real benefit will be the ability to benchmark business continuity capabilities between regions, countries, sectors and companies. All of this will enable us to move closer towards a global level of best practice. It should also speed up the removal of the silo mentality and approach by integrating the disciplines of business continuity with security, emergency and crisis management and ultimately compliance.

Finally, we really do need to have better global agreement on terminology and accepted practice. Until the English speaking countries agree, it is difficult to get common acceptance elsewhere. The role of ISO will certainly be of great value in this area.

A4C BUSINESS CONTINUITY PLANNING IN ASIA

Alan Craig FBCI – Thailand

Alan is Managing Director of Survive In Asia Ltd, based in Bangkok, Thailand, and provides business continuity consultancy and training services across Asia and Oceania.

Preamble

In the late 1990s, the author once had the good fortune to meet a past chairman of a major British banking group who was on a tour of bank operations in Asia. A very experienced and personable gentleman, the first line of his presentation in Thailand was something along the lines of: 'it's wonderful to be back in Asia'. At the post-presentation networking, I chatted with the chairman and mentioned – somewhat tongue-in-cheek – that there is no such place as Asia and perhaps he should use the name of the country he is actually in! The underlying point is relevant, however; sometimes the important detail can be missed by focusing on a bigger picture that might not even exist in reality.

The context

Introduction

Any topic using the term Asia seems to hint at a compact and relatively homogenous territory capable of discussion and summary within a single – and often brief – report. Whereas everyone knows that Asia is the largest continent with the biggest population, there seems to be a tendency – at least in 'the West' – to try to summarize Asia in the broadest terms.

Indeed, whereas reports on business opportunities or operations in China, Japan or India may run to many lines of monthly board minutes, countries such as Vietnam, Myanmar (previously Burma) and South Korea might merit no lines at all (for the record, these countries have populations of over 84, 50 and 48 millions, respectively). Japan is a member of the G8 group of countries; Nepal and Laos are among the countries with the lowest GDP per capita. But all of these countries listed are often included within that single business report entity: 'Asia'.

It is estimated[1] that by 2020, Asia will host the world's top four urban areas by population: Tokyo (37 million), Mumbai (25 million), Delhi (25 million), Dakka (22 million). In the top 10 are another two Asia cities: Jakarta (20 million) and Karachi (18 million).

This discussion excludes countries such as Russia and the Central Asian Republics (sometimes referred to as belonging to Eurasia) and is restricted to East Asia, South East Asia and South Asia.

Top transnational companies (TNCs) from developing Asia

The assumption often seems to persist that the multinational companies that operate in Asia come mainly from the developed economies. In fact, the position is quite a bit different.

In September 2005, UNCTAD reported that of the top 50 multinational or transnational companies with business operations in Asian countries, 39 are based in Asia, and four of those 39 rank among the 100 largest TNCs worldwide. The same source lists the five largest TNCs from Asia and Oceania (by foreign assets 2003) as:

1. Hutchison Whampoa, Hong Kong SAR, China (which is also ranked 16th globally)
2. Singtel, Singapore
3. Petronas, Malaysia
4. Samsung, Korea
5. China Ocean Shipping, China.

Business continuity planning within Asia – a generalized overview

Why is BCP in Asia an important issue?

The history, size and diversity of the Asian continent make it a very interesting and important topic of study in any context. However, in a book about business continuity planning, there has to be much more to the relevance than general interest. There are several reasons why we should all be concerned about the development of sound BCP principles and practice for organizations within the Asian continent. Those reasons include:

---

[1] www.citymayors.com.

1. Manufacturing supply chain – Asia is the major powerhouse in terms of providing component parts and finished goods across all commercial sectors. An interruption to the supply chain from supplier companies based in Asia could lead to significant problems for the purchasing organizations.
2. IT development – some countries within Asia are host to companies (sometimes large corporations in their own right) that provide major software and other IT management or development activities to outsourcing organizations. Usually the supplying companies are based in countries with an English speaking capability, such as India or the Philippines.
3. Service supply/CRM – on a similar basis, large-scale call centre activities, for example, are outsourced to companies in the same countries.
4. Food supplies and food security – Asia supplies many of the items now taken for granted on many of the dinner tables of the world.
5. Resource management – the main industrial economies within Asia are experiencing phenomenal growth, partly due to the above considerations, and partly due to their need to supply their own populations. The efficient use of scarce resources in further business or economic developments can legitimately be included in a wider BCM mandate; and as part of a country's wider aspirations. Energy and environmental issues in Asia are likely to be a major part of the global management of resources in the coming years.
6. Competition – over the coming years, companies in developing countries will become strong competitors to established businesses in developed countries, competing directly for the same business, no longer content to be just the low cost contributor in the value chain. In one way or another, efficient BCM may be a differentiator or competitive advantage for such competing organizations.
7. Humanitarian Issues – the human populations within developing countries in Asia are often exposed to natural disasters of cataclysmic proportions, leading to many deaths and injuries. Even without the terrible repetition of such catastrophic events, quality of life is often poor, accompanied by relatively high infant mortality rates and low life expectancy rates. Most developed countries and various international organizations, such as the United Nations and the European Community, regard assistance to such developing countries as being a high priority. In its own sphere of influence, BCM can contribute to this effort and help reduce unnecessary death, injury and suffering.

The Y2K experience

Working towards Y2K was not necessarily a positive experience for many companies based in Asia. The Y2K phenomenon was the first time many local companies – large or small – had been introduced to business continuity planning principles in general and contingency planning techniques in particular. Such companies were more or less forced to take part in the BCP for the 31 December 1999 to 1 January 2000 switchover. The impetus came mainly from partners, suppliers or customers who were foreign investors (and thus were under stricter regulatory compliance requirements in their home countries and moreover had to be seen to be protecting shareholders' funds). That Y2K turned out to be such a small event confirmed the suspicions of many business owners and organizational executives that BCP was an excessive requirement.

The same foreign direct investment (FDI) inputs and some organic initiatives are continuing to promote BCP in this new millennium but in general terms, companies in many Asian countries – and regrettably even subsidiaries or associates of large 'western' multinationals – lag far behind their western counterparts in terms of business continuity planning and practice.

Origins of a BCP within companies located in Asian countries

Analysis of any hard information available plus informal discussions with company managers suggests strongly that where rigorous business continuity planning exists within Asia-based companies, the likely sources of any BCP regime are TNCs with parent entities located within the highly regulated countries such as USA, UK, Europe, Australia and New Zealand. Such companies will likely 'import' a BCP template from another part of the organization and tweak it to a greater or smaller extent for local application.[2]

However, the largest number of TNCs operating within Asia comes from other Asian countries (see UNCTAD information above), which themselves do not yet have rigorous business continuity planning regimes.

The number of organically developed business continuity plans arising within the continent from non-TNCs remains very low in comparison to the highly regulated countries mentioned above. This aspect is indeed changing as various countries in Asia develop their own BCP and risk management standards and capability (see below); and also as 'local companies' seek partners – customers or suppliers – on a transnational basis and are thus obliged to upgrade their own business continuity processes and practices. However, in many cases the pace of BCP development and related issues seems painfully slow.

Some survey results concerning the development of BCP and related issues in Asia

The following snippets paint a very general picture (some other survey results are included within specific country overviews below):

[2] Many multinational companies from the West spend a lot of time, effort and resources developing specifically tailored business models or processes that reflect business requirements and the wider cultural aspects of the host country. However, it seems that business continuity planning processes are often 'imported wholesale' (with only minor amendments) from head office and indeed are frequently managed from head office.

1. A Gartner Group study indicated that the market for disaster recovery and business continuity planning in Asia-Pacific was worth US$360 million in 2000 and continues to grow at a CAGR of 30%.
2. An International Data Corporation (IDC) study suggested that the Asia-Pacific network security market (excluding Japan) reached US$264.3 million in 2001 and was expected to grow by 29% to reach US$340.9 million by the end of 2002. This level of annual growth was expected to continue for the foreseeable future.
3. A 2002 study by CMP Worldwide recorded that 71% of the enterprises surveyed had security as a top corporate priority, while only 38% actually implemented the intended security policies.

People do come first

In reports and analyses such as this, it is often too easy to slip completely into the cold jargon of the business continuity context. However, whatever events are discussed at whatever level, we must never lose sight of the fact that the incidents and disasters that occur often result in death and injury, sometimes on a massive scale. In addition, the survivors and family networks of those killed or injured often suffer terrible and long-lasting post-traumatic stress. For example, the Indian Ocean earthquake and tsunami killed up to 300000 and injured 500000 across Indonesia, Thailand, Myanmar, India, Sri Lanka and elsewhere. In the face of such numbers and the tragedies that lie behind them, corporate communications about contingency planning and crisis management might seem cold and inadequate. However, we can still hope that professional business continuity management principles and practice applied diligently can help reduce such numbers of dead and injured in future disasters. In any event, people do come first – life is never cheap.

Disasters and crises – the Asian profile?

The list of 'general' business continuity events, incidents, disasters or emergencies is long. In Asian countries, similar events and disasters manifest themselves. There are fires, thefts, assaults, car accidents, storms, floods, leaks, plane crashes, delayed events, insect problems, arson, fraud, corruption, riots, explosions – and so on. However, the range and scale of the *natural* disasters can be huge. And only in Asia do major ferry disasters involving the deaths of hundreds seem to occur every other month.

Bruce Swales is Regional Director for BELFOR in Asia. BELFOR is a major restoration company which gets to see (and fix) the disaster damage and devastation caused to business or industrial operations and equipment. He says: 'Throughout Asia, other than Singapore or Japan, BCP still remains a topic of interest to most companies but not of sufficient interest for the majority of companies to do anything about it! Despite the apparent increase in natural disasters (earthquakes and typhoons) companies still appear to believe that "it will never happen to me".' Bruce splits his time between Japan and Singapore!

He adds:

> In Taiwan, despite a strong local risk management movement, and several international insurance companies either pulling out of the market or critically reviewing their risks, manmade disasters (predominantly fires) still occur with monotonous regularity as they have done for many years. Major fires still regularly occur within the semiconductor and electronics industries, despite the lessons that were learnt by the industry following the two largest fires ever in that industry, which both occurred in Taiwan some 10 or so years ago. Some companies either have a BCP, or have commenced developing a BCP, but such companies appear to be in the minority.

OK, the fire is out, but what do we do next?

Even where a BCP exists, there are still mountains to climb. As Bruce Swales continues:

> One disturbing point that BELFOR regularly sees in companies that already have a BCP is that in most instances the BCP is seen to be reasonably well developed up to the point that the fire has been extinguished; the chemical spill has been removed or the flood waters have receded. But the plans are often extremely light on what needs to happen next in order to resume normal business operations fully within the shortest practical time. Emergency response teams will be well developed and trained, with comprehensive procedures, regular drills, etc. However, the necessary activities to rebuild the damaged infrastructure and resources, in an expedient manner, in order to resume normal business operations, are hardly touched upon. And, in almost every case, the option of using professional restoration or recovery services is never considered and the more expensive option of replacement prevails.

Another specific issue to be faced in the Asia context is the ability of the emergency services to respond promptly and professionally. The level of service is very high in some countries but woefully inadequate in others. Businesses and commercial operations have specifically to factor in emergency service response capability into their BCP work.

Piracy

Not a regular business continuity consideration, sea piracy is alive and well in the Malacca Straits, running between Indonesia, Singapore and Malaysia. This is a major shipping lane, and, for example, 80% of Japan's oil imports pass through the Malacca Straits. It is estimated that 50000 vessels a year use the Malacca Straits, ships which trade worldwide.

The three countries mentioned above are now committing navy vessels to patrol the area.[3] In addition, several private security companies from Britain and the US have entered the private navy business in the region, each hoping to earn the minimum $50000 security price tag per ship. In the past, piracy was purely commercial, focusing on ship and crew valuables and the cargo. Now, known terrorist groups are involved in the piracy activity. Currently, a great fear is that a piracy attack could take possession of a large LPG carrier and use it in a major terrorist attack.

Partner and investment risks

In addition to the usual business continuity fiscal and treasury risks which are run in a multicultural and multicurrency business operation, existing and prospective investors – especially from the developed countries – to many Asian countries have to undertake as much due diligence as is possible. It is not unknown for local partners in Asia to operate in such a manner that the foreign partner is eventually obliged to abandon much of the investment.

Five countries

China

China is the most populous country in the world and is set to become the world's largest economy within the next decade or so. Businesses from all over the world are flocking to China to take advantage of very low costs of production, especially labour, and to get access to the internal China market.

As a very large, geographically dispersed country, China – in one part or another – faces most of the business continuity risks and threats found in the Asia region with the notable exception of major terrorist activity. Due to the age of the working assets within industrial areas away from the Tier 1 cities, there are regular problems causing the deaths of many. The mining industry is still beset with major safety problems. The construction of the Three Gorges Dam will help prevent many of the deaths due to flooding of the Yangtze River (1931, 3.7 million dead; 1975, 80000 to 200000 dead; 1997 3000 dead, 14 million homeless).

Currently China has very little BCP capability, certainly of the locally developed variety. But, according to the Singapore Business Continuity Management Consortium (SBCM), 'China is expected to be the one of the fastest growing markets for

---

[3] A joint anti-piracy exercise was held off the island of Langkawi on 2 February 2007 by Thai and Malaysian marine police and the Japanese coastguard.

business continuity management services within Asia Pacific.' SBCM is targeting China for major opportunities for business continuity-related service and product companies. The SBCM will focus on opportunities in China's energy, finance, telecommunications and transportation sectors, specifically targeting Tier 1 cities such as Beijing, Shanghai and Shenzhen.

China has established its own new business continuity professional association, called the China Business Continuity Management Professional Committee. In October 2004, the association held its first meeting in the Beijing Friendship Hotel, very accurately titled: 'CBCM BCM 2004 – China's first seminar'.

India

The second most populous country in the world, like China, India is expanding its economy at a furious pace.

Parts of India experience massive flooding leading to huge problems. Terrorism is another major problem within India.

The IT (e.g. software development) and related services sectors (e.g. call centres) are major developing business interests outsourced by companies in developed countries which should require a fast-track in terms of parallel BCP development.

However, Gartner says 85% of Global 2000 enterprises have established a disaster recovery plan for core technology and infrastructure, but only 15% have a fully fledged business continuity plan. A 2002 KPMG survey on 'Business Continuity Management Preparedness in Indian Industry' showed that 79% of the respondents did not have a documented and tested BC plan.

As Nathaniel Forbes of Forbes Calamity Prevention in Singapore said recently in his blog: 'I confess I'm skeptical about BCP in India. I talked in the last 90 days with two companies in Mumbai that are both considering building commercial recovery sites. Both companies told me there were no commercial recovery facilities in India, that banks in India were "just discovering" BCP, that there are no full-time BCP consultants in India. That is, there are none of the indications of a contingency culture in India, yet.' Dr Dutta of telecom giant VSNL agrees: 'BCP in Indian companies is still a lot of hype. Companies merely talk about it because they want to look very principled and organized. But sadly, they do not follow the practices. Some use a half-baked solution where they use a DR site, but the image at the site is not updated.'

However, there is evidence that new disaster recovery facilities are beginning to come on-stream in India quite recently. One enterprising operation has located an Indian DR facility on the island of Mauritius. But regrettably there is no clear sign that India is ready to commit to developing its own BCP standard or to adhere to an international standard, despite compliance requirements from the Bank of India.

Japan

Home of the 10th largest population in the world, Japan is exclusively an island nation.

The country's political and financial capital, Tokyo, lives under the constant threat of large-scale damage from a major earthquake. Japan is highly sensitive to the threat of terrorist attacks.

Bruce Swales of BELFOR comments: 'Probably the country in Asia where we are seeing the fastest acceptance and commitment to developing a BCP within business is Japan. Whilst not too many Japanese companies currently have a full BCP, the majority of medium to large companies known to BELFOR in Japan is in the process of developing a BCP, or has top management commitment to developing a BCP.'

In a very recent report, Celent estimates that banks and brokerages in Japan will spend US$866 million on business resiliency in 2005, a figure that will grow to approximately US$886 million in 2007. More than 75% of financial institutions have some sort of business contingency protocol, as they develop their full BCP capability. Nevertheless, many firms still lack fully fledged BCP programme that address both the systems recovery and operational continuity aspects of disaster preparedness. Alternate sites for data backup and recovery are fairly common.

Singapore

A small island nation located at the tip of the Malay Peninsula, Singapore is listed at number 117 in the world population rankings.

As it is relatively well protected from the open ocean by the islands of Indonesia and Malaysia, Singapore experiences few natural disasters. However, Singapore has one of the highest rates of lightning activity in the world, leading to several deaths each year. In 2002/03 there were 33 deaths recorded as probably due to an epidemic of SARS. Threats to Singapore come mainly from outside. The annual burning of the land on some Indonesia islands causes huge black clouds over Singapore, leading to respiratory problems. Singapore is also very sensitive to any potential threat of terrorist activity arising from groups based in Malaysia or Indonesia.

According to Bruce Swales: 'In Singapore, 10 years ago we used to see a medium to large industrial fire almost on a weekly basis, but nowadays it is more like once or twice a year! All I can put this down to is improved risk management.'

The Singapore Standards, Productivity and Innovation Board (SPRING) has been pushing BCM strongly since 2002/3. The business continuity management (BCM) programme was initiated by SPRING to encourage organizations to take up BCM as part of good management practices. In July 2003, the SPRING standard on

'Requirements for Business Continuity Management' was launched. The objective was to provide organizations with a set of requirements that will lead them towards achieving BCM competence. In September 2005, the Technical Reference (TR19:2005) on BCM was launched to supersede the SPRING standard.

Singapore is well aware of the wider value of a professional BCP approach based on a solid standard such as TR19:2005. The government quotes:

> At the national level, a standard on BCM can improve Singapore's global image as the preferred business hub in Asia. It gives foreign investors greater assurance and confidence in the reliability and resilience of Singapore companies to deal with disasters and crises. By providing a strong base of resilient supporting industries, Singapore can attract more MNCs [multinational companies] and entrepreneurs to base themselves here. For local companies wishing to venture overseas, a standard on BCM also serves as a good internationalization tool. It assures our foreign partners of continuity in the supply of goods and services. This would greatly enhance the international competitiveness of Singapore.

There is a message there for any company or country.

Thailand

Thailand is the 19th most highly populated country in the world with 65 million inhabitants, Thailand is not the huge economic and industrial powerhouse that is India or China and is not the major financial centre that is Tokyo or Singapore. Thailand is, however, a very successful economy with considerable oil and gas reserves both in the Gulf of Thailand and upcountry. But its selection as a country worthy of inclusion in a business continuity analysis is due to a series of events that could lead to major impacts for many foreign company investments in Thailand.

Late in 2006, Thailand experienced a peaceful military coup to overthrow the government of Prime Minister Thaksin Shinawatra. The critical reason for the coup was the sale of several of Thailand's key telecommunications companies by the Shinawatra family to Temasek, the investment arm of the government of Singapore. The deal – worth around US$2 billion – was structured such that no tax of any kind was paid. Like many takeovers, the deal was complex but unlike many takeovers of this size, it involved several anonymous British Virgin Island companies. The whole story is worthy of a mystery novel but this is not the point of this reference.

One of the outcomes of the situation has been a series of decisions by the current government – appointed by the coup leaders – to plug all longstanding loopholes in Thai law regarding foreign companies and investment; and to bring in some new regulations. Many companies that have nominally Thai control but are foreign managed in practice – including 15 listed on the Stock Exchange of

Thailand – are likely to be affected by the changes and in a worst case scenario, some companies may lose their Thai incorporation. Those companies who did not take advantage of the relaxed attitude of the Thai authorities to past company incorporations will not of course be directly affected. However, the indirect effects may be felt much more widely.

This could be a classic business continuity scenario – changes in government regulations that affect the ability of a business to continue operations on a planned and predictable basis.

What is in the future? – risks and threats

In many senses the future will be more of the same. There will still be cross-cultural issues to deal with, different political systems, currency problems, different calendar systems, different values, completely different social structures, etc., both within Asia and between Asia and the other trading blocs. Fires will still occur, petty crime will still go on, economies will boom and bust, corruption will stay, illegal economic activities will continue, workplace problems will not go away – and so on. The basic 'stuff' of business and BCP will continue to provide the challenges that all organizations and businesses face. But there will be new or escalated challenges that have to be faced.

Natural disasters

Natural disasters will continue to play havoc throughout Asia and the worst effects will continue to be felt in the poorer countries, where economic migration takes millions of people every year from their inland villages to the relatively more economically successful coastal regions.

There will certainly be more floods, typhoons, hurricanes, mud-slides, etc. as these phenomena are linked to the annual climate cycle and the monsoon rains. There will be more earthquakes as much of coastal Asia is based along the 'Ring of Fire', the Asia-Pacific undersea fault-line. There may even be more devastating tsunamis, partly due to the Ring of Fire and partly due to weakening of the earth's crust around the Indonesian islands due to the previous earthquake which caused the devastating tsunami of 2005. Avalanches, lightning storms, volcanic activity, etc. – they all add to the sometimes frightening list of natural disaster threats that various countries in Asia face.

The huge humanitarian cost of such disasters will be overwhelming; the cost to the local economy will be immense. In cold business continuity terms, such natural disasters set major challenges from site selection to business recovery, not just the crisis management issues. But both the relative cheapness of semi-skilled labour in various Asian countries and the sheer size of the local markets mean that foreign direct investment will continue apace – both within Asia and from the developed countries to Asia.

Terrorism

Myanmar and North Korea are about the only Asian countries relatively untouched by terrorism, perhaps due to their totalitarian governments. Most other Asian countries have terrorist challenges to face – and the terrorists can come from sources such as religious groups, separatists or other political and ideological groups.

This of course is not a challenge just for Asia – the growth of terrorism is a worldwide phenomenon. In many ways, the Asian challenge is less as the terrorist groups or rebel groups restrict their activities to threats within their own country and their own peoples. However, the export of violence to other countries and other peoples within the local country is increasing. The Bali bombings in October 2002 and the Bangkok bombings in December 2006 are cases in point. Prior to these events, both locations felt themselves to be immune to terrorist violence.

The risks related to, and the impacts of, terrorist attacks and events are not dissimilar in effect to other risks, threats and impacts that the organization and the business continuity planner have to face. The human and economic price of terrorism has in many ways become just another cost of doing business, albeit a tragic one when it leads to the loss of life, or to injury.

Intellectual property

If Asia is the 'world's factory' producing massive quantities of industrial and consumer goods, toys and clothes, to name but a few, it is also where such items and more are relentlessly copied and sold on in markets and other more sophisticated outlets, often worldwide. The photocopying of textbooks is a major industry in Vietnam and China: pirate DVD film and software copies are found everywhere.

The equally relentless process of globalization will indeed help to resolve some of the IPR issues faced by major brand names and copyright holders. However, it is unlikely that the phenomenon of copying will ever be wholly eradicated. The copying of brand name and copyright items is a major industry in its own right.

Crying pandemic wolf?

In the early 2000s it was SARS, now it is the turn of HPAI (highly pathogenic avian influenza) to capture the attention of the world. Bird flu, as it is better known, seems to present a major danger of draconian pandemic effect, if the virus is passed from bird to human, and then human to human. In 1918, Spanish flu H1N1 (which was first publicly reported in Spain but was actually first diagnosed in the USA), killed up to 50 million people worldwide.

Not everyone is convinced of course, and SARS (severe acute respiratory syndrome) is often cited as one example when major crises were predicted but it was ultimately seen as a case of 'crying wolf'. In fact, SARS did have a major epidemic effect in China, where there were 774 deaths. By May 2003, mortality by age group was as follows: below 1% for people aged 24 or younger, 6% for those 25 to 44, 15% in those 45 to 64 and more than 50% for those over 65. In 2006, a systematic review of all the studies on the 2003 SARS epidemic found no evidence that anti-virals, steroids or other therapies helped patients. A few suggested they caused harm. SARS is still very much a threat.

However, currently, world attention is on bird flu. If a bird flu (H5N1 variety) pandemic becomes an imminent threat, it will have a huge effect on businesses continuity worldwide but perhaps particularly in Asia. The reasons include:

1. Asia generally, and China specifically, are perceived as the originating locations of the virus. Any travel and other restrictions imposed due to pandemic threat would likely be more severe in Asia and consequently this could have an impact on the global economy.

2. The above notwithstanding, attempts to migrate back to one's home area would be massive. As examples:

   (i) An estimated 6–7 million Filipinos live and work abroad, some 10% of the resident population and the Philippines government estimates that they send home US$12 billion every year.

   (ii) Local country populations would be impacted as workers migrate away from the industrial zones to their own home areas.

   (iii) Expatriate managers from TNCs – either within Asia or from developed countries – would also attempt to return to their home countries.

   (iv) Expatriate managers, perhaps particularly from the developed countries, may decide – due to the travel and other restriction issues mentioned above – to return to their home country at an earlier stage in the 'possible pandemic development process' than is necessary. The outcomes of this scenario would lead to major business continuity issues for the multinational business.

3. Even before any major death statistics are recorded such worker migrations could have a negative impact on the production of goods and services in Asia.

The above – and many other attempts to define 'what could happen' – are indeed scenarios only. There are many more such scenarios – some even more challenging in terms of business continuity. It is up to the business and the business continuity manager to select a spread of scenarios and plan accordingly.

Energy

There is at least one other future issue which will have a major influence on the continuity of some businesses and the failure of others (indeed, it may cause the failure of some countries), but these issues are not really within the remit of the business continuity manager as they involve geopolitical forces. The competition for energy – particularly oil and gas, and nuclear capabilities – will help drive whole new regional and global economic relationships. In Asia, the major economies such as China and India are competing strongly for oil available from existing sources. New oil and gas sources, such as in the sea around the highly contested Spratly Islands, are causing international tensions. The People's Republic of China (PRC), the Republic of China (Taiwan) and Vietnam each claim sovereignty over the entire group of islands, while Brunei, Malaysia and the Philippines each claim various parts. Several of the nations involved have soldiers stationed in the Spratlys and control various installations on different islands and reefs. The risk of more international tension exists in the East China Sea where Japan and China each claim the rights to billions of dollars worth of underwater energy reserves. That these disputes might erupt into something much more serious in the (near) future, as the availability of oil and gas diminishes, cannot be discounted.

Nuclear issues can lead to even more despondent scenarios for the future. The continent of Asia is bracketed by the two countries that are determined to develop a nuclear capability, seemingly under any circumstances. Iran and North Korea are under pressure from the international community to hold back from their nuclear development plans. On the one hand, possession of peaceful nuclear power generation capability can help ameliorate the problems mentioned above in the competition for the world's fossil fuel resources. On the other hand, the risk from badly constructed or managed nuclear power stations, or the risks from an aggressive use of nuclear weapons hardly bears thinking about, whether one is a business continuity professional or not.

Summary

Asia is the largest, most highly populated continent. However, the countries within Asia are very diverse. There is no discernible pattern among them concerning the development of business continuity planning principles and practices. In general the level of commitment to BCP is quite low.

The major economic powerhouses of China and India are experiencing massive growth and these countries will be even more major players in the global economy in the years ahead, a widespread lack of BCP capability notwithstanding. Japan remains a major financial and manufacturing centre and has foreign investments all over the world, again without having a major BCP legacy. The political situation in Thailand has caused a lot of investing companies to make contingency plans for their ensured survival but there is no real BCP presence in the country. Only Singapore is making a strategic effort to develop its own BCP standards to enhance its attractiveness for FDI and to assist the efforts of Singapore companies who themselves wish to invest overseas.

A4D   USEFUL INTERNATIONAL CONTACTS

This section includes representative details of a selection of organizations that will be of interest to business continuity management professionals. It is by no means exhaustive.

Professional certification and accreditation bodies

The Business Continuity Institute: www.thebci.com
The Disaster Recovery Institute International: www.drii.org
Association of Contingency Planners: www.acp-international.com

Emergency preparedness, business continuity and disaster recovery information exchange associations

There are large numbers of regional 'DRIE' (Disaster Recovery Information Exchange) groups throughout the world. These include:

www.drie.org
www.nedrix.com
www.drieottawa.org
www.drie-west.org
www.continuityforum.org.

Books, news and articles

www.continuitycentral.com
www.rothstein.com
www.contingencyplanning.com
www.drj.com

The London Business Resilience Group encourages business in business continuity planning and provides information about risk to London businesses. www.londonprepared.gov.uk.

Links and resources to brief descriptions of emergency management and business continuity resources

www.ala.org/ala/acrl/acrlpubs/crlnews/backissues2002/novmonth/crisisdisaster.
  htm
www.disaster-resource.com
www.nicic.org/Library/018191
www.birdflu-manual.com.

Organizations

American Society for Industrial Security (ASIS): www.asisonline.org
EPIX (Emergency Preparedness Information Exchange – provides links to national
  emergency preparedness organizations): epix.hazard.net
Florida Emergency Management: www.floridadisaster.org/County_EM/county_
  list.htm
(USA) Federal Emergency Management Agency (FEMA): www.fema.gov
International Association of Emergency Managers (IAEM): www.iaem.com
International Association of Fire Chiefs: www.iafc.org
International Association of Emergency Managers: www.ngdc.noaa.gov
International Federation of Risk and Insurance Management Associations (IFRIMA):
  www.ifrima.org
(USA) National Fire Protection Association: www.nfpa.org
(USA) National Association of Flood and Stormwater Management Agencies: www.
  nafsma.org
Risk and Insurance Management Society: www.rims.org

Glossary of general business continuity terms

ALARP   Of risk, A Level As Low As Reasonably Practicable.

Alert   A formal notification that an incident has occurred which may develop into a disaster.

Asset   Something of value; tangible premises, plant, equipment, people, intellectual property or intangible quality, e.g. reputation.

ATOF   (Recovery) At Time Of Failure.

ATOP   (Recovery) At Time Of Peak.

Alternative site   A standby location or locations from which critical activities may be resumed.

BS 25999   A UK BSI Standard for business continuity management.

ISO 27001   An ISO standard for information security, part of which references business continuity.

Backup site   See Alternative site.

Basel Accord (Basel II)   An agreement by international financial institutions on the financial risk assessment and the ratios between capital and risk.

Building denial   A situation in which premises cannot, or are not allowed to be, accessed.

Business continuity   Strategic and tactical capability of the organization to plan for and respond to incidents and business disruptions in order to continue business operations at an acceptable predefined level.[1]

Business continuity management   Holistic management process that identifies potential threats to an organization and the impacts to business operations that those threats, if realized, might cause, and which provides a framework for building organizational resilience with the capability for an effective response that safeguards the interests of its key stakeholders, reputation, brand and value-creating activities.[2]

---

[1] BS 25999–1:2006.
[2] BS 25999–1:2006.

The Definitive Handbook of Business Continuity Management, Second Edition.
Edited by Andrew Hiles FBCI. © 2007 John Wiley & Sons Ltd.

Business continuity plan (BCP)   Documented collection of procedures and information that is developed, compiled and maintained in readiness for use in an incident to enable an organization to continue to deliver its critical activities at an acceptable predefined level.[3]

Business continuity management lifecycle   Series of continuity activities which collectively cover all aspects of the business continuity management programme.[4]

Business continuity management programme   Ongoing management and governance process supported by top management and appropriately resourced to ensure that the necessary steps, are taken to identify the impact of potential losses, maintain viable recovery strategies and plans, and ensure continuity of products and services through training, exercising, maintenance and review.[5]

Business impact analysis (BIA)   Process of analysing business functions and the effect that a business disruption may have on them.[6]

CAR   FEMA's (q.v.) Capability Assessment for Readiness – the starting point for self-assessment under NFP 1600 (q.v.).

Cold site   An alternative facility that, although not fully equipped, will host the restoration of critical activities.

Contingency plan   A plan to deal with a specific set of adverse circumstances.

Crisis   An abnormal situation, or perception, which threatens the operations, staff, customers or reputation of an enterprise.

Critical activities   Those activities which have to be performed in order to deliver the key products and services which enable an organization to meet its most important and time-sensitive objectives.[7] Alternative: mission critical activities.

Damage assessment   An appraisal or determination of the effects of the disaster on human, physical, economic and natural resources.[8]

Disaster   Any (usually physical) event that threatens the viability of an organization.

Disaster management   Strategies for the prevention, preparedness and response to disasters, and the recovery of operations following disasters.[9]

Disaster recovery (DR)   An integral part of the organization's BCM plan by which it intends to recover and restore its IT, infrastructure and telecommunications capabilities following an incident.[10]

---

[3] BS 25999–1:2006.
[4] BS 25999–1:2006.
[5] BS 25999–1:2006.
[6] BS 25999–1:2006.
[7] BS 25999–1:2006.
[8] NFPA 1600.
[9] State Records New South Wales, Australia, Guidelines on Disaster Management, Section 2.
[10] Business Continuity/British Standards Institution Publicly Available Specification 56.

FEMA   US Federal Emergency Management Agency.

HACCP   Hazard Analysis Critical Control Point – a European requirement for risk assessment in the food industry.

Hazard   A theoretical exposure to danger (see also Threat).

HAZMAT   Hazardous Material.

HAZOP   Hazardous Operation.

HAZCHEM   Hazardous Chemicals.

Hot site   A facility equipped with whatever is necessary (including infrastructure) to provide rapid recovery of operations (usually refers to information and communications technology and work area provision).

Invocation   Act of declaring, to a contracted supplier of BC services, that their services will be used.

Maximum tolerable period of disruption   Duration after which an organization's viability will be irrevocably threatened if product and service delivery cannot be resumed.[11] Also referred to as Maximum Tolerable Outage (MTO) or Maximum Acceptable Outage (MAO).

NEMA   US National Emergency Management Association.

NFPA   US National Fire Protection Association.

NFPA   1600 US standard for disaster/emergency management programmes.

Recovery time objective   The time by which a pre-agreed level of operations has to be restored. The BS 25999–1:2006 definition is defective in that this may (but not necessarily) be the same as the maximum tolerable period of disruption.

Recovery point objective   The precise time to which data or transactions have to be restored (e.g. close of business previous day; start of day; or some point during the day).

Risk   A hazard or threat that has been assessed (weighted) as to the probability of it occurring to a specific asset. Alternative: The chance of something happening that will have an impact upon objectives. It is measured in terms of consequence and likelihood.[12]

Risk analysis   The quantification of threats to the enterprise or its essential operations or processes and the estimation of the likelihood of their occurrence.

Risk management   The systematic application of management policies, procedures and practices to the tasks of identifying, analyzing, assessing, treating and monitoring risk Alternative: The culture, processes and structures that are directed towards the effective management of potential opportunities and adverse effects.[13]

---

[11]   BS 25999–1:2006.
[12]   AS/NZS 4360: 1999, *Risk Management,* Standards Australia, NSW.
[13]   AS/NZS 4360: 1999, *Risk Management,* Standards Australia, NSW.

Service Level Agreement (SLA) An agreement between a service provider and its customer(s) specifying the scope, minimum acceptable quality and timeliness of the service.

Standby service Alternative site(s), facilities and/or resources that may be used in a disaster.

Stand down Formal announcement to cease alert status.

Threat A theoretical exposure to danger (see also Hazard).

Vital record Information, documents or data that are essential for recovery from a disaster.

Vital materials Supplies, equipment, etc. that are essential for recovery from a disaster.

Warm site A designated standby site, equipped and serviced to a level that will enable the enterprise to resume its essential operations and processes before their loss threatens the capability of the enterprise to fulfil its mission.

Wide area disaster A catastrophe affecting a large geographic area (e.g. major power outage, hurricane or flood) that destroys or denies access to public, telecommunications, transport or utilities infrastructure. Often civil or military emergency authorities will take control, thus limiting the actions possible by individual entities.

Work area recovery Restoration of office activity; a recovery site including desks, telephony and office systems.

Index

Indexed compiled by Terry Halliday